Health Care and Public Policy: An Australian Analysis

5th edition

George Palmer and Stephanie Short

First edition published 1989
Second edition published 1994
Third edition published 2000 by Palgrave Macmillan
Fourth edition published 2010
Reprinted 2013
Fifth edition published 2014
PALGRAVE MACMILLAN
15–19 Claremont Street, South Yarra 3141

Visit our website at www.palgravemacmillan.com.au

Associated companies and representatives
throughout the world.

National Library of Australia Cataloguing-in-Publication entry

Author: Palmer, G. R. (George Rupert), 1928- author.
Title: Health care and public policy : an Australian analysis / George Palmer, Stephanie Short.
Edition: 5th edition.
ISBN: 9781420256888 (paperback)
Notes: Includes bibliographical references and index.
Subjects: Public health—Australia.
            Medical policy—Australia.
            Medical care—Australia.
Other Authors/Contributors: Short, Stephanie D. (Stephanie Doris), 1956- author.
Dewey Number: 362.10994

Publisher: Kate Aylett
Project editor: Ingrid Bond
Editor: Gill Smith
Cover designer: Christabella Designs
Text designer: Friedo Ligthart
Permissions clearance: Jan Calderwood
Typeset in Bembo/11 pt by diacriTech, Chennai
Cover image: Shutterstock.com/Fransys
Indexer: Mary Russell

Printed in Malaysia

Internet addresses
At the time of printing, the internet addresses appearing in this book were correct. Owing to the dynamic nature of the internet, however, we cannot guarantee that all these addresses will remain correct.

Contents

Madhan B

List of figures

List of tables

List of abbreviations

AASW	Australian Association of Social Workers
ABF	Activity-based funding
ABS	Australian Bureau of Statistics
ACMA	Australian Communications and Media Authority
ACT	Australian Capital Territory
ACAT	Aged care assessment team
ACROD	Australian Council for Rehabilitation of the Disabled
ACTRAC	Australian Committee for Training Curriculum
ACTU	Australian Council of Trade Unions
ACHS	Australian Council on Healthcare Standards
ACHSM	Australasian College of Health Service Management
ACSQHC	Australian Commission on Safety and Quality in Health Care
AHMAC	Australian Health Ministers' Advisory Council
AHPRA	Australian Health Practitioner Regulation Agency
AHTAC	Australian Health Technology Advisory Committee
AHWAC	Australian Health Workforce Advisory Committee
AIDS	Acquired immune deficiency syndrome
AIHW	Australian Institute of Health and Welfare (until 1992, the Australian Institute of Health)
ALP	Australian Labor Party
AMA	Australian Medical Association
AMC	Australian Medical Council
AMPCO	Australasian Medical Publishing Company
AMWAC	Australian Medical Workforce Advisory Committee
AMWG	Access to Medicines Working Group
ANC	Australian Nursing Council
AN-DRG	Australian National Diagnosis Related Group
ANF	Australian Nursing Federation
ANMC	Australian Nursing and Midwifery Council
ANMAC	Australian Nursing and Midwifery Accreditation Council
ANPHA	Australian National Preventive Health Agency
ANRAC	Australasian Nurse Registering Authorities Conference
ANTA	Australian Natural Therapists' Association or Australian National Training Authority

ANU	Australian National University
AR–DRG	Australian Refined Diagnosis Related Group
ASMR	Australian Society for Medical Research
ATSIC	Aboriginal and Torres Strait Islander Commission
ATSIHWU	Aboriginal and Torres Strait Islander Health and Welfare Unit
AVCC	Australian Vice-Chancellors' Committee (Universities Australia)
BOO	Build, own, operate
BOOT	Build, own, operate, transfer
BUGA UP	Billboard Utilising Graffitists Against Unhealthy Promotions
CABG	Coronary artery bypass grafting (operation)
CAM	Care Aggregated Module
CAT	Computerised axial tomography
CDDS	Chronic Disease Dental Scheme
CDHP	Commonwealth Dental Health Program
CDNA	Communicable Diseases Network Australia
CEO	Chief executive officer
CFAC	Coalition on Food Advertising to Children
CHASP	Community Health Accreditation and Standards Project
CHF	Consumers' Health Forum
COAG	Council of Australian Governments
CPI	Consumer price index
DEETYA	Department of Education, Training and Youth Affairs
DEST	Department of Education, Science and Training
DHA	Commonwealth Department of Health and Ageing
DHC	District health council
DHFS	Commonwealth Department of Health and Family Services
DHSH	Commonwealth Department of Human Services and Health
DRG	Diagnosis related group
DSM	Diagnostic and Statistical Manual (of Mental Disorders)
DVA	Department of Veterans' Affairs
ECT	Electroconvulsive therapy
EEO	Equal employment opportunity
enHealth	Environmental Health Standing Committee
FFS	Fee for service
FPA	Family Planning Association
GDP	Gross domestic product
GP	General practitioner
GPSRG	General Practice Strategy Review Group
HACC	Home and Community Care (program)
HB	Health benefits (card)
HC	Healthcare card
HIA	Health impact assessment

HIV/AIDS	Human immunodeficiency virus/acquired immune deficiency syndrome
HIC	Health Insurance Commission
HMO	Health maintenance organisation (USA)
HPV	Human papillomavirus
HREOC	Human Rights and Equal Opportunity Commission (since 2009 known as the Australian Human Rights Commission)
HSD	Highly specialised drug
HWA	Health Workforce Australia
HWPC	Health Workforce Principal Committee
IHPA	Independent Hospital Pricing Authority
IIMS	Incident information management system
LHD	Local health district
LHN	Local hospital network
LOTE	Languages other than English
MA	Medicines Australia
MBS	Medical Benefits Schedule or Medicare Benefits Schedule. The two terms are used interchangeably.
ML	Medicare Local
MRI	Magnetic resonance imaging
MSAC	Medical Services Advisory Committee
NACAIDS	National Advisory Committee on AIDS
NACCHO	National Aboriginal Community Controlled Health Organisation
NAIHO	National Aboriginal and Islander Health Organisation
NCADA	National Campaign Against Drug Abuse
NDIS	National Disability Insurance Scheme
NHCDC	National Hospital Cost Data Collection
NHHRC	National Health and Hospitals Reform Commission
NHMRC	National Health and Medical Research Council
NHPA	National health priority areas or the National Health Performance Authority
NHRA	National Health Reform Agreement
NHS	National Health Service (Britain)
NHTAC	National Health Technology Advisory Committee
NHTAP	National Health Technology Advisory Panel
NHWDS	National Health Workforce Data Set
NHWT	National Health Workforce Taskforce
NMHS	National Mental Health Strategy
NMP	National Medicines Policy
NOHSC	National Occupational Health and Safety Commission
NOOSR	National Office of Overseas Skills Recognition

NPHP	National Public Health Partnership
NRAS	National Registration and Accreditation Scheme
NSW	New South Wales
NT	Northern Territory
NTB	National Training Board
OECD	Organisation for Economic Co-operation and Development
OHS	Occupational health and safety
OMA	Office of Multicultural Affairs
OOP	Out of pocket
OT	Occupational therapy
P3	Pharmaceuticals Partnerships Program
PBAC	Pharmaceutical Benefits Advisory Committee
PBS	Pharmaceutical Benefits Scheme
PHB	Pensioner health benefits (card)
PHERP	Public Health Education and Research Program
PHIAC	Private Health Insurance Administration Council
PHIR	Private Health Insurance Rebate
PHLN	Public Health Laboratory Network
PHRDC	Public Health Research and Development Committee
PIIP	Pharmaceutical Industry Investment Program
PISG	Pharmaceuticals Industry Strategy Group
PPP	Purchasing power parity
PSRS	Professional Services Review Scheme
QAHCS	Quality in Australian Health Care Study
Qld	Queensland
R&D	Research and development
RACGP	Royal Australian College of General Practitioners
RACP	Royal Australasian College of Physicians
RACS	Royal Australasian College of Surgeons
RANF	Royal Australian Nursing Federation
RB-RVS	Resource-based relative value scale
RCI	Resident classification instrument
RCS	Resident classification scale
RCT	Randomised controlled trial
RMO	Resident medical officer
RPBS	Repatriation Pharmaceutical Benefits Scheme
RSI	Repetitive strain injury
RUG	Resource utilisation group
SA	South Australia
SCC	Standards and Curriculum Council
SDR	Standardised death rate

SMHWB	Survey of Mental Health and Wellbeing
SNAP	Sub-acute non-acute (classification)
SRC	Standard Resident Contribution
SPP	Special purpose payment
STARTTS	Service for the Treatment and Rehabilitation of Torture and Trauma Survivors
TAFE	Technical and Further Education
Tas.	Tasmania
TGA	Therapeutic Goods Administration
TRD	Temporary-resident doctor
UHC	Universal health coverage
UNS	Unified national system (of education)
VACS	Victorian ambulatory classification
VET	Vocational education and training
Vic.	Victoria
VEETAC	Vocational Education Employment and Training Advisory Committee
VETAG	Vocational Education and Training Advisory Group
WA	Western Australia
WHO	World Health Organization

About the authors

George R Palmer is an Emeritus Professor in the School of Public Health and Community Medicine within the Faculty of Medicine at the University of New South Wales. He has written over 130 books, monographs and papers in the fields of statistics, economics, health policy, planning and financing. In 2008, Professor Palmer co-authored with Dr Tessa Ho, *Health Economics: A Critical and Global Analysis* (Palgrave Macmillan, UK).

Stephanie D Short is Professor and Head of the Discipline of Behavioural and Social Sciences in Health at the University of Sydney in the Faculty of Health Sciences. She has written extensively on the sociology of health care and is Convenor of HealthGov, an international network of regulators, professionals and researchers. In 2012, Professor Short co-edited with Dr Fiona McDonald, *Health Workforce Governance: Improved Access, Good Regulatory Practice, Safer Patients* (Ashgate, UK).

Acknowledgments

Author acknowledgments

Many colleagues provided us either with information or comment on the drafts of various sections and chapters for the first edition of this book. We would like to thank them for their valuable contributions.

In preparing the second edition, we were grateful to John Goss, James Green and Jacqueline Milne for providing useful and up-to-date data and policy information, to Annette Lahene for assistance with word processing and to Jill Lohmann, who provided expert assistance in updating many of the tables and figures and preparing the revised bibliography.

In preparing the third edition, we were most grateful for the invaluable assistance provided by Evelyn Sharman in all aspects of research and updating. We also acknowledged new sources of health policy material we drew upon extensively in writing this edition. The series *Healthcover*, produced by Ron Lord, was an excellent guide to contemporary policy developments. Most of the chapters in the 1998 book, edited by Gavin Mooney and Richard Scotton, *Economics and Australian Health Policy*, were used in our work.

In the lengthy task of producing the fourth edition, after a 10-year period of many changes in Australian health policy, we were most grateful for the skilled assistance of Lyn Broadway-Hill and Lynette Cowley with word processing, including the preparation of the numerous tables and figures. Sheryl Delacour undertook the onerous tasks of editing the bibliography and proofreading most of the chapters. She also provided very important insights based on her own contact with the health care system. Kate Masters, from the Health Sciences Library at the University of Sydney, provided valuable librarian assistance. Sue Brockway also provided expert and timely librarian assistance and Dr Kirsten Harley is thanked for valuable feedback and suggestions on the fourth edition. Dr Stephen Duckett kindly provided copies of his published and unpublished work, which we found invaluable. Substantial assistance was provided by Suchaya Thongyoo in research, updating and administration. We thank Drs Lynette Guy, Zhanming Liang, Evelyn Sharman, David Walker and Edith Weisberg for their input in specific fields of expertise. We thank also our most supportive and patient publisher, Elizabeth Vella.

In preparing the fifth edition, we are grateful to the professional team at Palgrave Macmillan: our publisher, Kate Aylett, publishing manager, Courtney Nicholls, project editor, Ingrid Bond, and editor, Gill Smith. As with the previous edition, we acknowledge the skilled assistance of Lyn Broadway-Hill with the text, tables and figures. Similarly, we are most grateful to Sheryl Delacour for proofreading and editing. Kanchan Marcus provided invaluable input, expertise and research assistance. Finally, we wish to acknowledge the exemplary data and statistics provided by the Australian Institute of Health and Welfare, on which we relied to write this edition.

George Palmer and Stephanie Short
January 2014

Publisher acknowledgments

The author and publisher are grateful to the following for permission to reproduce copyright material:

Table 6.1: 'Major steps towards implementation of the National Registration and Accreditation Scheme Timeline', by Pacey et al, 2012, reproduced by permission of the Publishers from 'A national scheme for health practitioner registration and accreditation: the case of Australia', in Short S and McDonald F (Eds), *Health Workforce Governance: Improved Access, Good Regulatory Practice, Safer Patients*, (pp 163–181), (Farnham: Ashgate, 2012). Copyright © 2012, **144**; Table 6.2: 'Professions regulated under the *Health Practitioner Regulation National Law Act 2009*', by Pacey et al, 2012, reproduced by permission of the Publishers from 'A national scheme for health practitioner registration and accreditation: the case of Australia', in Short S and McDonald F (Eds), *Health Workforce Governance: Improved Access, Good Regulatory Practice, Safer Patients*, (pp 163–181), (Farnham: Ashgate, 2012). Copyright © 2012, **145**; Figure 1.3: 'Respiratory tuberculosis: death rates, England and Wales 1850–1966', from *The Modern Rise of Population*, McKeown T, Academic Press, San Francisco, 1976, pp 93, 96, reproduced with permission from Elsevier, UK, **58**; Table 6.10: 'Dental Workforce: number per 100,000 population, remoteness areas, 2006, 2009 and 2010' from Health Workforce Australia 2013, *Australia's Health Workforce Series - Health Workforce by Numbers, HWA*, Adelaide, p 30, reproduced with permission, **189**; Table 6.7 'Employed registered and enrolled nurses: average total weekly hours worked, proportion working part-time and 50 hours or more per week, 2007 to 2011', from Health Workforce Australia 2013 *Australia's Workforce by Numbers: Health Workforce Australia*, Adelaide, reproduced with permission, **169**; Text extracts from *Bringing them Home, National Inquiry into the Separation of Aboriginal and Torres Strait Islander Children from Their Families*, Human Rights and Equal Opportunity Commission, Sydney, p 3 and p 658, **302**; Figure 8.3: 'HIV infecting a Helper T cell' sourced from *Better Health, better care, better life, Annual Report 2010/11*, Department of Health and Ageing (2011), reproduced with permission from Russell Kightley Media, **257**; Table 1.3: 'Expectation of life at birth and infant mortality rates in selected developed countries', 2010, based on data from *OECD (2013), Life expectancy and Maternal and Infant mortality*, reproduced with permission, **16**; Figure 1.2: Chart, 'Life expectancy and rise in life expectancy between 1983 and 2008 for OECD and other countries', based on data from *OECD (2011), Society at a Glance: OECD Social Indicators*, reproduced with permission, **17**; Table 10.1 'Public expenditure on health, percentage of total expenditure on health, selected OECD countries for which data was available, 2011', based on *OECD Health Data (OECD 2013)*, reproduced with permission, **366**; Table 1.2: 'Total health expenditure as a proportion of gross domestic product', based on data from *OECD Health Data (2013),* reproduced with permission, **6**; Table 4.1: 'Private health insurance: coverage of hospital treatment (%) Australia, 30 June 1984 to 30 June 2013', from *Industry statistics: Coverage of Hospital Treatment Tables Offered by Health Benefits Funds by State: Persons and Percentage of Population*, Private Health Insurance Administration Council website (2013), Canberra, **71**; Figure 1.4: Flowchart, 'Financing flowchart, Australian health-care system', adapted from Healy J, Sharman E and Lokuge B, 2006, *Australia: Health System Review 2006 (Health Systems in Transition, Vol 8, No 5, 2006),* World Health Organization (WHO), Regional Office for Europe 2006, Copenhagen, p 61, reproduced with permission, **21**; Figure 1.3: Flowchart, 'Organisational chart of the Australian health system', from Healy J, Sharman E and Lokuge B, 2006, *Australia: Health System Review 2006 (Health Systems in Transition, Vol 8, No 5, 2006),* World Health Organization (WHO), Regional Office for Europe 2006, Copenhagen, p 26, reproduced with permission, **20**.

The author and publisher would like to acknowledge the following:

Figure 9.7: 'Milestones in the life of the National Mental Health Strategy' based on data from Department of Health and Ageing, 2013, *National Mental Health Report, 2013: tracking progress of mental health reform in Australia 1993–2011, Commonwealth of Australia, Canberra*, **320**; Table 10.1: 'Summary of Commonwealth and state roles and responsibilities for health care', from *National Health Strategy, 1991b, The Australian Health Jigsaw: Integration of Health Care Delivery*, Issues Paper No 1, National Health Strategy, Melbourne, Commonwealth of Australia, **362**; Extract from Lees, M 1993, 'Time for a little leadership from Labor' says Democrats, *Healthcover*, vol 3, no 2, p 10, **164**; Figure 9.1: *Socioeconomic indices for areas (SEIFA) scores by health area, NSW, 2008*, Source: NSW Department of Health, (2009), **277**; Figure 8.4: 'Estimated number of deaths due to AIDS, 1960 to 2007, Epidemiological fact sheet on HIV and AIDS, core data on epidemiology and response, Australia, 2008', update, Source: based on data from *UNAIDS/WHO Working Group on Global HIV/AIDS and STI*, **257** (bottom); Figure 9.2: 'Universal Health Coverage Cube', based on World Health Organization 2010, *Health Systems Financing: The Path to Universal Health Coverage*, WHO, Geneva, **281**.

While every care has been taken to trace and acknowledge copyright, the publisher tenders their apologies for any accidental infringement where copyright has proved untraceable. They would be pleased to come to a suitable arrangement with the rightful owner in each case.

Preface

The last four decades have seen an upsurge of interest in health care reform. We have seen numerous reorganisations within the health sector, most notably in the United Kingdom and New Zealand, and at home, we have seen frequent changes in the financing, organisation and provision of health care. Policymakers, managers, clinicians and health care consumers are increasingly concerned about the cost and quality of health care, as evidenced by initiatives such as activity-based funding for hospitals, evidence-based medicine and clinical governance.

The common thread is that governments of all persuasions have been applying general management principles to health care, with the aim of providing quality health care services at the lowest possible cost. The Quality in Australian Health Care Study, completed in 1995, which reported on injuries and deaths occurring in Australian hospitals, provided a particular impetus for this concern with the twin concepts of quality and cost. Principles invoked in monitoring and managing the quality and cost of health services include the core concepts of effectiveness, efficiency and equity.

As financial restraint has played a more important role in the public policy environment, we have seen an increasing emphasis on managerial control and accountability. Within a context of increasing transparency in service delivery, there is greater emphasis on articulating the causal links between government inputs, outputs and outcomes. Over the last 30 to 40 years in teaching, conducting research and providing advice, we have become aware of a general tendency within governments to attempt to more satisfactorily align strategic policy goals, operational management and clinical accountability. Nowhere is this more evident than in the transition from historical budgets to activity-based funding, with the use of diagnosis related groups and other casemix measures. In short, colleagues in health are being expected to do more with less.

Despite the frequent ministerial pronouncements, numerous reports and associated protestations about significant changes in health care, it is to some extent a case of 'dynamics without change', as identified by Robert Alford in the United States in the 1970s. Indeed, in the 25 years since the first edition of *Health Care and Public Policy: An Australian Analysis* was published, we have been struck by the ongoing discrepancy between the rhetoric and the reality of health reform.

Of course, change is in the eye of the beholder. In-depth interviews with former senior executives in the New South Wales health system, conducted in association with the Australian College of Health Service Executives, indicated that the most common problems for health care managers were associated with managing in a context of constant change and uncertainty: lack of support and political interference. This phenomenon was characterised as centralised control and devolved responsibility. The trend towards short-term executive appointments, while providing a degree of flexibility for employers, tends to deny managers a sense that they can provide independent advice to ministers of health, free of fear or favour. The 1998 review of the General Practice Strategy unearthed low morale of general practitioners, related to falling incomes relative to their specialist colleagues. Nurses also recount working harder in hospitals and community settings, as hospitals are discharging patients 'sicker and quicker'. These problems with morale in health care are compounded by constant media reports about 'crises' in our system.

Do we have a more privatised health system now? Yes, there has been a modest shift from the public to the private arena, notably in the use of private hospitals and in services provided by private medical practitioners. Nevertheless, we still see about 50 million occasions of non-inpatients in public hospitals, which also provide the great majority of acute inpatient bed-days. The private hospitals, private health insurance companies and specialists continue to lobby for greater public subsidy of private health insurance, and the federal government rebate, which came into effect in 1999 under the Howard Government, achieved this objective. The causes and effects of this controversial private health insurance subsidy are given a prominent and close examination, along with the policies of the Rudd and Gillard Labor governments.

This edition of *Health Care and Public Policy* focuses on the main trends and the changes and challenges in the health care system in Australia in the new millennium. Medicare is still central to our health care system, hospitals and nursing homes continue to attract the bulk of health care expenditure, much health care remains uncoordinated, and private fee-for-service medical practice appears to be beyond criticism. Heart disease and cancer still dominate the public health agenda, and the health of the Aboriginal and Torres Strait Islander Peoples is still a national disgrace. Significant policy reform is much talked about but seldom achieved.

The two exceptions in the second half of the last century were the introduction of Medibank (reintroduced as Medicare in 1984) and the implementation of casemix-based funding in Australian hospitals. Medicare has been in place for 30 years and casemix-based hospital funding (now called activity-based funding) became mandatory for Commonwealth payments to the states and territories, under the National Health Reform Agreement of 2011.

Closer examination of these two periods of significant reform in health care policy suggests that changes in the broader political arena created the opportunities for health care reform. As Day and Klein (1992) in the United Kingdom and Tuohy (1999) in Canada have reminded us, broad structural change in health care is rare, and when it does occur, it is most commonly in response to a 'window of opportunity' created by the government of the day. In addition, governments open these windows onto 'landscapes' of health policy ideas that are in constant flux.

The most obvious structural change in Australia occurred in 1975 with the introduction of Medibank, a universal tax-based health insurance system. This significant health care reform was part of a broader platform of social policy reforms introduced by the Whitlam Government between 1972 and 1975. Medibank was an integral part of Whitlam's equity agenda, along with reforms in education, women's rights and so on.

The other significant health care reform, the introduction of casemix-based hospital funding in Victoria after the 1992 election, was also made possible by circumstances in the broader public policy arena, most notably political support for the Kennett Government in both houses of parliament, a large majority in the lower house and a substantial budget deficit.

In both cases, there was an historical conjuncture between the desire for change on the part of health policymakers and the opportunity for change created by the governments of the day. Additionally, the principles of Medibank and casemix were consistent with the philosophies of those particular governments (equity and fiscal prudence, respectively). An 'elective affinity' existed between the health policies chosen by the government and health policymakers' perceptions of what needed to be done.

All the 'tinkering' with private health insurance during the Howard Government (1996–2007) was, in our view, ill-conceived at best. The real problems are with the quality of care. In Australia, about 25 patients each day die as a result of hospital treatment for reasons that are avoidable. Nowhere was this more evident than in the Bundaberg hospital fiasco and in similar though less dramatic failures in other states.

The Rudd Government was elected in late 2007 with a mandate to 'end the blame game' between the federal and state and territory governments in Australia. To achieve this objective, it established the National Health and Hospitals Reform Commission (NHHRC). The commission's final report, released in 2009, undoubtedly provides an excellent review of policy issues and options, in the context of an ageing population and growth in chronic diseases and the rapidly increasing cost of medical and hospital care. On current trends, without significant policy changes, the proportion of GDP spent on health care was estimated in the report to rise from 9.3 per cent in 2003–04 to 12.4 per cent in 2032–33, a massive 33 per cent increase.

There were many commendable recommendations in the report. It adopted an appropriately cautious approach to massive extension of Commonwealth responsibilities in this area. All the essential expertise in the funding, planning and governance of hospitals lies with the states and territories. Despite the obvious problems the states and territories have experienced with these roles, the federal government needs to support them in improving their performance. A major change recommended to reduce the blame game was for the Commonwealth to assume all funding responsibility for primary care, including that of outpatients and accident and emergency services in public hospitals.

The commission proposed the creation of a national network of primary health care centres. It proffered that the centres would offer a comprehensive range of primary health care services, including 24-hour emergency care, and help ease the burden on public hospitals. It argued, also, for increased investment in health promotion and disease prevention. Moreover, the proposals to improve equity in access to dental care are long overdue. Our criticisms of the report relate mainly to omissions, most of which touch on the role of the medical profession, and on claims about not changing the balance between public and private funding for the next decade. Apparently, the rest of the world is envious of the fact that we have the balance right!

The other major issue in our system of financing and providing health care is the vital one of the equity or fairness achieved by these arrangements. In our view, it is the responsibility of the more fortunate and affluent members of communities to support less-fortunate citizens. A good deal of evidence supports the claim that societies with these values (emphasising social justice or fairness) achieve better health outcomes for their populations than the United States and others with very different, more individualistic, neo-liberal values.

Data on expenditure from the Organisation for Economic Co-operation and Development (OECD) shows the proportion of expenditure that is publicly funded across the OECD countries. In Australia, 68 per cent of our health care expenditure derives from taxation. In terms of public funding, this makes us fifth lowest in the OECD. The only nations that are worse, from our view, are the United States at the very bottom, and Switzerland, Greece and Portugal. The United Kingdom, France, Germany and other European countries achieve more equitable funding arrangements, with more than 80 per cent of expenditure being financed from taxation.

The high proportion of private funding in Australia is a reflection of the prevalence of high out-of-pocket payments for many specialist medical services, for medications and for most dental services. Similar considerations apply to the fees for private health insurance. In all these instances, private payments are made irrespective of the income and health status of the patients, subject to a limited amelioration as a result of safety nets and provisions for people in the lowest income brackets.

Here, we foreshadow the more detailed assessment in later chapters of the changes, in part based on the NHHRC report, that were actually implemented by the Commonwealth and state and territory governments via the National Health Reform Agreement of 2011. The principal omission was the failure to implement the NHHRC's recommendation for the takeover of all responsibility by the Commonwealth for primary care. This was due to opposition from state and territory governments, which, by 2011, were dominated by the Coalition parties.

Nevertheless, the National Health Reform Agreement did promote the use of activity-based funding for payments to the states and territories, a considerable increase in Commonwealth funding over a specified timeframe, and the creation of several new organisations to deal with funding, performance measurement and quality-of-care issues. Decentralisation of funding and management to local hospital networks was also included in the agreement, along with the formation of Medicare Locals.

With the change of federal government in September 2013, it is uncertain what changes in the agreement, if any, will be implemented by the Coalition.

In addition, in light of the failure of a largely self-regulated system of medical practice to assure the quality of hospital and other care, we are concerned that current policies do not address the need for the mandatory reporting of medical errors and misadventures. Indeed, we would like to see a future in which it is possible for patients to access league tables of the performance of individual hospitals and that of individual doctors and other health professionals.

George Palmer and Stephanie Short
January 2014

Introduction

This book provides the first comprehensive introduction to health services and health care policy in Australia. It explains what governments have done and what they can do about shaping Australia's health care system.

Although a number of very useful works examine particular health policy issues, there are two shortcomings in the Australian literature in this field. The first is the lack of a comprehensive coverage. While several very useful books concentrate on specific aspects of the health care system (see Bloom 2000; Boxall & Gillespie 2013; Crichton 1990; Hancock 1999a; Lin, Smith & Fawkes 2007; Mooney & Scotton 1998; Sax 1990), none of these provides a systematic account of all the important areas from a policy perspective. Gardner's (1989, 1992, 1997) edited collections did, to some extent, help to fill this gap.

The second shortcoming is the lack of a multidisciplinary framework within which past, present and future policy developments can be examined. Duckett's and Willcox's (2011) book, for example, offers a very useful description of the health care system in Australia, without much of the public policy analysis provided here. Our book, in providing such a framework, will be useful to doctors, nurses, social workers, health service managers, health planners, policy analysts and consumers. It explains how our complex and chaotic health system has developed, as well as the reasons for the current debates and conflicts in health care.

Our objective is to introduce students, clinicians, managers and policymakers to the political, economic and social contexts within which health policies develop. We explain what the term 'policy' means and stress that it is essential to be sensitive to the discrepancies between the 'model' and the 'reality' of policymaking. A major focus is the politics of health; for example, how the various interest groups influence health policymaking, how conflicts are resolved, and most importantly, what are the major political and other factors that limit the ability of governments to solve the numerous problems that arise in the provision of health services.

The fifth edition of *Health Care and Public Policy* draws on concepts, methods of analysis and data from political science, economics, sociology, epidemiology and public health. No single perspective or discipline can provide the basis for an adequate analysis of health care and public policy. Political science is particularly useful in analysing decision-making in health care, in identifying the main actors in the process and in examining the power relations between them. Economic analysis is vital in examining issues such as health insurance and health care financing, key issues in health policy debate in this century. Sociology is important because it reminds us that health care is a social enterprise, carried out by particular interest groups, that affects various groups in society in different ways. Who controls health services, what types of health insurance do Australians want, how can health services for disadvantaged groups be improved? Finally, concepts and tools from epidemiology and new public health are employed to ensure that our analysis of the health care system is tied closely to our understanding of health.

During the 1990s, we saw a plethora of firsthand accounts published in the health field by journalists, policymakers and academics. The most useful of these included the series *Healthcover*, produced by Ron Lord, which was an excellent guide to contemporary policy developments. Two other firsthand accounts stand out: that by Richard Scotton and Christine Macdonald (1993), titled *The Making of Medibank*, and Stephen Duckett's (1994) insider account of the introduction of casemix-based funding in Victorian hospitals.

In the broader field of government action and inaction, we found accounts by Paul Kelly (1992) from the *Australian*, former federal health minister Neal Blewett (1999) and John Menadue (1999), private secretary to former prime minister Gough Whitlam, particularly insightful. More recently, Paul Dugdale (2008) published a valuable practitioner's account of health policymaking in Australia. These insider accounts are an excellent source of information and insights about the realpolitik of health care and public policy reform.

We have also drawn heavily on the ideas of a number of overseas experts in health policy analysis. Notable among these have been the insightful accounts, from an international comparative perspective, of Ted Marmor with colleagues (2012) from the United States, Rudolf Klein (2009) from Britain and Carolyn Tuohy (1999, 2009) from Canada.

Is Australia moving in the direction of a privatised system of medicine along American lines, or is the Labor Party's Medicare policy simply the thin edge of the socialist wedge? Do Australians want a National Health Service–style health system or greater freedom of choice? Is entrepreneurial medicine going to replace the general practitioner in much the same way that supermarkets have replaced the corner store? This book provides the framework within which these and further issues can be discussed and analysed.

 The first three chapters outline the conceptual framework for analysis of Australian health care and public policy. **Chapter 1** is a brief overview of the Australian health care system and includes how health services are organised and financed, and the roles of the various levels of government. We emphasise the insights into the key elements of the system gained by examining how expenditure is distributed between the various sectors and the sources of the funding for these sectors, notably the Commonwealth, state and territory governments and the private sector. We also examine the performance of our system in an international context, and note that we perform fairly well using the conventional standards of life expectancy and infant mortality.

Chapter 2 addresses the question 'what is health policy?' It describes the five main stages in the public policymaking process: agenda setting, policy formation, adoption, implementation and evaluation, and the main interest groups involved in health policymaking. We discuss the three levels at which policies can be analysed: the decision-making level, the policymaking-process level and the structural level. In discussing the evaluation of health services, we focus on questions of effectiveness, efficiency and equity, and ask 'who benefits?' Are health services accessible to all, according to health need, and why are some groups, such as immigrants and Aboriginal and Torres Strait Island peoples, serviced so poorly? In this chapter we also introduce the copious general literature on public policy, which is often neglected by health policy analysts.

In **Chapter 3**, we examine the major theoretical perspectives in public policy analysis—including economic, political science, sociological and public health perspectives—and assess their strengths and weaknesses. Which groups have the most power in shaping health policy and why? We also note that the most useful approach to policy analysis, in our view, requires a combination of insights from all these disciplinary areas.

Chapters 4 to **9** address the major issues in current health care policy, and the ones that have attracted greatest public attention. **Chapter 4** examines health insurance and health care financing, the major focus for health policy debate in this country during the last 60 years. We sketch the background to the ongoing debates about Medicare and private health insurance, and place these within an international context. This chapter emphasises that issues of medical remuneration—how doctors are paid and how much they are paid—lie at the heart of health policy debate in Australia.

Chapter 5 focuses on issues relating to the organisation of health care services. The major focus here is on hospital provision, since the largest proportion of all expenditure on health goes to institutions. One of the main points to emerge from this chapter is that health insurance is often blamed for problems that emanate from other sources. A maldistribution of health care resources, inefficiencies in the provision of services, and dramatic cases of the provision of poor and life-threatening care are just some of the problems that have to be rectified through organisational reforms. In this chapter we also examine in some detail recent national policies dealing with public hospitals, including the move to activity-based funding, and the care of the aged and the provision of pharmaceuticals.

Chapter 6, the workforce chapter, focuses on those occupations in the health workforce that have major implications for the rest of the system. We examine a wide range of occupations, including medicine, nursing, the allied health professions, social work and dentistry. We look at the demand and supply for medical practitioners and refer to the transfer of nursing education to federally funded higher education institutions. Relevant reviews and recommendations with regard to alternative and complementary practitioners, and unpaid providers of health care, are also discussed within the context of the future health care needs of Australia's population. This chapter brings us up to date with international and national developments relevant to the health workforce. The tone for contemporary developments was set by the *World Health Report 2006: Working Together for Health*, with its emphasis on working together within and across countries. This global perspective is reflected in research on health workforce governance, which brings together concerns around the quality of education with issues of safety and the right to health. The Australian Health Practitioner Regulation Agency, established in 2010, is the overarching national registration and accreditation agency for the regulated health profession groups, which comprise over half a million registered health practitioners.

Technological developments continue to play an important role in generating increased costs of health care. In **Chapter 7**, we discuss developments that have significant implications for the health care system and policymaking; namely, the regulation and control of medical practice, entrepreneurial medicine, fraud and overservicing and 'unnecessary' surgery. The need for scrutiny of medical practices generally and for the further development of technology assessment in Australia is also emphasised. We also focus attention on variations in hospital service provision between areas and on medical overservicing, drawing particularly on research conducted by Professor Jeff Richardson.

Chapter 8 deals with the importance of public health. Although most health observers would agree that 'prevention is better than cure', there is still limited funding for preventative and health promotion strategies. Public health comprises less than 2 per cent of national health expenditure. Major initiatives in prevention and health promotion are discussed, including medical prevention, implementation of healthy lifestyle campaigns, and developments in line with the new public health approach, including reforms in tobacco regulation and taxation, developments in the field of illicit drugs, and strategies on HIV and AIDS. The Rudd Government devoted significant attention to encouraging healthy lifestyles, with a focus on alcohol misuse, tobacco control and obesity prevention. More significant, and lasting perhaps, was the legislation passed in 2012 that saw Australia become the first country in the world to implement plain packaging tobacco legislation. Of ongoing concern is the role played by industry groups in contributing to or addressing the harmful effects of alcohol, and ultra-processed foods and drinks.

Chapter 9 examines more closely health services for disadvantaged consumer groups—those groups that are disadvantaged within our current cultural, political and economic climate. A social justice perspective that views access to health and health care as a right, rather than a privilege, underpins this chapter. The universal health coverage framework promulgated by the World Health Organization is highlighted. Policy developments relevant to women, men, immigrants, Aboriginal and Torres Strait Islander peoples, people with mental health problems, people with intellectual and other disabilities, and older persons are given particular attention. In respect of people with mental health problems, we note how widespread these problems are in Australia. We emphasise concerns about the treatment of people with mental health problems, and with the practice of psychiatry, with its concentration on the use of drugs of dubious efficacy and safety. The chapter highlights the historic legislation to introduce the national disability insurance scheme, DisabilityCare Australia, in 2013, possibly Australia's most significant social policy reform since Medicare.

We assess recent research on the social determinants of health and Indigenous health in Australia, and in the context of globalisation, examine the renewed emphasis on primary health care in both developed and developing countries.

Chapters 10 and **11** explain how current conflicts and tensions might be resolved and how health policymaking processes might be improved. We note the increased attention to policy learning from other countries, and how some useful and some not so useful policy initiatives have been based on the experience of other countries. Particular emphasis is given to public accountability in health care, and we examine future health needs in the light of current trends and policies. We observe with regret that many of the most important policy issues, notably those associated with medical practice and quality of care, have often been neglected, while issues of lesser importance, such as the subsidising of private health insurance, have been the focus of considerable attention.

In **Chapter 10**, the strengthening of community and consumer participation in health care and the refurbishing of Commonwealth–state relationships are examined in some detail. In this chapter, the NHHRC report is highlighted. We welcome this thorough report but also identify some notable omissions, especially on the equity of the current financing arrangements. The report did not challenge the existing Medicare Benefits Schedule of fees, nor the predominance of fee-for-service medicine. We also examine the policy responses of the Commonwealth and state and territory governments to the report, as encapsulated in the National Health Reform Agreement of 2011. We welcome the fact that activity-based funding for public hospitals has, at long last, been adopted nationally, and that a consensus had been reached about the respective roles of the Commonwealth and state and territory governments in health matters.

In **Chapter 11**, we stand back from the current confusion and conflicts in order to take a broad view of the possibilities for future health policy developments in Australia. Ted Marmor's 2007 book *Fads, Fallacies and Foolishness in Medical Care Management and Policy* is highly relevant in assessing many policy proposals. We adopt a sceptical attitude to the gloom and doom predicted in some quarters by the ageing of the population. We note that the Australian media are especially prone to giving undue prominence to the views of uninformed critics, especially those ideologues who would prefer a highly privatised system of health care provision.

With this fifth edition of *Health Care and Public Policy* we welcome again the opportunity to contribute to a better-informed debate about the future of Australia's most commendable health care system.

The Australian health care system

The brief overview of the principal characteristics of the Australian health care system presented in this chapter introduces the institutions, services and providers and the organisational and funding arrangements that are the focus of health policy. In addition, we review the available evidence on the health status of the Australian population, and of the various groups that constitute it. The emphasis is on describing the health system as it exists in 2014 and foreshadowing the problems and issues that public policies have been designed to address.

It is not part of our purpose to present a vast array of statistical information. For an extensive and up-to-date coverage of facts and figures on the Australian health care system, the reader is referred to the biennial report of the Australian Institute of Health and Welfare (AIHW) (2012a) and its annual report, *Health Expenditure Australia* (2013b). We have provided a list of websites for obtaining the most up-to-date data and information on page 429.

In using the phrase 'health care system', we are conscious that the services, institutions and organisational arrangements we describe are concerned primarily with the treatment and care of those who are ill. For this reason, some people have referred to the 'illness care system' to identify these phenomena. However, if the purpose of the health care system is to undertake activities designed to promote the health status of the recipients—that is, to influence the outcomes associated with health services—there is no difficulty in continuing to use this well-established terminology. The word 'system' is also a convenient method of describing a collection of entities that are related to one another. It is not intended to imply that the relationships are of a coherent, integrated or systematic kind. Indeed, we demonstrate in later chapters that the relationships within the system typically do not possess these attributes.

The Australian health care system is the product of a diverse range of economic, social, technological, legal, constitutional and political factors, some of which are unique to Australia. Nevertheless, many of the characteristics of the system have been derived from other countries. The inevitable British influence from the beginning of European settlement continued to be highly significant in determining many aspects of the way health services were organised until after World War II, when there was considerable opposition from the medical profession and other groups to following the British example of introducing a national health service. The voluntary health insurance arrangements introduced in 1953 by a conservative government were based, in part, on similar systems that had become the dominant method of paying for health care in the United States.

The Canadian model of universal, taxation-funded health insurance formed the core of the Medibank scheme that commenced in 1975 and, after its early demise in the late 1970s, was resurrected in 1984 under the title of Medicare. The tendency to look to the United States as the source of technology, funding and organisational initiatives and the inspiration for new policies still exists in Australia. A notable example of this was the recent introduction of comprehensive casemix funding (now renamed activity-based funding) for all the larger Australian public hospitals. The United States' diagnosis related group system of patient classification has formed the basis of the locally developed classification (see **Chapter 5**). However, it is our perception that in recent years there has been an increased realisation among Australian health policy analysts and politicians that we must rely on our own innovations and solutions to improve our health care system in all its aspects. We explore in more detail in **Chapter 10** the issues associated with the transferability of health service policies between countries.

Expenditure on health services and sources of funds

To outline the characteristics of the Australian health care system in this chapter, it is helpful to present details of the expenditure on aggregate categories of services and the sources of funding of these services. It should be emphasised that official data in Australia is based on the financial year, from July 1 to June 30 of the following year. The financial year from 1 July 2012 to 30 June 2013 is then expressed by convention as 2012–13. It should also be noted that expenditure data may be expressed either in *current price terms*, which is without any adjustment for price changes as compared with other periods, or in *constant price values*. In the latter case, adjustments are made for price changes between the periods covered so that the impact of these changes is removed from the values.

Table 1.1, for the financial year 2011–12, enables us to highlight the relative importance of the specified health services as measured by the resources devoted to their provision, and the relative importance of each of the major sources of funding supporting these services. In particular, classifying by the source of funds shows the

Table 1.1 Total health expenditure, current prices, by area of expenditure and source of funds[a], 2011–12 ($ million)

| Area of expenditure | Government | | | | | | Non-government | | | | Total health expenditure | Percentage recurrent expenditure |
| | Australian Government | | | | State and local | Total | Health insurance funds | Individuals | Other[c] | Total | | |
	DVA	DHA and other	Premium rebates[b]	Total								
Total hospitals	1776	15 130	2630	19 536	22 905	42 441	6287	2450	2331	11 068	53 509	40.4
Public hospital services[d]	853	14 883	337	16 072	22 411	38 483	805	1117	1630	3552	42 034	31.8
Private hospitals	924	247	2293	3464	494	3958	5483	1334	701	7517	11 475	8.7
Patient transport services	151	55	75	281	2084	2365	179	351	96	626	2991	2.3
Medical services	837	17 278	502	18 617	–	18 617	1200	2955	1128	5283	23 900	18.1
Dental services	104	956	528	1587	718	2305	1261	4736	34	6031	8336	6.3
State/territory provider	–	–	–	–	718	718	–	20	22	42	760	0.6
Private provider	104	956	528	1587	–	1587	1261	4716	12	5989	7576	5.7
Other health practitioners	236	1061	250	1547	8	1555	599	1928	390	2916	4472	3.4
Community health and other[e]	1	1121	–	1122	5703	6825	1	115	149	265	7090	5.4
Public Health	–	1503	–	1503	663	2166	–	20	47	66	2232	1.7
Medications	467	8492	21	8980	–	8980	50	9733	78	9860	18 839	14.2
Benefit-paid pharmaceuticals	467	7963	–	8430	–	8430	–	1665	–	1665	10 096	7.6
All other medications	–	528	21	549	–	549	50	8067	78	8195	8744	6.6
Aids and appliances	2	425	204	631	–	631	488	2503	65	3056	3687	2.8

(continued)

Table 1.1   Total health expenditure, current prices, by area of expenditure and source of funds[a], 2011–12 ($ million) (continued)

Area of expenditure	Government						Non-government				Total health expenditure	Percentage recurrent expenditure
	Australian Government				State and local	Total	Health Insurance funds	Individuals	Other[c]	Total		
	DVA	DHA and other	Premium rebates[b]	Total								
Administration	43	485	460	988	300	1288	1100	–	2	1102	2390	1.8
Research	2	3854	–	3855	798	4653	–	5	281	286	4939	3.7
Total recurrent funding[f]	3619	50 357	4671	58 647	33 179	91 826	11 165	24 795	4599	40 560	132 386	100.0
Capital expenditure	–	336	–	336	5111	5447	–	–	2408	2408	7855	
Total health funding[g]	3619	50 694	4671	58 983	38 290	97 274	11 165	24 795	7007	42 968	140 241	
Medical expenses tax rebate	–	541	–	541	–	541	–	–541	–	–541	–	
Total health funding	3619	51 235	4671	59 524	38 290	97 815	11 165	24 254	7007	42 426	140 241	

Notes
(a) Tables show funding provided by the Australian Government, state and territory governments and local government authorities and by the major non-government sources of funding for health care. Values have been rounded.
(b) Includes the rebate on health insurance premiums that can be claimed either directly from the Australian Government through the taxation system or through a reduced premium being charged by the private health insurance fund (with a subsequent reimbursement to the fund by the Australian Government).
(c) 'Other' includes expenditure on health goods and services by workers' compensation and compulsory third-party motor vehicle insurers as well as other sources of income for service providers.
(d) Public hospital services exclude any dental services, community health services, patient transport services, and public health and health research undertaken by the hospital. Can include services provided off the hospital site such as hospital in the home, dialysis or other services.
(e) 'Other' denotes other non-institutional.
(f) Non-government capital consumption (depreciation) is included as part of recurrent expenditure.
(g) Total health expenditure has not been adjusted for the funding of non-specific tax expenditure.

Source: Data based on data from Table A3, Australian Institute of Health and Welfare 2013b, *Health Expenditure Australia 2011-12*, Health and Welfare expenditure series no.50, cat. no. HWE 59, AIHW, Canberra, pp. 71 & 79 (notes)

relative importance of the Commonwealth and state governments and of the private sector in financing the different aspects of health service provision.

The major role played by governments in financing health services in Australia is indicated by the fact that 69 per cent of total health expenditure was derived from this source in 2011–12. However, this proportion is relatively low by the standards of many other developed countries. For example, the comparable UK, Norwegian and Swedish values are over 80 per cent (OECD 2013). As we discuss in **Chapter 10**, this value raises important issues about the equity of health care provision and funding in Australia since out-of-pocket expenditure on health has a disproportionately larger impact on the finances of the poorest members of the community. Over 64 per cent of all government funding comes from the Commonwealth, with the Medicare payments in respect of medical fees and public hospital services being the items of greatest significance.

From a policy perspective, the expenditure data provide the basis for assessing, for example, where the objective of containing or reducing health care costs might be focused. Changes over time in the rate of growth of individual health expenditure categories may also alert governments and others to the need for policy-based interventions.

These data can also form the starting point for ascertaining whether too many resources are being devoted to certain types of services and too few to services that might yield greater benefits. Many policy analysts in Australia and elsewhere have pointed to the very high proportion of health expenditure devoted to institutional care. The 2011–12 financial year data indicate that 40.5 per cent of recurrent health expenditure was associated with this sector. The value somewhat underestimates the total resources devoted to institutions: most capital consumption and expenditure is for hospitals, some of the expenditure on medical services represents doctors' fees charged to private patients in public and private hospitals, and a proportion of pharmaceutical expenditure is also for the treatment of patients in hospitals.

As shown in table 1.1, the total recurrent and capital expenditure on health services in 2011–12 in current prices was approximately $140 billion, which represented about 9.3 per cent of Australia's gross domestic product (GDP) in that year. In comparing this value to those in the corresponding AIHW publications before 2007, it should be noted that the current value for total health expenditure excludes that for high-level (nursing home) aged care services. Expenditure on these services represented approximately 0.6 per cent of GDP in 2006–07 and 2005–06. The reasons for treating aged care facilities (nursing home) expenditure as part of social welfare expenditure are discussed in **Chapter 5**, including our reservations about the change.

The ratio of 8.9 per cent that total health expenditure represented of GDP in 2010 is slightly lower than that of most developed countries, with only the

Table 1.2   Total health expenditure as a proportion of gross domestic product and per person $US (PPP)[a] 2000, 2006, 2010: developed OECD countries

Country	2000		2006		2010	
	Health expd. GDP%	Per person $US (PPP)	Health expd. GDP%	Per person $US (PPP)	Health expd. GDP%	Per person $US (PPP)
Australia	8.1	2259	8.5	3168	8.9	3800
Austria	10.0	2898	10.2	3733	11.0	4457
Belgium	8.1	2245	9.5	3242	10.5	3965
Canada	8.8	2519	10.0	3672	11.4	4445
Denmark	8.7	2507	9.9	3573	11.1	4495
Finland	7.2	1853	8.3	2762	9.0	3239
France	10.1	2544	11.0	3435	11.7	4016
Germany	10.4	2677	10.6	3564	11.5	4349
Greece	8.0	1451	9.7	2606	9.5	2624
Iceland	9.5	2740	9.1	3267	9.3	3299
Ireland	6.1	1761	7.5	3182	9.3	3780
Italy	7.9	2028	9.0	2684	9.4	3019
Japan	7.6	1969	8.2	2604	9.6	3213
Netherlands	8.0	2340	10.0	4087	12.1	5028
New Zealand	7.6	1610	8.8	2389	10.2	3042
Norway	8.4	3043	8.6	4606	9.4	5413
Portugal	9.3	1654	10.0	2301	10.8	2767
Spain	7.2	1538	8.4	2545	9.6	3034
Sweden	8.2	2286	8.9	3191	9.5	3717
Switzerland	9.9	3221	10.4	4247	10.9	5299
United Kingdom	7.0	1827	8.4	2997	9.6	3422
United States	13.7	4791	15.9	7111	17.7	8247

Notes

(a) PPP = purchasing power parity; adjusts $US values according to the existing exchange rate of the local currency and its purchasing power in that country relative to the United States.

Source: Data based on OECD (2013a), *OECD. Stat Extracts*, <http://stats.oecd.org> accessed on 12 December 2013

United States (15.9 per cent) having a ratio that is substantially higher (see table 1.2). It should be noted that there are some differences in the way health expenditure is defined and estimated in each country. Of most importance is that other Organisation for Economic Co-operation and Development (OECD) countries include nursing home expenditure as part of health expenditure. The international agency attempts to make the data as comparable as possible but some definitional differences remain; these are unlikely to affect the comparisons in any important manner.

Butler (1998) presents long-term trends in health expenditure and funding in Australia and detailed international comparisons. Butler also carefully analysed some of the possible pitfalls in these comparisons, including the varying treatment of tax expenditures; that is, governments allowing certain outlays by individuals to be claimed as tax deductions. This work also provides an excellent summary of the factors that influence such trends and comparisons.

Figure 1.1 Proportion of recurrent health expenditure, current prices, by area of expenditure, Australia, 2011–12 (%)

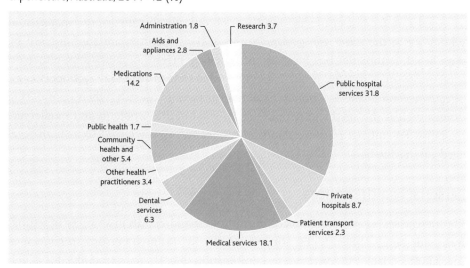

Source: Data based on Australian Institute of Health and Welfare 2013b, *Health Expenditure Australia 2011-12*, Health and welfare expenditure series no.50, cat. no. HWE 59, AIHW, Canberra, pp. 71 & 79 (notes)

Figure 1.1 displays some key data of table 1.1 in diagrammatic form. It is a useful summary picture of the relative contribution of each type of health expenditure to total recurrent expenditure on the health services. The domination of institutional care, medical expenses and medications in the health expenditure scene is clearly illustrated in the diagram, along with the much more modest contributions of public and community health.

Health care services

Hospital and aged care facility services

The hospital sector includes acute care public hospitals, private hospitals conducted on either a for-profit or a not-for-profit basis, mental hospitals administered by state health authorities, and other hospitals, including geriatric and rehabilitation hospitals and those for which the defence forces are responsible.

In general, hospitals are institutions that provide inpatient accommodation together with medical, nursing and other services. Most hospitals cater predominantly for patients whose treatment and care is of relatively short duration. As well as inpatient treatment, some hospitals also provide accident and emergency and outpatient clinic services. These short-stay, acute care institutions, both public and private, are the focus of many of the major policy and political issues discussed later. The category of public hospital services, which includes certain longer-stay public hospitals, repatriation and public psychiatric hospitals, accounts for approximately 31.8 per cent of all recurrent expenditure on health, with private hospitals being responsible for a further 8.7 per cent (table 1.1).

Aged care facilities cater for long-stay chronically ill patients, the majority of whom are in the older age groups. Some of these facilities are administered by state health authorities but most are operated by private organisations, either on a for-profit or a not-for-profit basis. The adequacy, quality and appropriateness of nursing home care is a policy issue that surfaces frequently when considering groups such as the aged and people with mental health problems and intellectual disability. For official purposes, nursing homes are now referred to as high-level aged care facilities.

Personal health services

Health services are provided outside institutions to individuals in a variety of settings by a wide range of health practitioners. Medically qualified persons, in general or specialist practice or in some cases a combination of both, are responsible for a high proportion of all these services. Most doctors in Australia work in private practice on a fee-for-service basis—that is, they are self-employed—but some are the salaried employees of hospitals, community health centres and related agencies provided by government and non-government organisations.

As table 1.1 indicates, health expenditure on medical services represented 18.1 per cent of total recurrent health expenditure in 2011–12, the largest individual item after hospital expenditure. This table also shows that most funding for medical services (78 per cent) is provided by the Australian Government under the Medicare program (see **Chapter 4**). Further details of medical staff and medical services are provided in **Chapters 6** and **7**.

Dentists, optometrists, physiotherapists, pharmacists and psychologists also provide personal health services, predominantly in private practice settings. Dental services account for the largest proportion of recurrent health expenditure (6.3 per cent) in this category; most of the funding is derived from direct payments by individuals. In recent years, there has been an increase in service provision by a range of practitioners, including chiropractors, naturopaths and acupuncturists, who would regard themselves as providing complementary or alternative health care services. The relationships between all these groups and the medical profession are discussed in **Chapter 6**.

Medications

Medications include prescription drugs subsidised by the Australian Government under the Pharmaceutical Benefits Scheme (PBS) and other medications that are available on a prescription but not included in the PBS. 'Over-the-counter' drugs available without a prescription make up most of the remaining items in this group.

As table 1.1 shows, total expenditure on medications is substantial and in 2011–12 represented 14.2 per cent of all recurrent expenditure. The Australian Government financed about 48 per cent of this expenditure, with the proportion paid for directly by individuals (mainly on non-PBS pharmaceuticals) making up most of the remaining expenditure. Further details of the PBS scheme are provided in **Chapter 5**.

Public health and community health services

The phrase 'public health' is used in a number of senses in the health services literature and elsewhere. For our purposes, we adopt the AIHW definition as those activities that are focused on communities and other groups of people, rather than on individuals. These services are usually provided by governments and include environmental health measures, health education, health promotion and other disease prevention activities, including immunisation programs. Public health and related activities of the Commonwealth and state governments are described below. Issues associated with disease prevention, health promotion and the 'new public health' are analysed in **Chapter 8**.

The need for a greater emphasis to be placed on the prevention of disease surfaces regularly in the policy prescriptions of governments and opposition parties. However, the expenditure on public health in Australia remains very modest. Table 1.1 indicates that in 2011–12, expenditure on these programs was 1.7 per cent of recurrent health expenditure.

Community health services, as defined by the AIHW, include non-residential services offered to patients in a community setting, usually by governments or voluntary organisations. Well-baby clinics, family planning centres and health services delivered to specific groups, notably Indigenous peoples, those with mental health problems, migrants and women are included in this category. (Since 2003–04, domiciliary care services funded under the home and community care (HACC) program have been transferred from health to welfare expenditure.) Table 1.1 indicates that 5.4 per cent of recurrent expenditure was devoted to community health and related services in 2011–12.

Organisational, administrative and financial arrangements—the roles of governments

A major influence on most aspects of health care is the presence of a federal system of government in Australia. There are six state governments, plus the Northern Territory and Australian Capital Territory governments, and a central (Commonwealth, federal or Australian) government. In addition, there is a system of local government, with over 560 local government areas in Australia.

Each of these three levels of government has various powers and responsibilities concerning health care, though the role of local government is a relatively minor one. As we indicate in later chapters, the Australian Constitution shapes and constrains these powers. However, the political processes, including which policies governments perceive as being desirable or expedient to implement, may be even more important in determining the responsibilities actually assumed by each level of government.

Differences between the major political parties, the Australian Labor Party (ALP) and the Coalition parties (the Liberal and National parties) in their stances on policy issues also have an important bearing on this matter. Generally, conservative (Coalition) Commonwealth governments have been more inclined than their ALP counterparts to perceive health as primarily a state responsibility. However, in the last days of the Howard Government in 2007 several initiatives were undertaken that ran counter to the usual stances of the conservative parties, including the attempted takeover of a public hospital in Tasmania. See **Chapter 4** for details of the reasons for these policy initiatives.

The principal responsibilities for health care by level of government as they exist at present are summarised below. In a later section, we indicate how many of these responsibilities are intertwined, both with one another and with the activities and roles of the private sector. It should also be noted that one of the major policy proposals of the ALP in the run-up to the 2007 election was to revamp Commonwealth–state relations, especially in the health area. Initially the

Rudd Government maintained the option of taking over all health funding if its proposed reforms were not met to its satisfaction. However, after the change of the leadership in 2010, the Gillard Government did not pursue this objective further.

Details of the initiatives undertaken to reform inter-government relations, including the establishment in 2008 of the National Health and Hospitals Reform Commission (NHHRC), the reports of the Commission and the package of health policy reforms agreed upon by the Commonwealth and the states in 2011 (the National Health Reform Agreement) are discussed at length in **Chapters 5** and **10**.

Commonwealth–state relationships

It is often claimed by those describing the Australian health care system that the Australian Government is primarily responsible for funding health services via health insurance arrangements and direct payments to the states, while the states are mainly responsible for the direct provision of services. There is a measure of truth in this generalisation; in particular, the financial dominance of the Commonwealth and its control over health insurance are the principal features of the central government's role in health in Australia.

It is important to emphasise, however, that health insurance and related aspects of the system have a direct impact on the provision of services, and the providers and consumers of these services. Thus, policies about hospital charges, including free hospitalisation under the Australian Health Care Agreements (formerly the Medicare Agreements), have had a profound influence on the practices and incomes of hospital-based medical specialists. Similarly, the methods of funding hospital and medical services and pharmaceuticals have a considerable impact on the finances of individuals in their roles as consumers and as taxpayers. They also generate much debate about the fairness and equity of the financial arrangements that support the health care system. These issues, including the political conflicts they have generated, are discussed in **Chapter 4**.

The Australian Government's roles in health care

Federal–state financial relations, as they affect health insurance and public hospitals, are introduced in the next section, and the policy issues these relationships raise form part of the subject matter of **Chapter 4**. The health insurance program, Medicare, constitutes a major part of the Australian Government's responsibility for health matters. The Department of Health provides policy advice to the minister for health about health insurance issues. Under the Abbott Government, the

Medicare program is administered by Medicare Australia as part of the portfolio of the Department of Human Services. The Department of Health remains responsible for Medicare policy.

Medicare Australia also plays a role in administering the payments and related aspects of a number of other Australian Government health programs including the Pharmaceutical Benefits Scheme (PBS), the Repatriation Pharmaceutical Benefits Scheme (RPBS) and the Private Health Insurance Rebate (PHIR).

Department of Health responsibilities include providing subsidies to patients and institutions under the nursing home benefits and assistance schemes, payment of domiciliary nursing care benefits and benefits to home nursing organisations, and subsidies to family planning and blood transfusion services. In addition, the department provides financial support for a wide range of national and state community health activities, health promotion and medical and health services research. Other responsibilities include the National HIV/AIDS Strategy, the National Drug Strategy, the National Mental Health Strategy and the National Women's Health Program.

A statutory authority, the Australian Institute of Health and Welfare (AIHW), collects health-related statistics and undertakes research into health status and the effectiveness of health technology. The institute is responsible to the Minister for Health and reports to the parliament through him or her.

A further important responsibility of the Commonwealth is the provision of hospital and medical services to eligible veterans, their widows and their dependants. These functions are administered by the Department of Veterans' Affairs (DVA), which has moved to a purchasing model. Instead of providing services directly, DVA now funds treatment by medical personnel, public and private hospitals and allied health providers. Veterans' hospitals (with one exception) were privatised, closed or transferred to state governments between 1992 and 1995. The Department of Defence provides for the health care of defence force personnel.

Other health activities of the Commonwealth include aspects of occupational health, principally of a research and educational nature, for which Safe Work Australia is responsible. Commonwealth services and funding directed specifically to the Aboriginal and Torres Strait Island communities are now administered by the Office of Aboriginal and Torres Strait Islander Health in the Department of Health. These are discussed in **Chapter 9**.

State/territory and local government responsibilities

The states and territories finance and/or provide directly a wide range of health services. Education and health are the major items in the budgets of all jurisdictions. In 2011–12, more than 53 per cent of the running costs and almost all of the capital costs of public hospitals were provided by the states (table 1.1). The financial and legal powers of the states over public hospitals would seem to enable their statutory health authorities to influence all aspects of the operations of these institutions. In the past, however, the willingness and capacity of most states to intervene in the internal affairs of hospitals has been limited. The constraints have included considerations of clinical autonomy, the political power of the medical profession and the inability to influence the referral patterns of doctors.

The degree of control that states have exercised over public hospitals has varied widely in the past. However, in the 1980s and 1990s, all states, largely for reasons of cost containment, sought to achieve more influence via the reform of funding methods, reductions in the total stock of beds, the redistribution of bed numbers and through other aspects of hospital planning such as role delineation and networking.

State psychiatric, geriatric and developmental disability hospitals receive almost all their funding from state governments, which normally have a direct responsibility for the administration of these institutions. As table 1.1 indicates, most of the funding for community health activities as defined above is derived directly from the states. State authorities, along with local health and other authorities, are responsible for environmental health protection in areas such as food safety, water quality control, atmospheric pollution control, waste disposal and occupational health and safety.

Other public health activities include immunisation programs, the surveillance of infectious diseases and the development of disease prevention campaigns. State health authorities participate in the National Drug Strategy and similar programs on a cost-shared basis with the Commonwealth. They also provide treatment and rehabilitation programs and health educational activities. The states are also responsible for the licensing and regulation of private hospitals and private nursing homes.

The individual states previously administered an extensive system of registration requirements for health professionals, including doctors, dentists, nurses, physiotherapists, optometrists and pharmacists. The legislation differed somewhat from state to state. However, since 2010 a national system of registration has been implemented. Representatives of the Commonwealth and the states and territories via the Council of Australian Governments (COAG) had agreed in 2008 to establish an Australian Health Practitioner Regulation Agency to oversee the work of national boards for each health professional group. Separate legislation in each state was passed to establish the new national system (see **Chapter 6** for further details of the national registration of health practitioners).

The organisation of the states' participation in health matters varies from state to state. All states, moreover, have undertaken major reorganisations of the system of health administration over the past 25 years. Most aspects of state responsibilities for health services are under the control of the health departments, called the Ministry of Health in New South Wales; the Department of Health in Queensland, South Australia, Victoria, Western Australia and the Northern Territory; the ACT Health Directorate in the Australian Capital Territory; and the Department of Health and Human Services in Tasmania. In all states and territories, frequent changes in the names and roles of the health authorities have taken place and these are likely to continue in the future.

These health authorities have planning and policy units designed to develop health plans and to formulate policies dealing with specific aspects of the states' roles in health. An increasingly important function has been the development and support of information technology and computerised health information systems.

Policies associated with the organisation of state administrative arrangements for health services, including the extent to which some of state responsibilities are delegated to smaller geographically based areas, are considered in **Chapter 5**, along with the national changes implemented in 2011.

Registered health insurance funds

The role of these private organisations, of which there were 38 at 30 June 2013, has varied considerably over time depending on the nature of the arrangements that governments have made for health insurance. During the periods when Coalition governments sponsored voluntary health insurance programs, the health funds were responsible for both medical and hospital insurance. Following the reintroduction of universal health insurance by the Commonwealth government in 1984, the health funds' main business has been to provide insurance to those who wish to have private patient status if admitted to a hospital.

However, ancillary coverage for dental, optical, allied health and other non-medical services has become increasingly popular. Since 2004, moreover, the funds have been allowed to provide some coverage of the gap between the charge for medical services and the reimbursement from Medicare.

The proportion of the population covered by private health insurance had continued to decline from approximately 64 per cent in 1983, prior to the introduction of Medicare, to a low point of about 30 per cent at the end of 1999 (Private Health Insurance Administration Council 1999). However, the measures introduced by the Howard Government in 1999, as discussed in **Chapter 4**, led rapidly to an increase in coverage to the current value of approximately 47 per cent (Private Health Insurance Administration Council 2013).

Private health funds and other private sector organisations, such as the manufacturers of pharmaceutical products, continue to be part of an important structural interest group in the health care arena.

The health status of the Australian population

The ultimate objective of providing health services should be the maintenance and improvement of the health status of the population. As discussed in **Chapter 3**, health services are demanded because of their expected effect on the health status of those who consume them. In practice, however, it is difficult to assess the impact of the provision of individual health services, technologies and facilities, or of the total health care system, on the health and wellbeing of the community. An important reason for this is that the concept of health is not easy to define and is impossible to measure directly (Hall & Masters 1986). In 1999, the New South Wales Department of Health (1999) released a document that relied on an integrated measure of health '… or the health quality of life that encompasses mortality, institutionalised morbidity, ability to carry out activities and in principle, mental and emotional well-being, over a defined period'.

In the absence of appropriate direct measures of health status, it has been necessary to resort to the use of surrogates such as mortality and morbidity measures. Death rates, appropriately standardised to take into account differences in the age distribution of the populations being compared, have been the most commonly used method of assessing health status despite the obvious limitations. These include the absence of a close relationship with disease patterns and feelings of wellbeing, since a good deal of morbidity is not associated with death; for example, many psychiatric problems. Moreover, there has been much concern recently about 'quality of life' issues, and debate about whether heroic attempts to prolong life 'at all costs' are justified.

Despite these problems, the mortality experience remains the most commonly used indicator of the health status of populations. It has the considerable advantage that death is easier to define and can usually be determined with a high level of precision. The two most commonly used mortality measures are the expectation of life at birth and the infant mortality rate. The former indicates the number of years a newborn child could expect to live if they experienced the current death rates at all ages in the future. In effect, the expectation of life provides a convenient summary measure of all these rates. In particular, its method of construction ensures that populations with different age distributions can be compared directly.

The infant mortality rate for a given period is the number of deaths of children aged less than one year, expressed as a rate per 1000 live births in the same period. The tendency to use infant mortality rate, especially when comparing different countries, reflects in part the belief that many infant deaths are avoidable, and that the rate may tend to reflect the overall effectiveness of the health care system.

Table 1.3 provides information about the expectation of life at birth for 18 developed countries. The infant mortality rate for each of the countries is also shown. For life expectation, Australia has among the highest values for both males and females.

Table 1.3 Expectation of life at birth and infant mortality rates in selected developed countries, 2010

Country	Expectation of life at birth (years)	Infant mortality rate (per 1000 live births)
Australia	81.8	4.1
Canada	81.0	4.9
France	81.8	3.6
Germany	80.5	3.4
Greece	80.6	3.8
Iceland	82.0	2.2
Ireland	81.0	3.8
Italy	82.4	3.4
Japan	82.9	2.3
Netherlands	81.0	3.8
New Zealand	81.0	5.5
Norway	81.2	2.8
Spain	82.2	3.2
Sweden	81.6	2.5
Switzerland	82.6	3.8
United Kingdom	80.7	4.2
United States	78.7	6.2

Source: Data based on OECD (2013a), *OECD. Stat Extracts*, <http://stats.oecd.org>, accessed on 12 December 2013

Our infant mortality rate, however, is higher than in 12 of the countries shown in the table. On the basis of both criteria Australia fares fairly well by international standards, although improvement is undoubtedly required for Aboriginal and Torres Strait Islander peoples. Life expectancy for Indigenous Australians is between 14 and 20 years less than the life expectancy of other Australians, and infant mortality rates for this group are three to five times higher than for the rest of the population (AIHW 2008a). The health and mortality experience of Aboriginal peoples is discussed further in **Chapter 9**.

Figure 1.2 shows in graphical form the data for life expectancies for a number of OECD and other countries (panel A). Panel B displays the progress the countries have made in respect of increases in life expectancy between 1983 and 2008. Australia shows up well on both indicators. The progress made with rising life expectancies is especially notable for a number of the lower-income developing countries, including Korea, Turkey, Indonesia and India.

The other important measure of 'health' is the degree to which there are differences in Australia between the various socioeconomic groups that comprise our diverse society. Unfortunately, comprehensive information on this issue is scarce, which may have considerable implications for health policymaking. In recent years, however, there has been a concerted effort to overcome the gaps and deficiencies in our knowledge about Aboriginal and Torres Strait Islander peoples and some progress has been made in this area.

Figure 1.2 Life expectancy and rise in life expectancy between 1983 and 2008 for OECD and other countries

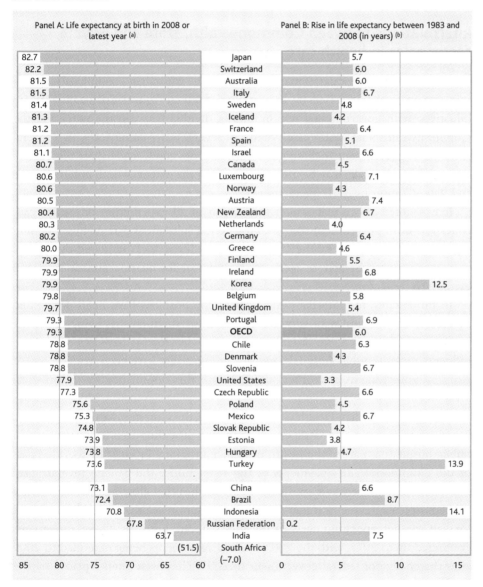

Notes

(a) 2009 for Chile, France, Mexico, Netherlands and Sweden; 2007 for Belgium and Canada

(b) 1990 for Chile, 1989 for Estonia and 1987 for Slovenia.

Source: Based on data from OECD (2011), *Society at a Glance: OECD Social Indicators* <www.oecd.org/els/ society at a glance.htm/>, accessed 28 January 2014

Several recent studies have demonstrated the presence of substantial differentials in mortality and morbidity experience between occupational and socioeconomic status groups. Research on geographical variations in infant mortality rates has also revealed major differences, which are probably related to socioeconomic status. Typically, high rates have been found in inner-city, low-income suburbs. These studies of socioeconomic and geographical variations in mortality are examined in **Chapter 9**.

Interrelations between Commonwealth, state and private sector roles in health care

As compared to other areas of major activity in the Australian economy, the health care system is characterised by a complicated mix of government and private initiatives, with governmental responsibilities divided between the states and the Commonwealth. The health care systems of several other countries with a federal structure of government, including the United States and Canada, share these characteristics, but Australia may be unique in terms of the extent of both public–private and state–Commonwealth interaction.

It was noted above that a high proportion of all expenditure on health care is derived from government sources. However, a substantial part of this spending represents subsidies paid by the Commonwealth for services rendered by doctors in private practice, by private aged care facilities or for pharmaceuticals provided by the private sector.

In most states, the internal policies of public hospitals have been dominated by their senior medical staff—doctors who identify themselves as being in private practice. In **Chapter 5**, we discuss the reasons why doctors have played such an influential role in public hospitals, and the attempts that have been made in recent years by governments and others to challenge this dominance by the medical profession.

Under the Australian Health Care Agreements, the Commonwealth made direct payments to the states to compensate them for providing free hospitalisation in public hospitals as part of the health insurance program. From 1981 to 1988, part of the Commonwealth's payments to the states under the general revenue tax-sharing arrangements was identified as being for health, following the termination of the hospital agreements under which the Commonwealth, from 1975, had paid for half the net operating costs of the state's public hospitals. These agreements continued up to 2011, with the 2003 to 2008 agreements being extended to 2009 after the change of federal government in 2007. They were then replaced by the financing arrangements set out in the National Health Reform Agreement of that year. Details of the Commonwealth–state financial agreements are discussed in **Chapter 4**.

Although most of the income received by doctors in private practice is provided by the Commonwealth, which also pays for medical education, all aspects of the legal control of the profession, including registration and the power to set fees, resided with the states until the national system of registration commenced in 2010. Similarly, the registration of private aged care facilities is a state responsibility, although a high proportion of the income of these institutions is derived from the Commonwealth subsidy.

The complex mixture of Commonwealth and state responsibilities for the provision, regulation and financing of health care is largely a product of the Commonwealth's assumption of responsibility for health insurance after World War II as part of a wider program of social welfare. The states at that time exercised extensive control over most aspects of the health care system. The social services amendment to the Australian Constitution passed in 1946 gave the Commonwealth wide powers to pass legislation dealing with hospital benefits and medical services, along with other social security benefits. The precise wording of section 51 (xxiiiA) of the Constitution is as follows:

> The provision of maternity allowances, widows pensions, child endowment, unemployment, pharmaceutical, sickness and hospital benefits, medical and dental services (but not so as to authorise any form of civil conscription) benefits to students and family allowances.

The civil conscription constraint on the power over medical and dental services had been insisted upon by the British Medical Association in Australia. Doctors had been concerned that the power over their services might be used to impose a national health service on the profession. The interpretation of the nebulous phrase 'civil conscription' became a matter for the High Court of Australia to determine.

Successive Commonwealth governments have been content to let the states retain most of the direct responsibility for health that lies outside the health insurance and financing areas. Nevertheless, the appropriate division of responsibility between the two levels of government continues to be a major policy issue. In **Chapters 4** and **10**, we examine the arguments for the notion that health should be primarily a state responsibility, and for the view that the Commonwealth must have a greater measure of involvement in health policymaking.

SUMMARY AND CONCLUSION

We conclude this chapter with diagrams of the principal components of the Australian health care system described above, and the most important relationships that exist between them. In figure 1.3, we present an organisational chart of the principal providers and funders of the system and their interactions. Governments supply either finance or

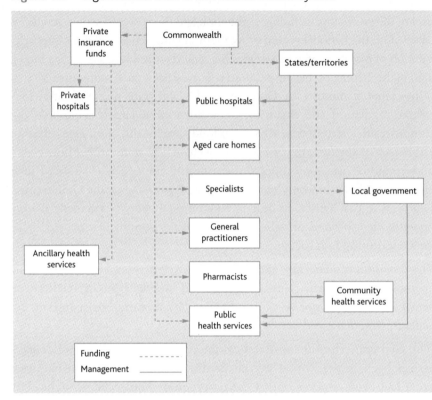

Figure 1.3   Organisational chart of the Australian health system

Source: Healy, Sharman & Lokuge (2006), p. 26

administrative oversight, including regulation and licensing arrangements, to the other individuals and organisations. The providers supply services, usually to individual patients, in the various contexts and receive payments from the several sources.

Figure 1.3 does not capture the other set of important relationships in the health care system, namely those showing the flow of funds between governments, other funders, providers and individuals. These are represented in figure 1.4. It should be noted that the population is divided into those who are patients in a given period and hence in receipt of provider services, and the rest of the population who are the beneficiaries of public health and certain community health services. Patients and the rest of the population may contribute to the flow of funds in the form of direct charges, private health insurance premiums and taxation payments.

A further perspective on the complexities of the health care system is provided by figure 1.5. This shows the ways a person with a health issue may encounter the various providers and institutions, incurring the possible treatment options. The diagram also shows the various outcomes, ranging from the resolution of the issue to placement in an aged care facility and death.

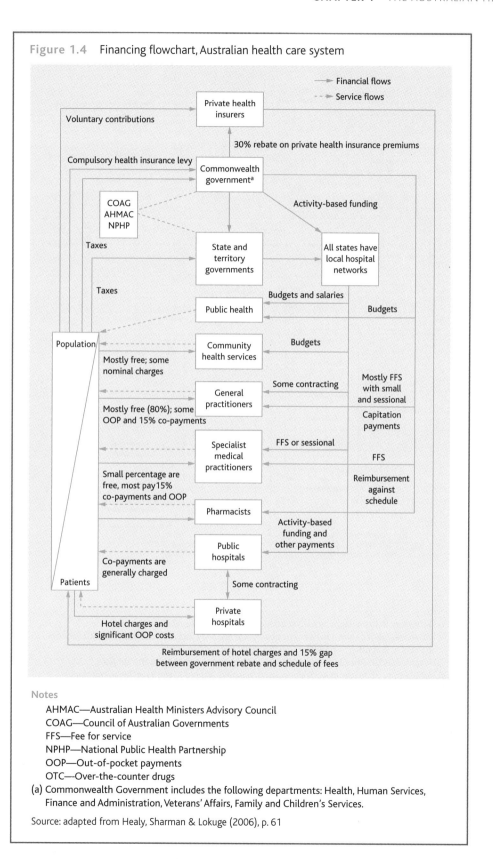

Figure 1.4   Financing flowchart, Australian health care system

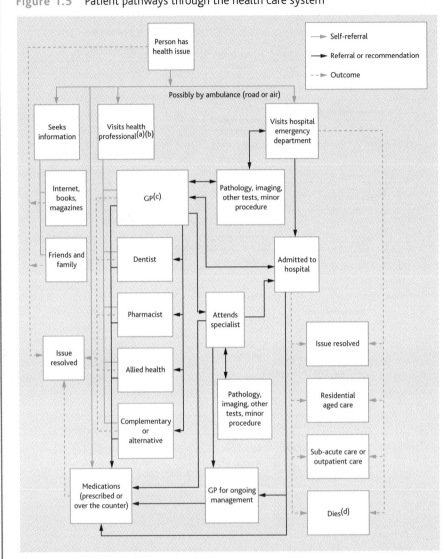

Figure 1.5   Patient pathways through the health care system

Notes

(a) This can include a telephone call to a health advice and referral service.

(b) The subcategories shown here are not complete and may include community health services and clinics, and other services for which a referral is not required.

(c) This includes GP-like clinics provided by hospitals and community health services.

(d) The majority of deaths in Australia occur in hospital, although death can be an outcome anywhere in the patient's path through the system or before any contact with the health system (such as in a motor vehicle accident).

Source: Based on Australian Institute of Health and Welfare 2012a, *Australia's health 2012*, Australia's health series no. 13, cat. no. AUS 156, AIHW, Canberra, p. 371

FURTHER READING

The Australian Health Care System (Oxford University Press 2011) by Stephen Duckett and Sharon Willcox provides a comprehensive and detailed account of all aspects of our health care system. All the topics we have discussed briefly in this chapter can be followed up in this excellent monograph.

The 2006 report by J Healy, E Sharman and B Lokuge in the WHO international series *Health Systems in Transition* also provides a useful summary of the main characteristics of the Australian health care system. Websites where these publications may be accessed are on page 429.

The various publications of the AIHW, the Commonwealth agency responsible for providing a wide range of data about most aspects of our health and welfare services, is the most important source of information that we have drawn on in compiling many of the statistics in this book.

The Australian Bureau of Statistics (ABS) provides up-to-date information on a wide range of demographic and economic phenomena, including a few that deal with health matters, notably a regular report on Australian private hospitals.

DISCUSSION QUESTIONS

1   A distinctive characteristic of the Australian health care system is our federal system of government. Summarise the principal roles and responsibilities of the Commonwealth and state/territory governments. What problems may be generated by the current distribution of responsibilities between the two levels of government?
2   The Australian system is also characterised by a complex interaction of public (government) and private funding and service provision. Some policy analysts regard this as a strength of our current arrangements and others as a weakness. What do you regard as being the main sources of this disagreement?
3   Drawing on the data presented in table 1.1, is it justified to conclude that we spend too much on institutional care and too little on public health and community health services? What further evidence might be needed to justify this conclusion?
4   The data presented in the chapter indicate that Australia performs well in relation to other countries using the criterion of life expectancy at birth, but not so well with regard to infant mortality. What are the problems with using either method as a measure of the performance of health care systems?
5   We have presented figures 1.3, 1.4 and 1.5 to summarise the principal characteristics of the provision and funding of Australian health services. How useful are these representations in promoting your understanding of the complexities of the system?

2

Public policy analysis and health care

The examination of Australia's health care system in **Chapter 1** revealed that two of the most important health policy issues relate to appropriate roles for public and private interests and for different levels of government. Much of the political controversy about health care arises from the fact that the federal government is responsible for financing a medical care system in which most services are provided by private practitioners. Since the central government pays for a high proportion of the total cost of health care, should it also have a major responsibility for policymaking and the overall planning of health services? Alternatively, should planning take place at state, regional or community level?

A policy analysis perspective is the best way to examine these and many other issues. The purpose of this and the next chapter is to develop a framework of ideas or concepts for thinking about health policy, which can then be applied to the various health care areas that make up the subject matter of the remainder of the book. This chapter explains what the term 'policy' means and reviews the main elements and questions that should be examined in reviewing each policy area. We consider the methods and approaches to policymaking and to policy analysis drawn from a range of disciplines, including the evaluation of policies. Of key importance in this endeavour is the construction of conceptual models designed to represent the relationships between a manageable number of common crucial factors that influence policy and the policymaking process across a range of areas and circumstances.

What is policy?

The term 'policy' is used in a variety of ways to cover many different types of statement, intention and action. 'Policy' may refer to the following:

- a very general statement of intentions and objectives—this interpretation is typified by the policy speeches of political leaders during parliamentary election campaigns. It includes statements such as 'Our policy is to introduce a comprehensive system of health insurance financed by taxation contributions'.

- the past course of actions of government in a particular area, such as economic, foreign or health policy—for example, 'Medicare has been the cornerstone of our health policy'
- a specific statement of future intentions such as 'Our policy will be to allow people to opt out of Medicare in order to take up private health insurance'
- a set of standing rules that are intended as a guide to action or inaction—for example, 'It is our policy not to interfere in those matters that are properly the responsibility of the states'.

Generally, the term 'health policy' embraces courses of action that affect the set of institutions, organisations, services and funding arrangements that we have called the health care system. It includes actions or intended actions by public, private and voluntary organisations that have an impact on health. The term includes political party policies that may be translated into government action at a later stage. Thus, policy may refer to a set of actions and decisions or to statements of intention. Government policy includes what governments say they will do, what they do and what they do not do.

Normally, the term 'public policies' is used when we are dealing with policies for which governments are primarily responsible. Public policies are carried out in the name of the people as a whole, with public resources, and they affect the public interest. The term 'public' implies that a distinction can be made between these activities and those of private individuals and groups (Forward 1974). It should be recognised, however, that some public policy analysts prefer to use a wider definition that embraces all policies that affect the public interest (Davis et al. 1988).

In the Australian health field, we are concerned primarily with government policymaking, although policies of private and non-governmental organisations such as private health insurance funds, private hospitals and the Australian Medical Association (AMA) impinge heavily on the overall policymaking process. Government health policymakers are found at federal, state/territory and regional levels of government and include ministers for health, heads of departments of health and other health authorities, and other senior officials.

The elements of a policy include the area affected, such as medical fees, health insurance or public hospitals; the objective or desired outcome, such as a reduction in hospital waiting lists; and the actions that have been or are to be taken, including the legislative, financial and administrative mechanisms involved in implementation.

Types of public policies

Public policies affect society in a variety of ways. Political scientists and others have made many attempts to categorise broadly these policies in a manner that will prove useful for analysing specific policy-related activities. One approach we have found useful for providing insights into health policy is that of Lowi. According to Lowi's (1964) typology, as adapted by Salisbury and Heinz (1970), there are four distinct ways in which public policies are perceived to affect individuals and organisations:

1 *distributive policies*, which consist of the provision of services or benefits to particular segments of the population. An example is the allocation of pensioner health benefit cards through the relevant Commonwealth agencies in order to make available a range of health services, such as pharmaceuticals, at no cost or at a reduced rate to pensioners. Distributive policies are characterised by the relative ease with which they can be adopted and implemented, since each policy can be implemented more or less in isolation from other policies, and without any noticeable reduction in the benefits provided to other groups.

2 *regulatory policies*, which involve the imposition of limitations or restrictions on the behaviour of individuals or groups. An example in the health field is legislation regulating the behaviour of registered health professionals, such as medical practitioners and nurses. Regulatory policies are reasonably specific and narrow in their impact. They determine who is restricted and who is given greater freedom.

3 *self-regulatory policies* are generally sought by an organisation as a means of promoting its own interests. Self-regulation may benefit an organisation directly or indirectly: being seen to be self-regulatory may enhance the official credibility of the organisation. A clear example of a self-regulatory policy is the establishment of the Australian Council on Healthcare Standards (ACHS), which accredits hospitals and aged care facilities on a voluntary basis. The AMA and the Australian Hospitals Association established this body in order to forestall government regulation. This self-regulatory principle applies equally to peer review, quality assurance and continuous quality improvement policies as developed by numerous health professions and organisations.

4 *redistributive policies*, which were characteristic of the 20th-century welfare state, consist of deliberate efforts by governments to change the distribution of income, wealth, property or rights between groups in the population. The Medicare health insurance scheme is one such case, since the cost of universal health insurance is financed in part through a compulsory income-tax levy and in part through other forms of taxation. Health insurance for the unemployed and low-income earners is therefore subsidised by higher-income earners.

In general, redistributive policies tend to provoke strong disagreement between sections of the population. Policies such as the creation of Medicare can divide the population into opposing groups: those with liberal or progressive political leanings, who favour redistribution, and those with more politically conservative attitudes, who believe that individuals and families should fend for themselves. Redistributive policies are relatively difficult to implement and even more difficult to maintain because there are always groups who gain and groups who lose when money and power are reallocated between groups. Those who possess wealth and power are understandably disinclined to give them up.

What is critical to this analytical schema is that different policies are perceived in different ways within the community. For example, when a government allocates funds in order to build a new teaching hospital, the action will proceed relatively unnoticed if it is seen as a distributive policy. If, however, it is perceived as a redistributive policy, critical opposition will be evoked among those who perceive that they are subsidising the new hospital. Thus, the same policy may be regarded as either distributive or redistributive according to the specific circumstances.

In addition, the four types of public policies are not mutually exclusive. A regulatory policy may also be redistributive. To illustrate, a registered occupation such as clinical psychology can expect to attract greater financial support from health insurance arrangements than non-registered occupations such as counselling and social welfare. We also note the caveat expressed by Hill (2013) that certain types of very important policies such as the making of war and the control of the economy do not find a place in the typology.

In spite of these and other reservations about the Lowi typology, we consider that it provides a useful basis for exploring the reasons why some health policies are implemented with a minimum of opposition while others encounter enormous opposition. As we shall see in later chapters, a distinguishing characteristic of the health field is the substantial resistance encountered to many proposed reforms that have been designed to promote the welfare of most members of the community.

What is distinctive about health policy?

What makes health policy different from other areas of policy and a subject worthy of being studied in its own right? Three elements are of critical importance. First, the medical profession's role in shaping and constraining health policy is without a counterpart in other policy areas. There is no equivalent to the medical profession in sectors such as education or social welfare. Second, the complexity of health care provision and the inability of individual consumers to distinguish between good- and poor-quality services pose special problems that render suspect the use of models derived from other areas of economic and social activity. It is inappropriate, for example, as we discuss in **Chapter 3**, to apply without substantial modifications policies based on competitive market mechanisms in the health field. Third, the nature of decision-making in health matters, where life and death issues may be involved, is associated with psychological stresses and distinctive expectations that lead the community to see health care and its providers as being 'different'.

These distinctive features of health policy indicate the need for considerable caution in applying to health the tools of analysis, interpretation and evaluation derived, for the most part, from other areas of policy. At the same time, the past tendency in Australia to ignore the existence of the formidable body of literature dealing with policy science, policy studies and policy analysis in the examination of health policy cannot only be described as unfortunate.

Special difficulties exist in health policy analysis, as compared to other areas of policy. These include the relative paucity of statistical material bearing on policy outcomes, the lack of well-developed theories and other evidence linking health care inputs to health status and consumer satisfaction, and the many factors that may influence these outcomes but that lie outside the control of policymakers. Some of these factors may be measurable but others may not be quantifiable. Critical information on the performance of individual hospitals and clinicians regarding the quality and other outcomes of specific interventions is still lacking. As we indicate in **Chapter 5**, considerable effort is currently being made to create systems to provide this information.

A comparison with economic policy analysis may be illuminating to illustrate the first of these difficulties. When we wish to evaluate policies dealing with inflation and unemployment, we do not first have to spend 12 months developing measures of these key variables. Readily available, up-to-date, reasonably valid series exist from which to draw for this purpose. Six years after the introduction of Medicare, it required a major research study to determine what had happened to the utilisation of medical services in Australia (Deeble 1991). It should be noted, however, that the availability and timeliness of data of this kind have improved considerably since then, largely due to the efforts of the AIHW.

Further difficulties in this field are illustrated by policies relevant to the acquired immune deficiency syndrome (AIDS), in which it is extremely difficult to isolate or measure sexual behaviour or intravenous drug use when examining the relative effectiveness of policies designed to alter sexual behaviour, intravenous drug use or both.

It is as well to recognise that some scholars wish to deny the existence of health policy as a separate, legitimate field of study. What we regard as health policy is seen by them simply as a small part of social policy mixed with a minor dose of economic policy, in that financing and health insurance issues complicate the subject matter slightly. Others argue on more radical grounds that Australia does not have a health policy, as indicated in the following quotation:

> There is not, nor has there ever been, any real health policy in Australia since Federation. There have been various policies about paying for medical or hospital treatment or about how to collect the money or how to distribute it, but even that has been mostly confused and dishonest.
>
> Opit (1984, p. 23)

It is desirable, in the interests of clear thinking, to recognise that there are important overlaps between social policy, economic policy and health policy. Social policy is concerned largely with the maintenance and distribution of income and the provision of welfare services such as housing and transport to specific target groups, including unemployed and older persons. While, in principle, health policy has a narrower focus—for example, meeting the health needs of a specified population—health insurance policies may be designed in part to cater for the same target groups as those catered for by the social welfare sector. Likewise, health policies may have significant budgetary implications for governments. Medicare, via its income redistribution effects, is an important aspect of economic and industrial relations policy, as well as health policy, for Commonwealth governments.

The definition, scope and objectives of policy analysis have been reviewed extensively by many writers, principally from political science, sociological and organisational theory perspectives (see, for example, Clegg & Dunkerley 1980; Dye 1976; Ham & Hill 1993; Heclo 1972; Hill 1997, 2013; Hogwood & Gunn 1984; Klein & Marmor 2008; Marmor & Klein 2012; Parsons 1995; Wildavsky 1979). It is not our purpose to review this literature, but it is important for policymakers and students with an interest in health to examine in considerable depth in this literature many of the broader issues that arise in health policy analysis; for example, those concerned with the exercise of power and authority and the role of the state.

Hill's (2013) review of policy analysis and the policy process is especially commended for its comprehensive coverage of the literature of this complex field. Similar considerations apply to the monumental work of Parsons (1995), which covers all aspects of the theory and practice of public policy. For a comprehensive review of public policy in all its aspects, the multi-authored *Oxford Handbook of Public Policy* (Moran, Rein & Goodin 2008) is recommended for any serious scholar in this field. Here and in later chapters, we are primarily concerned with explaining how some of the insights provided by these and other works may be applied to the health field.

The leading journal in the health policy field is *Health Affairs*. This journal is based in the United States and mainly deals with policy issues that are specific to that country. However, it also contains many policy writings that are of more general interest, some of which deal with policy issues in other health care systems and individual countries.

Questions associated with health policy analysis

Following are some of the main questions that may be asked about any health policy. The list is not exhaustive, but it should serve to convey some idea of the scope and content of our perspective.

- *What is the present policy?* In some cases, it may be a formidable task to establish the nature of the existing policy, since some governments have policies of inaction about certain areas and part of their political strategy may be to conceal the existence of a policy.
- *How, when and why did the policy come into being?* What influenced policymakers to adopt a particular course of action? What were the objectives of the policy?
- *Who are the policymakers?* Which, if any, interest groups do they represent? How do these groups endeavour to influence policymaking?
- *What stages and methods, including organisational arrangements and structures, have been used in the policymaking process?* What interested groups, if any, have been consulted? What sources and kinds of advice have been obtained?
- *Is the process of policymaking that has been adopted the best we can hope for?* How might it be improved?

(*continued*)

POLICY ANALYSIS

- *Is it good policy?* What has it achieved? Would a different policy be likely to yield better results? For whom?
- *Does the present policy need changing?* If so, is it feasible to change it? If so, in what ways?

Thus, health policy analysis includes studying all the different kinds of inputs to policy, the policymaking process and the outcomes of policy. It is also concerned with the broader issues of the economic, cultural and societal influences that impinge on the inputs, processes and outcomes of health policymaking.

As Hill and others argue, policy analysis is concerned with the description of existing policies and processes along with prescriptions about how policymaking might be improved. In this book, we endeavour to meet both of these objectives.

Corresponding to the variety of disciplines engaged in policy analysis is the great diversity of methods of analysis and evaluation that may be employed. These range from the techniques of literary, critical and historical scholarship, and the use of simple measurement and statistical measures, to deployment of the more complex techniques of cost–benefit and cost-effectiveness analysis, experimental design and multivariate analysis.

Policy analysis may usefully entail no more than an appraisal of the coherence, consistency and underlying logic of the published policy statements. Elaborate empirical or statistical analysis may not be required to demonstrate that the policies are muddled, that they lack clear objectives or that they contain elements that are logically inconsistent. It may also be readily established by resort to evidence that public policies have been focused on issues that affect only a very small proportion of the population while those problems that impact on much larger numbers have been neglected. Theoretical analysis may reveal that the intended outcomes of the policy are unlikely to be achieved because key causal factors have been ignored, or because it is demonstrated that the underlying theory on which the policy is based is fallacious. Much of the evaluation of economic policy is of this kind.

Levels of health policy analysis

Following Ham and Hill (1993, pp. 174–6), in health policy analysis we find it useful to acknowledge that there are three broad levels of analysis or emphasis within which studies can be carried out. First is a decision-making level within which analysts are concerned chiefly with identifying who makes decisions and how choices are made by individuals, and within government and other organisations. Second is a level that focuses on the health 'policymaking process', normally within government bureaucracies, and the actions and mechanisms whereby the agenda is defined and policies brought into practice. Third is the structural level in which analysis, criticism and evaluation of the existing health care system within its economic, political, social and cultural structures are the principal objectives.

Decision-making level

At the narrowest level of analysis, it is acknowledged that there are three different ways in which decisions can be made (Anderson 1984, pp. 8–11). These processes are important because they describe how the inputs into the policymaking process come about. Since decision-making involves a choice between competing alternatives, policy analysts are interested in understanding how this choice is made. Are decisions regarding government action made after a fully reasoned consideration of all options? Are the possible consequences associated with each option always examined? Alternatively, does decision-making resemble short-term crisis management more than even-handed rational decision-making based on relevant evidence?

It would appear that only a small proportion of decisions are made in a rational–comprehensive manner. That is, only some decisions are based on rational choice and consideration of all options. With *rational–comprehensive decision-making*, the method of achieving the specified objectives is selected when all possible methods have been taken into account. This requires a clear understanding of the objectives of the policy, comprehensive information about each alternative strategy and its advantages and disadvantages, and a rational, objective method of evaluation and decision-making.

It is generally accepted in the literature quoted in the policy analysis box on page 29, that policy decisions are more often made on an ad hoc or 'incrementalist' basis. *Incrementalism* is recognised as being descriptive of how policymakers make decisions in countries with political systems similar to our own. Incrementalism, or muddling through, involves making small adjustments to existing policies rather than reviewing all alternative strategies for achieving policy objectives. Incremental decision-making tends to yield politically safe, expedient and practical policy decisions. For political scientists such as Lindblom (1968), incrementalism is seen as not only inevitable, given the nature of the democratic political process, but also as desirable since it produces a minimum of policy disruption. Incrementalism tends to lead to conservative policies because the power of the most highly organised interests is strengthened, and the interests of groups with fewer resources tend to be neglected. In Australia, it has been suggested that 'incrementalism rather than innovation has been the norm in policy development' (Graycar 1978, p. 8).

Mixed scanning is the third type of decision-making process discussed in the policy literature. With *mixed scanning*, decision-makers utilise a 'compromise' approach, employing both rational–comprehensive choice and incrementalist decision-making processes (Etzioni 1967). Rational–comprehensive choice is brought to bear in establishing the major issues that require investigation and actions, while incrementalist decision-making is applied in choosing options within these areas. This method recognises the impossibility of considering all options but emphasises the scope for rational decision-making about some of the fundamental problems.

In general, we do not deal with this decision-making level of analysis in this book. We are concerned principally with the ways in which health issues are addressed rather than with the detailed analysis of discrete decision-making processes and decisions. Although several chapters examine aspects of decision-making in some detail, such as **Chapter 4** on health insurance, we have not tried to examine all health decision-making processes. To meet our objectives in this book, we are primarily concerned with the other levels of analysis, because it is policy action and inaction at the broader levels that shape and constrain decisions within health authorities, hospitals and other organisations.

The policymaking process

At the second level of policy analysis, we consider the governmental system within which policy decisions are made and implemented by the bureaucracies. Here we are interested in the content of policies and the process of policymaking within governments.

Policymaking has been conceptualised by analogy to an engine: the engine processes inputs such as petrol at one end and, at the other, converts these into outputs such as movement and noise. Such 'systems' thinking provides the analytical starting point for the field of study that focuses on the policymaking process. This idea was most influentially developed in Easton's (1965a, 1965b) work, which viewed policymaking as a dynamic system of inputs, processes and outputs. In this model, inputs include requests to deal with particular problems and expressions of support or, otherwise, for particular lines of action. In the conversion process or 'black box' of the policymaking process, these inputs are transformed into decisions and actions and hence outcomes. These outcomes then influence the inputs and the process, thus completing what is seen as an ongoing feedback cycle.

This systems approach is evident in the focus on outcomes-based measurement, evaluation and policymaking. Outcomes, as a term, derives from the principles of scientific management, particularly as applied to manufacturing processes that consider the inputs, outputs and outcomes of the production process. Systems thinking, as applied to management, is typified by the Ford assembly line. More recently, systems thinking has been applied to health and other service sectors of the economy. In the health industry, a 'health services output' refers to a change in the volume of services, such as surgical interventions of a specific kind provided to a population. These outputs are designed to achieve the outcome of improved health status.

Factories produce cars and other goods. Hospitals provide health care services (Fetter 1999). Thus, the hospital is conceptualised by analogy to an engine that can be 're-engineered'. This is the conceptual foundation for casemix classification systems and diagnosis related groups (DRGs) in particular (see **Chapter 5**).

The 'policy as process' perspective focuses on 'actors' in the policy system— those individuals and groups, including politicians, senior officials, doctors, private companies and community groups, who are active in the policy process. This approach focuses on the human relations of policymaking, as opposed to the mechanics. We emphasise, however, that this approach is limited in scope because important structural questions may be left unasked and unanswered. For example, why are the demands of some groups systematically more influential than those of others?

In figure 2.1, we have adapted Easton's basic systems model to foreshadow the higher-level factors that are discussed later in this chapter. Thus, the arrow running from the political system to inputs expresses the perception that governments, for example, try to influence the inputs, such as demands for policy changes. We have also introduced the interaction of 'society' with the political system, and the influence of society on inputs and outputs, to indicate that all these processes are shaped by the values and norms of the wider community and by economic and other forces (Kimberly & Zajac 1985).

Figure 2.1   A systems model of the policymaking process

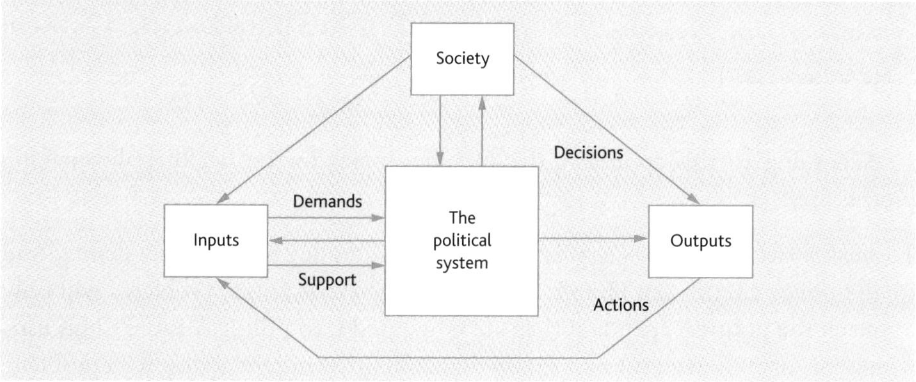

Source: adapted from Easton (1965a)

The limitations of the 'policy as process' level of analysis are discussed below, and in greater depth in the next chapter, where further insights from the fields of political science and sociology are utilised. However, this level of analysis does have considerable analytical power, particularly in describing how the stability of political systems is maintained.

One of the clearest expositions of the process approach to policy is found in the work of American political scientist James E Anderson (1984). This model is based on a 'sequential pattern of action' in the policy process, as illustrated in figure 2.2.

It is not always possible to identify each of these stages when examining actual cases of policymaking. Moreover, as Hill (2013) and Parsons (1995) emphasise, in the real world of policymaking the systems and stages models may be misleading in terms of what actually happens. Thus, there is a risk that a too-rigid application of the models for purposes of analysis may lead to distortion of a more complex reality. Nevertheless, in our view, as we indicate on the following page, these models provide a useful starting point and frame of reference for investigating complex policy issues, before introducing other factors that are not considered in the models, such as the impact of structural interests.

Figure 2.2   Key stages in the health policymaking process

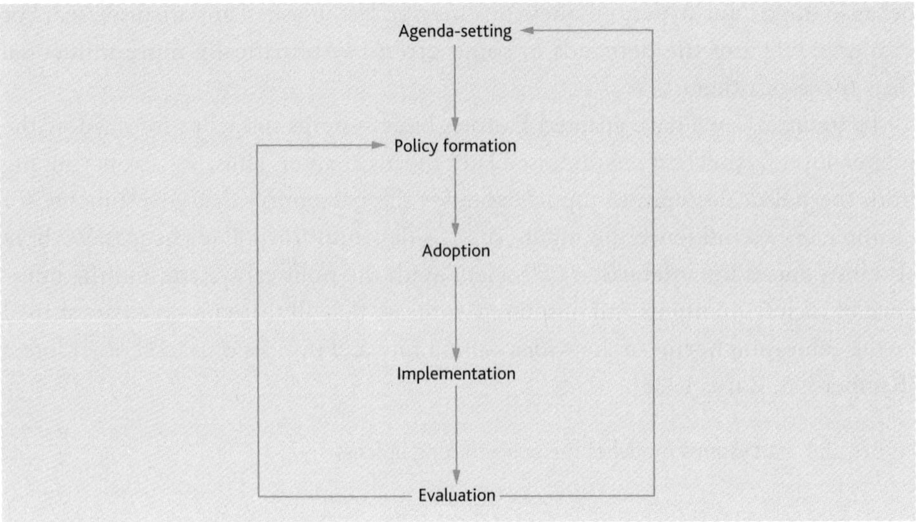

Source: Anderson (1984)

According to this approach, the five key stages in the health policymaking process are:

1   *problem identification and agenda setting*, in which policy problems are defined and the policy agenda set. Here it is acknowledged that public problems will only reach the political agenda if they are converted into political 'issues'. This usually occurs when an interest group demands government action on a problem, or when there is public disagreement over ways in which a problem should be addressed. A case in point is the issue of health insurance, which returns to our federal policy agenda frequently because of the persistence of strongly held and opposing views by powerful interest groups. The policy agenda generally includes those issues on which policymakers feel compelled to act. Agenda-setting will be discussed in some detail in **Chapter 8** on prevention and health promotion and when we examine new policymaking structures in **Chapter 10**.

2   *policy formation*, the stage in which policies are created or changed. Here we emphasise that the content of a policy cannot be understood apart from the political context within which it develops. It is useful to understand policy formation as a social and political process in order to conceptualise how policies are formulated (Milio 1988). The formation stage—also referred to as policy formulation, design or development—receives particular attention when we examine policies relating to issues such as tobacco industry regulation.

3   *adoption*, the stage when the policy is enacted or brought into force, for example, by state or federal legislation. Note, however, that new or changed public policies are often adopted by means of a decision of the Cabinet, or indeed of an

individual minister, without any legislative change if the existing legislation and administrative arrangements leave a good deal of discretionary power in the hands of the executive branch of government.

4 *policy implementation* includes the actions and mechanisms whereby policies are brought into practice; that is, where what is written in the legislation or policy document is turned into a reality. In this stage, the content of the policy and its impact on those affected may be modified substantially, or even negated. In analysing this stage in the policymaking process it is necessary to examine how, when and where particular policies have been implemented. As a starting point, it is useful to examine the relevant policy statements and policy documents. However, policy documents should not be accepted at face value as there is often a significant discrepancy between the rhetoric and the reality of policymaking.

5 *policy evaluation*, the final stage in the health policymaking process, includes monitoring, analysis, criticism and assessment of existing or proposed policies. This covers the appraisal of their content, their implementation and their effects. Moreover, evaluation is designed to help governments to implement policies in an effective and efficient manner.

This book makes considerable use of this level of analysis. For example, in **Chapter 4**, we start with a policy problem—the meeting of hospital and medical expenses by health insurance and related means—then we determine what policies governments have formulated, how policies were implemented and what impact they had on different social groups. In examining the process of policy formation, we look at the roles of key actors, interest groups, institutions and political processes. The aim is to understand how these interest groups affect what governments do, or do not do, concerning any particular issue.

The link between policy formation and implementation is an important aspect of the process because governments often encounter difficulties when attempting to translate intentions and promises into action. Implementation may be the most demanding aspect of policymaking because of the failure to anticipate opposition to the policy or because the financial, intellectual and other resources required for successful implementation have been underestimated. It is possibly the case that governments concerned with reforms, notably the Australian Labor Party in this country, have tended to underestimate the difficulties associated with implementing some policies. Traditionally, public servants work most effectively in administering existing programs. They may be less capable at organising and managing new endeavours.

Health policy evaluation requires critical examination of the impact of policies on outcomes such as health status, outcomes that are extremely complex and difficult to measure, as we have seen. Central to the policy evaluation process is the distinction between policy outputs and policy outcomes. Policy outputs include the things governments actually do: construct hospitals, provide infant health services, subsidise pharmaceuticals and so on. These actions are generally not difficult to measure. One can measure outputs in terms of bed numbers per 1000 of the population, numbers of visits to early childhood health centres or numbers of prescriptions. However, this does not tell us about the effects of these policies, including the impact they have on the health of the target population. While health services are the main output of the health care system, improvement in the health of the population is its principal objective. The distinction between health care provision and health status is, therefore, archetypal of the distinction between outputs and outcomes.

Fundamentally, policy evaluation requires that we know the objectives of a given policy, how it is to be implemented and what, if anything, has been accomplished towards attainment of policy goals. Further, we need to be able to distinguish between what occurred despite the policy and what occurred because of the specific policy. If the infant mortality rate in a given population decreased over a specified period was this due to upgrading of the maternity services at the local hospital, the establishment of a baby health clinic or improved maternal nutrition? Of course, policy evaluation may reveal that policies are not achieving their stated goals or that they have produced results that were not anticipated. In an ideal policy environment, evaluation is incorporated into the implementation process so that both the implementation process and policy outcomes are evaluated.

Health service evaluation generally focuses on two criteria: effectiveness and efficiency. We suggest that this is incomplete, however, unless we establish who benefits. Effective and efficient services may produce inequitable results in the sense that groups with relatively high levels of income and health status may benefit much more than those with lower levels of health status. Do particular policies yield services that are commensurate with variations in health status? Why do some groups, such as Aboriginal peoples, continue to have such a poor level of health status? The criteria of the fairness and equity achieved by the health care system's funding and related arrangements we view as being of critical importance to the overall evaluation process.

These questions will be discussed in greater depth as particular policy issues are addressed in later chapters. Cost-effectiveness analysis is discussed in **Chapter 5** in relation to pharmaceutical policy. Our analysis of technology assessment in **Chapter 7** also gives particular attention to the criterion of effectiveness. **Chapter 9** points to inequalities in health and ways in which the interests of disadvantaged groups can be furthered.

The structural level of analysis

At the structural level of analysis, we consider the wider social, economic and technological context within which the existing policymaking system operates. A broad analytical perspective, which is sensitive to the historical, sociological, economic and political structures that shape and constrain the policymaking process, is necessary in order to augment the other levels of analysis.

Particular attention is paid to the part played by major structural interests—that is, coalitions of powerful interest groups—in shaping the nature of the political debate and in determining which issues are included in the policymaking agenda. Economic interest groups, such as the tobacco and pharmaceutical industries, may play a largely hidden but crucial role in shaping the ways in which health issues are conceived and addressed. This analytical perspective recognises that policymaking may have as much to do with conflicts between entrenched structural interests and medicine's hegemonic position as with political lobbying and decision-making within the political system as it is customarily defined. This perspective also enhances the view put forward by political scientists that policymaking is inherently part of a political process, and that the role of evidence-based policymaking is subject to very important limitations (Marmor & Klein 2012).

The levels of policy analysis—an example

In interpreting the three levels of analysis, it is important to be clear that the scope of the analysis and the factors taken into account distinguish one level from another. For example, the same phenomenon—cigarette smoking—and the formulation and implementation of policies to control this behaviour may be examined at any one of these levels. An economic analysis, grounded in the rational–comprehensive model, would consider factors such as the price of cigarettes and the income of consumers, which affect the demand for this product at the level of decision-making by each actual or potential consumer, and hence for all consumers. Policy informed by this level has concentrated on increasing the price of cigarettes via excise duty and other taxes to reduce demand.

The 'policy as process' level of analysis would place the objective of reducing the consumption of cigarettes by taxation within the context of a policymaking process, and would consider the steps necessary to formulate, adopt, implement, evaluate and improve this process. The source of political demands for this specific policy, and an assessment of whether the policy would achieve government and community support, might also form part of the analysis.

The structural level of analysis approaches the issue of how to reduce the consumption of cigarettes by examining the dominant structural interests—cigarette manufacturers, tobacco growers and their allies such as advertising agencies—that benefit from the status quo. This status quo includes community attitudes towards smoking, along with the attitudes of politicians to the issue.

The demand of consumers for cigarettes, based on this level of analysis, is not a factor that exists in a vacuum. It is the product of a set of socially determined reactions to the activity of smoking, which have been carefully cultivated by the tobacco industry and related enterprises, including the media. The film industry has also played a notorious and longstanding role in this process. Thus, public policies that aim to decrease the consumption of cigarettes should also focus on how to challenge the power of the dominant structural interests and how to reshape community and political attitudes towards smoking behaviour. Initiatives such as the banning of smoking within buildings and the plain packaging of tobacco products fall within this category.

SUMMARY AND CONCLUSION

We have indicated that the term 'policy' is defined and used in a number of ways, but that it perhaps most generally conveys the notion of a course of action rather than any specific decision. Public policy generally refers to a course of action that has been undertaken or is proposed to be implemented by a government. However, it is important to recognise that government policy may also include consistent decisions to refrain from any action about an issue.

Policies may also be classified in several ways, including the general issues such as health insurance that are the focus of the policymaking activity. However, when part of the policy analysis objective is to understand why certain types of policy are subject to more or fewer obstacles than others, we regard the Lowi typology of distributive, redistributive, regulatory and self-regulatory policies as providing useful insights. Many actual or proposed health policies have obvious effects in redistributing income, power and status; it is hardly surprising, therefore, that policy reforms in this arena have proved exceedingly difficult to implement.

In reviewing the literature on policy analysis and the policymaking process, we have noted that much attention has been paid to developing simplified models of the process to facilitate our understanding of what is happening. Systems models featuring inputs, outputs and feedback loops in the policymaking process have been developed, frequently for this purpose. In addition, there has been an emphasis on dividing policymaking into several distinct stages for the same purpose. In keeping with all models designed to deal with complex realities, we emphasise the risks associated with the possibility of distorting what actually happens in the real world of politicians and other policymakers. Nevertheless, we have found that a judicious use of these models can prove effective in analysing specific policymaking endeavours.

Finally, we have indicated that health policy theory and analysis may be conceptualised as embracing three distinct focuses or levels. With a decision-making perspective, we can examine how specific decisions are made by individuals and within organisations that are relevant to policy formation and outcomes. At the second level, the focus is on the policymaking process. Here, the analysis concentrates on the ways in which governments convert demands from a variety of sources into health policy decisions and actions. The structural or macro level deals with the analysis and interpretation of the health care system, and the factors that influence health status, efficiency and equity, as the product of a range of social, economic and political forces. As an example, in **Chapter 9** we examine the role of pharmaceutical companies and psychiatrists in convincing communities to accept a disease-centred model of mental dysfunction that leads to an ever-expanding consumption of medications but for which evidence of its relevance is notably absent (Greenberg 2013; Moncrieff 2009).

We should emphasise, with Ham and Hill (1993, p. 174), that the study of health policy needs to consider all levels of analysis and, most importantly, the interaction between the different levels. We believe that an analysis dependent on one level alone is rarely sufficient. Precisely how many levels are investigated varies according to the nature of the problem. Critical analysis of health care and public policy, especially at the structural level, requires a framework that draws inputs from a number of disciplines, including economics, political science, sociology and epidemiology. It is to these perspectives that we now turn.

FURTHER READING

Michael Hill's 2013 book *The Public Policy Process*, 5th edition (Pearson Education), is possibly the most accessible, comprehensive and critical account of the literature of policymaking, its theory and applications. See also the publication that he has edited, *The Policy Process: A Reader*, 2nd edition (Prentice Hall/Harvester Wheatsheaf, 1997).

The chapter by Rudolf Klein and Ted Marmor (2008), 'Reflections on policy analysis: Putting it together again', in M Moran, M Rein and R Goodin (eds) *The Oxford Handbook of Public Policy* (Oxford University Press), provides an insightful account of the literature of policy analysis. In making sense of what governments do, they emphasise heavily the constraints imposed by the institutions within which governments operate, and the interests operating in the political scene. Klein from Britain and Marmor from the United States have written extensively about health policies in both countries; see also Marmor and Klein (2012).

Jeff Richardson's indictment of health policymaking in Australia 'Steering without navigation equipment: The lamentable state of Australian health policy reform', in *Australia and New Zealand Health Policy*, (2009, pp. 6–27), is one of the most important documents available on this topic. Richardson's contributions are discussed in some detail in **Chapter 10**.

DISCUSSION QUESTIONS

1   What do you regard as the most useful meaning of the word 'policy'? Why is it important to distinguish a policy from a decision?
2   Why are redistributive public policies the most difficult for governments to implement? Provide at least two examples of redistributive health policies that have been implemented in Australia in the past.
3   Why are self-regulatory policies highly regarded by many groups in the health sector and elsewhere? What are the advantages and disadvantages to governments of this approach to public policy?
4   Comment on Opit's statement made in 1984 that there has never been any real health policy in Australia. What can be assumed as his reasons for proffering this provocative claim?

5   It is often asserted that policy analysts may have two objectives: namely, to describe the nature of existing policies and to promote the adoption by governments and others of improved policies. Why do most policy analysts with a background in academia appear to emphasise the latter objective?

6   What are the advantages and disadvantages of the policy-as-process and the systems conceptualisation of policymaking?

7   Policies in Australia and elsewhere to reduce the prevalence of smoking have achieved notable success and possibly been the main factor in increasing the life expectancy of populations in developed countries in recent years. Discuss this statement in relation to the relative contribution of price changes for tobacco products versus measures to change community attitudes towards the activity of smoking.

3

Perspectives on health policy

In this chapter, we examine several perspectives and sets of generalisations about health, sickness and health care services. Taken in conjunction with our discussion in **Chapter 2**, these should facilitate the understanding of the nature of policy and policymaking, and assist in the critical analysis of the Australian health care system and of the public policies with which it is associated.

The sources of these perspectives include research evidence and analysis derived from many studies undertaken by economists, political scientists, epidemiologists, sociologists and health professionals. Our thinking about health policy issues has been influenced by the work and writings of Evans, Culyer, Marmor, Klein, Alford, Ham, Tuohy, McKeown and Freidson, together with the other public policy analysts discussed previously. This evidence will not be cited in detail; however, the bibliography on page 383 references a selection of what we regard as the most important of these studies.

As a starting point, it is productive to categorise the perspectives according to the disciplinary sources from which they have stemmed. Not surprisingly, the background of policy analysts has a marked influence on their appraisal of policy issues and especially on their recommendations about how policymaking and the outcomes of the process might be improved. In the first section below, we consider the perspectives and insights provided principally by economists. Next, contributions based on the work of political scientists and public policy specialists and sociologists are discussed. Perspectives arising out of the studies of epidemiologists and other health care researchers are summarised in the final sections. We strongly believe that good policy formulation and analysis needs a synthesis of material from all these disciplines.

Economic perspectives

Health economists are chiefly concerned with examining the determinants of health service utilisation and expenditure, health insurance and other financing arrangements, and alternative methods of organising and funding health institutions. A fundamental goal of economic analysis is to ensure that health services operate with maximum efficiency. The achievement of *technical efficiency* in the health area is defined as minimising the cost of producing a given level of output of health services. However, technical efficiency should not be considered in isolation from allocative efficiency.

For *allocative efficiency* to be present, the output of health services, and the distribution of this output between various health-related activities, should maximise the welfare of the recipients of these services. The evaluation of specific health services and programs, especially from these efficiency perspectives, and the analysis of the size, distribution and earnings of occupations within the health workforce, are further areas of interest to economists. The use of a specifically economic approach to health policy and services evaluation, including the techniques used, is discussed at length by Carter and Harris (1999).

Within a framework of scarce resources and competing objectives, economists depend heavily on two basic concepts, demand and supply, for describing and analysing the utilisation of goods and services. *Demand* is the quantity of a commodity that consumers would be prepared to purchase at a specified price. *Supply* is the quantity that providers are willing to offer for sale at the given price. In the simplest demand and supply model, all other factors that might influence consumption, such as income, are assumed to remain constant, and the relationship between demand and price for different values of each variable is described by a downwardly sloping curve, the demand function. Similarly, an upwardly sloping curve, the supply function, describes the relationship between prices and the quantities supplied. These two functions are illustrated in figure 3.1.

Figure 3.1   Market demand and supply curves

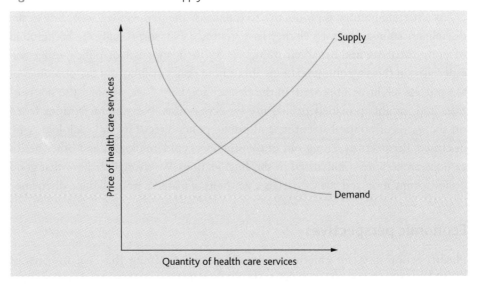

Consumers' preferences are assumed to be the underlying determinants of demand relationships, while costs of production underlie supply curves. At the point where the two curves for a given commodity intersect, the quantity demanded and the quantity supplied are obviously equal; the corresponding price, according to the assumptions of the model, has produced this position of equality or equilibrium.

In the recent past, those who extol the virtues of free markets and are critical of the attempts of governments to intervene in these markets have dominated economics, especially in the United States. Such economists are often referred to as economic rationalists or economic fundamentalists, especially by those who disagree with them. They belong to an approach to economic phenomena that is more accurately described as neoclassical economics (Stigler 1965).

Many economists with this approach have applied their prescriptions to the health services and have recommended a drastic overhaul of the methods of financing and providing health services. Typically they argue that the provision of free or heavily subsidised health services has led to the overuse of the services. They point to the phenomenon of moral hazard, that insurance may produce more instances of the events being insured against. Thus, a major policy thrust of neoclassical economics as applied to health care has been the advocacy of increased user charges as the appropriate response to the perceived problem of cost increases in the health sector. Accordingly, they advocate health insurance policies in which the consumers of services should bear some proportion of the cost of the services, including the notion that health insurance should only cover 'catastrophic' episodes (Feldstein & Gruber 1995). The conservative Harvard economist Martin Feldstein (1973) has also argued that there is a 'welfare loss from excess health insurance'.

Policies of this kind, often popular with governments faced by fiscal constraints, ignore the distributional and ethical issues associated with transferring income from the sick and often those on low incomes to the rest of the community. Further details of the limitations of applying naive economic models to the complexities of the health care sector are provided by Palmer and Ho (2008). The following quotation from Marmor and McKissick (2012, p. 72) is also relevant in highlighting the limitations of health policy analysis as undertaken by most economists:

> Economists, in particular, all too frequently practise a strain of policy analysis that treats the 'political part' of political economy as barely more than an afterthought.

It is important for those who draw upon the work of economists in policy analysis to be aware that many members of the discipline have queried the underlying assumptions and policy implications of various aspects of free-market neoclassical economics (Evans 1998; Keen 2001; Thurow 1983). One important claim of these economists is that the dominance or decline of the various schools of economic thought may have more to do with shifting political stances and power relations than new evidence or improved analytical techniques.

When applied to the health services, the division between demand factors and supply factors is useful as an organising framework, but only if we recognise the distinctive features of health care as a commodity and we are alert to the limitations of conventional economic theory.

A major difference between health care and other commodities is that the former is demanded by consumers only because of the expectation that it will promote health status; for example, by curing or alleviating an illness (Evans 1984). Services such as visits to doctors or treatments in hospital are valued by patients because of the anticipated improvement in health outcomes.

A further important difference between health care and other commodities is that the consumer generally lacks knowledge of the relationship between a health service and the desired outcome of better health status. A health care service is only of value to the consumer if it produces an improvement in the health status of the individual. Generally, the consumption of the health service per se is not valued, and the treatment, as in the case of surgical intervention, is often associated with much pain and discomfort.

With other commodities, whereby the consumer derives satisfaction from the characteristics of the service or commodity directly, lack of knowledge of the relationship between consumption and outcome does not arise. Thus, the user of a computer does not need to know the technical details of how the hardware and software operate, but they are able to determine fairly readily whether the tasks that the computer is capable of performing are worth the price established by the market. The provider of health care will have much more knowledge than the consumer of the likely impact on health status, or at least the patient perceives this to be the case. In these circumstances, the ability of the provider to influence the consumer's use of medical services is likely to be much greater than in other areas.

There is a substantial body of writing in health economics literature on 'supplier-induced demand' (Culyer & Evans 1996; Pauly 1994; Reinhardt 1985; Rice and Labelle 1989). The financial and other incentives present in a health care system, especially where fee-for-service is the predominant method of doctor remuneration, may serve to yield levels of use of certain services that do not correspond to those that maximise the welfare of patients. We return to this issue in **Chapter 7**.

Health care also differs from most other commodities because the onset of illness, disability or trauma is unpredictable for any individual. For example, if a person is seriously injured in a motor vehicle accident, that person's demand for health care will rise immediately from zero to an extremely high level. Health insurance is crucial in such instances because it protects consumers from the threat of economic uncertainty. At any time, moreover, the prevalence of disease and the risk of heavy financial outlays are very unevenly distributed across the community. Health insurance, therefore, has the objective of spreading these unequal risks over the relevant population (Nyman 2003).

Finally, in this regard, health care utilisation is characterised by the presence of effects external to the individual consumer. In infectious diseases, the most obvious case of this phenomenon, the failure of persons to seek treatment, may prejudice the health status of many others. It seems, however, that for a variety of altruistic and paternalistic reasons there is a general concern in the community about the level of consumption of health services by individuals (Culyer 1971).

Health care has been termed a 'merit good'—people gain satisfaction by subsidising the consumption of health services by others. It must be recognised, however, that the extent to which this is the case may vary widely from country to country and possibly within the same country at different periods. It is possible, for example, that the level of this concern has diminished recently in most Western countries. The decrease in the concern for other less-fortunate members of communities may have been carefully orchestrated by elite groups whose main objective is to lower their own taxes.

The conceptualisation of health care as a commodity, a perspective derived principally from the work of economists, helps us to understand the basis for many of the distinctive aspects of health systems and the policies associated with them. Thus, the extensive regulation of provider–patient relationships, including the registration of many health professionals, is likely to have been a response to the lack of knowledge of consumers about the effects of health care on health status. The existence of health insurance reflects uncertainty about the impact of illness and sharp fluctuations in demand for health services by individuals over time. Extensive subsidies or direct provision by governments of health services and/or health insurance are likely manifestations of external factors in consumption (Evans 1984).

The economic perspective we present here casts serious doubt on any attempt to explain the workings of the health care system by reference to a simple demand and supply model of the kind that many economists and politicians find appealing. More importantly, it implies that policy changes designed to produce or move towards a free market should be regarded with considerable scepticism, especially if their advocates reveal a lack of awareness of the special characteristics of health services set out above.

Whether more or less government regulation, support and intervention is required, and the form policy initiatives should take, are essentially empirical issues that can only be answered by reference to a detailed analysis of specific health service areas. Moreover, as we noted previously, since providers are able to exercise considerable influence over the 'demand' for their services, an emphasis on the factors underlying supply, rather than demand, is appropriate for analysing many policy issues, as we demonstrate in the following chapters.

The need to concentrate on the supply side has been recognised in the work of Enthoven (1988), an economist influential in promoting a managed competition model of health service delivery. This model recognises that competition between providers is the only aspect of the free-market model that can be applied successfully to health services. The notion of separating the roles of providers and purchasers of health services, whereby the purchasers are government or other organisations acting as agents for the final consumers, has achieved a good deal of popularity in a number of countries, including Australia (Scotton 1998b). We return to a discussion of the managed competition model in **Chapter 10**, and a critical analysis of the failure of the model to achieve governmental support here and elsewhere.

Other aspects of the health care system that we believe are very important in understanding health policy—in particular, the dominant but weakening position of the medical profession and the extent to which health care generates improvements in health status—will be discussed later in this chapter. Similarly, further perspectives are required to understand the source of the conflicts associated with many health policies in Australia, the frequent changes associated with several of them, and difficulties in implementing what are widely perceived to be desirable changes.

Political science perspectives

It was evident in our discussion of the Australian health care system that the distribution of health status varies widely between different groups when these are defined by factors such as socioeconomic status and geographic location. We also suggested that the distribution of resources between health services of different types—institutional, community health, curative, preventative—might differ markedly from the most efficient distribution, in the allocative or distributive sense of the term, in maximising health status. The reasons behind these problems are undoubtedly highly complex and are explored further in later chapters. Here, we wish to emphasise how political science perspectives may contribute to our understanding, in particular, of why changes in health care policies that might reduce or eliminate these and related problems have not been implemented.

Of the variety of approaches adopted by political scientists in interpreting health care and related social phenomena, the two that have been most influential in our opinion are those of Ted Marmor (1973) and Robert Alford (1975). Both writers have based their work on the United States' health care system, but the applicability of the underlying theories has been tested using British (Allsop 1984; Ham 1999) and Australian cases (Duckett 1984; Gardner 1997; Palmer 1978; Sax 1984; Short 1984, 1989). The work of Crichton (1998), Day and Klein (1992) and Tuohy (1994, 1999) has been crucial also in assisting us to understand when and how health care policy reform is most likely to occur.

Alford's thesis is that health policy reform and barriers to reform should be seen as the outcome of conflicts between three major health groups, or structural interests. Interest groups or stakeholders have a stake in the outcome of a policy. That is, they stand to gain or lose in some way from implementation of the policy. Structural interests are those alliances of interest groups that gain or lose from the health care system as it is currently organised. These alliances are described by Alford as the 'professional monopolists', the 'corporate rationalisers' and the 'community interest'.

The *professional monopolists* are principally the medical practitioners who have been able to secure the exclusive legal rights to undertake a range of diagnostic and therapeutic activities. Most importantly, this group, according to Alford, has been able to persuade the population that the knowledge and skills its members possess make a unique contribution to the health of the community. Doctors and their fellow professional monopolists, including other groups such as pharmaceutical and equipment manufacturers whose activities and incomes are linked closely to those of the medical profession, benefit from the health care system the way it is. Thus, they wish to retain the status quo and are usually very resistant to proposed changes in the system.

The group of *corporate rationalisers* consists of planners, administrators and some health professionals, including those with medical qualifications, whose interests are served by the promotion of greater efficiency, effectiveness and equity in the provision of health services. Corporate rationalisers would normally be members of the health service bureaucracy, though others such as politicians and academics may form part of this group. Consultants joined the ranks of the corporate rationalisers, particularly in the 1990s with cutbacks to planning and policymaking at the central levels in health authorities. More policy work has been contracted out, often to former senior health officers. Corporate rationalisers benefit from a reformed health care system, as their domains of responsibility increase with the implementation of policy reforms such as Medicare, casemix-based hospital funding and evidence-based health care.

The *community structural interest*, according to Alford, consists of a variety of organisations and agencies often representing single client groups, such as those with mental health problems, who have in common their desire to improve the health care available to the community. Australia has a wide variety of health pressure groups, which lobby politicians and members of the public and attempt to attract media support. These groups include the Australian Council of Social Service, CHOICE, the Health Issues Centre and the Consumers' Health Forum, which seek to promote community health and welfare. Their lobbying is usually directed towards ministers of health at federal or state levels, ministerial staff, members of parliament and public servants in departments of health.

Compared to the other structural interests in the Australian health care system, these groups are relatively diffuse, poorly financed and generally lacking in bargaining power in the political arena. The community interest is not necessarily furthered in the current organisation of health care in Australia.

The relationships between these three major groups are characterised by the professional monopolists (per Alford's description) as the dominant group, but with the corporate rationalisers seeking to challenge their position of dominance. The community interest is described by Alford as being repressed but with members of the group trying to become more influential. These structural interests may work together or in opposition in particular instances of policymaking and implementation. For example, Duckett's (1984) analysis of the origins of the Community Health Program pointed to a 'coincidence of interests' between corporate rationalisers and the community. Furthermore, corporate rationalisers and the community interest in Australia have allied themselves in defence of national health insurance for over 40 years (Jackson 1990).

We believe that this characterisation of structural interests in health care has a good deal of relevance to the analysis and interpretation of health policy in Australia from a structural perspective. In later chapters, this framework will be applied to several policy issues. Nevertheless, it is desirable to be aware of the possible weaknesses of the approach, especially when applied to the Australian scene.

First, the roles of government and of political parties as such are almost non-existent in Alford's work. The corporate rationalisers' group includes members of government bureaucracies but they are seen as pushing their own career interests rather than implementing the policies of governments. This analytical omission needs to be remedied; as revealed in **Chapter 4**, health insurance policies have been influenced considerably by which federal political party in Australia is in power.

Second, another important group in Australia consists of the trade unions of health employees, including the nurses' unions, which have become more militant since the mid-1980s. In Alford's model, trade unions may form part of the community interest, but their role is much more low-key than that which it may be more appropriate to assign them in the Australian environment. When Labor has been in power federally, especially during the period of the Hawke–Keating governments, the interests of the trade union movement as a whole were decisive in influencing the direction of health policy.

Third, doctors in Australia and elsewhere have become a more heterogeneous group than Alford's theory suggests. Although senior hospital specialists, together with the Australian Medical Association (AMA), continue to exercise a major influence of the kind Alford postulates, other medical groups with different values and goals, notably the Doctors' Reform Society, have become increasingly vocal. Unlike most members of the medical profession, who only become active when the prospect of reform is imminent, the latter groups actively seek major changes in the status quo.

Fourth, Alford presumes that the possession of superior knowledge and skills by doctors explains their position of dominance in health matters. While these attributes of doctors undoubtedly are an important aspect of their ability to exercise power, clearly there are many others, including hospital pharmacists, psychologists and physiotherapists, who possess a high level of specialised knowledge and skills but lack power. Other perspectives are required to provide a more comprehensive explanation of medical dominance, as we indicate below.

Political market for health policies

The role of government in health policy and the sources of the relative strengths and weaknesses of the various interest groups are given much more emphasis in the approach adopted by Marmor and others (Marmor & Christianson 1982). Drawing on the ideas of public choice theorists (Buchanan 1978; Downs 1967; Tullock 1976), Marmor describes health care policies as 'political goods', which are traded in a political marketplace for votes and financial support. Governments supply, at varying costs, health care policies that affect both individual consumers and those organised as interest groups. Demand for policies reflects the benefits that participants in the market expect to experience. In this model, bureaucrats also play an active role in the shaping of health care policies.

Each of these three groups—governments, bureaucratic suppliers and their constituents, who demand policies of various kinds—pursue their own objectives in the political marketplace. Governments and individual politicians wish to maximise their probability of being re-elected; bureaucrats wish to maximise their power, influence and career prospects. Consumers of health policies may have a generalised interest in more efficient health-related activities; for example, those that may improve their health status at no extra cost to themselves. Health providers may demand policies that preserve or augment their incomes, status and power.

According to Marmor, the value placed on any policy in the political market will reflect the interaction between these demand and supply relationships; this in turn reflects a power struggle between the relevant interest groups. Where the costs to governments of providing alternative policies are equal, the most highly valued policies will be those for which the demand is greatest. These policies are most likely to be implemented by governments, since the payoffs for governments and politicians in terms of votes and financial support will be largest.

One of the most important implications of this model is that the political market for health policies is unbalanced. Some participants will be able to exert much more influence over the market than others, partly because of their ability to offer more financial and other support to politicians and partly because of their ability to influence voters. In order to explain why certain participants in the political market will be motivated to exercise this power, Marmor points to the distinction between those who have a concentrated interest in a policy and those whose interests are diffuse.

In general, many health policies will have a direct and significant effect on the incomes of health care providers. This is especially the case with policies designed to contain costs or produce higher levels of efficiency, whereby substantial losses of earnings for individual doctors and health service employees will often result. The number affected by the policy may be small, but they have a strong incentive and often disproportionately large financial resources to oppose a policy of this kind. On the other hand, those who benefit from the policy—all taxpayers, for example—are numerically very large but their interest is diffuse. The benefit to any individual is small, and there will be little reason for the policy to find strong community support. Other things being equal, concentrated interests are likely to have more impact on the political market than diffuse interests.

The notion of an unbalanced market for health care policies provides further insights into the reasons why even health policy changes with considerable popular support are often very difficult to achieve, especially when the changes have a redistributive effect. This theory is consistent with and complements Alford's analysis of the barriers to health care reform. It has the advantage of identifying a more specific role for governments and of pointing to specific sources of the power attributed to the professional monopolists. In addition, it highlights reasons for the weakness of the community interest.

It is interesting to note that the distinguished United States health economist Victor Fuchs has applied the same principles to highlight the major obstacles to the reform of the American health care system by the Obama administration (Fuchs 2009).

Marmor differs from most other analysts who apply public choice theory to policy issues. These analysts typically criticise the role of governments as simply representing another interest group and hence argue for a lesser involvement of government in the national economy. Marmor is well known for his advocacy of a greater role for government intervention in the United States concerning health issues (Marmor 1973).

One problem with Marmor's theory of unbalanced political markets is that it does not explain the existence of policies that benefit primarily low-income groups, who lack power in the political market. It will be recalled that one of the properties postulated for health care as a commodity is that members of a community derive satisfaction from its consumption by other members of the community. The economic concept of health care as a 'merit good' helps to explain why policies such as the provision of free health care for the poor are successfully implemented when the demands of the relevant constituency are relatively weak.

Community activism in the health policy process

Australian research goes some way towards identifying the factors that facilitate or hinder community participation in the policymaking process (Short 1998). The study examined the development of the Consumers Health Forum of Australia, established in 1987, from its early origins in federally supported local community development work to its current status as a 'one-stop consultation shop' for the Commonwealth Department of Health. It has become the major national organisation representing the views of community and consumer groups on issues relating to health in an unbalanced political market that systematically favours the professional monopolists or the corporate rationalisers.

The study brought to light that the broader public policy agenda of the government of the day plays a crucial role in facilitating and/or resourcing community activism in the health policy process. Indeed, Short suggests that the high watermark of community activism in the health policy process (1987–1992), during the period of the Hawke–Keating governments, occurred due to an alliance of interests between a reformist minister (Dr Neal Blewett) and progressive public servants and community activists. It also suggests that the relative absence or weakness of these factors is likely to constrain or diminish the role of community activism in the health policymaking process.

Windows of opportunity and landscapes of health policy ideas

The work of Day and Klein (1992) in the United Kingdom and Hancock (1999b) in Australia also emphasises the importance of the broader public policy agenda.

In an analysis of health care politics, Day and Klein (1992) found it useful to distinguish between the politics of abnormal 'structural' change and the 'politics of adaptation'. This distinction between so-called 'constitutional' and 'distributional' dimensions of policy has also been utilised in the analysis of Canadian policy and politics (Tuohy 1994) and Crichton's (1998) analysis of the Australian and Canadian health care systems. Tuohy (1999) has also applied the same principles to her illuminating study of the different patterns of policy change in Britain, Canada and the United States. Her work is also an important exception to the fact that most international comparative studies are marked by superficiality and a lack of understanding of how each country's system actually operates (Marmor, Freeman & Okma 2009).

The *distributional dimension* of health policy relates to the allocation of tangible benefits and services across various interests in society. The *constitutional dimension*, sometimes referred to as the institutional mix, relates to the structure of the health care system itself, to the way in which it is organised and run, including the mix of hierarchy, market and peer control in decision-making structures. The *structural dimension*, or structural balance, includes the allocation of positions of influence within which policies are developed and implemented. This includes, most importantly, the relative influence of state actors, health care providers and private financial interests. The relative stability of health care politics is highlighted below.

Episodes of fundamental constitutional change have been relatively rare in the health policy arena, as Tuohy (1994, p. 249) suggests:

> Even more than is the case in most other policy arenas, the nature of politics within the health care arena has provided entrenched interests with the capacity to defend the status quo.

As we have seen, health care politics tend to be dominated by the medical profession and their allies, the professional monopolists. While there are times when this dominant medical power is challenged by public servants, hospital administrators, economists and other corporate rationalisers, generally the medical profession enjoys more influence in health care politics than the challenging corporate or repressed community interests do. Doctors and their fellow professional monopolists benefit, or believe that they benefit, from the constitution of the health care system the way it is. Thus, they wish to retain the status quo and are usually very resistant to proposed changes in the system. In this regard, note Marmor and Thomas's (2012) analysis of the relationship between governments and the medical profession that led them to conclude that the payment method for doctors adopted in any country is what the profession wants.

When structural change does occur in health care, it is more likely to result from exogenous factors—and particularly from developments in the broader political sphere (Tuohy 1994). As change is generated by external factors, episodes of structural change in health care are likely to arise independently of the evolution of policy ideas from health care per se. However, the impact of episodes of structural change is likely to be influenced by the prevailing climate of ideas within the health care system. Thus, the window of opportunity for structural change in the health care arena may be created and opened by factors in the broader political system. That window, however, will open onto a landscape of policy ideas about health care that is in a constant state of flux.

The particular structural changes that result will depend largely upon the landscape of health policy ideas. They will also depend upon how prevailing policy ideas—such as improved equity within communities, fiscal restraint and microeconomic reform—are absorbed and translated within the existing health care system. Indeed, analysis of the impact of research on policymaking indicates that ideas are more likely to affect policy development when they reinforce the values and goals of policymakers (Short, 1997b). Accordingly, when the outputs of the research process are compatible with policymakers' perceptions of the pragmatic realities of the time, they are more likely to be incorporated into policy.

Thus, the 'managed competition' experiment in health care introduced by governments in the United Kingdom, elsewhere in Europe and in New Zealand in the 1980s and 1990s, and advocated in Australia, was part of a larger public policy agenda of market-orientated reforms (Hancock 1999a). There was an 'elective affinity' between these two sets of policy ideas. Whether the new policies that emerge through this process represent desirable changes from the point of view of community welfare is a separate issue. In **Chapter 10** we question the underlying basis of the managed competition thrust, why it was not popular with governments in Australia, and how, along with 'managed care', the term was subject to much muddle and confusion (Marmor & Hacker 2007).

Between periods of structural change in health care, health care politics tend to be dominated by distributional issues and policies and by the constellation of actors and institutions within the health care structure. In Australia there is ongoing tension in the relative roles and responsibilities of the federal and state/territory governments. In the past, this came to a head every five years, when the Healthcare Agreements were renegotiated. Following the election of the Labor government in 2007, with its major health policy objective to eliminate the 'blame game' between the states and the Commonwealth, the roles and responsibilities of each level of government again surfaced as a major issue (see **Chapter 10**).

There were arguably two periods of structural change in health care politics during the 20th century in Australia. At other times, distributional issues, such as doctors' fees and hospital waiting lists (and incremental policy changes), are the norm. The most obvious structural change occurred in 1975 with the introduction of Medibank (now called Medicare) and the entitlement to health insurance for all eligible residents. This significant health care policy reform was part of the broader platform of social policy reforms introduced by the Whitlam Government between 1972 and 1975, and was crucial to that government's achievement of its equity agenda.

The other significant health care policy change, the introduction of casemix-based hospital funding in Victoria during the 1990s, was also prompted by changes in the broader public policy agenda. This was most notable in political support for the Kennett Government in both houses of parliament, a large majority in the lower house and a substantial budget deficit. In both cases, there was a historical conjuncture between the desire for change on the part of health policymakers and the opportunity for change created by the leader of the government of the day and the broader public policy agenda. Further discussion of casemix funding (now renamed activity-based funding), and the factors leading to its introduction and its recent application nationally, is presented in **Chapters 5** and **10**.

Sociological perspectives

Sociology augments the perspectives on health policy already discussed by providing additional insights into the societal and cultural bases of relations of domination and subordination in both the health care system and the broader community. Sociologists are concerned with equity; that is, with fair or just treatment.

Since Freidson's (1961, 1970b) important work on 'professional dominance', a major focus of research interest among health sociologists has been the power of the medical profession in shaping health care systems. For Freidson and for Willis (1989) in Australia, professional dominance is the analytical key to ongoing inadequacies in health policy. The medical profession dominates health care by enjoying professional autonomy—that is, freedom from outside scrutiny—through authority over other health occupations, and by shaping society's beliefs about health problems and how they should be managed. All three aspects of medical dominance have important implications for health policy.

Medicine is regarded as the archetypal 'professional' occupation. It enjoys a particularly high level of work autonomy or protection from outside scrutiny. Individual medical practitioners act as independent professionals, and they can only be evaluated by peers within the profession, through regulated patterns of peer review. This protection from outside evaluation or regulation means that doctors can, by and large, make clinical or technical decisions without being accountable to anyone outside the profession. Their privileged position is of relatively recent origin. It developed in the 20th century due to close links between the medical profession and elites in government and the public service. Furthermore, it has been suggested that the strength of these 'close links' can only be explained by the common upper-class origins of members of the profession and governing elites (Navarro 1978).

The medical profession's autonomy is strengthened by its traditional enjoyment of a legally supported monopoly over clinical practice. This protection from competing practitioners is illustrated by the fact that the medical profession has the exclusive authority, with a few exceptions, to hospitalise patients, to prescribe drugs and to order laboratory tests. Medicine's monopoly is also indicated by the fact that, again with some exceptions that have increased recently, the federal government's Medicare scheme will only reimburse patients for treatments carried out by registered medical practitioners.

Professional autonomy has important implications for health policy; doctors have the major influence on the type of health care we receive. This phenomenon is potentially problematic because, following Freidson, the perspectives and objectives of doctors and patients are not always compatible. Problems associated with medicine's clinical autonomy are further compounded by doctors' decisions often being affected by a 'technological imperative': if a method of treatment is available, doctors feel compelled to use it even if there is little evidence that it is effective (Mechanic 1976; Short 1985). The overservicing in surgical practice that we discuss in **Chapter 7** is an important manifestation of this imperative. Similar considerations apply to the use of drug therapy by psychiatrists, which we consider in **Chapter 9**.

Occupational dominance in health care is perhaps best characterised as a pyramid, with a powerful minority of doctors at the top controlling the work of other occupations beneath. This hierarchy also entails significant disparities in political influence, income, social status and educational level. As Willis (1989) has noted, 'Medicine dominates the health division of labour economically, politically, socially and intellectually' in Australia (p. 2).

Cultural authority, the third type of medical domination, is reflected in the fact that the medical profession, despite the setbacks it has suffered in recent years, continues to play a major role in determining many aspects of health policy in Australia. This includes the reason that some important issues—such as the rates of performance of certain questionable surgical procedures or information systems that link patient outcomes to the activities of individual medical practitioners—do not find their way onto the policy agendas of governments. It is doctors who often define health problems and shape decisions about how they should be managed. Thus, any analysis of community attitudes towards health and health care has to acknowledge that the views of the great majority of the population are dominated by the values and beliefs of the medical profession. In Australia, 'doctors are institutionalised experts on all matters relating to health' (Willis 1989, p. 3). When then prime minister Kevin Rudd in 2007 gave high priority to the reform of the Australian health care system, he followed this up with an extensive round of hospital visits where he mainly spoke to members of the medical profession.

Ethical considerations

We are mindful of an increasing tendency for health care analysts to argue that the major solutions to health policy issues in the future will involve wrestling with ethical considerations; that is, questions that relate to moral choices and rules of conduct. Certainly, there is a great deal of work to be done in applying ethical principles to health care problems. We acknowledge the importance of ethical considerations when questions relating to life and death are central—in issues such as abortion, surrogacy, genetic testing, cloning and euthanasia (Kuhse & Singer 1985; O'Sullivan, Sharman & Short 1999). Ethical considerations are also relevant when applied to health care decision-making and medical research (Health and Medical Research Strategic Review 1999; Mooney 1986; Rumbold 1986; Rutnam 1988). It is thus useful to distinguish between micro-level ethics, applicable to clinical decision-making between clinicians and patients, and macro-level ethics, relevant to the rights and responsibilities of governments and citizens (Bates 1999; Short 1997a).

Consider, for example, the case of an 85-year-old woman whose doctor suggests that she has an operation to remove her cancerous breast (a mastectomy). This situation raises ethical considerations for all parties affected by the decision: for the woman, her family and friends, health professionals, health administrators and taxpayers, who subsidise health services. The difficulty here is that codes of ethics such as the Hippocratic corpus are less useful in our modern society than in a more traditional society, because there is considerable disagreement across different sectors of the community over moral solutions. Is the medical practitioner obliged to do everything medically possible to treat the patient's cancer? Alternatively, is the doctor's major responsibility to relieve suffering? What if a nurse disagrees with the doctor's advice? Is the nurse morally obligated to support the medical practitioner's recommendation to operate? Should the nurse act as an advocate or representative for the patient?

We contend that the assertion of a single ethical point of view has limited utility in this instance because answers to these moral questions vary greatly between individuals, and between the different groups who have an interest in the outcome of the decision. For this reason, we find the notion of 'interests' to have considerably greater utility. The concept recognises that different groups often have different perspectives on a single problem, because they have different values or stand to gain or lose in different ways. An analysis based on interests rather than ethics recognises that differences of approach and emphasis in dealing with policy issues are inevitable and desirable.

In the above case, many economists will analyse the problem in terms of the 'preference functions' of the interested parties. This is based on the notion that people have a set of autonomous preferences that determines their choices when alternatives are presented to them. However, most health sociologists and political scientists will not assume that the patient is able to make a fully informed decision about their treatment, based on knowledge of all the possible treatment options, and the associated costs and benefits. Furthermore, sociologists and political scientists do not take for granted that patients make decisions based on their own value judgments about what is right or wrong.

The power relation between doctor and patient is crucial here (Short 1986a). Is the patient making an informed choice or is the doctor acting in a paternalistic manner; is the doctor making the decision on the patient's behalf because the 'doctor knows best'? These sociological and political considerations are significant because they acknowledge that what may be ethical for the patient or nurse may differ from the doctor's perception of ethical medical practice. Certainly, ethical considerations are necessary but not sufficient for a complete understanding of the problem and the solution.

The situation at Chelmsford Private Hospital in Sydney, where 24 people died during or after therapy in the infamous deep-sleep ward between 1962 and 1979, illustrates that ethical mechanisms, including peer review within the medical profession, are inadequate on their own (Bromberger & Fife-Yeomans, 1991). Similar considerations apply to the disasters in a number of public hospitals in Australia that emerged in the 2000s (van der Weyden 2005). These are discussed in **Chapter 5**. Such appalling failures of hospitals and health departments to protect health care consumers, along with the evidence that large numbers of hospital patients die each year from avoidable causes, point to the need for governments to implement a range of draconian measures to reduce or eliminate similar problems in the future. The mechanisms are discussed further in **Chapters 5** and **10**.

Interests

The theory of interests used here derives, in large part, from Lukes' (1974) three-dimensional theory of power. It has also been applied to analysis of British health policy by Allsop (1984) and Haywood and Alaszewski (1980), and in Australia by Hancock (1999b). Power refers to every possibility within a social relationship of imposing one's will, even against opposition. Domination, a specific type of power, refers to the possibility of finding a specific group of people to obey a directive (Weber 1978). In our view, the notion of interests is one of the most important conceptions in the study of health policy because it underlies every other perspective. Furthermore, it bears a direct relationship to the levels of policy analysis discussed in **Chapter 2**, and to the sources of medical dominance outlined above.

Specifically, the one-dimensional view is based on a 'subjective' conception of interests in which these are equated to consciously held and articulated preferences and grievances. At this level, interests are understood as policy preferences, so a conflict of interests is equivalent to a conflict of politically articulated demands. Attention is focused, therefore, on what particular individuals or organisations ask for in the health arena; from the political science perspective, the political demands made on the system. It has already been noted that the medical profession is well placed to make effective demands on the political system.

The two-dimensional view recognises, in addition, an objective conception of interests because it emphasises that attitudes and preferences are shaped by 'objective' conditions, which may be external to the consciousness of individuals or groups. This level is more complex than the one-dimensional view because it acknowledges that the most effective and insidious use of power often prevents an overt conflict of subjective interests from arising in the first place. It is important to study the ability of individuals or groups to control the issues placed on the policy agenda within the democratic political system. Mass media have a key role in bringing a concern to the attention of the public and in shaping the message (Bury & Gabe 1990;

Green & Thorogood 1998). We discuss agenda-setting in some detail in **Chapter 10**. Another concern is the establishment of the rules of the game—the ways in which issues on the agenda are handled.

As will be seen in later chapters, there are clearly areas of health policy that have been excluded from the political agenda or have not progressed beyond preliminary skirmishing. These relate to a wide range of non-decision-making areas in health policy, including issues such as the right to private practice in public hospitals, the setting of medical fees and the high rates of performance of a number of surgical procedures (see **Chapter 7**). The medical profession's power at this level of analysis results in the suppression of demands for change or challenges to medical dominance before they gain access to the relevant policymaking agenda.

The three-dimensional view recognises a conception of generalisable human interests, such as human rights, in addition to subjective and objective conceptions of interests. At this level, interests might be unarticulated or unobservable and, above all, people might actually be mistaken about, or unaware of, their own interests. We recognise the importance of hegemony; that is, the existence of sets of beliefs that operate to legitimise existing power relations. This gives powerful groups the ability to prevent parties from having grievances by shaping their beliefs, attitudes and preferences in such a way that they accept their role in the status quo, either because they see it as right, natural or unchangeable, or because they value it as beneficial.

It is here that the cultural authority of the medical profession and the capacity of doctors to generate demands for their services lie. Despite the alternative perspective offered by proponents of the new public health, issues such as pollution and alcohol abuse rarely reach the health policy agenda, whereas the waiting lists for elective surgery are a matter of constant concern. As in Britain, questions of priorities across a broad spectrum of health needs of the community hardly ever arise (Allsop 1984). Furthermore, the structure of our health care system—with its hierarchy of occupations, status and rewards—reinforces the power of professional monopolists and reduces the influence of challenging and repressed interests.

Epidemiological and public health perspectives

Although most politicians, administrators, clinicians and members of the public take the effectiveness of curative health services for granted, this has not always been the case. The first half of the 19th century has been characterised as a period of 'therapeutic nihilism', when there was systematic and vehement criticism of the effectiveness and humanity of medicine from members of the medical profession and the lay public (Black et al. 1984). It has also been claimed that it was not until 1910 that a random patient with a random illness consulting a random doctor had a better than 50-50 chance of benefiting from the consultation (Freidson 1970a). This sceptical attitude towards the effectiveness of medical care has received renewed support from epidemiological and public health sources during the past 30 years. As we note in **Chapter 7**, a challenging book by clinician Nortin Hadler (2008)

provides a well-documented account of the ineffective nature of a wide range of common medical, surgical and diagnostic interventions.

Epidemiologists study the determinants of the incidence and prevalence of disease. *Epidemiology* is the science concerned with the occurrence, transmission, control and natural history of diseases and risk factors. Public health, in contrast, is a broader and more eclectic field of study and practice. *Public health* refers to those efforts that are organised by society, through governments, to protect, promote and restore the health of a population. The emphasis is placed on a totality of endeavours, including those that impact on other systems such as housing and social welfare, and on activities that affect communities rather than individuals.

McKeown's contribution

Particularly influential in regard to the limited impact of clinical medicine on health outcomes is the work of Thomas McKeown (1976, 1979), a British doctor and demographer. McKeown's demographic research showed that decreases in mortality have arisen mainly from improvements in living standards, water supply, sanitation and nutrition, rather than from developments in medical science and technology. In addition, McKeown's data revealed that clinical medicine did not make any significant contribution to the reduction of mortality rates from infectious diseases such as respiratory tuberculosis until the second half of the 20th century, when antibiotic drugs and immunisation measures became widely available. This is illustrated in figure 3.2.

Many public health advocates influenced by McKeown's thesis now recognise that health services are not as important in determining health status as social, economic, dietary and other lifestyle and environmental factors. They claim that our

Figure 3.2   Respiratory tuberculosis: death rates, England and Wales, 1850–1966

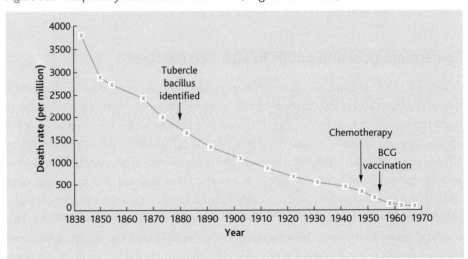

Source: McKeown (1976)

culture has overestimated the effectiveness of curative medicine and underestimated its limitations. The main thrust of the public health argument is the need to put the capacity of clinical medicine into perspective.

Public health proponents do not suggest that modern medicine is ineffective. They recognise, for example, that much medical intervention is concerned with reducing discomfort and disability, and that these goals are achieved with greater success than the reduction of mortality. What they do suggest is that society's investment in health services is inappropriately deployed because of its over-reliance on the 'engineering model' of clinical medicine and that other priorities, including a greater emphasis on the caring role, may be preferable.

Notable medical critics of the contemporary emphasis in health policy on curative medicine have included Cochrane (1972) and McKeown (1979) in Britain, and Leeder (1999), Powles (1973), Sax (1972) and Taylor (1979) in Australia. We classify these writers as public health advocates because they share Dubos's (1960, 1968) 'ecological' view of health and a common interest in epidemiology and public health. The main contention in Dubos's ecological perspective is that health is a 'mirage', or unattainable goal, and that significant improvements in health status cannot be achieved through medical means alone. This perspective stresses that health problems should be examined within an environmental, social and historical context because such domains are the basic sources of many of the problems.

The new public health

The new public health movement links 'traditional' public health concerns, which tend to focus on physical aspects of the environment such as clean air and water, food, infection control and occupational health and safety legislation, with broader social, economic and environmental factors. Many advocates of the new public health have been influenced by McKeown's thesis, as discussed above.

The new public health emphasises the need to draw on knowledge from different perspectives and the importance of a social movement as a stimulus, support and base (Fry 1987). This means that public health policy is not solely a health activity conducted by professionals. The loose network of groups and individuals that share this philosophy tends to emphasise health promotion, community participation and intersectoral collaboration. An intersectoral approach requires the coordination of policies and actions to achieve the maximum positive impact on the health of a community. It requires cooperation between governments, departmental officials, the private sector and non-government organisations in developing healthy public policies, as we examine in more detail in **Chapter 8**.

Cochrane's contribution

Archie Cochrane's (1972) influential work also helped to change health policy agendas in Britain and internationally. Cochrane, a clinical epidemiologist, linked the concepts of effectiveness and efficiency and attempted to develop an approach that would enable the National Health Service (NHS) in Britain to produce the best possible outcomes at the lowest cost for the British public. If two different services or practices result in the same improvement in health status—that is, they are equally effective when applied to a target population—the activity that produces the result at the lower cost is to be preferred; it is the more efficient activity. The promotion of efficiency, in this sense, does not necessarily imply the cutting of costs; it means producing the desired outcome with the lowest possible use of real resources. Cochrane, in fact, simply applied a basic economic criterion for optimum resource allocation to clinical medicine.

Cochrane claimed, moreover, that modern medicine was not necessarily ineffective but that its effectiveness had been 'under-investigated'. Cochrane advocated a cost–benefit approach in conjunction with the widespread use of randomised controlled trials to prevent the inefficient use of ineffective treatments and the inefficient use of effective treatments. It is of interest that the network of collaborating centres based in several countries, including Australia, that has grown out of evidence-based medicine developments is named the 'Cochrane collaboration'. Evidence-based medicine has increased in influence more recently, as reflected in our discussion in **Chapters 7** and **10**. However, we note also in **Chapter 7** that in using the Cochrane data we found that there is a conspicuous lack of reliable information bearing on the desirability or otherwise of a number of common surgical interventions. Similar considerations apply to the use of many psychotropic drugs, which we discuss in **Chapter 9**.

The main policy implications that flow from public health and epidemiological perspectives are the need:

- to shift the emphasis away from the provision of acute curative services and towards preventative public health strategies
- for reappraisal of the 'pastoral', or caring, role of medicine
- to evaluate critically and comprehensively the effectiveness and efficiency of medical practice.

These public health and epidemiological perspectives indicate, moreover, that the most important challenges 'to the ideological dominance of curative medicine in the sphere of health policy' have come from within medicine itself (Hart 1982, p. 436).

SUMMARY AND CONCLUSION

In this chapter our intention has been to outline key perspectives in health policy analysis that we believe have considerable descriptive and explanatory power when applied to particular aspects of policy in Australia. Either implicitly or explicitly, they form the background for the discussion of each of the policy areas and issues considered in the following chapters. Each perspective has a close relationship with a particular domain and is characterised by certain key issues, as illustrated in table 3.1.

Table 3.1   Theoretical perspectives on health policy

Perspective	Domain	Key issue	Main concepts
Economic	The economy	Efficiency	Demand, supply
Political	Politics	Policymaking	Reform, stability
Sociological	Society	Equity	Fairness, social justice
Epidemiological	Disease	Effectiveness	Morbidity, mortality

While each perspective has its own concepts and particular domain of reference, in practice all are closely interrelated. Thus, economists may use the concept of effectiveness and epidemiologists such as Cochrane are interested in efficiency. Clearly, the four perspectives listed in table 3.1 do not deal in the same way with the same policy issues. Nor are they able to answer the same historical or empirical questions. At the same time, however, there is no good theoretical reason for assigning economic issues exclusively to economics, political issues to political science, disease problems to epidemiology and social problems to sociology. These disciplines themselves can be viewed as cultural constructions produced by different groups of individuals and organisations, rather than reflections of distinct domains of social reality (Foucault 1972).

In the previous chapter we emphasised that health policy analysis must be multidisciplinary. Our approach requires input from all these perspectives to accommodate the complexities of the problems being addressed. Different problems, therefore, require the use of different perspectives and emphases. One example of this selection process will suffice before we move on to apply our framework to significant issues in health care.

When do we use Alford's 'structural interests' perspective and why? We have found that Alford's conceptual framework has greatest utility when we are attempting to explain barriers to health policy reform (Short 1998). Alford's approach is extremely useful in this problem domain because of the evidence that interest groups do 'work together' structurally within the policymaking system to oppose or to promote change. An example here is the way in which the Australian Medical Association, the health insurance industry and private hospitals, in the past, have been united in their opposition to Medicare and other desirable health reforms. We find it helpful, moreover, to talk about a collection of interest groups as being a 'structural interest' when we are referring to a particular structure, the health care system.

At the same time, we have acknowledged several limitations when applying Alford's framework to Australian health policy and argued that other perspectives are needed to answer further questions about possibilities for health care policy reform. This brought us to the broader public policy agenda and to recognition of the fact that health care reform is most likely to occur when windows of opportunity are created in the political arena by factors such as changes of government, election commitments and budgetary considerations.

FURTHER READING

Of the multiplicity of books dealing with health economics, most of which have been written for the United States academic market, we believe that the monograph by the Canadian health economist Robert Evans (1984), *Strained Mercy: The Economics of Canadian Health Care* (Butterworths) is still the most useful account of this complex and controversial subject. Most health economists in the United States, with some notable exceptions, subscribe to the doctrines of neoclassical economics that place considerable emphasis on free markets, user-pays principles and the alleged negative effects of health insurance and government regulation. Evans in this book devotes a good deal of attention to refuting their arguments and stressing the need for greater equity in health care funding and provision.

Robert Alford's 1975 *Health Care Politics: Ideological and Interest Group Barriers to Reform* (University of Chicago Press) has been one of the most effective in the discipline of political science in influencing the thinking of many health policy specialists, including ourselves.

The book jointly edited by TR Marmor and R Klein (2012), *Politics, Health and Health Care: Selected Essays* (Yale University Press), provides access to the perceptive views about health policy of two very knowledgeable academics and policy analysts. Marmor has written extensively about the health care system in the United States, while Klein has undertaken numerous studies of the British NHS. They are particularly scathing about the frequent appearance of fads in the literature of health services management and policy, which are often unrealistic in the claims made for them and which usually fade into oblivion when the next generation of fads is unveiled. They are also highly critical of the attempt to undertake policy analysis without paying at least equal attention to the political issues.

DISCUSSION QUESTIONS

1 What problems arise in applying the tools of economics to the problems of the health industry? Is the commodity 'health' just the same as any other commodity bought and sold in a market?
2 What do you understand by the phrase 'supplier-induced demand'? What are the implications of this concept for health policies such as those that focus on the use of co-payments to reduce demand?
3 How should ethical considerations influence health policy development and implementation?
4 Describe your understanding of the differences between ethics and equity as they apply to the health services.
5 We have emphasised in this chapter the notions of interests and power as key factors in understanding public policymaking about health. Do you agree with this 'world view'?

Health insurance and the financing of health services

The most distinctive aspect of any country's health care system is the set of arrangements in operation that reduce or eliminate the financial burden of illness experienced by individuals. All developed countries and many developing ones have implemented systems for meeting all or part of the medical and hospital expenses of members of their populations. The details of these arrangements, however, vary widely from country to country. For example, governments in the United Kingdom via the National Health Service (NHS) directly provide most health services to the entire resident population without significant charges; the expenditure incurred is financed out of general taxation and other government revenue.

At the other end of the spectrum of government involvement, in the United States most medical and hospital services are provided by private individuals and organisations, with the roles of governments being restricted mainly to subsidising costs borne by specific groups, notably the aged and the poor. Insurance to meet expenditure on health is made available by private health funds and the costs are paid for by individuals or, more commonly, by their employers. About 15 per cent of the population (some 47 million people) did not have any guaranteed protection against the costs of illness, which can run into many thousands of dollars in the case of major accidents and chronic illness. This situation is changing as the result of the Obama administration's Affordable Care Act (see page 64).

Other developed countries generally provide some form of health insurance for their entire populations. In many cases, this is administered and financed by a government agency; in other instances independent health funds are responsible for the insurance arrangements but they are subject to wide-ranging government regulations (OECD 1992; Reinhardt et al. 2004).

In most countries, health insurance, and the closely related questions of how health services are to be financed and how doctors are to be paid, have been contentious political issues at times of major policy changes. The reasons for conflicts associated with these changes are undoubtedly a consequence of the redistributive potential of policies in this area, and of the special role of the medical profession in the health care system and in the wider social and political arenas. It was noted in **Chapter 2** that redistributive policies are the most difficult to implement because of the opposition they generate from potential losers. When these losers include doctors, an affluent and well-organised group that is able to generate disproportionately large political demands, it is hardly surprising that many issues associated with health care financing produce political conflict.

What is of greatest interest is that in almost all countries, current health insurance and financing arrangements have not been the focus of longstanding political attention. Strong opposition to them from a major political party, or indeed from the medical profession as a whole, has not been a recurring political theme. The two notable exceptions are the United States and Australia. In both countries, health insurance has been the focus of a great deal of political activity for at least the past 50 years. In others such as Canada, there have been some recent attempts by conservative political parties in some provinces to alter the financing arrangements in light of budgetary problems and diminished public confidence in the system. Nevertheless, to date no fundamental changes have emerged (Tuohy 2009).

Attempts in the United States to establish some form of national comprehensive health insurance have been a consistent feature of administrations controlled by the Democrats since the presidency of Harry Truman, which began in 1945. Most Republicans, and the majority of the medical profession, have been opposed to any greater role for the federal government in health financing, especially if this would entail increased tax-funded expenditure. During the Reagan and Bush Senior administrations, any health initiatives that might increase government expenditure were regarded as unacceptable, but many groups were active from the latter part of the 1980s in endeavouring to devise schemes to provide health insurance coverage for the entire population.

The Clinton administration, elected in 1992, was strongly committed to a major restructuring of health insurance arrangements. However, because of concerted efforts by the main structural interests and opposition within the United States Congress, efforts to provide universal health insurance were notably unsuccessful. Nevertheless, they laid the foundation for the era of so-called managed competition, which led to dramatic changes in the way that health care is organised and doctors are paid. However, opposition to managed care from organised medicine, along with the excesses in restricting subscribers' entitlements practised by some for-profit managed care organisations, led to a backlash in the late 1990s.

With the election of President Obama in 2008, a new set of efforts to reform the dysfunctional and inequitable American health care system was initiated. This culminated in the signing into law of the Patient Protection and Affordable Care Act in March 2010. The Act provided for the extension of health insurance coverage to a high proportion of the currently uninsured via subsidies to those on lower incomes and increased regulation of the health insurance industry so that companies could not refuse to accept clients with pre-existing illnesses. The constitutionality of the important provision that non-insured persons would be required to take out health insurance or face a financial penalty was affirmed by the US Supreme Court in 2012.

The Republican Party bitterly opposed the legislation with absurd claims that it represented a takeover by the federal government of health care. However, so-called ObamaCare was generally unpopular with the electorate, with many people who enjoy good insurance coverage via their employers fearful that the new measures would only lead to higher costs and higher taxation.

The Australian experience is unique in that health has been a major political issue in many federal elections since 1969. There were fundamental shifts in health insurance policy following the changes of government in 1972, 1975 and 1983. The return to a conservative government in 1996 featured a substantial emphasis on bolstering the private health insurance and private hospital sectors but without any major changes to the universal publically funded health insurance and public hospital financing arrangements (see below). In the 2007 election, Labor's policy emphasised reform of the health care system, especially in regard to ending the blame game between the states and the Commonwealth over funding issues. When it came to office, the Rudd Government set up the National Health and Hospitals Reform Commission to provide advice and recommendations on many aspects of the funding of health services, and the relations between the state and federal governments in this policy area. The work of the commission and the subsequent policy initiatives of the Labor governments are discussed in **Chapters 5** and **10**.

Health insurance in Australia

It is not possible to understand the complexities of policy and political issues associated with health insurance in Australia without a basic knowledge of its historical development over the past six decades. Aspects of this history have been described in detail elsewhere (see, for example, Boxall & Gillespie 2013; Gillespie 1991; Gray 2004; Sax 1984; Scotton & Macdonald 1993). We summarise below the major milestones in health insurance policies.

Historical background

The first government-sponsored health insurance program in Australia, the Earle Page scheme, was introduced in 1953 by the Liberal–Country Party Coalition government. Essentially, the Commonwealth government subsidised private insurance by meeting part of the cost of rebates for medical expenses. The scheme was administered by private non-profit health funds, under conditions established by a national health act. Participation in the program was on a voluntary basis, but membership of a health fund was a necessary condition for receiving the government's subsidy for medical bills. Except for the government subsidy, the arrangements, with their heavy emphasis on the use of private health insurance organisations, were very similar to the system in the United States at that time.

The voluntary health insurance scheme was foreshadowed by the Liberal–Country Party Coalition while in opposition as an alternative to a national health scheme along British lines. The British Medical Association in Australia (later to become the Australian Medical Association, or AMA) had thwarted early moves in this direction by the Labor government, which lost power in 1949. Sir Earle Page, the then minister for health in the Coalition government, was a medical practitioner and had developed the health insurance program in close collaboration with the profession.

By the late 1960s, the Earle Page scheme had been subjected to much criticism owing to its failure to cover the entire population. This was due to the large gap in many cases between the fees charged by doctors and the refunds obtained from health funds, and because of the administrative complexity and costliness of the program. A committee set up by the government in 1968 to review the scheme (Committee of Inquiry into Health Insurance 1969) confirmed many of these criticisms.

Prior to the 1969 federal election, Labor had developed a credible alternative health insurance program based largely on the work of two health economists, Richard Scotton and John Deeble. This program was designed to cover the entire population and to be administered by a Commonwealth government authority. Furthermore, it would be funded entirely from taxation revenue, including a new health tax.

Medibank

After the victory of Labor at the 1972 federal election, the Whitlam Government set about implementing a health insurance program that incorporated the principles and characteristics developed by Scotton and Deeble. The program was strongly opposed by the AMA, private health funds and the opposition parties. The legislation to introduce Medibank, twice rejected by the Senate, was finally passed after a dissolution of both houses of parliament, a federal election in which health was again a major issue, and a joint sitting of both houses to resolve the continuing deadlock over this and other legislation (Scotton & Macdonald 1993).

The medical insurance aspects of Medibank were introduced on 1 July 1975, and a Commonwealth authority, the Health Insurance Commission, was established to administer the program, which was funded entirely from Commonwealth revenue. Later in 1975, after agreements with the states had been negotiated, free hospital care was made available in public hospitals as part of the program. This included free medical care with attending doctors being paid by the hospital on a salaried, sessional or fee-for-service basis. However, patients could still elect to be treated by their own doctor privately.

Return to voluntary private insurance

After the election of the Liberal–National Party Coalition in December 1975, the Fraser Government began the task of dismantling progressively the main features of Medibank. The first revision allowed for opting out of the government program by the purchase of private health insurance. Those who remained covered by the Health Insurance Commission were required to pay a levy of 2.5 per cent of their taxable income.

The last set of changes implemented by the Fraser Government in 1981 represented a return to a voluntary private health insurance program. The Commonwealth's subsidy was payable only to members of registered health funds. Contributions to the funds became eligible for taxation rebates. Free treatment in hospital as an inpatient or an outpatient was eliminated. Strong incentives were therefore put in place to induce people to take out private health insurance coverage and thus reverse the decline in fund membership that had occurred after the previous change. The preoccupation of Australian governments with bolstering private health insurance coverage is a continuing theme of health policymaking as we indicate on page 69.

Medicare

The election of the Hawke Labor Government in 1983 was followed by a return to a system of tax-funded health insurance administered by the Health Insurance Commission, now named Medicare Australia. Medicare, which was introduced on 1 February 1984, covered everyone normally resident in Australia and short-term visitors from countries with reciprocal health agreements. Free hospital care was again made available to all who chose this option, and the health funds were permitted to offer insurance to those who wished to become private patients in either private or public hospitals.

Initially, opposition to Medicare from the medical profession was relatively subdued as compared with the reaction to Medibank. The federal branch of the AMA indicated that, despite its continuing philosophical objections to compulsory health insurance, it would not actively oppose the direct billing option and centralising the administration of the program in a government agency (Repin 1984). The doctors' dispute that subsequently erupted in New South Wales was indicative of health insurance again providing the basis for a bitter political conflict between the government and sections of the medical profession.

Late in 1983, doctors became alarmed because a new provision of the Health Insurance Act (section 17) would make the payment of medical benefits for specified diagnostic services subject to an agreement between the hospital and the doctor rendering the service. The approval of the Commonwealth minister of health was required for the agreement. Guidelines for the agreement specified that the fee charged be no more than the schedule fee. Concern from the medical profession focused on the possibility that control of fees would be extended subsequently to all medical services provided in public hospitals.

The dispute was resolved by the Commonwealth and New South Wales governments making several concessions to doctors, including the repeal of section 17. Modifications to Medicare included the introduction of gap insurance as part of hospital insurance for medical services provided in hospitals to private patients. In New South Wales, fee-for-service payments to doctors for treating public patients were extended to all public hospitals, except the major teaching hospitals.

Coalition health insurance policies

During the 1987 federal election campaign, the Liberal–National Coalition's health policy indicated that the principal elements of Medicare would be repealed, with private health funds again providing medical insurance. Patients would be required to contribute much more in out-of-pocket payments. The Coalition appeared not to be certain about the details of critical points of the policy, especially regarding savings to the Commonwealth budget that could be achieved (Kelly 1992).

In the lead-up to the 1990 federal election, the Coalition again put forward a health policy document that would have altered drastically the national health insurance arrangements. Tax credits for health fund contributions were to be introduced and the health fund levy was to be abolished. The Coalition's health policy also included provision for each contributor to meet the first $250 of their medical expenditure each year.

The minister for health at the time, Dr Neal Blewett, was quick to point out that a revenue-neutral health scheme without losers was logically impossible to achieve. The Coalition's response was to drop the idea of a costed health policy statement and resort to a broad statement of principles. According to one chronicle of political events, this fiasco was even more damaging to the Coalition than its attempts to present an alternative to Medicare at the previous election (Kelly 1992).

The 'Fightback!' package introduced by the federal opposition late in 1991 contained a further health policy statement (Liberal Party of Australia 1991). Medicare would be retained but with increased private sector participation. A system of tax incentives for low-income earners and penalties for those on high incomes was foreshadowed to increase the proportion of the population covered by private health insurance for hospital cover. Direct billing would be eliminated for all except eligible pensioners. The medical fees aspect of the Fightback! health policy, involving the elimination of direct billing and increased co-payments by patients, was strongly criticised because of its potential to increase dramatically the aggregate fees charged by doctors at the expense of health fund contributors and patients (Scotton 1992b).

No doubt after realising that their health insurance policies had been unpopular at the previous three elections and possibly contributed to their defeat, the Coalition made the commitment in the 1996 election campaign to retain Medicare. Following their success and the appointment of John Howard as prime minister, the policies adopted in government concentrated on the private health insurance aspect of health insurance. To the surprise of some political analysts, the commitment to retain Medicare was kept during its term of office. Details of the Howard Government's changes to Medicare are set out below, along with those of the Rudd and Gillard Labor governments from 2007 to 2013.

Private health insurance

Before the introduction of Medibank, private health insurance was the predominant mechanism for paying for hospital and medical services in Australia. One of the most important effects of the move to compulsory tax-funded health insurance and hospital funding was to reduce substantially the role of private health insurance. However, private health insurance has continued to be available to meet all or part of the costs of private patient care in hospitals, and for other health care services such as dental and allied health. The pattern of heavy government regulation of private health insurance, introduced with the National Health Act passed in 1953 to implement the Earle Page voluntary health insurance scheme, has continued to the present time. A major aspect of the legislation was to enshrine the principle of community rating; that is, to ensure that premiums charged were not based on the risk of illness and the use of health services associated with individual members and their families. These risks vary widely; for example, they are greatly affected by age and family size. In general, community rating has led to the contribution rate for families being set at twice the rate for single persons, irrespective of the number of dependants covered. Variations in risk between different funds, based on the proportion of older members, have been addressed by the creation of a reinsurance pool to which all funds contribute.

In addition, the funds must adhere to several other constraints, including a waiting period before claims can be made, generally two months, except for pre-existing illnesses (12 months) and pregnancy (12 months). They must also include inpatient psychiatric, rehabilitation and palliative care services in their hospital coverage. They are prohibited from offering no-claim bonuses, discounts for non-smokers or insurance for nursing home care. They are not permitted to cover medical fee gaps except for the difference between the Medicare rebate and the scheduled fee for inpatient medical services to private patients. Regulation has also concentrated on the financial viability of the funds and the levels of reserves they are required to maintain.

The regulation of health insurance funds, including the registration of funds, is the responsibility of the Australian Department of Health aided by the Private Health Insurance Administration Council (PHIAC). Proposed changes in fees are also subject to the approval of the Commonwealth minister for health. PHIAC is a statutory authority that monitors the performance of the industry and provides data on the numbers and proportion of the population covered by the funds. Private health insurance is also the subject of health surveys conducted by the Australian Bureau of Statistics (2013a).

Coverage of the population by private health insurance

Coverage to meet hospital costs either as a private patient in a public hospital or in a private hospital is the most important measure of the role of private health insurance in the health policy context. In the 1982–83 financial year, prior to the establishment of Medicare, 65 per cent of the Australian population had some form of hospital insurance. By 30 June 1984, this proportion had declined to 50 per cent. It was hardly surprising that, faced with the health tax levy and the availability of free hospitalisation, many people, especially those in the lower-income groups, dropped their hospital insurance. Other reasons for the decline included the increases in contribution rates and large out-of-pocket payments (Industry Commission 1997).

Table 4.1 shows the fluctuations in population coverage from 30 June 1984 to 30 June 2013. The increase in the uptake of private health insurance, from the low point of 30.6 per cent at 30 June 1999 to the value of 47.0 per cent at 30 June 2013, is discussed below. The focus on private health insurance increased with the election of a Coalition government in March 1996. From 1 July 1997, under the Private Health Insurance Incentives Scheme, a tax rebate was introduced for contributors on low to medium incomes, along with an increase in the Medicare levy for persons on higher incomes without health insurance. These measures did not arrest the decline, with the percentage of the population covered for hospital insurance decreasing from 32 per cent at 30 September 1997 to 30.1 per cent at 31 December 1998 (PHIAC 1999).

The failure of the earlier measures led the Commonwealth government to introduce a massive 30 per cent subsidy for private health insurance to replace the earlier tax rebate from 1 January 1999, at a cost to the Commonwealth of approximately $1.6 billion. During the year, the hospital insurance rate edged up to the December 1999 value of 31.2 per cent.

After the failure of the large government subsidy to induce a substantial increase in the population covered by private health insurance, the Howard Government implemented a further modification to the rules of the game from July 2000. This was to link health insurance contribution rates to the age at which people took out a policy. Thus, people over 30 years would face a penalty, as compared to the contribution rate of younger people. This penalty amounted to a loading of 2 per cent for each year the person was over 30 when they took out private patient

Table 4.1   Private health insurance: coverage of hospital treatment (%), Australia, 30 June 1984 to 30 June 2013

Year	Percentage of population covered
1984	50.0
1985	47.7
1986	48.8
1987	48.3
1988	47.0
1989	45.5
1990	44.5
1991	43.7
1992	41.0
1993	39.4
1994	37.2
1995	34.9
1996	33.7
1997	32.1
1998	30.8
1999	30.8
2000	43.3
2001	45.2
2002	44.7
2003	43.8
2004	43.3
2005	43.1
2006	43.3
2007	43.9
2008	44.9
2009	44.9
2010	45.3
2011	45.9
2012	46.6
2013	46.9

Source: Private Health Insurance Administration Council (2013)

hospital insurance. The introduction of Lifetime Health Cover was supported by a large federally funded advertising campaign and it led to a marked increase in the coverage of private health insurance for hospital services. Since that time, the percentage of the population with private insurance has stabilised at between 43 per cent and 47 per cent, as table 4.1 indicates.

The other important policy initiative of the Howard Government was the introduction of MedicarePlus. There were three principal changes in the Medicare arrangements, which took effect shortly after the legislation was passed in March 2004. The first was a revised safety net procedure whereby those who had out-of-pocket payments above a certain threshold were able to access further medical rebates at a more generous level than would otherwise apply. Out-of-pocket payments are the difference between the Medicare rebate for the service and the actual charge met by the patient.

Under pressure from the minor parties, which held the balance of power in the Senate at that time, the threshold was set at $300 for those in receipt of a Commonwealth concession card or those on low incomes and entitled to family tax benefit. For the remainder of Medicare beneficiaries, the threshold was $700. When the threshold was reached, Medicare reimbursed further medical fees for out-of-hospital services at the standard rate plus 80 per cent of the difference between this rate and the fee met by the patient.

The government estimated that the annual cost of the new safety net concession would be $174 million by 2006–07. However, after less than one year of operation, the government noted that the annual cost was much higher and accordingly increased the thresholds to $500 and $1000. Furthermore, the main beneficiaries of the new measure were concentrated in higher income areas. This was hardly surprising in that large differences between medical charges and the Medicare schedule fee typically occur for private specialist services such as CAT scans, which are more frequently accessed by the relatively affluent members of the community.

The second element in MedicarePlus was the introduction of an incentive payment of $7.50 for bulk-billed general practitioner consultations in non-metropolitan areas for all children under 16 years and for concession cardholders. Bulk-billing rates in these areas of relative doctor shortage were generally lower than in the cities.

Finally, a new Medicare Benefits Schedule (MBS) item was introduced for the services provided by allied health professionals when these were part of a GP-sponsored multidisciplinary care plan. The MBS item covered up to five consultations by these professionals. The stated purpose was to improve the delivery of primary health care. For patients with complex health problems who would benefit from dental care, a subsidy was also introduced.

As an extension to the arrangement for allied health professionals, the government in 2006 introduced a special procedure to subsidise further the services provided by psychologists. The new procedure permitted up to 10 consultations in a calendar year to be reimbursed by Medicare when a GP created a mental health plan for the patient before making a referral to a psychologist.

In 2006, also, the private health insurance rebate of 30 per cent was increased to 35 per cent for enrollees between 65 and 69 years of age and to 40 per cent for those 70 years and older.

In the 2007 federal election campaign, Labor promised to continue the subsidy for private health insurance despite the fact that it had opposed the measure when it was introduced by the Coalition government. After its election, the Rudd Government in 2008 announced an important change to the penalty provision for those in higher income groups who did not take out private health insurance. The threshold taxable income of $50 000 at which the Medicare levy was increased to 2.5 per cent was raised to $100 000 for a single person and from $100 000 to $150 000 for family membership.

The other important change was that from 1 July 2012 the private health insurance rebate was means tested. For singles earning more than $84 000 and families earning more than $168 000 at that time, the rebate was progressively reduced so that no rebate was available when the earnings of singles were more than $130 000 and of families were more than $260 000. Corresponding increases in the Medicare levy for those on higher incomes without private health insurance were also introduced at the same time. These measures were strongly opposed by the Coalition parties then in opposition. They argued that the changes would lead to a massive exodus from private health insurance.

ANALYSIS OF HEALTH INSURANCE POLICIES

Health insurance has been the largest and most visible aspect of health policymaking in Australia over the 60-year period covered in this chapter. The outline of developments presented here has revealed a major difference between the major political parties about how the cost burden on users of health services should be met.

This disagreement has decreased since the decision of the Coalition parties prior to the 1996 federal election to support Medicare in the electorate. Nevertheless, the method and financial magnitude of assistance by the Howard Government, along with the means testing of the private health insurance rebate by the Labor government, indicated a continuing difference in the attitude of the main political parties to the respective roles of publicly and privately funded health insurance arrangements.

POLICY ANALYSIS

Political ideology and health insurance

In this section, we examine the factors that have contributed to the conflicts surrounding health insurance. These include the ideological positions of the major political parties and the interest groups supporting these parties, especially significant elements of the medical profession. We emphasise how policies in this area interact in a substantial way with the policies adopted to solve major problems of the economy, such as inflation and the size of the government's budget deficit.

The first issue is the source of the very different approaches to health insurance and the financing of health services. Traditionally, the conservative parties, the Liberal Party and the National Party (and their predecessors), have been wedded to a free-enterprise competitive model of an ideal set of economic relationships in which the role of government is kept to a relatively modest level. Consistent with this approach to policy measures, the model was designed to reduce the reliance on government expenditure to finance health insurance. Increasingly, however, the Coalition parties have been willing to undertake a more interventionist approach in economic and social issues, at least where the interests of their supporters and electoral popularity are at stake.

In Australia, there have been strong links between the conservative political parties and elite members of the medical profession. Indeed, as Willis (1989) has pointed out, many prominent conservative politicians, including several state premiers, have been doctors. Most members of the profession in Australia have seen their interests best served by a free-enterprise, private practice, fee-for-service model of medical service provision. In this model, the role of government is restricted to the payment of subsidies, together with protection of the profession's monopoly over major aspects of patient treatment.

The Australian Labor Party's thinking about the provision and funding of health services after World War II had been influenced heavily by the British Labour Government's decision to introduce the National Health Scheme (NHS). For most of Labor's long period in opposition in the federal parliament between 1949 and 1972, the party's health policy had consisted of vague statements about the desirability of implementing a national health service along the lines of the British scheme. In view of the wording of the 1946 constitutional amendment, which banned 'civil conscription' in the Commonwealth's powers concerning health services (see **Chapter 1**), and its narrow interpretation by the High Court in the late 1940s, it seemed highly unlikely that any attempt to move towards a national health service would have survived the inevitable legal challenge of the medical profession.

Labor's concern to change drastically the system of paying for medical and hospital services stemmed, in part, from the nature of the principal sources of its electoral support in this period: the trade union movement and those in lower-income groups. People of modest incomes, including many trade unionists, had relied heavily on the charity dispensed by doctors and hospitals in the period before the introduction of health insurance. The Earle Page scheme had yielded contribution rates that were too high for many of the poorer members of the community to afford. The tax deductibility of the contributions produced a further source of inequity since the net cost of insurance was higher for those on low incomes.

The Scotton and Deeble proposals for a universal tax-funded health insurance program, incorporating free hospitalisation and free medical care for patients whose doctors adopted the direct billing option, achieved the major equity objectives that underlay the national health service aspiration of Labor. Since the proposals left unaltered the private practice, fee-for-service basis of Australian medical practice, no legal challenge was likely to occur.

Most importantly, a similar system of medical insurance had been implemented successfully in Canada in the early 1960s. The Canadian scheme, and its acceptance by both the community and the medical profession, provided a model for what might happen in Australia. Increasing community dissatisfaction associated with the voluntary health insurance program, moreover, indicated that the new approach would be attractive electorally. The leader of the federal opposition, Gough Whitlam, therefore embraced universal health insurance in 1968 as a major aspect of Labor policy.

Sources of continuing political conflict

Major interest groups in Australia with a stake in health insurance have included the AMA, the private health funds and the Australian Private Hospitals Association. In the lead-up to the introduction of Medibank, these groups were bitterly opposed to the reform. Senior managers of health funds were undoubtedly concerned that their membership would decline substantially, as would their influence and incomes. Similarly, private hospitals expected that their role would diminish in the face of the availability of free services in public hospitals.

As we noted in **Chapter 3**, groups with a concentrated interest in health policy matters are able to have greater impact than the rest of the community. While their opposition to universal health insurance was overcome temporarily with the introduction of Medibank and Medicare, the same groups were instrumental in influencing the health policies of the Coalition parties for most of the period under consideration.

One important difference between the Canadian health insurance system and the Australian version may have played a significant role in the general acceptance of the former and the continuing conflict associated with the latter from the ranks of organised medicine. This was the method of paying doctors for medical services provided to patients in hospitals. Under the Medibank and the original Medicare arrangements, doctors (other than full-time salaried staff often in training posts) treating patients in public hospitals were normally paid by the hospital on a part-time salaried ('sessional') basis. For public patients, the only exception to this applied to smaller hospitals, mainly in rural areas, where fee-for-service payments (at the rate of 85 per cent of the schedule fee) were made by the hospital to attending doctors. Private patients continued to pay their doctors' fees directly.

In the Canadian scheme, all hospital patients are effectively private; they are billed directly by their attending doctors, who are not permitted to charge more than the scheduled fee, but they do not meet hospital charges.

Much of the medical profession's opposition to Medibank was based on the expected erosion of private practice in public hospitals and uncertainties about the future of private hospitals. Though the proportion of doctors on the visiting medical staff of public hospitals is relatively small, this group contains its most vocal, influential and affluent members. In all states except Queensland, doctors in this category, especially surgeons, have derived a good deal of their income from private patients in public hospitals. In these states, before the introduction of Medibank, hospital-based specialists, with few exceptions, treated public patients without raising a charge. They were referred to as 'honorary medical staff'.

Part of the problem for doctors was that their earnings per hour under the sessional payment arrangements were substantially less than what they would receive from fee-for-service treatment of private patients. Accordingly, any marked decrease in the number of private patients treated would reduce their incomes unless they were able to treat increased numbers in private hospitals. With the 'competition' from free public patient status in public hospitals, the future for private hospitals did not appear to be very promising.

In the aftermath of the doctors' dispute, the very generous sessional payments introduced in New South Wales and the extension of the fee-for-service option for public patient treatment, the financial advantages to doctors, especially surgeons and other procedural specialists, of treating private patients as compared to public patients were reduced but by no means eliminated.

After the introduction of Medicare, a substantial decline in the proportion of private patient usage of public hospitals was quickly observed. In the financial year 1982–83, 46 per cent of all bed-days in Australian acute care public hospitals were associated with private patients. For the first full financial year after the introduction of Medicare, 1984–85, the corresponding figure was 29 per cent (Commonwealth Department of Health 1987a). By 1997–98, a further fall to 9.4 per cent had taken place (AIHW 1999b). By 2011–12, the percentage had risen to about 12 per cent, reflecting the increase in private health insurance coverage after the year 2000 (AIHW 2013a).

We do not argue that the threat to medical incomes was the only source of opposition from the profession to universal health insurance. The early attempts of the Labor government between 1945 and 1949 to move towards some kind of national health service created an environment in which any action by subsequent Labor governments on health matters was interpreted by the more conservative members of the medical profession as the first steps towards a nationalised system. Declines over the past 30 years in the relative incomes of doctors, and possibly in their power and status within the community, may have also rendered them especially sensitive to and suspicious of further changes (Richardson 1984).

Another closely related source of opposition to Labor's health insurance policies was the potential impact on private hospitals, from which some doctors also derive substantial income. The reduction in private insurance posed a threat to the long-term viability of these institutions. As we indicate below, after the commencement of Medicare, private hospital utilisation in fact increased. Nevertheless, it is questionable whether the present levels of private hospital utilisation could be maintained in the longer term if substantial declines in private insurance coverage took place.

Labor's return to universal health insurance

The decision, made early in 1982, to introduce a health insurance program closely resembling Medibank seems to have been determined, in part, by the overriding economic objectives of moderating wage demands and reducing the rate of inflation. Of importance was the proposed role of Medicare in the Prices and Incomes Accord, originally negotiated between Labor and the Australian Council of Trade Unions (ACTU) late in 1982.

Under the accord, the unions agreed to exercise considerable restraint after the election of a Labor government in pushing for increases in wages and salaries. At the same time, it was noted that for most trade unionists the reintroduction of tax-funded universal health insurance would bring about a significant increase in their real income; that is, for those who did not take out private insurance. There was no doubt a perception within Labor that the frequent and confusing changes to health insurance by the Fraser Government had created an electoral climate in which Medicare would be a vote winner, both at the 1983 election and subsequently.

The attempts by the Coalition parties to develop alternative health insurance policies undoubtedly contributed to their defeat at the 1987, 1990 and 1993 elections. The decision of the Labor government in 1991 to reduce the benefit for GP services, thereby introducing a co-payment for direct-billed services, was perceived by some members of the federal caucus as threatening to blur this distinction for the electorate. This view prevailed eventually, and following the election of Paul Keating as the new leader and prime minister, the government subsequently reversed the major aspects of the original decision.

Objectives and effects of Medicare

The principal objectives of Medicare were more equitable financing arrangements, a redistribution of income to poorer members of the community, the extension of benefits to people not previously covered, greater influence over fees charged by doctors, more efficient administrative procedures, and an improved information system for monitoring medical service provision. In addition were the economic policy and political aims discussed above.

Achievement of several of these objectives was a direct and immediate consequence of the changeover to tax-based funding and universal coverage. In general, compared with the previous health insurance program, Medicare involved a substitution of the proportionate tax levy (with a lower income level below which no levy was paid) for flat-rate health fund contributions. Thus, the payments made by people for medical and hospital benefits became more directly related to their incomes. We note, however, that the increase in equity claimed for the change is based on a value judgment that depends, in turn, on the assumption that health care differs from other commodities, as we discussed in **Chapter 3**.

Extension of the direct billing option under Medicare was the means whereby greater influence over fees charged by doctors could be achieved. Medicare Australia makes a payment of 100 per cent of the schedule fee to the doctor for each service direct billed. The existence of this option places strong competitive pressure on doctors, especially GPs, to direct bill, in which case their patients make no payment, or to limit the gap between their fee and the refund payable to the patient.

About 76 per cent of all Medicare services were direct billed in 2011–12 (Medicare Australia 2013). It is not possible to assess how effective this process may have been in moderating increases in doctors' fees. However, charging fees that are much greater than the schedule fee is primarily a problem for medical services provided by specialists to private patients, often as part of hospital treatment. While 80 per cent of non-referred attendances (predominantly services provided by GPs) were bulk-billed in 2011–12, the corresponding values for specialist attendances, obstetrics and operations were 27.9 per cent, 41 per cent and 41.2 per cent respectively. Patients obtaining specialist care as private patients often face very large out-of-pocket payments. For a one-hour consultation with a psychiatrist, the fee charged may be $320 or more, with a Medicare rebate of only $221.

Centralising the processing of medical claims in Medicare Australia has undoubtedly achieved economies of scale in the administration of health insurance. It has also generated a comprehensive set of profiles of the practice patterns of doctors, enabling considerable potential for detecting fraud and overservicing. It is again not clear how much of this potential has been realised to date.

The claim by its opponents that Medicare would generate an increase in the number of people seeking admission to hospital seems to have been based on the assumption that a simple demand and supply model applies to health care without modification. According to this model, reducing the price of hospitalisation to zero would inevitably produce an upsurge in demand. Since the supply of beds and other resources is fixed in the short term, the upshot, it is argued, would be an increase in the number of people waiting to be admitted to public hospitals.

There are good reasons, as we discussed in **Chapter 3**, for believing that the 'market' for health services is dominated by supply-side factors. In particular, doctors and not patients make the decision to hospitalise. The use of a crude demand and supply model cannot be justified in these circumstances. Furthermore, between 1982–83 and 1984–85 (the full financial years before and after the introduction of Medicare), total occupied bed-days in public hospitals actually decreased from 17.1 million to 16.3 million (Commonwealth Department of Health 1987a). Since that time, with substantial growth in the Australian population, there has been a modest increase in public hospital bed-days to the value of 17.4 million in 2010–11 (AIHW 2012a).

The decrease in the rate of public hospital use after Medicare was implemented resulted, in part, from the decline in the ratio of private to public patients in public hospitals and a corresponding increase in the use of private hospitals. It should also be noted that several other factors—including nursing shortages and decreases in the supply of beds (partly resulting from the nursing shortage, partly a consequence of the hospital rationalisation policies to be discussed in **Chapter 5**)—all contributed to the decline in public hospital use and the problems experienced by some public patients in obtaining hospital treatment.

The principal effect of Medicare on health expenditure has been to produce a marked increase in the proportion funded by the Commonwealth government and initially a decrease in the proportion financed privately. In 1982–83, the Commonwealth financed about 27 per cent of all recurrent expenditure on health. By 1996–97, this value had risen to 47 per cent (AIHW 1999a). Since that time there has been a modest decline to 45 per cent (AIHW 2013b).

We explained previously how increased support for private insurance by subsiding contribution rates, either directly or by taxation credits, featured in all the policies developed by the Coalition parties in opposition between 1986 and 1993. The policymaking concern with private health insurance is perhaps surprising in light of the fact that only 8.7 per cent of recurrent health expenditure was financed directly from this source in 2011–12 (AIHW 2013b). About 50 per cent of health insurance fund finance was devoted to private hospitals in that year.

The official reason for the concern with private health insurance, as put forward by the Coalition government in the late 1990s, was the threat to the viability of private hospitals posed by the decline in the population covered by this form of health insurance. It was argued that a reduction in the use of private hospitals would flow over to increased pressure on public hospitals, for which the Commonwealth and the states share financial responsibility.

As we noted above, there was no sign of this having happened up to the 1997–98 financial year, with the decline in health insurance coverage being associated with increased use of private hospitals. Between 1993–94 and 1997–98, a time of much policymaking activity about health insurance by both Labor and Coalition governments, the proportion of patient days in private hospitals increased from 24.6 per cent to 26.9 per cent of all acute hospital patient days (AIHW 2009). This continued a trend that commenced with the introduction of Medicare.

During the same period, as shown in table 4.1, the proportion of the population covered by private health insurance declined from 39.4 per cent on 30 June 1993 to 30.6 per cent on 30 June 1998.

The reasons for this seemingly paradoxical result are not clearly understood. There is certainly evidence that the people who dropped out of private health insurance were the younger contributors, who, with the exception of women in the childbearing years, are not heavy users of hospital services (Industry Commission 1997).

The shift from having private patient status in public hospitals to using private hospitals has been the main factor in increasing the share of private hospital patient days. However, the reasons for this shift are by no means clear, and no hard evidence appears to have been generated about this important issue. It may have been because of effective marketing of private hospital services during a period when large hospital chains became much more influential than previously.

Since decisions about hospitalisation are influenced heavily by medical staff, including those who work in both private and public hospitals, the increase in private hospital usage may have reflected the doctors' perceptions of increasing problems in public hospitals, along with a deliberate strategy to reduce their dependence on the less financially rewarding public sector (Duckett 2008b). The privatisation and collocation activities of state governments, to be discussed in **Chapter 5**, have also contributed to the increased importance of private hospitals.

What is of considerable relevance in analysing policies that focused on private health insurance is that when each of the initiatives described previously was implemented, there was no evidence to support the proposition that the decline in the coverage of the population had posed a threat to either the public or private sectors. Accordingly, it has been argued that the decision of the Coalition government to spend initially $1.6 billion on subsidising private health insurance contributions by 30 per cent was at best premature, apart from the issue of whether there would be more cost-effective ways of supporting public hospitals (Duckett & Jackson 2000; Palmer 2000b; Richardson 2005; Willcox 2001). The cost of the subsidy had increased to $4.7 billion by 2011–12 (AIHW 2013b).

The future of health insurance

We wrote in 1993:

> The Coalition parties might be well advised in the future to concentrate on developing policies which address supply-side issues such as casemix funding … The leadership in these parties could also reflect on the wisdom of allowing their health policies in successive elections to be determined largely by inputs from free market economists and the AMA.
>
> Palmer & Short (1994, p. 78)

As we indicated previously, the Coalition parties by 1995 had recognised the popularity of Medicare with the electorate and the difficulties of providing a credible alternative. They had resisted calls from conservative state premiers, the AMA and others for the implementation of radical changes to Medicare. However, the concentration on private health insurance, including the very expensive subsidy of contributions, represented a continuation of elements of previous policies of the Coalition parties. It also served the interests of influential private sector groups, including private hospitals, health insurance funds and the AMA (Palmer 2000b).

In recent years there have been a number of claims, usually by conservative groups, that Medicare is unsustainable in the longer run since it is alleged that the ageing of the population will place greatly increased financial burdens on the health care system. As we argue in **Chapter 11**, the impact of increased life expectancy on health spending is likely to be much less than it is often assumed.

Support for Medicare from within Labor and from the trade unions will almost certainly ensure that Labor governments implement no changes that would affect the principle of universality and the taxation funding principle. Free hospitalisation, the direct billing option and the administration of the scheme by one government authority are also unlikely to be altered by future Labor governments.

Financing health services

In this section, we concentrate on the financial relationships between the Commonwealth and the states as they affect the health services. These relationships have been linked intimately with health insurance, since Commonwealth policies regarding public hospital charges and the payment of doctors can only be implemented with the cooperation of the states. Other aspects of financing health services, including state funding of hospitals, are more conveniently dealt with in the chapters that discuss overall policies in each subject area.

Before the introduction of Medibank in 1975, the Commonwealth government made payments to the states as part of its involvement in several programs. These included bed-day subsidies to the states to support public patients, including those for services provided to eligible pensioner patients under the Pensioner Medical Service arrangements that began in 1952, and those made under the Pharmaceutical Benefits Scheme, which subsidised the cost of drugs provided in public hospitals.

As part of the Medibank program, the Commonwealth agreed to meet half of the net operating costs incurred by the states in providing acute care hospital services. These payments replaced those made under the earlier arrangements, along with the cost to the states of introducing free hospitalisation. A major effect of the cost-sharing agreements was to increase the total financial support provided by the Commonwealth to the states for hospital services. By 1976–77, the first full financial year of the operation of the system, the Commonwealth's share of total recurrent costs of hospitals recognised under these agreements had risen to 44 per cent from the earlier values of about 25 per cent.

Medicare and Commonwealth–state financial arrangements

The Commonwealth did not change the identified health grant arrangements in conjunction with the introduction of Medicare, apart from implementing a change in the method of escalation to take into account differences between the states in population growth.

To compensate the states for the loss of fee revenue arising from the return to free hospitalisation and a reduction in the fees charged to private patients, a system of Medicare grants was initiated. These payments were also intended to reimburse the states for the expected increase in hospital bed utilisation. It was noted earlier in this chapter that the usage of hospitals actually declined after Medicare was implemented. As a result, the payments to some states were adjusted downwards to reflect the decrease.

The total absorption of identified health grants and Medicare grants in financial assistance grants to the states was originally foreshadowed by the Hawke Government elected in 1983. However, the Medicare Agreements for the five years from 1 July 1988 to 30 June 1993 provided for separate hospital grants to be made to the states based on their populations (Commonwealth of Australia 1992). These grants were subject to the proviso that the states maintain a minimum proportion of total bed-days in the state for public non-chargeable patients. Where the proportion was less than this minimum, the state incurred a financial penalty.

The Hospital Agreements entered into for 1 July 1993 to 30 June 1998 also provided for population-based block grants to the states, with bonuses and penalties to apply according to or in line with the proportion of total hospital bed-days represented by public patient bed-days. The agreement recognised that the use of undifferentiated bed-days for this purpose was unsatisfactory, and it was predicted that there would be a move to casemix-based measures to determine bonuses and penalties in the second year of the agreement.

When the 1993 to 1998 Medicare Agreements ceased on 30 June 1998, the 1998 to 2003 Australian Health Care Agreements came into effect (Bigg, Azmi & Maskell-Knight 1998). Despite the change in terminology, these agreements were based on a set of principles that have not changed significantly since Medicare was introduced. They require the states to provide reasonable access to public hospital services, free of charge and based on clinical need within a clinically appropriate period. Commonwealth funding for public hospitals was capped at the levels negotiated within the agreement, and the Commonwealth prescribed the outcomes required (Maskell-Knight 1999).

The agreements intended originally for the period 2003 to 2008 were extended to 30 June 2009 with the advent of the new federal Labor government in November 2007. The principles underlying the agreements were again largely unchanged, but with increased emphasis on the states being held accountable for meeting performance targets (Duckett 2004). Duckett noted that the initial negotiations leading to these agreements were subject to a good deal of acrimony, arising in part from the states all having Labor governments while the Coalition governed in Canberra.

In addition, the terms offered by the Commonwealth were significantly less generous than was the case with the previous agreement.

Discussion of the most recent changes to Commonwealth–state financial agreements is deferred until **Chapter 10** where the National Health Reform Agreement of 2011 is reviewed.

POLICY ANALYSIS

ANALYSIS OF FINANCING POLICIES

The financial relationships between the Commonwealth and the states in Australia, as they affect the health sector, have been dominated by the perceived need of the Commonwealth to influence the policies and practices of the states in order to implement its own policies, especially regarding health insurance. The financial resources of the Commonwealth, which derive from its income-tax powers, have enabled it to achieve its policy objectives by this means, not only in health but also across a broad range of other areas. Section 96 of the Australian Constitution enables the Commonwealth government to make grants to the states, now called special purpose payments (SPPs), under such conditions as it may determine. It therefore provides the legal basis for this method of exercising the powers of the Commonwealth.

The ability of the Commonwealth to force the states to implement policies to which they were opposed was illustrated by the original Medibank hospital cost-sharing agreements. The four states with conservative governments at that time were very critical of the federal Labor government's health insurance program, especially aspects affecting the public hospitals. Initially, each of these state governments refused to sign the hospital agreements because the conditions represented an unwarranted intrusion into an area of state responsibility. This objection was especially difficult to sustain in the case of Queensland, where the main condition, free hospitalisation, had been in operation for the previous 30 years! However, political pressure to accept the large sums of money being offered by the Commonwealth became too strong to resist; after a delay of up to four months all states had accepted the agreements.

Similar circumstances arose in 1981 with the Fraser Government's desire to eliminate free hospitalisation, using identified health grants to achieve this objective. All four of the state Labor governments introduced the hospital charges established by the Commonwealth, and adopted the criteria of the Commonwealth to determine eligibility for free treatment. Thus, the Commonwealth again assumed control of a very important aspect of state health policy.

The 1981 changes were accompanied by a good deal of rhetoric from the Commonwealth government about returning the responsibility for health services to the states. The identified health grants, and the full absorption of these into the financial assistance grants, were claimed to be consistent with this principle. Yet it is clear that the method of implementing these arrangements achieved the opposite effect by ensuring that it was the Commonwealth's underlying policy objective—the transfer of financial responsibility from the Commonwealth to individuals—that prevailed.

Health and health financing—where should responsibility lie?

Discussion in the previous section indicates that one of the most important policy and political issues associated with health in our federal system of government is which level of government should be responsible for the various elements of the provision and financing of health care.

The position espoused by the Fraser Government, when changes in health financing arrangements were introduced in 1981, that the Commonwealth should leave health matters to the states reflected in part the tensions experienced by the states with the health and other initiatives implemented by the Whitlam Government. These were seen as eroding a major aspect of the power and author-ity of the states, especially in respect of their public hospital systems. The political rhetoric of the conservative parties had made much of the alleged desire of Labor to centralise power in Canberra in pursuing its 'big government' agenda.

The claim by the Fraser Government that the states' constitutional responsibility for health policymaking and implementation should be restored is easy enough to refute. Since the Australian Constitution, as we have noted previously, gives the Commonwealth the power to legislate about the provision of hospital benefits and medical services, there is no legal basis for the claim that health care is a constitu-tional responsibility of the states. Moreover, the provision of section 96, that the Commonwealth may make grants to the states for purposes and subject to conditions that it determines, also indicates that one cannot appeal to the Constitution to sup-port the contention that the states should have the principal role in health matters.

What policies the Commonwealth chooses to implement in the health arena are not constrained by the Constitution but by assessments of the potential popularity of the initiatives, and the political demands for such policies emanating from the relevant interest groups. On the one hand, the fact that the Hawke Government had not wished to return to the flurry of health policymaking in areas such as hospital planning and community health that had characterised the Whitlam era reflected the perception that such policies would not receive significant support in the political climate of the time. On the other hand, the establishment of the National Health Strategy in 1990 and the National Health and Hospitals Reform Commission in 2008 indicated that the Commonwealth was prepared to consider further major health policy initiatives (Macklin 1990; National Health and Hospitals Reform Commission 2009a). These culminated in the National Health Reform Agreement of 2011 that spelled out in detail the respective responsibilities of the two levels of government. As we note in **Chapter 10**, the vague wording in the agreement about the Commonwealth having 'lead responsibility for primary care' leaves a measure of uncertainty about the responsibility for this key area.

It is also noteworthy that the 1993 to 1998 Medicare and 1998 to 2003 Health Care Agreements spelled out in detail the roles of both the Commonwealth and the states in implementing health policies in a wide range of areas, including mental health, quality assurance and casemix development.

The respective roles of the states and the Commonwealth again became the subject of political controversy during the 2007 election campaign when the Commonwealth government offered to take over and fund the Mersey Hospital in Tasmania. The hospital, under a state government plan, was to provide a restricted range of services only. It would also lose its intensive care unit. The hospital was situated in the marginal electorate of Braddon, held by the Liberal Party, and it was clear that the offer to support the hospital in order to maintain its existing services was primarily designed to influence the outcome of the forthcoming election.

A similar situation arose in Queensland where the federal Coalition government promised to intervene to establish local hospital boards, thereby reversing the Australia-wide trend towards the regionalisation of hospital and other health services that we discuss in **Chapter 5**. In this case, the federal government hoped to capitalise on a measure of discontent in non-metropolitan Queensland communities about the state Labor government's proposal to amalgamate a number of local government areas. The reversion to hospital boards was promoted as giving residents a greater degree of control over their local hospitals.

The incursion of federal government into state affairs represented a spectacular reversal of the conservative parties' traditional role as the defenders of 'state rights' against the attempts of Labor to centralise power and decision-making in Canberra. In this particular instance, the new policy stances of the Coalition government were notably unsuccessful. The Liberal Party lost the seat of Braddon, and the Coalition parties sustained a greater number of electoral losses in non-metropolitan Queensland than anywhere else in Australia.

When the rhetoric of constitutional responsibilities is set aside, the case for the states having the main role in health policy rests on the proposition that they are likely to make the best decisions about priorities and resource allocations in this field. Thus, the literature on fiscal federalism asserts that the most appropriate level of government associated with a particular function depends on the geographical scope of the activities and the presence or absence of national 'spillover' effects (Mathews 1980, p. 8).

Since health services yield benefits almost exclusively to the populations of the states in which they are located, it is clear that the geographical requirement for a predominantly state role is met. Moreover, direct spillover effects that might justify a Commonwealth role are difficult to establish except for potentially national epidemics. A lower health status in one state, due, for example, to inadequate hospitals, is unlikely to have direct implications for the health status of populations in other states.

Since, according to this argument, health is a major state responsibility with a substantial impact on state budgets, it has contributed (together with education) to a vertical imbalance in inter-governmental financial relations in Australia (Groenewegen 1979, pp. 172–4). It is claimed that with limited revenue sources, the states have been unable to devote sufficient funds to these activities. They have looked to the Commonwealth to provide extra revenue, but the Commonwealth, in making available additional funds, has applied conditions that have reduced the decision-making autonomy of the states. According to this argument, the upshot is likely to be a reduction in the quality of policymaking, because the states are better placed to make decisions in this area. It is also claimed that a greater reliance on specific-purpose federal grants will weaken controls over state expenditure to the extent that this is financed from other than state taxes and charges.

However, the notion of the fiscal federalists who believe that health policy-making will be superior if confined primarily to the states depends on a limited conception of the nature and determinants of health policies. If health policy implementation were a purely technical exercise of assessing health needs and of providing resources to meet those needs, it might be that the states, including local and regional organisations, would be best placed to undertake these activities. Nevertheless, it should be clear from the discussion of perspectives on policy in **Chapter 3** that policymaking is inevitably influenced by the demands of powerful structural interests in a political marketplace. Of these groups, it was also noted that sections of the medical profession had achieved a position of dominance.

In light of the belief that previous health agreements had not addressed the so-called blame game between the federal and state governments, the Rudd Government established the National Health and Hospitals Reform Commission early in 2008. The chief task of the commission was to put forward proposals designed to improve the relations between the two levels of government in health matters, based on an appraisal of how respective responsibilities should be defined and monitored. As we have noted above, the subsequent National Health Agreement of 2011, based with some exceptions on the National Health and Hospitals Reform Commission report, endeavoured to spell out these respective responsibilities.

SUMMARY AND CONCLUSION

Since the implementation of desirable changes in health policy in financial and other areas depends on overcoming resistance from the dominant structural interests, it does not follow that state governments will produce policies superior to those of the Commonwealth. Whether the Commonwealth is better placed to implement more equitable or more efficient policies in improving the health status of the population depends on the specific nature of the policy and the motivations of the Commonwealth to implement it. Nevertheless, there is a strong presumption that the Commonwealth is more capable of marshalling the resources needed for successful policy implementation when the big issues of the quality of health services, the balance between curative and preventative services, or how hospitals and doctors are to be made more accountable for their activities, are involved.

A strong Commonwealth motivation for policy initiatives arises out of its responsibility for meeting part or all of the costs of medical services. Even though there has been a major conflict between Labor and the Coalition about the precise form that assistance in pooling the cost of medical expenses should take, both groups accept the necessity for the Commonwealth to be involved. Indeed, the conception of health as an aspect of the social welfare system is enshrined in the Constitution. Pharmaceutical and hospital benefits and medical and dental services appear as Commonwealth responsibilities in the same sentence, together with widows' pensions, maternity allowances, child endowment and unemployment benefits (Palmer 1982, p. 14).

It is therefore inevitable that the Commonwealth government, as part of its social security role, will be heavily involved with health. Since the Commonwealth, irrespective of which parties are in power, pays or provides for the health care of at least some members of the community, including social services beneficiaries, it must have a continuing interest in the costs of providing health care and the policies that influence those costs.

The Hawke and Keating governments' decision to make payments to the states under the Medicare Agreements for hospital and other health services subject to detailed conditions, rather than absorbing them in the financial assistance grants to the states, recognised this reality. The 1993 to 1998 Medicare Agreements, with the more detailed conditions for Commonwealth funding that they included, may be seen as a further stage in this development. The Coalition government did not endeavour to alter these arrangements under the 1998 to 2003 and 2003 to 2008 Health Care Agreements.

FURTHER READING

Stephen Duckett's and Sharon Willcox's 2011 book *The Australian Health Care System*, 4th edition (Oxford University Press), provides a detailed account of the conflicts concerning health insurance in Australia and their sources in the different value systems of the major political groupings.

The early history of health insurance in Australia is discussed in the monograph by Scotton and Macdonald (1993), *The Making of Medibank: Australian Studies in Health Service Administration*, no. 76 (University of New South Wales). Richard Scotton, together with his colleague John Deeble, was the principal architect of Medibank and played a major role in its implementation, in conjunction with Bill Hayden, the minister for social security in the Whitlam Government.

Gwen Gray's 2004 monograph *The Politics of Medicare: Who Gets What, When and How* (UNSW Press) is a very readable account of the political aspects of policymaking about health insurance in Australia, with an emphasis on the policies of the Howard Government and their ideological underpinnings.

Anne-Marie Boxall's and James A Gillespie's book *Making Medicare: The Politics of Universal Health Care in Australia* (UNSW Press, 2013) is a vivid historical account and analysis of Medicare. It also calls for a fundamental rethink about health insurance arrangements in Australia in light of the episodic nature of care in a fee-for-service system and incentives for abuse of the system as doctors' incomes are generated by increasing episodes of care.

DISCUSSION QUESTIONS

1   Summarise the main reasons why health insurance has been a source of major political conflict over a long period in Australia.

2   We have seen that policymaking about the financing of health services has been highly politicised. Would it be feasible or desirable, as some have argued, to 'take the politics out of health care'?

3   What do you regard as the principal weaknesses and problems in the current system of public and private health insurance in this country?

4   Many people have argued in Australia and the United States for a one-payer system of health insurance. In your opinion, what are the advantages and disadvantages of such a system?

5   It has also been argued that the presence of a private health insurance option in Australia has the important advantage of providing the community with greater freedom of choice. Summarise the arguments that support or oppose this claim.

5

Organising health care services

This chapter examines the organisation, administration and funding of major elements of the health care system. The institutions and services covered include public and private hospitals, aged care facilities and pharmaceuticals. We emphasise the policies developed by the Commonwealth and state governments to influence the organisation, financing and quality of these services, and the factors that have shaped the development of these policies.

Since much of the policymaking and regulatory activities concerning health service institutions and other providers are the responsibilities of state governments and their health (or human services) departments, we also analyse the policies that have affected the roles and functions of Australia's various health authorities. The problems faced by the states in financing and controlling public hospitals, among other factors, have led to the reorganisation of all state health authorities at least once in recent years.

In addition, these authorities (excluding in Victoria) have needed to redefine the geographical divisions of their states, as a result of the Council of Australian Governments' (COAG) agreement between the Commonwealth and the states of August 2011. The National Health Reform Agreement (NHRA) prescribes that the states establish local hospital networks (LHNs) to manage the funding and provision of these services. It was agreed that in the case of Victoria the existing networks would be suitable to meet the same objectives. The agreement also included the nationwide introduction of activity-based funding of the larger public hospitals. Details of these organisational and funding arrangements are set out below.

Public hospitals

The attention devoted to public hospitals in this chapter reflects the large amount of total health care expenditure associated with these organisations, currently of the order of $42 billion, and the volume of public policymaking undertaken about the sector. We noted in **Chapter 4** that much of the political controversy generated by health insurance arrangements in Australia has centred on the payments made to doctors in public hospitals. In addition, for the community as a whole, the public hospital system is perceived as both the repository of detailed knowledge about all the illnesses that affect our species and a sanctuary to which we can turn when physical or emotional problems threaten to overwhelm us.

The problems that public hospitals experience—especially in respect of access, the quality, safety and appropriateness of the care provided and the resources made available to them—have set the scene for much of the policymaking of governments about this very important sector of the economy. State elections have often been dominated by opposition parties (of both sides) highlighting public hospital problems, especially long waiting lists and times. The success or otherwise of ministers for health has increasingly been measured by their ability to keep hospital and other health matters out of newspaper headlines. At the same time, both specialist medical practitioners and conservative economists may have tended to exaggerate the problems of public hospitals as they pursue their common objective of further privatisation of the hospital sector and reductions in the role of governments (Kasper 2009; Sammut 2011).

Summary of Australian public hospital characteristics

The Australian Institute of Health and Welfare (AIHW) publishes an annual report on Australian hospital statistics, the most recent of which at the time of writing was for 2011–12 (AIHW 2013a). It provides a detailed summary of the main features of the Australian public hospital system, including the number of hospitals, their types and location; the number of patient separations and their characteristics; and various funding and performance measures. Similar information is provided about the private hospital sector (see page 111).

It is not our objective in this chapter to present a large volume of data on the characteristics of the Australian hospital system. However, some basic facts about changes in the capacity and funding of the sector and movements in activity, notably in separations, bed-days and non-inpatient occasions of service, are essential for an understanding of the major policy issues.

The term 'public hospital' has been used by state health authorities to describe a wide variety of institutions, including state psychiatric and geriatric hospitals and hospitals for the developmentally disabled. In this chapter, we deal mainly with institutions that predominantly treat patients with acute problems that normally require a brief period of hospitalisation. In 2011–12, there were 736 acute public hospitals operating in Australia (table 5.1). It should be noted that there have been some increases in the number of beds in public hospitals in recent years, but these have just kept up with growth in the Australian population, as indicated by the numbers per capita.

Table 5.1 also indicates that recurrent expenditure, in constant prices, on public hospitals has increased from approximately $32 billion in 2007–08 to over $40 billion in 2011–12; that is, by nearly 26 per cent. The average rate of annual change in this measure over the period was 5.9 per cent.

The total number of patient separations from the hospitals in 2011–12 was 5.5 million, accounting for about 19 million patient days (table 5.2). (A separation is

Table 5.1   Public hospitals: capacity and expenditure, 2007–08 to 2011–12

	2007–08	2008–09	2009–10	2010–11	2011–12
Number of acute hospitals	742	737	736	735	736
Number of beds	54 137	54 382	54 812	55 789	56 582
Beds per 1000 population	2.66	2.61	2.57	2.57	2.60
Recurrent expenditure, constant prices, $million[a]	32 141	33 727	34 970	37 872	40 384

Note
(a) Expressed in terms of the reference year 2011–12

Source: Data compiled from four tables (2.1, 2.2, 4.8) in Australian Institute of Health and Welfare 2013a, *Australian Hospital Statistics 2011–12*, Health services series no. 50, cat. no. HSE 134, AIHW, Canberra

defined as the discharge from hospital to home, to another institution or death.) The number of separations has increased substantially in recent years from the value of 4.7 million in 2007–08 to 5.5 million in 2011–12; that is, by 17 per cent. However, due to reductions in the average length of stay of patients, the increase in patient days has been much more modest over this period, from 17.8 million in 2007–08 to 19 million in 2011–12, or 6.7 per cent.

Table 5.2   Public hospitals: separations and patient days, 2007–08 to 2011–12

	2007–08	2008–09	2009–10	2010–11	2011–12
Acute separations	4 608 000	4 748 075	4 916 330	5 114 373	5 329 166
Same day separations	2 342 455	2 438 918	2 548 838	2 660 640	2 777 380
Overnight separations	2 265 545	2 309 157	2 367 492	2 453 733	2 551 786
Sub- and non-acute separations	135 562	142 600	152 578	164 499	181 926
Total separations	4 744 060	4 891 023	5 069 288	5 279 132	5 511 492
Total patient days	17 835 944	17 889 182	18 102 746	18 487 019	18 991 036
Non-admitted occasions of service	41 255	41 989	42 081	42 526	45 315

Source: Data compiled from four tables (6.1, 7.1, 7.2, 7.3) in Australian Institute of Health and Welfare 2013a, *Australian Hospital Statistics 2011–12*, Health services series no. 50, cat. no. HSE 134, AIHW, Canberra

The acute public hospitals treat some sub-acute-care patients—mainly rehabilitation care, palliative care and geriatric evaluation and management care patients—along with non-acute maintenance care patients (AIHW 2013a, p. 244). However, the number of patient separations in these categories in acute public hospitals is now very low, representing only about 3.3 per cent of all public hospital separations in 2011–12.

A further important aspect of the data in table 5.2 is the considerable increase in non-inpatient occasions of service in public hospitals. These services include outpatient attendance, accident and emergency services, pathology and other diagnostic services, and pharmacy.

Public hospitals are also characterised by a considerable degree of diversity in terms of their size and roles. Table 5.3 shows the size distribution of public acute hospitals and 17 public psychiatric hospitals, together with the proportion of total public hospitals and total hospital beds in each category. It is noted that the great majority of public hospitals (71 per cent) are small institutions of 50 beds or fewer. Most of these are located in regional or remote areas of Australia (AIHW 2013a, table 4.7).

Table 5.3   Number of public acute and psychiatric hospitals by hospital size, 2011–12

Hospital size	Hospitals	Proportion of total public hospitals (%)	Proportion of total public hospital beds (%)
10 or fewer beds	217	28.8	1.6
More than 10 to 50 beds	318	42.2	13.3
More than 50 to 100 beds	71	9.4	8.8
More than 100 to 200 beds	65	8.6	16.6
More than 200 to 500 beds	57	7.6	30.1
More than 500 beds	25	3.3	29.5
Total	753	100.0	100.0

Source: Data from table 4.6 in Australian Institute of Health and Welfare 2013a, *Australian Hospital Statistics 2011–12*, Health services series no. 50, cat. no. HSE 134, AIHW, Canberra, p. 66

Table 5.4 shows the distribution of public hospitals according to their type and role, and their geographical location. The large principal referral hospitals and the specialist women's and children's hospitals are concentrated in the capital cities and the larger regional cities, along with the remainder of the larger hospitals.

Table 5.4   Distribution of public hospital type by location and average separations, 2011–12

Hospital type	Major cities	Regional	Remote	Separations (average)
Principal referral	53	26	1	45673
Specialist women's and children's	11	0	0	21956
Large	23	16	1	16871
Medium	20	63	0	6534
Small acute	0	114	41	1307

Source: Data from table 4.5 in Australian Institute of Health and Welfare 2013a, *Australian Hospital Statistics 2011–12*, Health services series no. 50, cat. no. HSE 134, AIHW, Canberra, p. 64

The 80 principal referral hospitals represent about 60 per cent of all public hospital beds in Australia and about 66 per cent of all public hospital separations. Most importantly, they include the major teaching hospitals, with their links to the university sector and their teaching and research roles. For this reason, and because they treat, on average, patients with more complex problems, they are also the most costly elements of the public hospital system.

In confronting the problems and policies associated with public hospitals including their management, the quality of the services they provide, their staffing and funding, it is very important that we do not lose sight of the great variety of roles and functions that individual hospitals perform. Thus, most of the plethora of methods proposed and adopted for monitoring and improving the quality of patient care, and for improving clinical governance, may not be relevant to the one-third of patient separations from the smaller hospitals.

Organisational arrangements

In the past, relatively autonomous boards of directors had administered most acute care public hospitals—the principal exceptions being some hospitals controlled by religious and charitable organisations and others administered directly by state health authorities. The autonomy of these boards varied considerably between the states and according to the size and role of the hospital. At one extreme, Queensland Health had exercised a high level of control over the hospital system since 1944 when all board members became appointees of the government (Heilscher 1980). In other states, notably Victoria and Western Australia, the boards had been less subject to government direction. The boards of major teaching hospitals, by virtue of the high status of their members, had enjoyed a good deal of autonomy, including the ability on occasions to frustrate the plans of health authorities.

Since the late 1970s, concerns about cost increases and the management of public hospitals, generated in part by Commonwealth inquiries, had made the states become much more active about intervening in the affairs of all these institutions (Commission of Inquiry into the Efficiency and Administration of Hospitals 1981; Hospitals and Health Services Commission 1974). The hospitals' heavy dependence on the states for finances, together with doubts about the efficiency of some institutions and budget overruns, had been the principal reasons for the change in the policies of the states.

The relationships between the state health authorities and the individual hospitals were subsequently affected by the belief, especially in the more populous states, that the public hospital systems might be better managed by a policy of delegating some of the functions of the state authority to agencies in geographically defined areas. In New South Wales, the policy led to the creation of a set of regional authorities in the early 1970s, with similar processes of decentralisation being implemented in other states. Further discussion of 'regionalisation' is set out on page 97. As we noted at the begining of this chapter, the movement has culminated in the recent creation of LHNs under the NHRA of 2011.

Problems of public hospitals

Several inquiries into the activities and performance of Australian hospitals over 40 years have highlighted a number of major problems. The first national study, undertaken by the Commonwealth Hospitals and Health Services Commission in 1973–74, drew attention to the imbalance in the numbers of beds per 1000 of population between inner-city and newly developed outer suburban areas in several states (Hospitals and Health Services Commission 1974). The report also found evidence of surpluses of beds in many rural areas. It was clear from the study that the states had failed to plan in developing their hospital systems for the large shifts in population distribution that took place after World War II. At the same time, the commission's report indicated that the total number of public and private hospital beds per 1000 of population, at that time about 6.3, was very high.

The Jamison Commission, established by the Fraser Government in 1979 to recommend changes in the Commonwealth's funding of public hospitals and health insurance, drew attention to an apparent lack of efficiency in the administration of hospitals and the absence of adequate statistical and management information systems (Commission of Inquiry into the Efficiency and Administration of Hospitals 1981). According to the commission, it was impossible to compare the efficiency of different hospitals because of the inability to measure in any meaningful way the outputs of hospitals and of treatment. The National Health Strategy (1991a) report on hospitals emphasised the need for reforms to improve the efficiency, equity and quality of services provided by both the public and private sectors. The report also drew attention to the need to reduce further the number of hospital beds per 1000 of population, which by 1990 had fallen to 5.0 from the peak of 6.5 in 1980.

Concerns about the quality of care provided in public hospitals have centred on insufficient effort being made to monitor and review the quality of medical care in most hospitals, despite the exhortations of health ministers and others over the past 30 years. A survey by the Australian Institute of Health (Renwick & Harvey 1988) revealed that extensive quality assurance activities in public hospitals were limited to a minority of institutions. Moreover, the Australian Council on Healthcare Standards, the organisation that implements a voluntary accreditation scheme for hospitals and other health facilities, did not begin to address quality issues until the late 1980s (Lapsley 2000). The organisation has since developed various clinical indicators such as wound infection rates and mortality rates associated with specific surgical procedures. Long waiting times for hospital admission for several elective procedures have raised questions about access to hospital services in the public sector.

Criticisms of public hospitals concerning quality of care issues, especially in Queensland, New South Wales and Victoria, escalated in the 1990s and 2000s. A national inquiry, which reported in 1995, indicated that about 16 per cent of all hospital admissions resulted in adverse outcomes, with an estimated 50 000 patients suffering a permanent disability and about 18 000 people dying each year

(Wilson et al. 1995). An Insight Report from *The Age* claimed that not only were the adverse outcomes continuing—and possibly underestimated in Victorian public hospitals—but also that a culture of cover-up was pervasive in many institutions (Birnbauer & Davies 1999).

Recently, there have been several extreme cases of dangerously poor quality of care in Australian public hospitals. The regional public hospital of Bundaberg in Queensland generated national headlines when it became evident that the director of surgery had provided treatment of dubious quality, possibly leading to the death of 16 patients (Thomas 2007). It also became clear that Queensland Health senior officials were initially less than forthcoming in pursuing enquiries into concerns raised by nursing staff about the activities of the surgeon. Furthermore, the registration process for the overseas trained surgeon implemented by the Medical Board of Queensland was highly flawed. Van der Weyden (2005), the editor of the *Medical Journal of Australia* at that time, has provided a comprehensive account of this and other scandals relating to hospital quality of care. The responses to these problems in Queensland are discussed below.

Other public hospital studies have criticised the lack of coordination and integration of the activities of individual hospitals, both with one another and with other elements in the health care system. Larger hospitals have tended to provide the most specialised and expensive services; in some instances justifying this process by reference to their roles as teaching hospitals (Enquiry into Hospital Services in South Australia 1983). Consequently, these services have been under-utilised in relation to the facilities and staff provided. A concentration of activities such as coronary artery bypass surgery at fewer sites may have yielded cheaper and higher quality services. The failure to integrate the activities of public hospitals with those of nursing homes, community health services and private medical practice has resulted in an overemphasis on hospitalisation and the inappropriate use of these expensive facilities.

The National Health and Hospitals Reform Commission, established by the Rudd Government in 2008, revisited yet again the problems of public hospitals. The final report of the commission made many recommendations for improving the quality performance of public hospitals (National Health and Hospitals Reform Commission 2009b). The policy responses of the federal government to this report, including the establishment of the Australian Commission on Safety and Quality in Health Care (ACSQHC), are discussed in the following pages.

Public hospital funding

The absence of appropriate mechanisms for allocating funds from governments to individual institutions was the focus of increasing attention in the early 1990s (National Health Strategy 1991a; Victorian Department of Health and Community Services 1993). The allocation methods predominantly attempted to maintain the financial position of each hospital in real terms in the face of rising prices and costs.

The information available to the state health authorities about each hospital was confined to crude measures of usage; for example, occupied bed-days, and of costs (costs per bed-day and per patient treated). Thus, it was not possible to develop criteria that related the funds to be provided to the outputs produced, which might have improved efficiency.

As we discussed in **Chapter 4**, reduced revenue to state governments from private patient fees in public hospitals, with the shift of these patients to private hospitals, put additional pressure on the states to contain public hospital expenditure. In some cases, the success in cost-reducing policies implemented by the states has been achieved at the expense of a more stressful environment for many hospital employees. There has also been an increasing tendency for the states to blame the Commonwealth for inadequate funding under the Health Care Agreements.

Policy responses

Much of the health policymaking activity of state governments since the early 1970s has represented responses to the problems outlined previously. Three types of policy change had as a major objective that of helping to resolve public hospital problems. The first has endeavoured to strengthen the capacity of the state health authority to plan and regulate hospitals and other health services for which it is responsible. The second has involved regulatory and planning activities designed to change the ways that hospitals operate in their internal activities and external relationships. The third type of policy response is concerned with how the funding of hospitals might be improved to achieve policy objectives such as increased efficiency and cost containment.

Organisation of the state health bureaucracies

The establishment of health commissions in New South Wales (1973), Victoria (1978) and South Australia (1981) was designed primarily to bring together all aspects of state health under one authority in the hope that coordination and integration of the activities of service providers would be improved. Commissions rather than larger departments were created because of the belief that the perceived greater degree of independence from government of the former would promote better relations with individual institutions. A need to 'depoliticise' health was seen as desirable by governments at that time.

In New South Wales, the Health Commission was abolished in 1982, with Victoria also reverting to a health department type structure in 1985. In the light of ongoing conflicts with the medical profession, particularly in New South Wales, it is significant that non-medical departmental heads replaced the two medically qualified commission chairpersons. It is also possible that the reinstatement of the departmental model signalled the recognition that health policymaking is inherently a political activity and that any attempt at depoliticisation is doomed to failure.

The second strand in the process of refurbishing state health authorities was 'regionalisation'. This term has been given a variety of meanings in the literature on health service organisations, but in the Australian context it is identified with the decentralisation and delegation of authority in the administration of health services (Palmer 1981). Various names have been assigned to the geographical and administrative entities, including regions, areas, districts and, most recently, networks. All embody the regionalisation principle of the decentralisation of decision-making and authority.

Under the NHRA, each state was required to establish LHNs by 1 July 2011. According to the agreement, the new structures will 'engage with the local community and local clinicians' and 'will directly manage public hospital services and functions'. They will receive directly Commonwealth and state funding. They will also implement national clinical standards as agreed between the Commonwealth and the states on the advice of ACSQHC. For each LHN, agreements will be produced in conjunction with the states (but not the Commonwealth) and will specify the number and mix of services to be provided, along with the level of funding based on activity-based funding and block grants.

Each LHN will have a professional governing council and a chief executive officer. The governing council members will be appointed under state government legislation by the state health ministers. The CEO will be appointed by the governing councils, with the approval of the state health minister.

Regionalisation

New South Wales was the first state to regionalise its health services, shortly after the formation of the Health Commission. Because of the size and geographical dispersion of the state's population, the government believed that offices located within each region would better respond to the needs of the region than would a central office located in Sydney. Over the next three decades, there have been several further reorganisations of the management of health services in the state.

The advent of the area health services program in Sydney, Newcastle and Wollongong in 1986 resulted in a lesser role for the regions, and the regional administrations in these cities were finally abolished in mid-1988. Entities called regions continued to exist in New South Wales outside the major cities. With the introduction of 22 rural district health services and boards in 1993, the regional offices were abolished shortly afterwards. Subsequently, 17 and, more recently, eight area health services replaced the former areas and districts. Following the change of state government in New South Wales in 2011, the Department of Health was renamed the Ministry of Health with the existing eight area health services being replaced by 15 local health districts (LHDs) and three specialty health networks. The LHDs meet the requirements of the NHRA.

Victoria also established regionalised systems of administration but, consistent with the smaller and more concentrated populations of the state as compared with New South Wales, there was less emphasis initially on geographical decentralisation and more on the rationalisation and delegation of administrative duties. The management, planning and oversight of Victorian public hospital and other state-funded services were decentralised to three metropolitan and five rural regions. These regions form part of the Department of Health that replaced the Department of Human Services after the change of government in 2011. Approximately 80 per cent of the department's staff is located in these regions. Following on from the NHRA, this structure did not need to change since it was agreed that it met the requirements of the NHRA.

Queensland adopted a system of regionalisation in 1991, having operated a highly centralised administrative system previously. Hospital boards were abolished at the same time. By 2007, the system consisted of three large regions divided into 21 districts. As a result of the NHRA, 17 hospital and health services were created to replace these regions and districts.

In South Australia, regionalisation, based originally on geographical 'sectors', was abolished in 1987. The South Australian Health Commission was replaced by the Department of Health in 1995 and two regions were created: Adelaide metropolitan and rural/remote South Australia. The metropolitan area was subsequently divided into two separate regions. Under the NHRA, three LHNs have been created for Adelaide, along with a country health network and a women's and children's health network. The Department of Health is now the Department of Health and Ageing.

In Western Australia, which adopted a purchaser–provider model, regional purchasing authorities were created, together with health district providers. After the NHRA, Western Australia established two metropolitan health services, a country health service for the remainder of the state and a child and adolescent health service.

In Tasmania, following a review in 1996–97, five statewide divisions, supporting service strands, replaced the regional structure of the Department of Health and Community Services. Subsequently, three area health services were created, retaining the same geographical boundaries when three Tasmanian health organisations were established after the NHRA. The state authority is now the Department of Health and Human Services.

In all states, the outcome of the most recent changes has been a reduction in the responsibility and staffing of the central health authorities, so that these bodies are designed to concentrate on their roles as managers, purchasers and regulators of the health care system. Whether these reforms, along with the revised funding model, will achieve the objectives of producing a better managed, more efficient and higher quality public hospital system, as well as the underlying reasons for their introduction at the behest of the Commonwealth government, are explored later in this chapter.

Regulation and planning of hospital activities

Almost all capital funds of public hospitals are derived from the state, and the development of new or expansion of existing facilities is dependent on the approval of the state health authority. Since the states also possess the legal power to close hospitals, in principle the capacity of governments to control the number and location of hospital beds is apparently unlimited.

The hospital rationalisation program conducted in Sydney in 1983 is the most striking example of a state government achieving a measure of geographical redistribution of beds in response to the imbalance between inner-city and outer suburban areas. In the exercise, two medium-sized hospitals were closed, and what had previously been a major teaching facility, Sydney Hospital, had its bed capacity and role reduced substantially. At the same time, bed numbers of several hospitals in the outer-western suburbs were increased. Hospital bed redistributions have also been undertaken in Melbourne and Adelaide.

Following the incorporation of the Concord Repatriation Hospital into the New South Wales public hospital system in 1993, a further rationalisation of hospitals in the Sydney metropolitan area was to be implemented. However, the local community vigorously opposed a major part of this process, the transfer of St Vincent's Hospital to the site of St George Hospital, and the government subsequently yielded to pressure. There is still a marked difference in the availability of hospital services between geographical areas in the state. The reasons for the persistence of this problem are explored in a later section.

Role delineation and networking are organisational arrangements designed to counter the tendency of hospitals to provide services that are not warranted by patient needs or by the capacity of the hospital, as indicated by its facilities, equipment and staffing. The health authorities in New South Wales and Victoria attempt to define the clinical services to be provided by each hospital, including the level of complexity of each service. The totality of these services and their complexity define the role of each institution. It is not clear at present whether the NHRA will change this arrangement.

Quality of hospital services

Policy responses by the states to the quality of care issues highlighted previously have varied greatly between the states. The mechanisms that have been implemented in New South Wales centred on the establishment in 2004 of a Clinical Excellence Commission. This commission, on which clinicians are heavily represented, has been given a diverse set of functions including:

- promoting and supporting improvement in clinical quality and safety in health services
- monitoring clinical quality and safety processes

- identifying, developing and disseminating safe practices in health care
- consulting with health professionals and members of the community
- providing advice to the minister and the director-general of health on all quality of care and related issues in the health services (Clinical Excellence Commission 2008).

According to the 2008–09 annual report of the Commission, a key activity has been establishing a reporting culture via the development of a system for recording sentinel events; that is, those that may reflect risks to patients. The reporting process is based on an incident information management system (IIMS). The commission sees the creation of this system, along with public reporting of risk-related events, as a major step forward in addressing the problems highlighted by the IIMS and overcoming the previous culture of concealment of clinical and other errors.

The response of the state government to the Bundaberg Hospital scandal in Queensland was far-reaching, with a number of Queensland Department of Health senior executives being replaced. Most importantly, a senior academic and former secretary of the Commonwealth Department of Health, Dr Stephen Duckett, was appointed to initiate a series of measures under the heading of clinical governance to avoid similar fiascos in the future, and to improve the safety and quality of care of hospital patients.

The policies developed as a result emphasised a distinct set of processes including culture change, organisational and accountability initiatives, and the creation of a statistical reporting system based on clinical indicators with a graphical presentation (Duckett 2007, 2009a, 2009b; Duckett et al. 2007, 2008). An important objective of culture change, mediated by educational programs, was to replace the previous climate of secrecy in Queensland health services with one of openness and accountability to the community.

A scathing report on many aspects of New South Wales public hospitals was published in 2008 (Special Commission of Inquiry into Acute Care Services in NSW Public Hospitals 2008). In possibly the most detailed and comprehensive report on a state public hospital system ever produced in Australia, Peter Garling revealed numerous problems about the safety and quality of care in public hospitals. They included the absence of medical staff and emergency departments in many smaller hospitals, a wide range of problems faced by clinical and management staff, and widespread discontent and demoralisation among all types of staff. Underfunding was perceived as a major issue by all hospital staff, but Garling was sceptical as to whether more money would cure some of the deep-seated problems, including considerable differences in efficiency between hospitals with similar roles.

The timing of the Garling report suggests that it was another important input into the development of the Commonwealth's reform initiatives from 2008 onwards. Given the size of the New South Wales public hospital system, and the possibility that a similar exhaustive study in other states would reach the same conclusions, it would have been impossible for Commonwealth policymakers to ignore the need for a drastic change in all aspects of the system.

In this regard, of considerable importance are the two new national authorities established by the NHRA, the National Health Performance Authority (NHPA) and the ACSQHC. The NHPA has been given the responsibility of providing 'clear and transparent quarterly public reporting of the performance of every Local Hospital Network (and) the hospitals within it'. The comparative analysis of performance across LHNs and the identification of best practice are also major responsibilities allocated to the NHPA.

The ACSQHC's role is to 'lead and coordinate improvements in safety and quality in health care by identifying issues and policy directions, and recommending priorities for action'. Important further responsibilities of the ACSQHC are to develop national clinical standards, to strengthen clinical governance and to recommend national datasets for quality and safety purposes.

Cost containment, efficiency and funding public hospitals

The period of rapid growth in the total expenditure of public hospitals from the late 1960s to the 1978–79 financial year, together with increased pressure from the Commonwealth to contain these costs (described in **Chapter 4**), led the states to restrict severely the funds they provided to their hospital systems. Though the hospitals had always been expected to keep within the budgets established by state health authorities, in practice, in the earlier period of more buoyant funding, the government normally met spending in excess of the budget allocation. In the more cost-conscious environment of the 1980s, the states were able to force the hospitals to keep within their budgeted allocations. However, in the period between 2007–08 and 2011–12, expenditure on public hospitals in real (constant price) terms again grew strongly, as table 5.1 indicates.

We noted previously that the total number of hospital beds in Australia has reduced substantially since 1980. The ratio of available acute hospital beds (including private hospitals) per 1000 of population was estimated to be 3.89 in 2010–11, or approximately 60 per cent lower than the ratio of 6.5 reported in 1980 (AIHW 2013a). The earlier value is inflated slightly by the inclusion of institutions that would no longer be regarded as acute hospitals. However, this hardly affects the conclusion that we now use acute hospitals much more frugally than was the case 30 or more years ago. We further analyse changes in the utilisation of hospital beds in the next section of this chapter.

Utilisation of hospital beds

An assessment of the implications of the reductions is, therefore, an important aspect of evaluating overall the effects of health policy in this area. In view of the evidence presented in government inquiries quoted previously that Australia had a substantial surplus of hospital beds in the 1970s and 1980s, and high utilisation by world standards, the reduced dependence on hospitals might be regarded as potentially beneficial to the community. However, further analysis of this vitally important issue is desirable, especially since the earlier work is now out of date.

The number of inpatient bed-days associated with all public acute and private hospitals per 1000 of population in 2010–11 was 920 compared to 1560 in 1979–80 (AIHW 2013a; Commonwealth Department of Health 1987a). The number of separations per 1000 of population increased over this period but was more than compensated for by substantial declines in the average lengths of stay of patients in these hospitals. The latter result occurred partly because of the reduced presence of non-acute patients in public hospitals and partly as a consequence of changed policies about patient management, including a considerable increase in day surgery in both public and private hospitals. The incentives created by casemix funding have undoubtedly contributed to both these changes (see below).

The underlying assumption of much recent policymaking about hospitals, that over-utilisation of hospitals is present in Australia, continues to be plausible based on a comparison with the United States. For the broadly comparable group of short-stay hospitals in the United States, there were 562 bed-days per 1000 of population in 2006 (National Center for Health Statistics 2008). (When comparing US data with Australian data bear in mind that approximately 12 per cent of the bed-days in Australian acute hospitals refer to same-day patients. Almost all cases of this kind are defined as ambulatory patients in US hospital statistics.) Other international comparisons are of limited value because in the United Kingdom and elsewhere in Europe there are many non-acute patients in geriatric wards in acute hospitals.

Two reasons for the relatively large number of patient-days per 1000 of population by the Australian community are high rates of several elective surgical procedures, and the tendency to admit patients with minor conditions who might be treated at lower cost as outpatients.

We noted previously that there had been a concentration of nursing home type patients in some country hospitals, especially in New South Wales, and one of the objectives of role delineation in that state was to convert some of these institutions into nursing homes. Resistance from local communities and medical staff has led to this policy being implemented slowly. However, as we noted above, non-acute patients decreased considerably by the mid-2000s. The care of older people and chronically ill patients in public hospitals is more costly than are any of the other options.

The success of the Commonwealth in shifting the emphasis in caring for the aged from institutions to hostels and other community-based care (see page 118 and **Chapter 9**) may have been decisive in reducing the problem of non-acute patients in acute hospitals.

The over-provision of elective surgery and the tendency to hospitalise patients with relatively minor conditions is a consequence of the absence of mecha-nisms within most hospitals for controlling the types of patient treated and for reviewing the appropriateness of admissions. It is important to bear in mind that hospitalisation is often one of a number of options, most admissions are not emergencies of a 'life and death' kind, and the present state of medical knowledge means that there is a great deal of uncertainty about the relationship between treatment and health outcome for many conditions (McClure 1982; Wennberg et al. 1980).

It may be assumed that inpatient admissions are normally the outcome of a decision made by a doctor in light of their assessment of the patient's clinical condition and many other factors, including:

- bed availability
- the likelihood that hospital-based treatment will lead to an improved outcome
- an assessment of alternative strategies and their likely outcomes
- the relative monetary or status rewards of hospitalisation to the doctor, and its alternatives
- accepted practices within the local medical community about the treatment of certain types of patient
- costs to and preferences of the patient (Palmer 1986).

These circumstances help to explain the great variations observed in hospitalisation rates, even between small areas in the same region. They provide ample justification for admission decisions being subjected to a peer review process (Wennberg et al. 1984). More recent work in the United States by Fisher and colleagues has arrived at the same conclusion (Fisher et al. 2003a, 2003b). They also point to the need to develop protocols for the treatment of specific conditions, especially concerning admission criteria.

In Australia, only a limited amount of work has been undertaken to assess the variation between areas in hospitalisation rates. The study of surgical rates by Renwick and Sadkowsky (1991) indicated substantial variations between the states in age-adjusted rates for several elective surgical procedures including tonsillectomies and lens implants. The study reported by Richardson (1998) indicated that for a large range of operations in Victoria, the variations between statistical local areas in age-standardised rates between the lowest and highest rates were often tenfold or more. See **Chapter 7** for further discussion of these results in relation to various surgical interventions.

The reluctance of hospital administrators and governments to require systems to control hospital admissions, and the difficulties experienced with role delineation, are further signs of the medical profession's power and its ability to resist reforms that might threaten its clinical autonomy. Governments have preferred to use the blunter policy instruments of restricting bed numbers and funding to achieve their objectives. The problem that then emerges is that these instruments, in conjunction with geographical imbalances and staffing shortages, lead to significantly longer waiting lists if they are not supported by admissions and hospital role policies and the organisational arrangements to sustain them.

State and Commonwealth health authorities have therefore promoted a range of methods for reducing reliance on acute hospitals. These have included day surgery centres, coordinated care programs and hospital-in-the-home initiatives (Walsh & de Ravin 1995, p. 28). It would be desirable in the future for the clinical governance movement to place a greater emphasis on admission criteria for procedures that hospital morbidity data suggest are over-serviced.

Sources of funding for public hospitals

The sources of funding for public hospitals are shown in table 5.5, together with changes in the relative importance of each source and the average rate of annual growth of the components for various periods over the financial years 2000–01 to 2010–11. Note that all the values are in constant prices.

It should be noted that the states and territories provide the highest proportion of finance for their hospital systems but the importance of the Australian government in this regard is considerable. In **Chapter 4**, we stated that the National Health Care Agreements (now the NHRA) form the basis of the federal government's support of public hospitals, through which the states agree to the conditions set by Canberra to obtain these funds, notably free hospital treatment of inpatients and outpatients. Non-government revenue mainly consists of the fees charged to private patients in these hospitals.

Table 5.5 also indicates that the share of funding met by each level of government has varied considerably over the last decade. The percentage met by the states and territories increased from 47.2 per cent in 2001–02 to a peak of 54.4 per cent in 2006–07, the last financial year of the Howard Government. As part of the 'blame game', the states protested vigorously that the Commonwealth had required them to find additional resources from their own budgets. Since that time there have been some increases in both Commonwealth and non-government funding so that the states' and territories' percentage of public hospital funding decreased slightly to 53.3 per cent for 2011–12.

Allocation of funds from states to public hospitals

Since the mid-1980s, state governments have begun considering the problem of how to improve the allocation of funds to hospitals. Costs per patient-day and per patient treated have varied widely between hospitals, but the higher cost hospitals have inevitably claimed that their mix of cases has been more complex, hence more costly. In the absence of detailed and meaningful information about the kinds of patients treated by each hospital, these claims could not be refuted. Thus, the problem of how to fund hospitals is closely linked with the measurement of performance.

The Victorian Department of Health sponsored studies in the mid-1980s to explore the use of the US system of diagnosis related groups (DRGs) to influence

Table 5.5   Recurrent funding of public hospitals[a][b], constant prices[c], by broad source of funds and annual growth rates, 2001–02 to 2011–12

Year	Government						Non-government			Total		
	Australian Government			State/territory								
	Amount ($m)	Growth (%)	Share (%)	Amount ($m)	Growth (%)	Share (%)	Amount ($m)	Growth (%)	Share (%)	Amount ($m)	Growth (%)	Share (%)
2001–02	10862	–	44.9	11407	–	47.2	1900	–	7.9	24169	–	100.0
2002–03	11513	6.0	44.4	12621	10.6	48.7	1804	–5.1	7.0	25938	7.3	100.0
Break in series												
2003–04	11567	–	42.8	13832	–	51.1	1651	–	6.1	27049	–	100.0
2004–05	12104	4.6	41.9	14791	6.9	51.2	1985	20.3	6.9	28880	6.8	100.0
2005–06	12005	–0.8	39.8	16047	8.5	53.3	2083	4.9	6.9	30134	4.3	100.0
2006–07	12285	2.3	38.4	17397	8.4	54.4	2270	9.0	7.1	31952	6.0	100.0
2007–08	13389	9.0	39.2	18299	5.2	53.6	2453	8.1	7.2	34141	6.9	100.0
2008–09	15148	13.1	42.0	18003	–1.6	50.0	2872	17.1	8.0	36023	5.5	100.0
2009–10	14404	–4.9	38.3	20263	12.6	53.9	2937	2.3	7.8	37604	4.4	100.0
2010–11	15811	9.8	39.6	20748	2.4	52.0	3350	14.1	8.4	39910	6.1	100.0
2011–12	16072	1.6	38.2	22411	8.0	53.3	3552	6.0	8.4	42034	5.3	100.0
Average annual growth rate (%)												
2001–02 to 2006–07	–	2.5	–	–	8.8	–	–	3.6	–	–	5.7	–
2006–07 to 2011–12	–	5.5	–	–	5.2	–	–	9.4	–	–	5.6	–
2001–02 to 2011–12	–	4.0	–	–	7.0	–	–	6.5	–	–	5.7	–

Notes

(a) Includes dental services, community health services, patient transport services, public health and health research undertaken by public hospitals

(b) Public hospital expenditure estimates for 2003–04 to 2011–12 are derived from Public Hospital Establishments (PHE) data published in Australian hospital statistics. These differ from the estimates included in other sections of this report that are derived from the National Minimum Data Set.

(c) Funding values are expressed in 2011–12 prices.

Source: Data from table A10 in Australian Institute of Health and Welfare 2013b, *Health Expenditure Australia 2011–12*, Health and Welfare expenditure series no. 50, cat. no. HWE 59, AIHW, canberra, p. 78

the allocation of funds to public hospitals (Department of Health, Victoria, and the Victorian Hospitals' Association 1987; Palmer et al. 1989). Duckett (2008c) examined the background to these studies in detail. The South Australian Health Commission also sponsored similar studies.

DRGs, developed at Yale University by Professors Fetter and Thompson, form the basis of the system of prospective payments, introduced in 1983 by the US government to pay hospitals for treating aged and disabled patients under their Medicare program.

The Commonwealth government in 1988 and 1989 introduced a Casemix Development Program as part of the Medicare Agreements with the states. Under the Casemix Development Program, a large number of studies were undertaken. These included a national hospital casemix costing study designed to estimate costs by DRG for funding and other purposes, and studies that led to the creation of an Australian version of DRGs, now referred to as Australian Refined DRGs (AR-DRGs). The classification has been revised regularly on the basis of clinical and statistical advice.

Two of the projects funded under the program were designed to examine how DRGs might be used for funding Australian hospitals (Palmer 1992a; Scotton & Owens 1990). The work by Scotton and Owens represented a proposal for direct payments, based on a set of DRG prices, to be made by the Commonwealth to individual public hospitals or to the states in respect of their public patients. Proposals for charging on a DRG basis for private patients in public and private hospitals were also included in the study by Scotton and Owens.

The DRG funding study by Palmer (1992) focused on how a total financial allocation for public hospitals might be distributed between the hospitals according to their number of separations. Each discharge would be weighted by the relative cost of the DRG for all hospitals within the scope of the system to which it was assigned. This budget allocation model for casemix funding was based on the implicit assumption that the states would continue to establish budgets for each individual public hospital, with Commonwealth funding to the states for hospital services continuing to be based on block per capita payments. The subsequent application of casemix funding by the states, until the recent national changes (see below), was based largely on these principles.

Early in 1993 in Victoria, a discussion paper on casemix funding for public hospitals was released (Victorian Department of Health and Community Services 1993). The document referred to how hospital budgets in Victoria reflected history rather than contemporary performance standards or patterns of demand, causing many perverse consequences, including unnecessary admissions in some areas and the presence of waiting lists in others.

From July 1993, part of the budget allocated to each public hospital in Victoria was based on the inpatient casemix of the hospital, with the remainder being paid in the form of grants to cover outpatients, teaching and research activities, and a fixed-cost component. Separate provision for an outlier funding pool was made to reduce the risk for hospitals, especially major teaching and referral hospitals, with higher proportions of more expensive patients within DRGs. A compensation grant to cushion the effects of the changeover to casemix payments for the less efficient hospitals was included in the arrangements initially.

A good deal of finetuning has taken place subsequently; for example, to set targets for hospital output and to reduce the ability of some hospitals to increase their measured throughput by redefining some ambulatory patients as inpatients. One of the consequences of casemix-based funding was an increase in the number of day-only admissions, most of which were medical rather than surgical. Casemix funding based on a classification of outpatient services was introduced subsequently (Victorian Department of Human Services 1998). Further details of the use of DRGs in Victoria are provided by Duckett, who was primarily responsible for the implementation of casemix funding in that state (Duckett 1995, 1998b, 2008c).

Evaluations of casemix funding in Victoria revealed large increases in the technical efficiency of hospitals, especially in the early years (Duckett 1995; Victorian Auditor-General's Office 1998). However, casemix funding was introduced in association with annual reductions of around 5 per cent in allocations to public hospitals, and the effects of casemix, both positive and negative, are difficult to disentangle from the budget cuts. Claims of a decrease in the quality of care are almost impossible to substantiate in view of the lack of methods of assessing comprehensively this elusive concept (Palmer 1996).

South Australia introduced comprehensive casemix funding in 1994, largely following the Victorian model but with some important differences. These included the payment for intensive care patients being unbundled from the DRG-based allocation. Casemix funding for Queensland hospitals was based originally on the Victorian model. However, a new funding model was announced in 2007 in which a population needs-based funding allocation is made to each region, and the hospitals within each region were funded based on their casemix profile (Queensland Department of Health 2007).

In New South Wales, the use of a needs-adjusted per capita formula to allocate most state health expenditure to the area health services, together with the delegation of funding allocation details to area authorities, acted as an obstacle to comprehensive DRG-based funding. Some area health services had embraced DRG funding enthusiastically, while others rejected the method despite exhortations from the NSW Department of Health. However, casemix funding was at last made mandatory for all area health services from 1 July 2008.

All Australian states and territories to varying degrees incorporated elements of casemix funding in their allocations to public hospitals prior to the changes based on the NHRA discussed on page 108. However, in an international review of casemix funding by Kimberly, de Pouvourville and d'Aunno (2008) it was noted that, compared with some other countries, the application of casemix methods to funding in Australia was still incomplete in that not all states and hospitals were covered. Moreover, Duckett (1998b) noted some inconsistencies in the costing of

DRGs that led to considerable discrepancies in payment rates for individual DRGs between the states.

All the work on DRG-based funding, including an annual costing study based on data that individual hospitals volunteered to submit, provided the foundations for the use of the method by the Commonwealth for allocating funds to state public hospitals. This was possibly the most important recommendation of the National Health and Hospitals Reform Commission that the Commonwealth government agreed to implement (see **Chapter 10**).

An interesting change was the decision by the Commonwealth authorities to rebrand casemix funding as activity-based funding (ABF). It was presumably believed that the term 'casemix' was prone to being misunderstood, especially by medical practitioners, and that the focus on 'activity' was a preferable way of promoting an understanding of the need to relate funding to the activities undertaken by hospitals in terms of the relative costliness of the groups of patients being treated. It should also be noted that the phrase 'activity-based funding' has for a number of years been applied in other countries to casemix or DRG funding.

The move to activity-based funding via the NHRA

The NHRA mandated that from 1 July 2012 the Commonwealth payments for public hospital services would be based on the AR-DRG classification in its latest version, whenever feasible. However, it was recognised that for some institutions, notably the smaller public hospitals, block grants should continue. To implement ABF, 'efficient' prices needed to be determined for each AR-DRG, based on the national costing study.

For the purposes of ABF, the Independent Hospital Pricing Authority (IHPA) has been established as an independent Commonwealth statutory authority. The main functions of the IHPA are to develop the national classification of activity (casemix); to determine the data to be supplied by the states, including the coding standards to be applied in generating the data; to specify the costing data and the standards for the costing of the services delivered by public hospitals; and to collect the cost data from LHNs through the states in order to determine the national efficient price per AR-DRG from these data. Other classifications and costings are also to be developed for other admitted patients, including non-acute and sub-acute patients, and for non-admitted patients.

The IHPA has also been allocated responsibility for the National Hospital Cost Data Collection (NHCDC) in conjunction with the states. The NHCDC was previously conducted by the Commonwealth Department of Health and Ageing.

The IHPA has not released publicly the details of the methods it has used in its costing studies, and whether it has implemented changes that overcome the limitations of the NHCDC in its earlier form. These limitations included the voluntary nature of hospital participation leading to possible biases in the estimates of costs and the use of quite primitive methods of allocating costs to individual patients for many hospitals.

Health policymaking by the states and territories has been influenced heavily by the need to resolve the continuing problems of public hospitals. As judged by popular perceptions and political responses, these problems may have worsened since the early 1970s, despite the enormous effort devoted to policy initiatives outlined above. However, part of the 'credit' for the creation of these perceptions must be attributed to sections of the medical profession, especially in New South Wales.

We noted in **Chapter 4** that one of the main reasons for the opposition of some influential doctors to both Medibank and Medicare was the effect on private practice in public hospitals. By discrediting the public hospitals, these doctors may have hoped to blame Medicare and to persuade members of the community to take out hospital insurance and be treated in private hospitals. If this were the case, their efforts were fruitless in respect of private health insurance prior to the changes in private health insurance arrangements initiated by the Commonwealth government in the late 1990s. However, as we discussed in **Chapter 3**, they were very successful in shifting private patients into private hospitals from the public sector.

Alford's (1975) perspective on health policy serves as a useful guide in interpreting the frequent modifications to the organisation of state health authorities, and the limited changes that these and associated inquiries have produced in the provision of hospital and other health services. Alford's basic thesis (**Chapter 3**) is that the health services are the scene of conflicts between two major groups, the professional monopolisers and the corporate rationalisers. In the Australian environment, these may be identified with hospital-based specialists and senior health authority executives respectively. Members of the former group wish to retain the status quo, while the latter perceive their interests as being served by the promotion of health planning and the achievement of a greater measure of rationality in resource allocation.

Where these conflicting structural interests are evenly matched, the result is described by Alford as a state of 'dynamics without change'; that is, much effort is expended in official inquiries, report writing and reorganisation of the bureaucracy but no changes take place in the delivery of health services. Alford views inquiries as being part of the problem, since they tend to legitimate the existing structures of power when a necessary condition for change is the elimination or modification of these structures.

Since the hospital board system in Australia had formed an important part of the structure (the boards of major teaching hospitals have especially been dominated by medical staff and their supporters), eliminating these boards in New South Wales and elsewhere was an important step in achieving fundamental reforms in the hospital system. From this standpoint, the most interesting organisational development of the past two decades has been the creation of area health services in New South Wales and similar organisations in other states, and the continuation of this process with the creation of local hospital networks as part of the recent Commonwealth-inspired reforms.

However, in regard to the numerous organisational changes in the states' health authorities, including the various versions of regionalisation, we are left with the sense that state governments resorted to these changes to convince the electorate they were doing their job of improving the services and responding to the manifest problems. The reality was that governments were unable to have much impact on the provision of hospital clinical services because the key decisions about the admission of patients, the type of care they received, and how the quality of the services was measured and monitored, mainly lay with the senior medical staff. Governments were reluctant to question medical autonomy and dominance because of their perception that politically they would lose if such a confrontation emerged.

The abolition of hospital boards and the creation of area health services may not have been a sufficiently comprehensive change to enable the implementation of further hospital system reforms. Indeed, the most important incentive for the implementation of far-reaching changes in the Australian health care system has emerged out of the drastic and life-threatening failures that have bedevilled Australian hospitals in recent years.

In our view, the responses to these events, and the clinical governance movement, have laid the foundations for a major shift in the culture of the relevant organisations and possibly a substantial change in the power relations between medical clinical staff and other stakeholders.

If the NHPA and the ACSQHC are staffed adequately and are able to establish good relations with clinical and other hospital staff, along with relevant clinical colleges, the scene is set for a major transformation of public hospitals in Australia. However, the achievement of cultural change in the sense of overcoming the tendency of all governments and their agencies to conceal outcomes that may be politically damaging is always likely to be a long and difficult process. It will require also, in our view, more than exhortations to ensure that medical staff change their behaviour to conform with the standards and guidelines about clinical practice that are issued by the relevant authorities.

The threat to the autonomy of medical decision-makers in hospitals posed by these new reforms and structures, notably the clinical governance movement, may generate a political response, especially given that the conservative parties are in power federally and in most states. We have noted previously the close links between the Coalition and the medical profession.

Scope for increased hospital efficiency

Reform of the funding of public hospitals by basing the states' financial allocations on the output of each institution as measured by DRGs, as discussed above, is a very important step in redistributing resources between hospitals, and possibly between the hospital sector and other areas. The results of studies of public hospitals in Victoria and New South Wales strongly suggested that there was considerable scope for policies of redistributing finances in those states (Palmer 1986; Palmer et al. 1992). For 12 of the larger non-teaching hospitals in Victoria, the variation in cost per inpatient treated between the lowest cost and the highest cost hospital was nearly 77 per cent. However, the casemix complexity (as measured by the DRG profile) of the highest cost hospital was only 11 per cent greater than that of the lowest cost hospital.

Similarly, among a group of major teaching hospitals in Sydney, the cost per inpatient treated was 35 per cent more in the highest cost hospital than in the hospital with the lowest cost, after standardisation for casemix differences (Palmer et al. 1992). There is a strong presumption that variations in efficiency of the hospitals were responsible for most of the cost differences.

The likely losers, particularly teaching hospitals, have resisted even more strongly changes in the method of funding hospitals, given the potential they create for redistributing resources, than other policy changes described here. From the standpoint of government, however, these measures possess the considerable advantage that implementation is much easier than the planning, regulatory and organisational changes that have been the focus to date of state government health policymaking. In general, governments seem to have been more successful in the past at influencing the behaviour of providers by funding measures than by the direct regulatory means they have been prepared to implement. Whether the implementation of ABF within the NHRA, as compared with the other reforms, produces the same outcome is an interesting question that should be monitored carefully in the future. We return to this issue in **Chapter 10**.

Private hospitals

Private hospitals are short-stay institutions, which, unlike public hospitals, do not receive a subsidy from state governments. Most of their revenue is derived from private health fund reimbursements of patient fees and direct payments by patients. However, medical services provided in private hospitals are subsidised by the Commonwealth government under the Medicare health insurance arrangements.

Data about private hospitals are included in the AIHW publication on hospital statistics (see, for example, AIHW 2013a) and also by the Australian Bureau of Statistics (see, for example, ABS 2013a).

As table 5.6 shows, in 2011–12 there were 281 private acute hospitals in Australia, including private psychiatric hospitals, and 311 freestanding day clinics. Table 5.6 also indicates the distribution of private hospitals and day clinics between the states.

There is considerable variation between the states in the relative importance of the private hospital sector. In 2011–12, the percentage of all acute hospital patient days in private hospitals varied as follows: 28 per cent in New South Wales, 32 per cent in Victoria, 40 per cent in Queensland, 33 per cent in Western Australia and 27 per cent in South Australia. (The value for Tasmania is not available for confidentiality reasons.) (AIHW 2013a, table 7.3). The relatively low value for

Table 5.6   Number of private hospitals, by state and type, 2011–12

	Acute and psychiatric hospitals	Free-standing day hospital facilities	All private hospitals
New South Wales	89	96	185
Victoria	79	85	164
Queensland	54	53	107
South Australia	28	26	54
Western Australia	22	35	57
Tasmania, Northern Territory and Australian Capital Territory[a]	9	16	25
Australia	**281**	**311**	**592**

Note

(a) These jurisdictions have been combined to meet privacy requirements.

Source: Based on table 1.1 in Australian Bureau of Statistics 2013b, *Private Hospitals Australia 2011–12*, cat. no. 4390.0, ABS, Canberra

New South Wales reflects the greater use of public hospitals by private patients in that state.

Private hospitals in total provided 1.26 available beds per 1000 of population in 2011–12. The average length of stay for private acute and psychiatric hospital separations was 2.7 days for all patients and 5.4 days for those who stayed overnight.

There are two main types of private hospital: those conducted by religious, charitable and community organisations on a not-for-profit basis (about 41 per cent of total private hospital beds) and those owned and controlled by commercial for-profit organisations (59 per cent of beds) (ABS 2013a). These figures indicate a substantial shift away from not-for-profit ownership compared with the situation 15 years earlier, when nearly 60 per cent of beds were in this category. Of the for-profit hospitals, some are owned by listed public companies and private hospital chains, and others are independently owned by the medical staff. The most important of the for-profit private hospital groups are Ramsay Health Care and Healthscope.

The private hospital sector has grown considerably in Australia over the last decade in absolute terms and relative to the public sector. In 2011–12, private hospitals accounted for 32 per cent of total patient days and 38 per cent of total separations in Australian acute hospitals (AIHW 2013a). The corresponding values for 1997–98 were 27 per cent of patient days and 32 per cent of total separations (AIHW 2008c). However, in the more recent period of 2007–08 to 2011–12, patient days in private hospitals increased by 12 per cent, while the corresponding value for public hospitals showed an increase of about 11 per cent.

Most private hospitals are relatively small institutions; approximately 70 per cent have 100 beds or fewer (ABS 2013a). Of the private hospitals in Australia in

2011–12, only 27 had more than 200 beds (ABS 2013a). However, their average size has grown in recent years as some smaller hospitals have gone out of existence and newer hospitals, especially those operated by hospital chains, are larger.

The Productivity Commission's 1999 *Report on Private Hospitals in Australia* provides further details of the private hospital industry, including measures of performance and the relationships between private hospitals, doctors and health funds. A detailed analysis of the costs of private hospitals as compared with public hospitals is also provided by the Productivity Commission in *Public and Private Hospitals: Research Report* (Productivity Commission 2009).

In the past, private hospitals catered predominantly for patients suffering from less complex problems than those treated in public hospitals. There has been a tendency in recent years, however, for some private hospitals to offer complex services such as cardiac surgery and intensive care and to provide accident and emergency services. Other private hospitals have specialised in treating specific types of patients, including those with psychiatric and drug-related problems.

Private hospital funding

Private hospitals depend for their financial survival on fees received from patients. The fees they charge, however, are influenced by the benefits provided by health insurance funds. Most people using private hospitals are covered by hospital insurance, usually at the 'top hospital' rate, but a surprisingly high 20 per cent reported having no hospital insurance (ABS 2013a).

If private hospitals, especially those with above-average costs, increase their charges significantly above the norm, the widened gap between the cost to the patient and reimbursement from the health fund may discourage people from using them. As observed previously, doctors primarily make decisions about hospitalisation; nevertheless, there are limits beyond which patients will not be prepared to incur additional out-of-pocket expenditure. Similarly, health funds are concerned that if their contribution rates become too high—for example, because of trying to cover a larger proportion of the charges of all private hospitals—they will face a loss of membership.

Hospital Purchaser Provider Agreements (HPPAs) were introduced under the provisions of the *Health Legislation (Private Health Insurance Reform) Amendment Act 1995*. Under these agreements the hospital must accept the HPPA as full payment by the fund for the episode of care, unless a patient co-payment is incorporated in that agreement (Productivity Commission 2009). Subsequent amendments to the legislation under the Howard Government were designed to address the concerns of some doctors that their clinical autonomy might be threatened by the arrangements.

Most of the major health funds now claim that they have entered into these agreements with most of the private hospitals in the jurisdictions that they cover. We are not aware of any studies that confirm this claim of the health funds. However, it is probably the case that most patients in private hospitals who are members of health funds either have no co-payment, or a known co-payment, in respect of their hospital insurance coverage.

However, the same situation does not necessarily apply in the case of the medical services they receive while hospitalised, whereby medical practitioners generally are able to charge well above the Medicare fee on which the reimbursement from the Commonwealth government is based. As a result, patients may face large out-of-pocket payments when the doctors' bills arrive. An exception to this is when a Medical Purchaser Provider Agreement (MPPA) exists. Provision for the creation of MPPAs was included in the 1995 legislation. However, few doctors appear to have signed on to these agreements.

Attempts by successive Commonwealth governments to promote the use of DRGs as the basis of payments incorporated in formal contracts between the funds and the hospitals were described earlier. The use of DRGs for this purpose seems to have been most successful in South Australia and Victoria, where there was comprehensive casemix funding in the public sector. The use of casemix-based payments for private hospital services was studied by Willcox (2005), who found that payments based on DRGs had been implemented only partially in this sector at that time.

Policy issues

The principal issues associated with private hospitals that have been the focus of public policy are:

- regulation by state governments, especially in regard to quality of care and ownership
- relationships with public hospitals and other services in the public sector, including privatisation and collocation
- rationalisation of private hospital activities
- regulation, planning and rationalisation.

Regulation by state governments

The regulation of private hospitals is a state government responsibility, with each state having passed legislation providing for licensing of these institutions. In the past, the main objective of the legislation was to ensure reasonable standards of accommodation and safety for patients and staff. Regulation has focused also on the wider issues of quality of care, possible surgical overservicing and health planning.

Quality of care and related concerns have arisen out of the widespread belief in public hospital and state health authority circles that standards of care in some private hospitals are inadequate. The evidence to support these beliefs is limited, though the occasional instances of surgical and other catastrophes including deaths, and the attendant publicity, have fuelled such concerns. Since small hospitals in both the private and public sectors typically lack a medical staff organisation, there are grounds for believing that incompetent, fraudulent or deranged doctors may continue to practice long after their peers would have rejected them in a more organised environment. A medical staff organisation as found in the larger public hospitals typically consists of a director of medical services, a departmental structure covering the main medical specialties and committees of the visiting medical staff dealing with matters of peer review, quality assurance and related matters. The absence of direct evidence about the quality of care, which we discussed when considering public hospitals, applies also, possibly with more force, to private hospitals.

It is reassuring that there has been a substantial increase over the past few years in the numbers of private hospitals that have been accredited by the Australian Council on Healthcare Standards. In 2007, 71 per cent of all private hospitals (excluding private free-standing day hospital facilities), representing 91 per cent of private hospital beds, were accredited (AIHW 2008b). An important incentive for private hospitals to seek accreditation is that some health funds pay higher benefits for care in accredited hospitals. However, the capacity of the accreditation program to assure quality of care in either public or private sectors is still very limited.

The possibility that surgical overservicing may be a greater problem in private hospitals than in public hospitals also served to make governments consider legislative and planning controls over this group of institutions (Senate Select Committee on Private Hospitals and Nursing Homes 1987). A relatively high proportion of procedures with some evidence of overservicing is provided in private hospitals. In Australia, for example, approximately 56 per cent of all tonsillectomies and 43 per cent of all cholecystectomies were carried out in private hospitals in 2007–08 (AIHW 2008c). The rate of performance of each of these operations is known to be high in Australia compared to other countries, and as will be seen in **Chapter 7**, these procedures have been the focus of overservicing concerns.

In New South Wales, the *Private Health Establishments Act 1982* contained a number of provisions for tightening controls over private hospitals. Compliance of any proposed hospital establishment or expansion with the department's planning guidelines was designed to ensure that additional private hospital beds were provided only in areas with a shortage of public hospital beds. It was no doubt believed that the expansion of the supply of beds in other areas might serve only to increase the overservicing problem.

The Private Health Establishments Act was not proclaimed until 1988. The long delay is yet another example of the difficulties of public policymaking in this field. After the legislation had been agreed, lengthy negotiations were conducted with the Australian Medical Association. These centred on the details of how doctors would inform their patients about their pecuniary interest in a private hospital, the aspect of the legislation to which the medical profession had been most opposed. The government originally proposed that admissions by doctors to hospitals in which they had a financial stake should be prohibited, but strong opposition from the profession led to the incorporation of a less stringent condition in the legislation.

With the introduction of Medicare and the doctors' dispute that followed in New South Wales, the state government did not wish to worsen the situation by proceeding with legislation at that time. The existence of the Private Health Establishments Act had been one of the many grievances referred to by doctors during the course of that dispute.

The Private Health Establishments Act and the state's policy of not approving significant expansions in the numbers of private hospital beds continued to concern sections of the medical profession. One of the conditions laid down by procedural specialists for their return to public hospitals was that the legislation be repealed. The Coalition government in New South Wales agreed to this after its victory in the 1988 election. This government also agreed to permit some larger private hospitals to be established provided there was a reduction in the number of smaller private hospitals.

In Victoria, the *Health Act 1958* was amended in 1982 to strengthen the legal power of the Health Commission to refuse to license a proposed private hospital on health planning grounds. Legislation was subsequently implemented to ensure that the broad type of care to be provided by a proposed private hospital must be approved in principle by the Victorian Department of Health before the plan could be implemented.

It should be noted that the Senate Select Committee on Private Hospitals and Nursing Homes recommended that state planning procedures should include the private sector within their scope, that doctors and their families should be prohibited from having any financial interest in private hospitals, and that medical financial interests in diagnostic facilities should be disclosed to patients (Senate Select Committee on Private Hospitals and Nursing Homes 1987). The committee also urged that state health authorities should control 'the proliferation of private hospital beds', pointing to the presence of occupancy rates of less than 50 per cent in certain areas, including the Sydney metropolitan area.

The expansion of the numbers of bed-days in private hospitals during the 1990s and 2000s in New South Wales and elsewhere in Australia has been achieved without private hospitals increasing substantially in number, but instead through increases in the size of hospitals and in occupancy rates (ABS 2013a).

The future of private hospitals

Because of the large number of very small private hospitals, policy proposals in the early 1990s emphasised the need to rationalise the private hospital sector. This included individual hospitals specialising in the provision of defined categories of services such as day surgery, or becoming aligned with hospital chains and thereby achieving improved managerial performance (National Health Strategy 1991a). Subsequently, the debate and policymaking affecting private hospitals has focused on private health insurance, as we indicated in **Chapter 4**.

There have also been moves to privatise some public hospitals and to collocate private hospitals on the campuses of large metropolitan teaching and referral hospitals. In recent years, the private hospital sector has looked increasingly to opportunities in providing public sector infrastructures and services. On the other hand, cash-strapped governments have been amenable to the use of both private sector management and capital. Details of the privatisation and collocation arrangements and the magnitude of their impact were provided by Foley (2000), who estimated that over 4000 privately financed acute hospital beds came on line between 1994 and 2000 in association with state public hospitals.

Under a 'build, own and operate' (BOO) arrangement, the private sector provides these services and the state government then purchases public hospital services for a specified period. At the end of this period, the private organisation retains ownership of the facility. A BOOT (build, own, operate and transfer) project is similar except that at the conclusion of the contract period ownership reverts to the state government. A number of BOO and BOOT hospital arrangements have been entered into in several states, especially by Coalition governments.

The future of private hospitals in Australia at present remains uncertain. Since the introduction of Medicare, their usage, relative to that of public hospitals, has increased. That the expected decline in private hospital use has not occurred is a product of the problems of public hospitals, especially the community's perception of difficulties in securing treatment in the public sector and of the concerted efforts of some doctors to direct patients to the private institutions.

The private hospital sector can be expected to continue to press for the elimination of free treatment in public hospitals and the introduction of a means test. If both the Labor and Coalition parties continue to endorse the availability of free hospitalisation in public hospitals for all who choose this option, the future of private hospitals may depend on their willingness to treat increased numbers of public patients on a contract basis.

A review of the costs of treatment in public and private hospitals indicated that on a casemix-specific basis some types of elective surgery patients are treated at lower cost in private hospitals (Duckett & Jackson 2000). Other patients, notably those admitted for childbirth, are cared for at lower cost in public hospitals. More recently, Duckett (2008b) has concluded that there is no clear evidence that either sector is more efficient than the other, especially given the different cost structures that prevail in each sector. It cannot be claimed that the greater reliance on private hospitals over the last 10 years has increased the overall efficiency of the Australian hospital system.

A similar finding was reached by the Productivity Commission in 2009. The report determined that the available data were not sufficiently comparable between the two hospital sectors to draw any substantive conclusion about their relative efficiency. It was again noted that the public and private hospitals had quite different cost structures. For example, the costs of medical services to public patients in public hospitals are met by the hospital, while in the private sector these fees are paid for by patients. Capital costs, also—notably the way depreciation is measured—differ greatly between the two types of hospitals.

The same conclusion was reached about comparisons of the quality of care. The report recommended that steps should be taken to improve the reliability of the cost and quality of care data for this and wider purposes.

Nursing homes and hostels for the aged

The terminology 'nursing home' and 'hostel for the aged' was used to describe the provision of accommodation and other services for aged persons with special needs prior to the passing of the Commonwealth government's Aged Care Act of 1997. This act replaced the older terminology with 'high-level aged care and low-level aged care facilities' for the two types of accommodation respectively. However, the most recent Commonwealth legislation, which amended the Aged Care Act in 2013, has eliminated partially the distinction between low-level and high-level aged care facilities (see page 124). In our discussion of the history of this health policy area we continue to use the older terminologies.

It was noted in **Chapter 1** that the AIHW no longer treats expenditure on nursing homes as health expenditure. Since 2007, it has included high-level aged care expenditure as part of welfare expenditure. Low-level aged care services (hostel accommodation services) were always counted as welfare expenditure. The reasons for the changed treatment of high-level care for expenditure data are also discussed later. For many statistical purposes, the AIHW combines the characteristics of both types of institutions; for example, in assessing the bed capacity of the aged care accommodation sector.

Our preference to continue to treat issues associated with residential aged care as an important aspect of Australian health policy is based on our view that all the major problems of ensuring the quality and safety of patient care are common to these and other health institutions. The compelling need for coordination of patient-related activities between residential aged care and acute care hospitals also points to these aged care facilities being included as part of health policy discussion and analysis. This has been the approach adopted by the National Health and Hospitals Reform Commission in its studies, as we discuss in **Chapter 10**.

The principal role of aged care facilities is to meet the needs of those members of the aged population who have chronic problems. Younger persons with disabilities, including those with developmental disability and mental health disorders, make up most of the minority of the remaining clients of these institutions. A few aged care facilities are managed by state governments, mainly in Victoria, and others are organised as part of the public hospital system, including institutions that may be referred to locally as geriatric hospitals or hospitals for the aged. In general, the state-run institutions cater for the poorer members of the community and those with special needs, such as psycho-geriatric patients. However, most aged care facilities are in the private sector, owned either by commercial for-profit enterprises or by non-profit religious, charitable and other community organisations.

For the financial year 2010–11, the non-profit group was responsible for 60 per cent of services, the for-profit sector 27 per cent, and state and local government providers the remaining 13 per cent. At 30 June 2011, the total number of permanent residents in aged care facilities was about 165 000 (AIHW 2012b). Of these residents, 57 per cent were aged 85 years or older and only 4 per cent were aged less than 65 years.

In the financial year 2006–07, total recurrent expenditure on those institutions defined by the AIHW at that time as 'high care residential care expenditure', was estimated at $6.1 billion, of which $4.6 billion or 75 per cent, was provided by the Commonwealth government (AIHW 2008e). Apart from a modest expenditure by state governments on these facilities, 4 per cent of the total, the remaining source of funds was the fees paid by or on behalf of residents (21 per cent). The AIHW has not, as yet, updated these values.

Bed capacity

We noted previously that the method of defining aged care accommodation adopted after the implementation of the *Aged Care Act 1997* means that it is not possible to compare the numbers of beds in aged care facilities for subsequent years with the capacity of the system in the earlier periods. Nevertheless, it is of considerable relevance in understanding the interaction between government policy and the providers of aged care services to review briefly the main features of bed capacity changes from the 1960s onwards. We revert here to the older terminology of 'nursing homes'.

There was a high rate of growth in total bed capacity during the 1960s and 1980s, although this has varied considerably from period to period and between the different types of nursing home. The growth rate was very high in the 1960s and early 1970s, mainly in the for-profit sector of 'participating' nursing homes. This expansion was clearly a direct consequence of the introduction of the Commonwealth subsidy for nursing homes in 1963.

Between 1973 and 1977, growth in the number of beds slackened off considerably but there was a further rapid expansion from 1977 to 1984, mainly within the group of non-profit organisations. From 1984 to 1997, the increase in total bed numbers was very modest. The policy emphasis in this period had changed to one of fostering alternatives to institutional care for aged persons, notably via the Home and Community Care (HACC) program. Details of this and other community programs for the aged are set out in **Chapter 9**.

Between 30 June 1998, when the new approach of including nursing homes and hostels in the one category of residential aged care was introduced, and 30 June 2011, the number of operational places (beds) increased from 139 917 to 185 482

(AIHW 2012b). The most recent period was characterised by a marked increase in the number of places from 2002 onwards.

In interpreting these data, it is important to note that the number of places available is largely determined by the Commonwealth government's decisions about funding allocations for aged care in its annual budget. These decisions determine the number of new places it will subsidise each year. In addition, aged care institutions typically operate with an occupancy rate of about 95 per cent of their allocated bed numbers. Hence, the number of patients in institutions is approximately 95 per cent of the operational places quoted previously. Community demand for nursing home and hostel accommodation at the subsidised rates has always been sufficiently high to ensure that almost all available places are filled.

Table 5.7 shows the trend in the number of people in residential aged care from 30 June 1999 to 30 June 2011.

In addition to highlighting the increase in the number of permanent residents associated with the increases in bed capacity funded by the Commonwealth government, table 5.7 also indicates how the growth in the numbers and proportions of residents in the 'old, old' demographic category of those 85 years or more has escalated over this period. These residents are likely to be those with the highest

Table 5.7   Aged care facilities, resident numbers, by type and numbers and percentages 85+, at 30 June 1999–2011

Year	All permanent residents	All respite residents	Permanent residents (85+ years)	Respite residents (85+ years)	Permanent residents (85+ years) (%)	Respite residents (85+ years) (%)
1999	132 420	2479	64 638	903	48.8	36.4
2000	133 387	2604	66 503	1034	49.9	39.7
2001	134 004	2604	67 402	1008	50.3	38.7
2002	136 507	2422	69 258	1035	50.7	42.7
2003	140 297	2549	71 397	1024	50.9	40.2
2004	144 994	2646	74 229	1097	51.2	41.5
2005	149 091	2819	77 285	1174	51.8	41.6
2006	151 737	3135	80 099	1334	52.8	42.6
2007	153 426	3123	82 871	1445	54.0	46.3
2008	157 087	3163	85 912	1487	54.7	47.0
2009	158 885	3404	88 030	1644	55.4	48.3
2010	162 597	3773	91 462	1787	56.3	47.4
2011	165 032	3969	93 841	1972	56.9	49.7

Source: Data from table 6.1 in Australian Institute of Health and Welfare 2012b, *Residential Aged Care in Australia 2010–11: A Statistical Overview*, AIHW, Canberra, p. 60

care needs. As table 5.8 shows, among permanent residents, the percentage in this group rose from 48.8 per cent in 1999 to 56.9 per cent in 2011.

Of the permanent residents in aged care facilities at 30 June 2011 it has been estimated that about 52 per cent suffered from dementia and therefore had special needs. The estimate is based on an appraisal of the clinical characteristics of potential residents as required for admission to an aged care facility using the Aged Care Funding Instrument (ACFI) (see page 123) (Department of Health and Ageing 2012). The AIHW provides more details about dementia in residential care patients in its 2012 publication *Residential Aged Care in Australia 2010–11: A Statistical Overview*.

Aged care facility funding and charging

The patient-day subsidy was originally based in 1963 on one level of benefit for ordinary care patients and a larger benefit for 'extensive' care patients; that is, those with more intensive nursing care and other needs as certified by a doctor. The benefit was payable in respect of all patients in nursing homes approved by the Commonwealth.

Considerable variation in nursing home benefits between the states reflected the differences in fees, as the benefit, and the required minimum patient contribution set at 87.5 per cent of the aged pension for a single person, was designed to cover the fees charged by 70 per cent of nursing homes in each state. The differences in fees, in turn, arose out of variations in staffing and other costs.

In this period there were also substantial differences between the states in payments for extensive care benefits, payments under the deficit funding arrangements available to not-for profit organisations (see below), and the proportion of beds in the types of institutions as defined by their ownership status (Howe 1983).

The changed policies put into effect by the Commonwealth government from July 1988 onwards mainly addressed the funding issue, although greater provision of hostel accommodation was foreshadowed. As well as eliminating the deficit funding arrangement that previously applied to non-profit institutions, a standard resident contribution (SRC) was phased in by 1991. The SRC was set at 87.5 per cent of the aged pension based on the previous arrangements. However, the Commonwealth benefit plus the standard patient contribution then established the level of the fee for all states. The Commonwealth achieved this objective of national uniformity by enforcing the same staffing standard in each state, and by introducing a five-category system of classifying patients' needs, as determined by a resident classification instrument (RCI).

The characteristics of the RCI were broadly similar to the resource utilisation groups (RUGs) used for nursing home funding in the United States (Duckett, Gray & Howe 1995). With the growing interest in casemix funding in Australia, the Commonwealth Department of Health decided to develop, test and cost a more comprehensive casemix system for nursing home patients (Rhys Hearn 1997). This resident classification scale (RCS), consisting of eight levels of service need, was introduced in October 1997, in conjunction with the other funding changes discussed below. It was designed to cover hostel funding as well as nursing homes using a single instrument.

Three reports in the 1990s played an important role in the further development of government policy about nursing home funding and charging. The two reports by Robert Gregory (1993, 1994) were part of a review and evaluation of recurrent and capital funding for nursing homes. These reports examined details of the patient classification system and how it might be improved for funding purposes to promote greater efficiency in the operation of nursing homes. They also explored the design of a funding system for hostels.

The third report was that of the National Commission of Audit (1996), which, in the light of projections of the increased proportion of the population in older age groups, predicted large increases in Commonwealth outlays for subsidising nursing homes unless radical funding reforms were implemented. The report recommended means testing of fees charged, and increased user charges including contributions from the estates of patients with significant assets.

The two elements in the new policy as originally proposed, and incorporated in the Aged Care Act of 1997, were the alteration of fee-charging arrangements and the introduction of an entry contribution. The 1997 changes permitted non-full pensioners, including self-funded retirees, to be charged up to $63.30 per day above the SRC, with the money generated being offset against the Commonwealth's payments and therefore representing savings to the government.

The second element in the government's new policy was the introduction of an entry contribution, subject to a means test and defined as an 'accommodation bond'. In effect, this was an interest-free loan to the nursing home proprietor, which, it was claimed, could be used to support capital development of the nursing home. The previous government had applied a contribution of this kind to hostels, and the policy change was justified on the grounds of bringing the two sectors with allegedly similar functions into line.

The size of the accommodation bond was to be based on an assessment by each nursing home of the assets, including the family home, of each resident. Apart from ensuring that each person was left with a minimum level of assets, there was no restriction on the amount that the nursing home could extract as a 'bond'. In the face of mounting community and political opposition to the policy, the measure was withdrawn shortly after its inception (Howe 1998). However, a maximum charge of $4000 was introduced as an entry fee.

Since the 1997–98 financial year, the tradition of governments and others producing or sponsoring reports on aged care has continued. Of these, the most important Commonwealth government sponsored report was the Review of Pricing Arrangements in Residential Aged Care (Hogan 2004). Professor Hogan recommended in his report the introduction of the accommodation bond for high-care residents. Based on estimates of the increasing demand for aged care places in the future, he recommended that increased charges on nursing home residents should be implemented for those who could afford to pay. He also saw an increased role for the private for-profit sector in addressing these future requirements. The report noted considerable variations in the efficiency of individual institutions, indicating the potential for performance improvement of the whole sector.

A key recommendation of the report was that the government should increase the number of places to 108 per 1000 of the population aged 70 years or more. Provision of places was 98 per 1000 in 2003 when the Hogan study was conducted. A further recommendation was that the RCS should be simplified; providers claimed that collecting detailed information on the needs and problems of each patient was unduly burdensome.

The Coalition government agreed in 2004 to use 108 places per 1000 as its planning target. Funding to expand the sector was increased substantially. However, the Coalition government decided not to revisit the contentious issue of accommodation bonds for high-level care residents. As a result of industry pressure, it also agreed to sponsor the creation of a simpler patient classification system. The new classification, the Aged Care Funding Instrument (ACFI), with three categories of aged care need, was phased in progressively from March 2008.

The National Health and Hospitals Reform Commission in its 2008 report recommended that the aged care sector be reformed significantly to meet the challenges of an ageing population with diverse needs. The federal Labor government then asked the Productivity Commission to develop detailed options to meet these challenges. The final report of the Commission, *Caring for Older Australians: An Overview*, was released in August 2011 and highlighted a large number of weaknesses of the system, including:

- delays in care assessment and limited choice of care providers
- limits on the number of bed licences and care packages
- unduly complex system that is difficult to navigate
- variable care quality across the system
- difficulties for providers in obtaining finance for high-care facilities
- concerns of providers about the low level of charges for high-level accommodation
- workforce shortages due to low wages and the burden of high administrative loads
- insufficient independence of the complaints-handling process from the Department of Health and Ageing, which is responsible for policy development and may experience conflicts of interest (Productivity Commission 2011).

The Productivity Commission's numerous recommendations for reform, based on these problems and other challenges, included:

- the development of an integrated package of reforms to create a simplified 'gateway' that would provide easily understood information about what was available for aged persons, assess their care needs and financial capacity to contribute to the cost of their care and their entitlement to approved aged care.
- the proposal that aged persons could choose to pay either a periodic charge or a bond for all residential care accommodation. It was also recommended that limits on the number of residential places and care programs should be phased out, and the distinction between low care and high care, along with that between ordinary and extra service status, should be removed.
- an Australian aged care commission should be responsible for safety and the accreditation of facilities, with existing safety and quality standards being maintained.

The Commonwealth government's response to these recommendations, following consultation with older Australians, their families and industry representatives, was contained in a document released in April 2012, *Living Longer, Living Better* (Department of Health and Ageing 2012). The document suggested that the most important recommendations of the Productivity Commission report would be implemented, and legislation to amend the Aged Care Act of 1997 was passed by the federal parliament in June 2013.

The main elements of the reform, for which additional funding of $3.7 billion over five years was provided for in the Commonwealth's projected budget estimates, included:

- an integrated home support program featuring more home care packages to facilitate the ability of aged persons to remain in their own homes, where possible, along with improved means testing arrangements for the packages
- the expansion of residential aged care facilities, with an emphasis on the underserviced regional rural and remote areas
- an improvement in the contentious issue of means testing of patients, to be achieved by combining the income and assets tests
- the elimination of the distinction between low-level and high-level care, thus opening up the option of high-level patients being able to pay a bond or meet an accommodation charge
- the establishment of a new Aged Care Financing Authority in August 2013, with the responsibility of providing independent advice to the Commonwealth government on pricing and financing issues associated with the aged care sector, and ensuring value for money for the recipients of aged care services. The authority is also required to monitor over time the impact of the *Living Longer, Living Better* reforms, including the impact of the financing arrangements on access to care, industry viability and the aged care workforce.

- improvement of the ACFI; the classification of all patients to establish their needs has not been altered, but the relevant criteria to ensure the evidence basis of the assessments have been clarified.

Aged care policy issues

Policies about residential aged care facilities need to be examined in the context of wider issues concerning the principal client groups cared for in these institutions, especially the aged and younger people with substantial disabilities. In this section, we consider the problems these facilities face, the policy responses of governments and the limitations of and further problems created by these responses. **Chapter 9** examines other aspects of the provision of services for older people, people with mental health problems and other patients who use aged care facilities.

Commonwealth government involvement with nursing homes originally stemmed from its funding of hospitals under the voluntary health insurance program of the 1960s. Early in the development of the scheme it was recognised that long-stay patients in hospitals became ineligible for insurance benefits. This was because of private health fund rules that determined the maximum number of days of hospitalisation per annum for which they would be responsible. To overcome this problem, the Commonwealth introduced a 'special accounts' arrangement whereby it met the costs of maintaining these patients in hospital. However, the cost of the special accounts procedure escalated rapidly, with the Commonwealth being under considerable pressure from the health funds and the states to extend and improve it. Commonwealth payments to the states for maintaining long-stay pensioner patients in public hospitals also increased rapidly.

Since long-stay patients were often kept in hospital because of a lack of alternative accommodation or because of their inability to pay the fees charged by private nursing homes, the Commonwealth decided to subsidise these fees. The Commonwealth believed this would be cheaper than paying hospital fees via the special accounts and the Pensioner Medical Scheme. Relief of the financial burden falling on nursing home patients and their relatives was a further objective.

The government may not have anticipated the extent to which the subsidy also served to stimulate the growth of the nursing home industry. This growth reflected partly the increased demand for accommodation at the lower net price after the payment of the Commonwealth benefit, partly the considerable increase in the number of aged people, and partly changing social attitudes. The last, in turn, were influenced by the increased participation of women in the workforce and their lessened availability for carrying out the traditional role of caring for ageing relatives in the unpaid sector. The period from the mid-1960s was also one in which large numbers of patients were discharged from state psychiatric hospitals. Many of these people gravitated to nursing homes, some of which were established to cater for this new clientele.

By the early 1970s, the rapid expansion in nursing home bed numbers, together with a trebling of the Commonwealth's expenditure on benefits compared with the first full year of operation of the scheme, led to a search for alternative policies. In this period, moreover, the questioning of the appropriateness of treatment in institutions, which had led to the discharge of many psychiatric patients, carried over to other settings including nursing homes. Reports of this period dealing with the problems of the aged and others with chronic illness invariably stressed the desirability of community-based, non-institutional care (Hospitals and Health Services Commission 1973; Sax 1972).

Controls on bed numbers approved by the Commonwealth were introduced in 1972 and these led to modest increases in bed numbers over the next five years. The deficit-funding arrangements for nursing homes run by religious and charitable organisations introduced by the Whitlam Government in 1974 were designed to strengthen the viability of the non-profit sector as an alternative to commercial institutions. At the same time, the Commonwealth began providing funds to these organisations to construct homes for the aged, including nursing home accommodation. As Sax (1984) observed, while one arm of government was endeavouring to limit the growth of nursing home beds, another was laying the basis for further expansion. Different branches of government have their separate constituencies generating demands for policies, and it is difficult in these circumstances to achieve consistency.

While other sectors remained relatively constant, the large expansion in deficit-funded beds between 1977 and 1983 may also have been associated with the federal government's decision in 1977 (reversed in 1981) to make the health insurance funds responsible for paying nursing home benefits to people covered by hospital insurance. No information was then available about the insurance status of residents of the various types of nursing home but it is reasonable to assume that many patients in the not-for-profit sector were relatively affluent and more likely to be members of health funds. Although the government's official policy remained one of curtailing the Commonwealth's growth of bed numbers (Committee on the Care of the Aged and the Infirm 1977), the lessened financial responsibility of the Commonwealth may have weakened the resolve to implement it.

It is of note that the expansion of bed numbers between 1977 and 1983 was associated also with a substantial increase in the proportion of total recurrent health expenditure devoted to nursing homes. This figure rose from 7.6 per cent in 1977–78 to 9.1 per cent in 1984–85. However, it had declined to 7.6 per cent by 1998–99 (AIHW 2007a). As we noted previously, high-level aged care is no longer included in health expenditure estimates. However, in 2005–06, total expenditure on high-level aged care of $6091 million would have represented a further decline to 7 per cent if it were included in health expenditure (AIHW 2007a, 2008b). The considerable expansion in hostel accommodation no doubt had a major impact on the use of high-level aged care accommodation by clients with lower clinical needs.

In addition, the reduction may in part be attributable to the introduction by the Commonwealth in 1988 of financial support for developing multidisciplinary geriatric assessment teams. These teams provide advice to the aged on their needs including their possible requirements for nursing home accommodation. Admission to an aged care facility in recent years is now subject to the recommendation of an Aged Care Assessment Team (ACAT).

Between 1981 and 1987, no less than eight major Commonwealth reports examined aspects of the nursing home industry including administration, planning and funding. These reports outlined many trenchant criticisms, including those related to the administration of the program, the absence of clearly stated goals and objectives and monitoring and evaluation procedures, and the lack of coordination with other Commonwealth programs and those of the states.

Also subject to adverse comments was the failure to promote objectives such as higher quality of care; the provision of assessment and rehabilitation services and the strengthening of alternatives to nursing homes, including hostel accommodation and home care; and the absence of a rationale for funding mechanisms. According to a survey of nursing home patients across Australia conducted in 1987, many were receiving inadequate or unsuitable care (Commonwealth/State Working Party on Nursing Home Standards 1988). A common theme of the reports was the presence in Australia of a very large stock of nursing home beds by world standards, combined with the perception of a shortage of accommodation, particularly in certain areas.

The Commonwealth government established the Office for Aged Care Quality and Compliance in 2006. Its role includes that of responding to complaints via an investigative scheme. Quality assurance is also the responsibility of the Aged Care Standards and Accreditation Agency, which provides a program of accrediting individual aged care providers. Both agencies are part of the Department of Health.

Evaluation of nursing home performance is difficult because of the limitations of information on certain crucial issues. Of these, the most important is that there is still no regularly collected and comprehensive information about the quality of care provided by aged care facilities. Thus, we do not know whether the large increases in total expenditure on nursing homes and other aged care services has been associated with an improvement in quality as well as with the increase in the number of beds.

Despite the efforts of the AIHW—as reflected in its annual report *Residential Aged Care in Australia* and biennial report *Australia's Welfare*—there is a paucity of data about the characteristics of nursing home residents, including their socioeconomic status and their satisfaction with the services provided. It is also not possible to track the path of clients between the various elements of the system; for example, between the extensive set of community programs and the accommodation options. Thus, the available data do not permit any estimates to be made of the success of programs such as HACC in meeting their fundamental policy objective of reducing the need for institutional services.

The abortive attempt to introduce an accommodation bond for nursing home residents to support capital expenditure in the sector was an example of health care policymaking based on limited evidence and dubious assumptions. As Howe (1998) pointed out in a detailed critique of the policy, the notion that accommodation bonds, which had been acceptable for hostel accommodation, could also be applied to nursing homes was fatally flawed on several grounds.

Hostels are, in essence, alternatives to conventional housing as a source of accommodation that residents freely choose. Realising assets, including the family home, as part of this process was therefore perceived as acceptable by the residents and the community. However, entry into an aged care facility is based on the need for specialised care and treatment, often after a period of hospitalisation.

Hence, there was an understandable community perception that patients entering these facilities were being asked to make a large financial contribution to acquire a basic health service. Important differences between the capital requirements in the two sectors also made the entry bonds as a free source of capital for nursing home proprietors much less justified than in the hostels' case (Howe 1998, p. 149). Nevertheless, as we noted previously, accommodation bonds for care in aged care facilities were included as an option for residents in the 2011 reforms, along with the option of paying only an accommodation charge. At the same time, the Commonwealth government set out for providers the details of how they must use the bonds for capital investment purposes (Department of Health and Ageing 2012).

The policies from which the 1997 Aged Care Act are derived, including the extensive 2011 amendments discussed above, are based on the notion that all aged care facilities have as their primary function the provision of accommodation. In our view, this perception has been driven mainly as a justification for seeking greater contributions from the clients. If aged care accommodation is perceived mainly as a substitute for home-based accommodation, why should 'residents' not pay more for the service? Apart from the accommodation bond issue, it can be seen as paving the way for the payment of higher fees by those with larger assets and income in the means tested environment. The principal objective of the policy can thus be regarded as reducing the burden on the government's budget, in the light of all the factors generating greater public expenditure.

We do not attempt to canvass here all the issues and value judgments that arise in promoting a greater application of the user-pays principle. In the case of aged care facilities, we perceive that a potential threat to the quality of life of their clients is implicit in the associated emphasis on these institutions providing accommodation. It would be surprising if some organisations, especially in the for-profit sector, did not interpret this focus as justifying a lesser emphasis on treatment and quality of care. Reductions in more qualified nursing and other staff, along with pressures for profit maximisation, may have contributed to the well-documented instances of poor quality and complaints that have bedevilled the industry in recent years (Office of Aged Care Quality and Compliance 2008).

The aged care facilities sector illustrates, albeit in an extreme form, many of the difficulties faced by a central government in implementing ideal policy models and in achieving other goals such as increased efficiency and cost containment. The central implementation issue is how to change the mix of services provided to patients when the principal instrument available is financial and the government has only a limited ability to influence effectively the delivery of services.

As we have seen, there is a similar problem with public hospitals, but the states are one level of government closer to the organisations they are endeavouring to influence. Moreover, over a long period, they have developed legal and administrative means to exercise direct influence. These are largely absent in the relationship between the Commonwealth and the direct providers of care including the aged care facilities. In addition, a major problem for policy in this arena is that of shifting the emphasis to other forms of delivery, including community health services. The Commonwealth's HACC program and a number of community programs for the aged have been developed recently by the Commonwealth Department of Health. These are discussed in **Chapter 9**. It is currently too early to judge how effective these may be in reducing the pressure on the aged care sector.

It must also be recognised that well-established commercial and voluntary organisations in the sector are likely to be much more successful in resisting expenditure cuts, or the redistribution of funds, than community health groups in securing the benefits of the change. Again, we must look to major structural changes as the necessary condition for much-needed policy reforms affecting the care of the aged and other clients of these facilities. Whether the latest round of policy initiatives in this area will produce this effect remains to be seen.

The pharmaceutical industry

The pharmaceutical industry in Australia is responsible for the manufacture, dispensing and prescription of medicinal drugs. Most of these activities are part of the private sector but the amount of government regulation and financial involvement in the industry is considerable (Industry Commission 1996). The main actors in the industry are the manufacturers, the importers of medicinal drugs, the wholesalers and the registered pharmacies responsible for dispensing drugs that can only be prescribed by a health professional and for other over-the-counter (OTC) drugs. Some drugs are also supplied by other retailers. The prescribers are mainly doctors, but dentists, practice nurses, midwives and optometrists also have limited prescription rights. Manufacturers and pharmacies are subject to detailed regulation under both Commonwealth and state legislation (see page 135). The National Medicines Policy (NMP) aims to bring together all these groups to ensure that consumers obtain medications of acceptable efficacy and safety, and that access to them is at a cost that they and governments can afford. In addition, the NMP has the objective of ensuring that the various elements of the pharmaceutical industry in Australia remain viable. The Commonwealth Department of Health is responsible for the implementation of the NMP.

The Pharmaceutical Benefits Scheme

The Pharmaceutical Benefits Scheme (PBS), which is administered by the Department of Health in conjunction with Medicare (now part of the Department of Human Services), subsidises drugs prescribed by doctors and other health professionals when these drugs are listed in the Pharmaceutical Benefits Schedule. Over 90 per cent of drugs available only through a doctor's prescription are present in the schedule.

The total expenditure on all medications for human consumption was $18.8 billion in 2011–12, or about 14.2 per cent of total recurrent expenditure on health (see table 1.1). The Commonwealth government, via the PBS, the Repatriation Pharmaceutical Benefits Scheme, and other minor drug subsidy arrangements, met about 45 per cent of expenditure on all medications in 2011–12, with the payments for medications by individuals representing almost all of the remaining expenditure (AIHW 2013b). Most of the latter type of expenditure is for non-PBS pharmaceuticals, together with the co-payments for PBS items (see page 139).

From 2000–01 to 2010–11, expenditure on medications in constant price terms grew at the rate of 8.3 per cent per annum (AIHW 2013b, table A8). This was the highest rate of growth of an individual item distinguished in AIHW data on health expenditure in Australia.

As table 5.8 indicates, the year-by-year growth of expenditure in constant prices on all medications has been highly variable over the period covered by these data, ranging from 2.5 per cent in the years 2004–05 to 2005–06 and 11.1 per cent in 2007–08 to 2008–09. The table also shows that expenditure on those medications that are not part of the PBS grew at the very high rate of 14.8 per cent over the period 2005–06 to 2010–11.

In order to determine the factors that generate increases in PBS expenditure, and for other purposes, the federal government established in 2010 the Access to Medicines Working Group (AMWG). This was the product of a memorandum of understanding between the government and Medicines Australia (MA), the industry group that serves to promote the interests of pharmaceutical manufacturing enterprises in Australia. The AMWG was given the responsibility, via a data working group (DWG), to monitor and report on PBS expenditure trends and the drivers of growth in expenditure.

In a report to the AMWG, the DWG noted that in respect of growth since 2007–08, the contribution of general and concessional prescriptions (see page 133) had fallen whereas the contribution of the highly specialised drugs (HSDs) program had increased (Department of Health and Ageing and Medicines Australia 2013). The HSD program applies mainly to the use of these drugs in public and private

Table 5.8 Annual growth in health expenditure, constant prices, by area of expenditure, 2003–04 to 2010–11 (%) (medications in bold)

Area of expenditure	Average annual growth								
	2003–04 to 2004–05	2004–05 to 2005–06	2005–06 to 2006–07	2006–07 to 2007–08	2007–08 to 2008–09	2008–09 to 2009–10	2009–10 to 2010–11	2000–01 to 2010–11	2005–06 to 2010–11
Total hospitals	6.0	3.7	5.3	6.5	7.4	4.6	5.9	–	5.9
Public hospitals/ public hospital services	6.7	4.4	6.0	6.9	5.5	4.4	6.0	–	5.7
Private hospitals	3.4	1.2	2.8	5.0	15.1	5.3	5.7	5.7	6.7
Patient transport services	6.2	-0.1	12.3	8.8	15.8	4.3	6.1	–	9.4
Medical services	5.3	0.2	4.9	8.3	7.5	4.7	5.9	4.4	6.2
Dental services	2.6	1.5	1.3	2.1	7.7	10.3	1.3	–	4.5
State/territory provider	4.9	-0.2	-2.6	5.1	11.5	-5.1	9.4	–	2.7
Private provider	2.3	1.7	1.8	1.8	7.3	12.0	0.5	–	4.7
Other health practitioners	2.6	3.5	5.6	3.2	-2.5	6.4	6.2	–	3.7
Community health and other	5.4	3.7	8.0	10.5	-0.7	3.3	5.8	–	5.3
Public health	11.1	-2.7	11.9	21.4	-4.2	-13.7	-4.2	–	1.5

(continued)

Area of expenditure	Average annual growth								
	2003–04 to 2004–05	2004–05 to 2005–06	2005–06 to 2006–07	2006–07 to 2007–08	2007–08 to 2008–09	2008–09 to 2009–10	2009–10 to 2010–11	2000–01 to 2010–11	2005–06 to 2010–11
Medications	8.1	2.5	8.1	8.3	11.1	7.2	12.7	8.3	9.5
Benefit-paid pharmaceuticals	5.7	2.7	2.8	7.8	9.4	7.3	1.6	6.5	5.8
All other medications	12.5	2.0	17.0	9.1	13.7	7.1	28.4	10.8	14.8
Aids and appliances	9.8	4.2	5.7	0.1	6.9	12.5	9.9	–	6.9
Administration	4.4	-4.1	-5.0	6.1	10.5	-8.5	-30.6	-2.8	-6.7
Research	7.8	13.0	9.2	12.0	29.3	10.8	-1.0	9.7	11.7
Total recurrent expenditure	5.9	2.5	5.5	7.2	7.8	5.0	5.3	–	6.1
Capital expenditure	15.8	8.0	11.9	-2.7	-0.4	-10.4	30.7	5.3	4.9
Total health expenditure	6.4	2.8	5.9	6.6	7.3	4.2	6.4	–	6.1

Source: Based on table A8 in Australian Institute of Health and Welfare 2012d, *Health and Expenditure Australia 2010–11*, Health and Welfare expenditure series no. 47, cat. no. HWE 56, AIHW, Canberra, p. 117

hospitals that have the appropriate specialist facilities for treating chronically ill patients. The program covers immunosuppressive agents, HIV/AIDS antiretroviral agents, pulmonary arterial hypertension agents and a number of other specialised, high-cost medications.

The report also estimated that drugs associated with the treatment of cancer, cardiovascular diseases and mental illness were responsible for about 62 per cent of all PBS expenditure.

PBS beneficiaries

Two main categories of beneficiaries exist under the PBS: concessional and general beneficiaries. *Concessional beneficiaries* are those in receipt of social security or Veterans' Affairs benefits who hold a pensioner concession card, a health care card, a Commonwealth seniors health care card or a DVA white, gold or orange card. Commonwealth seniors cards are available to self-funded retirees of an age when they would be entitled to an aged pension and are subject to a means test.

Concessional beneficiaries from 1 January 2013 were required to make a co-payment of $5.90 per prescription, with this amount being indexed to movements in the consumer price index (CPI). In addition, a safety net arrangement operates whereby once a total out-of-pocket payment for prescriptions of individuals or families reaches a threshold level in a calendar year, further prescriptions are free for the remainder of the calendar year. For 2013, the threshold was set at $354.

The remainder of the population, *general beneficiaries*, pay a maximum of $36.10 per prescription from 1 January 2013. A safety net scheme also applies to this group. For 2013, the threshold was set at $1390.60 per annum, with a payment of $5.30 for additional prescriptions. These patient contributions and the safety net levels are also indexed for variations in the CPI.

Administration of the PBS

In subsidising the cost of pharmaceuticals, the Commonwealth intervenes in the industry in four important respects. First, it decides which drugs are to be included in the schedule. Second, it negotiates via the Pharmaceutical Benefits Pricing Authority (PBPA) the prices paid to manufacturers for drugs included in the scheme. Third, the Commonwealth is responsible for assessing the efficacy, safety and cost-effectiveness of drugs under consideration for listing in the schedule. Fourth, the Commonwealth pays retail pharmacies for the cost of supplying drugs; these payments include a prescription fee. Each of these areas has been the subject of intensive scrutiny and policymaking activity by the Commonwealth, which has developed a complex set of administrative arrangements to deal with them.

Drugs listed in the PBS schedule are determined by the Minister for Health on the advice of the Pharmaceutical Benefits Advisory Committee (PBAC). This body is an independent statutory committee consisting predominantly of medical practitioners nominated by the AMA. It has established guidelines about the criteria for a drug to be listed or delisted; these include efficacy, toxicity, the potential for abuse and the price relative to similar drugs (Industries Assistance Commission 1986).

Until 1988, the Pharmaceutical Benefits Pricing Bureau recommended to the minister the price to be paid for each new item recommended for listing. The department then negotiated with the supplier of the drug to ensure that the agreed price was not significantly higher than that recommended by the pricing bureau. This bureau, consisting of a majority of departmental representatives, was replaced in 1988 by the PBPA, which has a broader representation of industry groups.

Before a drug can be listed, the manufacturer must make a submission to the Therapeutic Goods Administration of the Department of Health to establish its quality, efficacy and safety. Applications that meet the department's reporting requirements are then subjected to an extensive evaluation process involving the National Biological Standards Laboratory and the Australian Drug Evaluation Committee, a statutory committee whose members have expertise in medicine and/or pharmacology.

In the early 1990s, it was realised within the Department of Health that economic criteria based on an analysis of cost-effectiveness should play an important role in listing pharmaceutical items. Accordingly, a Pharmaceutical Evaluation section was established within the PBAC to devise guidelines about the data that the drug companies must submit to meet the cost-effectiveness criteria. Further details about the PBS and cost-effectiveness analysis are provided in Salkeld, Mitchell & Hill (1998).

Historical background

When the PBS began in 1948, the scheme applied only to a restricted list of so-called lifesaving drugs, but these were free to everyone. Pensioners, however, were eligible to receive a much more extensive range of drugs. In 1960, a patient contribution was introduced for non-pensioner patients, but the list of drugs was extended to cover the same range as the pensioner schedule. Contributions required from general patients were increased in subsequent years to reduce government expenditure on the scheme. The provision in 1982 of a concessional rate for those on social service benefits who were not eligible for free prescriptions was designed to lighten the financial burden on low-income earners following a large increase in the general contribution.

Increases in beneficiary contributions to prescription costs over the years, including the introduction of a charge for aged pensioners in 1991, reflected the Commonwealth government's concern about the escalating cost of pharmaceuticals. It should be noted, however, that charges for pensioners were compensated for by an increase in the relevant pensions of $2.50 per week at that time.

The same concern about cost increases in the PBS underlay the decision to charge additional amounts for premium brands when cheaper generic equivalents are available. A generic brand is one that is equivalent in chemical composition and bio-availability to the premium brand; that is, a drug for which a patent was held. Once the patent expires, generic manufacturers are able to supply the drug at a much lower price that the premium brand. The distinction between the two types of drugs was incorporated in the PBS formulary in July 2007 when an F1 category for patented single-brand medicines was created, along with an F2 category for generic medicines.

Large cuts in the prices paid by the Commonwealth for major drugs under the PBS occurred in 2012 and 2013 to slow down the rate of increase in this aspect of the government's budget for health services.

Pharmaceutical industry policy issues

The highly regulated nature of the pharmaceutical industry, which arises out of the very large subsidy paid by the Commonwealth, has been the source of various major disagreements between the government, manufacturers and pharmacists. The disputes have arisen principally out of the price-setting policies as they affect both the manufacturers and pharmacists. These policies determine a substantial part of their Australian-based incomes because of the major role of the PBS in the industry. The lengthy and detailed evaluation process has also been a matter of contention between the government and manufacturers. As a direct result of these disputes there have been several extensive inquiries into pharmaceuticals and the PBS (Industries Assistance Commission 1986; Pharmaceutical Manufacturing Industry Inquiry 1979), together with the Baume (1991) inquiry. The comprehensive Industry Commission Report (1996) on the pharmaceutical industry is discussed on page 136.

It has been generally acknowledged that the control the Commonwealth exercises over pharmaceuticals has led to prices for PBS products being much lower than in other countries (Harvey 1985; Reekie 1984; Salkeld, Mitchell & Hill 1998). The bargaining power of the department arises out of the ready availability of alternative drug therapies. Apart from a few drugs that represent major therapeutic advances, the department is able to delist or refuse to list a drug, knowing that a close substitute will continue to be available to patients (Industries Assistance Commission 1986, p. 95).

However, a recent report by Duckett (2013), from the Grattan Institute Health Program, has cast doubt on whether the prices paid for pharmaceuticals under the PBS are still too high. By comparing the prices paid for the same drugs in the New Zealand health care system, where a cap is set on total expenditure on medications, Duckett was able to demonstrate that savings of the order of $1.3 billion per annum might be achieved.

Since overseas-owned companies manufacture most pharmaceuticals, and a considerable proportion of the ingredients are produced in other countries, the policy adopted has led to large savings for the government and for consumers, without significant losses for Australian producers. The Industries Assistance Commission (1986, pp. 101–2) argued that for Australian consumers and taxpayers, the benefits from lower drug costs attributable to the PBS substantially exceeded the costs of delays in gaining access to new drugs and reduced local research and development, as well as adverse effects on exports that might be attributable to the pricing policies. Unsurprisingly, there has been little enthusiasm for 'free-market' policies in this area, which would lead to increased local prices compared to those in other countries.

The pharmaceutical manufacturing industry

The industry is responsible, along with importers and wholesalers, for the provision of the medications that are the subject of the PBS and for the other prescribed and OTC drugs that contribute to all expenditure on pharmaceuticals. Through the organisation Medicines Australia representatives of the industry play an important role in public policies related to the PBS.

Under the Pharmaceutical Industry Development Program (PIDP) introduced in 1987, support for research, development and production in the local manufacturing industry was provided by a new pricing arrangement named 'Factor [f]' (Bureau of Industry Economics 1991). Under this arrangement, companies that increased their research and development (R&D), as well as their production value added (PVA), were required to have the prices for their pharmaceutical products adjusted upwards by the PBPA.

Pressure from the Australian Pharmaceutical Manufacturers Association (now Medicines Australia) was largely responsible for the policy change. The association was able to demonstrate that, over the 1970s and 1980s in Australia, the manufacture and export of pharmaceutical products had declined significantly. In addition, the replacement of the old pricing bureau by the more independent PBPA indicated a greater willingness by the government to agree to higher prices for pharmaceutical products. Furthermore, the duration of drug patents was extended from 16 to 20 years.

The Industry Commission Report (1996) was critical of the Factor [f] program. The commission could find no evidence that this form of financial assistance to industry, which used increases in pharmaceutical prices to stimulate both production and R&D activities, was the most appropriate method of supporting the local industry. It pointed to the existence of significant confusion about whether the program was an aspect of industry policy or of health policy. In any case, the commission believed that there was no case for subsidising this industry (or any other industry), apart from the presence of the PBS and lower prices for pharmaceuticals that the government was able to achieve as the sole purchaser of listed items.

In response to the Industry Commission's report, the Commonwealth government introduced a new scheme, the Pharmaceutical Industry Investment

Program (PIIP), which operated from 1999 to 2004. However, the PIIP retained the same objectives as the original Factor [f] program of stimulating R&D and local production by supporting higher prices of PBS items manufactured by the participating companies.

The Pharmaceuticals Partnerships Program (P3) replaced the PIIP in 2004. The program differed from its predecessors in that it only provided funding to subsidise R&D expenditure. This program was a belated response to the Industry Commission's criticisms of the original Factor [f] scheme in that it removed the nexus between PBS prices and general industry support. However, the P3 was terminated in 2009 after providing about $150 million for R&D expenditure.

Prior to the end of the P3 program, the Commonwealth government established a Pharmaceuticals Industry Strategy Group (PISG) with terms of reference that included the examination of the drivers and barriers to increasing investment in R&D, for clinical trials and for manufacturing activity in the industry in Australia. The terms of reference also included the identification of strategies to overcome the obstacles to investment in this area. In its final report to the minister for innovation, industry, science and research, the PISG, writing in 2009 at the onset of the global financial crisis, emphasised the challenges faced by the industry and stressed the need for Commonwealth government support.

Support for aspects of the industry, notably in fostering clinical trials of pharmaceuticals, for which Australia possesses considerable expertise, was announced by the Rudd Government in 2013.

Retail pharmacy

Retail pharmacy is also extensively regulated. Thus, under state legislation, only qualified pharmacists may own pharmacies and there is a limit on the number that may be owned by any one individual. The most important restrictions arising out of the PBS are those relating to the remuneration of pharmacists for dispensing drugs.

The payments made by the Department of Health to pharmacists for PBS items consist of the 'price to pharmacist', which is based on the price negotiated with the manufacturer, including a notional wholesaler's mark-up, a mark-up percentage, a professional dispensing fee and other miscellaneous margins. The mark-up component and the dispensing fee vary according to whether the drug has already been prepared or requires further preparation by the pharmacist. The rates of remuneration to pharmacists are determined by the Pharmaceutical Benefits Remuneration Tribunal, which is required by legislation to set the rates based on principles 'appropriate for the fixation of award wages or salaries'.

The Industries Assistance Commission (1986) also favoured eliminating restrictions on discounting and surcharging, together with restrictions on the ownership of pharmacies, but the federal government, mindful no doubt of the expected hostile reaction of pharmacists, chose not to implement these recommendations. The promotion of a more competitive market, which would be likely to benefit consumers, as the Industries Assistance Commission argued, has not loomed large as a policy objective when opposed by strong, well-organised interest groups.

Problems in the use of pharmaceutical drugs

Overprescribing for the aged population has been perceived as a problem in Australia, and this was one of the reasons why the co-payment for pensioner patients was introduced in 1990. However, it would seem that actions such as continuing education programs about pharmaceuticals, which might influence directly the behaviour of doctors, are also needed. The role of drug manufacturers in promoting the prescribing of drugs must also be acknowledged as part of the problem. Evidence was provided to the Industries Assistance Commission inquiry that most of the information available to many doctors was derived from advertisements and the activities of drug industry representatives (Avorn et al. 1982; Harvey 1985).

Concerns about the incorrect use of pharmaceutical drugs in Australia, especially by older members of the population, led to the National Health Strategy (1992a) undertaking a study on this issue. The report concentrated on the consequences of drug use, including deaths and hospital admissions, and recommended the development of risk profiles to assist health professionals, carers and patients to recognise individuals at high risk of adverse effects. In addition, it recommended that a national pharmaceutical drug education program be established to provide information to health professionals and others to improve the prescribing, dispensing and administering of drugs. The development of quality assurance and audit processes, including outcome standards for drug use to support health professionals' decision-making, was also recommended.

In 1992, a report written for the National Better Health Program entitled *National Policy Action to Improve the Use of Medications in the Elderly* (Marr 1992) recommended that the use of pharmaceuticals by older people required urgent attention for a number of reasons, including the adverse consequences of inappropriate use, additional risks to people from backgrounds of languages other than English and the general costs. The report briefly reviewed the contributions to better drug use that could be made by the pharmaceutical industry, doctors, pharmacists, nurses, consumers and government. It is not clear what effect, if any, such reports have had on drug prescribing, education and related matters.

It has been estimated that in 1999–2000, about 150 000 hospital admissions in Australia were medication related (Runciman et al. 2003). Of these, up to three-quarters were potentially preventable. Runciman and his colleagues concluded, after an exhaustive study of the available data and published reports, that adverse drug events are common in the Australian health care system. Anti-coagulant, anti-inflammatory and cardiovascular drugs featured prominently in these events. They also argued that there was an urgent need to improve the reporting of these medication problems and to implement methods to reduce their incidence.

In the literature dealing with pharmaceuticals and the pharmaceutical industry increasing attention has been paid to the overselling of the benefits of prescribed drugs by the extensive marketing undertaken by the industry. Recent books on this topic include *Bad Pharma: How Drug Companies Mislead Doctors and Harm Patients* by Ben Goldacre (2013), *Pharmageddon* by David Healy (2012), and *The Myth of the Chemical Cure: A Critique of Psychiatric Drug Treatment* by Joanna Moncrieff (2009). These works carefully document the lack of efficacy of many widely prescribed medications, together with the risks associated with their use. We discuss Moncrieff's important monograph in **Chapter 9**.

The compelling evidence presented in these books, and in a number of other similar works, casts doubt on whether the fundamental aim of the NMP to ensure the efficacy and safety of prescribed medications is indeed being achieved in Australia. Are our regulatory bodies also being deceived by the pharmaceutical industry? It seems to us that the issue should be given high priority in health policymaking.

Co-payments

It was noted previously that co-payments, also described as patient contributions, now apply to all expenditure on PBS items, except in the case of the safety net for concessional beneficiaries. A major increase in patient contributions, including the removal of free pharmaceuticals for eligible pensioners, took place in 1993. The justification given by the Commonwealth government was that the considerable growth in the cost of the PBS experienced to date was placing an unsustainable burden on the federal budget. However, for people with chronic illness the cost of medications can be considerable, despite the safety net arrangements. It should be noted that about 17 per cent of the total cost of PBS medicines is met by the patients (AIHW 2013b).

Substantial co-payments in any health expenditure area raise important issues about the equity of the arrangements especially when those on low incomes, including pensioner patients, take on much of the expenditure. As we discuss in **Chapter 10**, the PBS is one example of the wider equity problem in the Australian health care system whereby a relatively high proportion of health expenditure is paid for by patients compared with most OECD economically developed countries, with the notable exception of the United States. It is salutary in this regard to note that the British National Health Service provides free medication for all its residents of more than 60 years of age.

SUMMARY AND CONCLUSION

This chapter has covered many of the most important institutions, services and products that constitute the health care system. Although the activities discussed here are disparate, many of the policy issues have a good deal in common. As we indicated in **Chapter 1**, each area represents a complex mixture of private and government initiatives, which influence heavily the pattern of services, funding, regulations and controls.

Commonwealth and state/territory policies about institutional services and pharmaceuticals have aimed to contain the use of, and expenditure on, these services and products. The policies have been based, in part, on the belief that further increases in real per capita expenditure would yield low or possibly negative benefits, and they result from strong pressure on governments of both political complexions to reduce their total spending. In addition, it has been one of the consistent policy objectives of governments to reduce the dependence on institutional care and to substitute, whenever possible, community-based health services for this care.

These policies and others designed to produce a more efficient utilisation of health care resources have been resisted by a variety of private interests in each sector, including doctors in private practice, who have been concerned about the quality of the care provided to patients and about their own incomes. Consequently, progress in implementing changes has been slow, but the overall objective of containing the growth of total government expenditure in most of these areas has, in general, been achieved.

In some instances, notably for public hospitals, considerable improvements in efficiency and productivity have also resulted, in part from the introduction of more rational methods of funding and information gathering. Relevant interest groups have no doubt stimulated perennial perceptions of a crisis in health care financing and provision but it is not possible to achieve cost-containment goals without some implicit or explicit rationing of services.

A notable exception to the achievement of cost-containment objectives has been the PBS, under which new and expensive drugs in areas such as the treatment of depression and cancer have proliferated. These technological developments have driven up total costs and the costs to government in spite of increased co-payments met by patients and the extensive use of cost-effectiveness analysis. We have also pointed to the literature on prescribed drugs that documents concerns about the efficacy and safety of many of these pharmaceuticals.

Increased dependence on the private sector, designed to save money in public hospitals for state and Commonwealth governments, may also have the unintended consequence of escalating the cost of medical services, including diagnostic procedures, as service provision and fee levels increase. This is a further area where above-average health expenditure levels have been concentrated in recent years.

An important factor bearing on the success of cost-containment and quality of care policies is the size and composition of the health workforce, which is examined in the next chapter.

FURTHER READING

The AIHW's publication *Australian Hospital Statistics 2011–12* (2013a) is a rich source of data on many aspects of the public hospital system, including on the conditions treated, the diagnoses of admitted patients, rates of performance of specific procedures and the waiting times associated with obtaining procedural interventions. All these data are available on the AIHW website, the address for which is listed on page 429.

Similar considerations apply to data on aged care facilities contained in the AIHW's publication *Residential Aged Care in Australia 2010–2011* (2012b), except that there is far less information on the clinical and other characteristics of patients in these institutions.

Some private hospital data are found in the *Australian Hospital Statistics* publication of the AIHW. However, more detailed information on this sector is provided by the ABS in its regular publication *Private Hospitals, Australia, 2011–12* (2013a).

The Garling Report on public hospitals in New South Wales (Special Commission of Inquiry into Acute Care Services in NSW Public Hospitals 2008) should be mandatory reading for everyone involved in the health care sector, especially for any remaining sceptics who believe the problems of the system may have been exaggerated by policy analysts and others.

DISCUSSION QUESTIONS

1   It had been argued, especially by medical staff and the federal Coalition parties in opposition, that the area health services in New South Wales should be abolished and replaced by traditional hospital boards. Prior to the September 2013 federal election it seemed that Tony Abbott favoured the restoration of hospital boards and hence the elimination of local hospital networks. What are the arguments for and against this proposal? Who might stand to gain and who might stand to lose if the proposal were implemented?

2   What, in your view, are the reasons that the many problems of our hospital systems, notably about quality of care and safety, have remained unresolved into the 21st century?

3   We have observed in this chapter the large number of reports on aged care facilities in Australia over the last 30 years. What may be the reasons for so much government attention being focused on nursing homes and related institutions?

4   Why have both Labor and Coalition federal governments resorted to the greater application of user charges, especially in areas as diverse as pharmaceuticals and aged care? What have been the advantages and disadvantages of these policies?

5   We have raised concerns about the efficacy and safety of some prescribed medicines. What evidence would be needed to assess the validity of these claims?

6

The health workforce

The health workforce is a large and expanding section of the Australian labour force, with over three-quarters of a million people employed in the health industry. Health workforce policies shape educational opportunities, registration requirements and employment prospects for employees in the health care system. Policies influence the supply of and the demand for health personnel. Governments have an implicit responsibility to provide employment for the employees or 'human capital' they have trained or encouraged to be trained (Evans 1984, p. 295). In this respect, human capital is different from other types of capital, such as equipment or land, because it cannot be stockpiled or ignored. Education policies in any one period have serious implications for policies regarding health care provision in the future, or at least until that generation of workers has retired or been retrained.

A surplus of an occupational group such as medical practitioners presents a much more difficult and long-lasting policy problem than shortfalls in particular occupations. For example, nursing shortages in Australia in the 1980s were reduced in a relatively short period by increasing the numbers of nursing graduates coming into the labour market from tertiary nursing courses and by recruiting qualified nurses from overseas. However, attempts to curtail medical workforce growth were less successful in the last three decades. The reduction of migration additions to the permanent medical workforce helped slow its growth from 18.3 per cent between 1986 and 1991 to 13.8 per cent between 1991 and 1996, as there was a perception of oversupply (AIHW 1998a, p. 183). However, the Australian medical workforce more than doubled between 1976 and 1996—from 21 150 to 44 000 practising—when the population increased by 30 per cent (Australian Medical Workforce Advisory Committee & AIHW 1998, p. 9). Later, between 2002 and 2006, the medical workforce rose steadily with an overall increase of 15.6 per cent (from 53 991 to 62 425), as the perception of oversupply shifted to a perception of shortages of general practitioners and in many specialties (AIHW 2009; Department of Health and Ageing 2008a).

In 2006, the Council of Australian Governments (COAG) agreed on a national health workforce reform package to ensure that the health workforce was better able to respond to the changing care needs of the Australian community, while still maintaining the quality and safety of health services. This included establishing the National Health Workforce Taskforce (NHWT), which undertook projects to inform development of practical solutions on workforce innovation and reform.

The NHWT functioned under the Australian Health Ministers' Advisory Council (AHMAC) and reported directly to the chair of AHMAC's Health Workforce Principal Committee (HWPC). During 2005–06, the Australian Medical Workforce Advisory Committee (AMWAC) and the Australian Health Workforce Advisory Committee (AHWAC) were disbanded because of a review undertaken by AHMAC. These profession-specific workforce committees were disestablished as a means to enable a more holistic multidisciplinary approach to considering health-related policy development and program review activity.

Further activities of COAG included the National Partnership Agreement on Hospital and Health Workforce Reform. This was an agreement between the Commonwealth and the states and territories to improve the efficiency of the health workforce and the capacity of hospitals. The agreement focused on four reform components:

- introducing a nationally consistent activity-based funding approach
- improving health workforce capability and supply
- enhancing the provision of sub-acute services
- taking the pressure off public hospitals (COAG 2007).

Subsequently, this led to the establishment of Health Workforce Australia (HWA) in 2010. This agency subsumed the activities of NHWT by managing major reforms to the Australian health workforce, taking responsibility for its work through workforce planning and research, education and training, and innovation and reform.

Public policy defines which employees are qualified to carry out which work in the health care system. It can be argued, for example, that there is no scientific or economic reason why one has to be a qualified medical practitioner to prescribe pharmaceuticals. The medical profession has a monopoly, with a few exceptions, in the area of drug prescription because it has convinced governments that this should be the case. Government regulatory policy determines what each occupation is allowed to do and therefore defines the boundaries between occupational territories. These boundaries are not fixed; they shift with technological change and changes in political influence within and between health occupations. As will be seen later in this chapter, an occupation may take over the occupational territory of another in a process referred to as 'occupational substitution'. Generally, there are four principal ways that governments intervene in the labour market to influence the size of the health workforce and to achieve other policy objectives: occupational regulation, education, governance and health care financing and organisation.

Occupational regulation

Statutory regulation of professional occupations is carried out by government agencies or delegated professional bodies. Traditionally in Australia, registration boards under the auspices of state and territory health authorities set educational and other requirements for 24 distinct health occupations including medical practitioner (registrable in all states and territories), osteopath (registrable in all states and territories except Western Australia) and Aboriginal health worker (registrable in the Northern Territory only). Progress with registering additional health occupations has been slow since 1982, when the Australian health ministers decided not to register any more occupations unless they could cause fatal injury to patients (Grant & Lapsley 1993, pp. 171–4). Health authorities also monitor postgraduate qualifications required for specialist registration and practice, such as those awarded by specialist medical colleges (see **Chapter 7**). Professional registration boards are responsible for endorsing accredited educational programs and for ensuring that only practitioners with appropriate qualifications and experience are given legal entitlement to practise in their particular health occupation. Registration boards are also responsible for minimum standards of competence and limits of liability for malpractice.

Table 6.1   Major steps towards implementation of the National Registration and Accreditation Scheme

1992	Legislation to support mutual recognition between the states and territories of professional qualifications (*Mutual Recognition Act 1992* (Cth))
1995	Establishment of the Australian Medical Workforce Advisory Committee, an entity of Commonwealth and state/territory governments to monitor medical workforce
2000	Establishment of the Australian Health Workforce Advisory Committee, an entity of Commonwealth and state/territory governments to monitor health workforce
2002	Release of the first *Intergenerational Report*, issued by the Commonwealth Treasury to address the long-term sustainability of government finances as the population ages
2004	Launch of the first national Health Workforce Strategic Framework (by health ministers) Ministers announce a decision to pursue a nationally consistent approach to medical registration
2005	Jayant Patel, 'Dr Death', who had been practising medicine in Bundaberg, Queensland, since 2003, emerges into the public arena
2005	Three reports are issued by the Productivity Commission (*Economic Implications of an Ageing Australia*, *Impacts of Advances in Medical Technology in Australia*, and *Australia's Health Workforce*) addressing issues of the relationship between economic development and health expenditure and workforce
July 2006	COAG decides to move towards establishing schemes for registration and accreditation for health professionals by July 2008
March 2008	COAG members sign the National Partnership Agreement to Deliver a Seamless National Economy and the Intergovernmental Agreement for a National Registration and Accreditation Scheme for the Health Professions
2009	*Health Practitioner Regulation National Law Act 2009* enacted in Queensland, Victoria and NSW
2010	*Health Practitioner Regulation National Law Act 2009* enacted in Australian Capital Territory, Northern Territory, Tasmania, South Australia and Western Australia
1 July 2010	Introduction of the National Registration and Accreditation Scheme for Health Practitioners

Source: Pacey et al. (2012)

A nationally uniform system of professional registration on a profession-by-profession basis was proposed for implementation in the early 1990s (AIHW 1992; Pacey et al. 2012). This would have provided considerable advantages over the traditional system, such as more uniform standards of professional practice, improved career mobility for health professionals and more comprehensive and reliable data about these occupational groups for the purposes of workforce evaluation and planning.

Although this system did not eventuate, in 2005 the Productivity Commission undertook a research study to examine issues affecting the health workforce, including the supply of and demand for health workforce professionals and proposed solutions for the Commonwealth government to ensure the continued delivery of quality health care. This study recommended a single national registration board for health professionals, as well as a single national accreditation board for health professional education and training. In response, in 2008 COAG signed an intergovernmental agreement on the health workforce as an initiative to improve Australia's health system. In 2009 and 2010 all Australian states and territories enacted the national law. Australia's National Registration and Accreditation Scheme (NRAS) was implemented in July 2010.

The Australian Health Practitioner Regulation Agency (AHPRA) is an overarching national registration and accreditation system for the regulated health profession groups. Those initially covered were chiropractors, dentists (including dental hygienists, dental prosthetists and dental therapists), medical practitioners, nurses and midwives, optometrists, osteopaths, pharmacists, physiotherapists, podiatrists and psychologists.

As table 6.2 shows, four occupations were added in July 2012. This national system aims to assist health professionals to move easily between states and territories,

Table 6.2   Professions regulated under the *Health Practitioner Regulation National Law Act 2009*

2010 entrants	2012 entrants
Chiropractors	Aboriginal and Torres Strait Islander health practitioners
Dental practitioners [a]	Chinese medicine practitioners
Medical practitioners	Medical radiation practitioners
Nurses and midwives	Occupational therapists
Optometrists	
Osteopaths	
Pharmacists	
Physiotherapists	
Podiatrists	
Psychologists	

Note
(a) Includes dentists, dental therapists, dental hygienists, oral health therapists and dental prosthetists.

Source: Pacey et al. (2012)

and to increase the flexibility, responsiveness and sustainability of the health workforce. It also aims to provide better safeguards to the public and address the shortages and pressures faced by the health workforce. AHPRA is a bold national initiative that is the envy of many in federated health care systems such as Canada and the United States.

Education and competency standards

Governments also intervene in the health labour market by providing subsidies for educational costs and by establishing educational standards for specific health occupations. The vast majority of Australian health personnel are educated in publicly financed institutions—universities, vocational education and training providers, and hospitals. Governments generally have limited influence in defining the nature of training and education necessary for each occupation, but in some instances, notably nursing, the government role has been decisive in determining educational requirements. A significant policy development in this regard was the transfer of nursing education from hospitals to universities. In 1984, the federal government announced that, by 1993, all pre-registration nursing education would be transferred completely from hospitals to tertiary institutions. This transfer was brought forward in New South Wales to 1985. This policy decision is of historical significance when we consider that the hospital-based system of nurse training had remained substantially unchanged in Australia since 1868, when Lucy Osburn established Australia's first school of nursing at Sydney Hospital. In the medical area, the federal government commissioned an inquiry into medical education and the medical workforce, which reported to the minister of health in 1988. Several universities, initially Flinders, Queensland and Sydney, subsequently developed graduate-entry medical courses. These developments are discussed later in this chapter.

The training reform agenda of the Hawke and Keating Labor governments was the main impetus for the development of competency standards and their application to vocational education and training in Australia. The principal aim was to make vocational training more responsive to industry needs. In this context, a competency is defined as a combination of attributes—such as knowledge, abilities, skills and aptitudes—underlying specific aspects of successful professional performance (Gonczi, Hager & Oliver 1990). Australia was not alone in moving towards a competency-based education and training system. Similar microeconomic reforms have taken place in the United Kingdom, the European Community, the United States and New Zealand, with the former West Germany's dual system having been established as a standards-based system in 1968. Australia's training reform agenda is determined largely by industry, the Commonwealth, state and territory ministers for education and training, and other advisory groups such as the Vocational Education and Training Advisory Group (VETAG). In 1989, the National Training Board (NTB) was established to endorse competency standards developed at both occupational and industry levels with a view to developing a more effective, efficient, responsive and coherent national vocational education and training system.

Later, the NTB amalgamated with the Australian Committee for Training Curriculum (ACTRAC) to form the Standards and Curriculum Council (SCC), which was then subsequently replaced by the Australian National Training Authority's (ANTA) National Training Framework Committee. In 2005, the responsibilities and functions of ANTA were transferred to the Department of Education, Science and Training (DEST). During this time, a new national training system was implemented in order to reform Australia's training system. This system resulted in all states and territories signing the 2005–08 Commonwealth–State Agreement for Skilling Australia's Workforce, under which the Commonwealth government provided almost $5 billion to support training systems over the three-year period (Department of Education, Science and Training 2006).

More recent work in this area includes the national strategy *Shaping our Future: Australia's National Strategy for VET 2004–2010* for the progression of vocational education and training (VET) in Australia (Australian National Training Authority 2004).

Work that seeks to connect the development of professional-level competency standards with higher education is relatively minor compared to the training reform agendas pursued at the vocational level. The link between competency standards in the professions and higher education has come from reforms in overseas skills recognition. When the Commonwealth, state and territory governments agreed to the establishment of the NTB they also endorsed the migrant skills reform strategy, which was part of the government's national agenda for a multicultural Australia. The strategy seeks to ensure greater efficiency in the use of the skills immigrants bring to Australia by shifting the recognition process from one based on equivalence of paper qualification to a competency-based one. The National Office of Overseas Skills Recognition (NOOSR), a branch of Australian Education International, was established to oversee this strategy.

The development of competency standards in the professions has progressed on a profession-by-profession basis. Nursing has been at the forefront in developing competency standards as the basis for gaining entry to or being recognised within the profession. In 1988, the Australasian Nurse Registering Authorities Conference (ANRAC) foreshadowed the creation of a national register of nurses. ANRAC competencies were recognised as forming the basis for registration of enrolled and registered nurses in all states and territories (AIHW 1992, pp. 112–13). Dietetics also has been at the forefront of developing competency standards. The Dietitians Association of Australia adopted an interim set of minimum standards for professional training in 1990.

The university sector has voiced concerns about the relevance of competency standards to higher education through Universities Australia. They note that higher education provides graduates with generalist and specialist knowledge bases, conceptual skills and other intangible attributes in addition to professionally specific competencies. There has been criticism that attention to the more easily described and measured competency standards, particularly for professional practice, may result in a lack of attention to the less tangible but highly valued outcomes of higher education. Nursing, in particular, has been embroiled in this debate. It is now widely acknowledged that competency-based minimum standards for registration purposes are but one part of the broader professional education agenda.

The migrant skills reform strategy encouraged the development of entry-level competency standards in numerous health professions, including chiropractic and osteopathy, dietetics, medical science, medical radiations science, nursing, occupational therapy, optometry, pharmacy, physiotherapy, podiatry, psychology, social work and speech pathology. The move towards competency-based standards led to a review of all panels and councils that make up the assessment network of the NOOSR, including the Australian Medical Council (AMC) and the Australian Nursing and Midwifery Accreditation Council (ANMAC). These bodies are mainly responsible for establishing the mutual recognition of qualifications (in accordance with the Commonwealth *Mutual Recognition Act 1992*) and competency standards across Australia, under the umbrella of AHPRA.

Health workforce governance

At an international level, the *World Health Report 2006: Working Together for Health* (WHO 2006) drew attention to the quantity and quality of health professionals in a health system being a significant facilitator of or barrier to health improvement. It highlighted the severe workforce shortages in almost 60 countries and called on national leadership and global solidarity to invest in the health workforce for the future in order to guarantee universal access to health care in every country.

Health workforce governance brings together disparate disciplines, including political science, law and sociology, to address a dynamic field of practice that crosses over traditional boundaries between the public, private and community sectors. 'Governance' derives from the ancient Greek term meaning 'to steer'. In the context of new public sector management, it refers to the contemporary government analogy of 'steering not rowing', of directing and controlling, as distinct from the hands-on management of service provision. In the public sector, it often means entering into contracts with funders and providers of services, rather than attempting to manage and deliver services directly.

In 2008, COAG provided funding for several health workforce initiatives including supporting the training of health professionals, establishing more streamlined training arrangements, and considering funding approaches and incentives to ensure clinical training is delivered in the most cost-efficient manner. This built on progress made with the introduction of statewide initiatives in clinical training in Victoria and Queensland. In light of COAG's decision to create a national workforce agency, with responsibilities in the planning, coordination and funding of clinical training across medical, nursing and allied health disciplines, the challenge is to develop a truly national system. This needs to meet the diverse needs of the jurisdictions (federal and state/territory governments), health services (predominantly in the public hospital sector), and education providers (universities, TAFE colleges and registered training authorities).

To manage these initiatives, COAG established HWA, operating across the health and education sectors. It attempted to cultivate a more sustainable workforce to meet community needs, especially in Indigenous, outer metropolitan, rural and remote communities. Health workforce shortages, and rigidities and inefficiencies in education and service delivery, constitute a significant constraint on the ability of Australia's health care system to meet community needs adequately. The Australian Health Ministers Advisory Committee and the subsequent Productivity Commission (2006) research report on Australia's health workforce highlighted this problem.

Commonwealth, state and territory leaders have recognised a significant under-investment in the health workforce: in doctors, nurses, midwives, allied health professionals, paramedics and researchers. The Rudd and Gillard governments worked with state and territory governments and professions and implemented numerous initiatives in the intersecting fields of education and training, accreditation, regulation and health care provision in innovative nationwide attempts to improve the efficiency of the health workforce. The Abbott Government has expressed the desire to review these initiatives and to focus on frontline clinicians and services, rather than planning or management per se.

Workforce challenges to be addressed include:

- ageing of the population and workforce
- reduced average working hours
- the ethical and sustainable recruitment of health professionals from overseas
- changing patterns of population health and disease
- rising community expectations regarding health care
- financial and labour market pressures.

A major focus of national attention for COAG was establishment of the National Registration and Accreditation Scheme in 2010. This is perhaps the most significant reform on the Australian health workforce landscape, as it brings nine jurisdictions and 15 professions together into a common health workforce governance framework.

Health care financing and organisation

Health care financing and organisation determine how many personnel are required in order to provide particular services. Changes in the structure of health care provision can have a profound impact on the demand for occupations affected by the change. Similarly, a decision to permit the reimbursement under health insurance arrangements of certain types of health professional services would affect considerably the demand for their services. Thus, the inclusion of optometric services in the Medibank program in 1975 had a substantial impact on the requirements for optometrists. Several occupations including physiotherapy, occupational therapy and speech pathology were included in 2004. The Enhanced Primary Care program, introduced in 1999 and replaced in 2005 by the Chronic Disease Management program, provides extra preventative care for older people and improves the coordination of care for people with chronic conditions and complex needs such as palliative care.

In 2006, in response to growing mental health issues in Australia, new Medicare items were included to support the public and health professionals in recognising and addressing mental health issues. This initiative was part of the Commonwealth government's scheme Better Access to Psychiatrists, Psychologists and General Practitioners through the Medicare Benefits Schedule (MBS) (Medicare Australia 2009b).

Other health occupations will continue to attempt to be included in the MBS. However, it appears that with limited funding through the tax-paying system, the items that succeed in being listed on the schedule involve issues of most concern or with a high burden on society, such as mental health, one of the national health priority areas. The services not covered by the MBS are usually marketed as desirable extras to promote the purchase of private health insurance.

Composition of the health workforce

In 2010 there were 737 400 workers in the health services industries, which is a 23 per cent increase since 2005 (AIHW 2012a). People in the health workforce work mainly in the health services industries, and comprised 7 per cent of the total labour force in 2010 (AIHW 2012a). By comparison, almost 550 000 people were employed in the health workforce in 2006. The health workforce increased by 12 per cent between 1996 and 2001, and by 23 per cent between 2001 and 2006.

One of the most interesting features of the health care workforce is the discrepancy between the numerical representation of different occupations and their relative political influence. Most striking is the fact that the dominant profession, medicine, accounts for just 10 per cent of health practitioners, while a less powerful occupation, nursing, comprises the largest proportion (40 per cent of all health personnel). Of significance also is the gender composition of the health workforce, as 76 per cent of those working in the health industry are women; this had not changed in the decade between 1996 and 2006 (AIHW 2009).

Figure 6.1 shows the number of persons employed in health and health-related occupations from the 2006 census, including the percentage change between 2001 and 2006. These are the most recent comprehensive figures currently available. The total paid health workforce comprised 6 per cent of Australian employees in 2006 (ABS 2006a). The figures in the graph do not include everyone employed in the health industry, such as clerical and cleaning staff. The figures also give no indication of the number of people who work in the voluntary sector of the health care system as unpaid providers of health care.

Figure 6.1 Persons employed in health occupations: number of workers per 100 000 population, Australia, 1996, 2001 and 2006

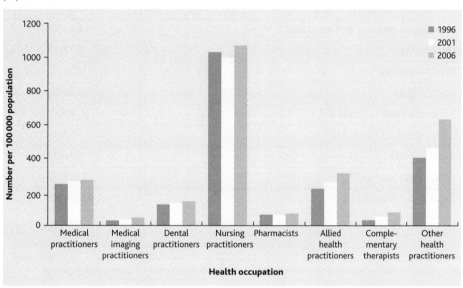

Source: Based on figure 2.1 in Australian Institute of Health and Welfare 2009, *Health and Community Services Labour Force,* National health labour force series no. 42, cat. no. HWL 43, AIHW, Canberra

Professional autonomy and prestige

The rhetoric of professionalism suggests that professions can be distinguished from other occupations because of traits such as education standards, levels of skill and professional ethics. Nevertheless, examination of the work practices of different occupational groups suggests that what primarily distinguishes professions from other occupations is the extent to which they have been able to achieve government-regulated autonomy over their work (Freidson 1970a). While occupational groups such as clerical assistants are accountable to their superiors, professionals have a high degree of autonomy and protection from outside evaluation within their occupational territory. In the health care workforce, doctors stand out as the profession with greatest autonomy. The other health occupations such as nursing, physiotherapy and clinical psychology are more accurately classified as 'semi-professions' because they do not have as much control over their own activities.

Table 6.3   Persons employed in health and health-related occupations, Australia, 2010

Occupation	2010
Generalist medical practitioners	44 600
Specialist medical practitioners[a]	29 300
Medical imaging workers	14 400
Dental practitioners	11 500
Dental associate professionals and assistants	27 000
Midwifery and nursing professionals[b]	236 000
Enrolled and mothercraft nurses	30 100
Nursing and personal care assistants	81 900
Pharmacists	19 200
Physiotherapists	20 400
Psychologists	21 500
Other allied health workers[c]	9900
Complementary therapists[d]	26 700
Social workers	20 400
Other health workers[e]	173 900
Total health workers	**766 800**

Notes
(a) Includes anaesthetists, internal medicine specialists, psychiatrists, surgeons and other specialist medical practitioners
(b) Includes midwifery and nursing professionals not further defined, midwives, nurse educators and researchers and registered nurses
(c) Includes dietitians, optometrists, orthoptists, chiropractors, osteopaths, occupational therapists, podiatrists, speech professionals and audiologists
(d) Includes health therapy professionals not further defined, massage therapists and personal consultants
(e) Includes health professionals not further defined, health and welfare service managers and nurse managers, medical laboratory scientists, occupational and environmental health professionals, other health diagnostic and promotion professionals, medical technicians, ambulance officers and paramedics, diversional therapists and indigenous health workers.

Source: Based on table 9.3 in Australian Institute of Health and Welfare 2012a, *Australia's Health 2012*, Australia's health series no. 13, cat. no. AUS 156, AIHW, Canberra, pp. 498–99

In 1983, Ann Daniel's survey of occupational prestige in Australia, which rated over 1000 occupations on a scale from one (highest) to seven (lowest), revealed that medical specialists enjoy the highest social status in the health field, with a rating of 1.5 (Daniels 1983). The rating scale revealed also that directors of nursing services have a prestige rating of 2.8, and that nursing has a lower occupational status than other predominantly female health professions, such as physiotherapy and occupational therapy.

Daniel's results indicate that the male-dominated professions, medicine and dentistry, have greater prestige than the predominantly female so-called semi-professions, such as social work and nursing. This gender factor is particularly important because these semi-professions are improving their professional status and receiving improved wages and working conditions (Short 1986b; Short & Sharman 1995; Short, Sharman & Speedy 1998). Concomitant with these changes is competition between occupations over occupational territories, as in the domain of childbirth. Indeed, in many ways these professions are rejecting their 'feminine' characteristics of obedience and subservience and adopting trade-union-type tactics, not unlike those used by professional associations such as the Australian Medical Association (Gardner & McCoppin 1989).

It is evident that the non-medical health professions aspire to the high levels of status, pay, job security and autonomy that the medical profession enjoys. It would also appear that the members of many health occupations are attempting to follow the medical profession along the path of professionalisation in order to attain similar rewards. We suggest, however, that medicine's dominance in health care is unlikely to see any serious challenge in the near future.

If it is acknowledged that part of the gap between the medical profession and the allied health professions can be explained by gender, then how can we explain the hierarchy within the allied health professions? Sociological research suggests that the social class background of members of these professions helps to explain this hierarchy. The prestige of occupations is determined by their members' access to 'wider bases of social power' (Johnson 1972). Medicine's dominant position was achieved historically because of the power of the men who transformed medicine into a profession. Traditionally, only 'gentlemen of independent means' enjoyed access to the learned professions of medicine, divinity and law, because others could not afford a university education. It remains to be seen whether the transfer of nursing education from hospitals to universities will decrease differences in status between nursing and the other predominantly female professions in the future. Competition between health occupations is also evident in competition over occupational territory, as the following case study illustrates.

OCCUPATIONAL SUBSTITUTION: THE CASE OF OBSTETRICS AND INDEPENDENT MIDWIFERY

Childbirth is a contemporary example of an occupational territory over which two occupations are competing. Should medical practitioners have a monopoly in this area or should nurses qualified in midwifery be allowed to practise as independent midwives, especially in relation to homebirth? This question is one of policy choice, and the implications for obstetric practice and the quality and costs of childbirth are far-reaching.

Competition between independent midwives and obstetricians over childbirth provides a vivid illustration of the broader social, political and economic context within which health workforce policy decisions are made. Independent midwifery has been on the formal policy agenda since 1984, when the Medicare Benefits Review Committee

(Layton Committee) recommended that Medicare benefits be extended to paramedical services such as independent homebirth midwifery. The Layton Committee commented that, of the many issues addressed, the question of payment of Medicare benefits for services provided by registered midwives 'generated the greatest depth of feeling and the strongest organised support' (NHMRC 1987, p. 3). However, the Layton Committee gave only qualified support to the services of midwives, because it was not satisfied that adequate back-up services were available in the event of complications arising during a homebirth delivery. The committee recommended, therefore, that a pilot program of homebirth be instituted to assess the feasibility, safety and ongoing costs of homebirths. This pilot program has not been implemented.

The possibility of independent midwives receiving government support to substitute for doctors in homebirth would require considerable policy changes at many levels of the health system (NHMRC 1987). Necessary changes in policy would include the following:

- permission for registered midwives to order and have access to the results of a range of routine antenatal and postnatal tests, such as ultrasound. At present only registered medical practitioners are permitted to order and interpret these and other tests.
- an appropriate rebate from Medicare for homebirth midwifery
- greater cooperation between homebirth practitioners and hospital staff to facilitate coordination in the event of a transfer during labour
- appropriate courses, probably through universities, to equip graduates of midwifery courses to practise as independent practitioners.

This list of necessary policy changes illustrates how entrenched medicine's monopoly over the provision of obstetric services is and how complex and protracted any breaking down of that monopoly would be.

While progress with midwife-managed birthing services in hospitals has been made under the Alternative Birthing Services Program introduced by the Commonwealth government in 1989, midwives are not funded to conduct homebirths in the program. Although midwives can manage births within selected hospitals, they still lack prescribing rights, they are unable to order diagnostic tests that would attract Medicare benefits and they lack access to most hospital services on the same terms as medical practitioners. Even midwives who do have the right to admit women under the Alternative Birthing Services Program 'rely on supportive doctors to ensure that women receive appropriate tests and medicines required during pregnancy' (Kelly, Chiarella & Maxwell 1993, p. 29).

On a related issue, a discussion paper on nurse practitioners released by the NSW Department of Health (1992) received very different responses from the nursing and medical professions. Responses to the discussion paper indicated that many nurses already viewed themselves as nurse practitioners working without direct medical supervision. One hundred self-employed nurses and 200 nurses who were employees viewed themselves as nurse practitioners (Kelly, Chiarella & Maxwell 1993, p. 24). Areas of nurse practitioner expertise included palliative care nursing, diabetes education, midwifery, women's health and rural and remote area nursing. In contrast, the discussion paper on nurse practitioners attracted criticism from some members of the medical profession.

The National Health Strategy (1992b) issues paper on general practice acknowledged that nurse practitioners could deliver some services more efficiently than general practitioners could. In practice, the determining factor as to who does what is often determined by the geographical, social, political and economic environment in which the work is done. For example, many rural and remote area nurses perform work otherwise performed by GPs.

Most people readily accept the nurse practitioner concept in remote areas of New South Wales where doctors do not choose to practise or provide services to disadvantaged groups of people (Coxhead 1992, p. 28).

Opposition to nurse practitioners from the medical profession is likely to continue, not least because of the 'very real threat to their income base in a number of primary health service areas' (Staunton 1992, p. 3). However, the discussion paper on nurse practitioners concluded that the issue should be viewed not as a takeover by either party, but rather as a natural integration of the responsibilities of doctors and nurses in the delivery of accessible and appropriate health care.

Enhancing the primary care role of registered nurse practitioners in specified areas that are not attractive to doctors is a policy option being considered by some state health departments, following the lead set in New South Wales. During the 1990s, the New South Wales Department of Health undertook a 'three-stage review of the role of nurse practitioners, followed by pilot projects at 10 sites' (Australian Medical Workforce Advisory Committee & AIHW 1998, p. 63). In 1996, evidence collected in the pilot projects indicated that nurse practitioners were 'feasible, safe and effective in their roles', and that they provided 'quality health services in the range of settings researched' (p. 63). The pilot study indicated also that 'an enhanced role and greater participation by registered nurse practitioners have the potential to relieve medical service provision measures in rural and remote areas and in public hospitals' (p. 59).

In 1999, the New South Wales Government passed legislation to establish nurse practitioner positions in selected areas of the state where there was demonstrated local need, local agreement and local support for them. In the same year, the Australian Medical Workforce Advisory Committee recommended that state and territory health departments should examine the possibility of developing procedures for employing nurse practitioners to fill designated areas of local service need in rural and remote areas: 'In remote areas specified by state health authorities as experiencing significant GP shortages, nurses have special powers for a limited range of prescribing and other activities normally undertaken by a GP' (Australian Medical Workforce Advisory Committee & AIHW 1998, pp. 49–50).

Over the coming years, the relevance and responsibilities of the nurse practitioner will become more formalised. From 1 January 2010, authorisation as a nurse practitioner or midwife practitioner requires evidence of completion of a master's degree relevant to the clinical practice context (Australian Nursing and Midwifery Council 2009). This formalised process requires nurses to show that they are able to meet the standards, competencies and performance indicators, and sustain knowledge, competence and experience at an advanced level.

Workforce planning

For workforce planning purposes it is most important to examine how health personnel are distributed in relation to the population they service. It is also necessary to examine changes over time so that shortages or surpluses can be anticipated and managed: 'Minimising over- and under-supply is an important goal if scarce resources are to be well used and essential services provided' (Australian Medical Workforce Advisory Committee & AIHW 1998, p. 17).

Figure 6.2 shows the number of health personnel per 100 000 population between 2001 and 2011. The number of nurses and doctors in the health workforce has increased compared to the size of the Australian population over the 10-year period. Since 2001, the per capita rate of GPs to population increased from 170.5 to 201.9 GPs per 100 000 persons. Table 6.4 reveals the distribution of doctors across states and territories in 2011. The Australian Capital Territory had the highest number of employed medical practitioners per capita (423/100 000 population), followed closely by the Northern Territory (420/100 000 population). New South Wales had the highest number of specialists, followed by Victoria.

In 2011, the per capita ratio of GPs to population in major cities (227.8 per 100 000) was twice that of remote areas (113.0 per 100 000), and considerably higher than the ratio of GPs in regional areas (144.9 per 100 000) (ABS 2011). The supply of doctors declined as remoteness increased.

Traditionally, workforce figures such as these have been derived from three main sources. First is the Census of Population and Housing, conducted every five years by the Australian Bureau of Statistics (ABS). This gives the most comprehensive data but is limited by the time lag between censuses and the processing and publication of results. In addition, the ABS conducts labour force surveys four times a year. The second main source of workforce data is derived from professional registers under the AHPRA umbrella. Figures from registration boards tend to differ from census data because health professionals may be registered but not practising, or appear in more than one occupational category. The third source is records from private organisations such as the AMA.

The Australian Institute of Health and Welfare (AIHW) relies on two principal sources of data: the ABS census and ABS labour force surveys. The former tends to produce lower health workforce estimates than the latter (AIHW 1998a, p. 181). Other sources of data about doctors include the Medicare provider database from the relevant Commonwealth authority, which includes data on Medicare providers from 1984–85 onwards; the Medical Directory of Australia, published by

Figure 6.2   Number per 100 000 population by health occupation, 2001 and 2011

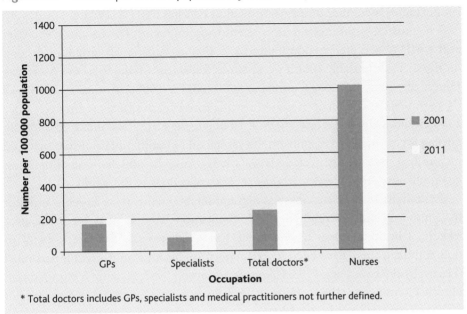

* Total doctors includes GPs, specialists and medical practitioners not further defined.

Source: adapted from Australian Bureau of Statistics 2013c, *Australian Social Trends, April 2013*, cat. no. 4102.0, ABS, Canberra

Table 6.4   Employed medical practitioners, by main occupation and states and territories, 2011

Main occupation	NSW	Vic.	Qld	SA	WA	Tas.	NT	ACT	Australia
Clinician	23 819	18 106	14 839	5964	7236	1709	895	1374	73 980
General practitioner	8136	6247	4941	2045	2371	625	308	378	25 056
Hospital non-specialists (salaried)	2933	1966	2226	689	1193	197	188	180	9576
Specialist	8032	6252	4603	2006	2312	572	192	481	24 475
Specialist in training	3880	3229	2480	1089	1105	269	163	275	12 491
Other	838	412	589	135	255	46	44	60	2382
Non-clinician[a]	1595	1307	789	365	431	105	77	183	4853
Total	25 413	19 413	15 628	6328	7667	1813	972	1557	78 833
No. per 100 000	352	351	349	386	326	355	420	423	353

Note

(a) Includes administrator, teacher/educator, researchers and other non-clinicians.

Source: Data based on supplementary table 1.3 in Australian Institute of Health and Welfare 2013c, *Medical Workforce 2011*, National health workforce series no.3 cat. no. HWL 49, AIHW, Canberra

the Australasian Medical Publishing Company; and the periodic workforce surveys conducted by a number of specialist medical colleges (AIHW 1998c).

The situation regarding workforce statistics is improving. The Labour Force Unit at the AIHW accepted responsibility for compiling a national minimum data set on the major registrable health occupations following a request by the Australian Health Ministers' Advisory Council in 1990 (AIHW 1998c). Annual figures on all the registrable health occupations in Australia have been available progressively since 1993. Additionally, a national medical labour force survey is conducted annually, nursing is now surveyed biannually, and several other health professions are surveyed on a rolling three-yearly cycle (AIHW 1998c). Australia now has one of the most comprehensive sets of health workforce data collections in the world.

Professions with well-established registration requirements are easier to monitor than more recently established health occupations. A case in point is the profession of health services management, for which reliable data are difficult to find. Although there have been several reports on health administration personnel (Harris, Maddern & Pegg 1998; Palmer & Stevenson 1982; Rawson 1986; Victorian Health Commission 1985), without introduction of a registration requirement precise figures will not be available.

Medical practitioners

The medical profession does not constitute a homogeneous workforce category. In general, the medical workforce consists of three modes of practice: specialist, general practice and salaried. The most significant divisions are between GPs and specialist doctors, and between salaried and non-salaried practitioners. Of the estimated 78 833 employed medical practitioners in Australia in 2011, the majority were males (60 per cent) working mainly in hospitals or private practice. Most clinicians in 2011 were working as general practitioners (34 per cent) or specialists (33 per cent) (Health Workforce Australia 2013) (see table 6.5).

We have stressed that the medical profession is the most powerful occupation in the health workforce, and that its power is far greater than its numbers or the money expended on doctors' incomes would suggest. For this reason, the medical profession attracts considerable policy and political attention. Oversupply of GPs, shortages in some medical specialties, maldistribution of medical personnel, length of medical education, medical curricula and registration procedures for immigrant doctors are the major medically related policy issues addressed in this chapter. Other important aspects of medical practice, including general practice developments, are examined in **Chapter 7**.

Between 2002 and 2006, the supply of full-time equivalent (FTE) medical practitioners increased from 271 to 290 per 100 000 population. However, during the same period there was a decrease of clinicians working in primary care, from 101 to 97 FTE per 100 000 population (AIHW 2009).

Table 6.5   Employed medical practitioners: demographics by state and territory, 2011

Characteristic	NSW	Vic.	Qld	SA	WA	Tas.	NT	ACT	Australia
Males	15 891	11 992	9941	4033	4754	1134	530	914	**49 221**
Females	9522	7421	5687	2295	2913	679	442	643	**29 611**
Mean age	46.6	45.2	44.5	45.4	44.5	46.1	42.9	45.8	**45.5**
Mean total hours worked	43.8	42.7	43.2	42.4	42.8	42.5	44.4	44.4	**43.2**
Work setting of main job									
Private practice	11 385	8556	6514	2657	3001	781	167	528	**33 596**
Aboriginal health service	125	37	110	31	86	n.p.	127	n.p.	**532**
Community health care services	388	453	309	139	210	43	39	43	**1625**
Hospital	11 023	8402	7099	2841	3534	803	495	686	**34 899**
Residential health care facility	55	42	42	16	23	6	6	5	**194**
Commercial/ business services	148	86	43	18	24	5	–	8	**333**
Educational facility	505	415	246	132	181	37	25	41	**1582**
Correctional services	35	16	8	5	13	n.p.	3	n.p.	**83**
Defence forces	96	31	91	20	16	n.p.	27	n.p.	**318**
Other government department or agency	183	111	110	63	75	21	29	80	**673**
Other	1470	1265	1055	407	505	110	52	116	**4999**
Total	**25 413**	**19 413**	**15 628**	**6328**	**7667**	**1813**	**972**	**1557**	**78 833**

Note
'n.p' is for 'not published' data, which cannot be released due to confidentiality issues.

Source: Data based on supplementary table 1.4 in Australian Institute of Health and Welfare 2013c, *Medical Workforce 2011*, National health workforce services no. 3, cat. no. HWL 49, AIHW, Canberra

Previously, the Commonwealth government attempted to control the number of doctors, considering that it was closely correlated with total health care costs (Podger 1998–99, p. 18). In 1995, the Commonwealth announced that it would negotiate with universities to reduce the annual intake to medical schools. Restrictions on medical school intakes and overseas-trained doctor entry were the two ways the

Commonwealth attempted to influence medical workforce supply. At the close of the century, there were policy initiatives in each of these areas because of the perception of oversupply. At the time, historical reasons for the oversupply of GPs included:

> too many medical graduates, too many medical immigrants, a slow-down in population growth since the 1970s, productivity growth through new technology, and changes in care patterns with shorter average patient stays in hospital and rising use of day surgery.
>
> Australian Medical Workforce Advisory Committee & AIHW (1998, p. 11)

Maldistribution was another key medical workforce issue believed to contribute to the oversupply of GPs. In 1996, there were 4000 primary care practitioners in urban areas and a shortage of about 500 in rural and remote areas (Australian Medical Workforce Advisory Committee & AIHW 1996a).

A specialist shortfall of 900 was estimated for rural and remote areas, though it was recognised that this figure needed to be quantified more accurately to account for visiting services and so on. Various sources of evidence indicated conclusively that supplier-induced demands existed in Australia and that this produced overservicing (Australian Medical Workforce Advisory Committee & AIHW 1998, pp. 39–43). Moreover, financial and other incentives provided under the Commonwealth government's General Practice Rural Incentives Program, as part of the General Practice Strategy, had limited success in attracting doctors to undersupplied areas. Policy responses in the mid-1990s

> tended to target GPs rather than specialists and have focused on training opportunities, continuing medical education, locum support, assistance with establishing/maintaining a practice and student medical school selection. Policy action in the specialist area has focused on increasing rural training positions.
>
> Australian Medical Workforce Advisory Committee (1996, p. 3)

In the 1996–97 Commonwealth government budgets, the Advanced Specialist Training Posts Program received funding to provide new specialist training posts in major rural centres (Australian Medical Workforce Advisory Committee & AIHW 1998, p. 57).

The dynamics of the medical workforce were to change again, as in the early 2000s shortages were emerging in the general practice workforce and remained in a range of medical specialties. The Commonwealth cap on medical school places to control the supply of the medical workforce in the mid-1990s may have contributed to this underinvestment in the medical and health workforce (Simoens & Hurst 2006, p. 29). The restriction of the number of undergraduate medical places was only one contributing factor; others included the unexpected reduction in hours worked across the medical workforce (AIHW 2008f).

Since 1996, state and territory health authorities had already identified 18 medical specialties experiencing shortages in the public hospital system (Australian Medical Workforce Advisory Committee & AIHW 1998). The inquiry into the surgical workforce conducted by Professor Peter Baume (1994) also identified shortages in public hospitals of some surgical specialties; for example, orthopaedics, ophthalmic surgery, plastic and reconstructive surgery, and ear, nose and throat surgery. Baume recognised that some of the reluctance of surgeons to work in the public hospital sector was economically driven; surgeons are most commonly paid by time in public hospitals, whereas in private practice they are paid by items of service.

In the medical specialties, there is constant tension between population demands from patients on waiting lists to receive services and the availability of those services across geographic regions, and between the public and private sectors. Macro funding constraints have led to national and state decisions about cost-effective allocation of specialist services, which conflict with local area desires for improved access (Australian Medical Workforce Advisory Committee & AIHW 1998, p. 15).

Government policies changed with the change of government in 2007. The Rudd Government's policies led to a sharp increase in medical school places to try to address shortages in the medium term and the use of international medical graduates to meet workforce needs in the shorter term, particularly in areas of geographic and specialty need. These approaches were supplemented by a strategic focus on the potential of health workforce reform to achieve productivity improvements (Carver 2008).

While women are over-represented in health care generally, they are under-represented in medicine. However, this is changing. The female proportion of the medical workforce increased from 19 per cent to 30 per cent between the 1981 and 1996 censuses (AIHW 1998a, pp. 184–5). This rising trend has continued: by 2002, the female proportion of the medical workforce was 32 per cent, and 34 per cent in 2006 (AIHW 2008f).

Nevertheless, women earn less than their male counterparts do, as they are more often employed in salaried positions rather than in private practice. In addition, female non-specialists in hospitals are predominantly resident medical officers and interns rather than salaried or other career non-specialists. On average, female medical practitioners also tend to work fewer hours. They are more likely to work part time, especially in the 30s and early 40s age groups, and they generally have a shorter economic working life. In 2006, female clinicians worked on average 36.6 hours per week, while male clinicians worked on average 46.2 hours per week (AIHW 2008f).

Women also specialise less frequently, and when they do it is in specialties such as psychiatry and dermatology, which are less well paid than more prestigious specialties such as neurosurgery. In 2006, 34 per cent of GPs and 22 per cent of specialist medical practitioners were female (AIHW 2008f).

Though the proportion of Indigenous medical students has been increasing, they still comprise less than 1 per cent of medical student intakes. In 2006, only 155 medical practitioners who were employed in medicine identified themselves as Indigenous. This accounts for 0.3 per cent of the medical workforce, whereas Aboriginal and Torres Strait Islander people comprise 2.5 per cent of the Australian population (AIHW 2006c). Change is expected to flow from policies implemented by several medical schools to increase medical training opportunities for students of Aboriginal and Torres Strait Islander origin and students from rural areas (National Health Workforce Taskforce 2009).

The role of the doctor and the way medicine is practised will continue to evolve. In 1995, the Australasian Cochrane Centre was established at Flinders Medical Centre in Adelaide as part of the International Cochrane Collaboration to prepare, maintain and promote evidence-based medicine. This centre was moved to Monash University under the leadership of the late Professor Chris Silagy in 1999. Australian governments expect that, over time, evidence-based medicine will reduce variation in practice, unnecessary treatment and underuse of some treatments, leading to improvements in the efficiency and effectiveness of the medical workforce (Australian Medical Workforce Advisory Committee & AIHW 1998, p. 29). In the closing years of the 20th century, increasing emphasis was placed on health outcomes. Divisions of general practice were moving to outcome-based funding models (Australian Medical Workforce Advisory Committee & AIHW 1998, p. 63). It is argued that

> Increased use of evidence-based medicine suggests potential for the existing [medical] workforce to be used more efficiently and effectively in achieving population health outcomes … Internet, other computer, and popular media access to evidence-based medicine will strengthen consumer knowledge and empowerment and change the doctor–patient relationship and the way medicine is practised.

> Australian Medical Workforce Advisory Committee & AIHW (1998, p. 29)

The focus of health care still revolves around primary care and the involvement of the medical workforce: 'Primary care is the foundation of our health care system, and successful health reform will depend on effective engagement with the primary care workforce' (Kidd 2009, p. 1).

In response to election commitments in 2007, the Rudd Government approved the establishment of the National Health and Hospitals Reform Commission (NHHRC) and a taskforce to develop a national primary health care strategy, which was implemented in 2010. It realised that successful reform of the health care system required effective involvement from general practice. The Rudd Government invested $1.1 billion towards the training of more health professionals, the largest investment ever made by the Commonwealth government towards the health workforce. In 2010, the Commonwealth and state health ministers agreed to collaborate in implementing a national strategic framework for primary health care through Medicare Locals and local hospital networks. We analyse this and related initiatives in **Chapters 10** and **11**.

We turn now to consider the pertinent issue of medical education.

Medical education

There have been two major Australian inquiries into aspects of medical education within the past four decades. The first, the Committee on Medical Schools, chaired by Professor Peter Karmel in 1973, made recommendations to the Australian Universities Commission on the need for new and expanded medical schools in light of the likely increase in demand for medical practitioners over the ensuing 20 years. At the time of the Karmel Report, the doctor-to-population ratio was 14 per 10 000 of the population; the committee stated that the ratio should increase to 18 per 10 000 by 1991 (Committee on Medical Schools to the Australian Universities Commission 1973). Following wide-ranging recommendations from the committee, the main recommendations acted on were increases in medical student intakes at the universities of Melbourne and Western Australia, and the establishment of an innovative medical school at the University of Newcastle. The fact that the projected doctor-to-population ratio of 18 per 10 000 was reached a decade before the expected time prompted in 1987 a further and more broad-ranging inquiry into both medical education and the medical workforce.

The Committee of Inquiry into Medical Education and the Medical Workforce (1988) (the Doherty Committee and Inquiry) was established in 1987 following a recommendation from the Australian Health Ministers' Conference in 1985. Of particular concern to the ministers was the rapid increase in the doctor-to-population ratio, 'the surge of specialism' since the 1960s and the maldistribution of medical personnel. A principle of primary medical care provision proposed by the Doherty Committee was that it was 'far better to have a few too many GPs than not quite enough' (Australian Medical Workforce Advisory Committee & AIHW 1998, p. 52). The pool of new Royal Australian College of General Practitioners fellows entering the labour market was cut back to 400 per year, and the net increase in the GP workforce declined from 594 in 1990–91 to 170 in 1995–96 and 150 in 1996–97.

Organisation for Economic Cooperation and Development (OECD) statistics from the mid-1990s showed 'medical workforce growth well in excess of population growth over many years for most OECD countries' (Australian Medical Workforce Advisory Committee & AIHW 1996a, p. 6). The oversupply of doctors in Australia was expected to continue until the year 2006, 'after which there will be a gradual convergence to 2019 when supply and requirements should balance' (p. 4). Medical school intakes have expanded over the decade, doubling from 1889 in 2003 to 3686 in 2012 (HWA 2013). The Australian Medical Workforce Advisory Committee and AIHW (1996a, p. 4) study found that reducing net additions to the medical workforce

> without addressing the internal imbalance that already exists within the workforce, could only be expected to exacerbate the mal-distribution and service delivery difficulties already evident within the workforce.

The specialist medical colleges determine the number of entrants into specialist training programs. The Baume Report (Baume 1994) received a somewhat hostile reaction from the Royal Australasian College of Surgeons when the college was criticised for the control it exercised over surgical workforce supply. Restrictive entry practices were discussed by the Australian Democrats in the federal parliament. Senator Meg Lees (1993, p. 10) referred to medical specialists as the 'great untouchables' of Australian health care:

> Their contribution and influence is enormous and yet in discussions on hospital efficiencies, improved productivity, better work practices and so on, the role of specialists is usually notable only by its absence. We hardly ever see, hear or read detailed analyses of the crucial issues surrounding medical specialists: the availability of training opportunities and the continuing restricted access into specialties for which there is increasing demand, the inequitable geographic distribution of specialists, their role in the management and manipulation of waiting lists, how much they are paid by the public system and whether or not we are getting better value for our money from them … We need to look seriously at the restrictive practices which currently govern entry into medical specialties because we need to know whether such practices are genuinely in the interests of Australians or exist simply to protect the incomes of specialists.

State governments are responsible for funding the training posts associated with specialist training programs. They can therefore reduce the numbers being trained compared to the numbers the colleges may wish to include in such programs. However, an expansion in numbers is more difficult for governments to achieve. When the Australian Orthopaedic Association has admitted fewer people into training programs than are needed to meet the needs in this expanding area, governments have been unable to intervene.

In the early 1970s, at the time of the Karmel Report, the AMA was supportive of the need for more medical graduates and the establishment of new medical schools. However, by the late 1970s, when the projected doctor-to-population ratio had been achieved, the AMA supported a 20 per cent reduction in intakes of students into medical schools (Best 1987). In 1987, the AMA recommended a 30 per cent reduction in medical school intakes to the Inquiry into Medical Education and the Medical Workforce. When the inquiry started, the president of the AMA, Trevor

Pickering, repeated the association's decade-long concern about Australia's rapidly growing oversupply of doctors.

It should be noted, though, that not all members of the profession shared the AMA's position. Of particular importance in this regard was the 'medical specialist/academic push which caucuses in the shadow of the National Health and Medical Research Council' and which had a significant influence on governments (Best 1987, p. 369). More specifically, the Australian Society for Medical Research advocates on behalf of medical and scientific researchers by lobbying governments, media, industry, philanthropic organisations and the public for increased funding for biomedical research and related activities. This interest group was particularly successful in influencing the Wills Committee report into health and medical research, as evidenced by the significant boost to biotechnology and genetic research in the 1999–2000 budget (Health and Medical Research Strategic Review 1999). The government committed itself to increase annual funding to the National Health and Medical Research Council from $165 million in the 1998–99 budget to more than $350 million in 2004–05.

It is noteworthy that the Commonwealth health authority and the AMA were in agreement about the need to reduce medical oversupply, but for different reasons. The AMA claimed that its chief concern was that underworked doctors would be unable to maintain their technical skills and competence. In contrast, the Commonwealth was concerned with the costs generated by medical oversupply, and by the inefficiencies created by the maldistribution of doctors. An excessive supply of doctors leads to overservicing and thus contributes to inefficiency (Commonwealth Department of Health 1981). While the AMA has wanted to reduce oversupply in order to preserve the workloads of its members, or their incomes, the department was then of the view that a reduction in medical personnel supply was warranted because of the problems caused by too many doctors providing too many services.

In light of these problems, the Committee of Inquiry into Medical Education and the Medical Workforce (1988) was given the following terms of reference to investigate the:

- effectiveness of current curricula and structures of medical undergraduate education
- effectiveness of current postgraduate training (including continuing education programs and specialist accreditation)
- provision of an appropriate supply of each broad category of medical practitioner
- selection of students for medical education
- the health, social and economic impact of the inquiry's major recommendations.

One of the principal submissions to the inquiry was prepared by the Commonwealth Department of Health in conjunction with the Australian Institute of Health. The joint study conducted for the inquiry found that Australia's total active medical workforce was 36 610 in 1987, and that the doctor-to-population ratio was higher than previously predicted—nearly 23 doctors per 10 000 of the population. It was noted that South Australia had the highest doctor-to-population ratios in all areas of medical practice, and that the Queensland ratios were the lowest. When the locational distribution of medical practitioners was examined, a large discrepancy between the number of doctors in capital cities and those practising outside capital cities became evident (Commonwealth Department of Health and Australian Institute of Health 1987). Of the active medical workforce, nearly 20 per cent received their basic medical qualifications overseas. The largest single method by which doctors from overseas gained permission to migrate was under the family reunion scheme.

Although the Doherty Inquiry only intended to receive written submissions from a range of individuals and organisations, significant pressure from community and consumer groups led to a series of person-to-person consultations with members of the committee. The submission from the Consumers' Health Forum (1987) recommended that students be trained within the primary health care model, which acknowledges that users of the health system have a central role in all aspects of health care planning and implementation. The Melbourne-based Health Issues Centre noted that consumer groups were not concerned so much with numbers of doctors, but with their selection, training and the type and quality of care they provide. Community groups indicated that practitioners should be more accessible to consumers, understand their role within the context of community care, incorporate teamwork, and acknowledge the role that individual consumers and communities play in identifying and meeting their own health needs. In short, community groups advocated wide-ranging changes to training programs in order to prepare medical practitioners for a more informed and critical consumer community (Szoke 1987).

The Committee of Inquiry into Medical Education and the Medical Workforce (1988) found general satisfaction with the technical competence of doctors but criticism of doctors' attitudes and values. It recommended that the training of Australia's medical students should be broadened to include more general practice and community medicine experience. It recommended also that medical graduates should serve a two-year internship instead of the current one year, and that the first year be spent in a metropolitan teaching hospital and the second in a smaller country or suburban hospital. The committee found that there was an overemphasis on hospital-based teaching at the graduate level, and that undergraduates risked being overwhelmed by the amount of medical information in medical curricula. The report recommended that students be exposed to general practice training early in their courses, and that they should undertake at least a month's experience in general practice or community health prior to graduation. It was also suggested that courses should emphasise the learning of 'principles' rather than 'compendia of facts'. A member of the committee, Neville Hicks, suggested that the report was notable because it paid serious attention to how a better primary care orientation could be introduced into medical education at undergraduate and postgraduate levels (Hicks 1988). However, the committee acknowledged that cost-generating recommendations would not be acceptable to the Commonwealth, and that the implementation of even minor incremental changes was unlikely given the attention and resources devoted to the restructuring of higher education at that time.

According to the committee, subjects not being addressed adequately in some medical schools included health problems associated with aged people, women, immigrant groups and people with disabilities, and aspects of illness prevention and health promotion. It was recommended also that all medical schools and universities should undertake regular curriculum reviews to ensure that students graduated with the knowledge, attitudes and skills needed for medical practice in the community.

The Australian health ministers responded to the Doherty Report in the following ways:

- improved data collection on the medical workforce
- the introduction of a second year of supervised practice for medical graduates before registration
- expansion of bridging courses for overseas-trained doctors seeking to pass the Australian Medical Council examinations for registration in Australia
- the requirement that overseas-trained doctors who passed the examination complete a year of supervised practice before registration.

On the issue of too many doctors and too many specialists in some specialties, it is noteworthy that the committee did not recommend any reductions in medical school intakes. This is hardly surprising. The political feasibility of reducing the size of medical schools is relatively low, given the power of the 'medical specialist/ academic push' referred to earlier. Instead, in 1992 the Australian health ministers decided to limit the number of overseas-trained doctors entering the Australian workforce permanently. In 1994, the then minister for health, Dr Carmen Lawrence, recognised that medical oversupply needed to be addressed with medical schools. In 1995, the Commonwealth government announced that it intended to reduce medical school intakes, a move which if implemented fully was to result in around 4500 fewer medical practitioners in the year 2025 (Australian Medical Workforce Advisory Committee & AIHW 1998, p. 6). On the issue of educational reform, three medical schools—Queensland, Flinders and Sydney—introduced a four-year graduate-entry medical degree rather than the standard six-year undergraduate program. From 1996, medical students at these three universities have needed to possess a first degree before undertaking the medical course, thus expanding their tertiary study to a minimum of seven years. The intention has been to attract a more mature and diverse range of students who have a stronger commitment to medicine as a career. Those applying for entry to the graduate-entry medical degree are expected to have a good first degree, adequate communication skills and an understanding of basic sciences.

By 1998, the seven undergraduate-entry medical schools also had schemes in place to select a proportion of students based on factors such as Aboriginal or Torres Strait Islander origin and rural home residence (AIHW 1998a, p. 185). As mentioned earlier, in 1995 the Commonwealth government negotiated with universities to reduce the annual intake to medical schools. To rectify the under-supply in rural and remote areas, $27 million over four years for six university departments of rural health was provided in the 1996–97 Commonwealth budget (Australian Medical Workforce Advisory Committee & AIHW 1998, p. 57). In addition, $210 million per year in real terms was furnished to provide opportunities for medical undergraduates and graduates to train and work in rural areas, along with funding for the John Flynn Scholarship scheme, which enables medical students to spend time training in a rural area (p. 57).

Experience shows that it is particularly difficult for governments to implement anything but minor incremental policy changes in the area of medical education. As Walsh (1984, p. 189), former dean of medicine at the University of New South Wales, predicted, 'the present basic system will continue but … changes will occur of a minor nature. They will be effected by those members of a conservative profession who were themselves educated in a well-tried system'.

Other occupational groups that have undergone significant scrutiny or change in recent years are nursing, health services management, the allied health professions, social work, public health, dentistry, alternative and complementary health care, and unpaid providers of health care. It is to these occupations that we now turn.

Nursing

Nursing is the largest and most dynamic occupation in the Australian health workforce. Political action on the part of nurses since the late 1970s has led to considerable and rapid change in two areas in particular—industrial relations and education. Three events in this period serve to highlight how fundamental the changes in the nursing workforce have been. First, in the national referendum in November 1983, members of the Royal Australian Nursing Federation (RANF) voted to remove the no-strike clause from their constitution. The second impor-tant policy decision, referred to above, was the Commonwealth government's announcement in August 1984 that all nursing education would be transferred from hospitals to tertiary institutions by 1993. The third significant event was the prolonged nurses' strike in Victoria in November and December 1986, when more than 17 000 nurses walked out of public hospitals to protest about delays in the resolution of their industrial claims. *The Age* newspaper in Melbourne reported that there was a 'revolution' in the hospitals (Hutton 1986, p. 28). By 1986, it seemed that the cheerful, selfless devotion of nurses, which had kept the public hospital system going for so long, could no longer be taken for granted. The 'Cinderella' occupation of the health care system had finally run out of patience (Short & Sharman 1995).

Between 2001 and 2005, the number of registered and enrolled nurses employed as nurses in Australia was estimated to have increased by 7.1 per cent, from 228 230 to 244 360, mainly a result of an 8.2 per cent increase in the number of employed registered nurses over the five-year period. The number of employed enrolled nurses also increased (2.3 per cent). In 2011, 93.7 per cent of nurses employed in Australia were registered nurses (Health Workforce Australia 2013).

Table 6.6 reveals a significant variation in the distribution of employed nurses among the states and territories. New South Wales, Queensland and Western Australia are below the national average (1081), while the Northern Territory and South Australia are well above the average. Nursing supply still appears to be evenly distributed across regions, ranging from 1234 FTE nurses per 100 000 in very remote areas to 1066 in major cities.

Table 6.6 Distribution of employed registered and enrolled nurses by states and territories, 2011

	NSW	Vic.	Qld	WA	SA	Tas.	NT	ACT	Australia
Number	79 351	78 159	55 128	28 430	26 920	7365	3470	4701	283 577
FTE per 100 000 population	972	1149	1053	1031	1351	1232	1497	1174	1081

Source: Data based on table 5.7 in Australian Institute of Health and Welfare 2012c, *Nursing and Midwifery Workforce 2011*, National health workforce series no. 2, cat. no. HWL 48, AIHW, Canberra, p. 41

Between 2001 and 2005, the nursing rate rose in all regions, with the largest increases occurring in outer regional areas, from 1059 to 1190, and very remote areas, from 957 to 1078 (up by 131 and 121 nurses per 100 000 population, respectively). These rises resulted from increases in nurse numbers being larger than population growth, compared to other regions and nationally.

Table 6.7 Employed registered and enrolled nurses: average total weekly hours worked, proportion working part time and 50 hours or more per week, 2007–2011

	Working hours								
	Average weekly hours			Part time (%)			50 hours or more (%)		
Year	RN	EN	All	RN	EN	All	RN	EN	All
2007	33.6	31.9	33.3	46.5	55.2	48.1	6.6	5.1	6.3
2008	33.7	32.2	33.4	46.1	54.7	47.7	6.8	5.1	6.5
2009	33.6	32.0	33.3	46.1	54.8	47.7	6.2	4.7	5.9
2011[a]	33.3	31.4	32.9	47.9	60.4	50.4	4.4	3.5	4.3

Note
(a) Data from HWA included 20 972 records (RN is a registered nurse; EN is a enrolled nurse).

Source: Health Workforce Australia (2013)

There were approximately 326 669 registered and enrolled nurses in Australia in 2011 (AIHW 2012c). Nursing is a dynamic industry. Although total nurse numbers were relatively constant during the 1990s, the nursing workforce has experienced a number of changes.

During the 1990s, part-time employment in nursing increased, particularly for women. The proportion of nurses working part time increased from 39 per cent in 1989 to 44 per cent in 1994 and remained at that level between 1994 and 1998 (AIHW 1998d). In 1995, 49 per cent of female nurses and 15 per cent of male nurses worked part time (AIHW 1997).

Between 2001 and 2005, on average, the population of both registered and enrolled nurses became older. In 2001, the average age of employed nurses was 42.2 years. In 2005, the average age was 45.1 years while in 2011 the average age dropped slightly to 44.5. The proportion of nurses who were aged 50 years or older decreased, from 35.8 per cent to 22 per cent over the same period (AIHW 2011d).

In the 1990s, nursing as an occupation became more attractive to men. The male proportion of the nurse workforce increased from 7.1 per cent in 1986 to 7.8 per cent in 1996. Male employment was highest in mental health nursing (34 per cent) and lowest in midwifery (less than 1 per cent) and private medical rooms (less than 1 per cent) (AIHW 1998d). Table 6.8 shows that the proportion of male nurses increased to 9.9 per cent in 2011 from 7.9 per cent in 2005. While nursing continues to be a female-dominated profession, with males comprising about 10 per cent of employed nurses, males are over-represented in senior academic and management roles.

Nurses work in a variety of environments—as clinicians, managers, educators and researchers—but the majority of nurses are clinicians in acute care hospitals. In 1995, almost two-thirds of registered nurses were employed in hospitals or day procedure centres, 13 per cent in nursing homes, 5 per cent in community health centres and 3 per cent in private medical rooms. The corresponding figures for enrolled nurses were 45 per cent in hospitals or day procedure centres, 34 per cent in nursing homes, 2 per cent in community health centres and 3 per cent in private medical rooms (AIHW 1998a, p. 186).

There has been little change in the profile of the employment sector for nurses. Between 2003 and 2005, approximately two-thirds of nurses were employed in the public sector (67.2 per cent in 2003, 65.4 per cent in 2004 and 65.9 per cent in 2005). During these years, nurses employed in the public sector worked, on average, 2.5 hours per week more than nurses employed in the private sector. Of the majority of nurses working in a clinical role in 2005, the largest proportions were employed in the areas of medical and surgical practice (31.5 per cent), aged care (15.3 per cent), critical care (14.4 per cent), midwifery (8.4 per cent) and peri-operative nursing (7.5 per cent).

The National Review of Nurse Education (1994) identified more than 25 nursing specialties. The committee's report also noted that 'trends to holistic professional practice, multi-skilling and collaborative teams are working alongside, sometimes

Table 6.8   Employed registered and enrolled nurses: age and sex, 2007 and 2011

	Registered and enrolled nurses 2007	Registered and enrolled nurses 2011
Number	263 331	283 577
Average age	43.7	44.5
% 50 years or older	33.0	38.6
% male	9.6	9.9

Source: Data based on table 3.1 in Australian Institute of Health and Welfare 2012c, *Nursing and midwifery workforce 2011*, National health workforce series no. 2, cat. no. HWL 48, AIHW, Canberra, p. 14

in opposition to, trends to specialisation and separated practice' (p. 56). Specialist nursing courses are provided at postgraduate level in universities, at certificate or advanced certificate level in hospitals, and by professional organisations and health care institutions. At the end of the 1990s, there was a national shortage in the specialised fields of operating theatre, critical and intensive care, neonatal intensive care, accident and emergency, midwifery, cardiothoracic and mental health nursing (AIHW 1998d). State shortages were also experienced in other areas. The AIHW (1998d, p. 1) points out that undertaking 'postgraduate training in these fields may involve significant costs for nurses, both in higher education courses and in income forgone during time out of the workforce while studying'.

The nursing labour force 'swings between undersupply and oversupply' (National Review of Nurse Education 1994, p. 115). Between 1992 and 1996, there was a significant rise in vacancies for registered nurses. Many nurses moved out of the labour force altogether, either permanently or temporarily, so attrition is high. In 1996, almost 20 per cent of Australian-born persons aged between 15 and 64 years with a highest qualification in nursing were not in the labour force. Significant leakage also occurs due to nurses obtaining employment in overseas countries and trained nurses leaving nursing for employment in other areas. In 1997–98, 815 nurses left Australia for long-term employment overseas, mainly in the UK, Ireland and the Middle East, and almost 2000 returned after an overseas stay of a year or more (AIHW 1998d). In 2004–05, 6619 nurses entered Australia and 4199 left for stays of 12 months or more, a net gain of 2420 nurses. However, these movements are not all for employment reasons, and therefore do not equate precisely to additions and losses from the nurse labour force.

Compared to the medical workforce, which makes extensive use of temporary-resident overseas-trained doctors to deal with workforce shortages, there is relatively low recruitment of overseas-trained nurses in Australia. In 1997–98, there was a drop in the number of persons with overseas qualifications assessed by the Australian Nursing Council as eligible to practise in Australia (AIHW 1998d).

In 1992, the Australian Nursing Council (now the Australian Nursing and Midwifery Accreditation Council) was formed as a national advisory body to establish and maintain a consistent approach to the regulation of nursing in Australia. It established and maintained competency standards, developed and maintained guidelines for the assessment and recognition of nurses qualified overseas, and achieved progress in the mutual recognition of qualifications across the states and territories.

In Australia, the main source of nursing recruitment is through the training of new graduates. However, the time required for students to complete training and enter the workforce is significant. Therefore, any acute change in the demand for nurses cannot be met by this group. An alternative short-term solution to the short supply of nurses is to recruit from overseas.

Nursing education

The apprenticeship-based Nightingale system, introduced to Australia by Lucy Osburn when she arrived in Sydney in 1868, remained substantially unchanged in Australia for some 100 years. Nurse training and education were examined by a series of reports from the 1940s and pressure for change developed as the century progressed (National Review of Nurse Education 1994, pp. 4–8). The contemporary foundations for radical reform in nursing education were cemented in the 1970s. Pressure from nursing reformers led the Commonwealth government to establish a Committee of Inquiry into Nurse Education and Training (1978), chaired by Dr Sidney Sax, an experienced health policy analyst. The Commonwealth minister for education asked the committee to give particular attention to the question of whether nursing education should take place in hospitals, educational institutions or both. The committee was asked to give particular regard to the implications of alternative forms of nursing education for the quality and cost of health services, the staffing implications in hospitals and educational institutions, the size and structure of the nursing workforce and the effects on the costs of the health and education sectors.

The Sax Committee's report acknowledged considerable problems with the hospital-based system of nurse training. In particular, the committee noted substantial variation in the type and quality of training received, both within and between states. Problems with hospital training cited by the committee included conflict between the service needs of hospitals and the educational needs of nursing students, lack of integration between classroom and clinical teaching, inadequate preparation for service tasks during training, inadequate study time, a lack of suitably qualified nurse educators, inadequate library and educational facilities, and too much task orientation. The lack of a separate budget for nursing training within hospitals was considered relevant to many of these problems. It was further acknowledged that introduction of college- or university-based education would alter the balance between Commonwealth and state funding in both the health and education areas. The committee made compromise recommendations, such as pilot schemes. While it did not recommend a complete transfer of nursing education to the tertiary sector, it placed the issue on the policy agenda.

The Australian Labor Party announced that it would establish 2200 nursing places in advanced education by 1985 if it were elected to government in the 1983 federal election. In August 1984, the Hawke Government subsequently announced that pre-registration nursing education would be transferred to the tertiary sector in Australia. The transfer took place between 1985 and 1993, varying between states and territories. Initially, the standard qualification was a three-year diploma in colleges of advanced education but the transfer was affected by changes in the higher education system. When the advanced education sector was abolished in the reforms of the then education minister John Dawkins through the establishment of the unified national system of education in 1989, nursing courses were moved to universities and the initial qualification for registered nurses was upgraded to a bachelor's degree (National Review of Nurse Education 1994).

At the end of 1993, once the transfer had been completed but changes were still unfolding, the Commonwealth government established the National Review of Nurse Education in the Higher Education Sector. The committee's report, *Nursing Education in Australian Universities*, made a number of conclusions and recommendations for consideration by policymakers. Some of the main conclusions were that:

- as education had come to the forefront, nursing culture would be transformed as a result
- the changes in education and career paths had moved ahead of actual opportunities for individual nurses, most of whom were in institutional employment
- a common national standard of funding for nursing places in universities (as is the case for other disciplines) should be established and phased in over time
- there was a need to strengthen research in nursing and the qualifications of academic staff
- management issues for university schools of nursing were likely to become increasingly important, as were the issues of quality assurance and benchmarking based on a best-practice approach
- university schools of nursing needed to establish closer and more effective relationships with various stakeholders, including health industry employers, the registering authorities and consumers of both health and education services.

The review produced a range of recommendations encompassing labour force planning; the public presentation of Department of Education data; careers and pathways, pre-registration clinical education; the undergraduate, postgraduate and specialist programs; beginning practitioners; clinical specialties; rural and remote area nursing; distance education; academic staff; nursing research; Commonwealth funding; and cooperation between health agencies and higher education institutions. The review also supported greater consumer involvement in the design, evaluation and implementation of nursing curricula. It stressed the need for greater cultural diversity in the nursing labour force and supported mechanisms to encourage recruits who were of Aboriginal and Torres Strait Islander descent and those from backgrounds with languages other than English (National Review of Nurse Education 1994).

Currently, training for nursing is provided by two sources: universities for registered nurses and VET institutions for enrolled nurses. Enrolled nurses can upgrade their qualifications to become registered nurses and this has been encouraged over the last decade through more varied training pathways, such as training packages that focus on competencies achieved either in a clinical setting or in the classroom (ANMC 2002a). This should be considered when looking at the slowing growth rate of enrolled nurse numbers compared to registered nurse numbers, because part of the change is a result of enrolled nurses upgrading their qualifications.

University-level general nursing courses required for initial registration as a nurse are usually of three or four years' duration when taken full time. The level of commencements in these courses was stable between 2001 and 2003 at around 8000 students per year, as was the level of completions at around two-thirds of the level of commencements. There was a decline in commencements in 2004, although completions flowing through from earlier course intakes continued to increase. Commencements in 2005 increased markedly, to 9578, while the number of completions, 5632, was similar to 2004.

The basic training for an enrolled nurse is shorter in duration than for a registered nurse. Enrolled nurse training varies across jurisdictions, although there is a national set of competencies (ANMC 2009). Enrolled nurse courses are generally Certificate III or Certificate IV level training programs and can take between one and two years to complete, depending on the level of theory mixed with clinical experience. In 2005, there were 13 815 students enrolled in VET nursing courses, and 5473 students completed their course in that year.

More recently, employers, nurses and consumers have turned their attention to the issue of continuing competence. International experience suggests that continuing competence may be linked to licensing in the future, with a professional portfolio used as a tool in a continuous quality improvement process. As an example, from January 2010, nurse practitioners were required to have a master's degree in their relevant field of expertise and evidence of continued training, knowledge and quality of service. There is, however, no convincing body of scientific evidence that supports the cost-effectiveness of the requirement to provide evidence of continuing professional education in protecting the public.

Professional nursing issues

In the 1980s, acknowledgment of widespread dissatisfaction within the nursing profession prompted the Victorian Department of Health and the Victorian branch of the Royal Australian Nursing Federation to establish the Committee of Inquiry on Professional Issues in Nursing (1988). The wide-ranging inquiry, chaired by the former commissioner of equal opportunity, Fay Marles, aimed to identify and rectify the underlying causes of the Victorian nurses' strike of 1986. Both parties in the dispute, the RANF and the government, acknowledged that basic professional issues needed to be resolved in order to ensure stability in the nursing workforce and in the state's health system. The terms of reference of the inquiry, which was limited to general registered nurses, included issues such as the changing role and nature of the nursing profession, perceptions regarding future roles for nurses, nursing salaries and conditions compared to those of other health care employees, and nursing education.

The submission to the Marles inquiry from the Royal Australasian College of Surgeons (Durham Smith 1987) indicated that the college did not support nursing's contemporary professional aspirations. According to the surgeons, every nurse need not be a fully trained professional. The college claimed that a second-level nurse, the state-enrolled nurse, was 'essential to provide for the bodily needs of the patient at the bedside' (Durham Smith 1987, p. 6). The college sought to encourage the training of enrolled nurses in programs within hospitals, and it expressed willingness to provide surgeons and anaesthetists to teach in hospital training programs. The college also recommended to the nursing profession and the government that it should reverse the decision to transfer nursing education to tertiary institutions. The college preferred the traditional system of hospital training, over which surgeons had more control.

The College of Surgeons' submission expressed concern that nurses were being educated by nurse academics who accentuated the scepticism felt by nurses about 'advice' from doctors. In addition, the college suggested that college-based education had destroyed the *esprit de corps* and loyalties that existed in the hospital-based system, which 'went such a long way to maintain harmony and understanding with medical and paramedical staff' (Durham Smith 1987, p. 6). This particular comment reflects a lack of awareness of nursing as a dynamic and developing occupation (Short, Sharman & Speedy 1998). The surgeons' submission acknowledged that there were some grounds for nurses' complaints about doctors, and nurses' lack of decision-making power in patient care. It was also acknowledged that nursing's role in decision-making may be vital. At the same time, it emphasised that one person must be in charge, the medical practitioner, who is ultimately responsible for diagnostic and treatment decisions. The college asserted that the medical practitioner was the 'natural' leader of the health care team, and that there should be a revival of trust and loyalty on the part of nurses. This medical view contrasts markedly with the attitudes of nurses that emerged from the study. The most important issues identified by nurses according to the Marles Report were:

- the increase in stress levels for nurses created by technological developments
- the need for nurses to play a greater role in decisions affecting them
- increasing tensions in nurse–doctor relations
- the major problem of overwork in a majority of settings

- resentment felt by nurses at the lack of recognition for their 24-hour service to patients in hospitals in contrast to the more limited demands on other professions
- the need for further education in every field, including basic and post-basic courses, in-service education and courses in non-metropolitan regions.

In acknowledging the stresses created by technological developments, the report noted that nurses were often excluded from decisions that affected them. Nurses emphasised that they were often expected to use technology for which they were inadequately prepared. New ethical dilemmas were also associated with technological developments. Nurses and doctors often clashed in their perspectives on ethical issues. This was related to nursing's emphasis on 'holistic' care, as distinct from treating the 'medical' condition. Priority issues included the question of when to institute radical treatment, when to resuscitate patients and the implementation of informed consent. Nurses believed that allowing a person to die with dignity was a crucial element in caring nursing practice. Nurses complained that the site of health care often determined which treatments and diagnostic tests were applied. If equipment and specialist medical expertise were available then they were likely to be used. In line with this technological imperative, nurses believed that treatment in city hospitals was generally more aggressive than in country regions, due to the availability of more advanced technology.

In areas such as occupational health and community nursing, in which nurses have higher levels of professional autonomy, this was seen as a source of job satisfaction according to the Marles Report. Nurses in areas such as intensive care also reported higher levels of job satisfaction due to the prestige attached to high technology and greater autonomy. Conversely, nurses expressed dissatisfaction in areas where their voices were not heard as equal members in a health care team. Both nurses and doctors acknowledged that relations between the two occupations had deteriorated in recent years. Nurses suggested that doctors should be educated to have a greater appreciation of nursing theory and practice, that decision-making processes should be reviewed and that changes in hospital administration could ease tensions between nursing and medicine. It was also noted that the 'God–handmaiden' relationship was more evident in country areas and between older male doctors and female nurses.

The 24-hour nature of nursing work sometimes caused tensions with other health professionals when the nursing role was not accorded the collegial status it merited. Many nurses felt that allied health professionals such as physiotherapists and social workers were performing functions that were part of nursing's unique generalist role. Competition over occupational territory with the allied health professions was more acute than with medicine, with which issues of power were more prevalent. Status difficulties were generally framed in terms of the higher respect accorded to the 'para-medical' professions by many doctors. Nurses saw remedies in educating professionals about nursing's contribution to patient care and in raising the status of nursing to that of the allied health professions through degree-level basic education and salary parity.

The findings of the Marles Report lend support to a body of nursing workforce research conducted in Australia and the United States, which concludes that pay and working conditions are not the major causes of dissatisfaction in nursing. Instead, nursing turnover and job dissatisfaction have been linked with political and organisational problems relating to nursing's under-representation in hospital decision-making and management (Cuthbert et al. 1992; Diers 1988; Fletcher 1986).

Indeed, Australian research suggests that nursing work was deskilled between 1970 and 1990, and that there is a link between job fragmentation, specialisation, deskilling and job satisfaction. For the majority of practising nurses, the modern hospital is a larger and more impersonal bureaucracy than in the past, and nurses are less able than other professions to retain a level of autonomy within this bureaucratic setting (Herdman 1998, p. 44). Participatory styles of management, effective communication among nurses, between nurses and with other employees, help and encouragement with continuing education, respect for nursing's perspective in decision-making, supportive nursing, and general administration emerge as important factors for the nursing profession. Indeed, research evidence suggests that nurses should play a more prominent role in all levels of health care decision-making in order to change health care practices. It is likely, for example, that nurses would give higher priority to extended care than their colleagues in the medical profession. Recurring shortfalls of registered nurses in high-dependency areas such as critical care and intensive care could be alleviated if nurses played a greater role in decision-making at all levels of the health care system. Contemporary nurses are overturning their traditional handmaiden role. In the opinion of one commentator, policymakers could 'improve the quality of care in hospitals by expanding the professional role of nurses and rejecting the notion that a hospital is a doctor's workshop' (McHarg 1984, p. 1).

Health services management

Generally, the occupation of health administration, or health services management, includes only those health employees who spend the majority of their time doing administrative tasks (Duckett & Price 1982). It includes chief executive officers (CEOs), general managers or deputy CEOs, people who hold corporate positions such as finance managers or managers of human resources, and directors or managers of a clinical service. The occupation also includes coordinators, project leaders, consultants and educators (Harris, Maddern & Pegg 1998). Since health services management does not have clear-cut entry guidelines or regulations regarding membership and exclusion, there are no reliable or comprehensive statistics on the health services management workforce in Australia. More recently, several studies have been conducted on aspects of the health services management workforce, including a 2006 study on senior health executives in the New South Wales public health sector (Liang 2008; Liang, Short & Brown 2006).

The first and most relevant study for our purposes was a survey of the health administration workforce in New South Wales, which collected statistics on the size and composition of the workforce, and established a system of classifying this occupation by type of organisation and by function and level of responsibility (Palmer & Stephenson 1982). Palmer and Stephenson noted particular difficulties in undertaking workforce planning in the health administration field because of the lack of clearly defined criteria for defining membership of the occupation, the heterogeneity of the roles of health administrators and the extent to which the occupational territory of health administration overlaps with clinical and other professional territories.

Health administration can be defined as the occupation responsible for the planning, organisation, direction, control and evaluation of the resources and procedures by which needs and demands for health care and a healthy environment are fulfilled through the provision of services to organisations and communities (Commission on Education for Health Administration 1975). More specifically, health administration activities include personnel management, financial management, committee work and public relations, policymaking and planning. The New South Wales study noted that a large proportion of health service administrators had assumed their roles largely on the basis of qualifications and experience in areas such as medicine and nursing. For other administrative positions, qualifications in areas of administration such as accountancy, or experience alone, were sufficient to secure senior health administration positions. Present-day senior health managers possess significantly higher education qualifications than those in the 1980s (Liang, Short & Brown 2006).

Palmer and Stephenson (1982) identified three streams in the health administration workforce, namely medical administration, nursing administration and general administration. The study noted also that health administrators worked in a wide range of institutional settings, including hospitals, community and public health services, and central and regional administrations of health authorities. The principal employing agencies were federal and state health authorities, semi-autonomous hospital boards and private organisations, including private hospitals and health insurance funds. In 1980, 52 per cent of health administrators in New South Wales were employed in public hospitals and 73 per cent in the public sector generally. At senior management level, 58 per cent were in the general administration stream, 24 per cent in medical administration and 18 per cent in nursing administration. When the overall health systems in New South Wales and Victoria were compared, it was evident that although the states have quite different organisational arrangements for the provision of health care, the number of administrators per million population for the two states was approximately equal (Duckett & Price 1982).

The second study of health administration, the *Report of the Working Party on Health Administration Education* (Victorian Health Commission 1985), recommended that the health administration workforce be studied every five years, that education focus increasingly on graduate entry, that locally based courses be developed, and that a pilot in-service training program be established. In a study in the same year, Rawson (1986) reported on the characteristics and educational needs of upper-level health administrators in Australia.

Grant's (1991) examination of the development of health administration education in Australia provides a useful overview of this changing occupation. Formal education for health services management began in 1948 with the establishment of the Institute of Hospital Administrators, now the Australasian College of Health Service Management (ACHSM), and the introduction of a distance education diploma. In 1956, with assistance from the WK Kellogg Foundation, the first master's degree in hospital administration was offered by a school of hospital administration, then the School of Health Services Management at the University of New South Wales. In 1959, the University of New South Wales took over the institute's course. While the majority of hospital administration students in the 1960s and early 1970s were general or financial administrators, since the mid-1970s the majority of candidates have come from clinical backgrounds in nursing, medicine or allied health. There has also been significant growth in the range of courses available. The Society for Health Administration Programs in Education provides information about courses in health services management offered by numerous universities in Australia.

Examination of the changing roles of health service managers in Australia at the close of the century indicated that they were experiencing workplace pressures similar to those experienced by managers in other industries. A survey of health service managers, conducted in 1998 for the then Australian College of Health Service Executives and the Society for Health Administration Programs in Education, indicated that managers were working longer hours and more intensely, and that this was affecting their health and wellbeing and their personal lives. The trend towards short-term appointments, while providing a degree of flexibility for employers, tended to deny managers a sense of employment security and hence financial security (Harris, Maddern & Pegg 1998, p. xiv). This concern was statistically more significant in Victoria and New Zealand, in the wake of rapid and significant changes to health care organisation and funding arrangements.

The 2006 study conducted by Liang and colleagues followed the career paths and experiences of senior health executives in the New South Wales health services between 1986 and 1999. There was significant turnover at the top, with senior health executives staying in their most senior positions for just over three years. The most common problems for health care managers were associated with managing in a time of change, uncertainty, lack of support and political interference (Liang, Short & Brown 2006). This political interference was characterised as centralised control and devolved responsibility, with the minister for health ultimately in control and health service managers held responsible for identifying, solving and fixing problems.

Health services management is unlike other professional occupations in health care, which require completion of a clearly defined educational program before a licence to practise is obtained. This is not unrelated to the fact that health administrators do not deal with health care consumers directly, as do other health professionals. A further obstacle to professionalisation is that the occupation of health services management covers a considerable diversity of tasks and levels of responsibility. The traditional involvement of medical practitioners, nurses and allied health professionals in many aspects of health administration has also hindered the emergence of health services management as a separate health profession with a distinctive educational preparation, occupational territory and system of licensing. However, it should be remembered that, while health services management represents only approximately 3 per cent of the total health workforce (and 5 per cent of the medical workforce), it exercises a degree of influence over the operations of the health care system that is significantly greater than its relatively small size might suggest.

The allied health professions

In 2012, the total number of allied health practitioners registered in Australia was 126788 (AIHW 2013f). The majority of allied health workers were psychologists (23 per cent), followed by pharmacists (21 per cent), physiotherapists (19 per cent), occupational therapists (11 per cent) and medical radiation practitioners (10 per cent). Between 2011 and 2012, the number of registered practitioners increased for all allied health professions (AIHW 2013f). National health surveys conducted by the ABS in 1989–90 and 1995 showed that consultation rates rose nearly 25 per cent for audiologists, dietitians, occupational therapists, social workers, speech pathologists and psychologists. It has already been noted that the allied health professions, including physiotherapy, occupational therapy, speech pathology, radiography, health information management (formerly medical records administration), podiatry (chiropody) and orthoptics, are female-dominated professions. For example, in 1998, approximately two-thirds of physiotherapists in private practice were female and the figure was even higher in the 45- to 64-year age group (76 per cent) (ABS 1999b).

Traditionally, women who accepted a role that was ancillary and subordinate to that of the medical profession carved out the allied health occupational territories. Medical practitioners made decisions and the 'paramedical' professions carried them out. The history of an allied health profession such as physiotherapy is one of a middle-class 'feminine profession' (Short 1986b). These professions are 'feminine' to the extent that their occupational cultures were shaped by what are traditionally regarded as female attributes such as nurturance, cooperation and selfless devotion.

While the situation may be changing, the feminine gendered nature of physiotherapy affects rates of practice. The majority of physiotherapists leave paid employment in their 20s and 30s in order to devote themselves to family responsibilities. Even recent graduates in these professions, like their counterparts in medicine and nursing, plan to have several children and to interrupt their careers while their children are young (Short 1986b). The majority would like to work on a part-time basis so that they can meet both professional and domestic responsibilities (Nordholm & Westbrook 1985).

In 1999, the ABS released the results of its first surveys conducted with private sector practitioners in three of the allied health professions: physiotherapy services (1999b), chiropractic and osteopathic services (1999c), and audiology and audiometry (1999d). A comprehensive survey of the allied health occupations, which was carried out by the Department of Labour and Immigration in association with the New South Wales College of Paramedical Studies in 1973, found a consistently high rate of therapists not practising. Non-practising rates ranged from 22 per cent in the case of speech therapy to 30 per cent in physiotherapy and 48 per cent in orthoptics. Of those practising in each profession, almost half were working part time, except for occupational therapy (Commonwealth Department of Labour and Immigration 1975). The 1981 census revealed that less than 60 per cent of the 7000 persons with physiotherapy qualifications were employed as physiotherapists (AIHW 1988c). There is no doubt that the rate of exit from these professions is related to the fact that they are female-dominated. These shortfalls can be counterbalanced with new entrants into the profession and with therapists resuming practice.

Podiatry, physiotherapy and pharmacy differ from the other allied health professions in that they provide greater opportunities for private practice and part-time work. Data for 1986 on allied health providers indicated that 76 per cent of podiatrists and 45 per cent of physiotherapists were employed in private practice, compared with 17 per cent of speech pathologists and 12 per cent of occupational therapists (National Health Strategy 1991b, p. 111). Private practice work is particularly attractive to women with family responsibilities because it provides more flexibility than salaried work. For female podiatrists and physiotherapists, and female professionals generally, family responsibilities are often combined with professional responsibilities and part-time work is the easiest way to manage both.

A significant trend in these and other female-dominated professions is their 'masculinisation'. More men are entering previously female-dominated professions. This trend has both positive and negative consequences for women in these professions. On the negative side, it is well known that men tend to gravitate towards higher paid managerial positions within feminine occupations, and in the case of physiotherapy, into the most lucrative areas of private practice—sports medicine and spinal manipulation. Second, in the past decades we have seen more and more male physiotherapists taking up financially rewarding opportunities while their female counterparts are restricted to part-time work because of their domestic responsibilities. Indeed, a very likely scenario is an increasing number of men owning private practices and an increasing proportion of women being employed on a part-time basis in private practice. On the positive side of the balance sheet, physiotherapy has asserted its independence from medicine much more strongly since the early 1970s, and this is related in part to the increasing proportion of men in physiotherapy who are ill at ease with the traditional subordinate role.

Occupational therapy's position in relation to medicine is similar to that of physiotherapy. During World War II, when occupational therapy became established, it was accepted that these therapists should work under the direction of the medical profession. Indeed, 'they deliberately sought the support of medical men in order to give the fledgling profession a sense of credibility and direction' (Anderson & Bell 1986, p. 26). Occupational therapy's success in achieving paramedical status within health care can be attributed to a high degree of patronage from the medical profession, and the fact that occupational therapy could only be applied under medical prescription. Thus, between 1946 and 1975 the position of president of the Australian Association of Occupational Therapists was filled by representatives from the British or Australian medical associations (Anderson & Bell 1988).

Data from the census on persons employed in selected health occupations and proportions by sex reveal that occupational therapy, physiotherapy, radiography and speech pathology comprise a majority of females. This contrasts with dentistry, medicine and pharmacy, which comprise a majority of males. The chiropractic and osteopathic professions are also male-dominated (76 per cent) (ABS 1999c). Notable, too, is the small size of the allied health occupations. Each is significantly smaller than nursing or even medicine.

While the allied health occupations have neither the influence of the medical profession nor the numbers of the nursing profession, they are usually in strong demand in the health workforce. Unacceptably high vacancy levels in the allied health occupations prompted the New South Wales government to establish a taskforce in January 1985 to examine recruitment difficulties for physiotherapy, occupational therapy, speech pathology and podiatry in the public health system. The taskforce found that recruitment difficulties were principally attributable to problems in attracting appropriate staff, rather than budgetary constraints. Vacancy levels in physiotherapy were particularly anomalous, given the apparent oversupply of registered physiotherapists.

In view of unacceptably high vacancy levels and unacceptably long waiting lists in the public sector, the Review of Recruitment Difficulties for Therapists in the New South Wales Public Health Sector (NSW Department of Health 1985) concluded that any simple demand-and-supply analysis based solely on present and target practitioner-to-population ratios was totally inadequate.

From previous studies of the female workforce and the class and gender composition of allied health professions, one can conclude that domestic factors such as marriage, childcare and family responsibilities restrict the mobility of these employees and their ability to participate in full-time employment in the public sector. An additional factor in podiatry and physiotherapy, in particular, is the availability of lucrative and flexible employment in private practice. This illustrates that workforce planners need to consider factors such as gender, marital status and childcare responsibilities in workforce analyses, and that professions with rights to private practice—such as medicine, podiatry and physiotherapy—are much more difficult to manage than occupations such as nursing and social work, which have more limited opportunities for undertaking private practice work.

However, growth was recorded within the allied health workforce between 1996 and 2001 (26.6 per cent). This growth continued between 2001 and 2006, by 27.9 per cent (14 222 workers).

Across allied health workers, the profession remained predominantly female (76.4 per cent), although the proportion of females within each occupation varied noticeably. Speech pathologists (97.2 per cent), occupational therapists (93.2 per cent), dietitians (91.9 per cent) and orthoptists (89.7 per cent) all had relatively high proportions of females compared with the overall average for allied health workers (76.4 per cent). Occupations with the lowest proportions of females were chiropractors (32.7 per cent) and orthotists and prosthetists (32.8 per cent).

In more recent years, in response to workforce demands, there has been an increase in the number of allied health assistants. In 2007, the Australian Physiotherapy Association (APA) recognised the role physiotherapy assistants play and the value they contribute. This resulted in a formal qualification, Certificate IV in Allied Health Assistance (Physiotherapy), and membership into the APA. The recognition of this relatively new occupation—allied health assistant—will raise new and interesting health workforce governance issues into the future.

On reflection, perhaps the most significant policy development for some allied health professionals was the inclusion of specific MBS items, which were incorporated into the Enhanced Primary Care program (now the Chronic Disease Management program) for physiotherapy, occupational therapy and speech pathology in 2004. In 2006, exercise physiology was added to the list of allied health professions included in the MBS, and in July 2012 Aboriginal and Torres Strait Islander health practitioners were added, on recognition of their status as a regulated health profession with AHPRA. Signficant also was the inclusion of psychology, occupational therapy and social work in medicine for the provision of GP-led mental health care plans. It is to social work that we now turn.

Social work

Social work is similar to the allied health professions in that social work's success in achieving university-level education and professional status has been attributed to its alliance with powerful members of the medical profession (Lawrence 1965). In social work, too, men are more likely to remain in the profession. Their over-representation at the top of the profession has been documented in Britain, the United States and Australia (Brown 1986). Social work differs from the allied health professions, however, in that it generally operates with greater freedom from medical control and interference. Social work is perhaps better able to avoid medical dominance as it straddles two policy areas, health and welfare.

The Australian Association of Social Workers (AASW) has been attempting to achieve a system of registration for decades. Nevertheless, a person has to be eligible for membership in order to be employed as a social worker. In addition, schools in Australian universities require accreditation by AASW in order to offer four-year degree courses in social work.

The social work profession has seen significant changes in the past decades. Social workers now deal with an increasing volume of welfare legislation, they work in 24-hour crisis counselling services in public hospitals, and there is increasing specialisation, with areas such as sexual assault and infertility having developed in recent years. Since the career structure and salaries in the public health system have not kept pace with changes in the profession, there has been a significant drain of social workers away from the health industry into welfare and other sectors. It appears that some social workers have taken their broad skills elsewhere, into areas such as health services management, human resources management and equal employment opportunities.

Public health

Public health is a perspective rather than a discrete profession. This perspective emphasises the promotion of health and the prevention of disease, and focuses on the health of populations rather than that of individuals. Public health has been subject to numerous reviews, policy developments and changes since 1985, when the Commonwealth minister for health appointed Dr Kerr White, a consultant to the US Rockefeller Foundation, to undertake an independent review of research and educational requirements for public health and tropical health in Australia. A wide range of specific problems preceded White's review. First was considerable uncertainty regarding the future of the School of Public Health and Tropical Medicine at the University of Sydney, the main educational centre for members of the public health workforce, which had been subject to numerous reviews in the preceding decade (Potter 1986). Second was a need for a review of national workforce requirements for public health research and education. In addition, there had been intense lobbying from politicians, academics and medical practitioners in Townsville for the establishment of a tropical medicine research unit at James Cook University. Finally, there was dissatisfaction with the level of funding for public health research as compared with biomedical and clinical research in Australia.

A number of the recommendations of White's (1986) report on research and educational requirements for public health were implemented. In 1986, the NHMRC formed a Public Health Research and Development Committee (PHRDC), the National Centre for Epidemiology and Population Health was established at the Australian National University, and responsibility for tropical health education was transferred to the University of Queensland. Through the Public Health Education and Research Program (PHERP), funds were also made available to permit the expansion of public health education at the universities of Adelaide, Western Australia, Newcastle and Monash. Following White's recommendations, all these training facilities were located within medical faculties in the various universities (Gifford 1988). Even though this assured consolidation of medical dominance in the public health field in Australia, White's report indicated that public health research should be multidisciplinary, rather than purely medical. It is also rather ironic that the Commonwealth placed the public health training programs under the control of medical faculties, which had contributed, both directly and indirectly, to the limited development of public health in the past.

In assessing the impact of White's review, it is of interest that his report recommended only three regional centres for public health research in Australia— Newcastle, Westmead and Adelaide. After intense lobbying from state health departments and interested universities, a more diffuse policy, one that satisfied a wider array of government and institutional interests, was implemented. At the time, concerns were raised about whether this decentralised public health education endeavour would be viable in the future, given the large amount of research funding required to sustain such a broad-ranging commitment.

At the time of White's review, there were only two postgraduate public health courses in Australia. Four years later, there were over 20 (Public Health Association of Australia 1989). The proliferation of postgraduate courses in public health and other concerns prompted the PHRDC to fund a report on the public health workforce in Australia. The report (Public Health Association of Australia 1990) started by making a strong argument for the relevance of a public health perspective for all personnel working in the health sector. As public health is an approach rather than an occupation, the study highlighted difficulties associated with estimating the nature, size and composition of the public health workforce.

The Public Health Association report (1990, p. 6) identified three major groups in the public health workforce. The first group consisted of highly qualified 'specialists' in public health who undertake teaching, research and consulting work at the forefront of public health. The study identified shortages of suitably qualified specialists in the fields of biostatistics, environmental health, epidemiology, health economics, health promotion, statistics and toxicology. The second group is commonly, but mistakenly, regarded as the public health workforce. It comprised public health practitioners, often with generalist postgraduate qualifications such as a Master of Public Health degree, who generally provide services directly to the public. The majority of graduates from these postgraduate courses are already employed in the health workforce and do not intend to undertake significant career changes. The third group consisted of approximately 300000 general health and associated workers whose jobs involved public health responsibilities on a regular or occasional basis.

The report on the public health workforce also identified a fourth group in the public health arena: consumers and community groups. Although not part of the paid public health workforce, consumers and community groups undertake many activities that support and enhance the public's health. The Public Health Association report acknowledged that these groups have an important part to play in public health research and training, and that the process of assessing and meeting their educational and training needs had only just begun. In 1990, the PHRDC funded a workshop on consumer participation in public health research (Matrice & Brown 1990). It noted that consumers and consumer groups have access to vital knowledge, which derives from their direct experience of health issues and problems. In 1992–93, the PHRDC supported a series of workshops for consumers, health professionals and researchers interested in consumer-based public health research.

Since White's report, we have seen a considerable reshuffling of public health cards in Australia. Between 1986 and 1993, the PHRDC of the NHMRC allocated over $18 million to scholarships, fellowships and public health research grants on a competitive basis, and institutional and organisational initiatives were funded through PHERP. This program supported postgraduate research and teaching programs in nine institutions, including the University of Sydney and the National Centre for Epidemiology and Population Health in Canberra. The proliferation of public-health-related courses in Australian universities was accelerated by the integration of former Colleges of Advanced Education into the unified university system after 1988.

In 1992, the review of the Public Health Education and Research Program undertaken by George Salmond, former director-general of the New Zealand Department of Health, recommended that public health networks be established in each state and territory, and that PHERP funds be used to support such networks. Salmond recommended that closer working relationships be developed between state health authorities, universities, industry, hospitals and other intersectoral interests, and that funds should be allocated on a competitive basis. The Commonwealth agreed to the continuation of the program by funding a maximum of eight centres for public health education and research under the aegis of existing schools or faculties, and a National Centre for International and Tropical Health.

The late 1990s saw federal government support for the establishment of a new medical school in Townsville, Queensland, and the completion in 1999 of the second review of the PHERP (Nolan, Bryson & Lashof 1999). Major achievements identified in the review included establishing two major national centres for public health (at the Australian National University and the University of Queensland) and the development of state-based consortia of universities delivering higher quality, more efficient and innovative public health training. The reviewers recommended that workforce development and research focus more specifically on national priorities, and that the two national centres (in Canberra and Brisbane) develop further partnerships based on priority health issues including inequities in health, occupational health, environmental health, food safety, oral health and injury prevention. The 1990s also saw implementation of most of the recommendations from the Review of the NHMRC (chaired by Peter Wills), which recommended a more systematic process for developing priority-driven research agendas in biomedical, clinical and public health research (Health and Medical Research Strategic Review 1999). Implementation of the Wills report recommendations expanded Australia's capacity to perform research relevant to population health; the effectiveness, efficiency and equity of the health system; and the integration of the results of priority-driven research into health policy and practice.

In 2006, the Australian Health Protection Committee (AHPC) and the Australian Population Health Development Principal Committee (APHDPC), two principal committees of AHMAC, replaced the National Public Health Partnership (NPHP). Originally, the NPHP had been responsible for identifying and developing strategic and integrated response to public health priorities in Australia. Public health priorities of the NPHP included addressing issues of healthy weight, communicable disease control, environmental health, injury prevention, child public health, information development, and workforce development and planning.

The AHPC focuses on broadening the membership of the Australian Health Disaster Management Policy Committee with the chairs of the Communicable Diseases Network Australia (CDNA), the Environmental Health Standing Committee (enHealth) and the Public Health Laboratory Network (PHLN). The APHDPC coordinates the national effort towards an integrated health development strategy that includes primary and secondary prevention, primary care, chronic disease and child health and wellbeing.

The dental workforce

The dental workforce operates within a confined occupational territory, that relating to the mouth and teeth (Nettleton 1992). While dentists have largely enjoyed autonomy from outside scrutiny in their own occupational territory, this is now changing. Recent and proposed reforms of dental policy and legislation are likely to affect the dental workforce significantly.

The dental workforce includes dentists, dental hygienists, dental therapists, oral health therapists, dental prosthetists, dental technicians and dental assistants. Dentists have authority over the work of the other dental occupations. In addition, dentists occupy influential positions as deans of dental faculties, directors of dental services, and heads of the dental auxiliaries divisions in TAFE colleges and on dental hygienists' examination boards.

In 2011, there were 18 803 registered dental practitioners of whom 14 179 were practising dentists (AIHW 2013d). Dentists comprised a majority of the workforce (75.4 per cent), followed by hygienists at 6.4 per cent and dental therapists at 6.2 per cent. Table 6.10 shows that the dentist to population ratio increased between 2006 (50.3) and 2011 (57.0) per 100 000 population.

Dental assistants, dental therapists and dental hygienists were almost exclusively female occupations (all over 87.9 per cent female), whereas specialists and prosthetists were the reverse. As in other lucrative health occupations with fee-for-service income, the dental profession is dominated by men. One study found that approximately 99.9 per cent of men in the dental workforce in New South Wales were working at the higher end of the hierarchy (dentistry, prosthetics and technicians), in positions of relatively high status and pay and with career prospects. However, the gender imbalance is slowly shifting, with 35.6 per cent of women employed as dentists in 2011 compared with 29 per cent in 2006.

Table 6.9   The employed dental workforce in Australia, 2009 and 2011

Dental workforce		
	2009	2011
Dentists	12 941	14 179
Dental therapists	1383	1165
Dental hygienists	1031	1206
Oral health therapists	651	1108
Dental prosthetists	1157	1145

Source: Data based on table 2.1 in Australian Institute of Health and Welfare 2013d, *Dental workforce 2011*, National health workforce series no. 4, cat. no. HWL 50, AIHW, Canberra, p. 5

Census statistics reveal that, in the past 30 years, more women have been entering the occupations of dentistry, dental technician and dental prosthetics at the upper end of the spectrum. However, there has not been a corresponding increase in the number of men entering the female-dominated occupations at the lower end. 'Feminisation' in the upper end of the hierarchy has not been matched by 'masculinisation' at the bottom. It appears that current salaries and conditions in the three female-dominated occupations are inadequate to attract male workers who already have access to wider employment opportunities.

The dental workforce is in a state of legal and administrative change. After World War II, dental technicians, who were dissatisfied with the low level of remuneration received from dentists, started to supply dentures directly to the public, which contravened the legal restrictions placed on them. These restrictions have now been removed. Dental therapists are usually employed to provide school dental services to children only. However, children have received dental treatment at the expense of other disadvantaged groups in society (Short 1995). Since the cessation of the Commonwealth Dental Health Program (CDHP) in December 1996, the waiting lists for routine dental treatment to health care cardholders and other eligible adults across Australia have soared. Only Queensland has supplemented the CDHP and some other states and territories have introduced co-payments for dental services to children and adults. To cope with the ever-increasing waiting lists in the adult population and as a response to the progressive 'greying' of Australia, more courses are now offered to train dental hygienists in Australia (Short 1998). This new 'oral health professional' can work in a variety of settings across a range of ages.

Dental policy development in response to increasingly recognised unmet need for dental care and significant difficulties in accessing this care is likely to continue to affect the dental workforce. The AIHW Dental Statistics and Research Unit projected an increasing demand for dental services 'from 65.5 million services in 2005 to 94.6 million services in 2020' (AIHW 2008i).

As in the medical and allied health professions, there is a shortage of dental personnel in rural and remote areas, with the number of dental workers per 100 000 population decreasing as remoteness increases (see table 6.10).

Table 6.10   Dental workforce: number per 100 000 population, remoteness areas, 2006, 2009 and 2011

Employed dentists by remoteness area[a]			
	Per 100 000 population		
	2006	2009	2011
Major cities	59.5	62.4	65.1
Inner regional	33.0	40.0	42.6
Outer regional	27.5	30.4	33.8
Remote/very remote	18.2	23.1	25.0
Australia[b]	**50.3**	**54.1**	**57.0**

Notes:
(a) In 2011 remoteness area was derived from remoteness area of main job where available; otherwise, remoteness area of principal practice is used as proxy. If remoteness area details were unavailable, remoteness area of residence was used. Records with no information on all three locations were coded to 'not stated'. In previous years, remoteness area of main job used.
(b) Includes dentists who did not state or adequately describe their location of practice and those who were overseas.

Source: Health Workforce Australia (2013, p. 30)

In response to the need for increased numbers of dentists, new centres have been established for training in dentistry, including Griffith University, La Trobe University, Charles Sturt University and James Cook University. This may go some way to ameliorate the lack of dentists, and the regional basis could improve the geographic distribution of dental personnel. However, it has been suggested that the projected increase in the number of dentists will not necessarily increase their capacity to meet dental care needs (AIHW 2008i).

It has been recognised that 'the aggregate shortage and maldistribution of the dental labour force create a substantial impediment to the improvement of oral health and dental care in Australia' (ARCPOH 2008). When we focus on the oral health of disadvantaged communities, we need to pay more attention to the balance of private and public provision of dental care. We also need to consider the impact of restrictions on the provision of oral health care by allied dental personnel and by non-dental personnel.

In the dental industry, fee-for-service accounts for 97 per cent of income (ABS 1999e). It is perhaps the most highly privatised area of health care. The majority of dentists (83 per cent) are private practitioners providing fee-for-service care. The small number of dentists working within the public health system contributes to difficulties in accessing dental care for many.

The reviews of dental legislation brought about by National Competition Policy reforms have had a significant impact on the dental workforce in Australia, with reduced legislative restriction on allied dental personnel roles. In Victoria, for example, dental therapists' employment in the public sector has been expanded to include the private sector.

There has been little integration of oral health care within primary health care and little oral health care is undertaken by non-dental personnel. In 2007, the Coalition implemented the Medicare Chronic Disease Dental Scheme (CDDS). By 2012, the CDDS had provided 21 million dental services to over one million Australians; however, the scheme was disestablished by the Labor government. In 2011–12, the Gillard Government responded to the National Advisory Council on Dental Health by announcing dental packages to treat 400 000 people on public waiting lists, boost the dental workforce and provide incentives for rural and regional dentists.

Given waiting lists for public dental treatment of over 650 000 people, and major policy proposals such as the National Health and Hospitals Reform Commission's proposed universal dental scheme, Denticare Australia (National Health and Hospitals Reform Commission 2009b), there is likely to be ongoing public concern and debate regarding the numbers, distribution and most suitable roles for dental and primary health care practitioners. Will increasing the number of dentists greatly improve equity in geographical access to dental care, affordability or increased recruitment of dentists into the public dental system? Given the predominance of private practice work in dentistry, perhaps not.

Alternative and complementary practitioners

'Alternative health care' is an umbrella term that applies to health practices that exist outside the orthodox health care system. For our purposes, the distinction between 'orthodox' and 'alternative' health care is partly one of government policy. Orthodox occupations, such as medicine and nursing, have gained government recognition, registration and support, while alternative occupations such as homoeopathy and naturopathy have not. It should be emphasised, however, that there is considerable diversity within alternative health care, which includes naturopathy, homoeopathy, aromatherapy, iridology, acupuncture, orthomolecular medicine and nature cure practice.

Definitions of what is 'orthodox', 'complementary' and 'alternative' vary over time, between countries and between states within countries. What is defined as alternative in one country may be considered orthodox in another. For example, although homoeopathy is classified as an alternative therapy in Australia, it has been an institutionalised part of the British National Health Service and legitimated by the Queen and her family. It is important to note, too, that chiropractic and osteopathy do not fit into the category of 'alternative'. They now have legal recognition and registration in all Australian states and territories, public support for four-and-a-half-year degree-level tertiary education programs and recognition for the purposes of workers' compensation and motor vehicle accident insurance. By our definition, chiropractic and osteopathy are 'complementary' rather than alternative health occupations. The term 'natural therapies' is used in order to refer to both alternative and complementary health occupations.

The professional association of natural therapists, the Australian Natural Therapists Association (ANTA), which represents a range of disciplines including chiropractic, osteopathy, naturopathy and acupuncture, is pressing for recognition and accreditation of all natural therapies in Australia. Since treatment by therapists accredited by this association is now recognised by about 30 private health insurance funds, ANTA sees this as an important preliminary step to registration for all its members.

Legislative change in the arena of alternative health care grew out of intensive lobbying by alternative practitioners, and an extensive series of inquiries between 1974 and 1977. The Senate Select Committee of Inquiry into Chiropractic, Osteopathy, Homoeopathy and Naturopathy (otherwise referred to as the Webb Committee) was established by the Whitlam Government and reported to the federal government in 1977. A significant change in policy that followed recommendations from this committee was the introduction of uniform legislation for the registration of qualified chiropractors and osteopaths in all states and territories. This change in policy was made possible because the Webb report defined chiropractors primarily as specialists in a limited occupational territory—that of spinal manipulation—rather than providers of a comprehensive system of alternative health care (Willis 1989).

Alternative health care has experienced increasing popularity in Britain, the United States and Australia. In Australia in 1977, approximately a quarter of a million new patients were visiting alternative practitioners every year (Boven et al. 1977); the Social Development Committee (1986) stated that nearly 400 000 Victorians visited alternative practitioners in 1986. In addition, the committee indicated that patients were positive about the services received and that they were broadly representative of the population as a whole. As mentioned previously, national health surveys conducted in 1989–90 and 1995 found a 23.6 per cent increase in the consultation rate for the group of health practitioners, which included alternative therapists. The Australian Health Survey 1977–78 indicated that, in a four-week period, as many as 356 000 people used or visited an alternative therapist. Wiesner

(1989, p. 18) noted that this number closely corresponds with those who sought advice from a chemist, a community nurse or a dentist.

In 2006, there were 16 354 workers within the complementary thera-pies workforce, representing a 47.2 per cent growth from 2001. This equated to 79 complementary therapies workers per 100 000 population. Massage therapists were the largest occupation in the group, comprising 50.8 per cent of the work-force (40 per 100 000 population). Naturopaths and natural remedy consultants were the next largest groups (18.5 per cent and 16.3 per cent, respectively). In total, massage therapists, natural remedy consultants and naturopaths comprised 85.6 per cent of complementary therapists. Massage therapists increased most in number between 2001 and 2006 (up by 66.6 per cent), followed by acupuncturists (up by 42.4 per cent).

The reasons for the increased popularity of alternative and complementary health care are both unclear and complex. A 'change in the cultural mood' is one possible factor, stemming from a growing disenchantment with 'scientific' medicine's monopoly in health care, and increasing willingness to acknowledge room for 'non-scientific' alternatives (Taylor 1984, p. 198). This reflects a broader cultural shift and the rise in consumerism in general. As the population is more highly educated than a generation ago, more people want to make informed con-sumer choices about health care instead of restricting themselves to the orthodox health system. In addition, studies suggest that the majority of people who use alternative therapies use them either in conjunction with orthodox medical treat-ments or when orthodox treatments have failed (Clavarino & Yates 1995, p. 264).

The increasing popularity of alternative modes can be explained, in part, by the superior quality of the client–practitioner relationship in alternative health care. Specifically, the Social Development Committee found that orthodox medicine was seen as unsympathetic and out of touch with current thought and feeling. Consumers are disillusioned with conventional medicine because of the superfi-ciality and brevity of the bulk of medical consultations (Taylor 1984). In Victoria, alternative practitioners were prepared to spend more time with their patients; the average consultation was just under 30 minutes. Alternative practitioners were more prepared to listen, and they showed more interest in the person's broad life situation than in purely physical problems. Furthermore, users of alternative health services were impressed with the focus on prevention and the apparent treatment of cause rather than symptoms. It is therefore argued that consumers are attracted to alterna-tive practitioners because of the superior quality of the healing relationship. One further possible reason for the increasing popularity of alternative health care is that it may be able to deal with some health problems more effectively than orthodox medicine. The use of acupuncture in pain management is one such example.

Do we have scientific evidence regarding the effectiveness of alternative modes of treatment? Alternative health care is in a catch-22 situation because it cannot gain further scientific recognition without scientific research, but it is unable to carry out scientific research because it does not have the educational base and funding neces-sary for undertaking such research. It is for this reason that government support for research on the effectiveness of alternative and complementary therapies is crucial for their future development. This is particularly true in the context of the increasing emphasis on evidence-based health care. Despite movement down this path, Clavarino and Yates (1995, pp. 268–269) point out that few studies examine client satisfaction. They cite several studies that indicate many people derive substantial benefits from alternative therapies, despite the lack of scientific evaluation of efficacy. While it has been shown that some alternative therapies cause harm, this has also resulted from orthodox medical treatments, such as use of thalidomide.

Perhaps the most fundamental difference between conventional and alternative practitioners is the difference in financial arrangements. When a consumer sees a registered medical practitioner, all or most of the fee is reimbursed through Medicare. In contrast, if an alternative practitioner is consulted there is no Medicare reimbursement at all, but there is total or partial reimbursement from some private health insurance companies. Consumers can claim rebates through Medicare for some alternative treatments such as acupuncture, but only if the treatment is provided by a qualified medical practitioner (Clavarino & Yates 1995, p. 261).

In Victoria, the Social Development Committee noted that 25 per cent of alternative health care clients were able to claim a refund through a private health insurance fund. Since individual consumers still have to pay all or most of the fees when receiving treatment from alternative practitioners, when free medical care is available, it is evident that the services of such practitioners are highly valued. In Australia at the current time, consumers do not have a real choice about which type of practitioner to consult, because the medical profession (and optometry) enjoy a near monopoly on reimbursement under Medicare. Allied health professionals are included in Medicare under medical referral in a limited number of programs only. Since it is considerably cheaper to consult a doctor than a chiropractor, there is a strong financial incentive to consult orthodox rather than complementary or alternative practitioners. The cost of treatment with alternative and complementary health care has made it a middle-class commodity.

From the consumer's point of view, the other major difference between orthodox health care and natural therapies is that there are no national registration and accreditation schemes governing the practice of natural therapies, other than chiropractic and osteopathy, and Chinese medicine practitioners (see table 6.2). The Webb Committee believed that the alternative therapies presented no major threat to the health of the community (Senate Select Committee of Inquiry 1977). This finding actually hinders the chances of these practitioners obtaining registration, since the Commonwealth and state health ministers in 1982 decided not to register any more health occupations unless there was a possibility that they could cause fatal injuries to patients. In Victoria, the Social Development Committee did not recommend registration of alternative practitioners because their educational standards were not subject to external scrutiny. Of particular relevance in this regard is progress during the 1990s in the establishment of higher education courses in alternative therapies at some Australian universities. In addition, an increasing amount of research is being conducted on the efficacy of vitamin, mineral, herbal and other complementary and alternative therapies. There is now also greater communication between orthodox, complementary and alternative practitioners.

Unpaid providers of health care

It is difficult to determine the extent of unpaid work in health care, including the role unpaid providers play in maintaining and furthering the health of the Australian population. There is a considerable body of sociological research on women as unpaid carers that suggests that we should include both paid and unpaid work in workforce analysis and planning (Baldock & Cass 1983; Finch & Groves 1983). Contemporary trends towards deinstitutionalisation and community care have stimulated this research, for there is increasing concern that many of these policies are only feasible because they shift the work from paid workers in health care institutions to more lowly paid or volunteer workers in the community.

This development extends the notion of occupational substitution to consider the reallocation of work from the paid section of the workforce to the unpaid sector and the concomitant analysis of the notion of 'volunteerism'. The community-based section of the health care system relies heavily on the use of unpaid work, in the form of work carried out by voluntary staff and in unpaid hours worked by paid staff. One effect of volunteerism, as a form of unpaid work, and the associated substitution of paid workers by volunteers, is a weakening of the industrial strength of paid employees in wage negotiations. This can lead to depressed wages and poor working conditions, particularly for those working in the non-government part of the community sector (Garde & Wheeler 1985; Paterson 1982). Many also believe that the use of unpaid workers in the community sector denies unemployed people access to jobs. Employment opportunities in the non-government community-based part of the health system are characterised by relatively poor pay and working conditions, limited training opportunities, extensive use of volunteers, weak industrial organisation and unreliable sources of funding. It would appear that community care can be a euphemism for the employment of unpaid or non-unionised employees.

The carer payment, administered by Centrelink, goes some way towards acknowledging the caring work carried out in the community by family members and friends. The carer payment assists people providing personal care and attention or constant supervision to friends or relatives who are frail and old, who have a disability or who suffer from a chronic illness. The spouse carer's pension, introduced in 1983, was subsumed by the carer pension in 1985 and extended to people caring for a near relative, not only a spouse, in the same home. Eligibility criteria were further extended in 1988 to include carers who were not near relatives of the person being cared for, and in 1991 to include carers who lived in an adjacent dwelling. This incremental widening of eligibility criteria for the carer pension occurred partly in response to lobbying from people caring for people living with AIDS.

The philosophy of philanthropy received renewed support from the Howard Government in the late 1990s. However, it should be remembered that large corporations and charities are more inclined to support heart-wrenching causes that involve sick children or so-called 'life-saving' procedures and technology, rather than stigmatised and socially contentious issues such as safe injecting rooms, hepatitis C or domestic violence.

SUMMARY AND CONCLUSION

The fields of professional regulation, education and employment have attracted much political attention in recent decades. Although we have seen considerable demands on workforce policymakers to make broad-ranging changes to the health workforce, these have generally been counteracted by considerable pressure from governments, health service managers and the medical profession to defend the status quo. Overall, workforce policy changes have been incremental rather than far-reaching. The most striking exception to this pattern is in nursing, where significant reforms have been achieved in nursing education. The historically significant transfer of nursing education from hospitals to tertiary institutions was only made possible because many women from nursing, the government and the public service worked together to lobby and work for reform (Kern 1986). Nursing was able to capitalise on its numbers in the health workforce and broad support within the political system to achieve a significant policy change.

The early 1990s saw progress towards the mutual recognition of professional qualifications across the Commonwealth, states and territories and the development of competency-based standards in a wide range of health professions, particularly nursing and dietetics. The other main policy development considered in this chapter is the issue of occupational substitution. The case of independent midwifery and obstetrics was analysed in some depth in order to show how the boundaries between occupations change over time. We demonstrated that there is increasing pressure from the female-dominated health occupations, and nursing in particular, to expand their roles. This can threaten occupations, such as obstetrics, that currently control these territories.

Other concerns include the emergence of new occupations such as allied health assistants who have varying levels of training, oversight and support.

It is sometimes attractive to governments to substitute one occupation for another, especially if the expanding occupation is paid less and is more responsive to government policies than the existing occupation. The implications for patient care are also considerable. Not only is it an issue of who can do the work, but also of how much it will cost the government and what the implications are for quality of care.

In terms of the medical workforce, we note the change in the discussion from concerns about oversupply to issues around medical shortages. With the election of the Rudd Government, policy orientation was directed towards 'what can we do about the shortage of doctors?' Will the Abbott Government perhaps be concerned about 'what can we do about the oversupply of doctors?'

The specific issue, of course, is that of the maldistribution between geographic and socioeconomic areas, and between particular medical specialities. The Rudd policy emphasised the shortage of specialists in rural areas, and the policy saw a significant increase in university places in medical schools. We have also seen the ageing and feminisation of the medical workforce, and the fact that medical practitioners do not work the long hours they used to. The power of the medical specialist and academic push would appear to be undiminished (Lewis 2005). The underlying issue is that no-one really knows how many doctors are needed. Perceptions of surplus and shortage are driven by underlying interests (Palmer & Ho 2008).

Lastly, the National Registration and Accreditation Scheme, implemented in 2010, marks significant progress in a national approach to health workforce governance (Pacey et al. 2012).

FURTHER READING

This field is in constant flux, so it is important to keep up to date with data from official sources including the ABS and the OECD. *Australia's Health*, published by the AIHW, provides a most useful update of data on the health workforce every two years.

The HWA *Health Workforce 2025* report (2012) is a useful overview of developments and challenges for the Australian health workforce, including continued reliance on overseas-trained professionals and the needs of international students. This is leading to a new definition of self-sufficiency that incorporates international students.

Conceptually no-one has had more influence on the social scientific study of the health workforce than the late US sociologist Eliot Freidson (1923–2005). His influential work *Profession of Medicine: a Study of the Sociology of Applied Knowledge* (Dodd Mead, 1970a) provided the conceptual basis for understanding the importance of the professions in contemporary society, and the role of medicine in particular at the apex of the division of labour in health care as the pre-eminent profession. Freidson re-conceptualised this work over the years, including more recently in *Professionalism: The Third Logic* (University of Chicago Press, 2001).

The seminal report *The World Health Report 2006: Working Together for Health*, by the World Health Organization, provides a global perspective on the health workforce, with a call for national and global leadership to address issues of workforce preparation, performance enhancement, attrition and migration. The report points to the crisis in human resources in developed and developing countries.

Chapter 7 in Palmer's and Ho's *Health Economics: A Critical and Global Analysis* (Palgrave Macmillan, 2008) provides a relevant analysis of health workforce economics and planning in a global context.

Short's and McDonald's *Health Workforce Governance: Improved Access, Good Regulatory Practice, Safer Patients* (Ashgate, 2012) covers issues relating to health workers, patient access to safe and quality services, and health policy. We refer with particular reference to Chapter 9, which provides a chronological overview of the National Registration and Accreditation Scheme, including the formation and implementation of the scheme.

DISCUSSION QUESTIONS

1 Australia has implemented a national system of registration and accreditation for health professionals. Examine the possible advantages and disadvantages of this set of reforms.
2 How do you envisage the health workforce of the future? What are the key challenges and changes?
3 How can we address maldistribution? What programs or incentives can be put in place to recruit recent graduates and health professionals to work in rural and remote areas for reasonable periods?
4 Consider the implications of health professionals migrating to work in Australia for (a) the health professionals themselves, (b) Australia and (c) the source countries and their respective health care systems. How can the ethical problems be addressed and resolved?

Medical services and technological change

In this chapter we provide further details of medical practice in the Australian health care system, including the relationship between doctors, other health professionals and Medicare; the problems of general and specialist practice; and the issues associated with the use of medical technology, predominantly by these health professionals. We highlight the considerable geographical variations, and possible overservicing, in the provision of specific surgical procedures, a largely neglected area in public policymaking dealing with the health care system.

General practice and specialist practice

Doctors in private practice, where most medical practitioners are engaged, may be either general practitioners (GPs) or specialists, with some overlap between the two categories. GPs normally represent the point of first contact with the health care system and treat the less serious conditions, which constitute the main reasons people seek medical care. In principle, when a GP considers that a patient may need more complicated treatment, including hospital-based treatment, the patient will be referred to an appropriate specialist.

The distinction between a GP and a specialist is that the latter holds a specialist qualification recognised by Medicare Australia, as part of its role in health insurance. It was noted in **Chapter 6** that specialist medical qualifications are normally obtained by meeting the requirements of a specialist college. The educational programs of the colleges are required to be approved and accredited by the Australian Medical Council.

From the standpoint of health insurance arrangements, doctors in private practice who are not specialists are defined as GPs if they meet one or other of several requirements. The vocational register of GPs maintained by Medicare Australia normally requires that the doctor be a fellow of the Royal Australian College of General Practitioners (RACGP) and has met the continuing education requirements of the college. A 'grandfather' arrangement allows doctors who were working as GPs before the change in Medicare requirements to continue doing so. As table 7.1 indicates, vocationally registered personnel provide most services of this kind.

Others who may access the higher content-based Medicare fees include members of the Australian College of Rural and Remote Medicine or those in approved training posts of the two colleges.

In the Australian system, although not in those of some other countries including the United States, health insurance payments are not made in respect of specialist services—that is, those designated as such in the Medicare Benefits Schedule (MBS) and performed by a doctor listed as a specialist—unless the patient has been referred by a GP. The GP acts as a 'gatekeeper' of access to medical services. A GP is under no legal obligation to refer a patient to a specialist. Some GPs, especially in rural areas, undertake surgical procedures such as appendicectomies. When GPs provide a service also undertaken by specialists, and if the service is one that GPs normally carry out, the MBS will contain a separate and lower fee for the service of the GP.

The constraints on the performance of specialist-type activities by GPs are in part accepted practice in the local medical community. Whether the GP has access to hospital beds is also an important determinant of their clinical role. It would be unusual for GPs to be given appointments as visiting staff of public hospitals in metropolitan areas, but such appointments are common in smaller country hospitals. Access by GPs to private hospitals, irrespective of their location, is also not unusual. A further inhibition on the performance by GPs of functions normally undertaken by specialists is the fear of legal action for negligence if a problem arises, especially in the case of surgical intervention.

The data presented in **Chapter 6** indicated that there are more GPs than any other type of doctor. Similarly, medical services for which Medicare payments apply are most numerous for GP attendances. About 36 per cent of all medical services for which Medicare benefits were paid came within this category in 2012–13 (Medicare Australia 2013). Medicare Australia also emphasises that lags in processing claims lead to the benefits paid in a given period being less than the number of services actually provided. In addition, GPs may provide other services and some specialists undertake GP activities.

Approximately 32 per cent of the value of all Medicare benefits paid in 2012–13 was for GP attendances (Medicare Australia 2013). The MBS fees associated with these services, on average, are lower than those for most other medical services. While not all GP services are defined in Medicare statistics, it is reasonable to assume that almost all un-referred attendances are attributable to GPs.

Table 7.1 shows the distribution of benefit payments by Medicare for each type of service. Note that the 'specialist attendances' category covers only those services provided by medical specialists not included elsewhere in the table; for example, under 'operations', 'anaesthetics', 'pathology total' and 'diagnostic imaging'.

The Medicare Australia statistics also reveal that the number of Medicare benefit claims processed in 2012–13 per head of the Australian resident population was 14.8, with the aggregate number of all Medicare-funded services being 344 million.

Table 7.1   Medical, nursing, allied health, optometric and dental services, benefits paid under Medicare, processed 2012–13

Type of service	Medicare benefit	
	$ million[a]	% of total[a]
Unreferred attendances, VR GP[b]	4908	26.4
Enhanced primary care	875	4.7
Other unreferred	145	0.8
Subtotal unreferred	**5928**	**31.8**
Practice nurse items	12	0.1
Total unreferred attendances	**5940**	**31.9**
Allied health	1290	6.9
Specialist attendances	1983	10.6
Obstetrics	198	1.1
Anaesthetics	397	2.1
Pathology total	2378	12.8
Diagnostic imaging	2703	14.5
Operations	1563	8.4
Assistance at operations	71	0.4
Optometry	367	2.0
Radiotherapy and therapeutic nuclear therapy	284	1.5
Miscellaneous	1393	7.5
Dental benefits	60	0.3
Total	**18 625**	**100.0**

Notes
(a) Figures have been rounded
(b) VR GP: vocationally registered general practitioner.

Source: Based on data from Medicare Australia (2013)

The average value of these benefits per head of population was $802, with an aggregate value of all benefits paid of $18.6 billion.

All these statistics have increased steadily in recent years. Thus, in 1997–98, the average number of claims processed per capita was 10.8, with the aggregate number of services being 202 million (Health Insurance Commission 1999). In that year, the average value of Medicare benefits per head of population was $357, with an aggregate outlay of $6.7 billion. Medicare services increased over twofold (2.24), and the aggregate expenditure on benefits in current prices increased nearly threefold (2.78) over the 15-year period.

It is also worth noting that in 2012–13, the aggregate Medicare benefits paid in respect of GP services was approximately $5.9 billion compared with about $11.2 billion for medical specialist payments, including pathology and diagnostic imaging (table 7.1). The numbers of active registered practitioners in each category are approximately 44 600 GPs and 29 300 specialists (table 6.3 on page 152). In respect of income for the two groups it should be noted that most GPs direct bill while many specialists charge well above the Medicare schedule fee. However, equipment and staffing costs for radiologists and pathologists are no doubt relatively high as compared with the other medical staff groups.

Table 7.1 also indicates the very high expenditure on the two areas of pathology and diagnostic imaging that combined make up 27.3 per cent of total Medicare expenditure on benefits. We return to these items below and the policy issues associated with these testing procedures.

General practice policymaking

Policymaking about medical practice in the early 1990s concentrated on general practice. With tight controls over the number of medical graduates entering specialist practice, the perceived oversupply of doctors at the time had mainly been reflected in the growth of the GP workforce. Moreover, the increased number of GPs correlated highly with the growth of Medicare benefits for GP services (Commonwealth of Australia 1992, p. 33). There were more GPs and they were providing more services.

A further incentive for public policymaking was the growth in so-called 'entre-preneurial medicine' in the 1980s. This development was based on 24-hour medical centres and had been a source of concern both for governments wishing to contain costs and for other GPs who perceived it as a threat to their incomes. The centres, concentrated in Sydney and Melbourne, often combined the provision of pathology services with primary medical care, and were sometimes owned by one entrepreneur, who employed a large number of salaried medical staff. Evidence surfaced of overservicing by these centres (Commonwealth of Australia 1985a; Health Issues Centre 1986).

The initial growth and popularity of entrepreneurial medical clinics suggested some dissatisfaction with traditional general practice within the community. More importantly, this development highlighted how vulnerable the fee-for-service system, coupled with generous health insurance payments, is to exploitation.

Major policy changes about general practice commenced with the introduction in 1989 of vocational registration by the Commonwealth government in collaboration with RACGP. The new set of medical benefits and fees became available to GPs who met the criteria for registration. The existing GP fees, which continue to be available to those not vocationally registered, were based solely on the duration of the consultation. The new items, with higher fees, are content-based descriptors of the services provided by GPs and are divided into four categories of increasing complexity. The higher-level fees also have minimum time requirements (Medicare Australia 2013).

Vocational registration and content-based fees were designed to encourage GPs to provide a higher quality of care. It was a condition of retaining registration that they should undertake continuing education and quality assurance activities. Moreover, it was believed that the new fee schedule would provide an incentive for GPs to undertake more extensive reviews of patients' conditions and their therapeutic needs.

The National Health Strategy issues paper on general practice (National Health Strategy 1992b) highlighted a number of problems including:

- GPs do not contribute in any systematic way to achieving national health goals and targets.
- There are many barriers to GP involvement in health promotion; for example, a lack of training and suitable educational tools.
- Many aspects of good-quality practice, such as consulting with other health professionals, are not recognised in the fee-for-service method of payment.
- Despite the greatly increased number of GPs, there are continuing difficulties in securing their services in some rural areas.

The paper made a number of recommendations designed to address these problems; many of them have been included in the Commonwealth government initiatives described below. The report marked the commencement of the general practice strategy.

In the 1992–93 Commonwealth budget, the enhancement of general practice was one of the main health policy developments (Commonwealth of Australia 1992). The specific measures for which Commonwealth funding was provided included a rural incentives package to encourage GPs to relocate to rural areas, local networks or divisions to be created to broaden the role of GPs, the development of a system of practice accreditation, and additional training funds to speed up vocational registration. The Commonwealth also commissioned and funded health services research aimed at strengthening general practice, including a general practice evaluation program.

It was also foreshadowed that alternatives to the current models for funding general practice activities would be explored with the Australian Medical Association (AMA) and the RACGP. Both these organisations endorsed a restructuring of general practice, and it was recognised that some shift from fee for service was required to facilitate a greater involvement of GPs in health promotion and related activities.

In the 1992–93 budget papers, the government's intention to improve access to the services of GPs but to reduce the rate of growth of the number of practitioners was emphasised. A tightening of the requirements for vocational registration was also foreshadowed.

The focus initially was on restricting the number of overseas practitioners who might qualify to work in Australia. Attempts were also made to reduce the number of entrants to Australian medical schools. In 1996, restrictions were placed on Medicare provider numbers to medical graduates by making their allocation dependent on possessing a relevant postgraduate qualification, including the fellowship of the RACGP, or being in a training program.

The Commonwealth government also fostered and funded the development of general practice 'divisions'. The objective was to promote local networks of GPs, who would be encouraged to share information and coordinate their activities with one another and with other health care providers. In 2010 there were 119 divisions of general practice, consisting of about 150 GPs each, in all parts of Australia (Davies 2010; Department of Health and Ageing 2010). These divisions were called the Australian General Practitioner Network. However, following on the creation of Medicare Locals (MLs) in 2012, the divisions of general practice were abolished (see below).

After the election of a Coalition federal government in 1996, a review of the general practice strategy was concluded in 1998 (Commonwealth of Australia General Practice Strategy Review Group 1998). The recommendations mainly addressed the strengthening of the program in the areas of GP involvement in preventative activities, and the embracing of quality improvement and cost-effectiveness measures. A further recommendation of major importance was the blending of fee-for-service payments with no-volume-related payments.

Other initiatives affecting GPs during the course of the Coalition government's period in office to 2007 included the introduction of allied health items for patients with chronic disease management plans developed by a GP, an increase from 85 per cent to 100 per cent rebate for Medicare GP services, the introduction of items for GP mental health care plans, together with the associated rebates for treatment by mental health professionals, mainly clinical psychologists.

In the context of the Labor government's return to power in 2007, the main initiative affecting general practice arose out of the National Health Reform Agreement (NHRA) of 2011 that required the creation by the Commonwealth of MLs by 1 July 2012.

MLs were linked in the agreement with the Local Hospital Networks (LHNs) that we discussed in **Chapter 5**. The MLs were designated as the GP and primary health care partners of the LHNs. The NHRA listed the main strategic objectives of the MLs as being:

- improving the patient journey by developing integrated and coordinated services
- providing support to clinicians and other service providers to improve patient care
- identifying the health needs of their local areas and the development of locally focused and responsive services, with an emphasis on identifying gaps in GP and primary health care services.

MLs, according to the NHRA, are required to be independent legal entities with strong links to local communities, health professionals and service providers. Linkages with state services that have similar primary care objectives, including services for people with serious mental illness and homeless people, are also mandated by NHRA.

Sixty-one MLs had been established by 2013, with the Commonwealth having budgeted $1.8 billion over five years for their support. This includes funding to GPs to assist with the provision of after-hours services.

In July 2012, the Australian Medicare Local Alliance (AMLA) was established to promote and publicise the activities of the MLs. AMLA has produced a series of policy papers bearing on primary health care, including coordination of health care, health promotion and disease prevention, and the social determinants of health.

A further initiative of the Commonwealth government bearing on general practice and related primary care items was the continuing restructure of the MBS for GP services. Since 1989 there have been four levels of GP Medicare benefits—designated in the MBS as A, B, C and D—with each having further subdivisions covering, for example, group attendance at aged care facilities (Medicare Australia 2013). However, one MBS item in each group corresponds to a standard GP encounter, and the sum of these four individual items makes up the great majority of GP attendances; hence the value of the aggregate benefit payments set out under 'unreferred attendance VR GP' in table 7.1.

Which item number the GP should use in claiming the benefit payment is determined by the complexity of the encounter, and in the case of levels B, C, and D, by the length of time of the encounter. For level B, the consultation is less than 20 minutes, for C at least 20 minutes, and for D at least 40 minutes. In 2012–13, item A (3) had a benefit payment of $16.60, B (23) a benefit of $36.30, C (36) a benefit of $70.30 and D (44) a benefit of $103.50, where the numbers shown in each case (3, 23, 36 and 44) are the individual MBS item numbers. New descriptors for B, C and D were introduced in 2010 that were designed to clarify which category should apply to a specific GP consultation. The stated objective was to increase the longer consultations for preventive care and chronic illness purposes.

What is of considerable interest is the number and percentage of GP services that fall within each category in 2012–13, as shown in table 7.2.

Table 7.2   Number of services for GP Medicare benefit items, Australia, processed 2012–13

Item	Number of services	Percentage of all services
3	2 782 240	2.7
23	86 903 539	84.3
36	12 395 029	12.0
44	1 048 740	1.0
Total	**103 129 548**	**100.0**

Source: Based on data from Medicare Australia (2013)

It is noteworthy that the great majority of GP encounters—over 84 per cent of the individual Medicare items listed—were for category B item 23, with a contact time of less than 20 minutes. The long consultation C item 36, designed to cover extended GP contacts with patients having chronic and more complex conditions, was cited in only 12 per cent of the encounters. The use of the short consultation A (3) and the prolonged consultation D (44) applied to less than 3 per cent and less than 1 per cent of cases, respectively.

In a careful analysis of long-term trends in consultation patterns, Taylor and colleagues (Taylor et al. 2010) concluded that, in recent years, there had been a marked decline in the relative use of level C consultations after a long period of increases. They attribute the decline to the focus of auditing by Medicare and the Professional Services Review Agency on long consultations; they also concluded that the decline could not be explained by the greater use of the special MBS items, such as those associated with chronic disease management. However, they did not canvass the possibility that in the earlier years some GPs were claiming payment for longer consultations when they did not meet the designated time and other requirements.

It should be noted that the Professional Services Review Agency of the Commonwealth Department of Health, established in 1994, is responsible for maintaining the integrity via auditing of both Medicare and the PBS. This includes an assessment of the appropriateness of the services provided by doctors and other health professionals that attract claims under these programs.

The picture that emerges from the data on GP consultation items in the MBS, and the trends over time in the use of the items, points to the difficulties of reconciling fee-for-service medical payments with the increased presence of chronic disease conditions in primary care patients. It is inherently a very gross procedure to allocate the great majority of GP consultations to effectively four price categories when one of these, B, dominates the rest. GP consultations may embrace a vast array of distinct types of patients, when classified by the obvious variables of age and sex, along with the great variety of diseases and other reasons for the encounters.

National Primary Health Care Strategy

The National Primary Health Care Strategy was released in 2010 (Department of Health and Ageing 2010). It emphasised the importance of general practice in the evolving primary health care system, stating it to be 'critical to the future success and sustainability of our entire health care system'. Key elements in the strategy are:

- improving regional integration between providers and services, based on Medicare Locals
- more extensive and innovative use of e-health, including MBS benefits for videoconference consulting outside metropolitan areas

- an increase in the intake of GP registrars
- a program of GP super-clinics funded by the Commonwealth Department of Health and Ageing.

In commenting on the strategy, Jackson (2013) notes that, in the three years to date, health care consumers will have observed little tangible change, and the general practice workforce still struggles to meet needs. Much of the activity associated with primary care has been devoted to the establishment of infrastructure. She also observes that there has been little reduction in the fee-for-service method of payment in which Australia lags well behind other countries in supplementing these payments with other methods of GP remuneration.

Specialist practice

Specialists practise in a wide variety of clinical areas. Classifications of specialties are based on several criteria, including the type of activity undertaken—for example, surgical, medical or diagnostic—and the body system that is the focus of the work. Approximately 40 specialties are recognised for medical benefits purposes, but a number of further sub-specialties may be distinguished.

A further distinction between specialists may be drawn according to whether they are primarily hospital based. Many specialists have public hospital appointments, but the amount of time they spend treating patients in hospital varies considerably depending on the nature of the specialty. All surgeons and anaesthetists heavily depend on the use of hospital facilities, while dermatologists, for example, may make very little use of such facilities in their practices.

Scotton estimated that, in 1994–95, the average net income of specialists, $168000, was precisely twice that of GPs at $84000 (Scotton 1998a). These values were based on an estimate of the number of full-time equivalent doctors in each category. The values quoted in table 7.1 for the Medicare benefits paid to each group in 2012–13 are broadly consistent with the continuing persistence of a large income differential between the two types of medical practitioners. Medicare benefits represent nearly 80 per cent of the total cost of medical services (AIHW 2013b).

It is possible that the emphasis of public policymaking on general practice issues has been in part a consequence of this wide disparity in incomes between the two groups and the perceived need to address the low morale of GPs; frequent reference is made to the latter in the above mentioned reports. Among this group of private practitioners there may be the expectation that only through government intervention will the unfavourable income balance be corrected. The introduction of a long-delayed resource-based relative value scale for fee setting is almost certain to have this effect, the main outcome in the United States.

The very high earnings of specialists, individually, may indicate that reforms are unlikely to be accepted, or even become a matter for negotiation, if they are seen as only likely to threaten these incomes. It must be recognised, of course, that the average income values conceal large variations between and within the various specialties. Procedural specialists, for example, are likely to be the large losers from any radical refurbishing of the MBS. In view of the aggregate benefits payments data, however, it may be surprising that the Commonwealth government has not placed more emphasis on policymaking to address problems, including the fee schedule relativities, where specialist practice is involved. Some of these problems are discussed in the remaining sections of this chapter.

Discussion of the special problems associated with the specialist practice of psychiatry, notably the increased reliance on drugs of dubious efficacy, is deferred until **Chapter 9** where we consider the problems of people with mental health problems.

Regulation and control of medical practice

In the past, medical (or medical practitioner) acts in each state provided the principal control over the practice of medicine, apart from special provisions under the hospitals and related acts that affect medical practice in public hospitals, as described in **Chapter 5**. Administered by medical boards, the medical acts, as well as providing for the registration of doctors, also contained mechanisms for the disciplining of doctors or their deregistration for incompetence, negligence, criminal conviction or unethical behaviour. Certain other activities, such as advertising and fee splitting, were prohibited under this legislation (but not in all states). From 1 July 2010, the Australian Medical Board acquired these responsibilities from the state boards and thus established uniform national procedures in respect of the control of medical practice.

Fee splitting occurs when a doctor to whom a referral is made agrees to pay a part of the fee to the referring doctor. Partners, assistants and locums are specific exceptions to this provision. Thus, if GPs and specialists work as partners in the same medical practice, the sharing of income within the partnership is not regarded as fee splitting. However, in some states, payment arrangements within partnerships must be disclosed to the medical board.

There are no legal restrictions on the ability of a doctor to establish a practice (or to acquire an existing practice) wherever they wish. As a consequence, there are many more doctors per head of population in some areas than in others. Thus, it was noted in **Chapter 6** that the doctor-to-patient ratio is much higher in capital cities than in the remainder of each state, particularly for specialists.

Fraud and overservicing

'Entrepreneurial medicine' may be regarded as the extreme manifestation of the potential for fraud and overservicing that our current system of paying for medical services facilitates. It is important to recognise that the distinction between these two activities is often not easy to make. Generally, medical fraud is taken to mean the receipt of a payment by a doctor when no service has been provided, or when the claim for payment refers to a more costly item than the service actually provided. Overservicing, on the other hand, refers to the provision of services that are 'not reasonably necessary for the adequate medical care of the patient concerned' (Commonwealth of Australia 1982a, p. 18).

However, determining what is 'reasonably necessary' often requires a fine clinical judgment. In many cases, there may be scope for legitimate differences of opinion, given the present state of development of medicine. It was observed previously that the considerable variations in hospital utilisation and in the performance of surgical procedures between different countries and areas is attributable, in part, to differences in the style of medical practice and to uncertainties about the likely outcomes of alternative strategies for patient management.

In the light of these variations, overseas policies, especially those in the United States, have addressed the issue of which levels of provision of specified services are the correct ones. The result has been a considerable emphasis on defining standards of practice and the establishment of clinical guidelines to achieve them (Harvey 1991; Renwick & Sadkowsky 1991). The upsurge of interest in outcomes research and evidence-based medicine in Australia and elsewhere is also a direct result of concerns about the appropriateness of aspects of clinical practice. However, there is not much available information to date that these guidelines and standards have an appreciable effect on the practices of doctors in the absence of organisational and financial changes.

Clearly, it must be regarded as unreasonable for a doctor to treat a patient in a given manner knowing that the treatment will not produce a beneficial outcome. Similarly, it is undoubtedly not reasonable to order tests when the results are not intended to be used subsequently to influence patient management. It might indeed be argued that if a doctor stands to gain financially in these instances, we are back in the area of fraud rather than overservicing.

Evidence of fraud and overservicing by some doctors was clearly demonstrated by the Public Accounts Committee of the Commonwealth in a lengthy inquiry started in 1982 at the request of the Fraser Government. We emphasise that by the current system we mean fee-for-service payments to doctors and the finance of these payments by health insurance schemes of the kind that have existed in Australia since 1953. Thus, much of the published evidence we have about the scope for fraud and overservicing is derived from the activities of doctors prior to 1982, and well before Medicare was introduced.

Evidence provided to the Public Accounts Committee, including reports of cases that were the subject of prosecution, revealed a wide variety of means whereby fraud and overservicing had taken place. The committee believed that the estimate of the cost of fraud and overservicing of $100 million per annum provided by the Commonwealth Department of Health probably erred on the conservative side (Commonwealth of Australia 1982a). However, the available data did not enable an accurate estimate to be made (Richardson 1987a).

In response to a report of the Commonwealth auditor-general, the then Commonwealth minister for health, Brian Howe, announced in 1990 that the government would draw up legislative proposals designed to enable the Health Insurance Commission to deal more effectively with fraud and overservicing. In the early 1990s, legislative and other steps were taken to facilitate the monitoring of doctors' ordering and other practices, especially in the areas of pathology and radiology, by the Health Insurance Commission, and to refer doctors suspected of excessive ordering to the Medical Services Committees of Inquiry. We indicated previously that the Professional Services Review Scheme (PSRS) took over this responsibility in 1994.

From a public policy perspective, overservicing poses the more important challenge in devising alternatives to present fee-charging, monitoring and surveillance arrangements. It is probable, moreover, that fraud is of lesser importance in generating increased costs in the health insurance system.

The principal test of whether a treatment or a procedure is reasonably necessary for a particular patient depends on its acceptability in the local medical community. Thus, if the more interventionist approaches to patient management are the norm in that community, city, region or state in Australia, it becomes difficult to sustain a claim of overservicing about an individual doctor who adheres to that norm. In practice, in the administration of health insurance legislation in Australia, the determination of reasonable necessity is left to the judgment of committees of experienced medical practitioners. Thus the PSRS, in determining whether an individual practitioner has indulged in overservicing, relies on the judgment of doctors on the agency who are appointed by the AMA. The detection of cases of potential overservicing has usually involved comparing the performance of individual practitioners with the average for a similar group of doctors.

It is questionable, however, whether the endorsement of the status quo implicit in this approach forms a satisfactory basis for policymaking in this difficult area. If it appears that the medical community as a whole accepts practices rejected elsewhere, or if the rates of performance of certain procedures, such as prenatal ultrasound, are unduly high by the standards of other regions or countries, there may be a strong case for some form of government intervention, especially when funding comes almost exclusively from the public sector.

'Unnecessary' surgery

The commonly used phrase 'unnecessary surgery', which carries the implication that the performance of all surgical interventions can be divided into two categories, may unduly simplify a complex set of issues (Bunker et al. 1977; Leape 1989). It is more useful to think in terms of degrees of justification for undertaking surgery when the variation depends on the nature of the procedure, including its risks and expected benefits; the clinical condition, age and other characteristics of the individual patient;

and other factors including the costs incurred. It is reasonable, however, to state that some operations should not have been undertaken because all available evidence indicated that the procedure would provide no benefit to the patient.

As demonstrated in the next section, the problems associated with surgery represent a special case of the more general problem of the assessment of medical technology. Nevertheless, it is useful, as the first step in this process, to examine the circumstances associated with specific high-volume surgical procedures that have been the focus of attention in the continuing debate about unnecessary surgery. Considerable scope for overservicing is associated to varying degrees with each of the procedures examined: appendicectomy, cholecystectomy, hysterectomy, tonsillectomy and coronary artery bypass grafting.

As we indicated in **Chapter 5**, Australian data concerning variations between areas in the provision of several of these procedures, together with data from other countries on the procedures, have been examined by Renwick and Sadkowsky (1991) at the AIHW, and by Richardson (1998). Reid has also investigated variations in the provision of several procedures between areas in New South Wales using diagnosis related groups (DRGs) (Reid 1995). These studies have confirmed the large magnitude of the variations, taking into account variations in the demographics of the populations being serviced. We have drawn on the Victorian data presented by Richardson (1998, table 10.2) for the procedures discussed in the following pages to illustrate the potential for overservicing in these cases.

Such substantial differences in the rates of performance of specific procedures could be the result of the residents of some areas being underserviced in the provision of adequate facilities and services. Nevertheless, the overwhelming evidence quoted in the above studies, and those of Wennberg (1998), Fisher and colleagues (2003a, 2003b) in the United States, point to the likelihood of substantial overservicing as the major causal factor in the face of clinical uncertainty (Fisher et al. 2003a, 2003b; Wennberg 1988). From an international perspective, McPherson from Britain has collaborated with Wennberg on the study of variations between areas in the use of common surgical procedures (McPherson et al. 1982).

In a recent paper, McPherson (2008) provided a history of small area variations research of the kind described above, and the implications for health policy. He notes that the work has inevitably cast doubt on the popular assumption that all surgical interventions are effective in promoting improved outcomes in the target populations.

Hadler (2008) also provides compelling evidence of the highly dubious nature of the empirical basis for many surgical and other interventions. His general thesis is that the recourse to treatments is grossly inflated in the United States by the combined efforts of providers, pharmaceutical companies and medical equipment suppliers, along with a gullible community.

Hadler, a distinguished rheumatologist, is especially critical of coronary artery bypass surgery, along with the newer substitute angioplasty. He analyses comprehensively all the clinical trials that have attempted to address the effectiveness of the procedures and concludes that for the great majority of patients subjected to surgical intervention, there are very modest discernible benefits in terms of increased life expectancy or even in reducing angina pain.

Hadler also comprehensively discredits or casts considerable doubt on a wide range of other medical and surgical treatments, such as surgery for lower-back pain, prostatectomy, screening for colorectal cancer, and a number of popular pharmaceutical products. His book should be required reading for all health policy analysts.

The data cited in the following pages have been based in part on studies conducted in the 1980s and 1990s. In the absence of evidence about changes in surveillance procedures, and in the light of more up-to-date information (cited below) about trends in the rates of performance of procedures in Australia, the picture presented is unlikely to have changed substantially since the earlier studies were performed. Comparisons with rates in the United States are appropriate in that it has been repeatedly demonstrated that these rates are substantially higher than in European countries that have been the subject of comparative studies (McPherson et al. 1982). It is important to bear in mind, however, that in some cases, differences between countries in the classification systems used for surgical procedures may affect the validity of comparisons.

Appendicectomy

The rate of performance of appendicectomies in Australia seems to be higher than in any other country for which relevant statistics are available, with the possible exception of Germany (Lichner & Planz 1971). The rate per 10 000 of population was 20.3 in New South Wales in 1986, compared with 11.3 in the United States in 1985 (National Center for Health Statistics 1987; NSW Department of Health, 1987a). The corresponding value in 2009–10 for Australia as a whole was 15.3 per 10 000 of population (AIHW 2008c), with the United States rate being almost unchanged at 11.5 per 10 000 in 2006 (National Center for Health Statistics 2008). It is possible that the high rate in Australia might reflect a difference in morbidity, associated, for example, with dietary habits, but there is no evidence to support this proposition.

An unusual characteristic of the earlier Australian data was the concentration of cases among adolescent females, for whom the rate was twice that for males in the same age group (Palmer & Jayawardena 1984). Since it has also been established that more appendixes that are normal are removed from females relative to males, a problem of differential diagnosis probably existed (Chang 1981). However, the more recent data for Australia indicate that the difference in surgical rates between young females and males is no longer present, suggesting that this example of unnecessary surgery has been reduced (AIHW 2008c).

The data presented by Richardson (1998) are based on age and sex standardisation of performance rates for residents of each statistical local area in Victoria for 1995–96.

They indicated that the standardised rates for appendicectomy varied by approximately 20-fold between the area with the lowest and the highest rate of use per head of population. The extreme values are affected by small numbers of hospital separations for the procedure in some areas. However, when the highest and lowest 25 per cent of area rates are removed, the highest of the remaining rates is still approximately 50 per cent more than the lowest of the remaining rates.

Since perforation of the appendix with a potentially fatal outcome may occur in some cases of appendicitis, it has been considered essential to remove the appendix when this disease is diagnosed. However, it is impossible to diagnose the disease with absolute certainty since several other conditions display very similar symptoms. Because of errors in diagnosis, it is inevitable that some appendicectomies will turn out to have been 'unnecessary' or 'negative' after the event in that no pathology would be detected in the tissue. The critical issue is to establish a standard for the percentage of cases where normal appendices are removed, and to establish mechanisms for monitoring compliance with this standard. When this percentage is exceeded, it is reasonable to assert that the performance of the doctors involved has been unsatisfactory and remedial action is required.

An article by Meeks and Kao (2008) from the University of Texas highlighted continuing controversies surrounding appendicitis and appendicectomies. After a comprehensive review of the literature, they highlighted the uncertainties associated with several key aspects of the management of this group of patients. These included the increased use of imaging methods, especially in terms of the relative cost-effectiveness of this expensive technique, the use of laparoscopic as opposed to open surgical methods, the management of appendicitis without surgical intervention, and the pros and cons of deferral of some emergency appendicectomies. The review concluded that there is a surprising lack of credible clinical trials data to resolve the controversies and recommended the support of well-conducted studies to provide definitive answers.

In a careful study of all appendicectomies conducted in an 11-year period in the Canadian province of Ontario, Wen and Naylor (1995) noted that higher diagnostic accuracy rates in individual hospitals were associated with larger perforation rates but these hospitals did not have higher death rates. They concluded that with appropriate management of perforated appendices, favourable outcomes could be achieved except for the very young and the aged. However, they stressed that the considerable variation in diagnostic accuracy rates between hospitals suggested that 'some proportion of appendicectomies could be safely avoided' (Wen & Naylor 1995, p. 1625).

The results of an important study from Norway by Hansson and colleagues (2009) challenged the conventional wisdom that a diagnosis of appendicitis should invariably lead to an appendicectomy. In a carefully controlled clinical trial, they established that for a group of patients treated solely with antibiotics, treatment efficacy was equal to that of the group on whom an appendicectomy was performed, but the serious complications rate was three times higher in the latter set of patients.

Cholecystectomy

The rate of performance of cholecystectomies is also high in Australia. The Australian rate per 10 000 of population was 23.7 in 2009–10, with the rate for females being nearly three times that of males (AIHW 2011e). The corresponding rate in the United States was 13.9 per 10 000 of population for all hospital discharges in 2006 (National Center for Health Statistics 2008). The female rate was slightly over twice as great as the male rate in the United States.

It is of considerable interest that in both Australia and the United States the rate of performance of the procedure increased substantially with the introduction of the laparoscopic technique in the late 1980s, as opposed to the traditional 'open' method (Legorreta et al. 1993; Rob, Corben & Rushworth 1998). For a health maintenance organisation in the United States studied by Legorreta and colleagues, there was an increase of 59 per cent in the rate per 1000 enrollees from 1988 to 1992.

In New South Wales, Rob and colleagues (1998) found a more modest increase of 24 per cent in the rate of performance of the procedure following the widespread adoption of laparoscopy. They concluded that the apparent lower threshold for surgery that had emerged needed further investigation. For Australia as a whole, nearly 90 per cent of cholecystectomies are now performed laparoscopically (AIHW 2008c). This is also the case in the United States.

The medical literature suggests that a consensus exists among doctors that removal of the gall bladder is the appropriate treatment for acute inflammation of this organ (cholecystitis), normally associated with the presence of gallstones. However, there is a good deal of controversy as to whether the presence of gallstones that do not produce symptoms should constitute a sufficient condition for the operation being performed (Gracie & Ransohoff 1982).

Doctors who favour a more aggressive approach argue that gallstones detected during routine examinations may cause problems for the patient when he, or more commonly she, reaches an age when the risks associated with surgery are greater. Those who advocate non-intervention in these circumstances point to the small but significant mortality associated with cholecystectomy, the potential for complications and the fact that few people with untreated gallstones die because of their gallstone disease. These conflicting attitudes towards elective surgery, together with errors in diagnosis, have contributed to the substantial variations in cholecystectomy rates between different areas and countries (Bunker 1985; McPherson et al. 1982).

For the Victorian data derived by Richardson (1998), the statistical area of residence with the highest rate had an age and sex standardised rate that was five times higher than the area with the lowest rate of performance of the procedure. Even when the highest and lowest 25 per cent of cases by area were eliminated, the highest rate was 33 per cent larger than the lowest rate. Again, the possibility of some surgical interventions being unnecessary is highlighted by these data.

Hysterectomy

The rate of performance of hysterectomies in Australia is high by the standards of many other countries, but lower than in the United States, where considerable concern has been expressed about possible surgical overservicing (Bunker 1985; Renwick & Sadkowsky 1991; Thompson & Birch 1981). In 2009–10, the rate per 10 000 of population (including males) in Australia was 13.9, compared with 19.1 per 10 000 of population in the United States in 2006 (AIHW 2011b; National Center for Health Statistics 2008).

It is clear from data on the diagnoses and age of patients who have had a hysterectomy in Australia that most are performed on premenopausal women for the relief of menstrual problems and for relatively minor pathology of the uterus; less than 4 per cent are for cancer of the uterus or cervix (Palmer & Jayawardena 1984). Sterilisation would appear to be an objective of the procedure in some cases. A more recent Australian study has confirmed that most hysterectomies in New South Wales and Victoria continue to be performed for the reasons cited above, and that there is considerable variation between geographical areas in its performance (Reid et al. 2000).

For this procedure, the basic decision-making problem is not primarily one of difficulties of diagnosis or uncertainties about the outcome of intervention or non-intervention. The problem is to balance the reduction of pain and discomfort associated with the cessation of menstruation and the risk of childbearing to the woman against the risk of mortality and complications arising from performing the procedure and its cost. Some hysterectomies might also be considered as unjustified in the sense that hormonal treatment, tubal ligation and more conservative procedures might be used with fewer risks and lower costs to achieve the same objectives.

For this procedure, the data of Richardson (1998) indicated that the highest age standardised rate per area resident was over 10 times larger than the smallest area rate. With the lowest and highest 25 per cent of rates removed, the highest rate of the remaining areas was 45 per cent larger than the lowest of the remaining rates.

Tonsillectomy and adenoidectomy

Tonsillectomies and adenoidectomies were the focus of one of the earliest attempts to measure variations between areas in the assessment of a surgical intervention. The work of Glover in this process is documented in the paper by McPherson (2008), whose own studies are discussed on page 210. Glover studied rates of tonsillectomy between counties and other areas in Britain during the 1930s and found that the rates of performance varied as much as 20-fold between the areas. The data also revealed that among 'well-to-do classes' the rates were threefold higher than for the rest of the population (Glover 2008). (The original article published in 1938 was reproduced in 2008 in the *International Journal of Epidemiology*.)

There was a considerable decline in the rate of performance of these procedures in Australia in the 1980s and 1990s as a result of the efforts of medical specialist groups and of state health authorities. Throat infection in children, associated with enlargement of the tonsils and adenoids, was the principal reason for removing these organs. The weight of medical opinion supported the view that in the majority of cases, there was no evidence that tonsillectomy was more effective than more conservative management in treating the conditions (Paradise 1981; Paradise et al. 1984; Wennberg et al. 1980). However, Paradise and colleagues (1984) found that in respect of very severe and recurring infections, modest improvements after surgery were found as compared with a control group in a clinical trial.

In recent years, the performance of these surgical interventions has increased substantially in Australia. In 2009–10, the number of tonsillectomy and/or adenoidectomy operations performed in Australia was 61 126 (AIHW 2011b) as compared with 47 583 in 2006–07 (AIHW 2008c). This substantial increase appears to be the result of the promotion of the procedures as a method of treating obstructive sleep apnoea in younger children (Lim & McKean 2009; Royal Australasian College of Physicians & the Australian Society of Otolaryngology 2008). However, in their Cochrane collaboration review, Lim and McKean (2009) found a lack of credible evidence to support the use of the interventions for this purpose.

It is not possible to compare the rate of performance of tonsillectomies and adenoidectomies in Australia with that of the United States because of the large number of outpatient cases not included in the US's inpatient hospital data. Day cases are covered in Australia's hospital data.

Tonsillectomy is one of the clearest examples of a surgical intervention with little justification for its performance in a high proportion of cases, since it does not produce the intended outcome. Since tonsillectomy is a relatively simple procedure, it is not surprising that about 54 per cent of all cases were operated on in private hospitals, with a high proportion being undertaken on a day-case basis (AIHW 2008c).

For tonsillectomies and/or adenoidectomies, the Richardson data indicate a 10-fold variation between the lowest and highest area rates. With the lowest and highest 25 per cent of cases removed, the highest rate of the remaining areas was 50 per cent greater than the lowest of the area of residence rates.

Coronary artery bypass grafting

Considerable attention has focused on coronary artery bypass grafting (CABG) because of the high cost per case and the uncertainties about its effectiveness. The use of this procedure has expanded dramatically in Australia and other countries since the mid-1970s. Between 1985 and 1994 in Australia, the rate per 10 000 of population for CABG operations increased by about 70 per cent (AIHW & National Heart Foundation 1999). Since 1994, however, there has been a slight decline in the rate of performance of the procedure, in association with a very large increase in angioplasty (see below).

The rate of performance of CABG in Australia was about three times that of Britain, Sweden, France and Germany but well below that of the United States in the 1980s (Jennett 1986). Based on the number of hospital separations where the procedure was performed, the rate per 10 000 of population in Australia was 10.9 in 2009–10, compared with 8.4 per 10 000 in the United States for 2006 (AIHW 2011b; National Center for Health Statistics, 2008). However, some differences in the classification of procedures between the two countries may affect these results. The high rates in Australia and the United States continue to be substantially larger than in the United Kingdom, where the total number reported for 2006 was 28 000, or approximately 4.5 per 10 000 of population. However, there were plans in the United Kingdom to increase this rate.

In most countries, there has been a considerable increase in the less invasive alternative to CABG, namely angioplasty, whereby blocked coronary arteries are cleared by a balloon inserted percutaneously. The procedure is usually accompanied by the insertion of a stent into the previously blocked area. In Australia in 2009–10, there were many more angioplasties performed than CABGs: 37 038 compared with 24 183.

Some evaluations of both CABG and angioplasty, mainly undertaken in the 1980s, suggested that the procedures significantly reduced mortality in only a small proportion of patients with coronary artery disease, those with left main disease (CASS Principal Investigators 1984; Veterans Administration Coronary Artery Bypass Surgery Cooperative Study Group 1984). However, the reduction in angina pain was substantial in some other patients.

Fox and others (2002), in a study conducted for the British Heart Foundation, also found that for patients with unstable angina, a comparison of conservative medical treatment with surgical intervention indicated that mortality rates were similar after one year in the two treatment groups. However, there was a significantly lower rate of severe angina in the intervention patients.

Where relief of angina symptoms could be achieved with drug therapy rather than a costly and potentially dangerous operation, the performance of this procedure should be regarded as unnecessary. In other patients, notably those in whom only one artery is affected, CABG may also be unnecessary (Hadler 2008; Williams 1985). Mortality rates may exceed 2 per cent even when performed in academic medical centres, and complications may lead to further surgical intervention in some cases. Neurological problems along with much pain and discomfort may also be the outcome (Arrowsmith et al. 2000). Selnes and colleagues (1999) found that, in older patients, a reduction in cognitive ability, along with increased risk of stroke, was associated with CABG procedures.

Technological developments in medicine

The effect of technological developments on the practice of medicine and hence on the total cost of health care may be one of the most important problems to be resolved by planners and policymakers in Australia and other countries over the next decade. It is widely believed that the experience of the past 30 years has demonstrated the potential for these developments to place considerable strains on the capacity of all economies to afford them. Consequently, even in the United States this prospect has led to consideration of the need to ration services (Aaron & Schwartz 1984).

For example, the so-called Oregon experiment was designed to ensure that the availability of specific services in that state for low-income patients was determined by the treatment priorities established by the whole community. It should also be pointed out that since many people are without health insurance in the United States, rationing by income level has always been present in that country.

Another cause for concern is that technological developments, in the context of fixed budgets set by governments, may distort the balance of resources devoted to the various aspects of the health care system. More money required to establish and support heart surgery may mean that fewer resources are available to develop community health services; additional technicians to staff the hospital's radiology department may mean that fewer nurses are employed in the medical wards.

Medical technology has been subjected to much criticism because of the perception in some quarters that, at worst, it may do more harm than good and that, in many instances, efficacy has not been demonstrated prior to its adoption (Banta & Russell 1981; Cochrane 1972; Office of Technology Assessment 1978; Relman 1979).

An impressive array of evidence reported mainly in medical literature and often based on the work of doctors has raised questions about a wide range of individual technological developments. These include antenatal foetal heart-rate monitoring, intensive care and coronary care units, computerised axial tomography (CAT), magnetic resonance imaging (MRI), chemotherapy for cancer and many of the more complex surgical procedures (Banta 1983; Husband 1985; Jennett 1986; Sandercock et al. 1985; Steinberg 1984). The book by Jennett, a British neurosurgeon, is of particular interest because of his well-argued support for the benefits of much high-technology medicine but also his frank recognition of inappropriate usage. Considerations of this kind have driven the evidence-based medicine movement discussed below.

What is technology?

Much of the debate about medical technology has concentrated on equipment of high capital cost, of which CAT and MRI have become the standard cases. There is no justification, however, for restricting the consideration of technology to high-cost equipment. Basically, a technology consists of the way that a set of factors of production, labour of various kinds, materials and capital equipment are brought together to generate an output; for example, patients treated or for whom a diagnosis is obtained. As judged from this standpoint, each medical service, no matter whether it is classed as diagnostic or therapeutic, including surgical and pharmaceutical, is the outcome of a technology involving a medical practitioner.

This definition of technology serves to emphasise that the equipment component should not be examined in isolation of the total system of diagnostic and therapeutic intervention. Thus, the appropriate assessment of the effectiveness or efficiency of a technology usually depends on the specification of all the circumstances of its deployment, including scale of operation, skills of the staff and the types of patient diagnosed or treated. Furthermore, the inclusion of the labour force in the definition leads to a consideration of the relationships between these people as a critical element in assessing performance associated with the technology (Daly & Willis 1987).

Problems in the use of medical technology

The problems associated with many diagnostic and therapeutic activities, including the surgical procedures discussed in the previous section, are often a product of their application to inappropriate types of patients. There are perhaps few existing medical technologies, even tonsillectomy, that do not benefit some patients. A necessary condition for effective medical practice is to determine who will benefit from the technology and to use it only on those patients.

For the more complex technologies, including heart surgery, a further problem is that the number of cases treated in individual institutions may be too small for the skills of the medical or nursing staff to be maintained, leading to the ineffective (and possibly dangerous) performance of procedures that are conducted more successfully elsewhere (Finkler 1979; Luft et al. 1979).

The cost problems that may be associated with medical technology point to an additional desirable condition for the use of technology: that it should be efficient as well as efficacious. For a technology to be efficient for patients, the additional benefits (reduced mortality and morbidity, improved quality of life) should exceed the additional costs associated with its application. When more than one technology will achieve the same level of effectiveness, the lowest-cost alternative should be deployed. Unfortunately, few medical technologies, with the exception of pharmaceuticals, have been evaluated using these principles and neither the patient nor the doctor has any incentive under the existing arrangements to consider the real costs before a medical service is provided.

Apart from the financial rewards for the doctor in a fee-for-service system, incentives for the overprovision of expensive technologies arise out of the marketing efforts of pharmaceutical manufacturers and equipment suppliers. This is the 'technological imperative' in medicine to use technologies if they are available and the medical ethos of doing 'everything possible' for the patient (Mechanic 1977; Richardson 1987b; Short 1985).

The 'career' of a medical technology

Many of the important issues associated with medical technology are highlighted in McKinlay's (1981) often-cited work on technological developments in medicine. He identified a lifecycle for incorporating innovations into medical practice based on ever-changing medical fashions rather than rigorous scientific testing and evaluation. Thus, a technology might pass through a seven-stage 'career' based on the activities and reactions of manufacturers, professionals, administrators and the media.

In the first stage, the 'promising report', the innovation will often be launched with a single enthusiastic report in the medical press or increasingly in the popular press based on small numbers of cases and little scientific evidence. It is becoming common for manufacturers and researchers to use sophisticated public relations techniques to 'sell' technologies to clinicians and to the public in this way.

In the second stage, 'professional adoption', support spreads from the original enthusiasts to widespread usage by doctors and others. This rapid diffusion is facilitated by peer pressure among professionals who are motivated to achieve technical breakthroughs, thereby winning the approval of their colleagues. Reports on the technology at this stage may cover larger numbers of cases but there is no attempt to relate the technology to the alternatives. For pharmaceuticals and equipment-based technologies, much of the information provided continues to be part of the marketing strategy of manufacturers and suppliers.

During the third stage, 'public acceptance and government support', the technology gains general approval and there is extensive belief in its effectiveness, despite the lack of evidence. At this stage, governments may be lobbied for support, and hospital-based technology may be the subject of charitable appeals. According to McKinlay, often the technology has made it once the government provides financial support or recognition.

For a time a technology becomes the 'standard procedure'; it is regarded as the most appropriate way of diagnosing or treating particular health problems even though evaluation will typically have been limited to observational reports. Any adequate evaluations with controls at this stage are confined to selected groups of patients in major teaching hospitals. Adverse reports that may surface will often be rejected by practitioners who, by now, have a strong stake in continuing to use the technology.

Some technologies may be subjected at the next stage to a randomised controlled trial (RCT), in which a comparison is made between the effects on the patients subjected to the technology and the outcomes for a randomly selected control group of the same types of patient. McKinlay notes that it is extremely difficult to conduct an RCT on a standard procedure because powerful interest groups and professional reputations depend on its continued use and perceived success.

When RCTs are implemented, they may reveal that the innovation is ineffective for most patients or no more effective than existing, and often cheaper, alternatives.

'Professional denunciation' may then result from the reporting of the trials, with the supporters of the technology endeavouring to explain away inconvenient conclusions by pointing to alleged defects in the methods or the lack of experience with clinical practice of those conducting the trials. The interests promoting the technology may attempt to produce more favourable results from further trials or they may develop new markets for it; for example, in other countries in the case of equipment and pharmaceuticals. McKinlay claims that the upshot of this stage will have little to do with the intrinsic worth of the innovation, but it will depend on the power of the interests that sponsor and maintain it.

In the final stage of 'erosion and discreditation', support for the technology declines and there is general acceptance of its limitations. Frequently, another rising star promoted by the same groups eclipses the technology. In some cases, proof of harmful side effects makes its continued use clearly untenable.

The history of discredited technologies provided by Jennett (1986), McKinlay (1981) and others, including the British Council for Science and Society (1982), suggests that many technologies pass through all seven of these career stages. However, as McKinlay emphasises, it is desirable to bear in mind that the concept of a career for a technology is an analytical tool and that individual cases may be more complex than the model suggests. An important application of these ideas is to suggest how the process of assessing technology might be improved so that the wasteful use of public and other resources can be reduced.

Technology evaluation and assessment

Medical technology evaluation is concerned with the determination of the efficacy, effectiveness and efficiency of the diagnostic, therapeutic and other tools used in medical practice. Ideally it requires a multidisciplinary approach in which clinical-medical, epidemiological, statistical and economic skills are deployed, using techniques such as the RCT, cost-effectiveness and cost-utility analysis to establish whether and how proposed technologies should be used (Drummond et al. 1987; Guyatt et al. 1986). The term 'assessment' denotes a more comprehensive process in which, for example, the social and political implications of technology are explored. It includes examination of factors that promote or impede the introduction of innovations (Banta et al. 1980).

Assessment should include reviewing the effects of the technology on the training needs of the workforce, and providing retraining and redeployment of staff made redundant by its introduction. These considerations are especially important when, for example, a major technological development such as a computerised hospital information system has a profound impact on the way that hospital records are collected and processed. The process of assessment should also draw on the lessons of the technology career model; for example, it is desirable to analyse the specific strategies that manufacturers may employ to promote and to have adopted a particular technology before it has been properly evaluated.

Management of technology assessment

Examples of the successful implementation of technology assessment programs are far from numerous. The most serious attempt to establish a program of this kind was the creation in the United States of the National Center for Health Care Technology in 1978. The centre was given an extensive mandate to undertake assessments of medical technology, which included economic, social and ethical elements as well as those of safety and efficacy (Jennett 1986). Its pronouncements carried considerable weight, since it provided advice to the US Department of Health and Social Security about whether services associated with certain technologies should be reimbursed under the US Medicare program.

It is a measure of the potential effectiveness of the program that the abolition of the centre in 1982 came after a vigorous campaign against it by the American Medical Association and the Health Industry Manufacturers' Association (Perry 1982). This response of doctors and equipment manufacturers, part of the medical-industrial complex (Relman 1980), might be regarded as an interesting variant of the professional denunciation stage of McKinlay's schema—if the assessment cannot be discredited, eliminate the organisation that produced it!

A similar fate was in store for the successor of the centre in the United States, the Office of Technology Assessment of the US Congress. Following the Republican Party's securing control of both houses of Congress in 1994, the office was abolished in 1995 (Leary 1995). The numerous and very valuable publications of the office are now available from the Princeton University website (see the list of websites on page 429). These include an extensive and detailed review of the assessment of health care technology in eight countries (Office of Technology Assessment 1995). Lessons gained from the studies are summarised in the chapter written by Battista and colleagues (Battista et al. 1995).

Management of health care technology in Australia

A large volume of information about medical and other technology in Australia is contained in the contribution of Hailey (1995) to the Office of Technology Assessment publication quoted above. The following account of Australian activities in this area draws on this work.

In Australia, the National Health Technology Advisory Panel (NHTAP) was established in 1982 to advise the Commonwealth government on the costs and effectiveness of medical technology. The committee had representatives from the Commonwealth and state and territory governments. It also included members of the medical profession, health insurance funds, hospitals and the manufacturing industry, together with a consumer representative and people with skills in health economics, biomedical engineering and 'medical evaluation' (Hailey 1995). A health technology division was created within the AIHW to undertake studies on technology assessment and to disseminate information, following the creation of the Australian Health Technology Advisory Committee (AHTAC) in 1990.

The studies of NHTAP and AHTAC concentrated on the review of overseas literature and the opinions of local professional organisations dealing mainly with expensive technology with high capital outlays. Much of the work was concerned with advising the government on whether and under what conditions these technologies should be introduced into Australia. The panel produced a report on MRI in 1983, recommending its introduction here but on a controlled basis, which prevented the rapid diffusion of the technology before its assessment (Commonwealth Department of Health, National Health Technology Advisory Panel 1983).

After the acceptance of these recommendations by the Commonwealth minister for health, NHTAP initially selected five public hospitals where MRI units were installed using Commonwealth funds. The medical benefits fee was designed to meet only the professional consultation component, and a Medicare benefit was not payable for MRI services provided outside the Commonwealth program. Data on the costs incurred and utilisation at each centre were subsequently collected. The policy of restricting MRI use in the private sector by the Medicare fees mechanism was subsequently overturned in 1998, following the election of the Coalition government in 1996. However, radiologists had to agree to accept a cap on total funding for imaging for a five-year period.

The assessment of proposals for the creation of liver transplant units, adult and paediatric heart/lung transplant units and a pancreas transplant service by the AIHW led to the establishment of nationally funded centres in each of these areas. Reviews were also completed of the laparoscopic and related minimum-access surgery approaches to the performance of a number of common procedures, including cholecystectomy (AIHW 1992; Hirsh & Hailey 1992).

Other developments in health care technology and assessment in Australia have been reviewed by Jackson (2007), O'Malley (2006) and Elshaug and colleagues (2007). The most important initiative was the creation in 1998 of the Medical Services Advisory Committee (MSAC). This organisation replaced the NHTAP. MSAC is charged with the responsibility of assessing whether individual new technologies should be allocated an item number in the MBS, and hence receive a medical benefit when the technology is eventually used. In creating the new committee, the government emphasised the need for an evidence-based approach to the assessment processes. Included in this category was the use of measures of safety, effectiveness and cost-effectiveness (Jackson 2007).

Jackson also stressed a number of limitations of the program of MSAC, including long delays in assessment and the lack of a basis for sponsoring clinical research as part of the assessment process. O'Malley (2006) expressed concerns that the focus on medical devices, often based on proposals from the industry, had rarely involved cost-effectiveness analysis. She also expressed concerns that the assessment process might lead to promising technological developments in medicine being underutilised.

On the other hand, Elshaug and colleagues (2007) were critical of the assessment strategy of MSAC since there was no basis whereby disinvestment in existing ineffective health care practices could be assessed and undertaken. Thus, the questionable procedural interventions we have discussed at length above would not be candidates for assessment and possible reduction. Elshaug and colleagues argue that the committee should have a responsibility for undertaking or sponsoring activities of this kind and be allocated additional resources for this purpose.

An extensive report entitled *Review of Health Technology Assessment in Australia* was published by the Commonwealth Department of Health and Ageing in 2010. The report's recommendations are designed to remedy the defects that have emerged in the program of health technology assessment in Australia. They include the speeding up of the assessments of MSAC by allowing sponsors of the technology to supply their own assessments for review, and to reform post-market surveillance of health technologies to strengthen patient safety and value for money for taxpayers (Department of Health and Ageing 2010). A key objective of the review is to address the regulatory burden on business that results from the technology assessment processes, responding to frequent criticisms from the relevant industries of the difficulties and delays they face in having their technologies accepted for funding purposes.

Policymaking issues

Despite the importance of medical practice in the Australian health care system, and the large volume of funds the Commonwealth and the states provide via health insurance and public hospitals to subsidise and support the services supplied by doctors, it is only very recently that coherent policies for dealing with the many problems outlined previously have begun to be developed. In the past, ad hoc policies have been devised to attempt to resolve individual problems as they have arisen. In this area, including medical technology deployment, policymaking has followed closely the Lindblom model of being disjointed and incremental (see **Chapter 2**).

There are several reasons for the problems with policymaking about medical services and technology. First, the state legislation that has controlled the activities of doctors has been concerned primarily with the registration of individual doctors and the control of their professional behaviour when this might constitute a threat to the welfare of patients or the reputation of the profession. With a few exceptions, the objectives of the legislation has remained unchanged since it was first enacted in the 19th century. It was not designed to deal with the complexities of medical practice as it has evolved in recent years. In particular, the legislation did not consider the possibility that forms of medical-practice organisation such as entrepreneurial medicine might develop, which needed regulation because of their scope in removing the ethical constraints on overservicing and dubious financial practices.

Second, the incentives for the states to introduce additional legislation were limited because the financial implications of further overservicing, apart from public-hospital-based activities, are borne by the Commonwealth. This did not rule out the possibility of more comprehensive state legislation but it meant that such legislation was unlikely to be given high priority by the states.

Third, a further constraint on legislative and organisational initiatives is the reluctance of governments to seek to implement further controls on the medical profession when significant elements in the profession may be opposed to these developments. The ability of doctors to be effective politically has been stressed repeatedly in this book. In the aftermath of the doctors' dispute of the mid-1980s, there has been an increased reluctance of both Commonwealth and state governments, Labor and Coalition, to become embroiled in a further major conflict.

In these circumstances, there is a strong temptation for governments to implement measures such as reductions in fees for pathology items and after-hours services, and agreements to cap total outlays for pathology and imaging. Such measures provide temporary relief from the cost pressures and are not seen as sufficiently threatening by most doctors to generate a major conflict. However, they do not address the underlying structural problems of the system.

The attempt to shift the balance of funding from fee-for-service to non-volume-related grants for general practice of the general practice strategy might be cited as a counter example. However, even the greatly expanded funding envisaged in the original Better Practice 1994–95 budget proposals of $200 million by the financial year 2000–01 would have represented less than 10 per cent of Medicare fee-for-service benefit payments in that year. We noted in table 7.1 that the item 'enhanced primary care', in which non-volume-related GP services are concentrated, was associated with Medicare benefits of $815 million in 2012–13, representing about 4.7 per cent of all benefits payments in that year. We noted also the comment by Jackson (2013) that Australia lags behind a number of other countries in developing non-volume-related payments for primary care doctors.

Fourth, the commitment to deregulation and privatisation in many areas of the economy in some measure has eroded the credibility of those who argue for additional controls over private practice and technology. Policy advisers and ministers who wish to promote interventionist policies need to convince sceptical colleagues that the 'market' cannot solve the problems and that tangible financial or other benefits will flow from the proposed initiatives.

It is unclear at present whether the global financial crisis of the late 2000s, and the profound questioning of the self-regulating properties of free markets that has ensued, will impinge on government policymaking in health services, including the critical issue of comprehensive assessment of existing technologies such as surgical interventions.

SUMMARY AND CONCLUSION

In the past, the division in responsibilities between the states, which possess the legislative and administrative means to control medical practice, and the Commonwealth, which bears a major part of the financial impact of the problems associated with this practice, has been perceived as an important obstacle to health policy reform. However, the general practice policy initiatives of the 1990s, based primarily on Commonwealth control over the medical benefits fee schedule and provider numbers, and the government's ability to fund access and quality-related projects, indicated that the Commonwealth has the capacity to act decisively in this area. How far it is prepared to exploit this potential, and the outcomes, is still an open question at present in the case of the attempted reforms of general practice.

With regard to medical technology, the Commonwealth, with the assistance of the states, is well placed to control the spread of high-cost items because of health insurance arrangements and the control of capital expenditure in public hospitals by the states. If no medical benefit is payable for a service produced by a technology, it is not feasible for the private sector to introduce it, at least in significant numbers, as demonstrated initially in the case of MRI. In any case, the Commonwealth can control or ban their importation, a strategy it has recently deployed to enable the evaluation of the quality of certain medical appliances before their use here.

It is quite another matter, however, whether the Commonwealth can resist the pressures that clinicians and equipment manufacturers bring to bear when an allegedly beneficial technology is being denied to the community. This has been the upshot of the MRI issue, whereby pressures from private radiologists, together with increased referrals to the public sector facilities, led to the decision to pay Medicare benefits for MRI procedures. It is extremely difficult, moreover, to prevent money raised by a charitable organisation, often at the instigation of hospital medical staff, from being used to acquire expensive items of equipment, irrespective of the appropriateness of the use of the technology (Short 1989). The need for new policymaking strategies concerning medical technology will be explored further in **Chapter 10**.

One outcome of these concerns has been the rapid development of the evidence-based medicine movement (Sackett, Richardson & Rosenbery Ward Haynes 1997). This movement has emphasised the application of randomised controlled trials to assess the efficacy and effectiveness of medical interventions. The regular production and dissemination of the results of these trials, and other relevant information drawn from academic literature, has also been a feature of the movement. The establishment by governments of centres such as the NHS Centre for Evidence-based Medicine at Oxford University, the Australasian Cochrane Centre at Monash University in Melbourne and other related centres in Australia has been designed to further the evidence-based medicine approach.

However, in reviewing the Cochrane studies of the surgical and related procedures discussed in this chapter, we were surprised to find that the usual conclusions derived from the available evidence about the effectiveness and efficiency of the interventions are that more and improved studies should be undertaken. It would seem that the evidence-based medicine movement, despite all it has promised, remains a work in progress.

The pursuit of the issues of fraud and overservicing was not a feature of the policies of the Coalition government during its period of office from 1996 to 2007. This is hardly surprising in light of the links between organised medicine and the Coalition parties, which we discussed in **Chapter 3**. Recent initiatives in this area of the Rudd and Gillard governments are discussed in **Chapter 10**, as well as their likely future, following the return to government of the Coalition parties in 2013.

FURTHER READING

We have already referred to the provocative book by Nortin Hadler, MD, *Worried Sick: A Prescription for Health in an Overtreated America* (University of North Carolina Press, 2008). In light of the data we have presented in this chapter about similar or higher rates of performance of some common surgical procedures in Australia, we are inclined to wonder what a comprehensive study of the kind Hadler has undertaken would reveal here.

Another book from the United States with a related theme is that of John Geyman, MD, entitled *The Corrosion of Medicine: Can the Profession Reclaim its Moral Legacy?* (Common Courage Press, 2008). Geyman's special focus is on corporatisation and the increased entrepreneurism of medical practice in the United States and its implications for the traditional moral role of the profession.

DISCUSSION QUESTIONS

1 Do you agree or disagree with the proposition that the rate of provision of some high-volume surgical procedures is a problem in Australia? Summarise the arguments and evidence supporting your position.
2 If a problem is perceived to exist about overservicing, what explanations can you offer for the failure of successive governments to take more action?
3 What is technology and what are the issues associated with its assessment?
4 What are the implications of the information presented in this chapter showing that specialist medical practitioners may earn on average at least twice the incomes of their GP colleagues? If this is seen as a problem, what measures might be implemented by governments to influence the situation.

8

Public health

Health departments in Australia invariably claim to be making increasingly significant commitments to public health in terms of both financial and organisational support. There are two main reasons for the increasing popularity of disease prevention and health promotion on the health policy agendas of Commonwealth and state and territory governments over the past three decades. The first reason stems from the fact that the therapeutic approach to health problems may be subject to the law of diminishing returns; that is, increased resources devoted to treatment produce progressively smaller increases in health status.

The second reason stems from the limitations of clinical medicine in dealing with the 'diseases of affluence', such as coronary heart disease, stroke, lung cancer and diabetes—diseases closely related to factors such as stressful living, tobacco smoking, diet, lack of exercise and environmental factors. While Australians can expect to live longer than in past generations, many people suffer from avoidable ill health because of the unhealthy nature of many modern environments, behaviours and health beliefs.

Disease prevention and health promotion

The terms 'disease prevention' and 'health promotion' are rarely defined explicitly and often used interchangeably. Both terms are encompassed in the dynamic term 'public health', which has been defined as an 'organised response by society to protect and promote health and to prevent illness, injury and disability' (National Public Health Partnership 1998). Public health is public in three senses of the word: for the public, by the public and in the public interest (Lin & King 2000).

Although there is considerable overlap between the terms 'health promotion' and 'disease prevention', health promotion includes wider strategies designed to augment health status in general rather than to prevent particular diseases.

> The term 'health promotion' has come to refer to a movement which gathered momentum in the 1980s. The movement is a radical one which challenges the medicalisation of health, stresses its social and economic aspects, and portrays health as having a central place in a flourishing life.
>
> Downie, Fyfe & Tannahill (1990, p. 1)

Additionally, each term implies a different relationship between health service providers and consumers. Preventative activities tend to be carried out by health professionals on particular clients or target groups. In contrast, health promotion engages individuals and groups in understanding and nurturing their own health (Milio 1988): 'Health promotion works with people not on them' (Brown & Szoke 1988, p. 37).

The World Health Organization (WHO) provided the inspiration for much of the emphasis on health promotion in Australia. In 1977, the 30th World Assembly of WHO decided that the main social goal of governments and WHO should be for all citizens of the world to attain a level of health permitting them to lead socially and economically productive lives. The International Conference on Primary Health Care, meeting in Alma-Ata in the former Soviet Union in 1978, called 'for urgent and effective national and international action to develop and implement primary health care throughout the world and particularly in developing countries' (WHO 1978, p. 6).

In the Declaration of Alma-Ata, the term 'primary health care' is used in two interrelated ways. It refers to a level of service provision: to essential health care that is made available in the community close to where people live and work. Primary health care is also a health care policy approach that seeks to extend health care beyond therapeutic care to health promotion; it is given low, although increasing, priority in our present illness-oriented health care system (Baum, Lennie & Fry 1992). Primary health care as a health care policy approach involves four basic principles: collaborative networking, consumer and community participation, balancing health care priorities between immediate and long-term needs, and partnership with the secondary and tertiary sectors (National Centre for Epidemiology and Population Health 1992). This broader meaning of the term links the provision of primary health care services with the objective of reorienting the health system towards health promotion rather than the treatment of disease (WHO 1986).

Australia was a signatory to the Health for All by the Year 2000 agreement when a global strategy for achieving this goal was adopted by member nations of the WHO in 1981. The Commonwealth Department of Health (1987b, p. 14) acknowledged that 'such an immense task cannot be achieved by governments alone'. Health promotion on this scale would only be successful if governments are joined by health professionals, businesses and communities in working together towards attainment of this social goal. The Commonwealth also acknowledged that empowerment of individuals and community groups to help themselves achieve better health through community development activities must accompany improve-ments in primary health care services, appropriate health professional education and development of relevant health information systems. Even 'health', in the narrow physical sense, cannot be separated from access to employment, income maintenance, housing and a healthy environment. Australia's commitment to the global strategy Health for All by the Year 2000 produced several important initiatives.

In March 1985, the then Commonwealth minister for health, Dr Neal Blewett, established the Better Health Commission with the aim of changing the basic direction of health policy in Australia from illness treatment to prevention. In May 1985, the Commonwealth Department of Health produced a draft plan, Advancing Australia's Health, to provide the Better Health Commission with material to assist its members in conducting their public inquiry. This influential document identified health goals and priority areas in line with the principles of strategic planning. The main health priority areas identified by the department were heart disease, injury, cancer and infectious disease (Commonwealth Department of Health 1985b).

Looking Forward to Better Health, the three-volume report of the Better Health Commission (1986a, 1986b, 1986c), specified that if 'the prevention of illness is to become a real rather than token commitment' then a level of fiscal commitment that involved federal agreements and legislative amendments would be required (1986a, p. ix). It also recommended that a new and independent body be established to provide leadership for better health and to act as a focus for health promotion and illness prevention. In light of its deliberations and in response to the evidence received, the Better Health Commission established taskforces to investigate three principal lifestyle-related causes of death and illness in the community: heart disease, nutrition and injury.

A Health Targets and Implementation ('Health for All') Committee was established, and its *Health for All Australians* report was the first national attempt to compile goals and targets for 'increasing the health status of all Australians and decreasing the inequalities in health status between population subgroups' (Health Targets and Implementation [Health for All] Committee 1988, p. 4). The priorities for action identified by the Health for All committee were nutrition, blood pressure (heart disease), the health of older people, injury prevention and cancer prevention. The original set of 20 goals and 65 targets was revised and refined in a subsequent report, *Goals and Targets for Australia's Health in the Year 2000 and Beyond* (Nutbeam et al. 1993). In its attempt to reorient Australia's health system to one focused more on health outcomes, the Australian Health Ministers' Advisory Council determined that a coordinated national effort in a selected range of areas offered the most potential for gain. The priority areas chosen for consideration were spelt out in the *Better Health Outcomes for Australians* report: heart disease, cancer, injury and mental health (Commonwealth Department of Human Services and Health 1994).

Further development of the strategic planning approach towards health promotion and disease prevention culminated in the national health priority areas (NHPA) initiative endorsed by Australian health ministers in 1996. The health ministers agreed to five national health priority areas—cardiovascular health, cancer control, injury prevention and control, mental health and diabetes mellitus—with a national report on each priority area to be prepared every two years. The first report was released in 1997 (AIHW & Commonwealth Department of Health and Family Services 1997). The national health priority areas initiative drew on expert advice from the National Health and Medical Research Council (NHMRC), the Australian Institute of Health and Welfare (AIHW), non-government organisations, clinicians and consumers. The initiative attempted to reduce the burden of illness with 'holistic' strategies that encompass the continuum of clinical care from prevention through to treatment and rehabilitation.

It is noteworthy that the five national health priority areas identified by the Australian health ministers in 1996 include the three core health problems identified by officers from the Commonwealth Department of Health in May 1985: heart disease, injury and cancer. During this 11-year period, policymakers and researchers inside and outside the Commonwealth health authority expended much epidemiological and other effort on preparing and publishing reports. Heart disease, cancer and injury are still central to the agenda. Other health problems, such as mental health and diabetes, were added to or removed from the list by ministers of health and others over the years. In retrospect, perhaps too much energy was expended on public health reporting rather than public health activity.

In 2007, the list of national health priority areas was increased to eight: arthritis and musculoskeletal conditions, asthma, cancer control, cardiovascular health, diabetes mellitus, injury prevention and control, mental health and obesity (ABS 2009a). It appears that over the years, the big three issues of public health concern remain heart disease, cancer and injury. There would appear to be a requirement to spend more time and energy on making progress with these three priority areas and a little less energy in defining and measuring the priorities for action on the public health agenda. We note also that until the election of the Rudd Government in 2007, most public health attention focused on attempting to increase the health status of all Australians, rather than decreasing inequalities in health status between population subgroups.

The fact is that public health continues to have a low priority when it comes to resource allocation. Figures on resource allocation completed for the National Public Health Partnership reveal that

> the proportion of total health expenditures devoted to public health and community health services *combined* was only marginally higher in 1995–96 than nearly 30 years earlier. The recorded increase (0.6 per cent) was entirely due to growth in the 'community health' category, a classification which includes some public health activities but also a range of personal care services.
>
> Deeble (1999, pp. 4–5)

In the financial years 1999–2000 and 2005–06, the public health proportion of total health expenditure remained basically constant at approximately 1.8 per cent to 1.9 per cent. As **Chapter 1** shows, the proportion of recurrent health expenditure in 2011–12 devoted to public health was a mere 1.7 per cent (AIHW 2013b). This confirms the continued low priority given to resource allocation for public health issues.

The Rudd Government included prevention along with public hospitals in the National Healthcare Agreements (2008–2013) with the states. This included better integration of preventative health care in the broader health system. The government also established the Australian National Preventive Health Agency (ANPHA) in 2011 with the aim of addressing the rising prevalence of lifestyle-related chronic diseases and encouraging healthy lifestyles, with a focus on alcohol, tobacco and obesity prevention. While the agency aimed to provide policy leadership and foster partnerships between governments, industries, community health promotion organisations and primary health care providers, progress was too easily stymied by industry bodies, such as the Australian Food and Grocery Council, and their lobbying efforts (Moodie et al. 2013).

For statistical purposes public health activities are defined as eight types of activities undertaken or funded by federal and state health departments that address issues related to populations, rather than individuals. These activities comprise:

- communicable disease control
- selected health promotion
- organised immunisation
- environmental health
- food standards and hygiene
- breast cancer, cervical and bowel cancer screening programs
- prevention of hazardous and harmful drug use
- public health research.

We have reliable expenditure data on these defined public health activities for the period specified in table 8.1, the decade up to 2011, as data were compiled on a consistent basis by all governments using a single data-collection protocol developed through the National Public Health Expenditure Project. Prior to June 2009, these data were provided under the auspices of the Public Health Outcome Funding Agreements. These agreements ceased on 30 June 2009 as federal government funding for public health programs was included within the specific purpose payments associated with the National Healthcare Agreement and through National Partnership payments. This dedicated public-health-activity expenditure reporting was halted in 2011, pending a review of the scope and content of the collection. As a result, subsequent public health expenditures are reported as total public health expenditure rather than as specific types of public health activities.

We can see that government expenditure on public health activities from 2000–01 to 2010–11 increased each year by about 4 per cent. All activities, with the exception of environmental health and public health research, showed real increases in expenditure, with the highest average annual growth rates evident for expenditure on prevention of hazardous and harmful drug use, organised immunisation and selected health promotion activities. Much of the growth in expenditure on organised immunisation resulted from costs associated with the implementation of the human papillomavirus (HPV) vaccination program.

Table 8.1 Total government expenditure on public health activities, constant prices, by activity, 2000–01 to 2010–11 ($ million)

Public health activity categories	2000–01	2002–03	2004–05	2006–07	2008–09	2010–11	Average annual growth rate, 2000–01 to 2010–11
Communicable disease control	223.5	258.8	282.0	284.2	299.7	294.4	1.8%
Selected health promotion	280.5	285.8	273.0	307.2	455.3	425.8	3.2%
Organised immunisation	268.6	346.2	413.4	485.3	661.1	490.0	6.0%
Environmental health	91.8	91.9	98.3	97.1	105.8	74.2	-2.5%
Food standards and hygiene	51.5	46.5	41.5	40.0	40.9	54.2	1.5%
Breast and cervical cancer screening programs[a]	187.7	185.9	225.6	265.1	338.0	253.0	2.8%
Prevention of hazardous and harmful drug use	143.9	157.4	199.9	207.4	273.8	283.7	7.1%
Public health research[b]	69.3	92.3	101.2	134.0	151.2	0.2	-44.7%
Public Health Outcome Funding Agreements administration[c]	0.3	0.3	0.3	—	—	—	—
Public health n.f.d[d]	—	—	—	—	—	71.9	—
Total	1250.0	1411.2	1535.4	1639.7	2274.2	1947.4	3.8

Notes

Data includes regulatory expenditures by the Therapeutic Goods Administration, Office of the Gene Technology Regulator and National Industrial Chemicals Notification and Assessment Scheme; constant price public health expenditure for 2000–01 to 2008–09 is expressed in terms of 2008–09 prices and cannot be compared with other tables in this report; data not reported for 2009–10; 2009–10 excluded from average annual growth rate calculations.

(a) Includes bowel cancer screening in 2006–07, 2007–08 and 2008–09

(b) For 2010–11, most expenditure on public health research has been reclassified as health research.

(c) In previous reports, direct expenditure incurred by the Australian Government in administering the PHOFAs was reported separately as it could not be specifically allocated to any of the core public health activity categories. For 2006–07, 2007–08 and 2008–09, this expenditure was treated as corporate overhead expenditure and apportioned across all categories.

(d) The government health expenditure national minimum data sets were introduced to this category in 2010–11; these had not been previously reported.

Source: Data based on table 4.21 in Australian Institute of Health and Welfare 2012d, *Health expenditure Australia 2010–11*, Health and Welfare expenditure series no. 47, cat. no. HWE 56, AIHW, Canberra, p. 75

Scope for disease prevention and health promotion

This chapter focuses on the analysis of three main public health approaches—the medical approach, the lifestyle strategy and the new public health perspective—and assesses the relative contributions that each is likely to make to improvements in the health of Australians.

In Australia and other developed countries, the most common diseases are chronic rather than acute. Instead of infectious diseases causing 30 to 40 per cent of mortality, as they did at the beginning of the 20th century, our mortality and morbidity patterns are dominated by chronic conditions. The most important causes of death in Australia are the so-called 'diseases of affluence'.

Australia's NHPAs are diseases and conditions that are given focused attention because of their significant contribution to the burden of illness and injury in the Australian community. The nine priority areas are arthritis and musculoskeletal conditions, asthma, cancer control, cardiovascular health, diabetes mellitus, injury prevention and control, mental health, obesity and dementia. In 2009, the leading causes of death were coronary heart disease for both males and females, followed by lung cancer for males and stroke for females (see figure 8.1) (AIHW, 2012a).

The leading causes of death in Australia are generally chronic conditions (AIHW 2012a). In 2009, the five major causes of death were coronary heart disease, lung cancer, stroke, dementia and Alzheimer's disease, and chronic lower respiratory diseases. Ischaemic heart disease, stroke and lung cancer remain the three leading causes of death over the last decade. Deaths due to dementia and Alzheimer's disease moved from the seventh leading cause in 1998 to the fourth leading cause in 2007 (ABS 2009a). Dementia was added to the NHPAs in 2012 due to growing recognition that dementia will be a major cause of disability for Australians in the future. The predicted rise in dementia prevalence can be attributed to the increasing longevity and ageing population. The growing evidence also indicates that medical conditions may increase the risk of dementia, while a healthy lifestyle may reduce the risk.

In 2012, 120 710 new cases of cancer were estimated to have been diagnosed in Australia and, it has remained the major underlying cause of death (the disease or injury that initiated the train of morbid events leading directly to death). The most commonly diagnosed cancers in 2012 were prostate cancer, bowel cancer, breast cancer, melanoma of the skin and lung cancer (AIHW 2012a). A total of 42 844 people died from cancer in 2010 in Australia, making it the second-most common cause of death. The ratio of deaths caused by cancer by gender was male 24 328 to female 18 516 (AIHW 2012).

If we turn to national cancer screening programs, the Coalition established the National Bowel Cancer Screening Program in 2006 for people at 50, 55, 60 and 65 years of age. In 2013, the Abbott Government promised to bring forward the implementation of biennial bowel cancer screening to encourage early detection for at-risk groups. The Coalition committed to invest over $46 million from 2015–2020

Figure 8.1 Trends in selected leading causes of death by sex, 1979–2009

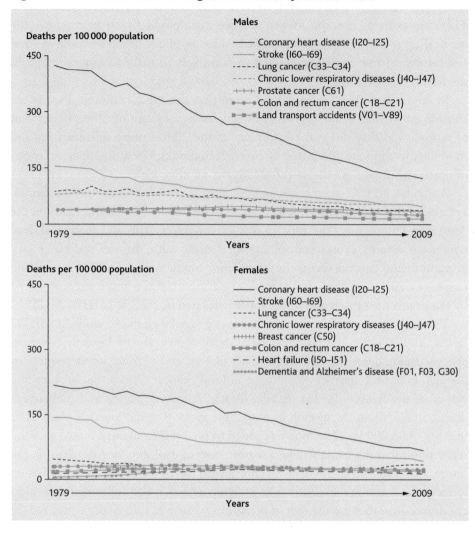

Notes:
(a) Causes selected to reflect the leading causes of death, by sex, from 1979-2009.
1. Leading causes groupings based on Becker, Silvi, Ma Fat et al. 2006.
2. Leading causes are determined by number of deaths by sex, each year. Causes that were consistently among the five leading causes of death by sex every year from 1979–2009 are for men: coronary heart disease, stroke, lung cancer and chronic lower respiratory diseases; and, for women: coronary heart disease and stroke. The remaining causes were among the five leading causes of death by sex for anyone of the years from 1979 to 2009.
3. Rates are age-standardised to the Australian population at 30 June 2001.

Source: Based on figure 2.20 in Australian Institute of Health and Welfare 2012a, *Australia's health 2012*, Australia's health series no. 13, cat. no. AUS 156, AIHW, Canberra, p. 94

for the implementation of the screening program for people aged between 50 and 74 years (Loughnane 2013, p. 14).

We turn now to consider the scope for disease prevention and health promotion in relation to chronic conditions. Results from the 2007–08 national health survey indicated that 77 per cent of the population reported having a long-term or chronic condition. Eyesight conditions remained the most commonly reported long-term disorders (52 per cent). Other commonly reported long-term conditions were arthritis (15 per cent), hay fever (15 per cent), asthma (10 per cent) and hypertensive disease (9 per cent) (ABS 2009).

The big cost groupings in health are cardiovascular diseases, cancer, nervous system disorders, musculoskeletal diseases, injuries, respiratory diseases, mental disorders and oral health. In 2001, the recurrent health expenditure for these groupings totalled approximately $50.1 billion (AIHW 2005).

The main evidence regarding the potential scope for prevention comes from the existence of differences in disease prevalence between different socioeconomic groups, sexes and ethnic groups. Although some commentators contend that the lowest levels of disease prevalence should be the objective of policymakers, more pragmatic observers realise that disease prevention is not the only or indeed the ultimate goal of public policy in Australia, or of the community in general. Health is 'a resource for everyday life, not the objective of living' (WHO 1986, p. 2). Although health is a highly valued social goal, it still has to compete with other policy goals, such as economic growth and the protection of civil liberties. Thus, it would be healthier for all Australians if a blanket speed limit of 80 kilometres per hour were applied to our roads. However, legislation of this kind would not be acceptable to the community. Motor vehicle manufacturers and oil companies would probably also object strongly to such a proposal.

Three approaches to public health

Examination of the politics of public health reveals that each strategy assigns responsibility for disease prevention to certain people and excuses others. The medical approach, the lifestyle approach and the new public health are the three most common perspectives on disease prevention and health promotion. These approaches are depicted in table 8.2 below. The *medical approach* locates the causes of disease within biology and places primary responsibility for prevention on the medical profession (Tesh 1981, 1988).

Lifestyle theory contends that the prevalent diseases of modern industrialised societies such as Australia are largely attributable to the way each individual chooses to live—how we work, eat, exercise and so on. Lifestyle, in this context, refers to the decisions that each individual makes in their daily life about their own individual behaviour. Although it is acknowledged that lifestyle choices are not always voluntary, the lifestyle approach implies that the responsibility for ill health rests primarily on the shoulders of individuals (Hetzel & McMichael 1987). It relies on action from health educators and health practitioners (including doctors).

The third perspective, the *new public health approach*, locates the aetiology of disease within the occupational and environmental context. It points to factors such as environmental pollution, unsafe and unhealthy working conditions, and the manufacture and marketing of unhealthy products such as tobacco and alcohol as among the major causes of disease (Doyal & Pennell 1983). This approach places a large part of the responsibility for ill health on the owners and managers of industry, such as tobacco growers and cigarette manufacturers. It calls for action on the part of governments and private and community organisations to create a healthier environment. In the remaining parts of this chapter, the current prospects for disease prevention and health promotion in Australia will be assessed within the framework of these alternative approaches.

Table 8.2   Approaches to disease prevention and health promotion

Approach	Responsible agent	Policy example
Medical	Doctors	Human papillomavirus vaccination
Lifestyle	Health educators and practitioners	Quitline
New public health	Governments, private and community organisations	National HIV/AIDS Strategy

The medical approach

The medical profession's approach to disease prevention is usually defined in terms of primary, secondary and tertiary prevention. Primary prevention consists of anticipating when diseases might strike and taking steps to prevent their occurrence. Vaccinations and immunisation for whooping cough, tetanus and human papillomavirus (HPV) fall into this category.

Secondary prevention entails intervening in the disease causality chain at an early stage when the victim may not be aware of its presence (Russell 1986). Important contemporary examples of effective secondary prevention in Australia include screening for cervical cancer, mammography screening for the early detection of breast cancer, and the prenatal diagnosis of chromosomal abnormalities leading to conditions such as Down syndrome.

Tertiary prevention is concerned with minimising the effects arising from existing disease or injury. It includes maintaining people with chronic health problems at an optimum level of independence and functioning. This type of prevention is a well-established part of health services in Australia; for example, in the prescription of anti-hypertensive drugs for persons at risk of a cerebrovascular accident (stroke). In the strategy of preventative medicine, the aim is to identify and help a vulnerable minority of individuals (Rose 1992).

The role of the medical practitioner as an agent of disease prevention has advantages and disadvantages (Sanson-Fisher et al. 1986). There are several reasons why medical practitioners may function as efficient agents of disease prevention. First, general practitioners are accessible to a significant proportion of the Australian community. About 82 per cent of the population consults a GP at least once a year (Deeble 1991). Second, people who visit doctors are generally representative of the population as a whole. Third, both patients and doctors see the doctor as an appropriate person to give advice on prevention. Fourth, patients visiting medical practitioners are likely to be responsive to such advice. Fifth, some evidence suggests that doctors can be effective in persuading patients to change unhealthy habits. Some areas in which GPs are potentially useful as agents of disease prevention include hypertension control, cervical cancer screening and immunisation. In addition, much attention has been devoted to the role of the GP in changing smoking and drinking behaviour. One such program was 'Smokescreen', a smoking cessation program designed specifically for use in general practice (Richmond et al. 1986). The Royal Australian College of General Practitioners (RACGP) provides useful online clinical resources, with ease of access to tools such as the Smoking Cessation Guidelines, as additional support to GPs and their involvement in such programs (Royal Australian College of General Practitioners 2007).

While both patients and doctors believe that prevention is an important and integral part of the doctor's responsibility, many doctors are not aware of the habits of the majority of their patients, even in the key areas of smoking behaviour and alcohol consumption (Sanson-Fisher et al. 1986). The reasons that may account for an absence of preventative effort include a lack of knowledge and skill in preventative medicine, a lack of appropriate and effective preventative measures and a lack of incentives for medical practitioners to undertake preventative measures. While the first two reasons are relatively self-evident and have their solutions in more prevention-oriented medical education and research, the third reason is crucial to this analysis and requires further examination.

It has been suggested that medical practitioners do not realise their preventative potential because they do not receive adequate encouragement or rewards from patients, medical colleagues or health insurance arrangements for carrying out preventative medicine (Sanson-Fisher et al. 1986). The disincentives are threefold. First, doctors may be concerned that prevention will result in a potential loss of patients. Patients may resent being told to stop smoking when they attend the doctor for a medical certificate and they may be tempted to see a different doctor. In addition, although there is evidence that patients think it appropriate that doctors provide preventative information, there is little research that reveals how patients react when doctors do intervene.

The second significant disincentive derives from lack of support from medical colleagues, which may, in part, derive from the curative emphasis in medical education. In medical practice, preventative activities are not perceived as being of high status.

The third obstacle to prevention is probably the most important currently. Doctors do not engage in preventative medicine on any significant scale because it is not financially advantageous to do so. The current fee-for-service system of paying, discussed at greater length in **Chapter 10**, encourages short consultations rather than longer consultations necessary for preventative counselling and education. Doctors working on a fee-for-service basis earn their income by treating or testing patients. Their role in the existing health care system is principally to react to illness, not to prevent it. Because most consultations carried out solely for preventative health purposes are not reimbursed under the current schedule of medical fees, largely because of the scope for overservicing, there are strong barriers to providing preventative services. As we indicated in **Chapter 7**, recent policy changes affecting general practice represent an attempt to make GPs more concerned with promoting health.

The lifestyle approach

For Victor Fuchs (1974), an influential health economist in the United States, lifestyle and personal behaviour are the major determinants of 'who shall live' in wealthy industrialised countries such as the United States and Australia. His major contention is that the connection between health status and medical care is not nearly as direct or immediate as most people believe. He further claims that medical care makes little impact on health differences between countries, and between different regions, sexes and socioeconomic groups. In Australia, this lifestyle emphasis was seen most clearly in the work of the Better Health Commission (1986a, 1986c). The commission's findings emphasised the importance of individual lifestyle in the chronic diseases that constitute the principal disease burden in Australia today, and concentrated on three health problems directly related to individual lifestyle: cardiovascular disease, nutrition and injury. Although these three areas were singled out for attention and taskforces were established on each one, the commission acknowledged that smoking was the leading cause of preventable illness and death.

Given that the Better Health Commission acknowledged that health promotion extends beyond the health care system, it is perhaps surprising that it concluded that individual lifestyle modification offered the greatest opportunities for disease prevention. The commission posited that smoking, diet, alcohol and physical activity were particularly important. Commentators have been critical of the emphasis on individual lifestyle because they contend that it is often accompanied by the ideology of 'victim blaming', which assigns responsibility to individuals for their illnesses (Crawford 1977; Taylor 1979). Many policy analysts reject this approach because it diverts attention from the social causes of disease in the structure of society (Labonte 1992). The lifestyle or behavioural strategy is based on an 'unrealistic behavioural model', according to Crawford (1977), because it ignores what is known about human behaviour and minimises the importance of factors such as the mass communications media that are outside the individual's control. The major limitation of the lifestyle strategy is that it presumes the actions of individuals to be based on largely rational decisions involving freedom of choice. It fails to take account of the social, political and economic forces that shape and limit individual choices.

The mass media play a significant role in shaping community attitudes and behaviour. Since the average Australian spends six to eight hours daily receiving information through print, broadcasting and the internet, it would be difficult to overestimate the media's impact on our perceptions of health and lifestyle.

The media has played a particularly important role in perpetuating demand for our principal drugs of addiction: tobacco, alcohol and pharmaceuticals (Stewart 1979). Although the media relies on health experts for information about health and lifestyle, the advertising industry spends a considerable amount of money to mould public perceptions. For example, beer manufacturers feature sporting heroes in promotional material because it creates an association in the public imagination between sporting success, health and beer.

Pharmaceutical companies are perhaps the most sophisticated players in the medical marketplace (Moynihan 1998). Media management is just one of the strategies they use in promoting their latest drugs and products. The public relations arms of pharmaceutical companies produce company-sponsored video news releases that feature media-friendly doctors and patients. These are fed via satellite directly into newsrooms, ready to be run as broadcast news. The business of medicine includes the sponsorship of scientific conferences, educational meetings, specialist advisory groups and patient foundations.

The public are not passive recipients of such advertising messages, however, partly because they receive messages from other sources as well. While we are confronted with the advertisers' socially constructed reality, we are also confronted with television programs such as *Grey's Anatomy* and magazines such as the *Australian Women's Weekly*, which project different perspectives on life and health. Other sources of information include the internet where 'do-it-yourself diagnosis' websites exist, allowing the public to enter symptoms or read about symptoms and diseases, while a generic diagnosis (or medical suggestions, including treatment options) is formulated for the user. Ultimately, public perceptions reflect the relative influence of these 'multiple realities' (Edelman 1977; Petersen & Lupton 1996; Showalter 1997; Windschuttle 1984).

Concrete socioeconomic factors such as education, income and occupation have a more significant impact on the health of Australians than individual choice. Sociologists emphasise that differences in lifestyle are not distributed randomly within the community (Lupton & Najman 1995; Short 1999). Obesity exhibits a social gradient; Australian states with the lowest levels of educational attainment, such as Queensland, experience the highest rates of obesity (Short 2004). Lifestyle variations are systematically patterned, with wealthy persons, Anglo-Australians, married people and members of religions such as the Seventh-day Adventist Church enjoying significant health advantages (Najman 1988). It is not an accident that those on lower incomes bear a disproportionate amount of the burden of non-fatal disease and have higher mortality rates, because they are 'least able to make informed choices and have the least power to control their own lives' (Taylor 1979, p. 237). Data available through the Social Health Atlas of Australia (Glover & Woollacott 1992) confirm the links between socioeconomic status and health: strokes, heart disease, lung cancer, hypertension, skin diseases and infectious diseases are more prevalent in lower income areas.

We should emphasise, however, that critics of the lifestyle approach do not condemn health education and lifestyle strategies per se. Rather, lifestyle strategies are most likely to succeed with people who bear the lowest burden of ill health and who have the greatest freedom to choose. Because people in the higher income groups have greater freedom to implement lifestyle changes in line with advice and information regarding diet and exercise, they are more likely to benefit from health education than are poorer people. Indeed, government emphasis on lifestyle strategy is likely to increase the disparity in levels of health between the rich and the poor (Holtzman 1979). This finding is particularly relevant for the state and territory health authority branches responsible for providing education and health promotion services (Harris, Sainsbury & Nutbeam 1999; Nutbeam 2008). Health education by itself is insufficient, as Taylor (1979, p. 240) argues:

> Informing people of the dangers of smoking is of little use while they are bombarded by propaganda to the contrary. Encouraging healthy dietary patterns is insufficient if healthy food is expensive, difficult to obtain and unhealthy eating patterns are promoted by a profit-oriented food industry. Asking people to drive carefully has little effect when they are provided with excessively powerful cars and motor-bikes whose gear ratios are specifically designed for rapid acceleration and while fast, reckless driving is glorified daily by the media (particularly television).

Health education is usually equated with lifestyle education, which provides information about one's body and how to look after it through diet, exercise and so on. However, there are two other types of health education that are less well known. The second provides information and advice about health services and how to utilise them. The third type provides information about policies, structures and processes in the wider environment that influence health (Draper et al. 1980). The lifestyle strategy is, therefore, only one strand within the broader field of health education. While the second type of health education is becoming more popular, the third type tends to be neglected because such interventions are unlikely to attract support from powerful vested interests and because, in part, of the naive attitude which 'denies that health has anything to do with politics' (Downie, Fyfe & Tannahill 1990, p. 29).

Anti-smoking Quit for Life campaigns were organised in several Australian states in the early 1980s (National Health Strategy 1993b, p. 101). The Sydney Quit for Life media-based campaign was funded largely by the NSW Department of Health. During 1983, the Quit Centre offered smokers a choice of six standard anti-smoking quit kits and a range of stop-smoking programs. Educational materials were also provided through telephone hotlines, shopping centres and other outlets. Evaluation of the program indicated that there were 83 000 fewer smokers in Sydney in the year following the campaign than in the previous year (Dwyer et al. 1986). The Sydney Quit for Life campaign is a good example of a lifestyle campaign that was implemented and evaluated with considerable rigour and success. These campaigns were so successful that the 'Quitline' still functions in each state and territory, providing free quit packs and over-the-telephone counselling assistance.

A further limitation of the lifestyle strategy emerges when it is assessed in economic terms; that is, when we ask whether the future benefits from lifestyle strategies justify present-day costs (Evans 1984). To answer this question it is useful to consider explicitly the steps in the lifestyle argument that lead from exhortation to implementation. It is frequently suggested, for example, that lifestyle programs such as physical education in schools will 'pay for themselves'. In isolating each step in the process, Evans has highlighted the number of causal links necessary to support lifestyle as a cost-reduction strategy, and the points at which it is vulnerable to criticism.

Economic evaluation of the lifestyle strategy suggests that it is not as efficient as strategies that target particular unsafe behaviours through regulation or taxation policy. For example, taxation of tobacco and alcohol appears to have a more substantial impact than an anti-smoking education program. With tobacco control, increasing taxation and the price of cigarettes appears to be the most effective public health strategy, as distinct from the medical approach and the lifestyle strategy (Collins & Lapsley 2008). Economists attribute the reduction in smoking rates to price rises. However, in **Chapter 3**, we acknowledge it is broader than the price component, which is important, but reduction is not as simple as that, as shown by the steady reduction in smoking rates rather than the link to pricing per se (see figure 8.2). Issues such as banning smoking in the workplace have played an important role. It is impossible to attribute the dramatic change that has taken place to any single factor.

It is difficult to evaluate education and lifestyle strategies generally, because education does not necessarily lead to long-term behaviour modification, and the lifestyle strategies do not necessarily lead to improved health status. Generally, it is easier to determine these links in a narrowly defined area such as drink driving because the connection between alcohol consumption and driving behaviour is well established. However, the linkages between exercise and heart disease are at best observed correlations, the causal significance of which is still uncertain. In most cases, the present state of knowledge about lifestyle and health is insufficient to establish hard and fast causal relationships.

A cynical observer might even suggest that lifestyle strategies increase rather than decrease health care expenditure because many lifestyle programs extend the scope and intensity of health care into the healthy community. Lifestyle education absorbs the energies of many in the expanding health workforce in activities that 'probably do no harm, may do some good, and offer the psychological rewards of the celebration of wellness' (Evans 1984, p. 283). This world view probably underpins the scepticism shared by many in the Abbott Government towards ANPHA. The underlying philosophy that health is an individual and parental responsibility, rather than a public good as such, is not consistent with support for the ANPHA.

The new public health approach

The new public health approach contends that the imperative of health policy, and public policy generally, should be the creation of an economy, a society and an environment conducive to the production of good health, as distinct from the production of disease (Klein 1983; South Australian Health Commission 1988; WHO 1986). The underlying logic of this strategy would require the transformation of society to be realised fully. Healthy public policies can be found in any sector of government or outside government (Pederson et al. 1988; Sylvan 1988). Healthy public policy transcends the boundaries of health departments and organisations.

In practice, this requires a close working relationship between Commonwealth, state and local governments, and between government departments and private and community organisations whose actions have an impact on health status. It calls for coordination of a wide range of policies, including health, welfare, housing and industry policies; that is, intersectoral policy collaboration. An example in Australia is the increase in lean-meat production by meat producers, a non-government policy leading to reduced fat consumption and better health for the community. A supportive 'healthy' government policy in this area might include a tax concession from the taxation department for lean-meat producers to encourage this trend. Such a policy would be a healthy public policy, even though it is not policy made directly by a health department. Intersectoralism is difficult to achieve, however, and there is often a naive belief in approaches that lie within the administrative rather than the political domain (Degeling 1995).

The term the 'new public health' is perhaps a misnomer as it was first coined during World War I. The WHO brought the term into contemporary prominence in 1986 with the Ottawa Charter for Health Promotion, subtitled 'Towards a New Public Health' (Baum 1998, p. 510).

More fundamentally, the philosophy of the new public health movement is consistent with the 1948 United Nations Declaration of Human Rights, Article 25, which states that 'Everyone has the right to a standard of living adequate for the health and well-being of himself [sic] and his family' (Asbeck 1949). The philosophy is embodied also in the Declaration of Alma-Ata (WHO 1978), in which human rights and social justice are core concerns. The Ottawa Charter (WHO 1986) reaffirmed social justice and equity as prerequisites for health, and advocacy and mediation as the processes for their achievement. The charter identified five action areas for health promotion: developing personal skills, creating supportive environments, strengthening community action, reorienting health services and building healthy public policy.

Supporters of the notion of healthy public policy emphasise that health is a fundamental human right and a sound economic investment. The Adelaide Recommendations on Healthy Public Policy (adopted at the Second International Conference on Health Promotion) in 1988 noted that trade unions, commerce and industry, academic associations and religious organisations have opportunities to act in the health interest of the community. It was suggested, therefore, that new alliances be formed to provide the impetus for health action (Commonwealth Department of Community Services and Health & WHO 1988). Four areas were singled out for action:

- supporting women's health
- developing integrated food and nutrition policies
- determining targets for reducing significantly the production, marketing and consumption of tobacco and alcohol
- developing 'new health alliances'.

The healthy public policy approach emphasises consultation and negotiation and requires strong advocates who can put health issues high on the agenda of policymakers, as illustrated by the anti-smoking movement. The Adelaide conference called for the fostering of the work of advocacy groups as a priority, in addition to helping the media to interpret complex health-related issues. This emphasis on 'new health alliances' or partnerships, especially with the private sector, featured prominently at the Fourth International Conference on Health Promotion, held in Jakarta in 1997 (WHO 1997).

The Fifth International Conference on Health Promotion, held in Mexico City in 2000, considered the resources and structures needed to develop and sustain capacity for health promotion at local, national and international levels. In 2005, the Sixth International Conference on Health Promotion was held in Bangkok, the latest in the series that began in Ottawa in 1986 and produced the Ottawa Charter on Health Promotion. Almost 20 years later, the world had changed greatly, due to the impact of globalisation, the internet, the greater moves towards private sector involvement in public health and the emphasis on a sound evidence-based approach and cost-effectiveness. From this, the new Bangkok Charter for Health Promotion was adopted to address rapidly changing global health issues. The four key commitments were to make public health:

- central to the global development agenda
- a core responsibility for all of government
- a key focus of communities and civil society
- a requirement for good corporate practice (WHO 2005).

Australian developments along new public health lines to be examined in this chapter include initiatives relating to Health for All, tobacco smoking, HIV/AIDS, drugs and occupational health and safety. We are not suggesting in this section that all these initiatives are solely new public health initiatives. For example, with the National HIV/AIDS Strategy, while the policy is consistent with the rhetoric of the new public health, considerable and increasing resources are devoted to medical treatments for people living with HIV/AIDS.

The new public health approach to key health issues

Health for all Australians

In the 1980s, the 'fiscal crisis of the state' (O'Connor 1973) was well understood by departmental officials and politicians, and apart from the provisions of the Wages and Incomes Accord—which focused mainly on Medicare—innovative and practical ideas in health policy were scarce. As a signatory to the WHO's (1981) Global Strategy for Health for All by the Year 2000, Australia was required to develop goals and targets for redressing health inequities and achieving overall improvements in health for the population.

In 1985 the then Commonwealth minister for health, Dr Neal Blewett, appointed the Better Health Commission to 'enquire into the current health status of the Australian population and recommend *national health goals, priorities and programs* to achieve significant improvements in illness prevention and health awareness' (Better Health Commission 1986a, p. xii, emphasis added). The Better Health Commission was asked to have regard to 'Australia's part in the World Health Organization's "Health for All by the Year 2000" initiative' (Better Health Commission 1986a, p. xiii).

The Commonwealth Department of Health (1985b) produced its own report, *Advancing Australia's Health*, before the Better Health Commission reported to the minister. With a strong focus on goals and epidemiologically measurable targets, the department's document symbolised the medical or epidemiological approach towards 'health for all' in the evolving public health debate (Whelan, Mohr & Short 1992).

The Better Health Commission's three-volume report (1986a, 1986b, 1986c) identified national health goals in three major areas: cardiovascular disease, nutrition and injury. It further proposed the establishment of a national body to promote health and a range of rather traditional lifestyle education strategies. The only new public health type of initiative (which was not acknowledged as such) was recognition of the relevance of community participation and advocacy. The commission recommended that 'a national community development fund be established to assist in and educate local communities about participation and advocacy projects' (Better Health Commission 1986a, p. 75). The Better Health Commission, in this context, drew attention to the proposed Consumers' Health Forum, but it did not link its proposed community development fund to the other proposed initiative.

The new public health terminology featured in the Health Targets and Implementation (Health for All) Committee's (1988) report to the Australian health ministers, entitled *Health for All Australians*. This report referred to WHO 'Health for All' principles of equity, community involvement, health promotion, intersectoral cooperation and primary health care, and ensuring appropriate infrastructure for the achievement of health goals. However, it further advanced the epidemiological goal-setting approach towards a national health promotion strategy by setting targets within a number of illness categories.

The Health for All committee, chaired by Stephen Leeder, Professor of Public Health and Community Medicine at the University of Sydney, found that major inequalities in health status continued to exist between sectors of the population according to socioeconomic class, gender and ethnicity, and that there was considerable scope for reducing the incidence and prevalence of many health problems through illness prevention and health promotion. The Australian health ministers agreed that there was a need for a national approach to health promotion and accepted the report's suggested priority areas: control of hypertension, improved nutrition, the prevention of injuries, the health of older people, the primary prevention of lung and skin cancer, and the secondary prevention of breast and cervical cancer. The Health for All committee established these priorities in the light of evidence regarding the seriousness of the problem, the feasibility of doing something now that was likely to be effective and the current lack of action. Thus, serious problems such as mental health were not included as priorities because it was not clear what needed to be done. Other major problem areas—including tobacco smoking, Aboriginal health and women's health—were excluded either because policy development and implementation were already in train or because the political or financial feasibility of tackling them was low. The committee acknowledged also that the changes suggested in the report could only occur if health were seen as a collective responsibility requiring collaboration between consumers, communities, industry and governments (Health Targets and Implementation [Health for All] Committee 1988).

In 1988, the Commonwealth allocated $39 million over a four-year period, on a cost-shared basis with the states for the National Better Health Program to be coordinated by national and state Health for All subcommittees. The program focused on supporting projects in the five areas of priority identified by the Health for All committee noted above. The evaluation of the program (Commonwealth Department of Health, Housing and Community Services 1992b) found evidence of considerable achievements by the National Better Health Program. These included progress towards developing a national food and nutrition policy; progress in implementing innovative health promotion projects, especially in the areas of nutrition and injury; and increased financial and administrative support for health promotion in most participating states and territories. Several areas of weakness were also identified, including the need for stronger policy direction and national coordination from the Commonwealth Department of Health, Housing and Community Services, and better integration of health promotion activities with mainstream health system activities.

In 1992, the National Better Health Program and the National Health Promotion Program were replaced by a newly created National Health Advancement Program. Funds of $6.1 million were allocated for major projects in the following areas: further refinement and application of national health goals and targets, incorporation of health impact assessment into a national policy on ecologically sustainable development, development of a national food and nutrition policy, and development of a coordinated injury prevention strategy.

In 1992, the Commonwealth Department of Health, Housing and Community Services commissioned Don Nutbeam, then Professor of Public Health at the University of Sydney, and colleagues to review Australia's health goals and targets and to set the health goals and targets for the 1990s. In their report, the numerous and diverse goals and targets were organised under four headings: preventable mortality and morbidity, health lifestyles and risk factors, health literacy and health skills, and healthy environments (Nutbeam et al. 1993). Of these four sections, the first two built on the previous set of goals and targets, while the last two reflected a shift towards the lifestyle and new public health approaches to health promotion. Michael Summers (1993, p. 9), from the Health Issues Centre, commented that 'it is a tremendous step forward in encouraging people to consider issues such as transport and housing, and not just doctors and hospitals, when they think about health'.

The *Medicare Agreements Act 1992* (Cth) provided for the Commonwealth and the states to agree on a new set of national health goals and targets by July 1994. The Medicare Agreements specified that the framework developed in the national health goals and targets consultancy provided an appropriate mechanism for pursuing outcome measurement and integration of the delivery of hospital and other services. The parties agreed to 'co-operate in monitoring and reporting on progress towards national health goals and targets ... [and] to actively participate in the development and implementation of health outcome indicators and measures' (Commonwealth of Australia 1992, p. 18). In 1993, the revised goals and targets (see Nutbeam et al. 1993) were subject to further consideration and refinement by the Australian health ministers, the Australian Health Ministers' Advisory Committee and the NHMRC.

At the National Health Summit in April 1993, Australia's health ministers agreed to develop a national health policy to establish national goals and targets for selected areas including cardiovascular disease, cancers, injury and mental health. The health ministers decided to develop action plans for implementation under the auspices of the Commonwealth with the involvement of the NHMRC and clinicians. This process evolved into the national health priority areas initiative that was endorsed by the Australian health ministers in 1996. As mentioned previously, the health ministers agreed to five national health priority areas: cardiovascular health, cancer control, injury prevention and control, mental health and diabetes mellitus.

There is no doubt that the many initiatives that followed in response to Australia's commitment to 'Health for All by the Year 2000'—including the Commonwealth Department of Health's (1985b) report; the Better Health Commission report, development of national health goals and targets; the National Better Health Program, revised goals and targets; and the National Health Advancement Program—have been a 'potent stimulus to the more general interest in [health] outcomes' (National Health Strategy 1993b, p. 28). There is doubt, however, about how much has been achieved in terms of developing a national strategy for the achievement of improved health outcomes and reduced inequities in health status. There is continuing tension between the proponents of different approaches towards disease prevention and health promotion, and between advocates of different priorities for action.

Since 1985 the Health for All agenda has fluctuated between narrow and broad lists of goals and targets, and across the full spectrum of interventions, including medical interventions, lifestyle projects and new public health initiatives.

When the Coalition government was elected in 1996, the then minister for health and aged care, Dr Michael Wooldridge, oversaw implementation of the Health Throughout Life Program on preventative health measures. This contained a set of targeted goals and outcomes that outlined measures designed to enhance the coordination of public health strategies and related research, including enhancing the public health role of the NHMRC.

The National Public Health Partnership, a five-year project, was established in 1997 to bring numerous public health initiatives under the one umbrella in order to strengthen public health infrastructure as a basis for program delivery and government investment. The partnership comprised representatives from the Commonwealth and state and territory public health services, with representatives from the NHMRC and the AIHW. New Zealand had observer status. While local government was not represented, an advisory group was established comprising key non-government organisations concerned with public health policy and service delivery. Initial priorities included legislative reform, workforce issues relevant to health promotion, environmental health and leadership, research and development, planning and practice improvement and national strategies coordination. The Legislation Reform Working Group of the partnership facilitated the publication of *Public Health Law* in Australia to stimulate discussion on key issues in public health legislative policy, including the regulation of disease and quarantine, immunisation, food, illicit drug laws and the regulation of alcohol and tobacco (Bidmeade & Reynolds 1997).

A second significant change has involved the 'broadbanding' of specific-purpose payments for transferring public health funding from the Commonwealth to the states and territories into bilateral public health outcome funding agreements. This meant that dollars allocated for specific 'vertical' programs such as the National Women's Health Program were pooled into block grants to each state and territory (Lin & King 2000). Before 1997–98, specific-purpose payments were made to the states and territories for HIV/AIDS, illicit drugs, women's health, cervical and breast cancer screening, alternative birthing, childhood immunisation, and a national education program regarding female genital mutilation. Essentially, the public-health-outcome funding agreements have seen these special payments pooled into a single public health fund to each state and territory. The aim is to provide greater flexibility at state and territory level, increased administrative efficiency and greater accountability for national public health outcomes.

Concern about Health for All focused on the social determinants of health at the turn of the 21st century. Worldwide interest in the population health consequences of the social and economic organisation of society and issues such as education, occupation and income, was fuelled by work conducted by epidemiologists and social scientists in Canada, under the auspices of the Canadian Institute of Advanced Research (Evans, Barer & Marmor 1994). Interest was fuelled also by longitudinal epidemiological studies conducted over several decades with civil servants in London by Michael Marmot and colleagues at the International Centre for Health and Society, as summarised in an influential document, *The Solid Facts* (Benzeval et al. 1995; Marmot & Wilkinson 1999; WHO Regional Office for Europe 1998). The solid facts referred to in the document are stress and social organisation, early life, the social gradient, unemployment, the psychosocial environment at work, transport, social support and social cohesion, food and poverty, social exclusion and minorities. With an individual risk factor such as smoking, for example, individuals who are marginalised from education, work and community are significantly more likely to smoke than their well-educated, employed and community-oriented peers.

The accumulation of epidemiological and social scientific evidence was fundamental to the establishment in Britain of the Independent Inquiry into Inequalities in Health, chaired by Sir Donald Acheson for the Blair Government (Acheson 1998), and of the Health Inequalities Research Collaboration, based at the National Centre for Epidemiology and Population Health at the Australian National University in 1998.

Australian collaboration focused on three issues—early childhood, work organisation and communities—in an effort to advise the Health Department on how to narrow the extent and spread of avoidable differences in health status, and to encourage the translation of research into policy and practice, with an emphasis on the health of disadvantaged groups and communities. Related Australian initiatives included the establishment of the Centre for Health Equity Training, Research and Evaluation by the NSW Department of Health (Harris, Sainsbury & Nutbeam 1999) and the publication of a book on the socioeconomic determinants of health by the Royal Australasian College of Physicians (1999).

In 2008, the final report of the Australia 2020 summit included the Long-term National Health Strategy. This topic was co-chaired by the then minister for health, Nicola Roxon. One of the main working groups focused on matters related to healthy lifestyles, health promotion and disease prevention. The working group put forward the following ambition: 'By 2020 we will have achieved a healthier lifestyle, through universal access to a clever wellness-focused evidence-based system with due regard to the environment in which we live' (Australian Government 2008). To achieve this goal it was recognised that there was a strong need for evidence-based preventative health policy and programs, a shift in focus from 'illness' in policy development to 'wellness', so that the concept of health prevention means an investment in wellness and wellbeing, as well as a focus on health policy that is integrated with broader government policies. The working group also discussed many other public health issues, including the health of Aboriginal and Torres

Strait Islander peoples, mental health, alcohol abuse, government accountability, preventative action, positive social marketing, and strengthening preventative health in the primary health care setting. These themes were evident in the rhetoric of the report of the National Health and Hospitals Reform Commission (2009b) with a focus on people-centred care, primary health care and chronic disease management, as discussed elsewhere.

Healthy cities

The WHO's concept of healthy cities provided an opportunity to apply the new public health perspective and the principles of the Ottawa Charter for Health Promotion (Ashton 1992a, 1992b; WHO 1986) at the local level. WHO's Healthy Cities Project was launched in 1986 and Australia was quick to develop its own healthy cities projects in line with the ideas emerging from WHO Europe. A submission from the Australian Community Health Association was successful in obtaining national health promotion funds to establish pilot healthy cities projects in the Illawarra (New South Wales), Canberra and Noarlunga (South Australia).

There was already some understanding and support for the healthy cities concept within the Commonwealth Department of Community Services and Health, largely because of the secondment of an officer to WHO Europe to assist with preparations for the 1988 Adelaide Healthy Public Policy Conference (Kaplan 1992). Hambly (1989, p. 12) suggests that Australia succeeded in gaining financial support for the pilot project because 'the key officers in the Commonwealth Department were very interested in obtaining some effective national program for health promotion. They liked the possibilities provided by Healthy Cities'. It may be relevant too that Dr Neal Blewett, the then minister for health, was keen to support constituencies for reform. The proposal succeeded in attracting approximately $655 000 for the three-year pilot period between 1987 and 1990 (Kaplan 1992).

In 1990, the National Better Health Program committed over $300 000 to Healthy Cities Australia for a two-year phase of network development. Related Australian initiatives included state coordination of similar projects in Queensland and South Australia, and the New South Wales–government-funded Healthy Cities Illawarra as a local project. The Municipal Association of Victoria's healthy localities projects were not linked to the national healthy cities network.

Waving or Drowning?—the evaluation of the national network phase of Healthy Cities Australia—noted that the national secretariat was slow to develop publicity and policy documents for the healthy cities in Australia (Whelan, Mohr & Short 1992). While contact between the secretariat and local projects was effective within the scale of the project, networking between projects was less than may have been expected. This, combined with the failure of the secretariat to incorporate Healthy Cities Australia as a national body, left the national network in a vulnerable position when funding for the project ceased with the end of the National Better Health Program in 1992.

Only 17 of over 800 local government areas in Australia were involved in formally designated healthy cities projects in 1992. Individual healthy cities projects around Australia were engaged in a wide range of activities, including community needs assessment, environmental projects, injury prevention and traditional lifestyle education activities. Innovative planning or local government projects were the exception rather than the rule. A range of strategies was used across the projects, including community development, social action and public relations.

The key principles of healthy cities, as outlined in the *Starting Out* manual produced by the national secretariat, are community participation in decision-making, collaboration between different sectors, working towards equity in health status between different groups, and improved ecological management (Healthy Cities Australia 1992). The evaluation reflected concern among many stakeholders involved in healthy cities at the uncertainty of the content of the project and the perception that it was 'something of an empty vessel, into which any policies, practices or techniques could be poured' (Whelan, Mohr & Short 1992, p. ii). As a health initiative directed at local communities and their governing councils, shires or municipalities, healthy cities had great potential to stimulate an active approach to the new public health at the local level. This potential was found to be realised in some projects, but to have been overtaken by suspicion and an opposition between health and local government officials and representatives in others. In Noarlunga, for example, the healthy cities project 'highlighted tensions between the different tiers of government, particularly between Local Government and larger "resource rich" federal and state Authorities' (Baum & Skewes 1992, p. 231, emphasis in original). Although the marketing of the health cities concept may have had some value, the crucial issue of what was precisely marketed remains obscure (Stanley 1987).

This brief overview of the pilot and network phases of the Healthy Cities Australia project has shown that there was continuing confusion about what the healthy cities concept actually meant in the Australian context, and deep-seated tensions between local government authorities and health authorities at state and federal levels. The Health Action Zone initiative in the United Kingdom is building on lessons gleaned from past failures and successes with healthy cities and other local health promotion projects (Jacobson & Yen 1998).

The concept of 'healthy cities' has evolved. In the Australia 2020 Summit held in 2008, it was proposed that the nation required 'smart cities and towns'. To achieve this, the following ambitions were expressed:

- Smart cities and towns aspire to be healthy cities promoted on the basis that there is a link between the nature of cities, environment and health.
- As a nation, Australia needs to plan for healthy cities using key planning tools—town planning, good architecture, and social modelling.
- We need to rethink how we plan and develop our cities. Tharangau, near Townsville, is a good example of urban planning that encourages healthy living and social and environmental integration.

■ Smart cities will support the measurement for wellness or a health rating that measures equity of access to things such as transport and healthy food, to help build healthy societies.

■ We need to better value the community and how it contributes to health.

Australian Government (2008)

Health impact assessment

While healthy cities projects attempt to facilitate healthy public policymaking, a health impact assessment (HIA) is a mechanism for limiting the development of 'unhealthy' public policies. Modelled on the environmental impact statement, it ensures that the impact on health is considered in the policymaking processes of non-health government portfolios.

Previously, the process of commissioning environmental impact statements before developments were allowed to progress had lost some credibility, because the proponent of a development chooses and pays the consulting firm that conducts the study. If a consulting firm is not in favour of the proposed project, another firm may be offered the contract (Higgins 1989, p. 29).

In the early 1990s, due to Australia's federal structure and the existence of different health authorities, the development of a comprehensive and coordinated national system of health impact assessment was not seen as feasible. The National Better Health Program moved towards incorporating health impact assessment into environmental impact assessment, based on recognition of the links between human health, social relations and the environment. Incorporating a health impact assessment into the process of environmental impact assessment provided the opportunity to improve a rather flawed system, rather than merely building onto it. A new public health rather than a technical approach was necessary if this opportunity was to be grasped (Summers 1992). With this in view, one of the four priorities of the National Health Advancement Program established in 1992 was the development of a methodology for undertaking environmental health impact assessments as part of a national policy on ecologically sustainable development. Several initiatives followed, including environmental health impact assessment protocols developed by the South Australian Health Commission, and guidelines developed by a NHMRC working party. None, however, became part of the regular activities of either environment or health services. More recently, integrated state-of-the-environment reports, which became mandatory in New South Wales and have been produced regularly by local government authorities in the other states and territories, have overtaken the idea of separate environmental health statements (Brown 1999).

In 2001, the National Public Health Partnership released HIA Guidelines. It was the first attempt to provide general guidance on the assessment of proposed developments and it acted as an introduction to HIAs as it was a relatively new process. These guidelines can be seen as the possible first step in attempting to formalise or 'streamline the process', as they set out to facilitate and promote the incorporation of HIAs into environmental and planning impact assessment, as well as assisting firms, communities and individuals who are involved in the preparation of HIAs (Commonwealth of Australia 2001).

HIAs have evolved rapidly over the last decade. Whereas once they were not deemed feasible, they are now seen as an important process of value to the community. The process considers the promotion of sustainable development by ensuring balanced considerations of the environment, human health impacts, policies and developments.

Tobacco control

As tobacco smoking is the leading cause of preventable illness and death in Australia, it presents policymakers with the greatest scope for prevention. About 40 000 Australians die each year through the use of tobacco—approximately 6000 from cancer, mostly of the lung, but also of the mouth, throat and kidneys; 9000 through damage to the blood vessels and heart; 3000 from non-cancerous lung disease; 20 000 from cerebrovascular accident (stroke); and 2000 from peripheral vascular disease. Tobacco smoking warrants examination in some detail because it has important lessons relating to potential legislative reform, and barriers to reform, in the healthy public policy arena.

Figure 8.2   Tobacco consumption by sex, 1945–2012

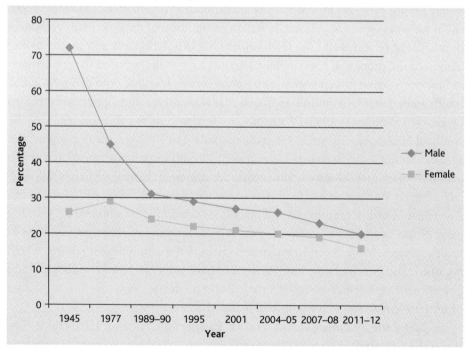

Source: Ministerial Council on Drug Strategy 1992, p. 12, and Australian Bureau of Statistics 2012, *Australian Health Survey: First Results 2012*, cat. no. 4364.0 55.001

The most powerful interest group in the tobacco-smoking arena has historically been the Tobacco Institute of Australia. The institute was funded by the four major Australian cigarette manufacturers: Rothmans, Philip Morris, WD and HO Wills and RJ Reynolds Tobacco. Much of its budget was spent on attempting to convince people, through marketing, talkback radio and television, that the connection between smoking and death had not been proven, and that every individual had the right to choose whether to smoke.

If community action groups such as Billboard Utilising Graffitists Against Unhealthy Promotions (BUGA-UP), the Non-Smokers Movement of Australia and Action on Smoking and Health have been successful, it is not merely because of their direct health messages. It is also because they use humour and high-profile protests to focus attention on the issues of tobacco advertising and promotion (Chesterfield-Evans 1983). In the last decades of the 20th century, these issues were put squarely on the health policy agenda, with an important milestone occurring when the Victorian government succeeded in introducing legislation banning billboard and cinema advertising and external displays, shopping centre promotions and 'giveaways'. One of the most important outcomes of the *Victorian Tobacco Act 1987* was the setting up of the Victorian Health Promotion Foundation (VicHealth), financed by a health promotion levy of 5 per cent on wholesale tobacco sales in order to fund health promotion projects. The foundation has made grants and sponsorships available to health, research, sport, recreation, art and cultural bodies for health promotion purposes. In the longer term, it is anticipated that these sponsorships will effectively end the association of tobacco with the arts in Victoria.

Action on the part of the anti-smoking movement has succeeded in keeping the issue of smoking on the agenda. Since the 1980s, we have seen small but significant policy developments in this area, including the banning of smoking on public transport, on aeroplanes and in workplaces. The price of cigarettes has risen sharply to encourage people to stop smoking. A significant defeat for the anti-smoking movement, however, occurred amid heated lobbying and debate in 1983 with the blocking of Western Australian legislation that proposed banning all forms of cigarette advertising and promotion. This defeat was contrasted with a successful example of reform, the South Australian *Tobacco Products Control Act 1986* (Chapman & Reynolds 1987). Major provisions of the act included the introduction of health warnings on cigarette packets, a ban on the sale of packets containing less than 20 cigarettes, an increase in the maximum fine for selling cigarettes to children under 15 and a ban on the distribution of sample cigarettes by tobacco companies. The reasons behind this success included the fact that South Australia has no significant tobacco industry. Tobacco is not grown or processed in South Australia, only sold and promoted. This left the tobacco industry at a significant electoral disadvantage, since it was unable to activate strong support within the state. In addition, the Labor government was in a secure position electorally at the beginning of a four-year term and the minister of health and community welfare had strong support from the cabinet, the ALP caucus and the electorate. At the same time, similar legislation, relating to the softening of penalties associated with prostitution and marijuana use, was receiving support from inside and outside the government. This political climate contrasted markedly with the West Australian situation in 1983, when the tobacco industry managed to create a considerable amount of community support for defeat of the legislation.

This comparison illustrates several factors that play a part in achieving or preventing legislative reform. It highlights, also, that a powerful interest group such as the tobacco industry can manipulate public opinion to serve its own interests, even when they are in conflict with the interests of the community as a whole. Although the Western Australian incident and a string of similar incidents left many observers pessimistic about the possibility of strong legislation being passed, the passing of the *Tobacco Products Control Act 1986* in South Australia indicated that the powerful lobbying strategy of the tobacco industry could be counteracted through significant counter-lobbying of community groups and health professionals. Similar tobacco acts that prohibited tobacco advertising, with the exception of point of sale, were introduced in Western Australia in 1990 and in the Australian Capital Territory in 1991. The health promotion foundations established in Victoria, South Australia, Western Australia and the Australian Capital Territory all receive funding, directly or indirectly, from taxation on tobacco (National Health Strategy 1993b, p. 37). The federal *Tobacco Advertising Prohibition Act 1992* reduced the disparity between the states and territories by leading to a ban on most forms of advertising and promotion from 1995 (National Health Strategy 1993b, p. 79).

An historic US court decision in 1988, in which a cigarette manufacturer was ordered to pay $495 000 damages to the husband of a woman who died from lung cancer, suggested that the legal power of the tobacco industry was waning (Sheehan 1988). The case was the first in over 300 lawsuits in which an American cigarette manufacturer was held liable for health damage caused by smoking. Hundreds of similar cases are now pending in the United States, and Australian lawyers and doctors say that it will make it easier for Australian claimants to sue tobacco companies for smoking-related illnesses. The case was seen as a potential landmark decision because it was the first in which it was proven that cigarette manufacturers knew more about the health risks of smoking than they had admitted publicly. It can also be seen as a partial defeat for the anti-smoking movement, which spent $3 million on the case, as it now appears that the health warnings on cigarette packets are sufficient to protect cigarette manufacturers from liability for health damage caused by smoking.

The issue of passive smoking was brought onto the political agenda by a community action group, the Non-Smokers' Movement of Australia, which had been campaigning for a smoke-free environment since 1977. The movement aimed to ensure that the non-smoker's right to clean air was protected and enshrined in legislation. The movement's successes included smoke-free transport on rail and bus routes, smoking bans on airlines, the introduction of non-smoking long-distance coaches, non-smoking taxis for passengers and drivers, occupational health and safety legislation to achieve a smoke-free working environment, and support for successful workers' compensation claims for health damage through exposure to smoke in the workplace. An out-of-court settlement for a Melbourne bus driver subjected to passive smoking at work brought the smoking issue into the occupational health and safety arena in Victoria in 1988. The case may have encouraged more employers to ban smoking in the workplace. In the settlement, Mr Sean Carroll, who was diagnosed with lung cancer, was awarded $65 000 based on his claim that his illness was caused by inhaling bus passengers' cigarette smoke. The settlement, which was reached after a three-day hearing of the Administrative Appeals Tribunal, was the first of its kind in Australia.

Because of this case, Australian courts ruled on numerous damages claims by non-smokers exposed to cigarette smoke in the workplace. This placed Australian employers under pressure to ban smoking in the workplace because of the risk of civil action by employees claiming that their health has been damaged by passive smoking. Much of the pressure on employers actually came from insurance companies, such as the Government Insurance Office, which were keen to avoid a flood of workers' compensation claims.

Smoking was banned initially in the Commonwealth Public Service, Telecom, Australia Post and a growing number of employer organisations. The legal situation for employers concerning the hazards of passive smoking was then unclear, however. As the Melbourne case was an out-of-court settlement, there was still room for a clear legal precedent on passive smoking in Australia. The court case brought by the Australian Federation of Consumer Organisations against the Tobacco Institute of Australia in the Federal Court of Australia focused the attention of policymakers, employers and the anti-smoking movement on one key question: 'Does scientific proof exist that passive smoking causes lung cancer, respiratory diseases in children and asthma attacks?' In his historic judgment in 1991, Justice Morling found 'compelling evidence that cigarette smoking causes lung cancer in non-smokers' (National Health Strategy 1993b, p. 34). In 1993, in the wake of the US government's decision to classify passive tobacco smoke as a 'Grade A' carcinogen, the equivalent of asbestos, the AMP society banned smoking in the public areas of its 14 shopping malls because of concerns about the health and legal dangers associated with passive smoking (Lewis 1993, p. 1).

The tobacco smoking issue indicates that the power of the tobacco industry has been eroded to some extent due to the combined efforts of many individuals, community action groups and professionals in the anti-smoking movement. Legislative reform in this area has been attributed principally to the work of community organisations (National Health Strategy 1993b). This issue illustrates that the influence of powerful interests can be counteracted if there is sufficient agreement within the community and sufficient demand for legislative reform from within the electorate.

The laws surrounding the issue of tobacco smoking have been dynamic in this century, with many enforced almost yearly since the early 2000s. In New South Wales alone these include:

- a ban on smoking in all enclosed workplaces and public places (except licensed hospitality venues) (2004)
- restrictions on the number of points of sale of tobacco products and requirement for separate retail tobacco licences (2004–05)
- a ban on advertising at point of sale (2005)
- graphic health warning labels for tobacco products introduced nationally (2006)
- a ban on the sale of fruit-flavoured cigarettes (2006)
- a ban on the sale of cigarette packets that can be divided into portions of fewer than 20 cigarettes (2006)
- a ban on smoking in vehicles when children under 16 are present (2007)
- hospitality venues becoming completely smoke-free in all enclosed areas, including pubs, clubs, bingo venues and casinos (2007)
- restrictions on the display of tobacco products, including the requirement to display a graphic health warning poster and limiting the size of tobacco product displays (2007) (Cancer Council 2009).

In 2012 Australia became the first country in the world to implement legislation to require tobacco products to be sold in plain packaging. The effects of plain cigarette packaging reforms show they are effective in reducing the rate and incidence of smokers. A study published in the *British Medical Journal* confirms that consumers perceive cigarettes to be of lower quality and are less satisfied by cigarettes than a year ago. Consumers were also more likely to quit smoking (Department of Health 2013). The legislation was challenged, unsuccessfully, in Australia's High Court. Subsequently, the tobacco industry expressed the view that they would use international law, trade agreements and copyright entitlements in order to attempt to challenge the veracity of the legislation above and beyond the Commonwealth of Australia.

HIV/AIDS

Few health issues have lent themselves as readily to the new public health approach as HIV/AIDS. It is one of the most serious and expensive public health problems that Australia—indeed the world—has ever faced (Blewett 1985). The WHO estimates that 30 million people throughout the world were living with HIV/AIDS in 2007. Since the start of the epidemic almost three decades ago, there have been approximately 25 million deaths from AIDS. Although the global epidemic of HIV has stabilised, there are unacceptably high levels of new HIV infection and AIDS-related deaths. The WHO has concluded that AIDS is a still-emerging epidemic that is 'out of control in many places'. The Southern African region continues to

Figure 8.3   HIV infecting a Helper T cell

Source: Department of Health and Ageing (2011)

have a disproportionate share of the global burden, as 67 per cent of people living with HIV are from sub-Saharan Africa (WHO 2008a).

Australia lies in a middle rank compared to other wealthy OECD countries that possess comparable surveillance systems. Infection with the virus generally interferes with the body's immune system, which makes the bearer more susceptible to a variety of severe infections and several unusual types of cancer. These associated infections and illnesses are fatal. By 2006, over 26 000 cases of HIV and 10 000 cases of AIDS had been recorded in Australia, with over 90 per cent of them being male.

Figure 8.4   Estimated number of deaths due to AIDS, 1990–2007

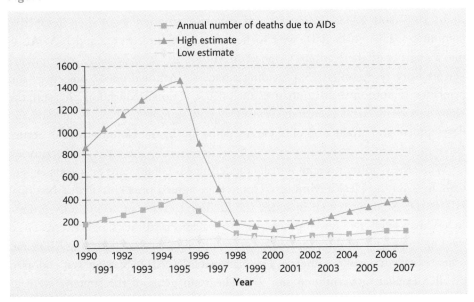

Source: UNAIDS/WHO (2008)

Since November 1982, when the first Australian case was diagnosed, a wide range of medical, lifestyle and new public health strategies has been implemented in an attempt to curb the spread of the virus. A detailed analysis of government responses indicates that Australia has been at the forefront of policy development in many ways (Commonwealth Department of Health 1986a). Australia was one of the first countries to acknowledge the potentially disastrous effects of AIDS and to implement initiatives in the areas of education, research and prevention. Australia was also first to test all blood supplies for the AIDS virus and it is one of the few countries that has established effective nationwide coordination of HIV/AIDS initiatives.

In 1984, the AIDS Task Force was established, under the chairmanship of Professor David Penington of the University of Melbourne, to advise health ministers on medical and scientific aspects of AIDS. In the same year, increasing public concern about exposure led to the establishment of the National Advisory Committee on AIDS (NACAIDS), chaired by Ita Buttrose. NACAIDS comprised representatives from high-risk groups, governments and the broader community and was established to advise the federal health minister on preventative education, social and legal implications and the provision of appropriate services for people with AIDS. The potential for conflict was, however, embodied in the two national advisory committees (Ballard 1989, p. 360). By 1986, Penington was calling for the testing of all high-risk groups, while the gay community was emphasising confidentiality and the need for preventative action. Neal Blewett 'basically supported Buttrose and the community sector against the medical model represented by Penington' (Altman 1992, p. 57). The medical model and the new public health approaches were engaged in a public debate, and the latter won.

In 1987 and 1988, Penington and Buttrose resigned from their respective committees. This enabled Blewett to fuse the AIDS Task Force and NACAIDS into a single body, the National Council on AIDS. This was the federal government's key advisory body on AIDS, providing advice on national needs, objectives and priorities. Commonwealth initiatives included a national education program, the Commonwealth AIDS Research Grants Program, support for blood screening, the development and production of blood screening kits by the Commonwealth Serum Laboratories, and contributions to initiatives operated by the states and territories.

While the Commonwealth initially funded all AIDS programs on a 100 per cent basis, in 1985 the Health Ministers' Conference agreed on a cost-shared National HIV/AIDS Strategy, which included the funding of relevant community groups. In a widely publicised development, the Australian Prostitutes Collective received funding to provide health promotion and counselling services regarding AIDS and other sexually transmitted diseases. The National HIV/AIDS Strategy was endorsed by all Australian governments in 1989. The twin goals of the strategy were to eliminate the transmission of HIV and to minimise the personal and social impact of HIV infection. The strategy comprised six programs or components: education, prevention, treatment, care and counselling, access and participation, and research and international cooperation.

The evaluation of the National HIV/AIDS Strategy pointed to the overall effectiveness of Australia's response to the epidemic (National Evaluation Steering Committee 1992). It noted that the epidemic appeared to have stabilised and that it was still mostly confined to men who have sex with men. Male homosexual sex accounted for 86 per cent of all HIV diagnoses (National Evaluation Steering Committee 1992, p. 8). Male homosexual sex and transmission through injecting drugs were the main modes of transmission for adults living with HIV/AIDS in Australia at the turn of the century (WHO 1998). The evaluation noted that the goal of minimising the personal and social impact of the epidemic had been constrained by finite resources and by the nature of the disease. It recognised that there were still problems with access to new drugs due to inefficiencies in Australia's drug evaluation system, as identified in Peter Baume's (1991) report. The evaluation noted also that the treatment needs of people with HIV/AIDS were growing as the range of available treatments became more complex, and that Australians had reacted largely with a high degree of tolerance, though discrimination remained an important issue. A study conducted by the New South Wales Anti-Discrimination Board (1992, p. 30) found that 'HIV and AIDS related discrimination is particularly extensive and pervasive in the provision of health care, including the services of GPs, hospitals, surgeons, dentists and allied health professionals'. In general, the evaluation concluded that Australia's response to HIV/AIDS had been a success, especially as the rate of increase in the number of people living with AIDS had slowed, and the spread of the virus had been largely confined to men who had sex with men. This success is supported by research on sexual and needle-sharing behaviour changes.

Community-based education projects and initiatives were established first by the gay community and then by people with haemophilia before the advent of the National HIV/AIDS Strategy. Community participation has been a major factor in government responses to HIV/AIDS in Australia. From the beginning, medical and scientific bodies consulted with groups with high-risk behaviours: men who have sex with men, haemophiliacs and recipients of blood products, intravenous drug users and their sexual partners, and prostitutes. Cooperation between medical practitioners, researchers and gay communities in Melbourne and Sydney in particular resulted in accurate reporting of the spread of the disease, and initiatives such as more liberal needle exchange programs and the greater availability of condoms.

In 1987, the controversial 'Grim Reaper' advertisement aimed to increase public awareness about AIDS and put AIDS on the public agenda. The Grim Reaper was an extremely successful initiative in terms of the 'symbolic uses of politics' (Edelman 1964). The campaign created the expectation in the public arena that the government should act on the issue and that it was responding in an appropriate way. This illustrates the proposition that any notion of an autonomous 'public opinion' is misplaced. With the Grim Reaper advertisement, the government cued the public towards the perception that everyone was endangered by the spread of AIDS, that it was a threat to the health of the general community as well as to groups with high-risk behaviours. Then it was perceived to be appropriate to spend considerable public funds to minimise the spread of AIDS. More cynical observers have suggested that this enabled AIDS to be given a much higher profile with health organisations and significantly more funding than it actually warranted. At the beginning of every epidemic, public health experts tend to exaggerate its importance since they have a stake in governments taking the epidemic seriously and providing funding for research and prevention.

The annual number of HIV diagnoses in Australia peaked in 1987. There followed 12 years of decline, after which the rate of diagnoses grew again to reach 983 in 2007 (after adjusting for multiple reporting). The annual number of AIDS diagnoses in Australia peaked in 1994 at 953 cases and then declined rapidly to 216 in 1999. The fall since 1996 was largely due to the introduction of effective combination anti-retroviral therapy, which delays progression from HIV infection to AIDS. The number of AIDS diagnoses has since remained relatively stable (UNAIDS/WHO 2008).

HIV/AIDS is more than just a health issue. Addressing HIV/AIDS needs political leadership to mobilise resources in a coordinated way across a broad range of fields. Partnerships need to extend beyond government to the private sector, civil society and community-based organisations to ensure an effective response to the disease and its impact. Thus, Australia is active both in advocacy at the political level and in activities designed to meet local needs and priorities. Australia has also been actively involved in helping other countries combat HIV/AIDS, approving a Global HIV/AIDS Initiative totalling $1 billion over the 10 years from 2000 to 2010.

Australia played a strategic leadership role internationally by belonging to the governing body of the Joint United Nations Programme on HIV/AIDS (UNAIDS) from 2005–06. The program was established in 1996 and is the leading advocate for worldwide action against HIV/AIDS. Australia continues to contribute over $5 million each year in core funding to assist UNAIDS to enable, strengthen and support an expanded response to the epidemic.

Other related participation by Australia is its membership on the board of the Global Fund to Fight AIDS, Tuberculosis and Malaria and it is a founding member of the steering committee for the Asia Pacific Leadership Forum on HIV/AIDS (APLF). Australia also initiated the Asia-Pacific Business Coalition on HIV/AIDS.

In 2007, Sydney was the host city for the Third Ministerial Meeting on HIV/AIDS. This meeting consisted of business and government leaders from around the region, who discussed greater private sector involvement in the fight against HIV/AIDS.

Australia also works within other international forums. It played an active role in the United Nations General Assembly Special Session on HIV/AIDS in mid-2001 to develop the Declaration of Commitment on HIV/AIDS and the follow-up high-level review meeting in 2005.

The Australian Government, formerly through AusAID and now through the Department of Foreign Affairs and Trade, continues to work with the World Trade Organization and WHO to improve the accessibility and affordability of essential HIV/AIDS drugs (Commonwealth of Australia 2009). In 2011, the *Annual Surveillance Report* on HIV-AIDS revealed a relatively steady number of HIV diagnoses at about 1000 over the previous five years. Australia's response to HIV has historically been successful; Australia maintains one of the lowest HIV prevalence rates in the world, at 0.1 per cent. The Sixth National HIV Strategy, endorsed by health ministers in 2010, highlights the need for prevention and investment in the long term to uphold a comprehensive response to HIV.

Drugs and alcohol

Increasing emphasis on the new public health approach is illustrated also by developments in the drug and alcohol field. Before the introduction of the Community Health Program in 1973, people with drug and alcohol problems were treated as psychiatric patients, predominantly in the psychiatric hospital system. Alcohol and other drug detoxification treatments and counselling services were available for psychiatric patients only (Committee of Review into Drug and Alcohol Services in New South Wales 1985). This inpatient psychiatric model changed from 1974, as the provision of community health services enabled people with mental health and/or drug and alcohol problems to be treated in the community.

Commonwealth funding for drug education projects increased considerably after the Special Premiers' Conference on Drugs, commonly referred to as the Drug Summit, in April 1985, when federal, state and territory government leaders agreed to provide an additional $100 million over three years on expanded initiatives in drug education, treatment, rehabilitation and research. The Drug Summit led to the establishment of the National Campaign Against Drug Abuse (NCADA), which embodied the new public health approach. The campaign involved intersectoral collaboration between the key sectors of health, education, law and enforcement, and entailed coordination between government, private and community organisations, including the Australian Federal Police, schools, the media, and community organisations such as the Wayside Foundation in Sydney's Kings Cross.

The NCADA aimed to minimise the harmful effects caused by the misuse of all drugs, both licit and illicit. This contrasted with earlier drug policies, which focused on regulating the supply of illicit drugs such as heroin, cocaine and marijuana. Commonwealth-funded national initiatives included national education projects; research, including the establishment of centres of excellence in Sydney and Perth; development of the National Drug Related Data Collection System; and 'The Drug Offensive', a public education and information campaign. The Drug Offensive was designed in three phases. Phase one aimed to raise public awareness about the drug problem by providing basic information on the abuse of licit drugs and the use of illicit drugs. In the second and third phases, specific drugs and specific groups in the community were targeted: young people, prisoners, Aboriginal peoples and women were singled out for special attention.

The community-based preventative approach to drugs and alcohol is of relatively recent origin and is best developed in New South Wales and Victoria. In New South

Wales, NCADA initiatives included the appointment of drug and alcohol community development officers, expansion of methadone maintenance programs, support for life education centres, an adolescent alcohol misuse campaign, and establishment of Jarrah House, the first specialist detoxification unit for women in Australia. These NCADA-funded education and preventative initiatives were administered through the departments of health, education, technical and further education, community services and corrective services.

The first three years of the program were reviewed by the first Task Force on Evaluation (National Campaign Against Drug Abuse 1989). The Second Task Force on Evaluation, chaired by Ian Webster, Professor of Public Health at the University of New South Wales, evaluated the six years of the NCADA, from 1985 to 1991 (Ministerial Council on Drug Strategy 1992). Expenditure on the NCADA for this period was over $247 million. As the campaign's major strengths, the report of the evaluation, *No Quick Fix*, identified the aim of harm minimisation, the greater policy attention paid to alcohol and other drug issues, and the new public health approach. The taskforce noted that community awareness had increased and that there had been a positive change in attitudes to the responsible use of alcohol and tobacco during the campaign. It indicated also that 'community development approaches will bring about the most effective and enduring outcomes for individuals and the whole society' (Ministerial Council on Drug Strategy 1992, p. xi). The weaknesses of the campaign included a lack of strategic goals and direction; the failure to achieve a harmonious partnership between the law, police, other enforcement agencies and the health sector; impediments to innovation; deficiencies in community consultation; and the continuing needs of disadvantaged social groups, especially women, Aboriginal and Torres Strait Islander peoples, and people from backgrounds with languages other than English.

The major recommendations of *No Quick Fix* were implemented in 1992, when the Commonwealth Government relaunched NCADA as a new five-year National Drug Strategy, with a strategic plan along with planning, administrative and organisational changes in federal, state and territory authorities. The three priorities identified in the evaluation of the NCADA, which were integrated into the National Drug Strategic Plan, were alcohol and violence, cannabis and psycho-stimulants. The program was reviewed in 1997 (Williams 1997) and the renewed program, the National Drug Strategic Framework: Building Partnerships, was put in place in 2002–03.

In 2003, the AIHW estimated that approximately 16 700 deaths were drug- or alcohol-related each year. The AIHW continues to collect data and reports on two broad categories of drug- and alcohol-related information. These include the prevalence and impact of drug and alcohol use within Australia, and service-related information detailing the characteristics of alcohol and other drug treatment services and their clients. The AIHW process for collecting and reporting service and population information was developed as a response to the information needs identified in the National Drug Strategy Framework.

The National Drug Strategy is a cooperative venture between Commonwealth and state governments and the non-government sector, which aims at improving health, social and economic outcomes for Australians by 'preventing the uptake of harmful drug use and reducing the harmful effects of licit and illicit drugs in our society' (Commonwealth of Australia 2004). This strategy has been operating since 1985, along with its predecessor, the National Campaign Against Drug Abuse. Both strategies were created from strong bipartisan political support and they involve a cooperative venture between the Commonwealth and state governments as well as the non-government sector. Within the AIHW, the Drug Surveys and Services Unit is responsible for analysing and reporting population-based drug and alcohol data and analysis, and reporting on alcohol and drug treatment services.

Occupational health and safety

Australia has been significant progress in occupational health and safety (OHS). Since the emergence of separate OHS acts across each of the Australian states and territories in the 1980s, with their own sets of regulations and guidance notes, there has more recently been intergovernmental agreement to establish a national approach to OHS legislation (Quinlan & Johnstone 2009).

In 2009, the Intergovernmental Agreement for Regulatory and Operational Reform in Occupational Health and Safety was signed to formalise cooperation between Commonwealth, state and territory governments. This was based on the concept of harmonisation between jurisdictions in relation to OHS legislation, with the implementation of appropriate governance arrangements to support these changes.

Contemporary changes have followed from a series of changes noted across each of the states and territories, with revision of their relevant legislations, regulations and standards. The traditional piecemeal approach to safety, and the lack of consistency across each of the jurisdictions, has made for difficulties for employers who operate across jurisdictions, and for workers who work across a variety of jurisdictions. Despite the variations, however, substantial gains have been made in reducing fatalities associated with work activity, as well as reducing injuries and illnesses (ASCC 2008).

Significant reforms in the OHS field in the mid-1970s and 1980s can be explained by a combination of factors. Contributing factors include unacceptably high levels of work-related fatalities and ill health, increasing costs to employers, and the inadequacies of old laws. It is noteworthy that the issue of occupational health was not brought onto the health policy agenda until the 1970s, when significant pressure from an alliance of groups representing workers' health interests gathered momentum. Between the mid-1970s and the mid-1980s, the trade union movement established workers' health centres in Lidcombe (Western Sydney), Melbourne, Brisbane, Newcastle and Wollongong (Biggins et al. 1989). Over this period, the 'workers' health movement'—a loosely organised social movement comprising individuals and groups from trade unions, the women's movement and health care—forced governments to act on longstanding OHS problems (Pearse & Refshauge 1987).

The promotion of workers' health and safety became a major health issue in Australia in the 1980s, with occupational health taking industrial as well as technical importance. In many countries, including Australia, solutions to OHS problems were framed in terms of participation by the workers, rather than solely manage-ment prerogative (Elling 1986).

The newer-style legislation protected many workers who were not covered by the old legislation and covered all aspects of health, since it placed a statutory duty on employers to provide a safe and healthy working environment. Previous legislation attempted to specify particular hazards and offences, an approach that was becoming 'hopelessly unwieldy' (Biggins 1987, p. 28).

Legislative reform was most intense during periods of Labor government in Victoria, South Australia, Western Australia, New South Wales and Queensland, when levels of worker organisation and influence were relatively high.

In 1985, new Victorian OHS legislation led to the establishment of a reformed OHS system. The Victorian *Occupational Health and Safety Act 1985* differed signifi-cantly from previous OHS legislation. It provided for trade-union-elected OHS representatives with powers to inspect, issue provisional improvement notices and stop work in dangerous instances. This innovative legislation was more effective than previous legislation because health and safety representatives were protected from victimisation for carrying out their responsibilities. Western Australia also introduced legislative reforms, similar to those in other states.

In the 1980s, Queensland continued to rely on old-style legislation due to considerable resistance from both employers and the National Party Queensland government (Quinlan 1987). In 1990, under the Goss Labor Government, Queensland reformed its legislation to bring it into line with the other states (Quinlan & Bohle 1991). In New South Wales, the introduction of occupational health and safety committees resulted in the concept of negotiation between workers and employers regarding safety issues in the workplace (Pearse & Refshauge 1987).

Since this time, WorkCover NSW has produced a revised OHS Act (2000) and regulations (2001), which expand on the duty of care requirements of employers to ensure that consultation takes place between them and their employees in relation to workplace safety. Other states have followed similar directions, with revision of OHS legislation to support a systems-based approach to safety and risk management practices to prevent workplace injuries and illnesses.

These changes followed legislative reforms across Australia that were influ-enced strongly by the British report *Safety and Health at Work: Report of the Committee 1970–72,* known as the Robens Report, which promoted the concept of self-regulation, with a concurrent involvement of workers and their organisa-tions. In the post-Robens period after the 1970s, greater focus on participative decision-making and training in OHS was introduced across most jurisdictions, aimed at promoting the value of recognising workers' interests in improving safety in the workplace.

In general, trade unions focused on strengthening their organisations' contributions in the belief that workers had the right to take greater control over their health and working environments to eliminate unhealthy working conditions:

> unions have moved away from a traditional concern with securing 'danger money' for members working in hazardous conditions, to negotiating with employers over the removal or control of the hazards themselves.
>
> Mathews (1985, p. iii)

The election of thousands of health and safety representatives in workplaces around Australia was perhaps the most positive innovation in the new-style legislation. Each employee-elected health and safety representative has legal powers and access to decision-making on OHS matters. This legislative reform acknowledged that workers needed certain rights protected by legislation in order to participate effectively in the promotion of their own health (Biggins 1987). These rights fell into three categories. First, the workers' 'right to know', to have access to information about hazards in the workplace, their effects and how they can be managed. Second, the workers' 'right to participate', to be involved in the formulation and implementation of OHS policies and procedures in the workplace. Third, the workers' 'right to refuse unsafe work', to assess the health implications of the working environment, stop the work if it is considered dangerous and call in a health and safety inspector to assess the situation. This third right attracted considerable opposition from employers, but the evidence suggests that employees have acted responsibly when it has been invoked (Biggins 1987).

Experience overseas and in Australia suggests that the OHS representative system works well (Biggins 1987; Biggins, Phillips & O'Sullivan 1991). There has been a marked decrease in the level of industrial disputes on health and safety issues, as most issues are resolved where they arise, in the workplace. Health and safety representatives also play a valuable role in helping to introduce new technologies, a situation that arises often in the health care system. Ideally, health and safety problems are addressed in the process of technological change so that the working environment can be made more effective and more compatible with the interests of the workers involved. Research indicates also that worker participation in OHS contributes positively to industrial relations (Biggins, Phillips & O'Sullivan 1991).

Evidence from Safe Work Australia—previously known as the Australian Safety and Compensation Council, which, in turn, replaced the National Occupational Health and Safety Commission (NOHSC)—shows that the incidence of illness and injury has been reducing across all jurisdictions of Australia. This has been particularly evident since the introduction of a participatory approach to the management of safety in the workplace.

Initially, national OHS priorities were back pain and disease, noise-induced hearing loss and chemical management. In 1991, the various premiers and chief ministers reaffirmed their commitment to bringing the myriad OHS rules and regulations into line and identified the areas in which occupational injuries and illnesses were most likely to occur: plant, certification of equipment, workplace hazardous substances, occupational noise, major hazardous facilities and manual handling. National strategies aimed at improving OHS performance across all states and territories agreed that a number of common goals needed to be achieved if these common OHS risks were to be adequately addressed. These target areas included a nationally consistent regulatory framework, comprehensive OHS data collection, a coordinated research effort, strategic enforcement, effective incentives, compliance support, practical guidance, OHS awareness and skills development (Safe Work Australia 2009).

It has been further claimed that a national approach that includes these core strategies has arisen over recent years in response to changes in economic and social patterns, such as changing employment arrangements, systems of work—including the growth of temporary employment (labour-hire arrangements)—new technologies, legal requirements and the changing demographics of an ageing workforce.

Critics of the national approach to a more consistent application of OHS laws across Australia have noted various definitional variations between current laws, such as differences in the definition of what is a 'deemed worker' and agreement over who is a contractor (Johnstone 2008). These issues have potential to create confusion when application of both federal and state laws might apply.

The ACTU suggests that attempts to apply a national approach to the management of OHS may weaken the employer's statutory duty to provide a safe and healthy workplace and thus make it more difficult to achieve successful prosecutions against unsafe work practices.

It has also been argued that self-regulation models embodied in the post-Robens-style OHS legislation would not work in changing political and economic climates because most employers would think that improving health and safety in the workplace is an economic cost they cannot afford (Merritt 1983). An expert in Australian OHS law, Adrian Merritt (1983), has argued that safety measures will only be implemented voluntarily when they contribute to company profits and when they decrease losses. She argued further that the only approach that will work is one based on strong government regulation that provides for vigorous enforcement of comprehensive OHS regulations by an enlarged inspectorate, backed by prosecution and heavy penalties. That way, employers would be forced to promote health and safety at work, since neglect of health and safety requirements would start to cost more than it saved.

In an era of economic change and uncertainty, there is potential for OHS risks to escalate in the workplace, since employers are likely to resist spending money on preventative measures, particularly when the benefits may be difficult to justify in the short term.

The role of the media

The mass media—press, television and radio—are 'possibly the most potent influence in our society' (Better Health Commission 1986b, p. 140). The invention of the internet in the early 1980s saw an explosion of web-based technologies, including electronic mail and the World Wide Web. These have increased media influence culturally, politically and economically over the last three decades. Participants from the health sector and the media at the Better Health Commission Workshop, 'The Role of the Media in Advancing Australia's Health', noted that the media have played a significant role in creating national and international markets for consumer goods produced by some of Australia's biggest companies. This has created a 'symbiotic relationship' between manufacturers, the media and advertisers, which actively promotes ill health through the marketing of products such as cigarettes and alcohol and foods with high concentrations of saturated fats, salt and sugar.

The *Lancet* series of expert papers on non-communicable diseases posits that transnational corporations are major drivers of non-communicable diseases as they profit from increased consumption of alcohol, ultra-processed ('junk') foods and other unhealthy products. It claims that policies are shaped by the corporate agenda. There is ample evidence that multinational corporations utilise similar strategies to the tobacco industry in order to undermine public health policies by biasing research findings, lobbying politicians and health professionals, co-opting policymakers, influencing voters and ignoring codes of conduct (Moodie et al. 2013). This powerful relationship between the media and the manufacturers of unhealthy products is further strengthened by the fact that advertising money pays for most of our media in Australia.

Advertising provides all the income for commercial television and radio and approximately 75 per cent of total newspaper income, and a 'large part of this revenue comes from the food, tobacco and alcohol industries' (Better Health Commission 1986b, p. 140). The food industry has particularly strong media ties. In the 1980s, between 45 per cent and 60 per cent of all advertising televised during the children's 4 pm to 6 pm time slot was for food products that were in direct conflict with current government priorities for better health and nutrition education. Why, then, did the Better Health Commission Taskforce on Nutrition recommend that the major strategy for achieving healthy dietary goals should be nutrition education and effecting change in food supply through increased liaison between health, industry, education and consumer bodies (Better Health Commission 1986b)? This differs markedly from the media workshop that recommended a ban on tobacco advertising and promotion, and the removal of restrictions on the advertising of condoms. The symbiotic relationship between the media, advertisers and food companies may partly explain the 'safe' recommendations made by the taskforce.

The Australian Medical Association (AMA) has stepped up its campaign to see alcohol advertising on radio and television banned and has criticised a number of advertisements that feature prominent sports stars, since they are seen to be contributing to Australia's underage drinking problem. Following a decision of the Federal Assembly of the AMA in 1988, AMA branches lobbied state health ministers to introduce a ban.

In 2002, the AMA endorsed other public health issues, such as the code of practice for car advertising. The Advertising Standards Bureau released tough new advertising standards to deter car advertising that glorified speeding and reckless driving, or motorcyclists not wearing helmets in advertisements. This resulted in graphic advertisements, endorsed by the federal government, which showed the wreckage of a car accident and its aftermath.

The AMA has also addressed the issue of unhealthy foods advertised on television, campaigning to ban the advertising of unhealthy food during children's viewing hours. It claimed that obesity was becoming more prevalent in children and urged the government to act on advertising that targeted children and unhealthy food, stating that obesity in childhood could lead to long-term health problems. It emphasised also that the media and the broadcast regulatory authorities have a significant role to play in attempting to combat this prominent public health problem.

The Commonwealth and state governments agreed on targets and goals for obesity reduction, especially in children, through the National Healthcare Agreements and National Public Health Partnerships. The AMA believed that junk food advertising to children could potentially undermine these efforts and recommended that the Australian Communications and Media Authority (ACMA) prohibit advertising of unhealthy foods during children's television viewing times.

The online campaign Coalition on Food Advertising to Children (CFAC) is aimed at putting more pressure on governments to remove junk food advertising from children's television.

Health professionals, public health experts and the community continue to raise concerns about the advertising and promotion of junk food. We note, however, that food advertising to children is one of the few issues raised in this book in which we have not seen significant public health progress over the last 25 years.

POLICY ANALYSIS

Health promotion is a striking example of a policy that is often not implemented because it may work counter to the economic interests of powerful groups. In addition, there is little incentive for health practitioners and administrators to support prevention. Indeed, there are very real incentives not to support it.

Analysis of legislative reform in the area of tobacco regulation revealed that healthy public policies can be introduced if there is a strong enough group to counteract the lobbying strategies of powerful vested interests. The work of community groups, including the Anti-Smokers' Movement of Australia, has been vital in the reform process, partly because they were able to keep the issue of tobacco smoking and health on the political agenda, and partly because community support for greater control over the tobacco industry was activated.

If a potential reform has support from all sectors of the community then it is much more acceptable to policymakers than a proposal that divides the community. If an issue is perceived as divisive then it is generally less acceptable to policymakers. If an issue threatens existing power, income or status hierarchies in a fundamental way, it is unlikely to attract support within the government (Edelman 1977). The medical approach to prevention tends to be more attractive to policymakers than other approaches because it is politically safe. Since the medical approach focuses largely on the individual patient, it tends to be less threatening to existing power relations than proposals for broad-ranging healthy public policies. The medical and lifestyle approaches tend to accept existing problems like smoking as given. The new public health movement calls for more fundamental social and economic changes.

Whether an issue attracts government attention at the stage of agenda-setting often depends on the way the issue is presented. If community activists and health professionals present an issue as threatening to powerful vested interests, it is less likely to receive support from policymakers than if it is presented as a consensual, or safe, issue. In the tobacco arena, we have seen a dramatic change in the way that legislative control of tobacco use has been perceived in just 20 years. During this period, the issue has changed from being a radical challenge to the power of multinational companies to being a safe and positive issue, as presented by the AMA. While the work of community action groups was crucial in placing the issue of smoking and health on the political agenda, the work of the AMA is likely to be equally crucial in achieving support for further legislative reforms.

The next question this chapter needs to examine is the feasibility of an expansion of health promotion activities in Australia currently. Supporters of the new public health are generally aware that governments and industry are unlikely to implement radical changes while the current political market is imbalanced in favour of provider and industry groups. It can, therefore, be argued that the broad-ranging social and economic changes that are required for any real progress in this area can only be achieved through collective political action. The new public health movement is utopian in the eyes of many healthy lifestyle proponents because it calls for a radical transformation of society in order to prevent disease. Such an outcome is highly unlikely in the current circumstances.

This helps to explain why governments tend to focus on preventative measures that can be implemented without too much political opposition, such as immunisation projects, breast and cervical cancer screening, healthy lifestyle campaigns and compulsory seatbelt legislation.

Uncertainty about the effectiveness of long-term measures also helps to explain why health promotion policies in general are seldom easy to realise. The imbalance between
(continued)

present costs and uncertain future benefits of many preventative measures explains, in part, the 'continuing frustration of the advocates of policies of prevention' (Klein 1983, p. 174). Moreover, it has been suggested that optimistic 'preventionists' are destined to experience 'inevitable disillusion' because the benefits of preventative strategies 'belong to the future and will, moreover, be diffuse and largely invisible' (Klein 1983, p. 177).

Prevention is not better than cure in every case. Individual interventions must be evaluated on their merits (Russell 1986). Cost-effectiveness analysis of the different strategies reveals that health promotion interventions that have proven to be relatively cost-effective are largely outside the clinical domain (Evans 1984). Taxation and regulation have been shown to be effective and cheap in controlling smoking and drink-driving behaviour and in encouraging the use of seatbelts. Efforts to influence such behaviour in a clinical or health education context are yet to be proved effective in the long term, and are certainly more expensive. Mass immunisation campaigns are cheaper and more effective than initiatives by individual medical practitioners. This is not to deny the existence of exceptions to this generalisation. Hypertension control and prenatal care are possible examples of cost-effective preventative medical interventions. Quit for Life is an example of an effective and efficient lifestyle strategy. This chapter has suggested, though, that the new public health strategy tends to offer greater scope for effective and efficient illness prevention and health promotion.

The tobacco smoking issue is a practical example of healthy public policy and constraints on healthy public policymaking (Blewett 1988). **Figure 8.2** indicates that the number of Australians who smoke decreased from an estimated 68 per cent of males and 28 per cent of females in the mid-1960s to approximately 25 per cent of males and 22 per cent of females in 1991 (Ministerial Council on Drug Strategy 1992, p. 12). This significant improvement is partly attributable to the implementation of policies concerning the regulation of cigarette advertising and promotion, and bans on tobacco smoking in public places. None of these initiatives would have been politically feasible even 20 years earlier because community attitudes would not have supported legislative reform. These reforms were only possible because of the work of the anti-smoking movement, a loose alliance comprising professional and community groups. This social movement was particularly important given the powerful interests associated with the tobacco lobby. The anti-smoking movement 'has so transformed societal attitudes that governments have now dared, and rightly dared, to act' (Blewett 1988, p. 12).

Policies relevant to tobacco consumption constantly evolve. Once again, community support for such policies is only raised as emerging evidence supports the detrimental effects of tobacco smoking. This issue has grown to the point where passive smoking has also become a major issue, with successful laws being implemented to protect members of the public, especially children. Examples include the ban of smoking in cars while children are present and the complete ban of smoking in enclosed areas of public venues, including pubs, clubs, bingo venues and casinos, in 2007 in New South Wales.

SUMMARY AND CONCLUSION

This chapter has indicated that, for a complex variety of reasons, the prospects for disease prevention and health promotion in Australia are limited. While there has been a great deal of rhetoric about preventative policies during the past decade, it is important to remember that funds for public health represent a small proportion of total health expenditure (less than 2 per cent). We emphasised that these strategies are difficult to implement because of economic and political considerations. A classic case of profits versus health is evident in attempts to prevent the harmful effects of tobacco, alcohol, and ultra-processed foods and drinks. The level of importance accorded to prevention and health promotion in public policy depends on the balance of forces between different interests and between competing policy objectives. It is further circumscribed by uncertainty about the effectiveness of many long-term public health strategies.

Nevertheless, there are some encouraging signs, including legislative reforms on tobacco smoking and the establishment of health promotion foundations in South Australia, Victoria, Western Australia and the Australian Capital Territory, and progress in controlling the spread of HIV/AIDs.

At the national level, significant progress has been made with the 2008–2013 National Healthcare Agreements, as prevention and health outcomes have been incorporated along with public hospital care. The emphasis on health outcomes in these agreements augurs well for the future of public health in Australia. In 2007, the Council of Australian Governments agreed to support wider objectives of better services for the community and social inclusion, especially closing the gap on Indigenous health and disadvantage. Two key priorities included closing the gap in life expectancy within a generation in Indigenous communities (by 2031) and halving the gap in mortality rates for Indigenous children under five by 2018. It is to these issues of equity, inclusion and social justice that we now turn.

FURTHER READING

The classic two-volume set *The People's Health* (Praeger, 2003) by medical historian Dr Milton Lewis is the definitive history of public health in Australia, from the beginning of European settlement in 1788 to the present. It analyses the medical, lifestyle and new public health approaches, including social justice and health in the new millennium.

The issue of tobacco control is the single-most important preventable source of illness and death in Australia. The influential *Costs of Tobacco, Alcohol and Illicit Drug Abuse to Australian Society in 2004/05* by two economists, David Collins and Helen Lapsley, provides evidence of the value of taxation as a public health strategy. It is a good model of economic evaluation and public health policy analysis.

Don Nutbeam's research on health literacy, published in 2008 as 'The evolving concept of health literacy', provides evidence of the social gradient at work.

The key priorities for action in the Commonwealth Department of Health and Ageing's *National Environmental Health Strategy 2007–2012* include emergencies and disasters, climate change, drinking water supplies, urban development and the lack of effective environmental health infrastructure in Aboriginal and Torres Strait Islander communities. This is a very useful resource for environmental health.

The *Lancet* paper 'Profits and pandemics' by Moodie et al. (2013) details the 2011 United Nations high-level meeting on non-communicable diseases and interventions to regulate the market to prevent harm caused by the unhealthy commodity industries.

The report *Advocacy and Action in Public Health: Lessons from Australia over the 20th Century* by Gruszin, Hetzel & Glover (2012) provides an invaluable historical snapshot of successes and achievements in Australia over the last century, including bringing communicable diseases under control, providing safe food and water, and curbing unhealthy behaviours such as smoking and drink driving.

DISCUSSION QUESTIONS

1 Do you agree that the media play a significant role in influencing health? If so, what strategies might be put in place to best utilise this tool to promote healthier lifestyles and environments?
2 The policies and laws surrounding tobacco smoking are evolving rapidly. Will they ever lead to the complete ban of cigarettes or is the government capitalising on taxes? Should taxes collected on the sale of tobacco be invested back into helping people to give up smoking?
3 Public health benefits the larger community. Why do you think it still remains a lower priority for governments? Is prevention always better than cure?
4 What role can and should industry groups play in preventing the harmful effects of tobacco, alcohol and ultra-processed foods and drinks?

9

Health services for disadvantaged groups

It has been discussed that equity is an important criterion in health service evaluation and policy development, together with effectiveness and efficiency. The principle of equity was the most significant component in the World Health Organization (WHO) Declaration of Alma-Ata in 1978, and in Australia's subsequent 'Health for All' strategy, as adopted by the Commonwealth government in 1981 and renewed in 1994. This strategy aimed to reduce inequalities in health status within the population and to achieve a more equitable distribution of health services.

It is notable that 30 years later, in 2008, the WHO chose to return to Alma-Ata, the capital of Kazakhstan in the former Soviet Union, to renew its commitment to equity and to launch the *World Health Report 2008: Primary Health Care (Now More Than Ever)* (WHO 2008c). As the title of this influential report implies, in the context of globalisation, glaring economic inequalities and stresses on social cohesion, health systems need to respond better and faster to the challenges of a changing world through a renewed commitment to 'the right to health care'.

Socioeconomic determinants of health and health care utilisation

We have highlighted the most significant inequalities in health status and health service utilisation within the Australian community based on socioeconomic status, urban or rural location, gender and ethnicity. People from disadvantaged backgrounds—as measured by income, education, living conditions or occupational status—have poorer health outcomes than those in advantaged groups. Poor people are more likely to have shorter life expectancies, higher levels of illness and lower utilisation of preventative health services (AIHW 2008a).

Socioeconomic gradients are evident, whether it be between socioeconomic status groups, such as professionals and workers, or between families of origin. Disadvantage affects people throughout life and into the next generation. These effects tend to entrench inequalities in health and wellbeing across the population (Hertzman 1999). Socioeconomic gradients of illness are evident in the National Health Surveys. People from lower socioeconomic backgrounds are more likely to smoke, exercise less, be overweight or obese, and have fewer or no daily serves of fruit. These are risk factors for many long-term health conditions such as respiratory diseases, lung cancer and cardiovascular diseases (ABS 2006b).

Among the long-term health conditions highlighted in the National Health Survey, those reported most often by disadvantaged groups were diabetes, diseases of the circulatory system (including heart disease and stroke), arthritis, mental health problems and respiratory diseases (including asthma). The survey also showed that socioeconomically disadvantaged groups reported more visits to doctors and hospital outpatient and accident and emergency services, but were less likely to use preventative health services such as dental care (ABS 2006b).

Socioeconomic gradients of illness for Aboriginal and Torres Strait Islander peoples are evident in a comprehensive report by the Australian Institute of Health and Welfare (AIHW 2008a). The report showed that relative to other Australians, the Aboriginal and Torres Strait Islander population is disadvantaged by a number of socioeconomic factors, including post-school educational qualifications, employment, income, living conditions and home ownership. This presents Indigenous Australians with lifelong disadvantage, placing them at greater risk of ill health, early death and reduced wellbeing. This situation has not changed significantly within the last decade.

Although, in recent years, the mortality rates of Indigenous Australians have slightly improved, data suggest that the gap in overall mortality rates between Indigenous and non-Indigenous Australians is widening. The welcome news is that the gap in mortality rates between Indigenous infants and other infants is narrowing (AIHW 2008a).

The National Health Strategy (1992d) research report on inequalities in health affirmed that good health is strongly influenced by socioeconomic status; in particular, what one earns and where one lives. The report, prepared by Allison McClelland, provided comprehensive evidence that a good income, higher education and full employment contribute significantly to one's chances of staying healthy and living longer. Perhaps the most important finding is that those who suffer the poorest health in Australia have the lowest incomes, and this is not simply because of unhealthy lifestyle choices. The association is more strongly related to work, or lack of it, and level of education. The achievement of post-school qualifications appears to have a particularly powerful positive influence on health beliefs and behaviours. Support from family and friends also contributes to good health.

On a more positive note, McClelland's report indicated that health care in Australia is reasonably accessible to all. Largely, people from disadvantaged backgrounds have good access to doctors and reasonable access to hospital services. This success story is mostly attributed to universal access through Medicare. The paper, however, pointed to one area of considerable inequity: a large number of people on low incomes find it difficult to afford dental care. As costly private health insurance is the only protection against large dental bills for most people, the National Health Strategy found that poor people and their children appeared to visit the dentist only in emergencies. Because of this report, and community consultations conducted by the Australian Council of Social Service and the Consumers' Health Forum, dental care initiatives were incorporated into the Australian Labor Party's health policy proposals before the 1993 election. In 1994, the newly appointed minister for health, Senator Graham Richardson, introduced the Commonwealth Dental Health Program. This program enabled the nation's 3.6 million health care cardholders to obtain access to emergency and basic dental care, free of charge, at an estimated cost of nearly $300 million in the first four years. The Commonwealth Dental Health Program was abolished in the Howard Government's first budget in 1996. This issue resurfaced under the Rudd Government, with the proposal for a publicly funded dental insurance scheme, Denticare, included as one of many proposals in the Report of the National Health and Hospitals Reform Commission (2009b).

Analysis of social class and mortality rates in the Australian population indicates that the death rates for males from the major causes of death are highest for men in the 'low' social class and lowest for men in the 'high' social class (McMichael 1985). The risk of dying before the age of 65 is highest for men in the lowest social class and lowest for men in the highest social class. Men in the 'low' social class have death rates for respiratory and digestive diseases that are approximately four times those of the comparable figures for men in the 'high' social class. Geographical factors often combine with socioeconomic factors in the development of inequalities in access to health and health services between urban, rural and remote areas in Australia (Titulaer, Trickett & Bhatia 1998, p. 128). Death rates among those living in rural and remote locations are higher than for those in capital cities and other metropolitan centres. Overall hospitalisation statistics show a pattern across regions similar to patterns of mortality. Generally, the rate of hospitalisation shows an incremental increase across the three zones (urban, rural and remote), with the rate in the remote zone much higher than in rural and metropolitan locations. Some of these differentials may be attributed to the much higher proportion of Indigenous people in rural and remote areas, who as a population group have comparatively poorer health status.

Because of Australia's large geographical size and the uneven distribution of its relatively sparse population, the provision of adequate services in any non-metropolitan area poses logistical and economic problems for health authorities. The more specialised secondary and tertiary health services are overwhelmingly concentrated in the state capital cities and in Canberra, the national capital. Health care consumers living in cities and large metropolitan centres, where larger hospitals are located, have greater access to medical technologies such as computerised axial tomography (CAT) scanners and coronary bypass surgery than do their counterparts in rural and remote areas.

Approximately 90 per cent of Australians live in urban areas, with only 3 per cent of Australians (1.8 million people) living in rural and remote areas in 2011 (ABS 2013c). There is no doubt that rural Australians experience some degree of disadvantage in gaining access to health care in comparison with their urban counterparts. Illness and mortality increase as one moves away from metropolitan centres to rural areas and remote locations (Titulaer, Trickett & Bhatia 1998). In recognition of this inequity, a number of federal initiatives were introduced with the needs of people in rural and remote areas clearly in view. These programs included the National Rural Health Strategy, the Rural Women's Health Program, the National Breast Cancer Screening Program, the National Aboriginal Health Strategy, the Northern Australia Social Justice Strategy and the Rural Incentives Scheme, which is part of the General Practice Strategy. These programs aimed to redress the shortage of GPs in rural and remote areas, encourage multipurpose health centres in rural areas, make services for people with disabilities and frail elderly people available in their own communities, and assist those waiting for elective surgery (Commonwealth of Australia 1992).

Inequalities in the utilisation of health services are also evident among subgroups of the population with different health needs. A notable instance of this is that the growth of health services has seen a disproportionate increase in expenditure 'directed towards the few, selected not so much by social class or wealth but by medical technology itself' (Mahler 1981, p. 10); for example, with a disproportionate amount spent on persons in the final months or years before death (Mahler 1981). A health care consumer with an acute physical problem resulting from a motor vehicle accident is much better served within the current health care system than a consumer with a chronic or disabling mental health problem such as schizophrenia.

Social determinants of health

Many factors influence people's health, such as genetics and personal behavioural choices. However, growing evidence suggests that health and illness are mainly influenced by our environment or context; that is, conditions in which people are born, grow, live, work and age, including the health system (WHO 2008d).

Recognising these factors provides a greater understanding of the environment, beyond the traditional yet still important physical environmental concerns with water, sanitation, air and so on. The influential factors in the human environment—such as the cultural, political, economic, psychological and spiritual contexts of our lives—are known in the literature as the *social determinants of health*. These factors are influenced by policy choices and they shape morbidity and mortality patterns. Social determinants are mainly responsible for health inequities. There is also increasing evidence that behaviours and the possibility of behavioural change are largely influenced by these social determinants (MacDonald 2005).

The WHO has vigorously promoted the social determinants of health approach. It was first implemented in Europe and, more recently, on a global scale. In its 2008 report *Closing the Gap in a Generation: Health Equity through Action on the Social Determinants of Health*, the WHO Commission on Social Determinants of Health found that while the 'poorest of the poor' have high levels of illness and early death, ill health is not confined only to the worst-off. Rather, in all countries at all levels of income, 'health and illness follow a social gradient: the lower the socioeconomic position, the worse the health' (WHO 2008d).

Studies show large health gaps not only between countries and between high-income and low-income groups within countries, but also even between regions of the same city, as revealed in area data indexed and analysed according to socioeconomic characteristics from the Australian Bureau of Statistics (ABS) (see figure 9.1). These indexes enable comparison of the social and economic conditions across Australia. Lower values indicate lower socioeconomic status. The Northern Sydney and Central Coast health area in Sydney, Australia's most populous city, had the highest index values in New South Wales. The most disadvantaged areas according to these indexes were the North Coast and Greater Western health areas, those with higher levels of unemployment and poverty, as illustrated in figure 9.1.

Figure 9.1 Socioeconomic indices for areas (SEIFA) scores by health area, NSW, 2006

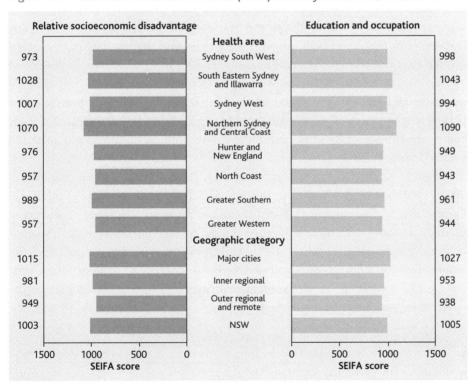

Source: NSW Department of Health (2009)

Overall, there is a considerable difference between major cities and regional and remote areas. Socioeconomic status decreases with increasing ruralism and remoteness. The Commission on the Social Determinants of Health argues that putting health inequalities right is a matter of social justice and an urgent 'ethical imperative'—something that should not be ignored (WHO 2008d).

Health inequalities are not only shaped by unequal distributions of material resources; they are also moulded by imbalances in the distribution of power and control. A sense of empowerment over life circumstances is the foundation for good health: people need to feel that they have at least some level of control over their lives, their jobs, their housing and their environments. Moreover, different groups have different opportunities to participate in political, economic, social and cultural relationships, organisations and structures. Which groups are more likely to experience social inclusion? People who do not face barriers to participation include people from high socioeconomic backgrounds, those from Australia's Anglo-Celtic ethnic majority group, and those who do not identify as Aboriginal or Torres Strait Islander (AIHW 2008a).

Social exclusion, or non-participation, stems from experiences of disempowerment, and generally gives rise to further adverse circumstances, such as low educational achievement and lower levels of service use, including using preventative health services. Typically, so-called behavioural health risk factors—such as smoking, poor diet, alcohol misuse and low levels of physical activity—are firmly embedded in the social exclusion and marginalisation that accompany structural imbalances in power. Sir Michael Marmot (2004), the London-based Australian epidemiologist, points, for example, to the fact that some people feel they do not have the same value as other people. This is the opposite of a human rights perspective, in which all people are accorded equal value. Social inclusion, agency and control are crucially important for the development of human potential and health (Marmot, 2004).

Social Inclusion: Origins, Concepts and Key Themes (Hayes, Gray & Edwards 2008), published by the Australian Institute of Family Studies as part of the Rudd Government's commitment to social inclusion, discusses a number of aspects of social exclusion. These include locational disadvantage, unemployment, intergenerational disadvantage, children at risk, child poverty, disability and its effects on employment, and homelessness, all of which can contribute to poor health outcomes. The following six government priorities were identified as part of the government's social inclusion agenda:

- addressing the incidence and needs of jobless families with children
- delivering effective support to children at greatest risk of long-term disadvantage
- focusing on particular locations, neighbourhoods and communities to ensure programs and services are getting to the right places
- addressing the incidence of homelessness
- increasing employment for people living with a disability or mental illness
- closing the gap for Indigenous Australians.

We examine now the theoretical foundation for this ethical imperative to 'close the gap'.

A social justice perspective

Injunctions such as 'health for all', 'social inclusion' and 'closing the gap' rest on the notion that what is available to some groups in the population should be available to all; access to health and health care is a right, not a privilege. This social justice philosophy, as developed by John Rawls (1972), prioritises the interests of the least advantaged groups in society. Policies designed within this social justice perspective can be regarded not so much as meeting the 'special needs' of disadvantaged groups but rather as guaranteeing basic rights to health and health care (Gifford 1986). Rawls' approach is problematic, however, when brought into practice because guaranteeing access to health care has the potential to impoverish a society (Daniels 1985). The preferred solution to this problem is to develop policies that favour equal access to health care for those with equal health need, which is essentially the principle of equal opportunity (McGuire et al. 1988). In this chapter, we focus on policies designed to improve access to health care for those groups at greatest disadvantage within Australia's current political and economic structure. These include groups such as Aboriginal and Torres Strait Islander peoples, who have less access to and control over political and economic resources than their non-Aboriginal counterparts.

The cost of health care is crucial to the notion of equality of access in health care because if two people face different costs in using a service—through factors such as direct payment for service, lost income, travelling expenses or waiting time—they have unequal access to that service (Le Grand 1982). Equality of cost of health care means that each health care consumer faces the same private 'cost' for each 'unit' of health care received; the Labor Party's Medicare policy enshrined equity of access in legislation: 'Central to the rhetoric of the Australian Labor Party is a desire to ensure that no person is precluded from gaining access to health care because of financial barriers; health care is a right not a privilege' (Duckett 1992, p. 138).

This link between human rights and health is of relatively recent origin. Following World War II and the Nuremberg Trials, where human rights abuses by medical doctors in the Nazi concentration camps were revealed, the medical profession has acted on an international level in an attempt to protect human rights. The Geneva Declaration, proclaimed by the World Medical Association in 1964, states that doctors should maintain the utmost respect for human life even under threat, and that they should not use their medical knowledge in ways contrary to the laws of humanity.

In 1994, the late Jonathan Mann, from the Centre for Health and Human Rights at Harvard University, led the first international conference on health and human rights. This 'new paradigm for medicine' recognised that human rights are an essential precondition for physical and mental health (Holst 1997, p. 73). We would add social health to this formulation and thus broaden the paradigm to health, rather than medicine.

In their positivistic sense, human rights are usually understood as enforceable claims on the delivery of goods, services or protection by the state. This process of enforceability proceeds at both the national and international levels, through idealisation, commitment and realisation. 'Human rights start out as moral rights and over time become to some extent enforceable rights in the positive law of different societies' (Eide et al. 1992, p. 385). The 1948 United Nations Declaration of Human Rights, Article 25, states:

> Everyone has the right to a standard of living adequate for the health and well-being of himself [*sic*] and of his family, including food, clothing, housing and medical care and necessary social services, and the right to security in the event of unemployment, sickness, disability, widowhood, old age or other lack of livelihood in circumstances beyond his control.

It is well to remember that whether these praiseworthy human rights declarations have the beneficial effect that their wording suggests depends on the interpretation, application and enforcement of the principles. More precisely, the implementation of human rights has to be exercised most of all in the national sphere, through the existence of:

- an independent judiciary
- a diligent representative government
- a vigilant, well-informed public.

Without these three necessary preconditions, human rights discourse is rhetoric rather than reality (Short 1997a). Moreover, citizen's rights are guaranteed by law only to the extent that they are protected by the citizenry's exercise of their obligation to participate in society. 'Rights are a protection from society. But only by fulfilling their obligations to society can the individual give meaning to that protection' (Saul 1997, p. 168). Social justice rests on rights and responsibilities.

Although Medicare and its predecessor, Medibank, were designed to ensure that all Australians have equal access to basic medical and hospital services on the basis of health need, disadvantaged groups often need further assistance in gaining access to general or mainstream health services. In addition, disadvantaged groups may require programs and services tailored to their specific needs. For example, an 'ethnospecific' health service is designed for and used by members of one particular ethnic group, such as Sudanese refugees. We here consider the following arguably disadvantaged groups: women, men, immigrants, Indigenous Australians, those with mental health problems, people with intellectual or psychiatric disabilities and older persons.

Universal health coverage

An emerging international concept of universal health coverage helps to bring many of these concerns together in a single conceptual framework or model. The *World Health Report: Health Systems Financing—The Path to Universal Coverage* (2010a) defines the three dimensions that constitute universal health coverage:

- access to good-quality needed services through a mix of prevention, promotion, treatment, rehabilitation and palliative care
- financial protection, so that no one faces financial hardship or impoverishment by paying for the needed services
- equity for everyone in the population and universality (WHO 2010a).

Thus, universal health coverage comprises three dimensions (figure 9.2): population coverage ideally reaching 100 per cent, the level of protection as a percentage of costs covered and the services being covered. The purpose of universal health coverage is to provide a framework for the equitable distribution of health services, particularly for marginalised groups. The WHO, the World Bank and many developing and donor countries have already adopted universal health coverage as their top health priority.

Figure 9.2   Universal health coverage cube

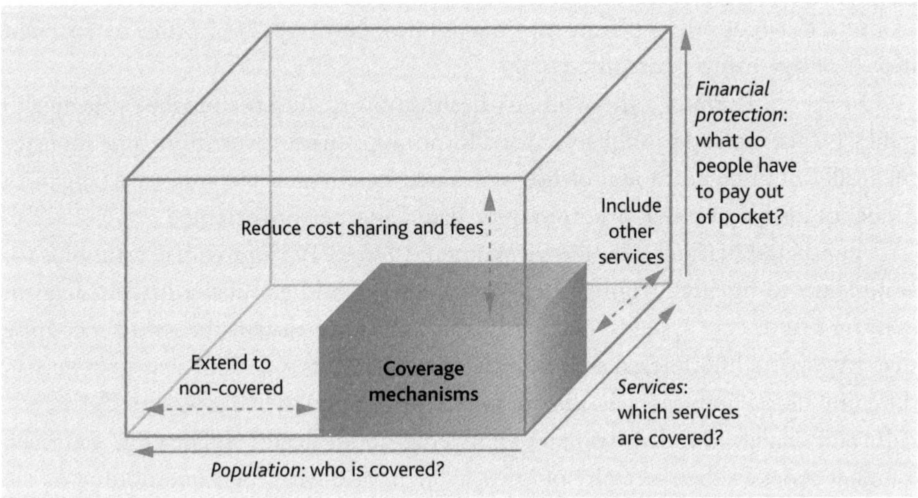

Source: Adapted from WHO (2010a)

Key WHO milestones in universal health coverage include:

- 1948: WHO Constitution
- 1978: Alma-Ata Declaration
- 2008: *Primary Health Care (Now More than Ever)* report
- 2010: *Health Systems Financing: The Path to Universal Coverage* report (Lin 2013).

In the Australian context, Medicare clearly satisfies these three dimensions, and this goes a long way towards explaining its popularity as a public policy (Boxall & Gillespie 2013). In this chapter we focus on the population dimension in universal health coverage: who is covered? We start with women.

Women

The women's health movement has produced some of the most active and vocal critics of existing health services since the late 1960s (Boston Women's Health Book Collective 1985; Broom 1991; Gray Jamieson 2013; Healthsharing Women 1990; Horsley, Tremellen & Hancock 1999; Ruzek 1978; Siedlecky & Wyndham 1990). During this period, women have been more successful than other consumer groups in reforming the health care system. The motivation for the high level of involvement of women in this activity is related to the fact that women are under-represented in the 'corridors of power' within the health care system, despite the fact that women are the major users and providers of health care services. The women's health movement has acted to change the existing health care system in three main ways: first, by having women's special needs recognised by policymakers and by emphasising that these needs are not restricted to their childbearing years or reproductive function; second, by establishing separate 'women-centred' health services, managed by and for women, to meet women's specific needs; and third, by attempting to reorient health policy more generally.

On the third strategy, the women's health movement has contributed to health policy by attempting to shift resource allocation priorities away from an expensive medically dominated model of hospital-based health care towards a participatory model of health care that is community-based and person-oriented.

The United Nations' Decade for Women, 1975 to 1985, provided a stimulus for complaints to be aired from women around the world about the inadequacies of existing health care systems. During this decade, governments began to recognise that a woman's life differed significantly from that of a man, and that women had different illness experiences that required sensitivity to women's special needs. A further change was that women's knowledge about health and healing was given a higher status in the hierarchy of knowledge in line with their questioning of the privileged status of medical knowledge about women's health (Doyal 1986).

The United Nations' Decade for Women closed with an international meeting in Nairobi, Kenya, which was attended by an Australian delegation of Aboriginal and non-Aboriginal women, led by Senator Pat Giles from Western Australia. Closer to home, the Decade for Women opened with an International Women's Year (1975) conference in Brisbane, entitled 'Women's Health in a Changing Society', and the end of the Decade for Women was marked by the second national conference on women's health in Adelaide in 1985 (Kerby-Eaton & Davies 1986a,b,c). The conference was organised around three themes: structural and political issues, such as women as providers and users of health care; women's reproductive role, which included issues such as new reproductive technologies and menopause; and social and economic issues, such as domestic violence and workplace health and safety. Then, in 1995, the Third National Women's Health Conference in Canberra focused on the health of Indigenous and immigrant women, implementing the National Women's Health Policy and changing patterns of working and living (Davis et al. 1996).

These developments saw women's health issues placed on the policy agendas of governments and organisations at community, state and territory, and national levels. The amount of discussion on women's health during this period was substantial. It is clear that many women in Australia have been working extremely hard to publicise women's health issues and to see that women's health policies have been developed and implemented. Since 1975, we have seen numerous national conferences on women's health, the Better Health Commission's National Workshop on Women and Health in 1985, state-based inquiries on women's health, and numerous seminars, forums and other community development activities that have identified major issues relating to women's health problems, women's experiences as consumers of mainstream health services and women's experiences as providers of health care. In addition, the Australian Health Ministers' Advisory Council established the Subcommittee on Women and Health in 1987, to report to the Australian health ministers.

At the federal level, the first initiatives in women's health were the funding of women's health centres under the Community Health Program in 1974, the appointment of Dr Stefania Siedlecky as the first medical services adviser on family planning in the same year, and the establishment of a women's health unit within the Department of Health in 1977. A women's health unit was established again by the Commonwealth government in 1985, and by state and territory governments in South Australia, New South Wales, Victoria, Western Australia and the Australian Capital Territory within several years. A large women's health policy unit was established in Queensland following the election of a Labor government in 1989. In 1995, a team of researchers based at the University of Newcastle in New South Wales was commissioned by the Commonwealth government to conduct the first Australian longitudinal study of women's health. The design allows for its continuation for 20 to 30 years. The intention is to survey three cohorts of young, middle-aged and older women at three-yearly intervals over this period.

Many Commonwealth program areas have a direct or indirect impact on women's health. These areas include child care, family support services for persons with disabilities, support for victims of domestic violence and sexual assault, aged care facilities and the National Women's Health Program. In addition, the federal Department of Health funds family planning associations through block grants to the states and supports a broad range of community and consumer health organisations, including the Australian Council of Social Service and the Consumers' Health Forum.

The significant policy initiative to come from the second national conference on women's health was the appointment for 12 months, from June 1987, of Liza Newby as special adviser on women's health to the then federal minister for community services and health, Dr Neal Blewett. Newby's major responsibility was to coordinate the development of a national policy on women's health through consultation with health authorities in the states and territories and with a broad range of community groups and health organisations. These consultations resulted in a discussion paper for community comment and response, the *National Policy on Women's Health: A Framework for Change*, released in 1988 (Commonwealth Department of Community Services and Health 1988a). The document set out 16 draft recommendations for establishing a framework within which strategies for a national policy on women's health could be developed. The issues of reproductive health, mental health, breast and cervical cancer screening and nutrition were adopted on an interim basis as priority health issues in the National Women's Health Program. Domestic violence and occupational health and safety were also singled out as issues that could provide illustrative models for a coordinated intersectoral approach to women's health problems, which would build on existing national and state and territory initiatives.

National Women's Health Policy: Advancing Women's Health in Australia was endorsed by the Australian Health Ministers' Conference in 1989 (Commonwealth Department of Community Services and Health 1989b), and the First National Women's Health Program was funded for $34 million over four years, to 1992–93. The policy and program were developed within a social or primary health care approach to health, which recognises that health is determined by social, cultural, economic and environmental factors as well as biological factors. Differences in health status are thus linked to gender, socioeconomic status, ethnicity and so on. The objective of the First National Women's Health Program was to provide funding for primary health care for women, focusing on improvements relating to the seven health issues identified in the consultation process as having priority:

- reproductive health and sexuality
- health of ageing women
- women's emotional and mental health
- violence against women
- occupational health and safety
- the health needs of women as carers
- the health effects of sex-role stereotyping.

Five broad structural areas of the health system were identified as needing action to improve the health of women:

- improvements in health services for women
- provision of health information and education for women
- provision of training and education for effective health care
- women's participation in decision-making
- research and data collection on women's health.

Most of the funding for the First National Women's Health Program was spent on providing improved primary health care services, including information and education services at local and state levels; some was spent on continuing education and training for health professionals. In addition, responsibility for implementing the National Women's Health Policy and Program was elevated to the Australian Health Ministers' Advisory Council Subcommittee on Women and Health, rather than a women's health branch within the department, as proposed in the policy.

In 1993, the Commonwealth reviewed the First National Women's Health Program, and the Second National Women's Health Program was funded until 1999, when the National Public Health Partnership played a more significant regulatory role at both federal and state and territory levels. Between 1989 and 1993, the principles of the National Women's Health Policy informed a number of other national initiatives, including the National Program for the Early Detection of Breast Cancer (National Advisory Committee for the Early Detection of Breast Cancer 1992) and the National Policy on the Screening for the Prevention of Cervical Cancer. The Alternative Birthing Services Program, established by the Commonwealth in 1989, also reflected the principles of the National Women's Health Policy. This Commonwealth program provided incentive payments to the states and territories to establish appropriate and safe midwife-managed alternative birthing services for women who chose not to give birth in a specialised hospital setting. It funded new or expanded birth centres in hospitals and community-based, midwife-managed prenatal and postnatal education and support services. In addition, the National Health and Medical Research Council (1992) resolved to develop a women's health strategy and implementation plan to ensure that the council's activity (including support for research, development of standards and guidelines, training and ethical policies and guidelines) took into account the goals and principles of the National Women's Health Policy.

At the state and territory level, what is most striking is the considerable variation in the commitments of resources devoted to women's health. Newby's research on women's health policies around Australia revealed that not all states and territories had developed health policies, programs and services for women (Commonwealth Department of Community Services and Health 1988a). Newby also found considerable differences between rural and city areas, which increased the uneven development of and accessibility to women's health services. In 1988, funding for women's health services was virtually non-existent in Queensland, Tasmania and northern Western Australia, and most extensive in New South Wales and South Australia.

Developments in women's health across the states

Here we consider developments in women's health services on a state-by-state basis. In New South Wales in the 1980s, the most significant event in women's health was the presentation of the report of the Women's Health Policy Review Committee to the minister in 1985. The major recommendations that were carried out included:

- the establishment of a women's health unit, under Carla Cranny, the first women's health adviser to be appointed by the New South Wales government
- the recruitment of women's health coordinators in seven regions of the state
- the provision of additional funds for sexual assault clinics in urban and rural locations
- development of a breast cancer mammographic screening program
- a cervical cancer awareness campaign
- initial funding for women's health centres in five new areas
- extended funding of existing women's health centres
- recruitment of women's health nurses and women's health education officers throughout the state.

Particularly innovative in New South Wales was the training of nurse practitioners and the establishment of 'well women's' clinics by the Family Planning Association. From 1976, nurse practitioners were trained to provide a wide range of health promotion services, including Pap smear collection, vaginal and pelvic examination and breast examination, issuing of oral contraceptives under authorisation, the fitting of diaphragms for contraception, pregnancy testing, counselling and general contraceptive advice (Meredith 1986). As the consumer response to nurse practitioners was very favourable, the Family Planning Federation of Australia initiated the first national course for nurse practitioners in February 1986. The next year, the NSW Department of Health decided to train nurse practitioners to work as women's health nurses in the community. Twenty women's health nurses were appointed in rural and outer urban areas to provide mobile breast and cervical cancer screening services and preventative health and counselling services. This development represented a significant challenge to the medical profession's monopoly over diagnostic and curative services. It also illustrates the way that initiatives in women's health policy can lead to significant reforms within the mainstream health care system.

South Australia, the other innovative state in the area of women's health policy, appointed Liz Furler as the women's adviser to the South Australian Health Commission in January 1984. This was the first appointment of a women's adviser within a health department in Australia (Furler 1986). The Office of the Women's Advisor in South Australia was an important role model for other appointments in women's health. From its inception, it ensured that women's health would not be isolated or relegated to the margins of health policy. By 1986, the office had become an integral part of the commission's decision-making processes. It was involved in all major policymaking committees, including environmental health, health promotion, occupational health and safety, staff development and equal employment opportunity.

The South Australian government then supported the establishment of a social health policy office that would act as a focus for mainstream health policies relating to intersectoral health development, primary health care and community health. The role of the Office of the Women's Advisor was extended to the broader population in October 1987 when the Social Health Office was incorporated into the Health Commission as a branch within the Planning and Policy Development Division. This contrasts with the Women's Office, which, in effect, acted as a ministerial adviser. In one sense, the Women's Office was incorporated into the mainstream, thus losing direct formal access to the chair of the Health Commission and the minister. However, these channels remained open on an informal basis.

In Victoria, development of a women's health policy gained momentum in late 1985, when the then minister for health, David White, established the Women's Health Policy Working Party to investigate women's health problems and to recommend measures to improve health services for women in Victoria. The work of this group began bearing fruit in the 1986–87 state budget, when funds were made available for the first fully funded women's health centre and the Women's Health Information Centre. In addition, the Women's Health Policy and Program Unit was established within the Victorian Health Department (Victorian Ministerial Women's Health Working Party 1987).

Victorian women have produced some of the most clearly articulated views on the politics of women's health in two very useful policy documents: *Why Women's Health?*, the discussion paper prepared by the Victorian Women's Health Policy Working Party in 1985, and *Why Women's Health? Victorian Women Respond*, published in 1987. The former document still offers one of the most incisive analyses of women's health policy published in Australia. The third section of the report is likely to be particularly useful for policy analysts because it places structural change at the centre of the policy agenda. It outlined a number of short- and long-term strategies for change. These included greater representation by women on hospital boards, community health centre boards and district health councils; changes within existing services to give increasing emphasis to women's health needs; additional specific-purpose health services for women; the introduction of an office of women's health; and support for local women's health groups.

Many of the recommendations in these reports were implemented between 1987 and 1992 (Southgate 1993). The Victorian Health Department established a Women's Health Policy Unit in 1987; women's health organisations, such as Healthsharing Women (1990, 1991), a statewide women's health information service, were funded through the Victorian Women's Health Program; a birthing services review was undertaken; and centres against sexual assault were funded. Following a change of government, the Victorian Liberal Government made no commitment to the existing women's health program. In 1992, the Women's Health Policy Unit was abolished, along with other units within the Victorian Health Department. Service support functions were transferred to regional offices where they were likely to receive a mixed response and varying levels of commitment. Reflecting on developments in women's health services since the *Why Women's Health?* discussion paper, Southgate (1993, p. 13) commented, 'Little did we realise that eight years after the question was asked of them, they would need to restate their case. It remains to be seen how successful women will be in holding onto what they have achieved'.

In January 1987, the West Australian government announced the establishment of the Women's Health Policy Unit, and by 1988 the state had a sexual assault centre, a women's health centre, programs to provide cancer screening services, and women's health services for women in outer suburban and rural areas. Western Australia has given particular support to the development of midwife-managed birthing services, both at home and in hospital.

Prior to 1989, the Queensland government provided no funding for women's health services at all. The only women's health centre in Queensland, in Brisbane, was funded through a national community health program grant from the Commonwealth. The pre-1989 National Party conservative Queensland government exhibited no commitment to women's health centres, advisers and so on. This left the Commonwealth in a difficult situation, since federal policy, in general, is one of non-involvement in direct health care delivery. While the Commonwealth was unable to fund women's services directly, it was possible to attach conditions to a proportion of grants to states and territories specifically for the development of women's health programs. However, this did not necessarily achieve the Commonwealth's national objectives for women's health, because the Queensland government could decide to channel the funds into mainstream clinical services, such as obstetrics and gynaecology. The situation changed considerably after the change of government in 1989, which led to the establishment of a Women's Health Policy Unit. A Queensland Women's Health Policy was developed following consultations with Queensland women in 1992 and 1993, and funding was provided to support women's health centres, health services for women in cities, regional and rural areas, and sexual assault and rape crisis services.

The family planning movement

The struggle by Australian women to control their own fertility has been a central issue in women's health since the 19th century (Siedlecky & Wyndham 1990). Formal birth control organisations were established in Australia in the 1930s and a formal movement for abortion law reform was developed after World War II. Commonwealth government support for state- and territory-based family planning associations dates back to 1971 and the early days of the modern women's liberation movement. The 'family planning movement' spread to all states with the establishment of family planning associations (FPAs), expansion of clinical and educational services and increased interest and influence from the medical profession (Siedlecky & Wyndham 1990, p. 169). Substantial government support came in 1974 when the Whitlam Labor Government allocated over $1 million for family planning activities. The Australian Federation of Family Planning

Associations was formally incorporated in 1975 and, in 1978, Wendy McCarthy was appointed as its first full-time executive officer. Medibank covered all family planning services provided by doctors, including abortion and sterilisation, from its inception in 1975.

> A system of health program grants was introduced to cover services provided by FPAs, which meant that FPAs no longer had to charge fees. With the lifting of the sales tax on contraceptives and inclusion of the pill on the pharmaceutical benefits list, most of the financial barriers to family planning were removed.
>
> Siedlecky & Wyndham (1990)

The Commonwealth's Family Planning Program aimed to make family planning accessible to all groups in the community, with special attention to the needs of adolescents, Aboriginal and migrant women, and women in rural and remote areas. The Commonwealth government continued to provide strong support for and commitment to family planning during the 1980s and early 1990s. Increased federal funding to the FPAs meant that they were able to 'increase the availability of appropriate services in the field of family planning for women of childbearing age', their original brief, as well as for other members of the community. It is important to recognise, also, that childbearing age ranges from 12 to 50. Women comprise over 50 per cent of the Australian population, and women of childbearing age over a quarter of the total Australian population. The FPAs, while recognising the special needs of this group of women, also acknowledge that appropriate services for women of childbearing age vary depending on their age, lifestyles and socioeconomic circumstances.

One particularly disadvantaged group is adolescent women for whom there is an increased risk of low birth weight and perinatal death with motherhood. While the greatest physical risks are to the baby, adolescent mothers are often severely financially and socially disadvantaged because their educational and employment opportunities are so restricted. For these women, the most appropriate services that FPAs can provide are comprehensive sexuality and reproductive health education and access to contraceptive information and services, so that they can make informed choices about their bodies and their future.

FPAs also provide special services for women in their 20s and 30s. Comprehensive contraceptive information and services are provided, in addition to a range of preventative health services. As breast and cervical cancer are the biggest killers of women in this age group, FPAs stress the importance of taking preventative measures to reduce the risks of developing cancer, such as regular Pap smears for cervical cancer and breast checks. Women in this age group are also counselled about the health benefits to themselves and their children of spacing births. As is the case for adolescent women, appropriate services for women of this age include the provision of information and services that offer a range of contraceptive choices and preventative health services and information. For women in their late reproductive years, FPAs provide services that make women aware of the risks to their health, and their children's health, of giving birth later in life. They also provide menopause counselling.

These services, together with the services and information designed specifically to meet the needs of young women, Aboriginal women, women living in rural and remote areas, migrant women, and women with physical and intellectual disabilities, are an integral part of Australia's health care system. They also reflect the FPAs' commitment to improving the status of women's health in Australia. This is achieved through providing appropriate clinical services for particular groups of women, health education that enables women to make informed choices about their bodies, and preventative services in crucial areas such as contraception, breast and cervical cancer, sexually transmitted diseases and HIV/AIDS. This broad and innovative range of women's health and reproductive services also enables the FPAs to play a vital role in postgraduate training for general practitioners and nurses around Australia.

Dorothy Broom's (1991) sociological investigation into Australia's 40 or more government-funded women's health centres reminds us of the twin aims of the women's health movement: to change the overall structure of a society that disadvantages women, while at the same time providing appropriate health services, health information and health education to individual women.

In 2007, the Rudd Government made a commitment to develop a National Women's Health Policy to improve the health and wellbeing of all women in Australia, and to implement policies to encourage the health system to be more responsive to the needs of women. It had been almost 20 years since the last National Women's Health Policy was developed (AIHW 2008a).

In 2009, the then Minister for Health and Ageing, Nicola Roxon, released the *Development of a New National Women's Health Policy: Consultation Discussion Paper*, commencing the first phase of consultations on the National Women's Health Policy. The consultations led to the National Women's Health Policy 2010, which aimed to improve the health of women, especially disadvantaged women who are at greatest risk for poor health. Other commitments made by the minister for health included the National Female Genital Mutilation Summit in 2012, which led to the announcement of the National Compact on Female Genital Mutilation, to collaborate across governments, sectors and communities about the illegal and harmful practice.

During the Gillard Government's term, health minister Tanya Plibersek welcomed the Pharmaceutical Benefits Advisory Committee's recommendation to include the RU 486 pill, or the 'abortion pill', on the Pharmaceutical Benefits Scheme (PBS) in 2013. This pill offers women a more affordable option and enables women to terminate a pregnancy medically rather than surgically. However, controversies surrounding the drug are also prominent. Pro-life activists complain that RU 486 will make abortions much easier, cheaper and quicker. On the other hand, politicians claim they have given women more choice and rights by including the pill on the PBS. Implementing policies and finding common ground among governments, right-to-life advocates, feminist community groups and reproductive health agencies is a constant challenge.

Women are the majority of health consumers, the majority of health service providers and the majority of carers in the Australian community. Governments recognise that improving the health of all Australian women will improve the health of the whole community.

Men

Although not traditionally considered a 'disadvantaged group' in general, there has been an emerging recognition of the need to consider the health issues of men. The primary reason for valuing the health of the men is the principle of equity, as all members of society are entitled to fair treatment without discrimination based on any features of social identity; that is, who they are as a person. Equity is not about competition between men and women, especially when there are significant disparities in health outcomes between groups of men in Australia. A focus on equity aims to reduce that gap and to ensure all men are healthy despite their social circumstances (AIHW 2008a).

Figure 9.3 Deaths in Australia, selected by sex, 2010

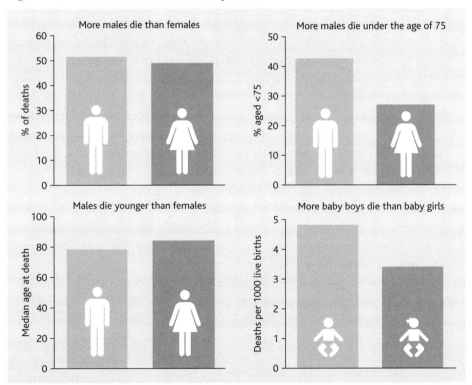

Source: Based on figure 2.18 in Australian Institute of Health and Welfare 2012a, *Australia's health 2012*, Australia's health series no. 13, cat. no. AUS 156, AIHW, Canberra, p. 87

While, overall, life expectancy for all Australians has increased over the past century, rates of men's mortality are still higher than those for women. In 2011, the median age at death was 78.4 years for males and 84.5 years for females (ABS 2013b). In addition, these rates have not improved to the same degree as female mortality (AIHW 2007). This statistic remains the same when looking at the differential between Indigenous men's health and Indigenous women's health. Mortality rates for Indigenous men across Australia are higher than those for any other demographic.

The group of Australian men who are most at risk of premature mortality are Aboriginal and Torres Strait Islander men. This group fares far worse than the rest of the male population. According to ABS 2012 data, Indigenous males born between 2005 and 2007 could expect to live to 67.2 years, 11.5 years less than the 78.7 years expected for non-Indigenous males (Australian Indigenous HealthInfoNet 2013). In 2011, the median age at death for Indigenous males ranged from 50.3 years for those living in South Australia to 58.5 years for those living in New South Wales (Australian Indigenous HealthInfoNet 2013).

In 2007, the Rudd Government announced that it would develop Australia's first National Men's Health Policy. This was followed up in June 2008 with the release of the paper *Developing a Men's Health Policy for Australia: Setting the Scene*. The paper marked the commencement of the consultation process for the first National Men's Health Policy. It outlined what the government wanted to achieve through the policy in a national and international context, some of the heath issues affecting men across the life course, the proposed principles on which the policy would be based, and the broad consultation process. The new Men's Health Policy was developed in parallel to the revised Women's Health Policy (AIHW 2008a).

Men and women play diverse roles in the Australian economy and society. They have different life experiences and health experiences due to biological (for example, genetic and hormonal), psychological, economic and social factors, including the roles they play at work, in the family and in the community. Obviously, some conditions (such as pregnancy and prostate disease) affect only women or only men; others are more prevalent in one sex or the other. Major depression is more prevalent among women, whereas deaths from suicide are more common among men. Some conditions may occur with equal frequency but men and women manage or experience them differently (AIHW 2008a).

The aim is for the policies to be complementary and based on similar principles; both will recognise gender as a basic determinant of health, which gives rise to different health outcomes for and different needs of men and women. Both policies arise from the current interest in policies that emphasise prevention, the unequal distribution of health and the social determinants of that unequal distribution, which are relevant for men and women. Each policy incorporates a gender-specific action plan that identifies practical activities to improve health outcomes across the life span.

The separate health needs of men and women are now on the national agenda. It will be interesting to see the extent to which the issues identified as most important in the draft National Men's Health Policy, developed under the Labor government in 1995, remain relevant. These include the relationships between socialisation and risk-taking behaviour in men and boys, socioeconomic status and men's health, and workplace health and safety. Men's mental health, substance use, sexual health and violence were also discussed.

Table 9.1 Differences between men's and women's death rates for age groups, 2011, Australia

Age group	Men	Women
0–19	1213	885
20–29	1145	467
30–39	1595	827
40–49	2878	1846
50–59	5973	3681
60–69	10935	6463
70–79	17317	11674
80–89	25339	26826
90–99	8697	17807
100 and over	235	1125

Note
Excludes deaths for which age at death was not stated.

Source: Based on Australian Bureau of Statistics 2011c, *Deaths, Australia 2011*, cat. no. 3302.0, ABS, Canberra

In 1999, the first state policy aimed at improving the health and wellbeing of men, *Moving Forward in Men's Health*, was developed by the NSW Department of Health. Then, in 2008, South Australia launched a policy that aimed to recognise health issues for men and suggested some principles and actions. In 2010, the Australian Government released the *National Male Health Policy* to promote health equity between male population groups through all life stages, as well as focus on preventative health measures and improve access to health care for men.

Immigrants

Australia is one of the most ethnically diverse countries in the world. Over a quarter (over 6 million) of its population was born overseas. At the 2006 census, one in seven Australians, or 61 per cent of people born overseas, was born in a non-English-speaking country. The largest non-English-speaking ethnic groups were from Italy, Vietnam, Greece and China (ABS 2007).

During the 1980s, the character and composition of Australia's immigrant population underwent significant change due to the unplanned increase of refugees from countries in conflict in South-East Asia, the Middle East and South America. Over the last three decades, South-East Asia, North-East Asia and Southern Asia have increasingly become the sources of both settler and long-term visitor arrivals (ABS 1999f). Overall, more than 100 different ethnic groups are represented in Australia's resident population, which is characterised by a rich diversity of cultures, religions, languages and dialects.

The second half of the 20th century saw three major periods in the history of Australian public policy towards immigrants (Martin 1978). In the 1950s and early 1960s, policies were based on the notion of assimilation; that is, the expectation that immigrants could blend into Australia's predominantly Anglo-Australian culture without undue strain on the part of the new settlers or significant change on the part of the Australian community. In the post–World War II period, immigrants were expected to reject their own languages and cultures in order to speak and act like Anglo-Australians.

From the mid-1960s to the early 1970s, policymakers began to acknowledge that immigrants had special needs. During this period, policies were dominated by the notion of integration. This philosophy recommended that the cultures of migrant groups be respected and maintained. The principal issues during this period were language, communication and cultural difference. The source of problems with immigration was believed to lie in the inadequacy or unsuitability of the settlers themselves. Immigrants were held responsible for the problems they confronted in Australia, and policies were designed to help immigrants adjust to the Australian way of life.

The mid-1970s saw federal commitment to a policy of multiculturalism, as outlined in Al Grassby's (1973) policy statement, A Multi-Cultural Society for the Future. 'Multiculturalism as an ideology calls for a celebration of cultural diversity as a continuing feature of Australian society' (Castles et al. 1988, p. 5). This policy approach acknowledges that cultural pluralism requires multi-ethnic political participation. Political participation on the part of immigrants was recognised as the only legitimate means by which disadvantaged ethnic groups might reverse the forces militating against them. This policy shift was made possible because established ethnic groups, such as those from Italian or Greek backgrounds, had become a political force in their own right. As a result, the more powerful immigrant groups claimed rights to power and participation, and demanded that the mainstream political system acknowledge their existence. Political action on the part of immigrant organisations was important because the ideology of multiculturalism often ignores the necessity of immigrant political participation over and above recognition of cultural diversity (Kringas 1984). While the policy approaches of assimilation and integration emphasised the transient nature of difficulties encountered by newly arrived settlers, the multicultural philosophy conceives of Australia as an ethnically diverse society in which all ethnic groups can make legitimate and permanent contributions to Australia's way of life.

It should be remembered also that immigrants are not evenly distributed within the Australian workforce. Although English-speaking immigrants have jobs similar to those of people born in Australia, immigrants from backgrounds with languages other than English (LOTE) are concentrated in the dirtiest, least-skilled and worst-paid jobs (O'Malley 1978). Immigrant women workers from LOTE backgrounds are concentrated in semi-skilled and unskilled jobs such as cleaning, process work and industrial 'dressmaking' (Facci et al. 1986). This results in immigrants from LOTE backgrounds having lower incomes and greater workplace health and safety problems than English-speaking Australians. Of particular concern is repetitive strain injury (RSI), a major workplace health and safety problem for working women and for women from LOTE backgrounds in particular (National Occupational Health and Safety Commission 1986).

The health of immigrants

Between the mid-1950s and mid-1970s, the main migrant health problems attracting the attention of medical practitioners were mental illness and stress, the social context of medical care, physical illness, hospitalisation, health care utilisation and alcoholism (Martin 1978, p. 155). Jean Martin noted that these problems were usually defined as problems within immigrants, not problems within the health care system. Medical research revealed that immigrants were vulnerable to mental health problems because of pre-migration experiences of deprivation and stress, and because of ignorance and fear, low standards of literacy, and alien cultural values and expectations. Since many immigrants experienced frustration and dissatisfaction when using mainstream health services during this period, this led to under-utilisation of health services. As immigrants stayed away from mainstream services, many health professionals were not exposed to many of the difficulties that immigrants encountered when utilising health services.

The tendency to 'blame the migrant' has been questioned since the mid-1970s, when emphasis was placed on changing the health care system in order to meet the needs of people from LOTE backgrounds. Martin's (1978) sociological analysis of developments in immigrant health care in Australia indicated that early responses were largely confined to implementing the minimal adjustment necessary to reduce the worst disruptions caused by immigrant patients through provision of interpreters in public hospitals. The New South Wales Association of Mental Health was singled out as particularly progressive in overcoming communication difficulties for immigrants, and the Hospital Interpreter Program of the New South Wales Health Commission was presented as a model plan for organisational change to meet immigrant communication needs.

For too long, Anglo-Australian health professionals have attempted to persuade immigrants to change in some way by educating them about healthy lifestyle, encouraging them to learn English and so on. In doing so, they rarely entertained the idea that immigrants could be the ones to solve their own problems.

Since the mid-1970s, the period of multiculturalism, there has been increasing acknowledgment of the need for ethnic communities to participate in the management of their own health problems. While the value of bilingual professionals and health care interpreters in developing sensitivity to the needs of immigrants within mainstream health care services is substantial, now there is more emphasis on immigrant participation and control. The concept of ethnic health services, or ethno-specific services, received endorsement from the Community Health Program in the mid-1970s. The Commonwealth's Community Health Program contributed to the first four community health centres designed specifically for immigrants, in Wollongong, Melbourne (two) and Sydney. Women's health centres and other community health centres have also fostered immigrant participation in their health care teams. There is no doubt that where ethno-specific health services and ethnic health workers and interpreters have been provided, there has been a proportionate increase in the use of health care services by Australians from LOTE backgrounds.

The Commonwealth government has been committed to identifying and addressing the needs of immigrants since 1986, when the minister for immigration and ethnic affairs presented guidelines for all Commonwealth departments and authorities to parliament. In keeping with this policy, a National Ethnic Health Policy Conference was held in 1988, with the theme, 'Health Policy for a Multicultural Australia: Towards a National Agenda'. This conference was the first stage in a program of community consultations to develop the health policy component in the national agenda for a multicultural Australia. The Department of Community Services and Health also sponsored a consultancy to review health service utilisation by ethnic Australians.

The Office of Multicultural Affairs in the Commonwealth Department of the Prime Minister and Cabinet produced two access and equity reports for the Commonwealth Department of Community Services and Health, in 1987 and 1988. The reports, *A Fair Go, A Fair Share* and the *Access and Equity Plan*, enabled the Office of Multicultural Affairs to monitor programs and services in order to assess where they were sensitive to the needs of immigrants. In addition, the reports facilitated the:

- establishment of data collection systems to evaluate the level of participation of diverse ethnic groups
- development of personnel practices to sensitise employees to a multicultural perspective
- delivery of services and implementation of programs in relevant community languages
- provision of opportunities for participation by clients in policy formulation and program delivery
- provision of administrative and legislative change, including arrangements with state and local governments and non-government organisations, for services with Commonwealth funding.

On the issue of immigrant participation in policy formation and service provision, it is perhaps ironic that people from LOTE backgrounds have been recruited into the health care team as interpreters, ethnic health workers and ethnic liaison officers, since many health professionals with overseas qualifications have been excluded from practising legally in Australia.

In the ongoing controversy over the registration of overseas-trained health professionals, and doctors in particular, one aspect of the question continues to attract public attention. This is the proposition that immigrants from LOTE backgrounds are being deprived of health care by health professionals who share their language and culture (Martin 1978). Furthermore, there has been little recognition of the underground immigrant health services provided by professionals from overseas excluded from registration in Australia. Thus, in the 1970s, Kunz (1975) noted that of the 370 medical practitioners from LOTE backgrounds who had arrived after World War II as refugees, staunch opposition from the AMA, together with government weakness and indifference, meant that more than one-third of these doctors were unable to gain registration. Of the two-thirds who did gain registration, approximately one-third of their working years 'were whittled away at unnecessary university courses and in menial occupations' (Kunz 1975, p. 115).

Providing opportunities to enable overseas-trained health practitioners to practise in Australia is a crucial element in the provision of culturally appropriate health services. The means by which this may be achieved include the valuation of overseas skills, the appreciation of non-British training models, the provision of accessible bridging courses, and the availability of supervised work experience. In her influential work on 'wasted skills', Iredale (1988) recommended that governments recognise the skills of immigrant health practitioners if they are serious about providing culturally appropriate services to Australia's multi-ethnic population. Since then, the various states and territories, led by New South Wales, moved forward in increasing opportunities for overseas-trained doctors to gain vocational registration in Australia, particularly after the completion of a period of service in rural or remote locations.

The *National Non-English Speaking Background Women's Health Strategy* (Alcorso & Schofield 1991) showed that immigrant women in Australia suffer specific health problems and have a worse health service experience than most Anglo-Celtic Australian women. The findings from this report were taken into account in the evaluation of the First National Women's Health Program and in the recommendations for the second program.

In surveying immigrant health policies in Australia, it is clear that the special needs of immigrants were not addressed until many years after the postwar immigration boom. Policies in the states of Victoria, South Australia and Western Australia were modelled on the New South Wales guidelines to a considerable extent. The Tasmanian, Queensland and Australian Capital Territory health authorities were considerably slower in responding to language and cultural barriers to health care. In Tasmania, for example, immigrants were forced to learn English (Mitchell 1988).

In 1992, an Ethnic Health Policy Unit was established within Queensland Health, with the intention of using affirmative action to improve services for people from LOTE backgrounds. Prior to this, the infrastructure for ethnic health in Queensland was non–existent (Sharan 1992). There were no ethnic health workers, health interpreters or ethno-specific services in the Queensland public health care system. In 1992, the Australian Capital Territory Department of Health introduced an Access and Equity Plan.

In New South Wales, guidelines to improve migrant access to hospitals were issued in 1983 and to community health services in 1984. This policy represented a breakthrough in immigrant health policy in Australia, for it was the first time that responsibility was placed on the system, not on the individual consumer. The guidelines noted that the provision of migrant health services rested on a new principle, 'the right of equality of access to health care services regardless of cultural origin or linguistic skills'.

Since 1983, when a memorandum was released by the then New South Wales premier, Neville Wran, there was a shift towards the mainstreaming of ethnic affairs policies in New South Wales. This policy shift was evidenced in reduced funding for ethno-specific services and renewed emphasis on encouraging immigrants to utilise generic or mainstream services. Mainstreaming as a policy development was conceived by the Ethnic Affairs Commission of New South Wales. The Department of Health's Ethnic Affairs Policy Statement, which was ratified formally in 1985, required, among other things, that the department report annually on its achievements in immigrant health. These guidelines were replaced in July 1987 by the NSW Department of Health's *Standard Procedures for Improved Access to Area and Other Public Health Services by People of Non-English Speaking Background* (NSW Department of Health 1987b).

Before the New South Wales immigrant health policy was introduced, there were no guidelines for improving the access of immigrants to mainstream health services. There was no interpreter or translation service; however, some immigrant health workers were employed in community health centres as part of the Community Health Program. The Healthcare Interpreter Service was established in 1977. It had extended to all metropolitan regions and the Illawarra and Hunter regions by 1980. The Health Information Translation Service was established in 1980 to provide written translated health information throughout New South Wales. Publications included a poster on immunisation and a brochure on Pap smears, which was translated into 17 languages.

Mainstreaming as a policy approach has developed at the federal level in conjunction with the Access and Equity Plan. In New South Wales, and increasingly in Victoria, South Australia and Western Australia, governments are implementing policies to ensure that the full range of mainstream health services are accessible and appropriate to all Australians, and that specially targeted ethno-specific services are provided where necessary. The National Health Strategy issues paper, *Removing Cultural and Language Barriers to Health*, noted that 'all state and territory health departments have either formal or informal policies to mainstream services' (1993c, p. 112). It noted also that a generalist approach is more cost-effective in the smaller states and territories. Only New South Wales made a firm policy commitment to the provision of ethno-specific services. While emphasising mainstream services, its Ethnic Affairs Policy Statement required specially targeted programs and services if it was apparent that generalist services were not providing adequate health care. The NSW Refugee Health Unit and STARTTS, the Service for the Treatment and Rehabilitation of Torture and Trauma Survivors, are two examples. These ethno-specific services largely act as a bridge to services in the generalist health system.

The differential health experience of immigrants

Almost a third of deaths registered in 2010 (43 100 deaths) were of persons who were born overseas, despite making up only 27 per cent of the resident population in 2010 (ABS 2013g). Males born in Poland had one of the highest SDR rates with 8.4 deaths per 1000 standard population, while males born in China enjoyed the lowest SDR rates. Death rates among people born overseas also varied by cause of death. For many causes, the rates were lower than for Australian-born people, lending support to the 'healthy migrant effect'. However, in some cases, they were not. Compared to the relevant death rate among Australian-born people, the rates were higher for:

- lung cancer among people born in the Netherlands, the UK and Ireland
- diabetes among people born in Croatia, Greece, India, Italy, Lebanon and Poland
- coronary heart disease among people born in Croatia and Poland
- influenza and pneumonia among people born in the UK and Ireland.

Migrants bring to Australia unique health profiles. Research has found that most migrants enjoy health that is at least as good as, if not better than, that of the Australian-born population. Immigrant populations often have lower death and hospitalisation rates, as well as lower rates of disability and lifestyle-related risk factors (Singh & de Looper 2002).

This 'healthy migrant effect' is believed to result from two main factors: a self-selection process that includes people who are willing and economically able to migrate and excludes those who are sick or disabled, and a government selection process involving certain eligibility criteria based on good health, education, language and job skills. This means that most people born overseas are in good health on arrival in Australia due to the rigorous health checks they undergo to be eligible for migration.

Migrants are often less exposed to harmful risk factors for cardiovascular and other non-communicable diseases in their countries of origin, before their relocation to Australia (Razum 2006). They may retain some of their advantage for such diseases long after migrating. It has been observed, though, that the migrant health advantage often diminishes with length of stay (AIHW 2006a).

Table 9.2 Standardised death rates (SDR) by selected country of birth, 2011

Country of birth	Males		Females	
	Number of deaths	SDR	Number of deaths	SDR
China	566	3.9	508	2.8
Croatia	537	6.3	314	3.7
France	111	8.5	61	3.4
Germany	931	6.5	912	4.2
India	391	4.3	358	3.4
Japan	32	5.9	53	3.6
Netherlands	857	6.3	722	4.6
Malaysia	161	4.2	144	2.9
Papua New Guinea	65	8.3	60	5.3
Poland	683	8.4	651	5.0
South Africa	252	5.0	235	3.8
United Kingdom	8028	7.0	7192	5.1
United States of America	197	8.9	127	6.4
Zimbabwe	28	4.2	24	3.0
Total overseas-born	**24 335**	**6.1**	**20 340**	**4.3**
Total	**75 330**	**6.8**	**71 602**	**4.9**

Source: Based on Australian Bureau of Statistics 2013g, *Migrant Data Matrices, 2013*, cat. no. 3415.0, ABS, Canberra

Despite these advantages, certain health risk factors and diseases are more common among some country-of-birth groups in Australia, reflecting diverse socioeconomic, cultural and genetic influences. Standardised death rates vary too between groups according to country of origin (see table 9.2).

Between 2003 and 2005, the overall annual death rate for people born overseas was 9 per cent below that for people born in Australia. However, rates varied between country of birth: people born in Vietnam had death rates almost half those of Australian-born people, those born in China had 30 per cent lower rates, and Italy 13 per cent lower. Rates for people born in the UK and Ireland, along with Germany and the Netherlands, were similar to the Australian-born death rate. Those born in Croatia and Poland had slightly higher rates.

Immigrants are certainly not a homogeneous group, and knowledge of the history of migration policies in Australia and of the various waves of migrants to arrive on our shores since 1788, is fundamental to any adequate understanding of health and access to health care in Australian society. We turn now to examine the health of Australia's first peoples.

Aboriginal and Torres Strait Islander Peoples

There is no doubt that the original inhabitants of Australia are the most disadvantaged group in Australian society. The statistics are stark, as shown in the following figures. In 2011, the unemployment rate for Aboriginal people (16 per cent) was considerably higher than for other Australians (5.7 per cent) (ABS 2011a). The median weekly income for Indigenous adults was much lower than that of their non-Indigenous counterparts. In the 2011 census, about one-quarter (26 per cent) of Aboriginal and Torres Strait Islander Peoples aged 15 years and over reported a non-school qualification compared with about half (49 per cent) of non-Indigenous people (ABS 2011b). Aboriginal people were more likely to live in improvised and/or overcrowded dwellings, and they are much less likely to own or be purchasing their own home (36 per cent) than other Australians (68 per cent) (ABS 2011b). Aboriginal people are also over-represented among the homeless or those at risk of being homeless. The imprisonment rate for Indigenous adults was more than 14 times that for non-Indigenous adults. Indigenous children are also over-represented in the juvenile justice system; in 1996, about 40 per cent of children in corrective institutions for children were Indigenous. In 1998, Indigenous children were four times more likely to be under care and protection orders and six times more likely to be on out-of-home placements (ABS & AIHW 1999).

This disadvantaged social and economic position has been compared to that experienced by Indigenous peoples in other postcolonial societies such as New Zealand, Canada and the United States (Saggers & Gray 1991). The report of the

Figure 9.4   Proportion of deaths, Aboriginal and Torres Strait Islander status, age group and sex, 2006–2008

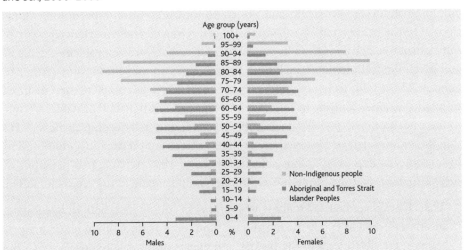

Notes
Deaths calculated as the proportion of all deaths registered for respective Aboriginal and Torres Strait Islander status.

Source: Based on Australian Bureau of Statistics 2010d, *The Health and Welfare of Australia's Aboriginal and Torres Strait Islander Peoples, Oct 2010*, cat. no. 4704.0, ABS, Canberra

Royal Commission into Aboriginal Deaths in Custody (1991) identified disadvantage and cultural breakdown as the root causes of the alarming number of Aboriginal deaths they investigated.

The Report of the National Inquiry into the Separation of Aboriginal and Torres Strait Islander Children from their Families, *Bringing Them Home,* was commissioned by the Keating Labor Government and presented to the Howard Coalition Government in 1997 (HREOC 1997). In the report, Sir William Deane, the then governor-general of Australia, stated:

> It should, I think, be apparent to all well-meaning people that true reconciliation between the Australian nation and its Indigenous peoples is not achievable in the absence of acknowledgment by the nation of the wrongfulness of the past dispossession, oppression and degradation of Aboriginal peoples.
>
> HREOC (1997, p. 3)

The two-year inquiry took evidence orally or in writing from 535 Indigenous people throughout Australia concerning their experiences of removal policies. The report suggests that between one in three and one in 10 Indigenous children was forcibly removed from their families and communities in the period from approximately 1910 until 1970 (HREOC 1997, p. 31). 'Most families have been affected, in one or more generations, by the forcible removal of one or more children' (HREOC 1997, p. 31).

Helen Siggers, a former registered nurse and director of the Aboriginal Education Centre at Monash University in Victoria, was in a position to compare Aboriginal students who had been removed from their families with those who had not. She observed that those not removed were more 'together as people', 'knew about their culture', 'had strong self-esteem' and 'positive (intimate) relationships (of some duration)'. On the other hand, those who had been removed had experienced 'years of self-destructive behaviour', an 'intensity of addictions', 'cardiac problems', diabetes and psychological problems, including the tendency to move from one partner to another. Those who were not removed were more likely to complete their planned university degree (Siggers, in HREOC 1997, p. 192). Michael Constable, a community health nurse in Ballarat, also observed 'a higher relationship turnover'. He told the inquiry that he observed the Stolen Generations on reaching adulthood to be 'chronically depressed' (Constable, in HREOC 1997, p. 192). It is perhaps not surprising then that the numerous recommendations made in the report included:

> That all health and related training institutions, in consultation with Indigenous health services and family tracing and reunion services, develop undergraduate training for all students in the history and effects of forcible removal.
>
> HREOC (1997, p. 658)

Health policy development in the area of Indigenous health should be accorded the highest priority compared with any of the other issues discussed in this book.

Indigenous people have the worst health status of any group in Australia for whom health statistics are available (ABS & AIHW 1999), as outlined below:

- Life expectancy at birth is considerably lower for Indigenous persons.
- In general, Indigenous mothers give birth at a younger age. Their babies are about twice as likely to be of low birth weight and more than twice as likely to die at birth than babies born to non-Indigenous mothers.
- Indigenous Australians die at younger ages than non-Indigenous Australians for almost every disease or condition for which information is available.
- Aboriginal adults are more likely to smoke and be obese than other Australian adults.
- Indigenous adults are less likely to drink alcohol than other Australians, but Aboriginal people who drink alcohol are more likely to do so at hazardous levels.
- Indigenous people are more likely than other Australians to report a variety of chronic conditions, such as asthma and diabetes.
- Indigenous persons are more likely to be hospitalised than other Australians. Dialysis (22 per cent) and respiratory disease and injury (8 to 13 per cent) are among the common causes of hospitalisation for Aboriginal people, but they are also more likely to be hospitalised due to conditions that are indicators of mental illness; for example, self-harm, substance abuse and suicidal behaviour.
- Aboriginal people are more likely than other Australians to be the victims of violence and to suffer intentional injuries resulting in hospitalisation. They are also over-represented in intimate partner homicides (20 per cent of victims and 22 per cent of offenders in 1989–96).

In conjunction with their worse health status, Indigenous Australians have private health insurance at only one-quarter the rate of other Australians (ABS 1999a). Thus, the Indigenous population has greater reliance on public hospitals and community services than non-Indigenous Australians (ABS & AIHW 1999).

Considerable evidence indicates, however, that Aboriginal people led a healthy life prior to European colonisation in 1788. Many Aboriginal people were massacred by the European invaders, and many more died with the rapid transmission of infectious diseases such as smallpox, measles, tuberculosis and venereal disease. The Aboriginal and Torres Strait Islander populations declined in numbers with colonisation and the consequent effects of dispossession from their land and sources of food. The mainland Aboriginal population, which has been living here for more than 40 000 years, declined dramatically from possibly as many as 500 000 in 1788 to a low point of 66 000 in 1933.

Statistics on the Aboriginal and Torres Strait Islander populations prior to 1967 are grossly inadequate. The census did not include the Indigenous population until 1971. Until then, policymakers did not know how many Aboriginal people lived in Australia, or how they were living, working and dying. As we discuss in **Chapter 10**, continuing problems with statistics on Aboriginal health have been addressed by the AIHW and the ABS. The ABS now has a standard procedure for identifying Aboriginal and Torres Strait Islander people, based on self-reported Indigenous origin and acceptance as such by the community in which they live.

Table 9.3   Age-standardised death rates, by Indigenous status, and Indigenous: non-Indigenous rate ratios, NSW, Qld, WA, SA and the NT, 2006–2010

Jurisdiction	Indigenous rate	Non-Indigenous rate	Ratio
NSW	962	598	1.6
Qld	1089	597	1.8
WA	1431	574	2.5
SA	1060	615	1.7
NT	1541	645	2.4
Total	1151	597	1.9

Notes
Rates per 100 000 are directly age-standardised using 2001 Australia standard population data; rate ratio is the Indigenous rate divided by the non-Indigenous rate; incomplete identification of Indigenous status underestimate true differences between both groups. Victoria was not included due to insufficient numbers of Indigenous participation.

Source: Based on Australian Bureau of Statistics 2010c, *Deaths, Australia, 2010*, cat. no. 3302.0, ABS, canberra

The Indigenous population was estimated by the 2008 Census as 517 200, or 2.5 per cent of the total Australian population (ABS 2008d). While Indigenous people comprise a higher proportion of the local population in the northern and central parts of Australia, the majority of Indigenous people live in the south–eastern part of the country in urban areas. It is notable, however, that one in four Indigenous Australians lives outside the urban areas compared to about one in seven non-Indigenous Australians (ABS & AIHW 1999). The 1995 National Health Survey included an enhanced Indigenous sample, enabling direct comparisons between Indigenous and non–Indigenous people at the national level. In 1999, the ABS and AIHW released a detailed report about the health and welfare of Aboriginal and Torres Strait Islander persons using data from national surveys, censuses and the collections of various Commonwealth, state and territory agencies. A number of other initiatives are expected to lead to improvements in the availability and quality of information about the Aboriginal and Torres Strait Islander population. These include the development and implementation of a National Aboriginal and Torres Strait Islander Health Information Plan and endorsement of the National Community Services Information Development Plan. Indigenous data collection has improved in recent years, but there is still a lack of good quality national statistics (AIHW 1998e, p. 28).

Ironically, the impact of introduced diseases increased with the establishment of settlements and missions. The practice of issuing food rations resulted in many

Aboriginal people abandoning their traditional way of gathering and hunting for food. This transition from a semi-nomadic way of life to a sedentary one led to problems with overcrowding, poor hygiene and sanitation and dietary changes that contributed to the current unsatisfactory socioeconomic and health situation for Aboriginal Australians. As Bartlett (1999, p. 5) points out:

> the widespread attitude in Australia from the last century until the 1940s tended to be that Aboriginal people would either die out if 'full blood' and be bred out if of mixed descent. Although we now see eugenics as highly unscientific, during this period various versions of eugenics received strong support from the academic community across a range of disciplines including medicine.

The past four decades have seen an increasing emphasis on self-determination in the demands placed on governments from Aboriginal communities and organisations. Limited land rights have been achieved at state and territory level, and significant progress has been achieved in the establishment of Aboriginal-controlled organisations such as Aboriginal legal services, land councils, housing associations and health services. The apparent intractability of Aboriginal social and economic problems forced the federal government to begin to support this move towards Aboriginal self-determination and self-management.

Until 1967, Aboriginal Australians 'were denied any form of self-determination or any degree of control over their own affairs, individually or collectively' (Refshauge 1982, p. 4). From the middle of the 19th century until the late 1960s, government policies were directed at segregation and then the assimilation of Aboriginal people into the Anglo-Australian society and way of life. During this period, policymakers presumed that the 'Aboriginal problem' would disappear as the Aboriginal population 'died out'. Assimilation was replaced by integration and then self-determination as Aboriginal people became more politically active in the mid-1960s. Aboriginal Australians were not given the right to vote until 1967, with the passing of a national referendum that gave the Commonwealth the power to legislate on Aboriginal issues. Even after 1967, when restrictive laws were abolished in all states except Queensland, virtually all organisations working for the 'welfare' of Aboriginal people were controlled and administered by non-Aboriginal people. During the mid-1960s, there was a massive exodus of Aboriginal people from rural areas into the cities in search of work. This had a considerable impact on rural and urban Aboriginal communities.

Aboriginal community-controlled health services

In documenting the history of the Redfern Aboriginal Medical Service, Andrew Refshauge, (1982) noted that the sudden influx of poor Aboriginal people into the cities exposed significant racism within the Euro-Australian population and public instrumentalities. By 1970, 'police harassment of the Black community had reached extremely serious proportions', and the European-controlled welfare organisations were either unable or unwilling to remedy the situation (Refshauge 1982, p. 4). At this time, the Sydney Aboriginal community identified the absence of accessible health services as one of the major problems confronting their community.

In this pre-Medicare era, Aboriginal people requiring medical attention had only two options open to them. They could visit a GP or the outpatients department of a public hospital. The first was virtually impossible for the majority of Aboriginal people, as most Sydney GPs at that time insisted on a cash payment before treating Aboriginal patients. As 98 per cent of Aboriginal people were living below the official poverty line, this meant that general practice care was inaccessible. The other option was almost as traumatic and degrading, because the overtly racist treatment of Aboriginal people in the local hospitals discouraged them from attending them, other than in cases of emergency. Indeed, employees at the Aboriginal Legal Aid Centre reported that 'many Aboriginals were prepared to die before being subjected to such humiliating treatment' (Refshauge 1982, p. 4). Aboriginal people in Sydney decided that they wanted to run their own health service. One of the first problems to be confronted was that there were then (and until very recently) no Aboriginal doctors. Instead, they enlisted the assistance of supportive non-Aboriginal medical practitioners such as the late Fred Hollows, associate professor of ophthalmology at the University of New South Wales, who went on to direct the National Trachoma and Eye Health Program.

The first Aboriginal medical service was established in Redfern, an inner suburb of Sydney, in 1971. The Redfern Aboriginal Medical Service was a historically important initiative as it was the first community-controlled medical service in Australia. The service was also unique because it was not managed by doctors or health professionals. Doctors were considered the least important members of the centres; the most important people were the patients, who also managed the service through the annually elected board of directors (Refshauge 1982). Since the service proved very popular with Aboriginal patients who had been subjected to discrimination and racism in the mainstream health care system, other Aboriginal communities have set up their own medical services. In addition, over 60 federally funded, community-controlled and independent Aboriginal medical services have been established around Australia. In 1985, federal responsibility for Aboriginal health was transferred from the Health Department to the Department of Aboriginal Affairs. It was later transferred to the Aboriginal and Torres Strait Islander Commission (ATSIC) and, in 1995, back to the Commonwealth Health Department. The Aboriginal health services attract additional funds for programs and services from state and territory governments, donations and non-government organisations.

The Aboriginal medical service initiative was ahead of its time in providing a broad range of coordinated primary health care services under one roof. The Redfern Aboriginal Medical Service has three main types of service: medical, dental and nutritional. It provides general practice, physician, ear, nose and throat, women's health, psychiatry and counselling services. The Redfern service also administers the

Murrawina preschool and a service for prisoners through the Long Bay Correctional Complex clinic. The dental clinic is responsible for dental health promotion, a dental practice, a specialist orthodontic clinic, staff training for Aboriginal dental assistants and mobile dental units that service the country areas of New South Wales. The third arm of the Redfern Aboriginal Medical Service, the nutrition program, supplies a weekly fruit and vegetable run to families at risk, a health improvement program, and welfare assistance with accommodation, transport and finances. Preventative, curative, dental and public health services are therefore provided for and controlled by Aboriginal people within a single integrated primary health care service.

Figure 9.5   Infant mortality rates, Aboriginal and Torres Strait Islander and non-Indigenous Peoples, 2001–2010

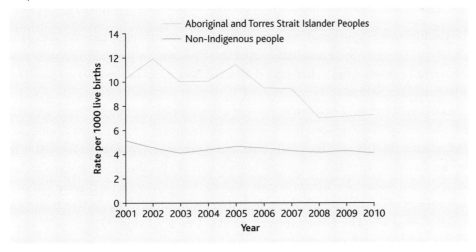

Notes
Includes deaths of people usually resident in New South Wales, Queensland, South Australia and the Northern Territory and excludes deaths for which Indigenous status was not stated.

Source: Based on Australian Bureau of Statistics 2010d, *The Health and Welfare of Australia's Aboriginal and Torres Strait Islander Peoples*, Oct 2010, cat. no. 4704.0, ABS, Canberra

The Central Australian Aboriginal Congress (commonly known as 'Congress') was established in Alice Springs by Aboriginal people in 1973. Medical, dental, rehabilitation and welfare services are made available by Congress in a community context for Aboriginal people in the Alice Springs region and outlying areas in central Australia. The Aboriginal health service in Alice Springs and five other health services give support to people living in more remote areas on a mobile basis. Congress acts as a forum whereby Aboriginal people are able to express their demands and grievances, and the means by which those demands can be channelled through to the relevant authorities.

Congress received funds from the Commonwealth Department of Health in 1985 for a research project to find out why central Australian Aboriginal women were dissatisfied with existing obstetric services. The researchers asked Aboriginal women what they wanted to do, how they wanted to have their babies and how they wanted to be treated. This was the first time that non-Aboriginal people had asked Aboriginal women where they wanted to have their babies. Prior to this, Aboriginal women were told that they had to give birth at the Alice Springs Hospital. Aboriginal women told Congress:

> We have lived by our Grandmother's Law for a long time now. Our Law has been violated since the white man came. Our babies die. Our women are shamed … We have no choice but to tell our story. We regret making known to all our sacred women's business. We talk in whispers about this Law but we want healthy babies and we want our Law. When you know our story you will know our shame and our sadness.

Duncan (1986, p. 17)

Clearly, some Aboriginal women wanted to provide and control their own childbirth service. The consultation enabled Congress to redefine the needs of Aboriginal women more in line with traditional Aboriginal beliefs and customs. The Aboriginal perception of 'borning' is not equivalent to non-Aboriginal lay perceptions of childbirth or the obstetric concept of parturition. Borning refers to a much broader and symbolic process that is inseparable from and integral to the Aboriginal Dreamtime, the Law, the land and its people (Duncan 1986). The Aboriginal way by the Grandmother's Law is directed and carried out by Aboriginal women in the security and ancestral tradition of the *Alukura*. Only women participate directly and assist in childbirth, which is conducted in a non-invasive, supportive, dignified and knowing way. The Grandmother's *Alukura* Law is a living tradition; it is a life source and base for future generations.

Congress sought support for the establishment of Congress *Alukura*, a culturally appropriate Aboriginal women's health care and borning centre, from the Departments of Health and Aboriginal Affairs. The basis of the Congress *Alukura* is the reassertion of the Grandmother's *Alukura* Law and its incorporation into borning and obstetric care. The Congress *Alukura* proposal received endorsement from the minister for health, and in 1987, the Department of Aboriginal Affairs approved funding for the Congress *Alukura* program. This enabled Congress to initiate a community-based program of care for Aboriginal women based on a social view of health. This includes maintaining and strengthening traditional law, culture and responsibilities in a program that aims to ensure that Aboriginal women will have culturally appropriate antenatal care, more information, more support during childbirth, improved postnatal care and better health outcomes.

The Congress *Alukura* consultation process serves as an important prototype of the way community consultation with Aboriginal people should be applied in the Aboriginal health policymaking process. In the 2010–11 financial year, about 3.7 per cent ($4.6 billion) of total health expenditure in Australia was spent on health services for Aboriginal and Torres Strait Islander people (AIHW 2013e, p. 6).

The main areas of expenditure were public hospital services (64.7 per cent), community health services (21.6 per cent), patient transport services (4.4 per cent) and private hospital services (2.3 per cent) (AIHW 2013e, p. 16). However, Indigenous people face a number of barriers to accessing health services and these cannot be dismantled by money alone. The barriers include 'distance, availability of transport, access to GPs and pharmaceuticals, the proximity of culturally appropriate services, proficiency in English, the extent of the involvement of Indigenous people in the delivery of health services, private health insurance cover and economic disadvantage' (ABS & AIHW 1999, p. 3).

The National Aboriginal and Islander Health Organisation, which operated as the umbrella organisation for Aboriginal community-controlled health organisations, evolved into the National Aboriginal Community Controlled Health Organisation in the early 1990s. In 1998, it attracted Commonwealth resources and became a national incorporated body with a secretariat in Canberra (Hunter 1999). This peak body assisted Aboriginal communities to establish their own community-controlled medical services, pressured governments to finance Aboriginal services adequately, and lobbied the federal government to exert its constitutional power to grant land rights to Aboriginal people throughout Australia. This representative organisation was overtly political, for it contended that Aboriginal health problems could only be resolved in a situation whereby Aboriginal peoples had:

- total control over Aboriginal affairs
- control of the resources and facilities required to solve the underlying problems
- inalienable title to land that can provide an economic and spiritual base for Aboriginal self-determination.

According to Dr Andrew Refshauge (1982), a former medical employee of the Aboriginal medical services and former health minister and deputy premier of New South Wales, the Aboriginal medical services see the solution to Aboriginal problems as being 'land rights and economic independence'.

Although the Aboriginal medical services are making a significant contribution to Aboriginal health, in the long term, strong financial commitment to a national public health strategy would be required to bring the health of Aboriginal people up to the standard of the non-Aboriginal population. Any such attempt 'must be aimed at alleviating Aboriginal poverty and powerlessness, at redressing the persisting effect of dispossession, and at eliminating discrimination' (Thomson 1984, p. 946). The key to Aboriginal health is self-determination. In October 1987, the Commonwealth minister for community services and health and the minister for Aboriginal affairs agreed that their departments needed to develop a national strategy on Aboriginal health.

The then Aboriginal Affairs minister Gerry Hand's (1987) statement to the federal parliament marked the beginning of a new and important era of national debate about Aboriginal policy. The statement, 'Foundations for the Future', showed that the government was willing to put on the political agenda, in the bicentennial year, the relationship between Aboriginal and non-Aboriginal Australians. Hand made an unequivocal assurance that changes would not be made unless they were endorsed by the Aboriginal and Torres Strait Islander communities. The policy statement acknowledged that 'Aboriginal people need to decide for themselves what should be done, not just take whatever governments think or say is best for them' (Hand 1987, p. 1). The minister reorganised the administration of the Department of Aboriginal and Islander Affairs under a national commission, ATSIC, and a system of regional councils. He also proposed recognising prior ownership of the Australian continent, and the development of a treaty or compact between Aboriginal and Torres Strait Islander peoples and non-Indigenous people.

In March 1990, the functions of the Department of Aboriginal Affairs and the Aboriginal Development Commission were incorporated into ATSIC. In effect, it represented a working experiment in greater Aboriginal and Torres Strait Islander participation in policy development and implementation in all policy areas, including health. The linchpin of the commission structure was the system of 60 regional councils comprising between 10 and 20 elected representatives from Aboriginal and Torres Strait Islander communities and organisations. ATSIC was run by a board of 20 commissioners, all of whom were Aboriginal people or Torres Strait Islanders. Seventeen of the commissioners were elected by the regional councillors in each of the 17 zones, and initially the chairperson and two other commissioners were appointed by the minister for Aboriginal affairs. ATSIC's first chairperson was Lowitja (Lois) O'Donoghue, a registered nurse.

The report of the National Aboriginal Health Strategy Working Party (1989) called for improved coordination between Commonwealth, state and territory and Aboriginal community-controlled organisations. In 1990, the Commonwealth, states and territories agreed to establish a National Aboriginal Health Strategy to develop health services for Aboriginal people on a national basis. Most of the funds were devoted to meeting public infrastructure needs such as housing, water, sewerage, electricity and roads. Funds were also made available for establishing new and upgrading existing Aboriginal-controlled health services. The principle of self-determination, which was articulated clearly in the National Aboriginal Health Strategy (1989), and later endorsed by the Royal Commission into Aboriginal Deaths in Custody (1991), 'does not discount the significance of the Aboriginal and Torres Strait Islander Commission and other government-funded structures but recognises them as enabling rather than driving; as necessary but not sufficient' (Houston & Legge 1992, p. 114). Responsibility for the primary health care of Aboriginal and Torres Strait Islander Peoples was transferred from ATSIC to the Commonwealth Health Department in July 1995, under the leadership of the then minister for health, Dr Carmen Lawrence.

The 1990s policy of reconciliation, which aimed to build bridges between Aboriginal and non-Aboriginal Australians, was seen by many Aboriginal people as a backwards step, because it sidestepped deeper and unresolved problems such as land rights, compensation and self-management. These unresolved issues re-emerged in 1992 in the wake of the High Court's Mabo decision, which recognised native title to the land on which Eddie Mabo, his community and their ancestors had lived for thousands of years. The native title debate was rekindled by the Wik decision, handed down in the High Court of Australia in 1996, which tackled the concept of coexisting title between native title and pastoral leases. The Wik decision stated that the granting of a pastoral lease did not necessarily extinguish native title rights, but whenever pastoralists' and native title rights were inconsistent, the pastoralists' rights would prevail. The Howard Government put forward a 10-point plan in response to the Wik native title debate consisting of 300 pages of amendments that aimed to alter the *Native Title Act 1993*. Despite the fact that supporters of the existing Native Title Act accumulated a large number of signatures and significant support around the country, the Howard Government incorporated its 10-point plan into the so-called 'Wik legislation', enacted in the *Native Title Amendment Act 1998*.

For decades, it has been known that Aboriginal and Torres Strait Islander peoples experience significantly more ill health than other Australians. They generally die at much younger ages and are more likely to experience disability and reduced quality of life because of ill health. The burden of disease and injury among Indigenous Australians in 2003 was 3.6 per cent of the total burden of disease in Australia, for a group that makes up 2.5 per cent of the total population. The leading causes of this burden were cardiovascular diseases, mental disorders, chronic respiratory disease, diabetes and cancer (Vos et al. 2007). This has generated public sympathy, but all too often it has been accompanied by the assumption that nothing really can be done about it because 'nothing ever changes' in Aboriginal health. The obvious fact that Indigenous Australians have suffered poorer health has put constant pressure on public policy.

For many years, the research community and the Aboriginal and Torres Strait Islander health service sector, as well as other support groups, have argued that the better provision of primary health care can lead to, and is already leading to, improvements in the health status of Australia's Indigenous Peoples. From the 1980s onwards, this view has generally formed the basis for Aboriginal and Torres Strait Islander health policy, with Aboriginal community-controlled primary health care services at centre stage (especially following the 1989 National Aboriginal Health Strategy) and state and territory governments committing to improving their own primary health care strategies for Aboriginal and Torres Strait Islander Peoples (AIHW 2008a).

In 2004–05, Aboriginal and Torres Strait Islander Peoples reported lower incomes than other Australians, higher rates of unemployment, lower educational attainment and lower rates of home ownership (AIHW 2007). The socioeconomic disadvantage experienced by Aboriginal and Torres Strait Islander Peoples compared to other Australians places them at greater risk of exposure and vulnerability to health risk factors such as smoking and alcohol misuse, and other risk factors such as exposure to violence. Numerous other aspects of the living, working and social conditions of Indigenous Australians, along with a reduced sense of control over their own lives, may help to explain the generally poorer health of Aboriginal and Torres Strait Islander Peoples.

The historic national apology to Indigenous peoples from the then prime minister Kevin Rudd in February 2008 marked a significant change in the federal government's attitude. It was received with considerable emotion by Aboriginal and Torres Strait Islander Peoples, many of whom viewed it as a new phase in relations with the government.

A policy analysis of three decades of Indigenous health policies in Australia, as evidenced by speeches and papers from prime ministers and ministers for health and indigenous affairs (Aldrich, Zwi & Short 2007) reveals a continued lack of consistency towards Indigenous health care policy by Australia's major political parties. This is counterintuitive or surprising, as one might have expected a convergence in the policies of the two major political parties over the years. Analysis of the policy discourses of Liberal–National and Labor governments between 1972 and 2001 reveals that competing philosophies and ideologies have been the driving factors in policy design, causing the emphasis of Indigenous health care initiatives to oscillate radically depending on the beliefs of the incumbent government.

It would appear that Aboriginal health has become something that governments and oppositions use

> to score points against each other. This may have had an adverse effect and may explain why we do not have the results we would expect given the amount of money that has been spent and the attention that has been given to Aboriginal health. We have not made the progress seen in comparative countries such as Canada and New Zealand and even in the USA.
>
> Kunitz (1994)

The lack of continuity in approach has had detrimental consequences, both for the health and wellbeing of Indigenous Australians and the morale of professionals who work to provide much-needed services. A classic example is ATSIC, which was a Labor Party initiative. In 2004, some eight years after the Howard Government was first elected, it disestablished the commission, so the progress that might have been made was stopped. This type of stop–start approach is not conducive to good policy or service development. It takes considerable time for policymakers and providers to develop trust with Indigenous communities. Too often, it would appear that as soon as progress is made, there is a change of government at the local, state or federal level, and progress is stalled again. This may very well reduce the willingness and ability of all parties to think and act long term.

Significant differences are apparent in the competing ideologies of the two major parties in relation to Aboriginal health over the last three decades of the

20th century. The conservative parties tend to attribute problems to individuals and families, and believe that the solutions lie with individuals and families through improving attendance at school and reducing alcohol and drug consumption. In contrast, the Labor Party has consistently taken a structural approach and emphasised structural issues such as land rights and self-determination. In 2007, the Northern Territory Emergency Response ('the intervention') was implemented by the Howard Government with aims to protect children, make communities safe and build a better future for people living in Indigenous communities in the Northern Territory. In 2011–12, the Gillard Government contributed to the National Partnership Agreement on Closing the Gap in Indigenous Health Outcomes. As a result, there were 37 regional Tackling Smoking and Healthy Lifestyle Teams promoting health, and the 'Live Longer', 'Health Heroes', 'Do Something Real' and 'Care for Kids' marketing campaigns had commenced by 2012. The federal government also negotiated with the Northern Territory government to develop the National Partnership Agreement on Stronger Futures (to replace Closing the Gap), with a particular focus on Indigenous groups in the Northern Territory to improve primary health care and access to allied health services.

On reflection, perhaps the key to addressing vital health concerns (such as closing the gap in life expectancy between Indigenous and non-Indigenous Australians) is a much-needed bipartisan approach, with the formulation of longstanding policies that remain in place irrespective of the prevailing political climate.

We are doing a disservice to Indigenous citizens with this stop–start ideological approach to health policy. We need a longer-term, consultative, bipartisan, evidence-based approach in order to close that gap.

People with mental health problems

It was estimated in 2007 that mental health problems affect more than 45 per cent of the Australian population in their lifetime (ABS 2010a). Young Australians, however, are most at risk of mental disorder. In 2007, more than one in four young adults aged between 18 and 24 years experienced a mental disorder (AIHW 2011f). Among young people, the most prevalent types of disorders were anxiety disorders, substance use and affective disorders. The figure declined steadily to 6 per cent for those in the population aged 65 years and over (AIHW 2011f). Many who experience a mental disorder will recover spontaneously. The vast majority of the others can be treated and will fully recover. Only a small number experience long periods of distress and disability. Nevertheless, the Human Rights and Equal Opportunity Commission (1993) (since 2009, the Australian Human Rights Commission) concluded that people with mental illness are among the most vulnerable and disadvantaged groups in the community, experiencing stigma and discrimination in many aspects of their lives.

A common theme in mental health services in Australia since the early 1980s has been the discharge of people with mental health problems from psychiatric institutions into the community (Australian Community Health Association 1989). New South Wales and Victoria were the first states in which mental health legislation was reformed in line with increased recognition of the rights of people with mental illness. In 1982, the minister for health in New South Wales established the broad-ranging Inquiry into Health Services for the Psychiatrically Ill and Developmentally Disabled, chaired by David Richmond. The resulting Richmond Report highlighted the need to develop separate policies and services for people with mental illness and developmental (intellectual) disabilities. In the field of mental health, a more balanced system of service provision was recommended, with greater emphasis on decentralised accessible community services, assessment, early intervention and family support. In the same year, the New South Wales government introduced new legislation relating to the care, treatment and welfare of people in the community who suffer from mental health problems.

The Richmond program in New South Wales and the principal new act, the *Mental Health Act 1983*, generally replaced the *Mental Health Act 1958*. This earlier act had become progressively outdated and inappropriate to the needs of people with mental health problems, their families and the community. The 1983 legislation gave renewed emphasis to the legal protection of people with mental health problems. This approach towards mental health legislation has been referred to as 'the new legalism', as it is critical of psychiatric coercion and concerned with strengthening the rights of those who seek to resist psychiatric treatment or incarceration (Unsworth 1987). The new legalism recognises that labelling those with mental health problems 'the mentally ill' is problematic, as the stigmatising labelling process and subsequent psychiatric treatment can magnify the original mental health problem. For this reason, it may be inappropriate to refer to people with mental health problems as 'the mentally ill'; however, the term is in common usage in the health system.

Most of the provisions of the 1983 Mental Health Act were implemented before the change of government in New South Wales in 1988. The Mental Health Review Tribunal was formed, and the *Protected Estates Act 1983*, which covers the management of the affairs of people judged to be incapable, had already come into effect. Under the Richmond program, between 1983 and 1988, many long-stay patients were transferred from state psychiatric hospitals into community-based accommodation, including about 300 people with mental health problems. The Labor government also proposed closing nine of the state's largest psychiatric hospitals.

People incapable of managing their own affairs are protected under the separate *Protected Estates Act 1983*. This act replaced the property provisions of the 1958 act and recognised that people may be incapable of managing their property or practical affairs for reasons other than mental illness. It also recognised that those who have mental health problems are not automatically incapable of managing their own affairs.

Section 5 of the *Mental Health Act 1983* defined the term 'mentally ill person' for the purpose of involuntary admission and detention only. It did not define mental illness in psychiatric terms or in the more general sense. The rationale behind this definition is that legal powers of detention and involuntary treatment should be restricted and that people with harmless mental disorders should not be locked away and treated without their consent. Thus, the definition specifies the types of behaviour due to mental illness that warrant legal detention either for the person's own protection or for the protection of other people in the community, or both. These behaviours are generally those that can cause serious bodily harm. They include attempted suicide, self-mutilation, physical neglect, certain acts of violence against others or their property and extreme harassment behaviour. Police officers were given new responsibilities under the act to enable them to take a person who had committed an offence to a psychiatric hospital rather than a police station, if the police officer perceived that it would be beneficial to the welfare of the person.

The Act also established a review board to regulate the performance of psycho-surgery and other treatments and to advance research in psychosurgery. It prohibits the carrying out of prolonged deep-sleep therapy and insulin coma therapy. The change of government in New South Wales in March 1988 saw the establishment of the Ministerial Implementation Committee on Mental Health and Developmental Disability, chaired by the eminent psychiatrist Dr William Barclay. The change of policy was reflected in the terms of reference and composition of the committee. The membership of 11 people included eight with professional training in the psychiatric field and one with professional expertise in developmental disability. In addition, a committee was formed, with Anne Deveson as the chairperson, to review the *Mental Health Act 1983*. Issues of particular concern to this committee included community treatment orders and electroconvulsive therapy (ECT).

Implementation of the Richmond program became an important election issue in New South Wales in 1988, with some legitimate concerns expressed. Staff and their unions from psychiatric institutions held rallies to protest the proposed closures and the opposition promised to keep the institutions open and to close down halfway houses in the community. After the election, the Coalition government promised to upgrade and keep open the hospitals marked for closure, and to review the state's *Mental Health Act 1983*.

Many professionals were concerned about the closure and running down of psychiatric hospitals. They saw many patients with longstanding or chronic mental disorders discharged into communities that were unprepared for or ill-disposed towards them. Some saw the growth of the anti-psychiatry movement as setting in reverse the hard-won progress achieved by psychiatry during the past half century. In addition, with the closure of psychiatric hospitals, time was needed for slow changes, since many people with mental health problems had been institutionalised for long periods. Of course, for new patients it may be better and cheaper not to be institutionalised; with adequate community services, they should not reach that stage in the first place. When the Richmond program was being implemented, approximately 70 per cent of psychiatric patients in psychiatric hospitals had chronic mental health problems of long standing. Some may have been suitable for discharge and intensive rehabilitation. A long-term follow-up of long-stay mentally ill patients discharged from New South Wales psychiatric hospitals indicated that the majority did well with supported, subsidised permanent housing in the community, and required low levels of mental health care (Andrews, Teeson & Hoult 1990).

British studies showed that if deinstitutionalisation were to be successful, the same amount of money and resources had to be made available in the community as were formerly channelled into institutions (Roth & Kroll 1986). In the case of the Richmond program, deinstitutionalisation could only be used as a cost-cutting exercise if it involved shifting costs to private nursing homes, boarding houses or hostels; that is, to the private sector, which heavily relies on the Commonwealth government for its financial viability.

The Richmond Report referred to the existence of approximately 4000 psychiatric and ex-psychiatric patients from state psychiatric hospitals living in nursing homes and boarding houses, most of which were in the private sector. The problem here, as discussed in **Chapter 5**, is that there is a good deal of evidence that the conditions of care in many private institutions leave much to be desired. This so-called process of deinstitutionalisation of psychiatric patients can actually mean a substitution of one sort of institution for another, prompting the grave suspicion that the process of substituting private facilities for public facilities has not been in the best interests of the patients concerned. The massive transfer of patients with mental health problems from the public sector to the private sector involved a corresponding shift in financial responsibility from the New South Wales government to the Commonwealth. The Richmond program was criticised then, because a program designed to meet the cost-cutting objectives of the state government was unlikely to be concerned with raising issues about quality of care and the appropriateness of placing people in institutions that did not involve the New South Wales government in any costs (Palmer 1984). Thus, the basic question of the most appropriate environment for the care of people with mental health problems was overshadowed by our health care system's public–private, Commonwealth–state financial arrangements, to be discussed further in **Chapter 10**.

In the context of the implementation of the Richmond program, it became clear that there was increased reliance on the for-profit community sector to provide services to former patients and increasing pressure on families to provide care. It was also evident that families were already providing care with little support. As the not-for-profit organisations were already facing demands for services from people discharged from institutions, they often had little choice but to refer people to the for-profit private sector. These problems highlight the need for health departments to evaluate the effects of programs such as the Richmond program and the effects of deinstitutionalisation on patients, their families and the community to ensure that standards are not compromised.

Victoria has also undertaken major reforms in mental health care, especially with the *Mental Health Act 1986*, and more recently with wide-ranging inquiries into psychiatric institutions. Significant elements of reforms in mental health care in Victoria include a bill of rights for consumers, a network of psychiatric advocates that supports consumer advocacy within hospitals and the broader community, and establishment of the Mental Health Review Board, which deals with appeals against involuntary detentions made under the act.

Since 1991 in South Australia, a single mental health authority, South Australian Mental Health Services, has been responsible for administering both hospital-based and community-based mental health services in the state. Queensland has also seen changes in the mental health field, partly in response to the Carter Commission of Inquiry into the infamous Ward 10B at the Townsville Hospital. An independent Mental Health Review Committee was established to monitor consumer rights and the quality of mental health services, and minimum standards for mental health services have been developed as part of the process of formulating a mental health policy for Queensland. We turn now to examine the national context.

Australia's National Mental Health Policy

In 1992, the Australian health ministers endorsed the National Mental Health Policy and agreed to implement a five-year national plan of action in mental health reforms (see figure 9.7). This followed endorsement of a Statement of Rights and Responsibilities by the Australian health ministers in 1991. The National Mental Health Policy and Plan and the Statement of Rights and Responsibilities formed the basis for the National Mental Health Strategy, which represents commitment by the state, territory and Commonwealth governments to improve the lives of people with mental illness. The National Mental Health Strategy reflects marked changes in mental health policy, with a shift in emphasis from institutional to community-based care, greater integration of mental health services with the wider health system, and closer links with other services such as housing, employment and income support. In short, the strategy advances the policy of mainstreaming of mental health services with the general health sector, with an emphasis on community-based treatment and support rather than institutionalisation.

The National Mental Health Strategy aimed to:

- improve the quality and range of assessment, treatment and rehabilitation services available to people with mental health problems
- advance the human rights of those with mental illnesses to prevent abuses
- destigmatise mental illness
- promote the mental health of the Australian population
- wherever possible, prevent the onset of mental health problems and mental disorders.

The National Mental Health Policy acknowledged that consumers and carers had an important part to play in implementing the reforms. A National Consumer Advisory Group was established, consisting of a primary consumer or carer from each state, territory and the Commonwealth, to provide advice to governments and ministers with the aim of ensuring adequate protection of consumer rights and meaningful consumer input to decisions on mental health. The National Mental Health Policy was revised in 2008, with renewed commitment from all Australian health ministers and ministers with responsibility for mental health to the continual improvement of Australia's mental health system.

In 2003, mental illnesses were among the 10 leading causes of disease burden in Australia, accounting for 13 per cent of the total burden of disease (AIHW 2006a). Long-term mental and behavioural problems include:

- anxiety disorders (including panic disorder, agoraphobia, social phobia, generalised anxiety disorder, obsessive-compulsive disorder and post-traumatic stress disorder)
- mood (affective) disorders (including depression, dysthymia, mania, hypomania and bipolar affective disorder)
- alcohol use disorders (including harmful use and dependence)
- drug use disorders (including harmful use and dependence).

In the 2004–05 National Health Survey, 11 per cent of all persons reported a long-term mental or behavioural problem. Half of all persons reporting mental and behavioural problems in 2004–05 National Health Survey reported mood (affective) problems, and 46 per cent reported anxiety-related problems. The proportion reporting a long-term mental or behavioural problem has increased over the National Health Surveys. In 1995 the proportion was 6 per cent, in 2001 it was 10 per cent, and in 2004–05, it was 11 per cent (after adjusting for age differences). This may reflect an increased willingness to report mental disorders (ABS 2006b).

While mental-health-related separations accounted for 4.5 per cent of all hospital separations in 2003–04, they accounted for 12 per cent of total days spent by patients in hospitals (AIHW 2006a). In 2004–05, principal diagnoses of depressive disorders (36 per cent), neurotic and stress-related disorders (17 per cent), mental and behavioural disorders due to alcohol (12 per cent) and schizophrenia (11 per cent) accounted for the largest proportions of mental-health-related hospital separations (AIHW 2006a). Expenditure on mental health services ($3 billion) accounted for 6 per cent of all health expenditure in 2000–01 (AIHW 2005). In 2003–04, expenditure on all hospital services (public and private) accounted for 34.8 per cent of total recurrent health expenditure. Of this expenditure on hospital services, 2 per cent was for public psychiatric hospitals (AIHW 2006a).

The National Mental Health Policy 2008 adopted a whole-of-government approach to mental health, first agreed to by the Council of Australian Governments

Figure 9.6 MBS-subsidised GP mental health encounters and services by age and sex, 2009–10

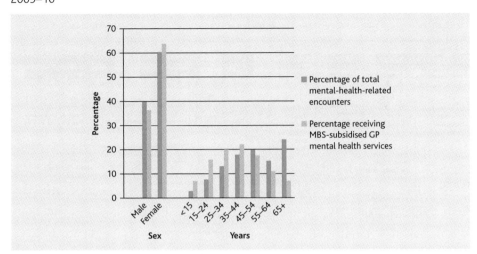

Source: Based on Australian Institute of Health and Welfare 2012e, *Mental Health Services-In Brief 2012*, cat. no. HSE 125, AIHW, Canberra

in July 2006, within the National Mental Health Strategy. It works towards ensuring that Australia has a mental health system that detects and intervenes early in illness, promotes recovery and ensures that all Australians with a mental illness have access to effective and appropriate treatment and community supports to enable them to participate in the community fully. It purports to be 'A system that supports efforts to prevent mental ill health, promotes resilience and lessens the stigma so often attached to mental illness' (DHA 2009a).

The National Health Strategy (1993d) issues paper on continuity of care for people with chronic mental health problems supported implementation of the national policy and proposed strategies for improving continuity of care, particularly for people with mental illness and psychiatric disability. Under the National Mental Health Strategy, the delivery of specialist mental health services remained the responsibility of state and territory governments; the Commonwealth worked with the states and territories to improve the delivery of services. The strategy encouraged the states and territories to reform legislative and financial arrangements for the people with mental illness. The then minister for health, housing and community services, Brian Howe, criticised psychiatric institutions as being inefficient and impractical, with some spending up to $75 000 per year per patient. In opening the annual congress of the Royal Australian and New Zealand College of Psychiatrists, he said:

> While most patients, 90 per cent, now live in the community, 80 per cent of state mental health budgets remain tied up in institutions. As a result there are insufficient funds for services in the community such as crisis management teams, respite care and supported accommodation.

Howe, quoted in Cant (1992)

Figure 9.7   Milestones in the life of the National Mental Health Strategy, 1991–2014

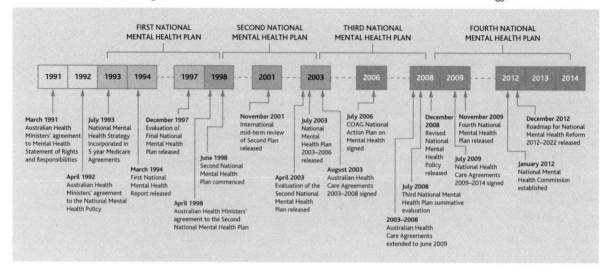

Source: Department of Health and Ageing (2013)

In the 1992–93 federal budget, the Commonwealth committed $135 million over six years to accelerate the process of mental health reforms by the states, including the integration of mental health services with the acute hospital and community care systems. A further $107 million was provided directly to the states and territories to support infrastructure reforms to reduce the size of separate psychiatric hospitals and to replace them with psychiatric units attached to general hospitals and a range of specialist services based in the community. This national approach to mental health policy and services was integrated into the Medicare Agreements signed in 1993. In 1998, the Commonwealth government committed funds to renew the National Mental Health Strategy to 2001, and the second National Mental Health Plan was put in place to implement the strategy (Commonwealth Department of Health and Aged Care 1997).

The anti-psychiatry movement

Since the 1960s, numerous researchers have focused critical attention on the dehumanising consequences of psychiatry and psychiatric institutions. In *Madness and Civilization*, the late historian and philosopher of ideas Michel Foucault (1967) suggested that psychiatry and mental institutions might be no more humane than the prisons and punishments that characterised treatment of the insane more than 200 years ago. This work, and the work of sociologists such as Erving Goffman (1968), has been attributed with providing 'much of the moral impetus' for the relatively recent trend towards deinstitutionalisation (Ingleby 1981, p. 12).

In his study of the 'career of the inmate' and the 'process of mortification' in mental asylums, Goffman (1968) pointed out that the various rationalisations for dehumanising patients were often generated by efforts to manage the lives of a large number of inmates in a restricted environment and on a small budget. Sociologists researching the experience of psychiatry report that many consumers are critical of prolonged drug therapies and psychiatric hospitalisation (Rogers, Pilgrim & Lacey 1993). Both appear to be of questionable benefit. Often, patients seem to recover despite psychiatric treatment, rather than because of it. In a particularly influential study, 'On being sane in insane places', David Rosenhan (1973) reported how psychologically normal investigators who presented themselves at mental hospitals with one single fabricated psychiatric symptom were committed to inpatient treatment for periods ranging from seven to 52 days, even though they behaved 'normally' following the initial deception. This study provided evidence that psychiatry was not always able to distinguish between the 'sane' and the 'insane' within the context of psychiatric hospitals.

In the 1960s and early 1970s, criticisms of psychiatric labelling and institutionalisation developed into what has been referred to as the 'anti-psychiatry movement'. The work of RD Laing, a British psychiatrist, was particularly influential in this movement since it brought into question society's definitions of 'sanity' and 'insanity' (Laing & Esterson 1970). Anti-psychiatry reversed the traditional labelling process of psychiatry and suggested that those labelled 'insane' might be more 'sane' than those who conform to their 'mad' society. Laing worked with other radical psychiatrists in developing alternative models of care, which allowed people labelled as schizophrenic to undertake 'voyages of discovery'. In Italy this developed into a national program of deinstitutionalisation and de-professionalisation of services for the mentally ill, which has come to be known as 'The Italian Experience' (Basaglia 1981).

In the United States, Thomas Szasz, a libertarian psychiatrist, denounced these community-oriented anti-psychiatry developments as 'creeping socialism' (Ingleby 1981, p. 8). Szasz argued that mental illness was a 'myth' because it did not have a physical reality like 'real' diseases. He argued that psychiatry posed an unjustified threat to individual freedom. The solution was to return to a contractual relationship between individual psychiatrists and patients and to the individual self-determination that would be achieved.

In the late 1970s and 1980s, feminists were particularly critical of ways in which psychiatry and mental health services reinforced women's inferior position in modern society. In particular, it was argued that psychiatry's definition of 'mental health' corresponded to the way in which males thought and acted (Chesler 1972). This means that women who are often socialised into being passive, submissive, dependent and insecure are more likely to be diagnosed as being 'mad'. Cross-national statistics on gender and psychiatric illness and hospitalisation confirm that women are diagnosed as mentally ill more frequently than men. In Australia, men and women have similar overall prevalence rates of mental disorder. However, after the age of 35 years, women are more likely to have a mental disorder. Women are more likely to experience anxiety disorders and affective or mood disorders such as depression, whereas men are more likely to experience substance abuse disorders. Women are also more likely to use services for mental health problems than their male counterparts (ABS 1998).

Also in the 1970s and 1980s, gay and lesbian interest groups attacked psychiatry's ideology and practices, with some success. In 1973 the American Psychiatric Association agreed to eliminate 'homosexuality' from its list of mental disorders, and the 1980 edition of the disease-classification manual, the Diagnostic and Statistical Manual of Mental Disorders (DSM-III), specified that homosexuality was a disorder of sexual functioning only when the person viewed their sexuality as an unwanted and persistent problem. Responsibility for the social construction of pathology had shifted, therefore, from the psychiatric profession to the consumer.

Many researchers have been critical of the threats to individual freedom posed by psychiatric treatments and mental institutions. Whereas early critiques focused on the effects of psychiatric treatment and institutionalisation on individual patients, more recent developments have looked at mental health problems within a broader social and political context, one that acknowledges the importance of the power of the psychiatric profession and the need to reform mental health services.

The main policy implication to emerge from the anti-psychiatry movement is that the distinction between 'sanity' and 'insanity', and the psychiatric diagnoses that result, are more culturally relative than the science of psychiatry has professed. The profession of psychiatry has constructed psychiatric diseases (labels) such as 'schizophrenia'. More precisely, the profession and these disease labels have been constructed together. Although this critical perspective does not deny that mental illness and suffering are very real, it points out that problems associated with psychiatric diagnoses and treatments threaten the self-esteem, dignity and autonomy of individual patients. Psychiatric diagnosis and treatment may be useless, harmful or destructive; that is, counter-therapeutic.

The second policy implication to emerge from the anti-psychiatry movement is philosophical support for deinstitutionalisation, given the unhealthy effects of psychiatric institutions, but as the discussion of the Richmond program indicated, it does not follow that all persons currently in institutions would be better off in the community. What is crucial is the manner in which deinstitutionalisation is implemented. Few would deny that some people will mental illness need asylum from the broader society, where they cannot cope. According to Michael Rosser, former secretary of the NSW Department of Health, 'domestic-style architecture built on a common campus like a university or housing estate' would have achieved many of Richmond's aims without increasing substantially the demand for staff and departmental costs (Rosser, quoted in O'Neill 1988, p. 9). Related to this is support for non-psychiatric approaches for people with emotional and behavioural problems. These policy analyses provided theoretical support for the development of community health facilities, crisis intervention centres, therapeutic communities and talking therapies in general.

It could be argued, however, that the influence of Foucault, Goffman, Szasz and others has made the pendulum swing too violently towards the anti-psychiatry and deinstitutionalisation positions. What was once portrayed as benevolent psychiatric practice is now presented as psychiatric punishment and moral imprisonment. Perhaps the main value of this critique of psychiatry is that it makes us examine the problems inherent in psychiatric treatment and institutionalisation, and it heightens awareness of the need to prioritise the dignity and freedom of each individual with a mental health problem. An unfortunate consequence of the excessive zeal for deinstitutionalisation is that people with mental illness have contributed greatly in Australia and elsewhere to the growing population of homeless people in the larger cities. Many people have experienced major problems by not being admitted as psychiatric inpatients when this type of care may have been the most satisfactory option.

An important feature of the reformed mental health legislation is the separation of policies relating to people with mental health problems from those relating to people with intellectual (developmental) disability. Under reformed legislation, people with intellectual, or developmental, disabilities are no longer subject to the same laws that apply to people with mental health problems, unless they also have mental health problems.

Until recently, data on the mental health status of Australians were minimal. From 1993–98, initiatives by the Commonwealth, states and territories under the National Mental Health Strategy led to the improved collection of data on mental health services. These are used to monitor the reforms in mental health service delivery introduced under the Mental Health Strategy (AIHW 1998a). Data for hospital admissions due to mental disorder or associated disability are now available, but there were no data about consumers of mental health services in community settings. Mental health was designated as one of the five National Health Priority Areas, and for policy and planning purposes, data about service delivery and mental health status is required for specific groups. In 1994, a workshop commissioned by the Commonwealth Department of Health and Family Services recommended that a national survey of mental health was needed and that the survey should comprise three components: adults, children and adolescents, and low-prevalence psychotic disorders such as schizophrenia. The department commissioned the ABS to conduct the adult component of the study in 1997. The results were published in *Mental Health and Wellbeing: Profile of Adults, Australia 1997* (ABS 1998) and were used to monitor initiatives of the National Mental Health Strategy. A National Youth Suicide Prevention Strategy was also implemented.

The field of mental health has attracted increased public and media attention over the last decade. Prominent lobby and service groups have been established, such as Beyondblue, the national depression initiative, and the Black Dog Institute, a community-oriented provider of specialist expertise in mood disorders, including depression, bipolar disorder and postnatal depression. The aims are to increase awareness of mental health problems in the community, to attempt to reduce the stigma or negative esteem attached to mental health problems, and to encourage people to seek professional advice from general medical practitioners or other mental health practitioners.

Disease-mongering

At the same time, increasing attention is being paid to the medicalisation of mental health and 'how the world's biggest pharmaceutical companies are turning us all into patients' (Moynihan & Cassels 2005). Work by Ray Moynihan, a regular contributor to the *British Medical Journal*, and others has examined how the medico-pharmaceutical industry has 'transformed' the way we think and talk about physical and mental health concerns. We discuss below the perceptive contribution of the British psychiatrist Joanna Moncrieff (2009) in *The Myth of the Chemical Cure: A Critique of Psychiatric Drug Treatment* to the issues associated with the construction of mental disorders. The industry is turning more of us into customers each year. The use of celebrities is now a standard way that the industry promotes its products and tries to alter public awareness, public thinking and public perceptions about illness.

One way that the companies and their marketing arms work is to try to redefine more and more people as sick in order to increase demand for their products. The United States is the epicentre for the 'selling of sickness', or 'disease-mongering'. The United States accounts for less than 5 per cent of the world's population but about 50 per cent of the pharmaceutical market. We are fortunate in Australia to have legislation that places a strict ban on direct-to-consumer marketing. However, so-called disease awareness programs, heavily influenced by pharmaceutical companies, are not banned and so marketing strategies are more subtle. The main implication from this awareness of disease mongering is the need to be more sceptical about the claims made about conditions, disease labels and treatments, pharmaceutical and otherwise.

It would be misleading in the context of the discussion of mental illness policies not to question further the status of psychiatry as a professional endeavour, as well as question the DSM, the long-awaited fifth edition of which was released in 2013. It might be claimed that our comments may be regarded as part of a new anti-psychiatry movement. The following discussion draws upon the excellent book by Joanna Moncrieff (2009) cited above.

The delivery of mental health services in the 19th and early 20th centuries was concentrated in large hospitals for the 'insane' ('asylums'), where treatment was mainly custodial except for the use on occasions of stimulants and sedatives. In addition, treatments such as ECT and lobotomy came into vogue in the latter part of this period.

Outside these institutions, psychiatry, especially as practised in the United States, went through two phases in the 20th century. Following the work of Freud and his followers, the profession was dominated up to the 1970s by psychodynamic techniques that stressed the role of early childhood development and experiences in generating mental disorders under the rubric of 'neuroses'. The 'talking cure' consisted of lengthy interactions in which patients were encouraged to express their recollections and accompanying emotions, especially in regard to matters of sexuality. The role of the psychiatrist was to listen patiently and encourage patients to reveal their innermost thoughts. In keeping with Freudian views, those patients with the more severe disorders, notably schizophrenia, were not seen as suitable cases for treatment.

This period was therefore one in which the psychiatric profession largely restricted its activities to the more affluent members of the community who could pay the large annual expenditure arising out of the psychodynamic approach. Public and private health insurance companies and governments were reluctant to subsidise the treatment methods. In Australia, Medicare placed strict limits on the number of occasions of service that would be subsidised in any year.

In the second period, from around the 1960s to the present, psychiatric practice has consisted almost exclusively of the dispensing of drugs. In this period, the antipsychotic drugs, notably chlorpromazine and haloperidol, which had been created in the 1950s, came into extensive use for the treatment of schizophrenia for patients mainly in psychiatric institutions. These drugs were apparently effective in mitigating the psychotic features of the illness including hallucinations and delusions. However, they had unfortunate side effects, notably tardive dyskinesia, a problem of balance that led to a characteristic and disabling style of movement of treated patients. The underlying theory of the efficacy of the medications was that they had a direct effect on the neurotransmitter dopamine, and that an overactivity of this agent was the underlying cause of the psychotic condition. However, the evidence to support the association between dopamine activity and schizophrenia has never been established (Moncrieff 2009, p. 93).

The development of antidepressants, notably fluoxetine (Prozac) in the 1970s by Eli Lilly scientists and its approval by the US Federal Drug Administration in 1987, opened the way for the next phase in the practice style of psychiatrists whereby the numerous people with so-called depression of varying degrees of severity became potential clients of these professionals, and of the drug companies. The latter focused on creating a wide range of selective serotonin reuptake inhibitors (SSRIs) of a similar kind to fluoxetine, but with sufficient difference in the underlying chemical structure so as not to breach the patents held by Eli Lilly. The development of the SSRIs was accompanied by claims that the underlying reason for the mental problem of depression was a deficiency in the neurotransmitter serotonin, and that this would be cured by the new drugs. A further class of drugs, selective serotonin noradrenalin reuptake inhibitors (SSNRIs), was created, which focused on the neurotransmitter noradrenalin, assumed also to be deficient in patients with depression.

As Moncrieff demonstrates by extensive reference to the research literature, there is no scientific basis for the claim that depression in its many forms is caused by deficiencies of either serotonin or noradrenalin. The basis of what she refers to as the 'disease-centred model of mental distress' is fatally flawed yet it has become an article of faith for most psychiatrists worldwide. It has the powerful implication that the treatment of patients with certain mental health problems can be undertaken by using chemical substances to address the underlying deficiency in their physiological and biochemical make-up.

As the title of Moncrieff's book indicates, the existence of a chemical cure is a myth. The existence of the myth serves the interests of both the psychiatric profession and the drug companies. For the former, it justifies a mode of practice that does not require the lengthy interaction and intellectual skills required by the psychodynamic approach. It also aligns psychiatry with mainstream medicine, in which drugs, notably antibiotics, do indeed cure an underlying disease process. For the pharmaceutical industry it opened up the enormous market, as described previously, for its products because of the high prevalence of mental distress.

Moncrieff does not deny that the mental state induced by either antipsychotics or antidepressants in the case of some patients is experienced as an improvement in their subjective feelings. She likens the effect to self-medication with alcohol by those with problems of anxiety and depression. Alcohol produces a short-term reduction in the painful mental states, but with the dire consequences that result from continued self-medication. With psychotropic drugs, including antipsychotics and antidepressants, the side effects may be equally disastrous, including an increased risk of suicide in some patients.

The other aspect of psychiatric practice relevant to mental health policy is the use of the DSM, developed and published by the American Psychiatric Association, and treated as a 'quasi-bible' by psychiatrists throughout the world. The DSM consists of a detailed list of symptoms, the presence of which is used to define a very large number of separate disease entities. The major criticism of this classification of mental disorders relates to the contention discussed previously that there is a pronounced bias in modern psychiatry to medicalise human suffering. *The Book of Woe: The DSM and the Unmaking of Psychiatry* by Gary Greenberg (2013) presents an eloquent, and indeed highly amusing, critique of the DSM along these lines. His central claim is that dozens of mental disorders do not exist and that the DSM-5 is a 'fiction of ideology'.

Greenberg presents a mass of evidence of how DSM decisions have created 'false epidemics' of over-diagnosis and over-treatment. He describes how the diagnostic threshold for bipolar disorder was lowered in 1994 to cover people without full-blown mania, but who have elevated moods that the DSM defines as 'hypomania', which Greenberg describes as 'exuberance'. As a result, bipolar diagnoses soared, as did prescriptions for mood stabilisers and antipsychotic drugs. Possibly the most alarming aspect of the over-diagnosis of bipolar disorder was the creation of a juvenile version of the disorder, for which Greenberg claims there was no solid evidence of its existence. He also notes that Joseph Biederman, the psychiatrist who was able to convince the profession and others of the existence of the disorder, had been paid about US$1.6 million in drug company money over the period 2000 to 2007 (Greenberg 2013, p. 86). Biederman was subsequently suspended from his position at Harvard University.

Greenberg and others are highly critical of the fact that, in establishing a diagnosis, a list of symptoms is set out, and the presence of an arbitrary number of these confirms the label that should be applied to the patient. If a person has five of the nine symptoms of depression they will be given the same diagnosis as a person who reports all nine of the symptoms. Moreover, unlike other categorisations of disease, such as the Australian Refined Diagnosis Related Groups, there is no attempt to assess the severity of the symptoms in the DSM; for example, by assigning a severity weight to each symptom.

An excellent example of the medicalisation of 'normal' behaviour, and its cultural correlates, is provided by Schizoid Personality Disorder 301.20 in the DSM-5. The diagnostic criteria are as follows (American Psychiatric Association 2013, pp. 652–5):

1 Neither desires nor enjoys close relationships, including being part of a family
2 Almost always chooses solitary activities
3 Has little, if any, interest in having sexual experiences with another person
4 Takes pleasure in few, if any, activities
5 Lacks close friends or confidants other than first degree relatives
6 Appears indifferent to the praise or criticism of others
7 Shows emotional coldness, detachment, or flattened affectivity
8 Four or more of these criteria leads to the allocation of an individual to this 'disorder'.

We note that the characteristics set out are strongly at variance with American culture, which emphasises the desirability of people having large numbers of friends with whom one constantly interacts. This provides one explanation of the popularity of Facebook, where the mark of success is to have hundreds or thousands of 'friends'. In addition, the symptoms also stress family life (values?) as the desirable norm. We might also note that the Buddhist monk who may spend years alone in meditative isolation would meet possibly all seven of the criteria, if there were anyone around to observe him. It is also by no means clear that individuals who display the characteristics listed, and the lifestyles they have chosen, are any less happy than the rest of the population.

Of considerable importance in the medicalisation of a pattern of behaviour that deviates considerably from social expectations is the use of the term 'schizoid' to describe the supposed disorder. The behaviour as expressed bears no relationship to the psychotic characteristics of schizophrenia; however, the use of this adjective sets the scene for the symptoms to be characterised as a mental disorder.

We have indicated that the issue of mental illness has received increasing attention by governments, as evidenced by the large number of reports and strategies that have emerged in Australia over the last three decades. These have largely consisted of statements designed to alert communities to the prevalence of mental health problems, to reduce the pervasive stigmatisation of those with such problems, and to recommend courses of action for potential sufferers to seek treatment.

As with others groups and policies that we have discussed in previous chapters, we are conscious of the point stressed by Alford (1975) that the multiplicity of reports on policy areas may be part of the problem since they may serve to entrench existing power relations; in this instance, the role of psychiatrists as experts. We have observed that the anti-psychiatry movement of the 1960s and 1970s threatened the credentials of the profession. The responses of organised psychiatry included the development of the DSM as a guide to diagnostic accuracy, and the associated movement to a pattern of treatment that focused almost exclusively on the use of drug therapy to cure the alleged deficiencies that created the disorders.

Thus, we propose that the development of policies regarding people who suffer from mental health problems should be informed by an awareness of the inadequacies of the disease-centred model of psychiatric practice. For this reason, we have cited the evidence provided by contributors such as Moncrieff that heavily criticises the myth of the chemical cure. We have also noted the important role played in psychiatric practice of the DSM, the criticisms of the underlying model and the critical role it has played in medicalising mental health problems. For all these reasons, and because of the troubling links between psychiatry and the pharmaceutical companies, it would seem very clear that reforms in the profession may be a necessary condition for improvement in the status of those suffering from mental health problems.

People with disabilities

Since 1981, the International Year of Disabled Persons, people with disabilities have been more vocal and political, both as individuals and through self-help groups and consumer advocacy organisations. In the ensuing decades, the disabled rights movement has made it clear that people with disabilities want to be treated as people first, people whose abilities matter more than their disabilities. During this period, the discourse of disability has moved from rehabilitation to human rights (Short 1981). The slogan of the disabled rights movement is 'Think Ability Not Disability'. In the context of public policy, a 'disability' is any restriction or lack of ability to perform an activity in the manner considered normal for a human being (WHO 1980). Disabilities can be physical, intellectual or psychiatric. Specific disabilities include hearing disability, blindness and print handicap, intellectual disability, psychiatric disability or severe multiple disabilities. People with disabilities are not necessarily sick. They do not want to be treated like patients. They do not want to be told how to live their lives. The message that came through very clearly in the International Year of Disabled Persons is that people with disabilities hate and fear being lumped together and hidden away in institutions (Short 1981). People with disabilities are demanding the right to make their own decisions and have equal access to educational and employment opportunities.

The emphasis in public policy in this area has shifted from 'paternalistic' or 'charitable' models towards a consumer-oriented approach, based on rights and accountability (National Health Strategy 1993d, p. 166). In 1983, the Commonwealth funded the Australian chapter of the advocacy group Disabled Peoples International and established the Disability Advisory Council of Australia, which provided direct advice to the government on behalf of people with disabilities. The Disability Advisory Council of Australia was replaced by the Australian Disability Consultative Council in 1994; it provides a consultative role to ministers. In addition, each state has an advisory body that represents the interests of people with disabilities. Information services have also been established, such as the Disability Information and Resources Centre in South Australia, which provide advice and information to people with disabilities and the general community.

People with disabilities and their families and supporters are also represented through state branches of peak, or umbrella, disability organisations. These include Disabled Peoples International (Australia), National Council on Intellectual Disability and National Disability Services, a wide range of parent groups, the national intellectually disadvantaged self-help network, and branches of the National Association of Intellectual Disability. This last organisation—the peak organisation representing people with intellectual disabilities, parents, friends and professionals—has expressed concern at the failure of some politicians and most of the media to distinguish between people who have an intellectual disability and those who are psychiatrically ill. The association stresses that the vast majority of people with an intellectual disability are not ill, either physically or mentally, and that they do not need hospitalisation or any other form of institutionalisation. Intellectual disability is an impairment of learning function; it is not an illness. In 1988, the New South Wales Council for Intellectual Disability protested to the then minister for health, Peter Collins, and argued through the media that reviewing mental health services and services for people with an intellectual disability under the one review committee, the Barclay Committee, was turning the clock back 20 years.

Results from the ABS (2009b) Survey of Disability, Ageing and Carers revealed that 4 million people, or 18.5 per cent of Australians, reported a disability in 2009. Both males and females reported similar rates of disability (18 per cent and 19 per cent respectively) (ABS 2009b). Most of this group identified a severe limitation or restriction as the main cause of their disability (87 per cent), with musculoskeletal disorders such as arthritis the most common cause. Mental or behavioural disorders were the cause of disability for only a small proportion (15 per cent). The majority of those with a disability (87 per cent) were limited to some degree (handicapped) in their ability to perform certain activities or tasks in relation to one or more of the following areas: self-care, mobility, communication, schooling or employment. Of the 1.1 million people with a profound or severe restriction, 56 per cent were female. Informal assistance to those who needed help because of disability or ageing was provided by 2.6 million Australians (ABS 2009b). The proportion of Australians with a disability has increased steadily since the ABS first conducted the survey in 1981, partly due to an ageing population. The disability rate ranged from 3.4 per cent of children under four years to 88 per cent of people aged 90 or older.

Results from the ABS (1990) Disability and Handicap Survey, 1988, revealed that the vast majority of people with disability were living in private households. Fewer than 9 per cent of people with 'handicaps' and approximately 6 per cent of people with disabilities lived in institutions. Persons with disabilities comprised nearly 93 per cent of people in institutional care. In addition, more than half of the people with disabilities were aged 75 years or more, and nearly two-thirds of these were women.

Traditionally, the Commonwealth government's responsibilities in relation to program development and service delivery for persons with disabilities have been threefold. First, it provides income maintenance through direct cash payments to people with disabilities. These cash payments include the disability support pension, the rehabilitation allowance and the mobility allowance. Second, it provides direct services to people with disabilities, mainly through the CRS Australia (formerly the Commonwealth Rehabilitation Service) program, which links the Commonwealth departments of social security, employment, education and training, health and community services, with the aim of coordinating the retraining needs of persons on pensions or allowances. Third, the Commonwealth provides subsidies to other organisations that conduct services for people with disabilities, primarily under the *Disability Services Act 1986* (which replaced the *Handicapped Persons Assistance Act 1974*). Income support, in the form of pensions and benefits paid to people with disabilities, is the major component of the Commonwealth's contribution.

In 1983, the Commonwealth Department of Social Security established the Handicapped Program Review as a means of identifying changes necessary for future policy development. After extensive consultations with people who have disabilities, their relatives and friends, and consumer groups and service providers, the review recommended that the Commonwealth focus primarily on improving the prospects of people with disabilities through developing independent living options, better training and employment opportunities, and realistic access to generic or mainstream community services.

In 1985, *New Directions*, the report of the Handicapped Program Review (Commonwealth of Australia 1985b), foreshadowed far-reaching changes in the nature of service delivery for people with disabilities in Australia. Perhaps, most importantly, the review signalled that an emphasis on independent living had taken over from the more traditional medical model that had shaped policies for developmental disability in the past.

The same year also saw the establishment of the Office of Disability, and in 1986 the Commonwealth government legislated, through the *Disability Services Act 1986*, to enable a more flexible approach towards people with disabilities. A simultaneous initiative was endorsement of a set of principles and objectives. This meant that all disability services seeking government funding in the future would be measured against these objectives and principles. Reforms in disability services consistent with these principles and objectives have been implemented steadily. Younger people with disabilities can now receive Home and Community Care services, and an innovative attendant care service that assists people in nursing homes with severe physical disabilities to move into the community. An income-test-free child disability allowance was introduced, and further income support initiatives were recommended in the Social Security Review (Commonwealth Department of Social Security 1988). Given the fact that disability continued to engender fear and ignorance among many people, a resource manual, *Disability, Society and Change* (Commonwealth Department of Community Services and Health 1988b), was made available through the Office of Disability for interested individuals and community organisations. Production and distribution of this manual was consistent with the department's policy of empowering people with disabilities themselves and those who support and advocate for them.

The Disability Reform Package, introduced in the 1990–91 and 1992–93 budgets, included changes in the pension system to remove disincentives to return to work; expanded services in the areas of rehabilitation, training and support; and increased benefits for transition to work (National Health Strategy 1993d). It attempted to enhance opportunities for people with disabilities to find meaningful employment in the community and discourage long-term dependence on income support.

State government responsibilities include the provision of programs for people with disabilities in the areas of education, health, family and community services, housing and transport. Local governments also provide support services for people with disabilities. A wide range of services for people with disabilities is provided by non-government organisations, including special schools, sheltered employment, residential accommodation, home care services, vocational training, social, sporting and recreational facilities, information services, publicity, advocacy, lobbying and representation.

An important feature of the Handicapped Program Review was the emphasis given to consumer perspectives and consumer outcomes; that is, to what consumers thought about the services and whether they benefited from them. Consumers with disabilities identified the following outcomes as the most important: a place to live, paid employment, being competent and self-reliant, participating in community activities, feeling secure, having choices in life, and having a positive image in the eyes of the community.

Persistent and effective lobbying on the part of many consumers with disabilities and their supporters, combined with support from politicians and public servants, led to the enactment of a significant piece of legislation, the Commonwealth *Disability Discrimination Act 1993*. This act makes discrimination against people with disabilities, including people with HIV/AIDS, illegal. The law applies in the areas of employment, education, services and facilities, clubs, sport and in the administration of Commonwealth programs. If a person is treated less favourably because of their disability, complaints can be lodged with the Disability Discrimination Commissioner, through the Australian Human Rights Commission. Although this law does not provide a solution to many problems encountered by people with disabilities, it does enable people who are discriminated against to seek some form of redress.

At the national and international levels, significant progress was made in 2008 when Australia was one of the first Western countries to ratify the United Nations Convention on the Rights of Persons with Disabilities. Ratification is a symbolic commitment to continue to make progress in disability law, policy and practices in Australia, especially in ensuring equal opportunity in education and employment, as well as addressing the inadequacies in supports and services for many persons with physical and other challenges and their families. Professor Ron McCallum, prominent advocate for Vision Australia and legal academic, was appointed inaugural rapporteur to the United Nations Disabilities Convention in 2009. In this position, he was responsible for reporting to the United Nations General Assembly on the recommendations and activities of the Committee on the Rights of Persons with Disabilities.

In 2013, the Gillard Government passed historic legislation to introduce the National Disability Insurance Scheme (NDIS), possibly Australia's most significant social policy reform since Medicare. The scheme will be implemented in all states and territories, with the objective of giving the power to individuals to choose the care they want. It is a welcome relief to people with disabilities and their families and carers, especially to people not covered by insurance schemes associated with motor vehicle accidents or workplace injury. The scheme is a most significant step forward in health for all, and evidence of Australia's renewed commitment to advancing the rights of persons with disabilities, and to ensuring that they are supported to contribute as productive members of society.

Older persons

Many policymakers, managers, clinicians and members of the public have a distorted and overly negative view of ageing and older people. The International Year of Older Persons, in 1999, attempted to redress the view that sees 'old people' as problems requiring considerable attention and resources. Russell's (1981) and Russell and Schofield's (1986) work on the sociology of ageing helps to dispel many distorted or ill-informed views about aged people in Australia. A major myth is that the escalating costs associated with the care of older people can be explained solely by the fact that an increasing proportion of the population is aged 65 years or more (Sax 1993). Increasing costs associated with older people are linked more closely with social and political changes than with physiological ageing as such. Political changes include increased government financial support for nursing homes, and social factors include compulsory retirement and higher rates of women's work-force participation. These social changes have led to a decreased ability to care for older parents at home. The so-called 'burden of illness' among the elderly has been exaggerated also. Even among those aged 75 years or more, incapacitating illness and disability are the exception rather than the norm. Many older people are not a burden to anyone; they are independent and resourceful and often contribute more to their families and communities than they receive in assistance.

The vast majority of people over 65 years of age do not live in institutions. In 2011, 94 per cent of people aged 65 and over lived in private dwellings and, for people aged 65–74 years, a further 2 per cent lived in non-private dwellings (ABS 2013d). The numbers increased with age for non-private dwellings to 6 per cent for 75 to 84 year olds and 26 per cent for 85 years and over (ABS 2013d). Older people living in non-private dwellings amounted to 180 300 people, of whom the vast majority were in aged care facilities (67 per cent) or accommodation for the retired (25 per cent). Indeed, the 2011–12 National Health Survey found that one-third (31.4 per cent) of older people living in the community rated their health as fair or poor (ABS 2013e). A very small minority of the older population suffers from a health problem such as dementia, which was estimated to affect one in 10 Australians aged 65 years and over in 2011. The majority of older people live independently in their own homes. Moreover, those needing assistance receive it overwhelmingly from their own families, rather than from professionals or volunteers. Female relatives, commonly wives and daughters (Kinnear & Graycar 1983), do most caring work in the community. This is reflected in the ABS (2013e) finding that women comprised 70 per cent of the primary carers who provided informal assistance to people with a disability in 2012 (ABS 2013e).

In 1985, existing federally funded services and programs for the aged were placed under one umbrella, the Home and Community Care (HACC) program. This program provides a comprehensive and integrated range of services within the community. It is the mainstay program for the frail aged and people with disabilities who wish to live at home. With HACC, existing programs such as home nursing, Meals on Wheels, allied health services and home care services were combined with new programs including assessment services, aged day-care services, sitting services, respite care and transport for aged people and people with disabilities, on a cost-shared basis with the states. The HACC program is administered by the states through different departments. A study conducted by the Social Policy Research Centre on the first 18 months of the HACC program in a single local government area in Sydney pointed to inadequate overall funding and problems with coordination in both the planning and provision of community support services (Fine 1992).

The HACC program helps those people living in the community who, in the absence of basic maintenance and support services, might otherwise be admitted to nursing homes and hostels before they need such an intensive level of health care. The program also supports those who care for these people, through the provision of support services such as respite care and the Domiciliary Nursing Care Benefit. An important principle of the program is consultation with service providers and users on the gaps in existing services and priorities for developing new types of service. In 1999, the Domiciliary Nursing Care Benefit was incorporated into the Care Allowance, broadening the eligibility criteria for carers.

Aged care policy developments

Two important policy developments have occurred in the last two decades. First, is a shift in balance from residential care to home-based care. In 1991–92, community care packages were introduced to provide a community alternative to residential care for the frail aged. Subsequently, in 1998 the then prime minister John Howard announced a $270 million staying home package of measures to encourage older Australians to stay at home with assistance from carers. To ensure that only those who are highly dependent are placed in residential care, multidisciplinary aged care assessment teams (ACAT) were established nationally.

Second, is the shift away from nursing home accommodation towards hostel accommodation, the latter catering for older Australians with less-intensive needs. Between 1989–90 and 1995–96, there was a 41 per cent increase in available hostel beds compared with a 3 per cent increase in nursing home accommodation.

The Commonwealth has continued to allocate additional funds to community services in recognition of the preference of many older people and people with disabilities to remain in their homes, and the need for a better balance between the resources provided for community services and institutional care. Anna Howe, former director of the Office for the Aged in the Commonwealth Department of Health, Housing, Local Government and Community Services, noted:

> The major outcome of the re-direction of aged-care policy in terms of service provision has been the expansion of community care and the containment of residential care, with a shift in the balance between nursing home care and hostel care within residential provision.

Howe (1992, p. 238)

From 1985–86 to 1990–91, the increase in recurrent Commonwealth expenditure on nursing home care was just 9 per cent. In contrast, expenditure on the HACC program grew by 95 per cent, and for hostels, the increase in recurrent expenditure was 127 per cent (Howe 1992, p. 238). Within the HACC program, some of the additional funds have been used for projects known as community options projects, or in some states, linkage or brokerage projects. Community options coordinators are responsible for assessing the needs of each individual client and arranging (or, where necessary, purchasing) the community services required. Community options projects extend choices to the individual consumer by assisting them to acquire services such as home modification, delivered meals or home care in a way that suits their individual preferences and needs. They have great potential but often the services are not available to be brokered for.

For each age group within the aged population, the rate of institutionalisation is lower for males and generally lower for persons who are married (ABS 1984). Married persons who require some assistance to live independently usually receive assistance from their spouses and so, in many cases, can continue to live in private accommodation. The majority of older men live with their spouses and are often cared for at home even when they have a serious or incapacitating illness. Since married women frequently outlive their husbands, many older women live alone and they are not cared for in the same way. This partly accounts for the high number of women, relative to men, living in institutions. A much higher proportion of married aged persons than unmarried aged persons live in private dwellings. Married people are more likely to live at home, and having a spouse is the most significant single defence against social isolation, public dependency and poverty (Rowland 1982). Australians who are married experience lower rates of death than those who are never married, widowed or divorced, but these differences are most pronounced for men (ABS 1997).

Australia has one of the highest rates of institutional care for older persons in the world (Parker 1987). This can be explained by the broad-ranging social and political changes discussed previously, particularly the remarkable growth of nursing home provision after 1962, when the Commonwealth subsidy for nursing homes was introduced. Detailed analysis of this situation, as presented in **Chapter 5**, indicates that the nursing home subsidy supplied the motivating force behind the boom in the nursing home industry, to the point where it dominated the development of Commonwealth policy for older persons.

Continuing problems with institutional care for older persons include the placement of older people with chronic long-term health problems in acute hospitals instead of nursing homes, and the presence of older persons in nursing homes owing to factors such as a lack of alternative accommodation and community services. The nursing home sector has also attracted criticism relating to standards of care. A survey carried out by the Australian Council on the Ageing and the Department of Community Services (1985) found that most older people regard a nursing home as the least attractive option for their care. Other forms of care, such as home care services and hostels, are much more popular with older people. This finding is particularly disturbing given that over 80 per cent of Commonwealth spending on aged care goes to nursing homes, which cater for only 4 per cent of the aged population. In a study of 24 homes, the Victorian Aged Services Peak Council

(1987) reported 'very distressing' results. Although 60 per cent of patients surveyed could not control their bladders or bowels, only 20 per cent were washed daily. Almost half the patients in the study were unnecessarily confined to wheelchairs.

Chris Ronalds' (1989a) influential issues paper, *I'm Still an Individual*, provided convincing evidence that the rights of older people living in nursing homes and hostels were often ignored, neglected or abused. Pooled clothing, abject boredom and lack of privacy were some of the widespread problems experienced by residents in the 85 nursing homes under investigation. Ronald's (1989b) final report to Peter Staples, minister for housing and aged care, helped to shape the national policy agenda for the 'residents' rights movement' in Australia, including introduction of a Charter of Residents' Rights and Responsibilities, a resident–proprietor agreement, and the establishment of aged consumer forums in each state (Gibson, Turrell & Jenkins 1993). In 1997, the Aged Care Standards and Accreditation Agency was established to ensure that residential aged care facilities achieved and maintained high standards of accommodation and care (Podger & Hagan 2000). The National Aged Care Industry Council, which represents the providers of residential aged care services in both the private and charitable sectors, also aims to improve standards and quality of care in residential aged care services (Healthcover 1999). These developments, combined with the resident-focused, outcome-oriented nursing home regulation system introduced in 1997, were designed to improve the standards of care in nursing homes and the quality of life of nursing home residents.

Maintaining one's home and the capacity to remain in one's familiar neighbour-hood are very important to older people (Keens et al, 1983). For most older people this is a realistic possibility, because the vast majority are neither poor nor disabled. However, for approximately 10 per cent of older people there are barriers to living independently. Barriers include inadequate housing, low income, physical disability, transport difficulties and lack of social support. Clearly, the needs of older people are not only health-related but also social and economic. Many older people live in nursing homes, hostels and retirement accommodation for reasons other than illness or disability. For those whose needs are health-related, policy responses should include provision for nursing in the home, home help, household maintenance and repairs, and home visiting. Deficiencies in any one of these areas can lead to the older person requiring other accommodation.

Examination of nursing homes and hostels in **Chapter 5** indicated that many inquiries and reports have stressed the desirability of appropriate levels of accommodation and services being made available for the 13.6 per cent of Australia's population that is aged 65 or more. It is projected that the percentage of the population aged 65 years and over will double to about a quarter of the population by 2056 (ABS 2008c). Moreover, it is estimated that 22 per cent of the total increase in health services expenditure between 1975–76 and 1996–97 can be attributed to the ageing of the population. In 1999, the then prime minister John Howard established a Ministerial Reference Group to develop a long-term National

Strategy for an Ageing Australia. The group was to be the vehicle for community consultation about the type of policies and programs needed to meet the demands of older people in the future. The Commonwealth government conducted coordinated care trials to address the health needs of older people who are chronically ill or disadvantaged (Fisher 2009). However, the then opposition shadow minister for health, Jenny Macklin, claimed that the coordinated care models being trialled were an insufficient policy response to the fragmentation of the financing and organisation of health and aged services that characterised the Australian health care system. According to Macklin, 'alternative financing models that systematically finance health and aged care services together' would be a more appropriate long-term policy approach to the ageing of the population (Healthcover 1999).

More recent aged care policies emphasise that a suitable range of adequately funded, easily accessible community services should be made available to make home life a realistic possibility for older people (Fine 2006). These policies also acknowledge that not providing a continuum of community care will be costly for governments, which have to provide or fund alternative accommodation, and for the women and families who have to cope with inadequate support services in the community. Costs will also be borne by older persons themselves, who may experience unnecessary social isolation, dependence and restrictions on their freedom (Keens, Graycar & Harrison 1983). In the 1990s, with growing residents' rights and increasing activism among older Australians, the issue of abuse and neglect of the elderly at home (McCallum, Matiasz & Graycar 1990) attracted greater attention from the community, professionals, managers and policymakers.

Disability, health and age

The relationship between disability, health and age is not necessarily straightforward, even though at first it may seem so because of the general tendency for the prevalence of certain health conditions and disability to increase with age (DHA 2008b). In the older age groups, illnesses affecting human functioning become more prevalent, including cardiovascular diseases, arthritis and dementia. People with disability in older age groups need more frequent assistance than do younger people, and with more core activities. Older people also have more health conditions associated with disability (AIHW 2005). Other factors that change the environment and circumstances of older people, such as loss of a spouse, technological change or surrendering a driver's licence, may also result in older people needing assistance with certain activities in order to support their capacity for community living.

The Survey of Disability, Ageing and Carers conducted by the ABS in 2003 (ABS 2004) found that 43 per cent (over 1 million persons) of the 2.3 million people aged 65 years and over living in households expressed a need for some form of assistance to help them stay at home. The most common type of need was property maintenance (29 per cent), followed by transport (22 per cent), housework

(20 per cent) and health care (20 per cent). Approximately 26 per cent needed some assistance with personal activities, such as self-care, mobility, communication, cognition or emotion, and health care.

The HACC program remains the main provider of home-based care services in Australia. In 2004–05, over 3000 agencies delivered HACC services (AIHW 2007). Nearly 60 per cent of their clients were referred to the program by formal services such as GPs, hospitals or other government or non-government organisations. The remainder were either self-referred or referred by family or friends (AIHW 2007). Overall, the HACC program provided almost 22 million hours of assistance to older people in 2004–05, over a third of this as centre-based day care, a service provided to groups (8 million hours), and nearly a quarter as domestic assistance (5 million hours). In addition, it provided over 10 million meals, 3 million one-way trips and $5 million in assistance with home modifications that help prevent injury in the home.

Community Aged Care Packages (CACPs) are funded by the Commonwealth government and began in 1992 as an alternative to low-level residential aged care. The program provides home-based care to frail or disabled older people living in the community, following an ACAT assessment and recommendation. It provides a package of assistance managed by a care coordinator. The latter manages the care needs of the recipients and arranges provision of numerous types of assistance, including personal care, domestic assistance, social support, assistance with meal preparation and other food services, respite care, rehabilitation support, home maintenance, delivered meals, linen services and transport. A recipient of CACP services is not excluded from receiving additional community care if required. For example, the program does not provide nursing services or allied health care, but these services are offered by the HACC program. An exploratory study (Karmel & Braun 2004) found that at least 35 per cent of CACP recipients were using at least one HACC service in the second half of 2002, and that 11 per cent of CACP recipients were using HACC nursing services.

In 2001, the Extended Aged Care at Home (EACH) pilot was implemented and became a fully established program in 2002. The EACH packages are funded by the Commonwealth government to deliver care at home to people who are otherwise eligible for high-level residential care. At 30 June 2006, there were 2580 available EACH packages and 2131 EACH recipients. EACH packages provide a similar range of care services as CACPs, with the addition of nursing and allied health care services. In 2005, EACH Dementia packages were also allocated. This program was specifically aimed to assist frail older people with dementia-related high-care needs. A care recipient on an EACH Dementia package could access the same types of assistance that are available to an EACH package care recipient. However, delivery of that assistance may be provided using a more flexible approach and strategies that are appropriate for people with dementia. In addition, EACH Dementia packages also provide access to dementia-specific specialist services and support (AIHW 2007).

The Living Longer Living Better package introduced by the Gillard Government offers older Australians more choice, control and access to health services they may need or want. The 10-year aged care package, introduced in 2011–12, aims to provide a sustainable and national aged care system that is fairer. It is projected that the Australian population will continue to age over the coming decades. This is not a new phenomenon, as it can be attributed to sustained low fertility levels and increasing life expectancy. Clearly, the challenges will not dissipate. On a positive note, though, it would appear that significant progress has been made over the last several decades in terms of shifting care priorities from residential care towards community-based care, and within the residential care sector, there has been a shift in the balance between nursing home care and hostel care. Both these trends are consistent with increased respect for the rights of older Australians, and consistent with the ethos of an ageing and caring community.

SUMMARY AND CONCLUSION

This analysis of health services and public policy developments relating to women and men, immigrants, Aboriginal people, people with mental health problems, people with disabilities and older persons has revealed that the existing health care system does not guarantee that all groups have equal access to health or health care. In developing policies, programs and services that aim to counteract this problem, three main strategies have been identified.

The first strategy aims to make existing generic or mainstream services more accessible and appropriate to the needs of disadvantaged groups. The second strategy focuses on the development of specific services for particular social groups. This strategy is most clearly developed in the areas of women's health and Aboriginal health, and is particularly well illustrated by the work of the family planning associations in each state and territory in Australia. These strategies are compatible with a social justice perspective towards health care. Both contend that health differentials between groups can be reduced if health care is made accessible to all, according to health need.

The third strategy does not take the unequal distribution of health status and health care services as its starting point; instead it asks how and why the inequalities have occurred. It suggests that mainstreaming and specific services do not provide an adequate prescription for change. This strategy locates inequalities in health within the social, political and economic structure of Australian society. In particular, it contends that the inequalities in health status between groups is the outcome of relations between these groups, relations characterised often by conflicts of interest and the unequal distribution of social, political and economic power. Thus, inequality is conceptualised in relational rather than distributional terms. This strategy is based on the contention, for example, that the deprivation, powerlessness and poor health status of Aboriginal and Torres Strait Islander peoples follow as a necessary consequence of relations with non-Indigenous Australians. In the relational, or structural, strategy, the main concern in public policy development is not the unhealthy or disadvantaged group per se, but the unequal social relations that are manifested in a variety of forms.

This third strategy implies that progress towards the achievement of greater equity, social justice and social inclusion will require the transformation of complex social, political and economic relations through which inequalities are constituted, and not just improving access to health care. It attempts to shift the balance of power within the health care system towards the more disadvantaged sectors of the community, and places organisational change at the forefront of policy development. The structural strategy advocates a wide range of changes in organisational structures and encouragement of greater representation of and participation by disadvantaged health care consumers at all decision-making levels in the health care system. The structural strategy has insights that are crucial to the success of policies designed to increase equity because it points out that realisation of the right to health can be achieved only if the need for health care is equalised. Although debate about which strategy to adopt in improving the health of disadvantaged groups will continue, perhaps the best policy solutions will incorporate aspects of all three strategies. Moreover, in 1999 with the International Year of Older Persons, it became evident that the social justice perspective and concomitant emphasis on human rights previously espoused by the women's health movement, Indigenous peoples, people with mental health problems, persons with disabilities and others, had spread to one more segment of the 'patient' population.

FURTHER READING

On a philosophical level, in order to understand inequalities in health and the moral imperative that underlies a social justice perspective towards health, we recommend reading the International Declaration of Human Rights and, in particular, Article 25. This articulates the fundamental 'right to health'. For a more recent enunciation of this commitment to equity and 'universal coverage', see the *World Health Report 2008: Primary Health Care (Now More Than Ever)* (WHO 2008c).

The methodology to understand and measure socioeconomic disadvantage in Australia has improved significantly in recent years through the work of the ABS. We particularly recommend the work by Adhikari (2006). Socioeconomic Indexes for Areas (SEIFA) were constructed by the ABS for the 2006 Census of Population and Housing to focus on particular aspects of socioeconomic status. The Index of Relative Socioeconomic Disadvantage (IRSD) combines indicators of disadvantage such as low income, high unemployment and low levels of education. A high IRSD implies that an area has few families with low income, few people with little or no training and few people working in unskilled occupations.

For further explanation of the debates around 'disease-mongering', we recommend work by Ray Moynihan, an independent journalist and a regular contributor to the *British Medical Journal*. In particular, see Moynihan's and Cassels' *Selling Sickness: How the World's Biggest Pharmaceutical Companies Are Turning us All into Patients* (Nation Books, 2005).

We also recommend the 2010 WHO report *Health Systems Financing: The Path to Universal Health Coverage*. This details actions required by low-, middle- and high-income countries to move towards universal coverage and to improve health outcomes.

The United Nations Economic and Social Commission for Asia and the Pacific, *Regional Survey on Ageing 2011: Australia* reports comprehensive information on the Commonwealth government's approach to ageing in terms of population ageing and senior Australians.

DISCUSSION QUESTIONS

1   Which group, or groups, is most disadvantaged in Australian society? Why?
2   Which socioeconomic group is over-represented among the medical specialists who oversee the health care system in Australia?
3   Explain why the health gap between adult Indigenous Australians and non-Indigenous Australians is widening, while the health gap between Indigenous and non-Indigenous babies is decreasing.
4   What are the three key strategies adopted by policymakers in attempting to meet the health care needs of disadvantaged groups?
5   To what extent does Australia's health care system satisfy the three dimensions of universal health coverage?

10

Reforming health policymaking, delivery and financing

In designing health policy initiatives, governments, their advisors and other policy analysts may draw on a wide range of information and data sources. Comparative studies of health institutions and policies in other countries have formed an important basis for proposed policy reforms in many jurisdictions. The underlying rationale for this approach is that policies that have worked successfully in one or more countries may provide similar benefits in one's own environment, despite there being important differences in the institutions, history and cultural norms of the countries being compared.

Marmor and colleagues (2009) have indicated that the 1990s and 2000s have experienced an upsurge in comparative studies of health policies, engendered in part by the provision of health data by international agencies, notably the Organisation for Economic Development (OECD) and the World Health Organization (WHO) (Klein 2009; Marmor, Freeman & Okma 2009). However, these writers on policy learning from other countries have been at pains to point out the limitations and pitfalls of what, on the face of it, appears to be a promising method of improving the policymaking process in each country. We return to this issue later in the chapter.

Health policy initiatives and changes—a comparative analysis

In Australia, several major proposed or implemented health policy changes have drawn heavily on the experience of other countries. Prior to World War II, as we noted in **Chapter 1**, the characteristics of the Australian health care system were largely derived from the British system. These included the heavy reliance on fee-for-service (FFS) payments to doctors, the absence of health insurance arrangements except for those provided by friendly societies, and the very limited involvement of governments in financing the provision of medical and hospital services. For the poorer members of communities, free treatment, especially in hospitals, was largely at the discretion of members of the medical profession acting in a charitable capacity.

Following the creation of the British National Health Service (NHS) in 1948, and its antecedents, notably the Beveridge Report on social welfare of 1942, the

Australian Labor government of the time in the early postwar years moved towards the creation of a similar system in Australia. As we noted in **Chapter 4**, these efforts were thwarted by the conservative opposition, along with the British Medical Association in Australia. In what must rank as one of the most bizarre judicial decisions in Australia's history, the High Court ruled that the requirement for doctors to sign a form requesting free medicines for patients constituted 'civil conscription' and was thus unconstitutional. No further attempts were made to follow Britain down the nationalised health service path.

We also observed in **Chapter 4** that the voluntary health insurance program introduced by the conservative government in 1953 followed closely the pattern of health insurance arrangements in the United States, with the management of the system residing with a multiplicity of private health insurance funds, although with rather more government regulation of the industry than was present in the United States.

With the return to power of the Labor government in 1972, the scheme then called Medibank relied heavily for its main characteristics on the Canadian system of health insurance, with all Australian citizens being covered by the government-funded scheme, which included free hospitalisation in public hospitals. As we indicated in **Chapter 4**, there was much more opposition to the introduction of the program in Australia than in Canada because of the growth of private health insurance organisations under the previous regime, and because of the almost complete absence of private hospitals in Canada. Many Australian specialists with links to private hospitals were apprehensive about the threats to their income if the existence of private hospitals, and of private practice in public hospitals, was threatened by the new arrangements.

We conclude this section on external inputs to Australian health policymaking with two further and contrasting examples from the United States: managed care and casemix funding, now called, as we noted previously, activity-based funding.

Managed care and managed competition

Although the terms 'managed care' and 'managed competition' correspond to health care policy arrangements that are in some measure distinct, for our present purposes it convenient to ignore these finer distinctions. As we discussed in **Chapter 2**, the term 'managed competition' was coined by the economist Alain Enthoven (1988).

Enthoven recognised that the attempts to introduce more competitive elements into the financing and provision of health services had to recognise that it was the decisions of providers that were of critical importance. As we have emphasised previously, in the context of doctor dominance and supplier-induced 'demand' it is the decisions of the medical profession that have the overwhelming influence in determining usage and expenditure on health services. Thus, in the attempt to achieve increased efficiency, attention needed to be focused on the providers and the financial intermediaries.

In the United States, the abortive attempt of the Clinton administration to introduce universal health coverage, based on a managed competition model, later evolved into the managed care era (Marmor & Hacker 2007). Hacker and Marmor point out, however, that there has existed considerable confusion in the United States about what the phrase 'managed care' actually means: 'Because managed care is an incoherent subject, most claims about it will suffer from incoherence as well' (Marmor & Hacker 2007, p. 27).

Hacker and Marmor argue convincingly that, along with many other catch-phrases that have become commonplace in the language of health policy and health services management, the purpose of the terms 'managed care' and 'managed competition' had more to do with convincing the target audiences of the desirability of implementing certain changed funding and organisational arrangements rather than clarifying the precise details of the proposed policy reforms.

In Australia, the health economist Richard Scotton, who had been prominent in designing Medibank and Medicare, has argued strongly for the principles of managed competition to be applied to the Australian health care system (Scotton 1998b). He outlined a system in which public and private budget-holders, funded on a capitation basis, would contract with public and private providers to offer their services to the residents of relatively large geographical areas. The budget-holders would therefore be placed in a situation in which they competed with one another for clients and accordingly would be under pressure to achieve greater efficiency in their operations.

The details of Scotton's well-argued case are not our concern here. What is important in the context of policymaking reform in Australia is that federal governments of both political persuasions have displayed no interest whatsoever in the managed competition proposal.

The reasons for the lack of impact of the Scotton proposals, except in academic policy circles, are presumably because of the dramatic changes that were envisaged for the main actors in the Australian health policy scene. The managed care and managed competition proposals all have at their core the substitution of capitation payments to the financial intermediaries for the existing arrangements. Capitation involves an annual rate per contributor or member of a defined population. While this would not necessarily entail a shift from FFS payments to capitation for doctors, the perceptions of doctors that this would happen would undoubtedly have provoked the vigorous opposition of the medical profession to the changes. Similar considerations apply to the private health funds. The incentives for increased competition between them would also be perceived as putting at risk the viability of some of them, which is indeed part of the rationale of the managed competition model.

Activity-based funding

We have discussed the development and application of activity-based funding (ABF) in Australia for public hospitals at some length in **Chapter 5**, culminating in its universal application for this purpose, as agreed to under the National Health

Reform Agreement of 2011. In this section we treat this very important policy initiative as an example of an import from the United States that was successfully implemented in this country. As we also noted in **Chapter 5**, early work on intro- ducing casemix that was based on diagnosis related groups (DRGs) for funding in Australia commenced in the late 1980s. One of us (George Palmer) had been invited by the Yale group to spend the 1987 academic year working with them on several casemix research projects.

It was evident that Professor Robert Fetter, the leader of the group, was keen to promote the use of DRGs in other countries. From our discussions, he realised that Australia possessed the data and the technical expertise to be able to introduce a casemix program fairly quickly. Fetter made available the computer software to group the hospital discharge data into the existing DRG system. He also agreed to make time available for further visits to Australia aimed at convincing government officials and others of the potential of DRGs for hospital funding and other purposes. An important convert from one of these discussions was Stephen Duckett, at that time a senior official of the Victorian Department of Health (Duckett 2009c).

Fetter and Palmer also organised a conference on casemix at the University of New South Wales in 1988, which was opened by the then Commonwealth minister for health, Dr Neal Blewett. Commonwealth government financial support for a casemix development program, linked to the Medicare agreements between the Commonwealth government and the states, followed shortly afterwards.

Opposition to the use of casemix for funding purposes from the medical profession was fairly widespread. The most common theme was that DRGs were based on United States clinical practice and that they would not work in Australia because medicine was practised very differently in this country. However, a further source of medical opposition that surfaced from time to time was that a group of operations researchers, mathematicians and economists would be unable to devise a system that properly classified the diverse activities of their profession. This belief ignored the fact that inputs from many practising clinicians had been drawn upon in creating the original DRG system in the United States.

The election of the conservative Kennett Government in Victoria in 1993 was a further critical element in the application of DRGs in Australia for hospital funding. Prior to that time, despite the research that had established the feasibility of using casemix in Australia, and how the approach might be applied to funding hospitals in the very different organisational and financial arrangements as compared with the United States, there had been no examples of casemix use in practice for this purpose.

The Kennett Government was elected with a large majority in both houses of parliament. It possessed a mandate to balance the state budget, which had incurred a large deficit under the previous administration. When early in its term of office the government announced cuts of the order of 5 per cent per annum over three years in all public sector activities, including health services, there was relatively little opposition.

The responsibility for securing public hospital budget cuts was assigned to the newly appointed director-general of health, John Patterson, an economist who had devised policies for charging for water in a public sector system. Several people, including Stephen Duckett and Helen Owens, introduced him to the use of DRGs for funding purposes. Duckett had been instrumental in funding the first Australian study of DRGs referred to in **Chapter 5** and Owens, along with Scotton, had co-authored the monograph on DRG funding sponsored by the Commonwealth (Duckett 1995; Scotton & Owens 1990).

Patterson and Duckett were able to convince the government that the most efficient and equitable way of spreading the budget cuts between hospitals was via the use of DRG funding. In other circumstances, a redistributive policy of this kind would have been bitterly contested by the potential losers, including doctors, managers and other hospital staff. However, the health department was able to move quickly to implement the policy without any major political or technical problems emerging.

In the light of the successful application of activity-based funding in Victoria and subsequently South Australia, we may ask why did its national application take almost 20 more years to come to pass? We are not aware of any clear answers to this question. However, we note that Dr Blewett moved on from his post in 1990, and that the federal Labor government concentrated on refining the DRG system, creating the Australian Refined DRGs (AR-DRGs), with the underlying assumption that further work on funding applications was the responsibility of the individual states. Finally, the health priorities of the conservative Coalition government elected in 1996 did not extend to the further pursuit of national activity-based funding.

The other relevant development was the continuing opposition to the use of casemix for funding in the New South Wales Health Department. Part of the reservations about the application of this new method of hospital funding stemmed from the fact that the department had devoted considerable resources to securing greater equity between geographical areas in the allocation of health service funding. The method used was based on that applied in the British NHS developed by the Resource Allocation Working Party (RAWP), which essentially applied age- and sex-adjusted mortality rates in the various areas as a surrogate for relative rates of morbidity. As we have indicated previously, the decentralisation of funding responsibilities to areas in the state also complicated the acceptance of casemix allocations. In any case, the issue of reconciling activity-based funding with greater resource allocation equity between areas may not be capable of any precise resolution.

Comparative data on health systems performance

The examples cited have been based on the attempt to achieve radical reforms in the target country by drawing on what has been perceived to work elsewhere. We have seen that Australia managed to attain universal health insurance coverage by drawing on the Canadian example and a better method of funding hospitals based on the US research into and application of casemix funding. However, in a sense, a more fundamental application of comparative data is to attempt to rank the performance of different countries using a variety of criteria. We noted in **Chapter 1** that life expectancy and infant mortality rates have traditionally been used for this purpose, and that the performance of the Australian health care system ranks fairly well using these measures.

The use of data on the aggregate performance of health care systems was a potent factor in the efforts of President Obama to reform aspects of the health insurance arrangements in the United States, which culminated in the passing of the Affordable Health Care Act of 2010. Supporters of the need for reform were able to point to two salient facts: first, that life expectancy in the United States was significantly lower than in most other developed OECD countries, along with infant mortality rates that were substantially higher than those in other comparable countries; second, that the rate of health expenditure per person was more than twice as great in the United States than elsewhere in OECD countries. Coupled with the fact that the system in the United States left around 47 million residents without insurance coverage, it was obvious, except to most members of the Republican Party and their supporters, that drastic reform was needed.

Problems in the Australian health care system

The review of health policy and the characteristics of the Australian health care system presented in the previous chapters indicate the presence of many major problems. We are indebted especially to Professor Jeff Richardson of Monash University for a number of very perceptive papers he has written about health policy in Australia (Richardson 1999, 2005, 2009; Richardson & Segal 2004).

In his 2005 paper, Richardson made a fundamental distinction between policies that deal with marginal, largely irrelevant issues and those that address (or should address) major, often life-threatening, problems of our health care system. In the former category, he places the flurry of policymaking about private health insurance that characterised the Coalition government's policies in the late 1990s and early 2000s. In the latter, he stresses the failure of successive governments to deal adequately with the well-documented failure of hospitals to achieve acceptable levels of performance in relation to quality of care, including the prevention of the numerous instances of mortality and morbidity associated with hospitals documented in **Chapter 5**.

Richardson also remarks on the compelling evidence about the wide variations between areas in the provision of specific high-volume surgical services and the surprising lack of interest of governments and others in understanding and dealing with the problem and its implications for patient welfare and economic efficiency. We discussed this problem and the closely related issue of technology assessment in **Chapter 7**.

We agree that both these problems ought to be afforded high priority in health policymaking. The other high-priority policy area concerns the relations between the federal and state governments in respect of the financing and management of health services. The establishment in 2008 of the National Health and Hospitals Reform Commission (NHHRC) by the Rudd Government was designed to provide major input into policymaking in this area. The importance of establishing the best model of Commonwealth–state relationships is closely bound up with the achievement of major structural changes in our health care. We argued previously, in **Chapter 4**, that a greater role for the central government in health matters may be a necessary but not a sufficient condition for major reforms to be implemented. We explore later in this chapter the extent to which the health reforms of the Rudd and Gillard governments may have addressed some of these problems.

The other major problem in our existing methods for funding and providing health services concerns the equity and fairness of these arrangements. Because of the complexity of this issue, and its relationship to our evaluation of the very important final report of the NHHRC, we defer our extended discussion of equity to a later section.

Other problems in the health care system include:

- a continuing relative neglect of prevention, health promotion and other aspects of community health provision, and a perception that people with chronic illnesses, including older people and those with psychiatric disorders, are not well served by the current organisational and funding arrangements
- the proliferation of untested and often very expensive medical technologies
- large differentials in health status between the various socioeconomic and ethnic groups, including deplorable measures of health status in the Indigenous population
- increases in the use of and expenditure on medical services, including diagnostic services, which may reflect increases in the size of the medical workforce and the heavy reliance on FFS doctor remuneration, exacerbated by a grossly outdated Medicare Benefits Schedule
- limited involvement of consumers in policymaking, research and service delivery, and the perception that provider interests are dominant
- frequent reorganisations of health authorities and innumerable reports on the system, but little evidence of improvements in efficiency or health status as a consequence
- a sense of considerable demoralisation among doctors, nurses and other health professionals, and extensive deskilling in departments of health.

The problems listed above are not unique to Australia but because of our federal system, and the relatively large private sector role in health service delivery, we may suffer from more problems than a number of other comparable countries. Because of these and other differences, it is also doubtful whether the methods adopted or recommended in other countries for resolving the problems can be applied here, at least without considerable modification.

It should be a source of considerable concern that the existence of many of these problems, as shown in earlier chapters, was recognised in the early 1970s, and many of the Commonwealth and state policy initiatives since then have been aimed at their resolution. The reasons that these initiatives have failed to achieve their objectives requires further analysis; this is the logical starting point for the attempt to suggest how policymaking might be improved. However, it would be misleading to give the impression that the intervening years have been totally lacking in health-related achievements.

From 1983 to 2010, the two measures of health status discussed in **Chapter 1** have recorded considerable improvements: both male and female expectations of life at birth have increased by six years, while the infant mortality rate has declined by nearly 50 per cent (OECD 2013). Unfortunately, it is not possible to determine the relative contributions to these impressive gains of greater access to and better quality of medical and other health services, of preventative measures induced by the health care system, and of other factors, such as higher living standards, which are not products of the system.

Overseas and local evidence suggests that the reduced incidence of coronary artery disease, the principal source of increased life expectancy, is associated mainly with improved smoking and dietary habits, while the decline in infant mortality is a product of the better management of the newborn. No doubt a multiplicity of reasons contributed to the decline in Australia in the prevalence of smoking and the consumption of saturated fats. Health-related policies, including the development of community health services and health promotion activities, may have made at least a modest contribution to these changes.

We are also well aware of the principle that a large number of factors contribute to the health of populations, including, most importantly, social class and status (Evans, Barer & Marmor 1994; Marmot 2005). Indeed the dismal performance of the health care system in the United States, outlined on page 347, cannot be solely attributed to the inadequacies of the health insurance and financing arrangements in that country. Glaring inequalities in income, social status and power are likely to have had a direct influence on the poor health status of many underprivileged groups, notably the African–American population.

Constraints on policymaking

The failure to solve the many problems facing the Australian health care system might be attributed to the absence of appropriate policymaking structures, to the incompetence of those responsible for formulating and implementing policies, to the strength of the forces resisting change, or to some combination of these and other factors. In general, the political science and sociological perspectives discussed in **Chapter 3** have stressed the power of the groups opposed to changes, including the dominance of the medical profession, as a key causal factor.

Political scientists have also emphasised the difficulties of implementing rational–comprehensive models of policymaking and have tended to agree with the view articulated by Lindblom (1968) (see **Chapter 2**) that incremental adjustments to existing policies are both desirable and inevitable. Economists, epidemiologists and systems scientists have pointed to the need for more evaluative and analytical studies and for improved data to provide a basis for better policymaking. Either implicitly or explicitly, they have adopted the position that a more rational process of policymaking can be achieved.

In our view, it is possible to improve on the policymaking and health care structures that exist at present, and some of the more promising options will be discussed below. However, there is considerable evidence, based on our experience and that in other countries, that the powerful structural interests that stand to lose from many desirable policy initiatives are able to achieve considerable success in thwarting the efforts of governments to implement reforms. For this reason, the nature of the new structures to be created must be established, in part, by reference to how they will impinge on the current distribution of power within the system. We believe the attempt to find purely technical solutions to health care problems is doomed to failure, since these, by definition, do not consider who stands to lose from the proposed policy and what actions they may take to retain or restore the status quo.

Inclusion on the policy agenda

Following the analysis presented in **Chapter 3**, we take as our starting point the fact that whether certain policies are formulated and implemented depends on the strength of the demands for these policies and the power of the interest groups promoting or opposing the policies. Most importantly, the analysis of the concepts of power and interest indicated that issues might not reach the policy agenda (that is, being under active consideration with a view to being implemented). This is because the agenda is controlled by those who have an interest in retaining the status quo, and because often the people who stand to benefit from policy initiatives accept the status quo (Haywood & Alaszewski 1980; Lukes 1974).

The dominance of medical and other groups is not challenged because these groups have shaped the beliefs and preferences of large sections of the community. Since most policy initiatives that are desirable from a community interest standpoint are likely to have a detrimental influence on some powerful group, it is perhaps surprising that any major redistributive reforms are ever implemented!

Is it possible to deduce from these perspectives and from previous Australian experience what are the specific conditions for the successful generation and implementation of new health policies? Unfortunately, as we observed previously, most of the theoretical material we have discussed, including that of Alford and Marmor, is at its best when explaining why desirable policies are not implemented.

These writers, in general, have relatively little to say about possible solutions based on examples of successful policy implementation. Nevertheless, a few guidelines for maximising the success of policy initiatives may be derived from this background.

Exclusion from the policy agenda, as noted previously, is often a major barrier to be overcome before successful policymaking can be undertaken. For this reason, we need to consider the necessary conditions for an issue to reach the agenda. It is important to bear in mind, however, that a policy may fail to be effective because of problems at subsequent stages of the policymaking process, notably that of implementation.

In the Australian context, many major policy initiatives become part of a policy agenda when a political party includes the item as part of its proposals for future changes. By a major policy initiative, we mean a proposal that, if adopted, would represent a substantial break with previous methods of managing the issues that form the subject matter of the policy. Changes of this kind, rather than incremental adjustments to existing policies, are required to solve many of the problems listed previously.

In the health arena, the inclusion of compulsory tax-funded health insurance on the policy agenda of Labor in the late 1960s is the most notable example of a change in direction of this kind, culminating in the introduction of Medibank in 1975 and its resurrection as Medicare in 1984 (Scotton & Macdonald 1993). The reasons behind the inclusion of Medibank as a major aspect of Labor Party policy at that time included widespread discontent with the voluntary insurance scheme, the comprehensive critique of the Earle Page scheme provided by Scotton and Deeble (1968), and their detailed construction of a plausible and potentially politically attractive alternative. In addition, after a long period of conservative government, there was a realisation within Labor that substantial social policy changes were expected by and acceptable to the community.

The efforts of the Coalition government, the Australian Medical Association and the voluntary health funds to keep health insurance off the political agenda, a strategy that had worked well after the introduction of the Earle Page scheme, were no longer effective in the face of this combination of circumstances. It is clear, however, that the conjunction of favourable conditions characterising this example may be extremely difficult to replicate. It might be concluded, also, that the prospects for a major change, if opposed by powerful groups, are only likely to be favourable if at least some of these conditions or other equally important factors are present.

In a climate of severe restrictions on government expenditure, a further important reason for an item being included in the policy agenda is the prospect that the initiative will produce savings for the government; for example, by shifting the costs elsewhere or by promoting greater efficiency. The climate of opinion emphasising microeconomic reform, which developed in Australia in the late 1980s, may have been critical in persuading the Commonwealth government to examine alternative methods of financing and managing hospitals, such as those undertaken as part of the Casemix Development Program.

The successful implementation of casemix funding in Victoria acted as an example to some of the other states to pursue a similar policy. As noted in **Chapter 5**, there were varying degrees of support from governments in the other states for the introduction of casemix funding.

These examples of how health issues have been taken up by political parties and governments emphasise the circumstances in which initiatives for action have come from politicians; although, as in the case of universal health insurance and casemix, building on the work of academics and other researchers. It should be emphasised, however, that some policymaking reflects a response to issues that have become the focus of public attention.

Newspaper headlines about dying patients being transported by ambulance between several hospitals before they could be admitted are likely to provoke quick responses by governments to improve the effectiveness of accident and emergency services. In the case of new technologies, we have already observed (see **Chapter 7**) how good publicity about an alleged therapeutic or diagnostic breakthrough may generate enormous pressures on governments to accept and fund the innovation before it has been properly evaluated. Clearly, the degree to which an issue has been able to command the attention of the public is a potent determinant of whether it is included on the policy agenda.

The issue attention cycle

Downs (1972) has suggested that many issues progress through a regular pattern of changes in the intensity of the attention devoted to them. Using the example of public perceptions of ecological issues, he distinguished a five-stage process in which the issue moves from being of interest only to those who are directly involved to a wider public perception of the existence of a crisis requiring immediate remedial action. Subsequently, there is a realisation of the problems associated with resolving the issue, including the costs to taxpayers and specific interest groups. At this stage, the media may no longer see the issue as being newsworthy, as the public's concern moves on to other topics. The issue then gradually disappears from the public arena, even though the problem may remain largely unresolved. In the final 'post-problem' stage, there may be occasional but modest resurgences of interest.

The existence of an issue attention cycle serves to highlight the needs and pressures for interest groups and governments to expedite the policymaking process while the intensity of public demands for action remains high. At the same time, the fluctuations in public attention and the rapid shifts from one issue to another place considerable obstacles in the path of careful, well-designed policymaking.

The health care field, perhaps because of its potential to be a rich source of newsworthy stories, may be especially susceptible to the issue-attention-cycle phenomenon. A review of the daily press in Sydney and Melbourne over the past few decades indicates that the following health issues, with potential policy implications, have achieved a considerable degree of prominence over short periods: quality of care in nursing homes, hospital waiting lists, overspending of hospital budgets, unnecessary surgery and other overservicing, doctors' incomes and fees, nurses' working conditions and the cost of health insurance. Most of these issues appear to resurface regularly with much the same prominence as in their earlier appearances. This may represent further evidence of the unchanging nature of the underlying problems, the absence of effective policymaking and the strength of the forces opposing change.

The word 'crisis' has appeared periodically in newspaper headlines about hospitals for at least the last 30 years in Australia. This may have more to do with how some of the stakeholders hope to achieve their objectives or how journalists perceive what is newsworthy than about the state of the hospital system at any particular time.

Improved policymaking and policymaking structures

The processes of health policy formulation and evaluation in Australia are divided between the state and federal health authorities, the political parties and other organisations including tertiary educational institutions with an involvement in the health area. Governments, especially the Commonwealth government, have established a variety of advisory committees to assist them when specific health problems and issues have arisen. It was noted previously that typically the impact of these committee reports has been limited because of the failure of the process to address the deep-seated structural problems of the system. It was also observed that part of the purpose for governments of establishing ad hoc inquiries of this kind is the symbolic one of giving the appearance of taking action on an issue.

It is clear that the many problems summarised at the beginning of this chapter can only be resolved if there is a commitment by governments to address the underlying structural problems. The political costs of further inaction in the health field have possibly become sufficiently high, and the demands for change from significant community groups sufficiently strong, that this commitment is emerging for both state and Commonwealth governments.

As indicated previously, the most important policy-related development following the election of the Rudd Labor Government in 2007 was the creation of the NHHRC. The main issue that the commission was asked to address was that of Commonwealth–state responsibilities as they affected public hospitals. The federal Labor Party, in the lead-up to the 2007 election, foreshadowed the takeover of responsibility for the public hospital system if the states did not improve their performance in this area. However, its wide-ranging terms of reference allowed the NHHRC to make recommendations about most aspects of the financing and provision of health services in Australia, subject to a number of important constraints discussed on page 367. We defer until the end of this chapter a review and evaluation of its final report, and its relationship to the health policy changes that were enacted by the Labor government and which, in respect of hospitals, were outlined in **Chapter 5**.

Health services quality and outcomes

A major gap in the data required for better policymaking is the absence of reliable and meaningful information about the quality of health care and the outcomes of care and treatment. We indicated in **Chapter 5** that there are continuing concerns about the quality of hospital and aged care facility care. In both areas, the studies discussed in that chapter provided evidence to justify these concerns. There is an important need to assess outcomes, such as mortality and morbidity rates, in a way that can attribute these outcomes to the treatment and care received, especially on an institutional- and provider-specific basis.

In an ideal situation for patients, it would be possible for each person contemplating hospital admission to be able to access online the performance of the hospital and the medical staff involved in the recommended treatment. Such a system would make much more meaningful the notion of choice that is largely absent even for private patients at present. For many epidemiologists and economists, outcomes measure the true performance of the health care system and its components. However, the technical and conceptual difficulties in implementing policies of this nature, along with the inevitable opposition by providers, are formidable.

As we noted in **Chapter 5**, concerns about quality issues led most state governments to introduce organisations and techniques to address the problems. These were based in part on the clinical governance movement created in Britain following the Bristol hospital scandal (Scally & Donaldson 1998; Smith 1998). The original thrust of clinical governance was to put in place structures in hospitals that would identify problems of this kind before calamitous outcomes ensued. The need for clinical standards, for processes to assess clinical competence, for data to monitor doctors' personal performance and the ways that staff concerned about patient safety can make their concerns known have all been emphasised in state health department documents (Queensland Department of Health 2013; Victorian Department of Health 2013). In addition, emphasis was placed, as we noted in **Chapter 5**, on the need to create cultures of openness to replace those of secrecy and cover-up that have often characterised many hospitals and health departments.

Despite the large volume of literature that has been generated by the clinical governance movement, it is difficult to determine how much improvement in patient safety has been generated by the processes and procedures, along with the exhortations, that have been put in place. We note with regret that in Britain another appalling example of bad patient care was uncovered in the NHS hospital at Stafford, despite the lengthy experience with clinical governance in that country. The final report on the affair was published in 2013 (Francis 2013). The report highlights the usual deplorable deficiencies in hospital and clinical management, including a culture of cover-up at all levels. Among the numerous recommendations were included criminal sanctions to make revelations of poor quality of care mandatory in the NHS.

Policymaking and management within governments

It was noted previously that in the 1980s there was a tendency for senior appointments in some state health authorities to be made from outside the health services. Governments, it seems, had accepted the proposition that no special knowledge of the health services was required for senior management and policymaking purposes in this area. It is understandable, in light of the problems experienced by the health services over the past decade, that governments should have looked to new types of managers to solve these problems.

However, our analysis of the complexities and unique features of the health care system, coupled with our interpretation of the sources of the barriers to change, suggests that generalist managers who concentrate exclusively on the techniques of management are unlikely to be effective in resolving the underlying structural problems. Nor does a lack of knowledge of the nature and history of health organisations, services and issues seem to be a desirable qualification for management and policy development in this highly complex arena! (We have also noted with interest that managerialism has been included by Marmor (2007) in his provocative critique of 'fads, fallacies and foolishness' in health care management and policy.)

There is some evidence that, more recently, especially in making new senior management and policy appointments to health authorities, knowledge and experience in health have again become important criteria for filling these positions. Since, as we have argued, many of the problems of the health services stem from the existing distribution of power, the responsibility for change lies firmly with governments acting within the political arena. Similarly, better policymaking is likely to flow from the endeavours of those who have a detailed knowledge of the structural interests, the pressure groups and the power relations within the health services.

Fee-for-service and other forms of doctor remuneration

It was observed in **Chapter 4** that the FFS method of doctor remuneration has been an important source of conflict between governments and the medical profession in Australia. Federal Labor governments have indicated their desire to reduce FFS payments in public hospitals. The decline in the numbers of private patients in these hospitals, and hence of FFS, following the introduction of both Medibank and Medicare, was a major reason for the opposition of doctors to these schemes. This factor has also contributed to the increasing medical support for private hospitals that has characterised the 1990s and 2000s.

The method of doctor remuneration is critical in health care policy because of the potential impact on the number of medical services provided, on doctors' incomes and on the costs to governments and to patients. It is also important because of the style of practice it may generate and of the possible effects on the relationships between the principal actors in the health care system. Generally, doctors have preferred the FFS system because of their expectation that their incomes would be higher and because of their perception that their autonomy is maximised, compared with other payment methods. Governments have often preferred to pay doctors on a salaried basis for much the same reasons. They have wished to reduce the total cost of health care and to exercise more control over the profession.

FFS is likely, given the ability of doctors to influence the use of their services, to lead to the provision of more services than alternative forms of remuneration such as a salary or capitation payments. Whether a tendency to provide more or fewer services because of a change in the payment method is desirable depends, in part, on a judgment about the existing level of provision. In the Australian situation, where the prevalence of FFS may have exacerbated the overservicing problem, any extension of this method of doctor remuneration needs to be justified on other grounds or subjected to careful controls.

In primary medical care as provided by GPs, it is inevitable that disease prevention activities will be inhibited where the FFS mode prevails. In general, fee schedules do not account adequately for the longer consultations that may be required for health educational and counselling activities. Similarly, we noted in **Chapter 7** that there seems to be a strong association between FFS and the receipt of much higher levels of remuneration by surgeons and other specialists who undertake procedural interventions, compared to GPs and other doctors who are responsible for other forms of therapy.

It is to be noted, however, that these problems associated with FFS, which derive from the encouragement of certain types of medical activities and the discouragement of others, are partly the product of an inappropriate fee schedule and the patterns of fee-charging practices that have evolved over a considerable period and that the schedule reflects.

In Australia, where the Commonwealth government may (or may not) lack the constitutional power (or the political will) to fix the actual fees charged by doctors, it is clearly very difficult to alter drastically the fee schedule used to determine health insurance payments. Patients will face large out-of-pocket payments for those services for which the schedule fees are decreased but when doctors do not reduce the fees they charge. It is presumably for this reason that the Commonwealth has not given high priority to the restructuring of the entire fee schedule even though the anomalies and inequities it contains are well recognised.

There would seem to be two possible strategies that governments might pursue in Australia to overcome the problems associated with the heavy reliance on FFS as the principal method of doctor remuneration. The first is to promote the growth of other forms of doctor payments, notably salaried and capitation payments. Comprehensive community health centres are vehicles to achieve this change in emphasis. We noted in **Chapter 7** that a tentative move had been made in this direction in the recent reforms of general practice funding whereby grants for the provision of specified services are replacing FFS. However, the overall impact of these changes has to date been very modest. The Abbott Government was unlikely to pursue further changes in this area.

The second strategy is to accept the existing FFS emphasis, and possibly its extension in public hospitals, at least in the short term, but to require the implementation of several reforms and safeguards that would eliminate or reduce the detrimental effects of this method of doctor remuneration. Of the possible reforms in the system of payments, the most important are the restructuring of the fee schedule along the lines indicated previously, and gaining the adherence of doctors to the schedule. Other changes include the introduction and strengthening of utilisation review programs in hospitals, designed to reduce the incidence of overservicing and inappropriate admissions.

Both strategies are likely to be resisted by sections of the medical profession. As indicated previously, whether either strategy will be adopted in the near future depends on the strength of the community's demand for change and the political costs to governments, particularly the Commonwealth government, of further inaction. The promotion of community participation and the community interest may also be a necessary condition for achieving a much-needed redistribution of power in the health care system. In the next section, we consider how the power of the community interest might be increased.

Strengthening community and consumer participation

In previous chapters, we indicated that enhancing community and consumer participation in decision-making about health, health care and health policy has become widely recognised as an important way to deal with health policy challenges. Broad structural change requires consumer advocacy, community education and political debate about health issues within the broader community. Clinicians, health service managers and policymakers cannot change the health policy agenda by themselves; they need a strong base of community support from which to work.

Community participation has been encouraged by the Commonwealth government and some states in Australia. Its formal origins can be traced to 1973 and commencement of the Community Health Program, which supported community health centres, women's health centres and community-controlled Aboriginal medical services with community-elected boards of management. More recent participatory and advocacy mechanisms included district health councils in Victoria, health and welfare councils in South Australia, the Consumer Advisory Network of Western Australia, the district health forums of Tasmania, the Health Issues Centre in Melbourne, the Public Interest Advocacy Centre in Sydney and the national Consumers' Health Forum (CHF), located in Canberra.

The CHF, established in 1987, is the major national organisation representing the views of community and consumer groups on issues relating to health. The forum was established in line with recommendations from the review of community participation in the Commonwealth Department of Health (1985a). The initiative started with a petition by community and consumer groups to the minister for health requesting greater consumer representation in health in order to balance the views of professionals, governments and industry in the political arena. Milio (1988) observed that there is perhaps no other country in the world where an organisation such as the CHF, representing consumer interests, has such direct access to national policymakers.

The principle behind the CHF is that the best way to ensure better representation of the repressed community interest is through resourcing and networking consumer and community organisations that have an interest in health issues. This acknowledges that interest groups with concentrated interests, such as the Asia Pacific Endometriosis Alliance or the British Maternity Alliance (see Matrice & Brown 1990), are well placed to articulate and strengthen the interests of their members. It enables 'substantive representation', as representatives of these concentrated interest groups can articulate and further the interests of their constituencies (Marmor & Christianson 1982). It also acknowledges that the community interest is repressed because the existing structure guarantees that its interests will not be furthered unless an extraordinary amount of political and organisational energy is expended to counteract its structural disadvantage (Short 1998).

There are significant practical advantages associated with ensuring active community participation in decision-making about health and health policy. Strengthening the community interest improves community awareness and understanding about health and the determinants of ill health; it also strengthens the voice of disadvantaged groups within the health care system and helps to ensure that services are made accessible and appropriate to community needs. It can produce a more balanced political market within the policymaking arena in relation to health care professionals and other powerful interests within the health arena. The importance of the anti-smoking movement in enabling the passing of reformist legislation regulating tobacco advertising and promotion is a case in point. Similarly, a well-organised women's health movement created a political climate that enabled initiatives such as women's health centres to gain broad public, and hence government, support.

There is, however, a traditional resistance on the part of clinicians, managers and policymakers towards direct public accountability. Many are sensitive to any public criticism and are not predisposed to advocacy structures. Health ministers and senior public servants can be selective in responding to community pressure, since a strong and powerful consumer voice can prove a powerful ally in the political marketplace. It should be remembered, though, that effective community participation involves representing the repressed community interest. It does not mean co-opting community groups in order to further the interests of either clinicians or managers.

The Australian experience to date has shown that problems can arise with consumer and community involvement. One such case occurred in the Illawarra region in the years 1986 to 1987, when administrators in the Illawarra Area

Health Service financed an appeal to raise $1.5 million in public donations to buy a radiotherapy machine for the Wollongong Hospital. The need for such a device, which had relatively high running costs, for a relatively small hospital was questionable.

Examining the political process behind the Illawarra Cancer Appeal-a-thon revealed that the Illawarra Area Health Service, with help from the local media, supported community involvement in this instance to add weight to its request for funding from the New South Wales Department of Health for a new building at the Wollongong Hospital (Short 1989). This case illustrates the fact that community perceptions and consumer demands are easily manipulated by more powerful interests in the health system.

Numerous community and consumer organisations have participated in consultation processes that have left them disappointed, frustrated, cynical and wary of future involvement. Participation by consumer and community groups in government consultation processes has meant significant contributions of their time, expertise, resources and energy, often with minimal outcomes (Cameron 1987). The term 'community involvement' is usually applied to instances when community members participate in the planning, administration or evaluation of health programs and services without necessarily furthering their own interests.

Developing effective participatory mechanisms and structures requires careful planning, with attention given to the nature of representation and accountability and the briefing, training and access to information of representatives (Health Targets and Implementation [Health for All] Committee 1988). It is also important to note that some attempts at community participation have failed miserably, either because of political misuse of the process or inattention to the above matters.

Consumer and community participation in the Australian health care system is analysed usefully around the twin concepts of 'representation' and 'accountability'. A key factor in ensuring successful consumer and community participation strategies is the selection of representatives. It is critical that representatives be chosen by consumer and community groups, and that they be accountable to their own constituents. In the case of the area health board initiative in New South Wales, this was not the case. Although the boards might be seen to be representative of community groups, such as women or immigrants, they were not selected by these groups and they are not accountable to them. Similar considerations may apply to the local hospital networks created by the National Health Reform Agreement of 2011.

Accountability means 'answering to' or, more precisely, 'having to answer to', and this usually refers to those agents who control resources, sanctions or votes (Marmor & Morone 1980). Accountability tends to flow upwards in the bureaucratic health system generally; moreover, many so-called consumer representatives are not accountable to the public they represent. A community representative appointed by a health minister, an ethics committee or a hospital board can be seen merely as a political appointment or 'token' representative if they are not accountable to the constituency they are supposed to represent.

Efforts to improve consumer representation in the health policy development process have often failed to include this necessary mechanism of consumer accountability. Significant problems result from the fact that nothing binds the majority of consumer representatives to the preferences of the community they represent. The CHF provides perhaps the greatest potential for furthering the interests of the community. Although bodies such as the CHF do not claim that those selected by the community are totally representative of any or all groups in the community, they are nevertheless more representative than any contemporary alternatives.

The NSW Department of Health introduced formal mechanisms to enhance consumer or community representation in the form of health councils in the late 1990s, and in 1984 New South Wales was the first state to establish an independent health care complaints unit (Walton 1993, 1998). Since then, Victoria and Queensland have developed complaints commissions that operate on a conciliation model of health services dispute resolution. The Victorian and Queensland commissions focus primarily on conciliation, leaving the investigations and legal prosecutions of health practitioners to the individual registration boards.

Eventually all states and territories were required, as a result of the 1993–1998 Medicare Agreements, to establish a complaints body to resolve health care complaints. These complaints bodies have also been given the role of recommending improvements in the delivery of hospital services for which the Commonwealth provides financial assistance. It is questionable, in the light of continuing hospital scandals, how effective these units have been in meeting their objectives.

As a result of many criticisms of the New South Wales complaints unit, including long delays in investigating complaints, the New South Wales Health Care Complaints Commission replaced it in 1993. The commission lies outside the jurisdiction of the NSW Department of Health. It played a valuable role in investigating the scandals regarding patient care and cover-ups at the Camden and Campbelltown hospitals in that state.

Ideally, consumer and consumer organisations can work together to further their common interests on issues such as equity of access to health care. Collaboration between community, consumer and clinician groups also offers great potential as a constituency for reform within the health care system. The Friends of Medicare Campaign launched in 1999, for example, brought together an alliance of partners to protect Medicare: the Public Health Association of Australia, the Health Issues Centre, the Australian Nurses' Federation, the Doctors' Reform Society, the Women's Health Network and the Australian Council of Social Service. Another notable instance of collaboration between consumers, community groups and clinicians is the alliance established between the Health Issues Centre, CHOICE and the Royal Australasian College of Physicians around a shared interest in health policy and health systems financing reform.

Commonwealth and state government roles in health care

We indicated previously that before its election in 2007, the Labor Party had promised to end the 'blame game' between the Commonwealth and state governments regarding health services, and to take over all responsibility for public hospitals if the states did not improve their performance. We explore in this section the historical background to the issue before we present our discussion of the final report of the National Health and Hospitals Reform Commission, established in 2008 to make recommendations about these relationships and other policy matters.

The appropriate roles of the Commonwealth government and of the states in health care matters have frequently emerged in previous chapters as an unresolved issue. As indicated previously, considerable attention was given to this issue by the National Health Strategy, which produced comprehensive evidence about the mixed and inconsistent separation of responsibilities for health care delivery and finance between the two main levels of government (National Health Strategy 1991b). Table 10.1, which is reproduced from the National Health Strategy document *The Australian Health Jigsaw: Integration of Health Care Delivery*, summarises the relationships in several key areas as they existed at that time, and illustrates the magnitude of the problem. There had been little change in these responsibilities in the meantime (National Health and Hospitals Reform Commission 2008a). It is still, at the time of writing (October 2013), too early to judge whether the 2011 reforms will have much impact on the relationships between the states and the Commonwealth on health matters. This uncertainty is exacerbated by what changes to the National Health Reform Agreement legislation and its implementation may be undertaken by the Abbott Government.

We noted in **Chapter 4** that the Commonwealth, as a result of its central position in the implementation of health insurance policies and as part of its social security role, has exercised considerable influence on the health care activities of the states. In particular, a major aspect of public hospital policy, the level of fees charged and the basis on which free hospitalisation is provided, has been determined by successive Coalition and Labor federal governments.

The intrusion of the Commonwealth into what are perceived to be the responsibilities of the states has attracted much criticism, largely along the lines also noted in **Chapter 4**—that the states are better placed to be aware of the needs of the communities they serve. However, this approach, as we have indicated previously, ignores the fact that policymaking and planning are not simply technical exercises of assessing health needs and deploying resources to meet those needs.

We have also argued that the Commonwealth, because of its heavy financial involvement and powers, is more likely than the states to be willing and able to marshal the resources required to implement substantial shifts in the direction of health policy. In view of our perception of the pressing need for many reforms in the organisation, financing and delivery of health services, a strong Commonwealth involvement in all aspects of health care policy is considered to be vital. Thus, if

Table 10.1   Summary of Commonwealth and state roles and responsibilities for health care

Service area	Commonwealth only	States only	Mixed Commonwealth and states
Acute hospital inpatients	• Provision of medical benefits to private patients in public and private hospitals • Partial funding of pharmaceutical costs in private hospitals • Regulation of health funds • Operation of veterans' hospitals and private hospitals	• Determining mix and location of services • Policy on medical remuneration in public hospitals • Regulation of private hospital ownership and location	• Funding public hospitals (40% Commonwealth, 48% state, 12% private) • Policy objectives and service entitlements set by Australian Health Care Agreements • Various private patient fees set following Commonwealth–state consultation • State responsible for administration
Medical services	• Funding of part or all fees charged to individuals • Funding of Aboriginal medical services • Funding of university medical schools	• Policy on medical remuneration in public hospitals for public patients • Funding of medical services provided in community-based services • Registration of medical practitioners	• Joint funding of non-inpatient medical services in public hospitals as part of conditions of Australian Health Care Agreements. State determines service level and administers service.
Pharmaceuticals	• Policy, funding and administration of pharmaceuticals provided in community pharmacies	• Policy and administration of pharmaceuticals provided in public hospitals • Regulation of ownership, standards, etc., of community pharmacists and pharmacies	• Joint funding of public hospital pharmacies as part of conditions of Health Care Agreements. State determines service level and administers service.
Community health, allied health and home care	• Direct funding of individuals of domiciliary nursing care benefit • Regulation of health funds that reimburse for allied health • Purchasing of services for veterans • Funding of doctors in community health centres via the Medicare Benefits Schedule	• Funding, policy and administration of community health services, child and family health services, community palliative care, alcohol and drug services, and other community-based services	• Joint funding, policy and administration of HACC • Joint funding of outpatient allied health services via Medicare Hospital Grant • Commonwealth funding of post-acute and palliative care services specifically in Health Care Agreements. States propose specific services for funding; Commonwealth approval is needed.
High-dependency living support	• Funding and administration of state hostels • Funding, policy, standards, monitoring of private and voluntary sector nursing homes and of private sector hostels • Direct funding of intense community support programs via HACC (Commonwealth-only funds) • Funding of psychiatric and community services for veterans	• Regulation, standard setting and monitoring of nursing homes, hostels and other supported accommodation undertaken by some state governments • Funding, policy and administration of some palliative care services • Funding, policy and administration of psychiatric hospitals	• Joint funding of state-operated nursing homes, with Commonwealth direct benefit funding to nursing homes States responsible for administration • Joint funding of geriatric hospitals and nursing-home-type patients in public hospitals, and palliative care via Health Care Agreements • Joint funding and administration of geriatric assessment teams and services

Service area	Commonwealth only	States only	Mixed Commonwealth and states
Mental health	• Funding of part or all of fees charged by private psychiatrists • Funding of psychiatric drugs through PBS • Funding, policy and administration of Commonwealth Rehabilitation Services • Provision and purchase of services for veterans	• Policy, funding and administration of dedicated psychiatric facilities • Registration of mental health professionals • Regulation and standards monitoring of private hospitals, residential facilities and supported accommodation	• Joint funding of acute psychiatric services provided in general hospitals as part of Health Care Agreements • Joint funding, policy and administration of HACC
Prevention, public health	• Operation of some dedicated national campaigns • Food standards regulation • Operation of Australian radiation laboratories	• Funding, regulation, policy and administration of public health programs (e.g. sanitation, immunisation)	• Joint funding, policy and administration of women's health screening, national better health, youth health services, AIDS, drug education programs
Other provisions, services and programs	• Recognition of medical specialties for benefits purposes • Provision of aids and appliances via stoma and limbs scheme • Research funding, policy and administration via National Health and Medical Research Council • Administration of acoustic laboratory • Some dental services funded through the Medicare Benefits Schedule • Regulation of health funds' dental provisions • Dental services to veterans • Funding of Royal Flying Doctor Service	• Registration and regulation of health professionals • Funding, policy and administration of aids and appliances • Some direct funding of medical research • Specialised child and family health services provide developmental services • Various dental schemes funded and administered: school dental, dental hospital, pensioner denture, low-income dental, etc.	• Joint funding of transfer of nurse education to colleges—states administer program • Blood transfusion service jointly funded by Commonwealth and state • Funding, policy and administration of ambulance services, other patient transport schemes

Notes

Some details in table 10.1 have been updated to reflect the very limited changes that have taken place between 1991 and 2010. The terminology of 'nursing homes and hostels', which applied at the time of the original report, has not been changed to 'aged care facilities'.

Source: National Health Strategy (1991b)

the role of the Commonwealth was simply to provide financial assistance to the states, a situation that the states have favoured and Commonwealth governments at times have also found attractive, the prospects for changes in the current status quo would be very modest.

In this case, it is clear that achieving the objectives of the original program, especially the development of prevention and health promotion and of comprehensive multidisciplinary health centres, will not take place without further Commonwealth funding and, most importantly, detailed guidelines from the Commonwealth about how the program should be developed. This issue has also surfaced again following the creation of the NHHRC and its report, discussed later in this chapter, and recent policy developments in this area (see below).

The problems with the Commonwealth's aged care facilities subsidy program were also discussed previously. In this case, the Commonwealth, with total financial and administrative responsibility for the program, has often lacked the ability to influence the range and quality of the services provided to patients, even though it provides most of the funding for these institutions. In addition, we noted that it was difficult to achieve the Commonwealth's objective of shifting the emphasis from nursing home care to community health services when the primary financial and administrative responsibility for these services lies with the states. The future and impact of the reforms of the aged care sector we discussed in **Chapter 5** (enacted into law in the last days of the Labor government in 2013) that were designed to address these problems remain unclear at present.

It is difficult to establish ideal models of the appropriate relationships between the Commonwealth and the states in health matters that cover all areas of health service provision. The proposals about Commonwealth–state relationships recommended by the NHHRC are discussed on page 368, along with the policy changes they engendered. At this stage we note that the thrust of the Rudd Government's policy to eliminate the blame game between the two levels of government in the Australian federal system was possibly utopian.

When funding flows to the health services from both sets of government, it will always serve the short-term political interests of each level of government to blame the other level for the failings of the system. The original proposal for the Commonwealth to take over all funding of primary health care (including hospital non-inpatient services) would have eliminated one important dysfunctional aspect of the current arrangements. However, this change was not pursued in the 2011 agreement between the Commonwealth and the states.

Values and equity

We strongly believe that it is the responsibility of the more affluent and fortunate members of communities to support the more vulnerable members of society. In respect of health services, this value inevitably translates into the need for some redistribution of income from the more affluent and often healthier people to those who are sicker and poorer. There is much evidence, moreover, to support the proposition that countries that adhere more closely to these values achieve better outcomes for all their communities than those that adhere to other value systems (Evans & Stoddart 1990; Evans, Barer & Marmor 1994).

We recognise that, in Australia, the political conflicts about health insurance policies that we described at length in **Chapter 4** were, in part, a reflection of the conservative parties' espousal of a value system that emphasises personal responsibility in health affairs, along with that of freedom of choice (Duckett 2008b). As Gray (2004) has documented in detail, this value position was consistently advocated by John Howard, the former prime minister, throughout his lengthy political career. It serves to explain, moreover, the preoccupation with supporting private health insurance that characterised his term of office.

We argued in **Chapter 3**, however, that an analysis in terms of values is incomplete if we do not recognise the structural interests that serve to gain from promoting a given value position. Previously, we identified elements of the medical profession, private health funds, private hospitals, pharmaceutical companies and health appliance suppliers as the major components of this structural interest group.

How does Australia perform, given the value position we have advocated and its implications for the goal of promoting a more equitable system of health policies? We believe that there is a good deal of scope for improvement in the current arrangements for the funding and provision of health services, and that insufficient attention has been devoted in Australia to what we regard as a major problem. We present the following evidence to support this claim.

Vertical equity is the principle that those of higher incomes should contribute more to the financing of the health care system than those who are less affluent. Horizontal equity occurs when individuals of similar incomes make similar contributions to the funding of the system. When a progressive taxation system is the main method of funding the provision of health care, the system is likely to be more equitable than when other financial arrangements are present. Based on this principle, it would be expected that countries that rely mainly on funding from taxation—that is, public funding—would achieve a greater degree of equity in the ways their health services are funded than those that rely on other sources of finance.

Based on these principles, and the value systems that underlie them, the Belgium health economist van Doorslaer and his English colleague Wagstaff have undertaken a series of international comparative studies, funded by the European Union, in the ECuity Project (Wagstaff & van Doorslaer 1997; van Doorslaer et al. 1999). They were able to confirm empirically the above hypothesis. To determine the degree of equity achieved by a number of European countries and the United States, they used an index of progressivity devised by Kakwani (1977) to measure the impact of taxation scales in redistributing income.

Unsurprisingly, the National Health Service in the United Kingdom achieved a high positive index value and the system in the United States a negative value for the Kakwani index. In general, those other countries of Europe—notably Norway, Ireland and Italy—that rely predominantly on taxation to fund their health care systems did well on the measure. Switzerland and the Netherlands, which use private health insurance as a major source of funding, achieved low levels of equity. In general, there was a close relationship between the proportion of funding from public sources in each country and the index of equity.

Table 10.2 shows the proportion of public funding for a number of the more advanced OECD countries. It is noted that 14 of the 20 countries listed have a higher proportion of public funding than Australia. We believe that these data, along with the results of the ECuity Project, raise serious doubts about the equity of the

Table 10.2 Public expenditure on health, percentage of total expenditure on health, selected OECD countries for which data are available, 2011

Country	Percentage
United States	47.8
Switzerland	64.9
Portugal	65.0
Greece	65.1
Ireland	67.0
Australia[a]	67.8
Canada	70.4
Spain	73.0
Finland	75.4
Austria	76.2
Germany	76.5
France	76.8
Italy	77.8
Iceland	80.4
Sweden	81.6
Japan[b]	82.1
New Zealand	82.7
United Kingdom	82.8
Luxembourg[c]	84.0
Norway	84.9

Notes
(a) 2010 value
(b) 2010 value
(b) 2009 value

Source: based on OECD (2013b) *OECD Health Statistics 2013—Frequently Requested Data*, <www.oecd.org/els/health-systems/oecdhealthdata2013-frequentlyrequesteddata.html>, accessed on 12 December 2013

current funding methods in Australia. The reliance on private health insurance and the large out-of-pocket payments for many medical and dental services and for pharmaceuticals are specific manifestations of how we deviate from a fair distribution of the cost of supporting our health care system. The poorer and sicker members of our community are clearly disadvantaged by these arrangements.

The inequitable features of the Australian health care system have been analysed comprehensively and compellingly in a book chapter by Duckett (2008b), in which he points to the concentration of private health insurance among the more affluent members of the population and notes that private health insurance in Australia 'is a product that obliterates one's reliance on public sector services and circumvents public sector constraints' (Duckett 2008b, p. 185). He indicates that many medical specialists provide services in both the private and public sectors and are therefore able to influence waiting times for many procedures in the public sector. These long waiting times produce a strong incentive for many people to acquire health insurance to subsidise their treatment in the private sector, which happens to be much more remunerative for the specialists!

The term 'equity' is also often applied to the relative ability to access health services by specific population groups. For example, if health services are lacking in rural and remote geographical areas then it can be stated that the distribution of those services is inequitable. Similarly, if persons of low incomes experience problems in accessing certain services (such as dental services) that are readily available to the more affluent members of the community, it is reasonable to point to a lack of equity in the system of provision.

Clearly, equity in the funding sense discussed above and equity in provision are closely linked. High co-payments for medications, which contribute to overall funding inequity, may reduce access to drugs vital to those with chronic illnesses. As we noted previously, a visit to a private psychiatrist for a patient with a chronic mental health problem may incur a fee of $320 or more, with a Medicare rebate of about $220. Thus, we regard an equitable system of financial arrangements as being a necessary but not a sufficient condition for achieving equity in access to services of the appropriate kind. We examine below how this vital issue of ensuring an equitable system of health funding and provision is dealt with in the report of the National Health and Hospitals Reform Commission.

Evaluation of the final report of the NHHRC

We have stressed in earlier chapters our cynicism about the extensive resort to the commissioning and production of reports by governments. This position was partly based on our review of the history of reports in areas such as hospitals and aged care, and our perception that little lasting change was achieved as a consequence of these numerous and often costly activities. We are also very mindful of the thesis put forward by Alford (1975) that the reports themselves may be part of the problem, since they tend to confirm and strengthen the existing power relations in our society. We have already posed the question about the NHHRC of whether it will form part of the solution to the numerous problems outlined in this chapter or whether it will enhance the underlying problems.

At present, we are cautiously optimistic about the impact that the work of the NHHRC may have in generating profound reforms in the Australian health care system. We have been impressed by the overall quality of the research, empirical evidence and conceptual analysis on which the 2009 report, *A Healthier Future for All Australians: Final Report of the National Health and Hospitals Reform Commission*, and its recommendations are based. In this regard, it was fortunate that two of Australia's leading health policy analysts, Dr Stephen Duckett and Dr Sharon Willcox, were appointed to the commission. Both people have published extensively in highly regarded local and international journals on many aspects of health policy. It is evident, moreover, from the vast amount of material presented, that the NHHRC was very well resourced, with access to highly competent support staff.

The coverage of a wide range of health care issues is particularly impressive. Data and analysis are presented on the lack of efficiency in hospital performance; avoidable deaths in hospitals; the equity and access problems of severely disadvantaged groups, notably Indigenous people; those suffering from mental illness and other chronic conditions; and the residents of isolated and other rural communities. Important topics such as the health workforce and how its performance might be improved, a greater emphasis on disease prevention and health promotion, the need for improved primary health care services, and improved coordination of health care services delivered by different providers, are examined and analysed in a compelling way. The report makes a strong case for further policy initiatives by governments and others. The need for the financial support to foster access to basic dental services is given considerable emphasis.

It is important to be aware that the report contains 123 individual recommendations, accompanied by suggestions about how many of them might be implemented. Our summary of what we regard as the most important recommendations is, of course, highly subjective and reflects our values, priorities and political realities (see Klein & Marmor 2008). We follow this summary with a review of these recommendations in light of the problems that we and others have outlined previously. This review focuses on certain notable omissions from the report—especially on funding, equity and medical practice issues—and we analyse the possible reasons for the omissions.

Summary of the significant recommendations

The following recommendations are the ones we have selected as the most important from the final report:

- the Commonwealth government to take full responsibility for the funding and planning of all aspects of primary health care, including all community health services and outpatient services in public hospitals

- the Commonwealth government to assume full responsibility for providing universal access to basic dental care
- the Commonwealth government to assume sole responsibility for all public funding of aged care services
- the Commonwealth government to be responsible for allocating activity-based payments to the state and territory governments for all the services they provide using casemix classifications. The casemix funding systems would be developed and applied on a national basis.
- the Commonwealth government to pay 100 per cent of the efficient cost of public hospital outpatient services using an agreed casemix classification
- the Commonwealth government to meet 40 per cent of the efficient cost of every public patient admission to a hospital, sub-acute or mental health care facility, and every attendance at a public hospital emergency department. An extension to 100 per cent funding of these services over time is also recommended.
- the expansion of Medicare ('Medicare Select') to provide greater consumer choice, greater provider competition and better use of public and private resources. It is recommended that hospital and health plans be established to deliver on Medicare entitlements.
- an agreement between governments on a new Healthy Australia Accord, which would clearly articulate the agreed and complementary roles and responsibilities of all levels of government in improving health services and outcomes for the Australian population.

Although they do not involve a comprehensive takeover of all health financing from the states in the short term, the funding recommendations, if implemented, would create an environment in which many of the dysfunctional elements in the current arrangements, especially regarding primary care, would be eliminated or reduced.

Other important recommendations include the development and strengthening of institutions, notably the Australian Commission on Safety and Quality in Health Care, to set standards and monitor the quality of all health services. The need to improve the reporting of information bearing on quality and safety is also emphasised, along with the development of electronic patient records. The setting up of a national authority for health promotion and disease prevention initiatives is also recommended.

In respect of equity of access matters, a good deal of attention, very appropriately, is paid to the problems of the most disadvantaged groups: Indigenous people, people with mental health issues and residents of remote rural areas. We welcome also the recommendation, as part of the reform of primary care, proposing the reactivation of the comprehensive multidisciplinary community health centre concept.

Problems that the report does not address

When we review our statement of high-priority problems, as set out in this chapter, it is evident that, in many instances, the report either avoids the underlying issue, pays only limited attention to it or rejects the notion that the problem exists.

No mention is made of the problem of substantial and unexplained variation in the provision of specific services to the residents of similar geographic areas. We have examined this issue in detail in **Chapter 7**, and it forms a large part of Richardson's exploration of neglected but significant policy phenomena (Richardson 2005). In Robert Evans' eloquent phrase, it represents 'the dog in the night time' (Evans 1990) or alternatively 'the elephant in the room'.

No mention is made of the possible overprovision of surgical and diagnostic services. There is an implicit assumption in most of the report that all medical interventions are desirable (relatively cost-effective?), and that equity of access to services means that all residents are entitled to receive these interventions based on 'need'. The only qualification made to this perception was that a relatively minor space in the report is allocated to recommendations for the further development of clinical guidelines and educational or other initiatives to promote their use. These recommendations include the creation of a National Institute of Clinical Studies. There were a few very cautious comments about the Medicare Benefits Schedule in respect of the criteria for adding new items and of giving access to more provider groups, but there were no recommendations for its total restructuring, which is sorely needed.

In our view, however, the major weakness of the report is that there was no attempt to address the glaring inequities generated by Australia's current funding arrangements, with their heavy emphasis on private health insurance; large co-payments for many medical, pharmaceutical and aged care services; and the incentives that the insurance system creates for recourse to private hospital and private medical care, which is largely unregulated and unsupervised. It was emphasised earlier that, compared with the pervasive values of solidarity and communitarianism that underpin health care funding models in Europe, the heavy reliance on private funding in our country achieves neither vertical nor horizontal equity.

From our value perspective, the most questionable statement in the whole report is the following: 'We want to see the overall balance of funding through taxation, private health insurance and out-of-pocket contributions maintained over the next decade' (National Health and Hospitals Reform Commission 2009b, p. 121). The only justification for this statement is that the current balance of public and private funding affords 'greater personal healthcare choices'. We might well add 'for the more affluent members of our community'. Clearly, this recommendation might be restated as a proposal that the numerous sources of financial inequity we and others have highlighted should not be addressed for a decade except as they affect the access to services of specific disadvantaged groups.

The reasons for these omissions are clear. It was not seen as a role of the commission to make recommendations touching on what might be described as politically sensitive issues about which the previous federal government may or may not have chosen to intervene. The issue of what to do about the large, ill-conceived and inequitable subsidy of private health insurance, inherited from the Howard Government, immediately comes to mind.

All aspects of medical practice, including the structure of the Medicare fees schedule, control of the fees charged by doctors in private practice, and the implementation of strict criteria for the admission and treatment of public hospital patients, fall in the same category of political sensitivity.

We have emphasised previously that no government wishes to confront the medical profession unless it becomes essential to achieve other politically popular objectives. The creation of Medibank in the mid-1970s is the most important example in Australia's history.

However, it may be impossible for any government to avoid a major conflict with organised medicine if unsustainable cost escalation and community interest pressures produce a situation whereby more far-reaching reforms than those of the NHHRC become politically acceptable. The failure of the limited reforms proposed by the NHHRC, and subsequently adopted by the Commonwealth and state governments, to be implemented successfully—leading, for example, to a recurrence of the gross failures to protect the safety of hospital patients that have been recognised recently—would undoubtedly contribute substantially to these pressures. In our final chapter, we return to this and related issues.

Summary of the policy responses to the report

We have discussed the policy initiatives of the Commonwealth Labor government resulting from the NHHRC report, along with other inputs, in our earlier chapters, notably in **Chapter 5** in respect of hospital organisational and funding reforms. Here, for convenience, we summarise the main changes. These arrangements formed the basis of the National Health Reform Agreement of 2011, which was entered into via the Council of Australian Governments, and became law as a result of legislation passed by the Commonwealth and state and territory legislatures:

- Commonwealth funding for public hospitals is to be allocated using so-called 'efficient prices' for each AR-DRG, when the size and scope of the hospital is appropriate to this procedure, defined as activity-based funding. Smaller hospitals will continue to be allocated block grants.
- The Independent Hospital Pricing Authority has been established to determine the efficient prices, based on hospital costing studies.
- The Commonwealth and the states have agreed to establish local hospital networks in defined geographical areas to manage the hospitals and other health services, including the activity-based funding and block grants.

- Two further organisations have been created: the National Health Performance Authority and the Commission on Safety and Quality in Health Care.
- The Commonwealth has agreed to provide substantial extra funding to the states for public hospitals, including at least $16.4 billion in growth funding from 2014–15 to 2019–20.
- The Commonwealth is to establish Medicare Locals to coordinate activity between general practitioners and primary health services.
- The agreement recognises that the states are the system managers of public hospitals while the Commonwealth has full responsibility for aged care. The Commonwealth has 'lead responsibility' for GP and primary care (Department of Health and Ageing 2011).

The Abbott Government does not seem likely to wish to alter the agreement in any substantial way, and major changes would undoubtedly be opposed by the states, including the four largest states with Coalition governments. The Abbott Government has signalled that it may delay the full implementation of the Commonwealth's financial commitment. In addition, it wishes to review the functions of Medicare Locals. It is also believed in informed circles that the government will abolish the National Health Performance Authority as part of its general review of government agencies of this kind.

POLICY ANALYSIS

In the light of the very recent establishment of the National Health Reform Agreement, the limited time the new agencies have been in existence and the uncertainties generated by the change of federal government in 2013, any detailed analysis of the outcomes of the policy changes would be premature. However, several aspects of the agreement call for comment.

The comprehensive implementation of activity-based funding is long overdue. While the agreement only applies to Commonwealth funding, it is highly likely that the states will use the same method of allocating funds to local health networks for their share of funding.

The reference to *efficient* prices as the basis of activity-based funding is unclear. Interpreted literally it would imply that the costs of the most efficient hospitals would form the basis of cost-derived prices. However, in the reports of the Independent Hospital Pricing Authority there is no indication that the previous procedure of averaging all costs per AR-DRG of the reporting public hospitals has been changed.

On the matter of the Independent Hospital Pricing Authority being allocated responsibility for collecting costing data from hospitals, we would prefer that a vitally important inherently statistical collection of this kind should be the responsibility of the Australian Bureau of Statistics (ABS). This agency has the main expertise in Australia in undertaking complex collections of data, using advanced survey methods, notably carefully designed probability samples using stratification by size and other characteristics of the population elements. It is also obvious that a collection of this kind should be compulsory for all selected hospitals based on the powers in this regard of the ABS, rather than continuing to be a voluntary survey.

We do not wish to be unduly critical of the emphasis placed in the agreement on the decentralisation of management and funding authority to local hospital networks. However, the main justification provided for the initiative is that these networks will be better placed to assess and respond to the interests of local communities than a central authority based in the capital city. However, two issues are raised by this argument. First, previous experience with largely autonomous hospital boards suggests that the interests of board members in their capacity as local business owners and professionals predominate. Such groups may wish to make their local hospitals larger, more lavish in terms of services and more expensive. In these circumstances, the repressed consumer, patient and community interest may not be strengthened, especially since the composition of the local hospital network councils rests with state governments of varying political persuasions.

Second, as Marmor (2007) points out, there is a complete lack of evidence that the decentralised model of hospital decision-making works better than the alternatives. The basis of the model may constitute a further example of the fads and fallacies to which health care management is especially prone. Understanding the needs of local communities and their preferences requires specialised knowledge of epidemiological, demographic and sample survey techniques that are hardly available, even in the capital cities, at the local level. These are roles that the properly resourced central authority should exercise.

The roles of Medicare Locals in promoting improved relationships between general practice and the other, predominantly state-controlled, aspects of primary and community care provision are not clearly defined. As we have indicated in **Chapter 7**, they have evolved out of the Divisions of General Practice, but we are not aware of documentation related to what these entities have actually achieved in practice. The overarching problem with the Medicare Locals is that GPs in a predominantly fee-for-service system are under intense pressure to service a flow of patients as quickly as possible. They are hardly in a position to allocate much time and energy to liaise and collaborate with the state-run primary care services, which have very different personnel, funding arrangements and objectives.

The agreement is to be commended for spelling out in some detail the responsibilities of each level of government. However, the points we have made above suggest that there is much room for improvement in the methods used, and in the organisations established or foreshadowed, with their far-reaching roles and responsibilities.

SUMMARY AND CONCLUSION

In this chapter, we have examined a range of problems and issues relevant to the question of how the Australian health care system might be reformed. We have reiterated our findings in earlier chapters that many major problems exist in our system of health care funding and provision, and that these include a number that have been recognised for many years in numerous government reports, health service research studies and other writings of policy analysts and academics.

We have emphasised the problems associated with the drastic risks and poor quality of care experienced by many hospital patients, the remarkable variations in the medical services provided to residents of different local areas, and the questionable rates of provision of certain high-volume elective surgical procedures. We have pointed also to the uneasy relationships between the Commonwealth and state governments in respect of heath care funding and provision, and the negative implications for the community of the consequent blame game.

We have also highlighted the evidence that despite the existence of universal health insurance, the mixed system of public and private funding, along with aspects of private medical practice, produce an inequitable system in which the income levels of community groups have a considerable impact on their access to hospital and medical care.

In keeping with the insights afforded by the work of political scientists and sociologists, which we reviewed in **Chapter 3**, we have analysed the reasons why the responses to these problems by governments have been limited or non-existent. We have identified the power of the structural interests to resist change, in part by convincing governments, the media and communities that it would be politically unpopular and disruptive to introduce reforms.

In reviewing how these obstacles to desirable reforms might be overcome, we have emphasised the need to strengthen the community interest as a countervailing power to those of provider interests. It is an open question as to how influential this currently repressed interest may become in the future.

We reviewed the main recommendations of the final report of the National Health and Hospitals Reform Commission. We observed that the report has many positive features, including its recommendations for changing the responsibilities and accountabilities of governments, with the central proposal being the takeover of all funding responsibility for primary care by the Commonwealth.

It was noted, however, that politically sensitive issues, notably those that may affect the Commonwealth government's relationship with the medical profession and other powerful interest groups, along with the funding and provision inequities generated by the subsidy of private health insurance and the resort to the private sector, have been largely ignored.

The responses to the report and other inputs led to the National Health Reform Agreement, the mains details of which as they affect hospitals were discussed in **Chapter 5**. We noted with the regret that the takeover of all primary care funding was not incorporated in the agreement as a result of opposition from the states. We have also queried some of the institutions to be established under the agreement and their roles and responsibilities. Nevertheless, the comprehensive use of activity-based funding and the detailed spelling out of the respective responsibilities of each level of government are to be commended.

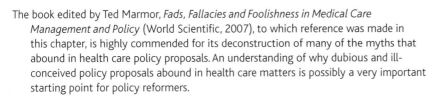

FURTHER READING

The book edited by Ted Marmor, *Fads, Fallacies and Foolishness in Medical Care Management and Policy* (World Scientific, 2007), to which reference was made in this chapter, is highly commended for its deconstruction of many of the myths that abound in health care policy proposals. An understanding of why dubious and ill-conceived policy proposals abound in health care matters is possibly a very important starting point for policy reformers.

Marmor's and Klein's *Politics, Health, and Health Care: Selected Essays* (Yale University Press, 2012) provides a great deal of insight into health policy successes and failures across a wide range of countries and issues.

DISCUSSION QUESTIONS

1   Three of the highly acclaimed policy initiatives in Australia in recent times have been activity-based funding, evidence-based medicine and clinical governance. Examine the proposition that each of these phrases may or may not fall in the category of 'fads and fallacies' as these terms are used by Marmor.
2   We have questioned at some length the overall equity of the Australian health system as it is currently organised and funded. Do you agree or disagree with the position we have taken?
3   How feasible would it be to implement policies that introduced a greater degree of fairness into our system?
4   What reforms, if any, of the provision of medical services in Australia, including the methods of paying for these services, may be feasible?

11

The future

Our purpose in discussing possible future changes in key factors that influence the Australian health care system, the principal focus of this chapter, is not to attempt to predict the future. Rather, the purpose is to suggest the likely outcomes, based on the analysis of this book, if governments do not formulate and implement appropriate policies. Our basic thesis is that health care problems, especially financial and political problems, will inevitably worsen in the absence of major policy initiatives. In addition, we examine the closely related question of how reforms designed to meet a variety of social, economic and health status objectives, including those highlighted in **Chapter 10**, might be promoted.

Key future trends

Of the factors we have chosen to examine here, the ageing of the Australian community—the increase in the numbers and proportion of the population in the older age groups—is the only one lying largely outside government influence. Even in this case a massive shift in immigration policy could conceivably reverse the current trend; however, this change is regarded as being too unlikely to warrant further consideration. All the other factors, to varying degrees, are capable of being influenced by government actions. Thus, the policy responses may, in principle, concentrate directly on these influences or on their effects.

The ageing of the population

At 30 June 2012, 14 per cent of the Australian population was aged 65 years and over (ABS 2013b). According to current population projections, by the year 2056 this value is projected to increase to between 23 per cent and 25 per cent (ABS 2008c). Of the Australian population at 30 June 2012, the proportion who were 85 years of age or older (the 'old old') was 1.8 per cent. The ABS population projections indicate a dramatic increase in this group to between 4.9 per cent and 7.3 per cent in 2056.

These projections are based on a specific set of assumptions about future trends in fertility, mortality and immigration rates, which may or may not be met. Nevertheless, this vast shift in the age composition of the population, including a corresponding decrease in the proportion in the younger age groups, poses special problems for the health services because of the very high use of these and aged care facilities by the 'old old'. Nevertheless, we must be cautious about over-interpreting these projections.

In the past, there has been a somewhat naive tendency to predict doom and gloom for the health services and for government budgets, on the basis of projections of the numbers in the older age groups (National Commission of Audit 1997). We pointed out previously that the basic fallacy here is that current associations between advanced age and expenditure on health services are unlikely to apply to current cohorts when they reach these age groups. Increases in the proportion of the population in the older age groups reflect the fact that the age-specific death rates at each age have fallen. According, it is highly likely that age-specific morbidity rates have also decreased. It is these rates that influence the usage and expenditure on health services. As Fuchs (1984) has argued, the years to death are the most important determinant of expenditure; with increased life expectancy, expenditure in a given age group is likely to decrease. Based on this and a number of other assumptions, Richardson and Robertson (1999, p. 349) concluded from their empirical analysis that there is considerable doubt about whether age- and sex-based need has been or will be a major determinant of the use of and expenditure on health services.

As we asserted in **Chapter 5**, in respect of aged care facilities, the ageing of the population has been a convenient method of arguing for policies whereby public sector expenditure is reduced and greater responsibility is placed on individuals and the private sector. However, it is important to emphasise that many of the difficult health care problems, with important ethical and resource usage implications about the appropriateness of continued treatment and of quality of life during and after therapy, are concentrated in the older age groups.

The proliferation of medical technology

The experience of the past 30 years indicates the remarkable ability of the medical technology industry to devise new methods of diagnosis and treatment of disease. Despite the doubts about the effectiveness and efficiency of many of these developments, in general they have been embraced with considerable enthusiasm, especially by hospitals and their medical staff. The technological imperative in medicine, the association of high technology with the status of hospitals, the fee-for-service payment arrangements and the demands of a public conditioned to expect miracle cures represent some of the main reasons for this relatively uncontrolled expansion. In the absence of greater government intervention, there is every reason to believe that the proliferation of costly, marginally effective technology will continue in the future, in Australia and elsewhere.

The supply of doctors

We documented in **Chapter 6** that the supply of doctors in Australia has increased substantially since the early 1970s, and that this expansion is projected to continue in the future, although at a slower rate. We recognised previously, however, that the shift from a perception in official circles of a surplus of medical staff in the mid-1990s to one of a shortage in the latter part of the 1990s, and subsequently, may have had more to do with the change of government in 1996 than with an objective assessment of population requirements. The focus in federal Labor government policy, and the recommendations of the National Health and Hospitals Reform Commission (NHHRC), has stressed the use of nurses and of allied health staff as a substitute for their medical colleagues. As we emphasised in **Chapter 6**, there is clearly a need for the improved planning of health workforce requirements before we contemplate drastic increases in the numbers of doctors.

The results of the availability of more doctors include the likelihood, in the absence of other changes—for example, in fee-charging arrangements—that over-servicing may escalate and that, consequently, there will be further problems in constraining the growth in total health care expenditure.

Other likely developments

Other probable future trends include increased demands from non-medical workers in health care, especially nurses, for improved remuneration and working conditions and greater influence in health care decision-making; a greater level of consumer and community awareness of health issues, together with further pressures from the emerging community structural interest for the system to be more responsive to this interest; and a greater measure of militancy from some doctors as threats to their position of dominance and to their incomes and status escalate.

It might also be predicted that governments will continue to be under pressure to restrict their spending as the demands of influential and wealthy groups for taxation cuts continue to be articulated. Nor is the popularity of small government philosophies likely to diminish. These include the views emanating from members of the 'New Right' in Australian politics, who have had a direct influence on some members of the medical profession. There are some signs, however, that this influence may be diminishing.

If these outcomes were to eventuate, the conflict between demands for additional resources and the difficulties faced by governments in finding extra funding would obviously accelerate. This set of circumstances, in association with the considerable scope for political conflict posed by the often irreconcilable demands of doctors, community groups and health service employees, would place great strains on the whole system. Of course, other largely unpredictable factors such as the state of the economy might change this pessimistic scenario. The hope for a substantial increase in the allocation of resources to the health sector, following strong growth in the Australian economy up to 2008, was diminished more recently as a result of the global financial crisis. However, Australia did not fall into recession, as most other countries did after 2008, so there remains some scope for further increases in health expenditure as a proportion of gross domestic product.

Given that government funds, restrained by current deficits, are likely to fall short of those required to meet all the demands on the system, further rationing of health care provision is inevitable. The need for rationing could lead to demands for a more comprehensive system of government control and ownership, the National Health Service (NHS) solution, or for the operation of competitive market mechanisms such as those envisaged in the managed competition purchaser–provider separation scenario. These conflicting demands would form an additional basis for bitter political dissension.

Possible solutions

The initiatives discussed in previous chapters, including the National Health Reform Agreement, and the associated changes in funding arrangements—notably the national use of activity-based funding for public hospitals to achieve increased efficiency—may help to ameliorate the worst effect of the resource-scarcity problem. In addition, a greater concentration of resources in community health services and in disease prevention and health promotion activities may eventually ease the pressures on the health care system. It was stressed, moreover, that if the pressures on governments to achieve economies in the provision of health services became sufficiently compelling, issues that had previously been ignored, such as placing further constraints on the fees charged by doctors and their hospital admission practices, might become part of the policy agenda.

It was pointed out earlier that the supply of doctors and the proliferation of expensive technology were the two future changes that could be affected by public policy. At the same time, shortages of specialists willing to work in the public sector—especially in disciplines such as orthopaedics, ophthalmology and psychiatry—which affect problems of access for public patients, can only be resolved in the short term by importing overseas-trained specialists on a contract basis.

In respect of the other potential driver of future cost increases, developments in medical technology, the policy requirement is for improved and more extensive evaluation of medical technology of all kinds using a variety of techniques, including cost-effectiveness and cost-utility analysis (Carter & Harris 1998). In the current enthusiasm for evidence-based medicine, it would be unfortunate if we lost sight of the fact that new technologies should only be adopted if the additional benefits they yield exceed the additional costs of providing those benefits.

In previous chapters, however, we indicated that the willingness and the capacity of governments to intervene in these areas were limited because of the strength of the interests involved in both sets of developments. Nevertheless, it is clear that policies designed to influence both these factors should be afforded high priority by governments.

The perspectives on health policy discussed in **Chapter 3** and elsewhere, especially those of Marmor and colleagues (1973, 1976, 1980) and Alford and colleague

(Alford 1975; Alford & Friedland 1985), suggest that further structural changes that, for example, reduce the dominance of the medical profession and produce a greater measure of balance in the political market for health care policies are the necessary conditions for the achievement of many of these much-needed reforms.

As we indicated in **Chapter 10**, for the councils of local hospital networks and similar organisations, a policy of substantive community representation needs to be implemented whereby the groups selected for this role possess concentrated interests in consumer-based aspects of health and are well placed to further those interests. Furthermore, the individuals chosen as representatives should have an adequate understanding of the interests of the groups they represent and they should possess the personal skills to present the case for those interests. They should also be accountable to the people they represent and have adequate training and support.

However, a substantial strengthening of the repressed community interest in the health arena is unlikely to take place solely as a result of the actions of governments and their bureaucracies. The material on the composition of the councils, as set out in the National Health Reform Agreement, does not appear to give much weight to community interests. The members of the health bureaucracies, to achieve their own objectives, may see the promotion of this interest as a useful short-term method of countering the influence of the structural interest of providers, especially if this process favours policies that lead to the containment of costs. Nevertheless, the presence of vigorous community groups may equally well be perceived as a threat to their authority by governments and public servants. The aims of the community interest and of the corporate rationalisers are not always in agreement.

The development of women's health centres and other initiatives concerning women's health that have taken place since the early 1970s suggest that the existence of a well-organised and popular social movement may be an essential requirement for the achievement of major reforms. The success of the women's movement in placing a large range of other social issues, including equal pay and equality of employment opportunities, on the policy agendas of governments also supports this conclusion. Whether the existing health consumers' organisations will be able to develop into a social movement of this kind is not clear at present.

More radical reforms? Beware of false prophets!

From the perspectives of health care reformers at the extremes of the political spectrum, our proposals will appear very modest. Thus, we do not regard a nationalised health service, along the lines of the British scheme and of some other European countries, as being a feasible option for Australia. In Britain almost all specialist doctors are salaried employees of the NHS, and all GPs are paid either on a 'per patient' capitation basis or they receive a salary. Apart from the possible constitutional barriers to these arrangements in Australia, the attempt to impose such a system here would gain little support from the community and would be opposed strongly by the great majority of doctors. Contrary to the beliefs of some members of the medical profession, no significant groups in Australian politics have advocated a nationalised health service in this country for at least the past 50 years.

It is also clear that many of the major problems faced by the Australian health care system are still present in Britain, including the dominance of the curative hospital-based model and the absence of quality monitoring techniques more than 60 years after the NHS was created (Allsop 1984; Ham 1999). The rationale for reforms in the NHS, such as greater accountability for resource use and quality by clinicians, based on the clinical governance movement, and the emphasis on provid-ing evidence of effectiveness among the criteria for prudent purchasing of health services, may be seen as attempts to come to terms with these problems (Lugon & Secker-Walker 1999). We have noted previously that about 10 years after the Bristol Royal Infirmary paediatric cardiac scandal during the 1990s, and the promotion of clinical governance to minimise patients' risks in NHS hospitals, equally dramatic instances of appalling patient care emerged at the Mid Staffordshire NHS Trust hospital in England, as documented by the Francis report referenced in **Chapter 10**.

The Coalition parties in Australia may continue to seek alternatives or modifica-tions to Medicare, especially in the light of their commitment to reduce the federal deficit on coming to power in 2013. Despite the commitment of the Coalition to preserve Medicare, which was kept during its term of office between 1996 and 2007, there is possibly a lingering belief among the more conservative Coalition politicians that means tests for public hospital admission, the elimination of direct billing and larger co-payments for patients represent the way forward.

More radical moves than those contemplated to date by the Coalition parties, such as the establishment of a competitive private market for health care, have been promoted by some economists and doctors in both the United States and Australia (Kasper 2009; Lindsay et al. 1986). At their worst, these are based on the belief that a substantial increase in the costs borne directly by consumers of health services will decrease demand and total expenditure without any significant detrimental effects. The capacity of providers to generate demand is either denied or ignored in these proposals.

Depending on the level of 'small' or 'no government' ideology associated with these prescriptions, provision for the poor and the chronically ill becomes a residual social welfare responsibility for governments, or a matter for the private charity of doctors and other providers. Free-market solutions of these kinds are not likely to find much support in Australia, outside the ranks of the ideologues, unless there is a dramatic worsening of the current state of the health care system. Nevertheless, they are often given considerable prominence in the media and elsewhere.

In this regard, may we make a plea for commentators on health policy matters, including journalists and the media generally, to take a more critical approach to the nostrums that are being continually touted as solutions to the latest alleged health care 'crisis'. The first question to ask is what interests do the proposers represent and what do they stand to gain from the course of action they are recommending? The second question is what is the evidence that the proposal(s) will provide a greater benefit to the community than other options including the status quo? In addition, it is often highly relevant to inquire about the qualifications and experience of the self-appointed expert on health policy.

The existence of more radical proposals for health system changes may serve as a useful reminder to all the actors in the Australian scene that the much less drastic set of reforms considered here may represent the best set of compromises that can be expected. Given the nature of Australian society and its political parties, the structural dominance of the medical profession and the history of controversy surrounding health insurance, it is very unlikely that the level of conflict within the system will diminish in the future. It is in all our interests to ensure that this conflict is not destructive.

Bibliography

Aaron, HJ & Schwartz, WB 1984, *The Painful Prescription: Rationing Hospital Care*, The Brookings Institution, Washington DC.

Abel-Smith, B 1997, *Choices in Health Policy: An Agenda for the European Union*, Dartmouth, Aldershot.

ABS—see Australian Bureau of Statistics

Acheson, D 1998, *Independent Inquiry into Inequalities in Health Report*, Stationery Office, London.

Adams, AI 1974, 'The state of health services—International comments: Developments in Australia's health services', *International Journal of Epidemiology*, vol. 3, pp. 5–7.

Adhikari, P 2006, *Socioeconomic Indexes for Areas: Introduction, Use and Future Directions*, cat. no. 1351.0.55.015, Australian Bureau of Statistics, Canberra.

AIHW—see Australian Institute of Health and Welfare

Alcorso, C & Schofield, T 1991, *The National Non-English Speaking Background Women's Health Strategy*, Australian Government Publishing Service, Canberra.

Aldrich, R, Zwi, A & Short, SD 2007, 'Advance Australia Fair: Social democratic and conservative politicians' discourses concerning Aboriginal and Torres Strait Islander Peoples and their health 1972–2001', *Social Science and Medicine*, vol. 64, no. 1, pp. 125–37.

Alford, RR 1975, *Health Care Politics: Ideological and Interest Group Barriers to Reform*, University of Chicago Press, Chicago and London.

Alford, RR & Friedland, R 1985, *Powers of Theory: Capitalism, the State, and Democracy*, Cambridge University Press, Cambridge.

Allsop, J 1984, *Health Policy and the National Health Service*, Longman, London.

Altman, D 1992, 'The most political of diseases', in E Timewell, V Minichiello and D Plummer (eds), *AIDS in Australia*, Prentice Hall, Sydney.

American Psychiatric Association 2013, *Diagnostic and Statistical Manual of Mental Disorders*, Fifth Edition, American Psychiatric Association, Arlington.

Andersen, TF & Mooney, G 1990, *The Challenge of Medical Practice Variations*, Macmillan, London.

Anderson, B & Bell, J 1986, 'Female dominated occupational therapy: Deliberate strategy or historical coincidence', *Proceedings of the Women Workers in Health Care Conference 1985*, Sydney.

Anderson, B & Bell, J 1988, *Occupational Therapy: Its Place in Australia's History*, New South Wales Association of Occupational Therapists, Sydney.

Anderson, JE 1984, *Public Policy-Making*, 3rd edition, Holt, Rinehart & Winston, New York.

Andrews, G, Teeson, M & Hoult, J 1990, 'Follow-up of community placement of the chronic mentally ill in New South Wales', *Hospital and Community Psychiatry*, vol. 41, no. 2, pp. 184–8.

ANMC—see Australian Nursing and Midwifery Council

Arrowsmith, JE, Grocott, HP, Reves, JG & Newman, MF 2000, 'Central nervous system complications of cardiac surgery', *British Journal of Anaesthesia*, vol. 84, pp. 378–93.

Asbeck, FM (ed.) 1949, *The Universal Declaration of Human Rights and Its Predecessors, 1679–1948*, EJ Brill, Leiden.

ASCC—see Australian Safety and Compensation Council

Ashton, J (ed.) 1992a, *Healthy Cities*, Open University Press, Buckingham.

Ashton, J 1992b, 'Now is the time for critical debate', *Health for All 2000*, vol. 4, no. 2, p. 8.

Australian Bureau of Statistics 1984, *Handicapped Persons Australia 1981*, 2nd edition, cat. no. 4343.0, ABS, Canberra.

Australian Bureau of Statistics 1990, *Disability and Handicap, Australia, 1988*, cat. no. 4120.0, ABS, Canberra.

Australian Bureau of Statistics 1996, *Deaths, Australia, 1996*, cat. no. 3302.0, Australian Bureau of Statistics, Canberra.

Australian Bureau of Statistics 1997, *Deaths, Australia*, cat. no. 3302.0, ABS, Canberra.

Australian Bureau of Statistics 1998, *Mental Health and Wellbeing: Profile of Adults, Australia 1997*, cat. no. 4326.0, Australian Bureau of Statistics, Canberra.

Australian Bureau of Statistics 1999a, *National Health Survey: Aboriginal and Torres Strait Islander Results Australia, 1995*, cat. no. 4806.0, Australian Bureau of Statistics, Canberra.

Australian Bureau of Statistics 1999b, *Physiotherapy Services, Australia 1997–98*, cat. no. 8552.0, Australian Bureau of Statistics, Canberra.

Australian Bureau of Statistics 1999c, *Chiropractic and Osteopathic Services, Australia 1997–98*, cat. no. 8550.0, Australian Bureau of Statistics, Canberra.

Australian Bureau of Statistics 1999d, *Audiology and Audiometry Services, Australia 1997–98*, cat. no. 8554.0, Australian Bureau of Statistics, Canberra.

Australian Bureau of Statistics 1999e, *Dental Services, Australia 1997–98*, cat. no. 8551.0, Australian Bureau of Statistics, Canberra.

Australian Bureau of Statistics 1999f, *Australia Now—A Statistical Profile*, ABS, Canberra.

Australian Bureau of Statistics 2004, *Survey of Disability, Ageing and Carers (SADC) 2003*, cat. no. 443.0, Australian Bureau of Statistics, Canberra.

Australian Bureau of Statistics 2006a, *Census of Population and Housing: A Picture of the Nation*, cat. no. 2070.0, Australian Bureau of Statistics, Canberra.

Australian Bureau of Statistics 2006b, *National Health Survey 2004–05, Summary of Results in Australia*, cat. no. 4364.0, Australian Bureau of Statistics, Canberra.

Australian Bureau of Statistics 2007, *2006 Census Tables: Australia*, Australian Bureau of Statistics, Canberra.

Australian Bureau of Statistics 2008a, *Private Hospitals Australia, 2006–07*, Australian Bureau of Statistics, Canberra.

Australian Bureau of Statistics 2008b, SEIFA: Socio-Economic Indexes for Areas, Australian Bureau of Statistics, Canberra.

Australian Bureau of Statistics 2008c, *Population Projections Australia, 2006–2101*, cat. no. 3222.0, Australian Bureau of Statistics, Canberra.

Australian Bureau of Statistics 2008d, *Year Book Australia, 2008*, cat. no. 1301.0, Australian Bureau of Statistics, Canberra.

Australian Bureau of Statistics 2009a, *Causes of Death 2007: National Health Priority Areas*, cat. no. 3303.0, Australian Bureau of Statistics, Canberra.

Australian Bureau of Statistics 2009b, *Disability, Ageing and Carers, Australia: Summary of Findings*, cat. no. 4430.0, ABS, Canberra.

Australian Bureau of Statistics 2010a, *Year Book Australia, 2009–10*, cat. no. 1301.0, Australian Bureau of Statistics, Canberra.

Australian Bureau of Statistics 2010b, *Measures of Australia's Progress, 2010*, cat. no. 1370.0, Australian Bureau of Statistics, Canberra.

Australian Bureau of Statistics 2010c, *Deaths, Australia, 2010*, cat. no. 3302.0, Australian Bureau of Statistics, Canberra.

Australian Bureau of Statistics 2010d, *The Health and Welfare of Australia's Aboriginal and Torres Strait Islander Peoples, Oct 2010*, cat. No. 4704.0, Australian Bureau of Statistics, Canberra.

Australian Bureau of Statistics 2011a, *Labour Force Characteristics of Aboriginal and Torres Strait Islander Australians, Estimates from the Labour Force Survey*, cat. no. 6287.0, Australian Bureau of Statistics, Canberra.

Australian Bureau of Statistics 2011b, *Census of Population and Housing: Characteristics of Aboriginal and Torres Strait Islander Australians, 2011*, cat. no. 2076.0, Australian Bureau of Statistics, Canberra.

Australian Bureau of Statistics 2011c, *Deaths, Australia, 2011*, cat. no. 3302.0, Australian Bureau of Statistics, Canberra.

Australian Bureau of Statistics 2012, *Australian Health Survey: First Results, 2012*, cat. no. 4364.0.55.001, Australian Bureau of Statistics, Canberra.

Australian Bureau of Statistics 2013a, *Private Hospitals, Australia, 2011–12*, cat. no. 4390.0, Australian Bureau of Statistics, Canberra.

Australian Bureau of Statistics 2013b, *Population by Age and Sex, Australia, 2012*, Australian Bureau of Statistics, Canberra.

Australian Bureau of Statistics 2013c, *Australian Social Trends, April 2013*, cat. no. 4102.0, Australian Bureau of Statistics, Canberra.

Australian Bureau of Statistics 2013d, *Reflecting a Nation: Stories from the 2011 Census, 2012–2013*, cat. no. 2071.0, Australian Bureau of Statistics, Canberra.

Australian Bureau of Statistics 2013e, *Australian Health Survey: Updated Results, 2011–2012*, Cat 4364.0.55.003, ABS, Canberra.

Australian Bureau of Statistics 2013f, *Disability, Ageing and Carers, Australia: Summary of Findings*, 2012, cat. no. 4430.0, ABS, Canberra.

Australian Bureau of Statistics 2013g, *Migrant Data Matrices, 2013*, cat. no. 3415.0, Australian Bureau of Statistics, Canberra.

Australian Bureau of Statistics 2013h, *Measures of Australia's Progress, 2010*, cat no. 1370.0, ABS, Canberra.

Australian Bureau of Statistics and Australian Institute of Health and Welfare 1999, *The Health and Welfare of Australia's Aboriginal and Torres Strait Islander Peoples 1999*, cat. no. 4704.0, Australian Bureau of Statistics, Canberra.

Australian Community Health Association 1989, *Review of the Community Health Program*, 2nd edition, Australian Community Health Association, Sydney.

Australian Council on the Ageing & Department of Community Services 1985, *Older People at Home*, Australian Government Publishing Service, Canberra.

Australian Government 2008, *Australia 2020 Summit—A Long-term National Health Strategy*, Australian Government, Canberra.

Australian Health Ministers 1992, *National Mental Health Policy*, Australian Government Publishing Service, Canberra.

Australian Indigenous Health InfoNet 2013, *Health Facts: Overview of Australian Indigenous Health Status 2012, Mortality*, Australian Indigenous Health InfoNet, Edith Cowan University, Perth.

Australian Institute of Health and Welfare 1992, *Australia's Health 1992: The Third Biennial Report of the Australian Institute of Health and Welfare*, AIHW, Canberra.

Australian Institute of Health and Welfare 1997, *Nursing Labour Force 1993 and 1994*, AIHW, Canberra.

Australian Institute of Health and Welfare 1998a, *National Medical Workforce Data Collections: Discussion Paper*, AIHW, Canberra.

Australian Institute of Health and Welfare 1998b, *International Health—How Australia Compares*, AIHW, Canberra.

Australian Institute of Health and Welfare 1998c, *National Medical Workforce Data Collections, A Discussion Paper*, July, AIHW, Canberra.

Australian Institute of Health and Welfare 1998d, *Nursing Labour Force 1998*, AIHW, Canberra.

Australian Institute of Health and Welfare 1998e, *Australia's Health 1998*, The Sixth Biennial Report of the Australian Institute of Health and Welfare, AIHW, Canberra.

Australian Institute of Health and Welfare 1999a, *Australian Hospital Statistics, 1997–98*, AIHW, Canberra.

Australian Institute of Health and Welfare 1999b, *Health Expenditure Australia, 1996–97*, AIHW, Canberra.

Australian Institute of Health and Welfare 2005, *Health System Expenditure on Disease and Injury in Australia, 2000–01*, 2nd edition, AIHW, Canberra.

Australian Institute of Health and Welfare 2006a, *Australia's Health 2006*, AIHW, Canberra.

Australian Institute of Health and Welfare 2006b, National Mortality Database, AIHW, Canberra.

Australian Institute of Health and Welfare 2006c, *Medical Labour Force 2006*, AIHW, Canberra.

Australian Institute of Health and Welfare 2007, *Australia's Welfare 2007*, AIHW, Canberra.

Australian Institute of Health and Welfare 2008a, *Australia's Health 2008, 11th Biennial Report*, AIHW, Australian Government Publishing Service, Canberra.

Australian Institute of Health and Welfare 2008b, *Health Expenditure Australia 2006–07*, Health and Welfare Expenditure Series no. 35, AIHW, Canberra.

Australian Institute of Health and Welfare 2008c, *Australia's Hospital Statistics, 2006–07*, Health Services Series no. 31, AIHW, Canberra.

Australian Institute of Health and Welfare 2008d, *Public Health Expenditure in Australia, 2006–07*, Health and Welfare Expenditure Series no. 34, AIHW, Canberra.

Australian Institute of Health and Welfare 2008e, *Residential Aged Care in Australia, 2006–07: A Statistical Overview*, AIHW, Canberra.

Australian Institute of Health and Welfare 2008f, *Medical Labour Force 2006*, AIHW, Australian Government Publishing Service, Canberra.

Australian Institute of Health and Welfare 2008g, *Nursing and Midwifery, Labour Force 2005*, AIHW, Australian Government Publishing Service, Canberra.

Australian Institute of Health and Welfare 2008h, *Dentist Labour Force in Australia, 2005*, AIHW, Adelaide.

Australian Institute of Health and Welfare 2008i, *Projected Demand for Dental Care to 2020*, AIHW, Adelaide.

Australian Institute of Health and Welfare 2009, *Health and Community Services Labour Force*, AIHW, Canberra.

Australian Institute of Health and Welfare 2011a, *National Health Workforce Data Set: Allied Health Workforce 2011*, Cat. no. HWL 51, AIHW, Canberra.

Australian Institute of Health and Welfare 2011b, *National Health Workforce Data Set: Dental Workforce 2011*, Cat. no. HWL 50, AIHW, Canberra.

Australian Institute of Health and Welfare 2011c, *National Health Workforce Data Set: Medical Practitioners 2011*, Cat no. HWL 49, AIHW, Canberra.

Australian Institute of Health and Welfare 2011d, *National Health Workforce Data Set: Nursing and Midwifery Workforce 2011*, Cat. no. HWL 48, AIHW, Canberra.

Australian Institute of Health and Welfare 2011e, *Australian Hospital Statistics 2009–10*, Health Services Series no. 40, AIHW, Canberra.

Australian Institute of Health and Welfare 2011f, *Young Australians: Their Health and Wellbeing 2011*, cat. no. PHE 140, AIHW, Canberra.

Australian Institute of Health and Welfare 2012a, *Australia's Health 2012*. Australia's health no. 13, cat. no. AUS 156, AIHW, Canberra.

Australian Institute of Health and Welfare 2012b, *Residential Aged Care in Australia 2010–11: A Statistical Overview*, AIHW, Canberra.

Australian Institute of Health and Welfare 2012c, *Nursing and Midwifery Workforce 2011*, National health workforce series no. 2, cat. no. HWL 48, AIHW, Canberra.

Australian Institute of Health and Welfare 2012d, *Health Expenditure Australia 2010–11*, Health and welfare expenditure series no. 47, cat. no. HWE 56, AIHW, Canberra.

Australian Institute of Health and Welfare 2012e, *Mental Health Services—In Brief 2012*, cat. no. HSE125, AIHW, Canberra.

Australian Institute of Health and Welfare 2013a, *Australian Hospital Statistics 2011–12*, Health services series 50, cat. no. HSE 134, Australian Institute of Health and Welfare, Canberra.

Australian Institute of Health and Welfare 2013b, *Health Expenditure, Australia, 2011–12*, Health and Welfare expenditure series 50. cat. no. HWE 59, AIHW, Canberra.

Australian Institute of Health and Welfare 2013c, *Medical Workforce 2011*, National health workforce series. cat. no. HWL 49, AIHW, Canberra.

Australian Institute of Health and Welfare 2013d, *Dental Workforce 2011*, National health workforce series no. 4, cat. no. HWL 50, AIHW, Canberra.

Australian Institute of Health and Welfare 2013e, *Expenditure on Health for Aboriginal and Torres Strait Islander People 2010–11*, cat. no. HWE 57, AIHW, Canberra.

Australian Institute of Health and Welfare 2013f, *Allied Health Workforce 2012*, National health workforce series no. 5, cat. no. HWL 51, AIHW, Canberra.

Australian Institute of Health and Welfare & Australian Health Ministers' Advisory Council 1995, *National Health Information Development Plan*, Australian Government Publishing Service, Canberra.

Australian Institute of Health and Welfare & Commonwealth Department of Health and Family Services 1997, *First Report on National Health Priority Areas 1996*, AIHW and Commonwealth Department of Health and Family Services, Canberra.

Australian Institute of Health and Welfare & Department of Health and Ageing 2007, *Older Australia at a Glance*, 4th edition, Australian Government, Canberra.

Australian Institute of Health and Welfare & National Heart Foundation 1999, *Cardiac Surgery in Australia 1994*, Cardiovascular Disease Series no. 9, AIHW, Canberra.

Australian Medical Association 2009, *AMA calls for ban of junk food advertising on children's TV*, media release, Australian Medical Association, 30 April, available at <https://ama.com.au/media/ama-calls-ban-junk-food-advertising-children%E2%80%99s-tv>.

Australian Medical Workforce Advisory Committee 1996, *The Medical Workforce in Rural and Remote Australia*, Australian Medical Workforce Advisory Committee, Sydney.

Australian Medical Workforce Advisory Committee & AIHW 1996a, *Australian Medical Workforce Benchmarks*, Australian Medical Workforce Advisory Committee, Sydney.

Australian Medical Workforce Advisory Committee & AIHW 1996b, *Female Participation in the Australian Medical Workforce*, Australian Medical Workforce Advisory Committee, Sydney.

Australian Medical Workforce Advisory Committee & AIHW 1998, *Medical Workforce Supply and Demand in Australia: A Discussion Paper*, Australian Medical Workforce Advisory Committee, Sydney.

Australian National Audit Office 1993, *Medifraud and Excessive Servicing*, Health Insurance Commission, Australian Government Publishing Service, Canberra.

Australian National Training Authority 2004, *Shaping our Future: Australia's National Strategy for VET 2004–2010*, Australian Government, Canberra.

Australian Nursing and Midwifery Council 2002a, *National Competency Standards for the Enrolled Nurse*, Australian Nursing and Midwifery Council Incorporated, Canberra.

Australian Nursing and Midwifery Council 2002b, *Principles of Assessment of National Competency Standards*, Australian Nursing and Midwifery Council Incorporated, Canberra.

Australian Nursing and Midwifery Council 2009, *National Competency Standards for the Nurse Practitioner*, Australian Nursing and Midwifery Council Incorporated, Canberra.

Australian Safety and Compensation Council 2002, *National OHS Strategy 2002–2012*, Australian Safety and Compensation Council, Australian Government, Canberra.

Australian Safety and Compensation Council 2008a, *Notified Fatalities Statistical Report: July 2008 to December 2008*, Safe Work Australia, Australian Safety and Compensation Council, Australian Government, Canberra.

Australian Safety and Compensation Council 2008b, *Work-Related Traumatic Injury Fatalities, Australia 2005–06*, Safe Work Australia, Australian Safety and Compensation Council, Australian Government, Canberra.

Australia's Health Workforce 2009a, *Registration and Accreditation Scheme for the Health Professions*, Australian Health Ministers' Advisory Council, Melbourne.

Australia's Health Workforce 2009b, *National Partnership Agreement on Hospital and Health Workforce Reform*, National Health Workforce Taskforce, Australian Health Ministers' Advisory Council, Melbourne.

Australia's Health Workforce Online 2009, National Health Workforce Taskforce, accessed 19 October 2009, <www.nhwt.gov.au/nhwt.asp>.

Avorn, J, Chen, M & Hartley, R 1982, 'Scientific versus commercial sources of influence on the prescribing behaviour of physicians', *The American Journal of Medicine*, vol. 73, pp. 4–8.

Baldock, CV & Cass, B (eds) 1983, *Women, Social Welfare and the State*, Allen & Unwin, Sydney.

Ballard, J 1989, 'The politics of AIDS', in H. Gardner (ed.), *The Politics of Health: The Australian Experience*, Churchill Livingstone, Melbourne.

Banta, HD 1983, 'Some aphorisms concerning medical technology', in JR Gray and BJ Sax Jacobs (eds), *The Technology Explosion in Medical Science*, Spectrum, New York.

Banta, HD 1995, 'Health care technology as a policy issue', *Health Care Technology and its Assessment in Eight Countries*, pp. 1–13, US Congress, Office of Technology Assessment, US Government Printing Office, Washington, DC.

Banta, HD & Russell, LB 1981, 'Policies toward medical technology: An international review', *International Journal of Health Services*, vol. 11, pp. 631–52.

Banta, HD, Behney, CJ & Willems, JS 1980, *Towards Rational Technology in Medicine: Considerations for Health Policy*, Springer, New York.

Barer, LM, Thomas, EG & Stoddart, GL (eds) 1998, *Health, Healthcare and Health Economics*, John Wiley, Chichester.

Bartlett, B 1999, 'Health services development and Aboriginal health', *New Doctor*, Summer, pp. 5–10.

Basaglia, E 1981, 'Breaking the circuit of control', in D Ingleby (ed.), *Critical Psychiatry: The Politics of Mental Health*, Penguin, Harmondsworth.

Bates, PW 1999, 'Health law, ethics and policy: Challenges and new avenues for the 21st century and the new millennium', *Medicine and Law*, vol. 18, pp. 13–46.

Battista, R, Banta, HD, Jonsson, E & Gelband, H 1995, *Health Care Technology and its Assessment in Eight Countries*, Office of Technology Assessment, Washington, DC.

Baum, F 1998, *The New Public Health: An Australian Perspective*, Oxford University Press, Melbourne.

Baum, F 2002, *The New Public Health*, 2nd edition, Oxford University Press, Melbourne.

Baum, F & Skewes, A 1992, 'Noarlunga', in J Ashton (ed.), *Healthy Cities*, Open University Press, Buckingham.

Baum, F, Lennie, I & Fry, D (eds) 1992, *Community Health: Policy and Practice in Australia*, Pluto Press with Australian Community Health Association, Sydney.

Baume, P 1991, *A Question of Balance: Report on the Future of Drug Evaluation in Australia*, Australian Government Publishing Service, Canberra.

Baume, P 1994, *A Cutting Edge: Australia's Surgical Workforce 1994*, Australian Government Publishing Service, Canberra.

Becker, R, Silvi, J, Ma Fat, D, L'Hours, A & Laurenti, R 2006, 'A method for deriving leading causes of death', *Bulletin of the World Health Organization*, vol. 84, no. 4, pp. 297–304.

Benzeval, M, Judge, K & Whitehead, M (eds) 1995, *Tackling Inequalities in Health: An Agenda for Action*, King's Fund, London.

Best, J 1987, 'Suffering the surfeit of doctors, Professor Doherty?', *The Medical Journal of Australia*, vol. 146, pp. 367–9.

Better Health Commission 1986a, *Looking Forward to Better Health, Volume 1, Final Report*, Australian Government Publishing Service, Canberra.

Better Health Commission 1986b, *Looking Forward to Better Health, Volume 2, Final Report*, Australian Government Publishing Service, Canberra.

Better Health Commission 1986c, *Looking Forward to Better Health, Volume 3, Final Report*, Australian Government Publishing Service, Canberra.

Bidmeade, I & Reynolds, C 1997, *Public Health Law in Australia: Its Current State and Future Directions*, Australian Government Publishing Service, Canberra.

Bigg, I, Azmi, S & Maskell-Knight, C 1998, 'The Commonwealth's proposal for the 1998–2003 health care agreements', *Australian Health Review*, vol. 21, no. 2, pp. 8–18.

Biggins, D 1987, 'The politics of occupational health', *Current Affairs Bulletin*, August, pp. 27–31.

Biggins, D 1988, 'Focus on occupational health: What can be done?', *New Doctor*, no. 47, pp. 6–10.

Biggins, D, Abrahams, H, Farr, T & Kempnich, B 1989, 'The role of the Workers' Health Centre', *Journal of Occupational Health Safety—Australia and New Zealand*, vol. 5, no. 4, pp. 317–25.

Biggins, D, Phillips, M & O'Sullivan P 1991, 'Benefits of worker participation in health and safety', *Labour and Industry*, vol. 4, no. 1, pp. 138–59.

Birnbauer, B & Davies, J 1999, 'Public hospital errors exposed', *The Age*, 21 November, p. 1.

Black, N, Boswell, D, Gray, A, Murphy, S & Popay, J (eds) 1984, *Health and Disease: A Reader*, Open University Press, Milton Keynes.

Blewett, N 1985, Ministerial statement, 25 May.

Blewett, N 1988, 'Health for all Australians: A national initiative to improve Australia's health', paper presented at the Second International Conference on Healthy Public Policy, Adelaide, April.

Blewett, N 1999, *A Cabinet Diary: A Personal Account of the First Keating Government*, Wakefield Press, Kent Town.

Bloom, A (ed.) 2000, *Health Reform in Australia and New Zealand*, Oxford University Press, Melbourne.

Boston Women's Health Book Collective 1985, *The New Our Bodies Ourselves*, Penguin, New York.

Boxall, A & Gillespie JA 2013, *Making Medicare: The Politics of Universal Health Care in Australia*, UNSW Press, Sydney.

Boven, R. et al. 1977, 'New patients to alternative health care', cited in Senate Select Committee of Inquiry into Chiropractic, Osteopathy, Homeopathy and Naturopathy (1977), *Report*, appendix 6, Australian Government Publishing Service, Canberra, p. 298.

Braithwaite, J, Healy, J & Dwan, K 2005, *The Governance of Health Safety and Quality*, Commonwealth of Australia, Canberra.

Brennan, TA, Leape, LL, Laird, NM, Hebert, L, Localio, R, Lawthers, AG, Newhouse, JP, Weiler, PC & Hiatt, HH 1991, 'Incidence of adverse events and negligence in hospitalised patients, Results of the Harvard Medical Practice Study 1', *New England Journal of Medicine*, vol. 324, pp. 370–6.

British Council for Science and Society 1982, *Expensive Medical Techniques*, Council for Science and Society, London.

Britt, H, Bhasale, A, Miles, DA, Meza, A, Sayer, GP & Angelis, M 1996, 'The sex of the general practitioner: a comparison of characteristics, patients, and medical conditions managed', *Medical Care*, vol. 34, no. 5, pp. 403–15.

Broadhead, P 1985, 'Social status and morbidity in Australia', *Community Health Studies*, vol. ix, pp. 87–97.

Bromberger, B & Fife-Yeomans, J 1991, *Deep Sleep: Harry Bailey and the Scandal at Chelmsford*, Simon & Schuster, Sydney.

Broom, D 1991, *Damned If We Do: Contradictions in Women's Health Care*, Allen & Unwin, Sydney.

Brown, S 1986, 'Gender and social work', *Proceedings of the Women Workers in Health Care Conference 1985*, Sydney.

Brown, S & Szoke, H 1988, 'Health promotion: The Victorian context', *Health Issues*, no. 14, pp. 35–9.

Brown, V 1999, 'A ground-truthing ecologically sustainable development', in S Buckingham-Hatfield and S Percy (eds), *Constructing Local Environmental Agendas: People, Places and Participation*, Routledge, London.

Bryson, L, Adamson, L and Lennie, I 1992, *The Corporate Context for Community Health*, Australian Community Health Association, Sydney.

Buchanan, JM (ed.) 1978, *The Economics of Politics*, Institute of Economic Affairs, London.

Bunker, JP 1985, 'When doctors disagree', *The New York Review*, 25 April, pp. 7–12.

Bunker, JP, Barnes, BA & Mosteller, F 1977, *Costs, Risks and Benefits of Surgery*, Oxford University Press, Oxford.

Bureau of Industry Economics 1991, *The Pharmaceutical Industry: Impediments and Opportunities, Program Evaluation, No. 11*, AGPS, Canberra.

Bury, M & Gabe, J 1990, 'Hooked? Media responses to tranquiliser dependence', in P Abbott and G Payne (eds), *New Directions in the Sociology of Health*, Falmer, Brighton.

Butler, JRG 1998, 'Health expenditure', in G Mooney and R Scotton (eds), *Economics and Australian Health Policy*, Allen & Unwin, Sydney.

Cameron, L 1987, 'Taking the "con" out of consultation', *Health Issues*, no. 12, pp. 17–19.

Cancer Council 2008, Coalition on Food Advertising to Children, CFAC, Cancer Council NSW, Sydney.

Cancer Council 2009, *Smoking and The Law*, The Cancer Council NSW, Sydney.

Cant, S 1992, 'States told to improve care of the mentally ill', *The Australian*, 4 May, p. 2.

Carter, R & Harris, A 1998, 'Evaluation of health services', in G Mooney and R Scotton (eds), *Economics and Australian Health Policy*, Allen & Unwin, Sydney.

Carver, P 2008, *Self Sufficiency and International Medical Graduates—Australia*, National Health Workforce Taskforce, Australian Health Ministers' Advisory Council, Melbourne.

CASS Principal Investigators 1984, 'Myocardial infarction and mortality in the coronary artery surgical study (CASS) randomised trial', *New England Journal of Medicine*, vol. 310, pp. 750–8.

Castles, S, Cope, B, Kalantzis, M & Morrissey, M 1988, *Mistaken Identity: Multiculturalism and the Demise of Nationalism in Australia*, Pluto Press, Sydney.

Chang, AR 1981, 'An analysis of the pathology of 3003 appendices', *Australian and New Zealand Journal of Surgery*, vol. 51, p. 169.

Chapman, S & Reynolds, C 1987, 'Commentary: Regulating tobacco—the South Australian Tobacco Products Control Act, 1986. Its development and passage through parliament', *Supplement to Community Health Studies*, vol. XI, pp. 9–15.

Chassin, MR, Kosecoff, J Park, RE, Winslow, CM, Kahn, KL, Merrick, NJ, Keesey, J, Fink, A, Solomon, DH & Brook RH 1987, 'Does inappropriate use explain geographic variations in the use of health services? A study of three procedures', *Journal of the American Medical Association*, vol. 258, pp. 2533–7.

Chesler, P 1972, *Women and Madness*, Avon, New York.

Chesterfield-Evans, A 1983, 'Buga-up (Billboard Utilising Graffitists Against Unhealthy Promotions): An Australian movement to end cigarette advertising', *New York State Journal of Medicine*, December, pp. 1333–4.

Chrisopoulos, S & Teusner, DN 2008, 'Dentist labour force projection 2005 to 2020: The impact of new regional dental schools', *Australian Dental Journal*, vol. 53, no. 3, pp. 292–6.

Clavarino, A & Yates, P 1995, 'Fear, faith or rational choice: Understanding the use of alternative therapies', in GM Lupton and JM Najman (eds), *Sociology of Health and Illness: Australian Readings*, 2nd edition, Macmillan, Melbourne.

Clegg, S & Dunkerley, D 1980, *Organisation, Class and Control*, Routledge and Kegan Paul, London.

Clinical Excellence Commission 2008, *Annual Report, 2007–2008*, Clinical Excellence Commission, Sydney.

COAG—see Council of Australian Governments

Cochrane, AL 1972, *Effectiveness and Efficiency: Random Reflections on Health Services*, Nuffield Provincial Hospitals Trust, London.

Collins, DJ & Lapsley, HM 2008, *The Costs of Tobacco, Alcohol and Illicit Drug Abuse to Australian Society in 2004/5*, Commonwealth Attorney-General's Department, Canberra.

Commission of Inquiry into the Efficiency and Administration of Hospitals 1981, *Final Report vols 1–3*, (Chairperson, JH Jamison), Australian Government Publishing Service, Canberra.

Commission on Education for Health Administration 1975, *Report of the Commission on Education for Health Administration*, (Chairperson, JP Dixon), vol. 1, Health Administration Press, Ann Arbor.

Commission on Social Determinants of Health 2008, *Closing the Gap in a Generation: Health Equity through Action on the Social Determinants of Health. Final Report of the Commission on Social Determinants of Health*, World Health Organization, Geneva.

Committee of Inquiry into Health Insurance 1969, (Chairperson, JA Nimmo), *Report*, Australian Government Publishing Service, Canberra.

Committee of Inquiry into Medical Education and the Medical Workforce 1988, (Chairperson, RL Doherty), *Australian Medical Education and Workforce into the 21st Century*, Australian Government Publishing Service, Canberra.

Committee of Inquiry into Nurse Education and Training 1978, (Chairperson, S Sax), *Nurse Education and Training*, Australian Government Publishing Service, Canberra.

Committee of Inquiry into Rights of Private Practice in Public Hospitals 1984, *Final Report*, (Chairperson, D Penington), Australian Government Publishing Service, Canberra.

Committee of Inquiry on Professional Issues in Nursing 1988, *Report of the Study of Professional Issues in Nursing*, (Chairperson, F Marles), Health Department of Victoria, Melbourne.

Committee of Review into Drug and Alcohol Services in New South Wales 1985, (Chairperson, CB Kerr), *Final Report*, NSW Government Printing Service, Sydney.

Committee on Medical Schools to the Australian Universities Commission 1973, *Expansion of Medical Education*, (Chairperson, P Karmel), Australian Government Publishing Service, Canberra.

Committee on Safety and Health at Work 1972, *Safety and Health at Work: Report of the Committee 1970–72*, (Chairperson, Lord Robens), Her Majesty's Stationery Office, London.

Committee on the Care of the Aged and the Infirm 1977, *Report*, Australian Government Publishing Service, Canberra.

Commonwealth Department of Community Services and Health 1988a, *National Policy on Women's Health, A Framework for Change*: *A Discussion Paper for Community Comment and Response*, Australian Government Publishing Service, Canberra.

Commonwealth Department of Community Services and Health 1988b, *Disability, Society and Change*, Office of Disability, Canberra.

Commonwealth Department of Community Services and Health 1989a, *Issues Paper 'I'm Still an Individual': A Blueprint for the Rights of Residents in Nursing Homes and Hostels*, Department of Community Services and Health, Canberra.

Commonwealth Department of Community Services and Health 1989b, *National Women's Health Policy: Advancing Women's Health in Australia*, report presented to Australian health ministers in Burnie, 21 March, Australian Government Publishing Service, Canberra.

Commonwealth Department of Community Services and Health and World Health Organization 1988, *Healthy Public Policy*, report on the 2nd International Conference on Health Promotion, Adelaide.

See also Department of Health and Ageing for more recent publications.

Commonwealth Department of Health 1981, *Annual Report of the Director-General of Health 1980–81*, Australian Government Publishing Service, Canberra.

Commonwealth Department of Health 1984, *Revised Estimates of Medical Manpower Supply*, Australian Government Publishing Service, Canberra.

Commonwealth Department of Health 1985a, *The Review of Community Participation in the Commonwealth Department of Health*, Department of Health, Canberra.

Commonwealth Department of Health 1985b, *Advancing Australia's Health: Towards National Strategies and Objectives for Health Advancement*, Draft Plan, Department of Health, Canberra.

Commonwealth Department of Health 1986a, *Australia's Response to AIDS*, Australian Government Publishing Service, Canberra.

Commonwealth Department of Health 1986b, *Health Maintenance Organisations: A Development Program under Medicare*, Australian Government Publishing Service, Canberra.

Commonwealth Department of Health 1987a, *Health Statistical Supplement 1986–87*, Australian Government Publishing Service, Canberra.

Commonwealth Department of Health 1987b, *Annual Report 1986–87*, Australian Government Publishing Service, Canberra.

Commonwealth Department of Health and Aged Care 1997, *The National Mental Health Report*, Australian Government Publishing Service, Canberra.

Commonwealth Department of Health and Aged Care 1999a, Division of general practice website, accessed 21 November 1999, <www.health.gov.au:80/hsdd/gp/html>.

Commonwealth Department of Health and Aged Care 1999b, *Health Online: A Health Information Plan for Australia 1999*, Commonwealth of Australia, Canberra.

Commonwealth Department of Health and Australian Institute of Health 1987, *Inquiry into Medical Education and Medical Workforce*, Department of Health, Canberra.

Commonwealth Department of Health and Family Services 1998a, *General Practice: Changing the Future through Partnerships, Report of the General Practice Strategy Review Group*, Commonwealth Department of Health and Family Services, Canberra.

Commonwealth Department of Health and Family Services 1998b, *General Practice Education: The Way Forward, Report of the Ministerial Review of General Practice Training*, Commonwealth Department of Health and Family Services, Canberra.

Commonwealth Department of Health and the Hospitals and Health Services Commission 1976, *Review of the Community Health Program*, Australian Government Publishing Service, Canberra.

Commonwealth Department of Health, Housing and Community Services 1992a, *Caring for Rural Communities: Budget 1992–93*, Australian Government Publishing Services, Canberra.

Commonwealth Department of Health, Housing and Community Services 1992b, *Towards Health for All and Health Promotion: The Evaluation of the National Better Health Program*, Australian Government Publishing Service, Canberra.

Commonwealth Department of Health, National Health Technology Advisory Panel 1983, *Nuclear Magnetic Resonance Imaging*, Department of Health, Canberra.

Commonwealth Department of Human Services and Health 1994, *Better Health Outcomes for Australians: National Goals, Targets and Strategies for Better Health Outcomes in the Next Century*, Australian Government Publishing Service, Canberra.

Commonwealth Department of Labour and Immigration in Association with the NSW College of Paramedical Studies 1975, *Survey of Four Paramedical Professions, Professional and Technical Manpower Study no. 3*, Australian Government Publishing Service, Canberra.

Commonwealth Department of Social Security 1988, *Towards Enabling Policies: Income Support for People with Disabilities, Social Security Review, Issues Paper No. 5*, Australian Government Publishing Service, Canberra.

Commonwealth of Australia 1982a, *Medical Fraud and Overservicing, Progress Report*, Joint Committee of Accounts, Australian Government Publishing Service, Canberra.

Commonwealth of Australia 1982b, *In a Home or at Home, Report from the House of Representatives Standing Committee on Expenditure*, (Chairperson, LB McLeay), Australian Government Publishing Service, Canberra.

Commonwealth of Australia 1985a, *Parliamentary Public Accounts: Committee Report*, Australian Government Publishing Service, Canberra.

Commonwealth of Australia 1985b, *New Directions: The Report of the Handicapped Program Review*, Australian Government Publishing Service, Canberra.

Commonwealth of Australia 1992, *Health Care for All Australians: 1992–93 Reforms, Budget Related Paper no. 8*, Australian Government Publishing Service, Canberra.

Commonwealth of Australia 1993, *Agreement Between the Commonwealth of Australia and the State of New South Wales in Relation to the Provision of Public Hospital Services and Other Health Services from July 1993 to 30 June 1998*, unpublished document, Canberra.

Commonwealth of Australia General Practice Strategy Review Group 1998, *General Practice: Changing the Future through Partnerships*, Commonwealth of Australia, Canberra.

Commonwealth of Australia 2001, *Health Impact Assessment Guidelines*, Australian Government, Canberra.

Commonwealth of Australia 2002, *National OHS Strategy 2002—2012*, National Occupational Health and Safety Commission, Canberra, available at <www.nohsc.gov.au/nationalstrategy>.

Commonwealth of Australia 2004, *The National Drug Strategy: Australia's Integrated Framework 2004–2009*, Ministerial Council on Drug Strategy, Australian Government, Canberra.

Commonwealth of Australia 2008, *Social Inclusion: Origins, Concepts and Key Themes*, Australian Institute of Family Studies, Australian Government, Canberra.

Commonwealth of Australia 2009, *Australia's Global HIV/AIDS Initiative*, AusAID, Australian Government, Canberra.

Commonwealth of Australia 2010, *Australia to 2050: Future Challenges, Intergenerational Report: Overview*, Commonwealth of Australia, Canberra.

Commonwealth/State Working Party on Nursing Home Standards 1988, Development of Resident Classification System, unpublished paper.

Consensus Development Conference 1984, 'Coronary artery bypass grafting', *British Medical Journal*, vol. 289, pp. 1527–9.

Consumers' Health Forum 1987, *A Consumer Focussed Medical Education, Submission to the Commonwealth Government Inquiry into Medical Education and the Medical Workforce*, Consumers' Health Forum, Canberra.

Costa, C 1988, letter to the editor, *The Sydney Morning Herald*, 8 June, p. 19.

Council of Australian Governments 2007a, *National Healthcare Agreement*, Council of Australian Governments, Canberra.

Council of Australian Governments 2007b, *National Action Plan for Mental Health 2006–2011: Progress Report 2006–07*, Australian Health Ministers' Advisory Council, Canberra.Coxhead, J 1992, 'Nurse practitioners: Breaking new ground', *The Lamp*, September, pp. 27–32.

Council of Australian Governments 2013, About COAG, accessed at www.coag.gov.au/about_coag.

Coxhead, J 1992, 'Nurse practitioners: Breaking new ground', *The Lamp, September*, pp. 27–32.

Crawford, R 1977, 'You are dangerous to your health: The ideology and politics of victim blaming', *International Journal of Health Services*, vol. 7, pp. 663–80.

Crethar, M, Phillips, J, Stafford, P & Duckett, SJ 2009, 'Leadership transformation in Queensland Health', *Australian Health Review*, vol. 33. no. 3, pp. 357–64.

Crichton, A 1990, *Slowly Taking Control? Australian Governments and Health Care Provision, 1788–1988*, Allen & Unwin, Sydney.

Crichton, A 1998, 'Children of a common mother: A comparative analysis of the Australian and Canadian health care systems to 1995', *Australian Studies in Health Service Administration*, no. 83, School of Health Services Management, University of New South Wales, Sydney.

Culyer, A 1971, 'The nature of the commodity "health care" and its efficient allocation', *Oxford Economic Papers*, vol. 23, pp. 189–211.

Culyer, A 1980, *The Political Economy of Social Policy*, Martin Robertson, Oxford.

Culyer, A & Evans RG 1996, 'Mark Pauly on welfare economics: Normative rabbits from positive hats', *Journal of Health Economics*, vol. 15, pp. 243–51.

Culyer, A & Horesberger, B 1982, *Economic Medical Evaluation and Health Care Technologies*, Springer-Verlag, Berlin.

Cuthbert, M, Duffield, C & Hope, J 1992, *Management in Nursing*, Harcourt Brace Jovanovich, Sydney.

Daly, J & Willis, E 1987, 'The social relations of medical technology: Implications for technology assessment and health policy', in J Daly, K Green & E Willis (eds), *Technologies in Health Care: Policies and Politics*, Australian Government Publishing Service, Canberra.

Daniel, A 1983, *Power, Privilege and Prestige*, Longman Cheshire, Melbourne.

Daniels, N 1985, *Just Health Care*, Cambridge University Press, Cambridge.

Davies, PK 2010, 'Divisions of general practice: will they transform or die?' *Medical Journal of Australia*, vol. 193, pp. 75–77.

Davis, A & George, J 1993, *States of Health: Health and Illness in Australia*, 2nd edition, Harper and Row, Sydney.

Davis, G, Wanna, J, Warhurst, J & Weller, P 1988, *Public Policy in Australia*, Allen & Unwin, Sydney.

Davis, J, Andrews, S, Broom, DH, Gray, G & Renwick, M 1996, *Changing Society for Women's Health: Proceedings of the Third National Women's Health Conference, 17–19 November 1995*, Australian Government Publishing Service, Canberra.

Day, P & Klein, R 1992, 'Constitutional and distributional conflict in British medical politics: The case of general practice, 1911–91', *Political Studies*, vol. 11, no. 3, pp. 462–78.

Deeble, J 1986, 'Comment on the economics and financing of hospitals in Australia', *The Australian Economic Review*, 3rd quarter, pp. 73–4.

Deeble, J 1987, 'Health care under universal insurance: The first three years of Medicare', unpublished paper presented to the Australian Medical Writers' Association, Canberra.

Deeble, J 1988, 'Contribution for health insurance forum', in JRG Butler and DP Doessel (eds), 'Economics and health, 1987', *Australian Studies in Health Service Administration*, no. 63, University of New South Wales, Sydney.

Deeble, J 1991, *Medical Services through Medicare*, Background Paper no. 2, National Health Strategy, Melbourne.

Deeble, J 1999, *Resource Allocation in Public Health: An Economic Approach, a Background Discussion Paper for the National Public Health Partnership*, National Public Health Partnership, Melbourne.

Degeling, PJ 1995, 'The significance of "sectors" in calls for urban public health intersectoralism: An Australian perspective', *Policy and Politics*, vol. 23, no. 4, pp. 289–301.

Degeling, PJ, Baume, P & Jones, K 1993, 'Staging an official inquiry for policy change', *Policy and Politics*, vol. 21, no. 4, pp. 259–73.

den Exter, AP (ed.) 2008, *International Health Law. Solidarity and Justice in Health Care*, Maklu, Antwerp.

Department of Education, Science and Training 2006, *Commonwealth–State Agreement for Skilling Australia's Workforce*, Department of Education, Employment and Workforce Relations, Canberra.

Department of Health 2013, Plain packaging of tobacco products, accessed at <www .health.gov.au/internet/main/publishing.nsf/Content/tobacco-plain>.

Department of Health and Ageing 2007, *National Environmental Health Strategy 2007–2012*, Commonwealth Attorney General's Department, Canberra.

Department of Health and Ageing 2008a, *Audit and Health Workforce in Rural and Regional Australia*, Department of Health and Ageing, Canberra.

Department of Health and Ageing 2008b, *Enhanced Primary Care Program*, Department of Health and Ageing, Canberra.

Department of Health and Ageing 2008c, *Annual Report, 2007–08*, Department of Health and Ageing, Canberra.

Department of Health and Ageing 2009a, *National Mental Health Policy 2008: Foreword*, the Hon. Katy Gallagher MP, Department of Health and Ageing, Canberra.

Department of Health and Ageing 2009b, *Extended Aged Care at Home Packages*, Department of Health and Ageing, Australian Government, Canberra.

Department of Health and Ageing 2009c, *Review of Health Technology Assessment in Australia*, Department of Health and Ageing, Canberra.

Department of Health and Ageing 2010, *Annual Report, 2009–10*, Department of Health and Ageing, Canberra.

Department of Health and Ageing 2011, *Better Health, Better Care, Better Life. 30 Years Fighting HIV/AIDS, Annual Report 2010/11*, Commonwealth of Australia, Canberra.

Department of Health and Ageing 2012, *Living Longer. Living Better: Aged Care Reform Package*, Department of Health and Ageing, Canberra.

Department of Health and Ageing 2013, *National Mental Health Report 2013: Tracking Progress of Mental Health Reform in Australia 1993–2011*, Commonwealth of Australia, Canberra.

Department of Health and Ageing and Medicines Australia 2013, *Trends and Drivers of Pharmaceutical Benefits Scheme Expenditure; Report for the Access to Medicines Working Group*, Department of Health and Ageing, Canberra.

Department of Science, Education and Training 2006, *Commonwealth–State Agreement for Skilling Australia's Workforce*, Department of Education, Employment and Workforce Relations, Canberra.

DHA—see Department of Health and Ageing

Diers, D 1988, 'Nursing and shortages', unpublished paper prepared for the National Invitational Workshop on the Nursing Shortage, February, Washington DC.

Doessel, DP (ed.) 1990, *Towards Evaluation in General Practice: A Workshop on Vocational Registration*, Department of Community Services and Health, Canberra.

Doessel, DP (ed.) 1993, *The General Practice Evaluation Program: The 1992 Work-in-Progress Conference*, Australian Government Publishing Service, Canberra.

Donato, R & Scotton, R 1998, 'The Australian health care system', in G Mooney and R Scotton (eds), *Economics and Australian Health Policy*, Allen & Unwin, Sydney.

Downie, RS, Fyfe, C & Tannahill, A 1990, *Health Promotion: Models and Values*, Oxford University Press, Oxford.

Downs, A 1967, *Inside Bureaucracy*, Little, Brown, Boston.

Downs, A 1972, 'Up and down with ecology: The issue attention cycle', *The Public Interest*, vol. 28, pp. 38–50.

Doyal, L 1986, 'Promoting women's health', in E Kerby-Eaton and J Davies (eds), *Women's Health in a Changing Society*, vol. 1, conference proceedings, Adelaide.

Doyal, L & Pennell, I 1983, *The Political Economy of Health*, Pluto Press, London.

Draper, P, Griffiths, J, Dennis, J & Popay, J 1980, 'Three types of health education', *British Medical Journal*, vol. 281, pp. 493–5.

Drummond, MF, Stoddart, GL & Torrance, GW 1987, *Methods for Economic Evaluation of Health Care Programs*, Oxford University Press, Oxford.

Dubos, R 1960, *Mirage of Health*, Allen & Unwin, London.

Dubos, R 1968, *Man, Medicine and Environment*, Pall Mall, London.

Duckett, SJ 1984, 'Structural interests and Australian health policy', *Social Science and Medicine*, vol. 18, pp. 959–66.

Duckett, SJ 1992, 'Financing of health care', in H Gardner (ed.), *Health Policy: Development, Implementation and Evaluation in Australia*, Churchill Livingstone, Melbourne.

Duckett, SJ 1994, *Reform of Public Hospital Funding in Victoria*, Australian Studies in Health Service Administration Series, no. 77, School of Health Services Management, University of New South Wales, Sydney.

Duckett, SJ 1995, 'Hospital payment arrangements to encourage efficiency: The case of Victoria, Australia', *Health Policy*, vol. 34, pp. 113–34.

Duckett, SJ 1996, 'The new market in health care: Prospects for managed care in Australia', *Australian Health Review*, vol. 19, no. 2, pp. 7–22.

Duckett, SJ 1998a, 'Economics of hospital care', in G Mooney and R Scotton (eds), *Economics and Australian Health Policy*, Allen & Unwin, Sydney.

Duckett, SJ 1998b, 'Casemix funding for acute hospital inpatient services in Australia', *Medical Journal of Australia*, vol. 169 (supplement), pp. S17–S21.

Duckett, SJ 2004, 'The Australian Health Care Agreements', *Australian and New Zealand Health Policy*, vol. 1, no. 5.

Duckett, SJ 2005a, 'Private care and public waiting', *Australian Health Review*, vol. 29, no. 1, pp. 87–93.

Duckett, SJ 2005b, 'Living in the parallel universe in Australia: Public Medicare and private hospitals', *Canadian Medical Association Journal*, vol. 173, pp. 745–7.

Duckett, SJ 2005c, 'Australia', in R Gould (ed.), *Comparative Health Policy on Asia–Pacific*, Maidenhead, Open University Press, pp. 91–121.

Duckett, SJ 2007, 'A new approach to clinical governance in Queensland', *Australian Health Review*, vol. 31 (suppl. 1), pp. 515–19.

Duckett, SJ 2008a, 'Design of price incentives for adjunct policy goals in formula funding for hospitals and health services', *BMC Health Services Research*, vol. 8, p. 72.

Duckett, SJ 2008b, 'The continuing contest of values in the Australian health care system', in AP den Exter (ed.), *International Health Law Solidarity and Justice in Health Care*, pp. 177–89.

Duckett, SJ 2009a, 'Are we ready for the next big thing?', *Medical Journal of Australia*, vol. 190, no. 12, pp. 687–8.

Duckett, SJ 2009b, 'Transforming clinical governance in Queensland Health', in J Healy and D Dugdale (eds), *Patient Safety First: Responsive Regulation in Health Care*, Allen & Unwin, Sydney.

Duckett, SJ 2009c, 'Casemix development and implementation in Australia', in JR Kimberly, G de Pouvourville and T d'Aunno (eds) (2009), *The Globalization of Managerial Innovation in Health Care*, Cambridge University Press, New York.

Duckett, SJ 2013, *Australia's Bad Drug Deal: High Pharmaceutical Prices*, Grattan Institute, Melbourne.

Duckett, SJ, Collins, J, Kemp, M & Walker, K 2008, 'An improvement focus in public reporting: The Queensland approach', *Medical Journal of Australia*, vol. 189, pp. 616–7.

Duckett, SJ, Coory, M & Sketcher-Barker, K 2007, 'Identifying variations in quality of care in Queensland hospitals?' *Medical Journal of Australia*, vol. 187, pp. 571–5.

Duckett, SJ, Daniels, S, Kamp, M, Stockwell, A, Walker, G & Ward, M 2008, 'Pay for performance in Australia: Queensland's new clinical practice improvement payment', *Journal of Health Services Research and Policy*, vol. 13, no. 3, pp. 174–7.

Duckett, SJ, Gray, L & Howe, A 1995, 'Designing a funding system for rehabilitation services', *Australian Health Review*, vo1. 18, no. 3, pp. 30–44.

Duckett, SJ & Jackson, T 2000, 'The new health insurance rebate: An inefficient way of assisting public hospitals', *Medical Journal of Australia*, vol. 172, pp. 439–44.

Duckett, SJ & Price, PM 1982, 'A Victorian comparison', Appendix B in GR Palmer and AG Stevenson (eds), *The Health Administration Workforce in New South Wales*, Australian Studies in Health Administration, no. 44, University of New South Wales, Sydney.

Duckett, SJ & Ward, M 2008, 'Developing "robust performance benchmarks" for the next Australian Health Care Agreement: The need for a new framework', *Australian and New Zealand Health Policy*, vol. 5, no 1.

Duckett, SJ & Willcox, S 2011, *The Australian Health Care System*, 4th edition, Oxford University Press, Melbourne.

Dugdale, P 2008, *Doing Health Policy in Australia*, Allen & Unwin, Sydney.

Duncan, P 1986, 'The Congress Alukura by the grandmother's law', *Health Issues*, August–September, pp. 17–20.

Dunt, D 1982, 'Recent mortality trends in the adult Australian population and its principal ethnic groupings', *Community Health Studies*, vol. vi, pp. 217–22.

Durham Smith, E 1987, 'Submission to inquiry on professional issues in nursing by Royal Australasian College of Surgeons', *RACS Bulletin*, July, pp. 5–7.

Dwyer, J 2004, 'Australian health system restructuring: What problem is being solved?' *Australia and New Zealand Health Policy*, vol. 1, pp. 1–6.

Dwyer, T, Pierce, JP, Frape, G, Chapman, S, Chamberlain, A & Burke, N 1986, 'Evaluation of the Sydney "Quit for Life" anti-smoking campaign', *Medical Journal of Australia*, vol. 144, pp. 344–7.

Dye, TR 1976, *Policy Analysis*, University of Alabama Press, Alabama.

Easton, D 1965a, *A Systems Analysis of Political Life*, John Wiley, New York.

Easton, D 1965b, *A Framework for Political Analysis*, Prentice Hall, New York.

Edelman, M 1964, *The Symbolic Uses of Politics*, University of Illinois Press, Urbana.

Edelman, M 1977, *Political Language: Words that Succeed and Politics that Fail*, Academic Press, New York.

Eide, A, Alfredsson, G, Melander, G, Rehof, LA & Rosas, A 1992, *The Universal Declaration of Human Rights: A Commentary*, Scandinavian University Press, Oslo.

Elling, RH 1986, *The Struggle for Workers' Health: A Study of Six Industrialised Countries*, Baywood, Farmingdale, New York.

Elshaug, AG, Hiller, JE, Tunis, SR & Moss, JR 2007, 'Challenges in Australian policy process for disinvestment from existing ineffective health care practices', *Australia and New Zealand Health Policy*, vol. 4, p. 23.

Enquiry into Hospital Services in South Australia 1983, *Report*, (Chairperson, S Sax), South Australian Health Commission, Adelaide.

Enthoven, A 1988, *Theory and Practice of Managed Competition in Health Care Finance*, Elsevier, Amsterdam.

Etzioni, A 1967, 'Mixed-scanning: A "third" approach to decision-making', *Public Administration Review*, vol. xxvii, pp. 385–92.

Evans, RG 1984, *Strained Mercy: The Economics of Canadian Health Care*, Butterworths, Toronto.

Evans, RG 1990, 'The dog in the night time: Medical practice variations and health policy', in TF Andersen and G Mooney, *The Challenge of Medical Practice Variations*, Macmillan, London.

Evans, RG 1998, 'Towards a healthier economics: Reflections on Ken Bassett's problem', in LM Barer, EG Thomas and GL Stoddart (eds), *Health, Healthcare and Health Economics*, John Wiley, Chichester.

Evans, RG & Stoddart, GL 1990, 'Producing health, consuming health care', *Social Science and Medicine*, vol. 31, no. 2, pp. 1347–63.

Evans, RG, Barer, LM & Marmor, TR (eds) 1994, *Why Are Some People Healthy and Others Not? The Determinants of Health of Populations*, Aldine De Gruyer, New York.

Facci, F, Seniuk, S & Vella, A 1986, 'Migrant women's health in the Illawarra: Service or disservice?', in E Kerby-Eaton and J Davies (eds), *Women's Health in a Changing Society*, vol. 2, conference proceedings, Adelaide.

Feldstein, MS 1973, 'The welfare loss of excess health insurance', *The Journal of Political Economy*, vol. 81, pp. 251–80.

Feldstein, MS & Gruber, J 1995, 'A major risk approach to health insurance reform', *Tax Policy and the Economy*, vol. 9, pp. 103–30.

Fetter, RB 1999, 'Casemix classification systems', *Australian Health Review*, vol. 22, no. 2, pp. 16–34.

Finch, J & Groves, D (eds) 1983, *A Labour of Love: Women, Work and Caring*, Routledge & Kegan Paul, London.

Fine, M 1987, 'The sad story of the regulation of private hospitals', *New Doctor*, Summer, no. 46, pp. 28–9.

Fine, M 1992, *Community Support Services and Their Users. The First Eighteen Months*, Reports and Proceedings no. 100, Social Policy Research Centre, University of New South Wales, Sydney.

Fine, M 2006, *A Caring Society? Care and the Dilemmas of Human Services in the 21st Century*, Palgrave Macmillan, Houndmills, Basingstoke.

Finkler, S 1979, 'Cost-effectiveness of regionalisation: The heart surgery example', *Inquiry*, vol. 16, pp. 264–70.

Fisher, ES, Wennberg, DE, Stukel, TA, Gottlieb, DJ, Lucas, FL & Pinder, EL 2003a, 'The implications of regional variations in Medicare spending. Part 1: The contents, quality and accessibility of care', *Annals of Internal Medicine*, vol. 138, pp. 273–87.

Fisher, ES, Wennberg, DE, Stukel, TA, Gottlieb, DJ, Lucas, FL & Pinder, EL 2003b, 'The implications of regional variations in Medicare spending. Part 2: Health outcomes and satisfaction with care', *Annals of Internal Medicine*, vol. 138, pp. 288–99.

Fisher, KR 2009, *Whose Values Shape Social Policy?: Policy Process Limits To Economic Rationalism*, VDM Verlag Dr Müller, Germany.

Fletcher, A 1986, 'The nursing problem detection study', *Australian Health Review*, vol. 9, pp. 78–81.

Foley, M 2000, 'The changing public/private balance', in A Bloom (ed.), *Health Reform in Australia and New Zealand*, Oxford University Press, Melbourne.

Forward, R (ed.) 1974, *Public Policy in Australia*, Cheshire, Melbourne.

Foucault, M 1967, *Madness and Civilization: A History of Insanity in the Age of Reason*, Tavistock, London.

Foucault, M 1972, *The Archaeology of Knowledge*, Tavistock, London.

Fox, KA, Poole-Wilson, PA, Henderson, RA, Clayton, TC, Chamberlain, DA, Shaw, TR, Wheatley, DJ, Pocock, SJ 2002, 'Interventional versus conservative treatment for patients with unstable angina or non-ST-elevation myocardial infarction: the British Heart Foundation RITA 3 randomised trial. Randomized Intervention Trial of unstable Angina', *The Lancet*, vol. 360, pp. 743–51.

Francis, R (Chairperson) 2013, *The Mid Staffordshire NHS Foundation Trust Public Inquiry, Final Report*, The Stationery Office, London.

Freidson, E 1961, *Patients' Views of Medical Practice*, Russell Sage, New York.

Freidson, E 1970a, *Profession of Medicine: A Study of the Sociology of Applied Knowledge*, Harper & Row, New York.

Freidson, E 1970b, *Professional Dominance: The Social Structure of Medical Care*, Aldine, Chicago.

Freidson, E. 2001, *Professionalism: The Third Logic*, University of Chicago, Chicago.

Fry, D 1987, 'The "new" public health', unpublished paper, Australian Community Health Association, Sydney.

Fry, D & King, L 1985, *National Community Health Accreditation and Standards Project: Final Report*, School of Public Health and Tropical Medicine, University of Sydney, Sydney.

Fry, D & Lennie, IG 1987, 'Review and accreditation of community health centres', *Australian Health Review*, vol. 10, pp. 29–33.

Fuchs, VR 1974, *Who Shall Live? Health, Economics, and Social Choice*, Basic, New York.

Fuchs, VR 1984, 'Though much is taken—Reflections on ageing, health and medical care', *Milbank Memorial Fund Quarterly*, vol. 62, pp. 143–55.

Fuchs, VR 2009, 'The proposed government health insurance company: No substitute for real reform', *The New England Journal of Medicine*, vol. 360, pp. 2273–5.

Furler, E 1986, 'Women and health: Radical prevention', in E Kerby-Eaton and J Davies (eds), *Women's Health in a Changing Society*, vol. 1, conference proceedings, Adelaide.

Garde, P & Wheeler, L 1985, *Hard Labour: The Community Services Industry*, NCOSS Issues Paper no. 5, Council of Social Service of New South Wales, Sydney.

Gardner, H (ed.) 1989, *The Politics of Health: The Australian Experience*, Churchill Livingstone, Melbourne.

Gardner, H (ed.) 1992, *Health Policy: Development, Implementation and Evaluation in Australia*, Churchill Livingstone, Melbourne.

Gardner, H (ed.) 1997, *Health Policy in Australia*, Oxford University Press, Melbourne.

Gardner, H & McCoppin, B 1989, 'Emerging militancy? The politicisation of Australian allied health professionals', in H Gardner (ed.), *The Politics of Health: The Australian Experience*, Churchill Livingstone, Melbourne.

Garling, P 2008, *Final Report of the Special Commission of Inquiry: Acute Care Services in NSW Public Hospitals*, NSW Government, Sydney.

Geyman, J 2008, *The Corrosion of Medicine. Can the Profession Reclaim its Moral Legacy?*, Common Courage Press, Maine.

Gibson, D, Turrell, G & Jenkins, A 1993, 'Regulation and reform: Promoting residents' rights in Australian nursing homes', *Australian & New Zealand Journal of Sociology*, vol. 29, no. 1, pp. 73–91.

Gifford, S 1986, 'Better health for groups at risk: Special needs or basic rights?', *Community Health Studies*, vol. x, pp. 411–14.

Gifford, S 1988, *A Review of Post-graduate Public Health Training in Australia*, Public Health Association of Australia and New Zealand, Canberra.

Gillespie, JA 1991, *The Price of Health: Australian Governments and Medical Politics 1910–1960*, Cambridge University Press, Cambridge.

Gillett, S, Parslow R, Scoles D, & Renwick, M 1991, *Hospital Utilisation and Cost Study, 1987–88*, Australian Institute of Health: Health Services Series no. 1, Australian Government Publishing Service, Canberra.

Glover, JA 2008, 'The incidence of tonsillectomy in school children', *International Journal of Epidemiology*, vol. 37, pp. 9–19.

Glover, JA & Woollacott, T 1992, *A Social Health Atlas of Australia*, cat. no. 4385.0, Australian Bureau of Statistics, Canberra.

Goffman, E 1968, *Asylums*, Penguin, Harmondsworth.

Goldacre, B 2013, *Bad Pharma: How Drug Companies Mislead Doctors and Harm Patients*, Fourth Estate, London.

Gonczi, A, Hager, P & Oliver, L 1990, *Establishing Competency-based Standards in the Professions*, Australian Government Publishing Service, Canberra.

Gracie, WA & Ransohoff, DF 1982, 'The natural history of silent gallstones', *New England Journal of Medicine*, vol. 307, pp. 798–800.

Grant, C 1991, 'Accreditation, evaluation, and review in Australian programs: The end of the beginning?', *Journal of Health Service Administration Education*, vol. 9, no. 2 (Spring), pp. 181–90.

Grant, C & Lapsley, HM 1993, 'The Australian Health Care System, 1992', *Australian Studies in Health Service Administration*, no. 75.

Grassby, A 1973, *A Multi-Cultural Society for the Future, Immigration Reference Paper*, Commonwealth Department of Immigration, Australian Government Publishing Service, Canberra.

Graves, EJ & Kozak, LJ 1998, 'National hospital discharge survey: Annual summary 1996', *Vital Health Statistics*, vol. 13, no. 140, p. 6.

Gray, G 2004, *The Politics of Medicare: Who Gets What, When and How*, UNSW Press, Sydney.

Gray Jamieson, G 2013, 'Reaching for Health', *Australian Health Review*, vol. 37, CSIRO Publishing.

Graycar, A (ed.) 1978, *Perspectives in Australian Social Policy*, Macmillan, Melbourne.

Green, J & Thorogood, N 1998, *Analysing Health Policy: Sociological Approaches*, Longman, New York.

Greenberg, G 2013, *The Book of Woe: The DSM and the Unmaking of Psychiatry*, Penguin, New York.

Gregory, RG 1993, *Review of the Structure of Nursing Home Funding Arrangements, Stage 1*, Aged and Community Care Service Development and Evaluation Reports, no. 11, Australian Government Publishing Service, Canberra.

Gregory, RG 1994, *Review of the Structure of Nursing Home Funding Arrangements, Stage 2*, Aged and Community Care Service Development and Evaluation Reports, no. 12, Australian Government Publishing Service, Canberra.

Groenewegen, P 1979, *Public Finance in Australia: Theory and Practice*, Prentice Hall, Sydney.

Gruszin, S, Hetzel, D & Glover, J 2012, *Advocacy and Action in Public Health: Lessons from Australia over the 20th Century*, Australian National Preventive Health Agency, Canberra.

Guyatt, G, Drummond, M, Feeny, D, Tugwell, P, Stoddart, G, Haynes, RB, Bennett, K & Labelle, R 1986, 'Guidelines for clinical and economic evaluation of health care technologies', *Social Science and Medicine*, vol. 22, pp. 393–408.

Hadler, N 2008, *Worried Sick, a Prescription for Health in an Overtreated America*, University of North Carolina Press, Chapel Hill.

Hailey, DM 1995, 'Health Care Technology in Australia', in US Congress, Office of Technology Assessment, *Health Care Technology and its Assessment in Eight Countries*, pp. 19–55.

Hall, J & Masters, G 1986, 'Measuring outcomes of health services: A review of some available measures', *Community Health Studies*, vol. x, pp. 147–55.

Ham, C 1999, *Health Policy in Britain: The Politics and Organisation of the National Health Service*, 4th edition, Macmillan, London.

Ham, C & Hill, M 1993, *The Policy Process in the Modern Capitalist State*, 2nd edition, Harvester Wheatsheaf, Hemel Hemstead.

Ham, C & Towell, D 1985, 'Policy theory and policy practice: An encounter in the field of health service management development', *Policy and Politics*, vol. 13, pp. 431–45.

Hamblin, R 2007, 'Publishing "Quality" measures: How it works and when it does not', *International Journal of Quality Health Care*, vol. 19, pp. 183–6.

Hambly, M 1989, *Healthy Cities in Canberra: Report of Project*, Healthy Cities Canberra, Canberra.

Hancock, L (ed.) 1999a, *Health Policy in the Market State*, Allen & Unwin, Sydney.

Hancock, L 1999b, 'Policy, power and interests', in L Hancock (ed.), *Health Policy in the Market State*, Allen & Unwin, Sydney.

Hand, G 1987, *Foundations for the Future: Policy Statement*, Australian Government Publishing Service, Canberra.

Hansson, J, Körner, U, Khorram-Manesh, A, Solberg, A & Lundholm, K 2009, 'Randomised clinical trial of antibiotic therapy versus appendicectomy as primary treatment of acute appendicitis in selected patients', *British Journal of Surgery*, vol. 96, pp. 476–81.

Harris, E, Sainsbury, P and Nutbeam, D (eds) 1999, *Perspectives on Health Inequity*, Centre for Health Equity, Training, Research and Evaluation, Social Health Research Unit and the Australian Centre of Health Promotion, Sydney.

Harris, M, Maddern, J & Pegg, S 1998, *The Changing Roles and Careers of Australian and New Zealand Health Service Managers*, College Monograph no. 6, Australian College of Health Service Executives, Sydney.

Hart, N 1982, 'Is capitalism bad for your health?', *The British Journal of Sociology*, vol. 33, pp. 435–43.

Harvey, R 1985, 'Submission to the Industries Assistance Commission Inquiry into Pharmaceutical Products', unpublished paper, Canberra.

Harvey, R 1991, *Making it Better. Strategies for Improving the Effectiveness and Quality of Health Services in Australia*, Background Paper no. 8, National Health Strategy, Melbourne.

Hayes, A, Gray, M & Edwards, B 2008, *Social Inclusion: Origins, Concepts and Key Themes*, Australian Institute of Family Studies, Department of the Prime Minister and Cabinet, Canberra.

Haywood, S & Alaszewski, A 1980, *Crisis in the Health Service: The Politics of Management*, Croom Helm, London.

Health and Medical Research Strategic Review 1999, *The Virtuous Cycle: Working Together for Health and Medical Research*, AusInfo, Canberra.

Health Insurance Commission 1999, *Quarterly Report, September 1999*, Health Insurance Commission, Canberra.

Health Issues Centre 1986, *Medical Business Entrepreneurial Style*, Health Issues Centre, Melbourne.

Health Targets and Implementation (Health for All) Committee 1988, *Health for All Australians, Report of the Health Targets Committee to Australian Health Ministers*, Australian Government Publishing Service, Canberra.

Health Workforce Australia 2012, *Health Workforce 2025*, HWA, Adelaide.

Health Workforce Australia 2013, *Australia's Health Workforce Series - Health Workforce by Numbers*, Health Workforce Australia, Adelaide.

Healthcover 1999, vol. 9, no. 2, pp. 1–2.

Healthsharing Women 1990, *The Health-sharing Reader: Women Speak About Health*, Pandora, Sydney.

Healthsharing Women 1991, *Women and Surgery 1990: Conference Proceedings*, Healthsharing Women, Melbourne.

Healthy Cities Australia 1992, *Healthy Cities Australia: Starting Out*, Australian Community Health Association, Sydney.

Healy, D 2012, *Pharmageddon*, University of California Press, Berkeley and Los Angeles.

Healy, J & Dugdale, D (eds) 2009, *Patient Safety First: Responsive Regulation in Health Care*, Allen & Unwin, Sydney.

Healy, J, Sharman, E & Lokuge, B 2006, *Australia: Health System Review 2006*, World Health Organization, Regional Office for Europe 2006, Copenhagen.

Heclo, H 1972, 'Review article: Policy analysis', *British Journal of Political Science*, vol. 2, pp. 83–108.

Heilscher, LA 1980, 'Cost control in Queensland hospitals', in RL Mathews (ed.), *Hospital Funding*, Australian National University, Canberra.

Herdman, E 1998, 'Knowledge without power: The professionalisation of nursing', in H Keleher and F McInerney (eds), *Nursing Matters: Critical Sociological Perspectives*, Churchill Livingstone, Sydney.

Hertzman, C 1999, 'Population health and human development', in DP Keating and C Hertzman (eds), *Developmental Health and the Wealth of Nations: Social, Biological and Educational Dynamics*, The Guilford Press, New York, pp. 21–40.

Hetzel, B & McMichael, A 1987, *The LS Factor: Lifestyle and Health*, Penguin, Melbourne.

Hiatt, HH 1987, *America's Health in the Balance: Choice or Chance?*, Harper & Row, New York.

Hicks, N 1988, 'Medical education inquiry', *In Touch*, Newsletter of the Public Health Association of Australia and New Zealand, vol. 5, pp. 2–4.

Higgins, E 1989, 'The true impact of environmental studies', *The Weekend Australian*, 16–17 December, p. 29.

Hill, M 1997, *The Policy Process in the Modern State*, 3rd edition, Prentice Hall/ Harvester Wheatsheaf, Hemel Hempstead.

Hill, M (ed.) 1997, *The Policy Process: A Reader*, 2nd edition, Prentice Hall/Harvester Wheatsheaf, Hemel Hempstead.

Hill, M 2013, *The Public Policy Process*, 5th edition, Pearson Education, Harlow.

Hills, B 1989, *Blue Murder*, Sun Books, Melbourne.

Hirsh, NA & Hailey, DM 1992, *Minimum Access Surgery*, Australian Institute of Health, Canberra.

Hogan, W 2004, *Review of Pricing Arrangements in Residential Aged Care*, Commonwealth of Australia, Canberra.

Hogwood, BW & Gunn, LA 1984, *Policy Analysis for the Real World*, Oxford University Press, Oxford.

Holst, E 1997, 'The role of health professionals in promoting human rights', *Human Rights and Health Professionals: Towards an Education Program for the Asian Region*, Psychosocial Trauma and Human Rights Program, Centre for Integrative and Development Studies at the University of the Philippines, Quezon.

Holtzman, N 1979, 'Prevention: rhetoric and reality', *International Journal of Health Services*, vol. 9, pp. 25–39.

Horsley, P, Tremellen, S & Hancock, L 1999, 'Women's health in a changing state', in L Hancock (ed.), *Health Policy in the Market State*, Allen & Unwin, Sydney.

Hospitals and Health Services Commission 1973, *Report on a Community Health Program for Australia*, Australian Government Publishing Service, Canberra.

Hospitals and Health Services Commission 1974, *A Report on Hospitals in Australia*, Australian Government Publishing Service, Canberra.

Houston, S & Legge, D 1992, 'Aboriginal health research and the National Aboriginal Health Strategy' (editorial), *Australian Journal of Public Health*, vol. 16, pp. 114–5.

Howe, AL 1983, 'Commonwealth expenditure on nursing home care: An analysis of interstate variations and the case for equalisation', *Social Security Journal*, December, pp. 24–35.

Howe, AL 1992, 'Participation in policy making: the case of aged care', in H Gardner (ed.), *Health Policy: Development, Implementation and Evaluation in Australia*, Churchill Livingstone, Melbourne.

Howe, AL 1998, 'The economics of aged care: Achieving quality and containing costs', in G Mooney and R Scotton (eds), *Economics and Australian Health Policy*, Allen & Unwin, Sydney.

Howe, AL & Preston, GAN 1985, *A Comparative Analysis of Nursing Home Patient Populations in Australia*, Occasional Paper in Gerontology, National Research Institute of Gerontology and Geriatric Medicine, Melbourne.

HREOC—see Human Rights and Equal Opportunity Commission

Hsiao, WC, Braun, P, Yntema, D & Becker, ER 1988, 'Estimating physicians' work for a resource-based relative-value scale', *New England Journal of Medicine*, vol. 319, no. 13, pp. 835–41.

Human Rights and Equal Opportunity Commission 1993, *Human Rights and Mental Illness: Report of the National Inquiry into the Human Rights of People with Mental Illness*, vols. 1 and 2, Australian Government Publishing Service, Canberra.

Human Rights and Equal Opportunity Commission 1997, *Bringing them Home, National Inquiry into the Separation of Aboriginal and Torres Strait Islander Children from Their Families*, Human Rights and Equal Opportunity Commission, Sydney.

Hunter, P 1999, 'The national Aboriginal community controlled health organisation', *New Doctor*, Summer, pp. 11–12.

Husband, E 1985, 'Role of the CT scanner in the management of cancer', *British Medical Journal*, vol. 290, pp. 527–9.

Hutton, B 1986, 'Revolution in our hospitals', *The Age*, 12 November, p. 28.

Industries Assistance Commission 1986, *Report: Pharmaceutical Products*, Australian Government Publishing Service, Canberra.

Industry Commission 1996, *The Pharmaceutical Industry*, Australian Government Publishing Service, Melbourne.

Industry Commission 1997, *Private Health Insurance*, Industry Commission, Canberra.

Ingleby, D (ed.) 1981, *Critical Psychiatry: The Politics of Mental Health*, Penguin, Harmondsworth.

Iredale, R 1988, 'Wasted skills: Recognition of overseas qualified health practitioners', paper presented to the National Ethnic Health Policy Conference, April, Adelaide.

Jackson, CL 2013, 'Our first National Primary Health Care Strategy: 3 years on, what change for general practice?', *Medical Journal of Australia*, vol. 198, no. 11, pp. 581–2.

Jackson, T 1990, 'Review of health care and public policy', *Journal of Health Politics, Policy and Law*, vol. 15, pp. 677–9.

Jackson, T 2007, 'Health technology assessment in Australia: Challenges ahead', *Medical Journal of Australia*, vol. 187, pp. 262–4.

Jackson, T & Sevil, P 1997, 'Problems in counting and paying for multidisciplinary outpatient clinics', *Australian Health Review*, vol. 20, no. 3, pp. 38–59.

Jacobson, B & Yen, L 1998, 'Health action zones—Offer the possibility of radical ideas which need rigorous evaluation', *British Medical Journal*, vol. 316, p. 165.

Jago, H 1982, 'How Sydney Hospital has survived to fight today', *Sydney Morning Herald*, 5 May, p. 30.

Jennett, B 1986, *High Technology Medicine: Benefits and Burdens*, Oxford University Press, Oxford.

Johnson, T 1972, *Professions and Power*, Macmillan, London.

Johnstone, R 2008, *Harmonising Occupational Health and Safety Regulation in Australia: the First Report of the National OHS Review*, Working Paper 61, Regulatory Institutions Network, Australian National University, Canberra.

Kakwani, N 1977, 'Measurement of tax progressivity: An international comparison', *Economic Journal*, vol. 87, pp. 71–80.

Kaplan, L 1992, 'Healthy cities in Australia', in J Ashton (ed.), *Healthy Cities*, Open University Press, Buckingham.

Karmel, R & Braun, P 2004, *Statistical Linkage across Aged Care Programs: An Exploratory Example*, Australian Institute of Health and Welfare, Canberra.

Kasper, W 2009, *Radical Surgery: The Only Cure for New South Wales Hospitals*, Centre for Independent Studies, Sydney.

Keen, S 2001, *Debunking Economics. The Naked Emperor of the Social Sciences*, Pluto Press Australia, Sydney.

Keens, C, Graycar, A & Harrison, J 1983, 'Ageing and community care', *New Doctor, Impact and Social Alternatives*, Joint Issue, September–October, pp. 23–8.

Kelly, JG, Chiarella, M & Maxwell, C 1993, 'Nurse practitioners: A new direction for health care delivery', *Healthcover*, April–May, pp. 24–9.

Kelly, P 1992, *The End of Certainty: The Story of the 1980s*, Allen & Unwin, Sydney.

Kelly, P 1994, *The End of Certainty: Power, Politics and Business in Australia*, Allen & Unwin, Sydney.

Kerby-Eaton, E & Davies, J (eds) 1986a, *Women's Health in a Changing Society*, vol. 1, conference proceedings, Adelaide.

Kerby-Eaton, E & Davies, J (eds) 1986b, *Women's Health in a Changing Society*, vol. 2, conference proceedings, Adelaide.

Kerby-Eaton, E & Davies, J (eds) 1986c, *Women's Health in a Changing Society*, vol. 3, conference proceedings, Adelaide.

Kern, A 1986, 'Health for All by the year 2000: Setting the scene in Australia 1985', in E Kerby-Eaton and J Davies (eds), *Women's Health in a Changing Society*, vol. 3, conference proceedings, Adelaide.

Kidd, MR 2009, 'What impact will the Australian Government's proposed national health care reforms have on Australian general practice?', *The Medical Journal of Australia*, vol. 191, no. 2, pp. 55–7.

Kimberly, JR & Zajac, EJ 1985, 'Strategic adaptation in health care organisations: Implications for theory and research', *Medical Care Review*, vol. 42, pp. 267–302.

Kimberly, JR, de Pouvourville, G & d'Aunno, T (eds) 2008, *The Globalization of Managerial Innovation in Health Care*, Cambridge University Press, New York.

King, V & Short, LM 1999, 'Overcoming geographic barriers through contemporary education of allied oral health professionals', *Proceedings of 5th National Rural Health Conference, Leaping the Boundary Fence–Using Evidence and Collaboration to Build Healthier Rural Communities*, Adelaide Convention Centre, Adelaide.

Kinnear, D & Graycar, A 1983, 'Non-institutional care of elderly people', in A Graycar (ed.), *Retreat from the Welfare State: Australian Social Policy in the 1980s*, Allen & Unwin, Sydney.

Klein, R 1983, *The Politics of the National Health Service*, Longman, London.

Klein, R 2009, 'Learning from others and learning from mistakes: Reflections on health policy making', in TR Marmor, R Freeman and KGH Okma, (eds), *Comparative Studies and the Politics of Modern Medical Care*, Yale University Press, New Haven.

Klein, R & Marmor, T 2008, 'Reflections on policy analysis: Putting it together again', in M Moran, M Rein and R Goodin (eds), *The Oxford Handbook of Public Policy*, Oxford University Press, Oxford.

Kringas, P 1984, 'Really educating migrant children', in J Jupp (ed.), *Ethnic Politics*, Allen & Unwin, Sydney.

Kuhse, H & Singer, P 1985, *Should the Baby Live? The Problem of Handicapped Infants*, Oxford University Press, Oxford.

Kunitz, SJ 1994, *Disease and Social Diversity: The European Impact on the Health of non-Europeans*, Oxford University Press, New York.

Kunitz, SJ & Brady, M 1995, 'Health care policy for Aboriginal Australians: The relevance of the American Indian experience', *The Australian and New Zealand Journal of Public Health*, vol. 19, pp. 549–58.

Kunz, E 1975, *The Intruders: Refugee Doctors in Australia*, Australian National University Press, Canberra.

Labonte, R 1992, 'Heart health inequalities in Canada: Models, theory and planning', *Health Promotion International*, vol. 7, pp. 119–28.

Laing, RD & Esterson, A 1970, *Sanity, Madness and the Family*, Penguin, Harmondsworth.

Lapsley, H 2000, 'Quality measures in Australian health care', in A Bloom (ed.), *Health Reform in Australia and New Zealand*, Oxford University Press, Melbourne.

Lawrence, J 1965, *Professional Social Work in Australia*, Australian National University Press, Canberra.

Lawson, J, Brown, JH & Oliver, TI 1978, 'The dental health revolution: The dramatic improvement in dental health of school children in the northern metropolitan region of New South Wales', *Medical Journal of Australia*, vol. 1, pp. 124–5.

Leape, LL 1989, 'Unnecessary surgery', *Health Services Research*, vol. 24, pp. 351–407.

Leary, WE 1995, 'Congress's science agency prepares to close its doors', *The New York Times*, 14 September, p. 26.

Leeder, S 1999, *Healthy Medicine: Challenges Facing Australia's Health Services*, Allen & Unwin, Sydney.

Lees, M 1993, '"Time for a little leadership from Labor" says Democrats', *Healthcover*, vol. 3, no. 2, pp. 8, 10–11.

Legorreta, A, Silber, JH, Constatino, G, Kobylinski, RW & Zatz, SL 1993, 'Increased cholecystectomy rate after the introduction of laparoscopic cholecystectomy', *Journal of the American Medical Association*, vol. 270, no. 12, pp. 1429–32.

Le Grand, J 1982, *The Strategy for Equality: Redistribution and the Social Services*, Allen & Unwin, London.

Le Grand, J, Mays, N & Mulligan, J 1998, *Learning from the NHS Internal Market*, King's Fund, London.

Lewis, D 1993, 'Smoking and shopping: Not in these malls', *The Sydney Morning Herald*, 13 January, p. 1.

Lewis, JM 2005, *Health Policy and Politics: Networks, Ideas and Power*, IP Communications, Melbourne.

Lewis, MJ 2003, *The People's Health*, Praeger, Westport.

Liang, Z 2008, *Health Reforms and Australian Senior Health Executive Workforce: Characteristics, Competencies and Challenges*, VDM Verlag, Saarbrücken.

Liang, Z, Short, SD & Brown, CR 2006, 'Characteristics and employment status of senior health managers in the 1980s, 1990s, and early 21st Century: Implication for future research and education development', *The International Journal of Health Administration*, vol. 23, no. 3, pp. 281–302.

Liang, Z, Short, SD, Howard, PF & Brown, CR 2006, 'Centralised control and devolved responsibilities: Personal experiences of top-level health executives on the implementation of area health management model in NSW 1986–99', *Asia Pacific Journal of Health Management*, vol. 1, no. 2, pp. 44–50.

Liberal Party of Australia 1991, *Fightback! It's Your Australia: The Way to Rebuild and Reward Australia*, Liberal and National Parties, Canberra.

Lichner, EA & Planz, M 1971, 'Appendicectomy in the Federal Republic of Germany: Epidemiology and medical care patterns', *Medical Care*, vol. 9, pp. 311–18.

Lim, J & McKean, MC 2009, 'Adenotonsillectomy for obstructive sleep apnoea in children', *Cochrane Database of Systematic Reviews*, Issue 2. Art. no.: CD003136.

Lin, V 2013, Universal Health Coverage, WHO Western Pacific Regional Office at Deeble Institute Symposium 2013, Australian Healthcare and Hospitals Association, Canberra.

Lin, V & Duckett, SJ 1997, 'Structural interests and organisational dimensions of health system reform', in H Gardner (ed.), *Health Policy in Australia*, Oxford University Press, Melbourne, pp. 64–80.

Lin, V & King, C 2000, 'Intergovernmental reforms in public health', in A Bloom (ed.), *Health Reform in Australia and New Zealand*, Oxford University Press, Melbourne.

Lin, V, Smith, J & Fawkes, S 2007, *Public Health Practice in Australia: The Organised Effort*, Allen & Unwin, Sydney.

Lindblom, CE 1968, *The Policy-making Process*, Prentice Hall, New Jersey.

Lindsay, CM 1986, *Policies and Prescriptions: Current Directions in Health Policy*, Centre for Independent Studies, Sydney.

Lofgren, H 2002, *Generic Drugs. International Trends and Policy Developments in Australia*, working paper, Melbourne Centre for Strategic Economic Studies, Melbourne.

Loughnane, B 2013, *The Coalition's Policy to Support Australia's Health System*, Liberal and National parties, Canberra, available at <www.liberal.org.au/latest-news/2013/08/22/tony-abbott-coalitions-policy-support-australias-health-system>.

Lowi, T 1964, 'American business, public policy, case-studies and political theory', *World Politics*, vol. 16, pp. 677–715.

Luft, H 1981, *Health Maintenance Organisations: Dimensions of Performance*, John Wiley, New York.

Luft, H, Bunker, JP & Enthoven, AC 1979, 'Should operations be regionalised? The empirical relation between surgical volume and mortality', *New England Journal of Medicine*, vol. 301, pp. 1364–9.

Luft, H 1980, 'Assessing the evidence on HMO performance', *Milbank Memorial Fund Quarterly, Health and Society*, vol. 58, pp. 501–36.

Lugon, M & Secker-Walker, J 1999, *Clinical Governance: Making it Happen*, Royal Society of Medicine, London.

Lukes, S 1974, *Power: A Radical View*, Macmillan, London.

Lupton, GM & Najman, JM (eds) 1995, *Sociology of Health and Illness: Australian Readings*, 2nd edition, Macmillan, Melbourne.

McCallum, J, Matiasz, S & Graycar, A 1990, *Abuse of the Elderly at Home: The Range of the Problem*, Joint Publication of the National Centre for Epidemiology and Population Health, Australian National University, Canberra, and Office of the Commissioner for the Ageing, Adelaide.

McClelland, A 1991, *In Fair Health? Equity and the Health System*, Background Paper no. 3, National Health Strategy, Melbourne.

McClure, W 1982, 'Toward development and application of a qualitative theory of hospital utilisation', *Inquiry*, vol. 19, pp. 117–35.

MacDonald, JJ 2005, *Environments for Health: A Salutogenic Approach*, Earthscan, London.

McEwin, R & Ring, I 1979, 'Factors affecting health service usage', Proceedings of the 12th Scientific Meeting of the Royal Australian College Of Medical Administrators, Royal Australian College of Medical Administrators, Melbourne.

McGuire, A, Henderson, J & Mooney, G 1988, *The Economics of Health Care: An Introductory Text*, Routledge & Kegan Paul, London.

McHarg, M 1984, 'Nurses seek new order', *Australian Hospital*, no. 86, June, p. 1.

McKeown, T 1976, *The Modern Rise of Population*, Elsevier, London.

McKeown, T 1979, *The Role of Medicine: Dream, Mirage or Nemesis?*, Basil Blackwell, Oxford.

McKinlay, JB 1981, 'From promising report to standard procedure: Seven stages in the career of a medical innovation', *Milbank Memorial Fund Quarterly Health and Society*, vol. 59, pp. 374–411.

McLean, J & Walsh, MK 2003, 'Lessons from the Inquiry into Obstetrics and Gynaecology Services at King Edward Memorial Hospital 1990–2000', *Australian Health Review*, vol. 26, pp. 12–23.

Macklin, J 1990, *The National Health Strategy: Setting the Agenda for Change*, Background Paper no. 1, National Health Strategy, Melbourne.

McMichael, AJ 1985, 'Social class (as estimated by occupational prestige) and mortality in Australian males in the 1970s', *Community Health Studies*, vol. ix, pp. 220–30.

McNair, P & Duckett, SJ 2002, 'Funding Victoria's public hospitals: The casemix policy of 2000–2001', *Australian Health Review*, vol. 25, pp. 72–98.

McNamara, P 2005, 'Quality-based payment: Six case examples', *International Journal for Quality in Health Care*, vol. 17. pp. 357–62.

McPherson, K 2008, 'Commentary on Glover and tonsillectomy. Health care variations then and now', *International Journal of Epidemiology*, vol. 3, no. 1, pp. 14–23.

McPherson, K & Bunker, JP 2007, 'Cost, risks and benefits of surgery: A milestone in the development of health service research', *Journal of the Royal Society of Medicine*, vol. 100, pp. 387–90.

McPherson, K, Wennberg, JE, Hovind, OB & Clifford, P 1982, 'Small area variations in the use of common surgical procedures: An international comparison of New England, England and Norway', *New England Journal of Medicine*, vol. 307, pp. 1310–14.

Mahler, H 1981, 'The meaning of "Health for All by the year 2000"', *World Health Forum*, vol. 2, pp. 5–22.

Marmor, TR 1973, *The Politics of Medicare*, Aldine, Chicago.

Marmor, TR 2007, *Fads, Fallacies and Foolishness in Medical Care Management and Policy*, World Scientific, Singapore.

Marmor, TR & Christianson, JB 1982, *Health Care Policy: A Political Economy Approach*, Sage, Beverley Hills.

Marmor, TR & Hacker, JS 2007, 'How not to think about managed care', in TR Marmor (ed.), *Fads, Fallacies and Foolishness in Medical Care Management and Policy*, World Scientific, Singapore, pp. 27–53.

Marmor, TR & Klein, R 2012, *Politics, Health and Health Care, Selected Essays*, Yale University Press, New Haven.

Marmor, TR & McKissick, GJ 2012, Medicare's future: Fact, fiction and folly, in TR Marmor and R Klein, *Politics, Health and Health Care, Selected Essays*, Yale University Press, New Haven, pp. 53–88.

Marmor, TR & Morone, JA 1980, 'Representing consumer interests: Imbalanced markets, health planning and the HSAs', *Milbank Memorial Fund Quarterly, Health and Society*, vol. 58, pp. 125–62.

Marmor, TR & Thomas D 2012, 'Doctors, politics and pay disputes: Pressure group politics revisited', in TR Marmor and R Klein, *Politics, Health and Health Care, Selected Essays*, Yale University Press, New Haven, pp. 255–73.

Marmor, TR, Wittman, DA & Heagy, TC 1976, 'Politics, public policy and medical inflation', in M Zubcoff (ed.), *Health: A Victim or Cause of Inflation?*, Prodist, New York.

Marmor, TR, Freeman, R & Okma, KGH 2009 (eds), *Comparative Studies and the Politics of Modern Medical Care*, Yale University Press, New Haven.

Marmor, TR, Freeman, R & Okma, KGH 2012, 'Comparative perspectives and policy learning in the world of health care', in TR Marmor and R Klein, *Politics, Health and Health Care*, Yale University Press, New Haven, pp. 297–318.

Marmot, M 2004, *The Status Syndrome: How your Social Standing Affects your Health and Life Expectancy*, Bloomsbury, London.

Marmot, M 2005, 'Social determinants of health inequalities', *The Lancet*, vol. 365, Issue 9464.

Marmot, M & Wilkinson, R (eds) 1999, *Social Determinants of Health*, Oxford University Press, Oxford.

Marr, R 1992, *Report and Recommendations for National Policy Action to Improve the Use of Medications for and by the Elderly*, National Better Health Program, Canberra.

Martin, J 1978, *The Migrant Presence: Australian Responses 1947–1977*, Allen & Unwin, Sydney.

Maskell-Knight, C 1999, 'The health care agreements: Risk-sharing and opportunities for reform', *Healthcover*, vol. 9, no. 1, February/March, pp. 29–33.

Mathers, C & Harvey, R 1988, *Hospital Utilisation and Costs Study, Vol. 2: Survey of Public Hospitals and Related Data*, Australian Government Publishing Service, Canberra.

Mathews, J 1985, *Health and Safety at Work: Australian Trade Union Safety Representatives Handbook*, Pluto Press, Sydney.

Mathews, R 1980, *Revenue Sharing in Federal Systems*, Australian National University, Canberra.

Matrice, D & Brown, V 1990, *Widening the Research Focus: Consumer Roles in Public Health Research*, Consumers' Health Forum of Australia, Canberra.

Maynard, AR 1975, *Health Care in the European Community*, Croom Helm, London.

Mechanic, D 1976, *The Growth of Bureaucratic Medicine: An Inquiry into the Organisation of Medical Care*, John Wiley, New York.

Mechanic, D 1977, 'The growth of medical technology and bureaucracy: Implications for medical care', *Milbank Memorial Fund Quarterly Health and Society*, vol. 55, pp. 61–78.

Medicare Australia 2009a, *Medical Benefits Statistics*, Medicare Australia, Canberra.

Medicare Australia 2009b, *What Medicare Covers*, Medicare Australia, Canberra.

Medicare Australia 2013, *Medical Benefits Statistics, Group Reports*, Medicare Australia, Canberra.

Medicare Benefits Review Committee 1985, (Chairperson, RA Layton), *First Report*, Australian Government Publishing Service, Canberra.

Medicare Benefits Review Committee 1986, (Chairperson, RA Layton), *Second Report*, Australian Government Publishing Service, Canberra.

Meeks, DW & Kao, LS 2008, 'Controversies in appendicitis', *Surgical Infections*, vol. 9, no. 6, pp. 553–8.

Menadue, J 1999, *Things You Learn Along the Way*, David Lovell, Melbourne.

Meredith, L 1986, 'Liberating women's health', in E Kerby-Eaton and J Davies (eds), *Women's Health in a Changing Society*, vol. 3, conference proceedings, Adelaide.

Merritt, A 1983, 'Australian law on occupational health and safety—An up-to-the-minute report about what's not really happening', *New Doctor*, September/October, pp. 33–6.

Milio, N 1988, *Making Policy: A Mosaic of Australian Community Health Policy Development*, Commonwealth Department of Community Services and Health, Canberra.

Ministerial Council on Drug Strategy 1992, *No Quick Fix: An Evaluation of the National Campaign Against Drug Abuse*, Ministerial Council on Drug Abuse, Canberra, Commonwealth of Australia.

Mitchell, G 1988, *Health Policy for a Multicultural Australia*, Department of the Prime Minister and Cabinet, Office of Multicultural Affairs, Canberra.

Moncrieff, J 2009, *The Myth of the Chemical Cure: A Critique of Psychiatric Drug Treatment*, Palgrave Macmillan, Basingstoke.

Moncrieff, J 2013, *The Bitterest Pills: The Troubling Story of Antipsychotic Drugs*, Palgrave Macmillan, Basingstoke.

Moodie, R, Stuckler, D, Monteiro, C, Sheron, N, Neal, B, Thamarangsi, T, Lincoln, P & Casswell, S 2013 'Profits and pandemics: Prevention of harmful effects of tobacco, alcohol, and ultra-processed food and drink industries', *The Lancet*, vol. 381, pp. 670–9.

Mooney, G 1986, *Economics, Medicine and Health Care*, Wheatsheaf, Brighton.

Mooney, G & Scotton, R (eds) 1998, *Economics and Australian Health Policy*, Allen & Unwin, Sydney.

Moran, M, Rein, M & Goodin, R (eds) 2008, *The Oxford Handbook of Public Policy*, Oxford University Press, Oxford.

Morrissey, M & Jakubowicz, A 1980, *Migrants and Occupational Health: A Report*, Social Welfare Research Centre Report no. 3, November, SWRC, Sydney.

Moynihan, R 1998, *Too Much Medicine: The Business of Health and its Risk for You*, ABC Books, Sydney.

Moynihan, R & Cassels, A 2005, *Selling Sickness: How the World's Biggest Pharmaceutical Companies Are Turning Us All into Patients*, Nation Books, New York.

Najman, J 1988, 'Health and the Australian population', in J Najman and J Western (eds), *A Sociology of Australian Society*, Macmillan, Melbourne.

National Aboriginal Health Strategy Working Party 1989, *A National Aboriginal Health Strategy*, Aboriginal and Torres Strait Islander Commission, Canberra.

National Advisory Committee for the Early Detection of Breast Cancer 1992, *Program Information Statement*, National Program for the Early Detection of Breast Cancer, Canberra.

National Campaign Against Drug Abuse 1989, *The National Campaign Against Drug Abuse, 1981–88: Evaluation and Future Direction*, Australian Government Publishing Service, Canberra.

National Center for Health Statistics 1987, National Hospital Discharge Survey, 1985, unpublished computer tape, Washington, DC.

National Center for Health Statistics 2008, *National Hospital Discharge Survey, 2006*, United States Government, Maryland.

National Centre for Epidemiology and Population Health 1992, *Improving Australia's Health: The Role of Primary Health Care, Final Report of the Review of the Role of Primary Health Care in Health Promotion in Australia*, Australian National University, Canberra.

National Commission of Audit 1996, *Report to the Commonwealth Government*, Australian Government Publishing Service, Canberra.

National Commission of Audit 1997, *Report to the Commonwealth Government*, Australian Government Publishing Service, Canberra.

National Evaluation Steering Committee 1992, *Report of the Evaluation of the National HIV/AIDS Strategy*, Australian Government Publishing Service, Canberra.

National Health and Hospitals Reform Commission 2008a, *Beyond the Blame Game*, National Health and Hospital Reform Commission, Canberra.

National Health and Hospitals Reform Commission 2008b, *A Healthier Future for all Australians, Interim Report*, National Health and Hospitals Reform Commission, Canberra.

National Health and Hospitals Reform Commission 2009a, *The Australian Health Care System: The Potential for Efficiency Gains, A Review of the Literature*, National Health and Hospitals Reform Commission, Canberra.

National Health and Hospitals Reform Commission 2009b, *A Healthier Future for all Australians—Final Report of the National Health and Hospitals Reform Commission*, Commonwealth of Australia, Canberra.

National Health and Medical Research Council 1987, *Report of the Working Party on Homebirths and Alternative Birth Centres*, National Health and Medical Research Council, Melbourne.

National Health and Medical Research Council 1992, *Report of the 114th Session*, Australian Government Publishing Service, Canberra.

National Health Strategy 1991a, *Hospital Services in Australia: Access and Financing*, Issues Paper no. 2, National Health Strategy, Melbourne.

National Health Strategy 1991b, *The Australian Health Jigsaw: Integration of Health Care Delivery*, Issues Paper no. 1, National Health Strategy, Melbourne, Commonwealth of Australia.

National Health Strategy 1991c, *Spending on Health: The Distribution of Direct Payments for Health and Medical Services*, Background Paper no. 7, National Health Strategy, Melbourne.

National Health Strategy 1992a, *Issues in Pharmaceutical Drug Use in Australia*, Issues Paper no. 4, National Health Strategy, Melbourne.

National Health Strategy 1992b, *The Future of General Practice*, Issues Paper no. 3, National Health Strategy, Melbourne.

National Health Strategy 1992c, *Improving Dental Health in Australia*, Background Paper no. 9, National Health Strategy, Melbourne.

National Health Strategy 1992d, *Enough to Make You Sick: How Income and Environment Affect Health*, Research Paper no. 1, National Health Strategy, Melbourne.

National Health Strategy 1992e, *A Study of Hospital Outpatient and Emergency Department Services*, Background Paper no. 10, National Health Strategy, Melbourne.

National Health Strategy 1993a, *Health that Works: Workplace Reform and Best Practice in the Australian Health Industry*, Work in progress report, National Health Strategy, Melbourne.

National Health Strategy 1993b, *Pathways to Better Health*, Issues Paper no. 7, National Health Strategy, Melbourne.

National Health Strategy 1993c, *Removing Cultural and Language Barriers to Health*, Issues Paper no. 6, National Health Strategy, Melbourne.

National Health Strategy 1993d, *Help Where Help is Needed: Continuity of Care for People with Chronic Mental Illness*, Issues Paper no. 5, National Health Strategy, Melbourne.

National Health Strategy 1993e, *Healthy Participation: Achieving Greater Public Participation and Accountability in the Australian Health Care System*, Background Paper no. 12, National Health Strategy, Melbourne.

National Health Workforce Taskforce 2009, *Clinical Training: Governance and Organisation*, Health Workforce Principal Committee, Melbourne.

National Heart Foundation 1988, *Coronary Artery Bypass Graft Operation*, National Heart Foundation, Canberra.

National Heart Foundation 1992, *Cardiac Surgery 1990*, Report no. 28, National Heart Foundation, Canberra.

National Occupational Health and Safety Commission 1986, *Repetition Strain Injury: A Report and Model Code of Practice*, National Occupational Health and Safety Commission (Worksafe Australia), Canberra.

National Occupational Health and Safety Commission 1988, *NOHSC Annual Report 1986–87*, Australian Government Publishing Service, Canberra.

National Public Health Partnership 1998, Memorandum of Understanding between the Commonwealth and States and Territories to Establish the National Public Health Partnership, National Public Health Partnership, Canberra.

National Review of Nurse Education 1994, *Nursing Education in Australian Universities, Report of the National Review of Nurse Education in the Higher Education Sector, 1994 and Beyond*, Australian Government Publishing Service, Canberra.

Navarro, V 1978, *Class Struggle, the State and Medicine*, Martin Robertson, London.

Nettleton, S 1992, *Power, Pain and Dentistry*, Open University Press, Buckingham.

New South Wales Anti-Discrimination Board 1992, *Discrimination—the Other Epidemic: Report of the Inquiry into HIV and AIDS Related Discrimination*, New South Wales Anti-Discrimination Board, Sydney.

NHMRC—see National Health and Medical Research Council

Nolan, T, Bryson, L & Lashof, J 1999, *Independent Review of the Public Health Education and Research Program*, Commonwealth Department of Health and Aged Care, Canberra.

Nordholm, L & Westbrook, M 1985, 'Career development of female physiotherapists: Stage four of a longitudinal survey', *Australian Journal of Physiotherapy*, vol. 31, pp. 10–15.

NSW Department of Health 1983a, *Guidelines to Improve Migrant Access to Hospitals*, circular no. 83/60, NSW Department of Health, Sydney.

NSW Department of Health 1983b, (Chairperson, D Richmond), *Inquiry into Health Services for the Psychiatrically Ill and Developmentally Disabled*, parts 1–3, NSW Department of Health, Sydney.

NSW Department of Health 1984, *Guidelines to Improve Migrant Access to Community Health Services*, circular no. 84/248, NSW Department of Health, Sydney.

NSW Department of Health 1985, *Report of the Therapy Task Force, Review of Recruitment Difficulties for Therapists in the New South Wales Public Health Sector*, NSW Government Printer, Sydney.

NSW Department of Health 1987a, NSW hospital inpatient statistics 1986, unpublished computer tape, NSW Department of Health, Sydney.

NSW Department of Health 1987b, *Standard Procedures for Improved Access to Area and Other Public Health Services by People of Non-English Speaking Background*, circular no. 87/163, NSW Department of Health, Sydney.

NSW Department of Health 1992, *Nurse Practitioners in New South Wales: The Role and Function of Nurse Practitioners in New South Wales, A Discussion Paper*, June, NSW Department of Health, Sydney.

NSW Department of Health 1999, *Framework for Managing the Quality of Health Services in New South Wales*, New South Wales Department of Health, Sydney.

NSW Department of Health, Population Health Division 2006, *The Health of the People of New South Wales—Report of the Chief Health Officer*, NSW Department of Health, Sydney, available at <www.health.nsw.gov.au/publichealth/chorep/>.

NSW Department of Health 2009, *Health in Hunter New England, Social Determinants of Health, Socio-economic Indices by Health Area*, Health eRESOURCE, Hunter New England.

Nurses and Midwives Board 2009, *National Competency Standards for the Nurse Practitioners*, Nurses and Midwives Board New South Wales, Sydney.

Nutbeam, D 2008, 'The evolving concept of health literacy', *Social Science and Medicine*, vol. 67, no. 12, pp. 2072–8.

Nutbeam, D, Wise, M, Bauman, A, Harris, E & Leeder, S 1993, *Goals and Targets for Australia's Health in the Year 2000 and Beyond*, Department of Public Health, University of Sydney, report prepared for the Commonwealth Department of Health, Housing and Community Services, Australian Government Publishing Service, Canberra.

Nyman, JA 2003, *The Theory of Demand for Health Insurance*, Stanford University Press, Stanford.

OECD—see Organisation for Economic Co-operation and Development

Office of Aged Care Quality and Compliance 2008, *Report on the Operation of the Office of Aged Care Quality and Compliance, 1 July to 31 December 2007*, Office of Aged Care Quality and Compliance, Canberra.

Office of Technology Assessment 1978, *Assessing the Efficacy and Safety of Medical Technologies*, Office of Technology Assessment, Washington DC.

Office of Technology Assessment, United States Congress 1995, *Health Care Technology and its Assessment in Eight Countries*, accessed 10 April 2009, <www.Princeton.edu/~ota/html>.

O'Connor, J 1973, *The Fiscal Crisis of the State*, St Martin's Press, New York.

O'Malley, P 1978, 'Australian immigration policies and the migrant dirty-worker syndrome', in R Birrell and C Hay (eds), *The Immigration Issue in Australia*, La Trobe University, Melbourne.

O'Malley, SP 2006, 'The Australian experiment: The use of evidence based medicine for the reimbursement of surgical and diagnostic procedures 1998–2004', *Australian and New Zealand Health Policy*, vol. 3, pp. 10–23.

O'Neill, J 1988, 'New health boss plots out the path of his scalpel', *Sydney Morning Herald*, 9 July, pp. 8–9.

Opit, L 1984, 'Viewpoint', in M Tatchell (ed.), *Perspectives on Health Policy*, Australian National University, Canberra.

Opit, L & Gadiel, D 1982, *Hysterectomy in New South Wales: An Evaluation of its Use and Outcome*, Office of Health Care Finance, Sydney.

Organisation for Economic Co-operation and Development 1992, *The Reform of Health Care: A Comparative Analysis of Seven OECD Countries*, Organisation for Economic Co-operation and Development, Paris.

Organisation for Economic Co-operation and Development 1997, *Health Data 1997: A Software for the Comparative Analysis of 29 Health Systems*, Organisation for Economic Co-operation and Development, Paris.

Organisation for Economic Co-operation and Development 2008, OECD Health Data, CD ROM version, OECD, Paris, <www.oecd.org/health/healthdata>.

Organisation for Economic Co-operation and Development 2011, *Society at a Glance: OECD Social Indicators*, OECD Publishing, doi: 10.1787/soc_glance-2011-en.

Organisation for Economic Co-operation and Development 2012, *OECD Health Data*, CD ROM version, OECD, Paris, <www.oecd.org/health/healthdata>.

Organisation for Economic Co-operation and Development 2013a, *OECD. StatExtracts*, <http://stats.oecd.org>, accessed on 12 December 2013.

Organisation for Economic Co-operation and Development 2013b, *OECD Health Statistics 2013-Frequently Requested Data* <www.oecd.org/els/health-systems/oecdhealthdata2013-frequentlyrequesteddata.htm> accessed on 12 December 2013.

O'Sullivan, G, Sharman, E & Short, S (eds) 1999, *Goodbye Normal Gene: Confronting the Genetic Revolution*, Pluto Press, Sydney.

Owens, H 1998, 'Health insurance', in G Mooney and R Scotton (eds), *Economics and Australian Health Policy*, Allen & Unwin, Sydney.

Pacey, F, Harley, K, Veitch, C, Short, S 2012, 'A national scheme for health practitioner registration and accreditation: the case of Australia, in S Short and F McDonald (Eds), *Health Workforce Governance: Improved Access, Good Regulatory Practice, Safer Patients*, (pp. 163–181), Ashgate, Surrey.

Palmer, GR 1978, 'Social and political determinants of changes in health care financing and delivery', in A Graycar (ed.), *Perspectives in Australian Social Policy*, Macmillan, Melbourne.

Palmer, GR 1979, 'Health', in A Patience and B Head (eds), *From Whitlam to Fraser: Reform and Reaction in Australian Politics*, Oxford University Press, Melbourne.

Palmer, GR 1981, 'Regionalisation: Models and recent New South Wales experience', *Australian Health Review*, vol. 5, pp. 16–21.

Palmer, GR 1982, 'Commonwealth/state financial relationships and the financing of health services', in PM Tatchell (ed.), *Economics and Health, Proceedings of the 3rd Australian Conference of Health Economists*, Australian National University, Canberra.

Palmer, GR 1984, 'The issue of privatisation and related problems in the public health sector', *The Lamp*, vol. 41, pp. 32–3.

Palmer, GR 1986, 'The economics and financing of hospitals in Australia', *Australian Economic Review*, vol. 3, pp. 60–2.

Palmer, GR 1987, 'Health maintenance organisations for Australia?', *Current Affairs Bulletin*, vol. 64, pp. 24–30.

Palmer, GR 1989, 'Health insurance and financing', in B Head and A Patience (eds), *From Fraser to Hawke*, Longman Cheshire, Melbourne.

Palmer, GR 1992a, *The Implementation of Output-based Financing of Hospitals in Australia—Phase 1: Report to the Department of Health, Housing and Community Services*, Centre for Hospital Management and Information Systems Research, University of New South Wales, Sydney.

Palmer, GR 1992b, 'Casemix and the funding of hospitals in national health systems: An exploration of problems and issues based on recent Australian experience', Proceedings of the Annual Working Conference, Patient Classification Systems, Europe, September, Brno.

Palmer, GR 1996, 'Casemix funding: Objectives and objections', *Health Care Analysis*, vol. 4, pp. 185–93.

Palmer, GR 1997, 'Future directions for health policy in Australia. Many problems, new feasible solutions?', in AH Harris (ed.), *Economics and Health, Proceedings of the 18th Australian Conference of Health Economists*, Australian Studies in Health Service and Administration no. 81, University of New South Wales, Sydney.

Palmer, GR 2000a, 'Evidence-based health policy making, hospital funding and health insurance', *Medical Journal of Australia*, vol. 172, pp. 130–3.

Palmer, GR 2000b, 'Government policy making, private health insurance and hospital efficiency issues', *Medical Journal of Australia*, vol. 172, pp. 413–14.

Palmer, GR, Aisbett, C, Ng, L-M & Lohmann, J 1992, *Casemix Costs in Seven Sydney Teaching Hospitals—Round 2*, Centre for Hospital Management and Information Systems Research, University of New South Wales, Sydney.

Palmer, GR, Aisbett, C & Reid, B 1997, *Evaluating the Performance of the Australian National Diagnosis Related Groups, Report to the Commonwealth Department of Health and Family Services*, Centre for Hospital Management and Information Systems Research, University of New South Wales, Sydney.

Palmer, GR & Freeman, J 1987, 'Comparisons of hospital bed utilisation in Australia and the United States using DRGs', *Quality Review Bulletin*, vol. 13, pp. 256–61.

Palmer, GR & Ho, MT 2008, *Health Economics: A Critical and Global Analysis*, Palgrave Macmillan, Basingstoke.

Palmer, GR & Jayawardena, Y 1984, *Information Systems for Hospital Bed Utilisation Review*, Australian Studies in Health Service Administration no. 50, University of New South Wales, Sydney.

Palmer, GR & Short, SD 1994, *Health Care and Public Policy: An Australian Analysis*, 2nd edition, Macmillan, Melbourne.

Palmer, GR & Short, SD 2000, *Health Care and Public Policy: An Australian Analysis*, 3rd edition, Macmillan, Melbourne.

Palmer, GR & Stevenson, AG 1982, *The Health Administration Workforce in New South Wales*, Australian Studies in Health Administration no. 44, University of New South Wales, Sydney.

Paradise, JL 1981, 'Tonsillectomy and adenoidectomy', *Pediatric Clinics of North America*, vol. 28, pp. 881–92.

Paradise, JL, Bluestone, CD, Bachman, NZ, Colborn, DK, Bernard, BS, Taylor, FH, Rogers, KD, Schwarzbach, RH, Stool, SE & Friday, GA 1984, 'Efficacy of tonsillectomy for recurrent throat infection in severely affected children. Results of parallel randomized and nonrandomized clinical trials', *New England Journal of Medicine*, vol. 310, pp. 674–83.

Parker, RA 1987, *The Elderly and Residential Care: Australian Lessons for Britain*, Gower, London.

Parsons, W 1995, *Public Policy. An Introduction to the Theory and Practice of Policy Analysis*, Edward Elgar, Cheltenham.

Paterson, HM 1982, 'Voluntary work in Australia', *Australian Bulletin of Labour*, vol. 8, pp. 95–103.

Pauly, MV 1994, 'A re-examination of the meaning and importance of supplier-induced demand', *Journal of Health Economics*, vol. 13, pp. 369–72.

Pearse, W & Refshauge, C 1987, 'Workers' health and safety in Australia: An overview', *International Journal of Health Services*, vol. 17, pp. 635–50.

Pederson, AP, Edwards, RK, Kelner, M, Marshall, VW & Allison, KR 1988, *Coordinating Healthy Public Policy: An Analytic Literature Review and Bibliography*, Department of Behavioral Science, University of Toronto, Toronto.

Perry, S 1982, 'The brief life of the National Center for Health Care Technology', *New England Journal of Medicine*, vol. 307, pp. 1095–100.

Petersen, A & Lupton, D 1996, *The New Public Health: Health and Self in the Age of Risk*, Allen & Unwin, Sydney.

Pharmaceutical Manufacturing Industry Inquiry 1979, (Chairperson, JT Ralph), *Report*, Australian Government Publishing Service, Canberra.

PHIAC—see Private Health Insurance Administration Council

Plunkett, A & Quine, S 1996, 'Difficulties experienced by carers from non-English-speaking backgrounds in using health and other support services', *The Australian and New Zealand Journal of Public Health*, vol. 20, no. 1, pp. 27–32.

Podger, A 1998–99, 'Govt "committed to the sustainable balance" between public and private', *Healthcover*, vol. 8, no. 6, Dec–Jan, pp. 16–20.

Podger, A & Hagan, P 2000, 'Reforming the Australian health care system: The role of government', in A Bloom (ed.), *Health Reform in Australia and New Zealand*, Oxford University Press, Melbourne.

Potter, JD 1986, 'Editorial: The Kerr White Report', *Community Health Studies*, vol. x, pp. 77–8.

Powles, J 1973, 'On the limitations of modern medicine', *Science, Medicine and Man*, vol. 1, pp. 1–30.

Private Health Insurance Administration Council 1999, *Coverage of Hospital Insurance Tables Offered by Registered Health Benefits Organisations by State: Persons and Percentage of Population*, Private Health Insurance Administration Council, Canberra.

Private Health Insurance Administration Council 2008, *Industry Statistics: Coverage of Hospital Treatment Tables Offered by Health Benefits Funds by State: Persons and Percentage of Population*, Private Health Insurance Administration Council, Canberra.

Private Health Insurance Administration Council 2013, *Industry Statistics,* Coverage of hospital treatment tables offered by health benefits funds by state: persons and percentage of population, Private Health Insurance Administration Council, Canberra.

Productivity Commission 1999, *Report on Private Hospitals in Australia*, Commission Research Paper, AusInfo, Canberra.

Productivity Commission 2006, *Australia's Health Workforce, Research Report*, Productivity Commission, Australian Government, Canberra.

Productivity Commission 2009, *Public and Private Hospitals: Research Report*, Productivity Commission, Canberra.

Productivity Commission 2011, *Caring for Older Australians: An Overview*. Report no. 53, Final Inquiry Report, Productivity Commission, Canberra.

Public Health Association of Australia 1989, *1989–90 Directory of Postgraduate Public Health Training in Australia*, Public Health Association, Canberra.

Public Health Association of Australia 1990, *Workforce Issues for Public Health*, Public Health Association, Canberra.

Queensland Department of Health 2007, *Annual Report, 2006–07*, Queensland Department of Health, Brisbane.

Queensland Department of Health 2013, *Blueprint for Better Healthcare in Queensland*, Queensland Government, Brisbane.

Quinlan, M 1987, 'Return of OHS legislation in Queensland: An update', *The Journal of Occupational Health and Safety—Australia and New Zealand*, vol. 3, pp. 292–3.

Quinlan, M & Bohle, P (eds) 1991, *Managing Occupational Health and Safety in Australia: A Multidisciplinary Approach*, Macmillan, Melbourne.

Quinlan, M & Johnstone, R 2009, 'The implications of de-collectivist industrial relations laws and associated developments for worker health and safety in Australia, 1996–2007', *Industrial Relations Journal*, vol. 40, no. 5, pp. 426–43.

Rawls J 1972, *A Theory of Justice*, Clarendon Press, Oxford.

Rawson, G 1986, *Senior Health Service Managers: Characteristics and Educational Needs*, Australian Studies in Health Service Administration no. 57, University of New South Wales, Sydney.

Razum, O 2006, 'Commentary: Of salmon and time travelers—musing on the mystery of migrant mortality', *International Journal of Epidemiology*, vol. 35, pp. 919–21.

Reekie, WD 1984, 'Drug prices in the UK, USA, Europe and Australia', *Australian Economic Papers*, vol. 23, pp. 71–8.

Refshauge, A 1982, *Aboriginal Medical Service: An Introduction*, Aboriginal Medical Service, Redfern.

Refshauge, C & Duckett, S 1976, *A Report on Physiotherapists in Australia, 1973–1974*, Australian Physiotherapy Association, Melbourne.

Reid, BA 1995, 'Hospital Admission Rate Variations between Areas in New South Wales: A Study Based on Diagnosis Related Groups', PhD thesis, University of New South Wales.

Reid, BA, Aisbett, CW, Jones, LM, Mira, M, Muhlen-Schulte, L, Palmer, G, Reti, L & Roberts, R 2000, *Relative Utilisation Rates of Hysterectomy and Links to Diagnosis*, Commonwealth Department of Health and Aged Care, Canberra.

Reid, M & Solomon, S 1992, *Improving Australia's Rural Health and Aged Care Services*, Background Paper no. 11, National Health Strategy, Melbourne.

Reinhardt, U 1985, 'The theory of physician-induced demand: Reflections after a decade', *Journal of Health Economics*, vol. 4, pp. 187–93.

Reinhardt, U, Hussey, PS & Anderson, GF 2004, 'U.S. health care spending in an international context', *Health Affairs*, vol. 23, pp. 10–25.

Relman, A 1979, 'Technology costs and evaluation', *New England Journal of Medicine*, vol. 301, pp. 1444–5.

Relman, A 1980, 'The new medical-industrial complex', *New England Journal of Medicine*, vol. 303, pp. 963–70.

Renwick, M & Harvey, DR 1988, 'A view of quality assurance in Australian hospitals through rose-coloured glasses?', paper presented to the Annual Conference of the Public Health Association, Brisbane.

Renwick, M & Sadkowsky, K 1991, *Variations in Surgery Rates*, Australian Institute of Health: Health Services Series no. 2, Australian Government Publishing Service, Canberra.

Repin, G 1984, 'The AMA's attitude to Medicare', *Australian Health Review*, vol. 7, pp. 31–3.

Rhys Hearn, C 1997, *Development of a Single Instrument for the Classification of Nursing Home and Hostel Residents, Report*, vol. 1, Aged Care Research and Evaluation Unit, University of Western Australia, Perth.

Rice, T & Labelle, RJ 1989, 'Do physicians induce demand for medical services?', *Journal of Health Politics, Policy and Law*, vol. 14, pp. 587–600.

Richardson, J 1984, 'Incomes of private medical practitioners and their control', in M Tatchell (ed.), *Economics and Health 1983*, Australian National University, Canberra.

Richardson, J 1986, 'Regulation or reprivatisation of the health care sector: Which path should Australia follow?', in CM Lindsay, *Policies and Prescriptions: Current directions in health policy*, Centre for Independent Studies, Sydney.

Richardson, J 1987a, *Financial Incentives and Entrepreneurial Medicine. Problems and Solutions*, Australian Studies in Health Service Administration no. 61, University of New South Wales, Sydney.

Richardson, J 1987b, 'Economic assessment of medical technology: Problems and solutions', in J Daly, K Green & E Willis (eds), *Technologies in Health Care, Policies and Politics*, Australian Government Publishing Service, Canberra.

Richardson, J 1991, *The Effects of Consumer Co-payments in Medical Care*, Background Paper no. 5, National Health Strategy, Melbourne.

Richardson, J 1998, 'The health care financing debate', in G Mooney and R Scotton (eds), *Economics and Australian Health Policy*, Allen & Unwin, Sydney.

Richardson J 1999, 'Evidence based policy: Can we move on?', *Healthcover*, vol. 9, pp. 39–41.

Richardson, JR 2005, 'Priorities of health policy: Costs shifting or population health', *Australia and New Zealand Health Policy*, vol. 2, no. 1, accessed 10 March 2009, <www.anzhealthpolicy.com/html>.

Richardson, JR 2009, 'Steering without navigation equipment: The lamentable state of Australian health policy reform', *Australia and New Zealand Health Policy*, vol. 6, no. 27, pp. 6–27.

Richardson, J & Robertson, I 1999, 'Ageing and the cost of health services', *Policy Implications of the Ageing of Australia's Population*, Productivity Commission and Melbourne Institute of Applied Economic and Social Research, conference proceedings, AusInfo, Canberra.

Richardson, J & Segal, L 2004, 'Private health insurance and the PBS: How effective has recent government policy been', *Australian Health Review*, vol. 28, pp. 34–47.

Richmond, RL, Austin, A & Webster, IW 1986, 'Three year evaluation of a programme by general practitioners to help patients to stop smoking', *British Medical Journal*, vol. 292, pp. 803–6.

Rob, M, Corben, P & Rushworth. R 1998, 'The impact of new technology on cholecystectomy rates in New South Wales', *Journal of Quality Clinical Practice*, vol. 18, no. 4, pp. 263–74.

Rogers, A, Pilgrim, D & Lacey, R 1993, *Experiencing Psychiatry: Users' Views of Services, Issues in Mental Health Series*, Macmillan, in association with Mind Publications, London.

Ronalds, C 1989a, *I'm Still an Individual: A Blueprint for the Rights of Residents in Nursing Homes and Hostels*, Commonwealth Department of Community Services and Health, Canberra.

Ronalds, C 1989b, *Residents' Rights in Nursing Homes and Hostels: Final Report*, Australian Government Publishing Service, Canberra.

Rose, G 1992, *The Strategy of Preventive Medicine*, Oxford University Press, Oxford.

Rosenham, DL 1973, 'On being sane in insane places', *Science*, vol. 179, pp. 250–8.

Roth, M & Kroll, J 1986, *The Reality of Mental Illness*, Cambridge University Press, London.

Rowland, D 1982, 'The vulnerability of the aged in Sydney', *Australian and New Zealand Journal of Sociology*, vol. 18, pp. 229–47.

Royal Australian College of General Practitioners 2007, *Smoking Cessation Guidelines for Australian General Practice*, Royal Australian College of General Practitioners, Melbourne.

Royal Australasian College of Physicians & the Australian Society of Otolaryngology, 2008, *Indications for Tonsillectomy and Adenotonsillectomy in Children*, A Joint Position Paper of the Paediatrics & Child Health Division of the Royal Australasian College of Physicians and the Australian Society of Otolaryngology Head and Neck Surgery, Brisbane.

Royal Australasian College of Physicians, Health Issues Centre & Australian Consumers' Association 1999, *Response to the Senate Inquiry into Public Hospital Funding*, Royal Australasian College of Physicians, Sydney.

Royal Australasian College of Physicians 1999, *For Richer, for Poorer, in Sickness and in Health: The Socioeconomic Determinants of Health*, Royal Australasian College of Physicians, Sydney.

Royal Commission into Aboriginal Deaths in Custody 1991, *Towards Better Health, National Report: Overview and Recommendations* (Commissioner, E Johnston), vol. 4, Australian Government Publishing Service, Canberra.

Rumbold, G 1986, *Ethics in Nursing Practice*, Balliere Tindall, London.

Runciman, WB, Roughead, EE, Semple, SJ & Adams, RJ 2003, 'Adverse drug events and medication errors in Australia', *International Journal for Quality in Healthcare*, vol. 15, (supplement), pp. i49–i59.

Russell, C 1981, *The Aging Experience*, Allen & Unwin, Sydney.

Russell, C & Schofield, T 1986, *Where it Hurts: An Introduction to Sociology for Health Workers*, Allen & Unwin, Sydney.

Russell, LB 1986, *Is Prevention Better than Cure?*, Brookings Institution, Washington DC.

Rutnam, R 1988, 'Ethics in medical research: Australian developments', *Community Health Studies*, vol. xii, pp. 127–33.

Ruzek, S 1978, *The Women's Health Movement*, Praeger, New York.

Sackett, DL, Richardson, WS & Rosenbery Ward Haynes, RB 1997, *Evidence-Based Medicine: How to Practice and Teach EBM*, Churchill Livingston, London.

Safe Work Australia 2009, *Research and Emerging Issues*, Commonwealth of Australia, Canberra.

Saggers, S & Gray, D 1991, *Aboriginal Health and Society: The Traditional and Contemporary Aboriginal Struggle for Better Health*, Allen & Unwin, Sydney.

Salisbury, R & Heinz, J 1970, 'A theory of policy analysis and some preliminary applications', in I Sharkansky (ed.), *Policy Analysis in Political Science*, Markham, Chicago.

Salkeld, G, Mitchell, A & Hill, S 1998, 'Pharmaceuticals', in G Mooney and R Scotton (eds), *Economics and Australian Health Policy*, Allen & Unwin, Sydney.

Sammut, J 2011, *How! Not How Much: Medicare Spending and Health Resource Allocation in Australia*, Centre for Independent Studies, Sydney.

Sandercock, P, Molyneux, A & Warlow, C 1985, 'Value of computed tomography in patients with stroke: Oxfordshire Community Stroke Project', *British Medical Journal*, vol. 290, pp. 193–7.

Sanson-Fisher, RW, Webb, GR & Reid, ALA 1986, 'The role of the medical practitioner as an agent for disease prevention', Appendix 2, in Better Health Commission, *Looking Forward to Better Health*, vol. 3, Australian Government Publishing Service, Canberra.

Saul, JR 1997, *The Unconscious Civilisation*, Penguin, Melbourne.

Sax, S 1972, *Medical Care in the Melting Pot: An Australian Review*, Angus & Robertson, Sydney.

Sax, S 1984, *A Strife of Interests: Politics and Policies in Australian Health Services*, Allen & Unwin, Sydney.

Sax, S 1985, 'Community Health in Australia: A Position Paper', unpublished paper, Australian Institute of Health, Canberra.

Sax, S 1990, *Health Care Choices and the Public Purse*, Allen & Unwin, Sydney.

Sax, S 1993, *Ageing and Public Policy in Australia*, Allen & Unwin, Sydney.

Scally, G & Donaldson, LJ 1998, 'Clinical governance and the drive for quality improvement in the new NHS in England', *British Medical Journal*, vol. 317, pp. 61–5.

Scott, R 1993, 'National uniformity is in sight', *Sydney Morning Herald*, 3 June, p. 14.

Scotton, RB 1992a, 'Demand side socialism and managed competition: Do they add up?', in C Selby Smith (ed.), *Economics and Health, 1991, Proceedings of the Annual Conference of the Australian Health Economists Group*, Public Sector Management Institute, Monash University, Melbourne.

Scotton, RB 1992b, 'Coalition's health policy: An opportunity missed', *Healthcover*, vol. 2, no. 1, pp. 10–16.

Scotton, RB 1998a, 'The doctor business', in G Mooney and R Scotton (eds), *Economics and Australian Health Policy*, Allen & Unwin, Sydney.

Scotton, RB 1998b, 'Managed competition', in G Mooney and R Scotton (eds), *Economics and Australian Health Policy*, Allen & Unwin, Sydney.

Scotton, RB & Deeble, JS 1968, 'Compulsory health insurance in Australia', *Australian Economic Review*, 4 October, pp. 9–16.

Scotton, RB & Macdonald, CR 1993, *The Making of Medibank*, Australian Studies in Health Service Administration Series, no. 76, University of New South Wales, Sydney.

Scotton, RB & Owens, H 1990, *Case Payment in Australian Hospitals: Issues and Options*, Public Sector Management Institute, Monash University, Melbourne.

Selnes, OA, Goldsborough, MA, Borowicz, LM & McKhann, GM 1999, 'Neurobehavioural sequelae of cardiopulmonary bypass', *Lancet*, vol. 353, pp. 1601–6.

Senate Select Committee of Inquiry into Chiropractic, Osteopathy, Homeopathy and Naturopathy 1977, (Chairperson, EC Webb), *Report*, Australian Government Publishing Service, Canberra.

Senate Select Committee on Private Hospitals and Nursing Homes 1987, *Report*, Australian Government Publishing Service, Canberra.

Sharan, A 1992, 'Ethnic health in Queensland', *Health Issues*, September, pp. 33–5.

Sheehan, P 1988, 'Cigarette firm loses smoker's death case', *Sydney Morning Herald*, 15 June, p. 17.

Short, LM 1987, 'The gender division of labour in dental health care', paper presented to the Women Workers in Health Care Conference 1987, Sydney.

Short, LM 1995, 'Oral health care in Australia—A public health perspective' (editorial), *Australian Journal of Public Health*, vol. 19, no. 1, pp. 5–6.

Short, LM 1998, 'Oral health for the elderly', *Australasian Journal on Ageing*, vol. 17, no. 3, August, pp. 107–8.

Short, LM & Riordan, P 1996, 'It's their right not to fluoridate, but is it right?' (editorial), *Australian and New Zealand Journal of Public Health*, vol. 20, no. 6, p. 563.

Short, SD 1981, 'An holistic approach towards disabled persons and their rehabilitation', *Australian Journal of Physiotherapy*, vol. 25, no. 5, pp. 145–7.

Short, SD 1984, 'The Medical Profession and the Shaping of the Health Care Systems in Britain and Australia', Master of Science dissertation, Bedford College (University of London).

Short, SD 1985, 'The war against cancer: A sociological study of cancer treatment', *New Doctor*, no. 35, pp. 25–8.

Short, SD 1986a, 'Medical authority: A sociological analysis of the power relation between doctors and patients in cancer treatment', in JL Sheppard (ed.), *Advances in Behavioural Medicine*, vol. 3, Cumberland College of Health Sciences, Lidcombe.

Short, SD 1986b, 'Physiotherapy: A feminine profession', *Australian Journal of Physiotherapy*, vol. 32, pp. 241–3.

Short, SD 1989, 'Community participation or manipulation? A case study of the Illawarra Cancer Appeal-a-thon', *Community Health Studies*, vol. xiii, no. 1, pp. 34–8.

Short, SD 1997a, 'On the tension between individual health rights and public health responsibilities' (editorial), *Australian and New Zealand Journal of Public Health*, vol. 21, no. 3, pp. 246–7.

Short, SD 1997b, 'Elective affinities: Research and health policy development', in H Gardner (ed.), *Health Policy in Australia*, Oxford University Press, Melbourne.

Short, SD 1998, 'Community activism in the health policy process: The case of the Consumers' Health Forum of Australia, 1987–96', in A Yeatman (ed.), *Activism and the Policy Process*, Allen & Unwin, Sydney.

Short, SD 1999, 'Why do poor people behave so badly?', in E Harris, P Sainsbury and D Nutbeam (eds), *Perspectives on Health Inequity*, Centre for Health Equity, Training, Research and Evaluation, Social Health Research Unit and the Australian Centre of Health Promotion, Sydney.

Short, SD 2004, 'Fat is a fairness issue', *Griffith Review*, vol. 4, pp. 95–100.

Short, SD & McDonald, F 2012, *Health Workforce Governance: Improved Access, Good Regulatory Practice, Safer Patients*, Ashgate, Farnham.

Short, SD & Sharman, E 1987, 'The nursing struggle in Australia', *Image: Journal of Nursing Scholarship*, vol. 19, pp. 197–200.

Short, S & Sharman, E 1995, 'Dissecting the contemporary nursing struggle in Australia', in GM Lupton and JM Najman (eds), *Sociology of Health and Illness: Australian Readings*, 2nd edition, Macmillan, Melbourne.

Short, SD, Sharman, E & Speedy, S 1998, *Sociology for Nurses: An Australian Introduction*, 2nd edition, Macmillan, Melbourne.

Showalter, E 1997, *Hystories: Hysterical Epidemics and Modern Media*, Columbia University Press, New York.

Siedlecky, S & Wyndham, D 1990, *Populate and Perish: Australian Women's Fight for Birth Control*, Allen & Unwin, Sydney.

Simoens, S & Hurst, J 2006, *The Supply of Physician Services in OECD Countries*, OECD Health Working Papers no. 21, OECD, Paris.

Singh, M & de Looper, M 2002, *Australian Health Inequalities: 1 Birthplace*, Bulletin no. 2, AIHW cat. no. AUS 27, Canberra.

Smith LR 1980, 'Aboriginal vital statistics: An analysis of trends', *Aboriginal Health Bulletin*, vol. 1, Australian Government Publishing Service, Canberra.

Smith, LR 1982, 'Aboriginal health and Aboriginal health statistics', *Aboriginal Health Project Information Bulletin*, vol. 1, pp. 14–24.

Smith, PC & Street, A 2006, 'Concepts and challenges in measuring the performance of health care organisations', in AM Jones (ed.), *The Elgar Companion to Health Economics*, Edward Elgar, Cheltenham.

Smith, R 1998, 'Regulation of doctors and the Bristol inquiry', *British Medical Journal*, vol. 316, pp. 1539–40.

Social Development Committee 1986, *Inquiry into Alternative Medicine and the Health Food Industry*, (Chairperson, JC Dixon), Victorian Government Parliamentary Papers, 1985–87.

Society for Health Administration Programs in Education 1992, *Management Education Directory (Health Services) 1992–1994*, Society for Health Administration Programs in Education (SHAPE), School of Health Sciences, La Trobe University, Bendigo.

Soderlund, N 1994, 'Product definition for healthcare contracting: An overview of approaches to measuring hospital output with reference to the UK internal market', *Journal of Epidemiology and Community Health*, vol. 48, no. 3, pp. 224–31.

South Australian Health Commission 1988, A *Social Health Strategy for South Australia*, South Australian Health Commission, Adelaide.

Southgate, J 1993, 'Why women's health: Where to now?', *Health Issues*, vol. 34, March, pp. 11–13.

Special Commission of Inquiry into Acute Care Services in NSW Public Hospitals (Chairperson, P Garling) 2008, *Final Report*, vol. 3, New South Wales Government, Sydney.

Spencer, A, Teusner, D, Carter, K & Brennan, D 2003, *The Dental Labour Force in Australia: The Position and Policy*, Australian Institute of Health and Welfare (Population Oral Health Series No. 2), cat. no. POH 2, AIHW, Canberra.

Stanley, A 1987, '"Healthy Cities" workshop', *Health Issues*, no. 11, pp. 19–21.

Staunton, P 1992, *The Lamp* (editorial), September, p. 3.

Steinberg, E 1984, *Nuclear Magnetic Imaging Technology: A Clinical, Industrial and Policy Analysis*, Office of Technology Assessment, Washington DC.

Stewart, B 1979, 'Drugs and the media', *Australian Journal of Alcoholism and Drug Dependence*, vol. 6, pp. 83–5.

Stigler, GL 1965, *Essays in the History of Economics*, University of Chicago Press, Chicago.

Summers, M 1992, 'Health impact assessment', *Health Forum*, September, pp. 3–4.

Summers, M 1993, 'Rewriting Australia's health goals and targets', *Health Issues*, vol. 34, pp. 8–11.

Swerissen, H & Duckett, SJ 2007a, 'Federalism and health: Negotiating the problems of "fiscal squabbles", "waiting" and "waste"', in S Barraclough and H Gardner (eds), *Analysing Australian Health Policy: A Problem-Oriented Approach*, Elsevier, Marrickville.

Swerissen, H & Duckett, SJ 2007b, 'Health policy for a long lived society', in A Borowski, S Encel and E Ozanne (eds), *Longevity and Social Change in Australia*, UNSW Press, Sydney.

Sylvan, L 1988, 'Healthy public policies', *Health Forum*, May/June, no. 5, pp. 12–14.

Sydney Morning Herald 1999, 'Recovery, a way off for hospital operations', 13 September, pp. 37, 40.

Szoke, H 1987, 'Medical education and medical workforce inquiry', *Health Issues*, no. 11, pp. 14–16.

Taylor, CR 1984, 'Alternative medicine and the medical encounter in Britain and the United States', in JW Salmon (ed.), *Alternative Medicines: Popular and Policy Perspectives*, Tavistock, New York.

Taylor, MJ, Horey, D, Livingston, C & Swerissen, H 2010, 'Decline with a capital D: Long-term changes in general practice consultation patterns across Australia', *Medical Journal of Australia*, vol. 193, pp. 80–3.

Taylor, R 1979, *Medicine Out of Control: The Anatomy of a Malignant Technology*, Sun Books, Melbourne.

Tesh, S 1981, 'Disease causality and politics', *Journal of Health Politics, Policy and Law*, vol. 6, pp. 369–90.

Tesh, S 1988, *Hidden Arguments: Political Ideology and Disease Prevention Policy*, Rutgers University Press, New Brunswick.

Thomas, H 2007, *Sick to Death*, Allen & Unwin, Sydney.

Thompson, JD & Birch, HW 1981, 'Indications for hysterectomy', *Clinical Obstetrics and Gynecology*, vol. 24, pp. 1245–58.

Thomson, N 1984, 'Australian Aboriginal health and health-care', *Social Science and Medicine*, vol. 18, pp. 939–48.

Thomson, N 1991, 'Review of Aboriginal health status', in J Reid and P Trompf (eds), *The Health of Aboriginal Australia*, Harcourt Brace Jovanovich, Sydney.

Thurow, LC 1983, *Dangerous Currents. The State of Economics*, Random House, New York.

Titulaer, I, Trickett, P & Bhatia, K 1998, *Rural Public Health in Australia—1991*, Australian Institute of Health and Welfare, Canberra.

Tomlinson, B 1992, *Report of the Inquiry into London's Health Service, Medical Education and Research*, Her Majesty's Stationery Office, London.

Townsend, P & Davidson, N (eds) 1982, *Inequalities in Health: The Black Report*, Penguin, Harmondsworth.

Tullock, G 1976, *The Vote Motive: An Essay in the Economics of Politics with Applications to the British Economy*, Institute of Economic Affairs, London.

Tuohy, C 1994, 'Response to the Clinton proposal: A comparative perspective', *Journal of Health Politics, Policy and Law*, vol. 19, no. 1, pp. 249–54.

Tuohy, C 1999, *Accidental Logics: The Dynamics of Change in the Health Care Arena in the United States, Britain and Canada*, Oxford University Press, Oxford.

Tuohy, CH 2009, 'Canada: health care reform in comparative perspective', in TR Marmor, R Freeman and KGH Okma, (eds), *Comparative Studies and the Politics of Modern Medical Care*, Yale University Press, New Haven.

Turner, L & Short, SD 1999, 'George Rupert Palmer—DRG Carrier and Champion', *Australian Health Review*, vol. 22, no. 2, pp. 86–102.

Turpin, T 1989, 'Occupational health and safety, and rehabilitation: The experience of migrant women in Victoria', paper presented to the National Ethnic Health Policy Conference, April, Adelaide.

UNAIDS/WHO 2008, *Epidemiological Fact Sheet on HIV and AIDS: Core Data on Epidemiology and Response—Australia*, UNAIDS/WHO Working Group on Global HIV/AIDS and STI Surveillance, Geneva.

United Nations Economic and Social Commission for Asia and the Pacific 2011, *Regional Survey on Ageing 2011: Australia*, Department of Health, Canberra.

Unsworth, C 1987, *The Politics of Mental Health Legislation*, Clarendon Press, Oxford.

van der Weyden, M 2004, 'The "Cam affair": An isolated incident or destined to be repeated?', *Medical Journal of Australia*, vol. 180, pp. 100–1.

van der Weyden, M 2005, 'The Bundaberg Hospital scandal: The need for reform in Queensland and beyond', *The Medical Journal of Australia*, vol. 183, pp. 284–5.

van Doorslaer, E, Wagstaff, A, van der Burg, H, Christiansen, T, Citoni, G, Di Biase, R, Gerdtham, UG, Gerfin, M, Gross, L, Häkinnen, U, John, J, Johnson, P, Klavus, J, Lachaud, C, Lauritsen, J, Leu, R, Nolan, B, Pereira, J, Propper, C, Puffer, F, Rochaix, L, Shellhorn, M, Sundberg, G & Winkelhake, O 1999, 'The redistributive effect of health care finance in twelve OECD countries', *Journal of Health Economics*, vol. 18, pp. 291–313.

Veterans Administration Coronary Artery Bypass Surgery Cooperative Study Group 1984, 'Eleven-year survival in the Veterans Administration randomized trial of coronary bypass surgery for stable angina', *New England Journal of Medicine*, vol. 311, pp. 1333–9.

Victorian Aged Services Peak Council 1987, *Quality of Care in Nursing Homes*, Health Vision, Melbourne.

Victorian Auditor-General's Office 1998, *Acute Health Services Under Casemix: A Case of Mixed Priorities*, Auditor-General, Melbourne.

Victorian Department of Health 2013, *Annual Report, 2012–13*, Department of Health Victoria, Melbourne.

Victorian Department of Health and Community Services 1993, *Victoria's Health Reforms, the First Step: Casemix Funding for Public Hospitals, Discussion Paper*, Health Policy and Programs, Department of Health and Community Services, Melbourne.

Victorian Department of Health and the Victorian Hospitals' Association 1987, *Diagnosis Related Groups*, Department of Health, Victoria, Melbourne.

Victorian Department of Human Services 1998, *Victoria—Public Hospital Policy and Funding Guidelines 1998–99*, Department of Human Services, Melbourne.

Victorian Department of Human Services 2008, *Annual Report, 2007–08*, Department of Human Services, Melbourne.

Victorian Health Commission 1985, *Report of the Working Party on Health Administration Education*, Health Commission of Victoria, Melbourne.

Victorian Health Department 1992, *The Mental Health Act: A Practical Guide*, Office of Psychiatric Services, Melbourne.

Victorian Ministerial Women's Health Working Party 1987, *Why Women's Health? Victorian Women Respond*, Health Department, Melbourne.

Victorian Women's Health Policy Working Party 1985, *Why Women's Health? Discussion Paper*, Health Department Victoria, Melbourne.

Vos, T, Barker, B, Stanley, L, & Lopez, A 2007, *The Burden of Disease and Injury in Aboriginal and Torres Strait Islander Peoples 2003*, School of Population Health, University of Queensland, Brisbane.

Wagstaff, A & van Doorslaer, E 1997, 'Progressivity, horizontal equity and reranking in health care finance', *Journal of Health Economics*, vol. 16 no. 5, pp. 499–515.

Wakefield, M, Hayes, L, Durkin, S & Boland, R 2013, 'Introduction effects of the Australian plain packaging policy on adult smokers: a cross-sectional study', *British Medical Journal*, vol. 3, no. 7, <doi:10.1136/bmjopen-2013-003175>.

Walker, D, Short, SD, Tennant, M et al. 2006, 'Factors influencing the development and uptake of the oral health role of Aboriginal Health Workers', NSW Aboriginal Health Workers State conference 21–22 September, Sydney.

Walsh, J & de Ravin, JW 1995, *Long-Term Care, Disability and Ageing*, Institute of Actuaries, Sydney.

Walsh, R 1984, 'Medical education in Australia', in M Tatchell (ed.), *Perspectives on Health Policy*, Australian National University, Canberra.

Walton, M 1993, 'The operation of NSW's proposed new Health Care Complaints Commission', *Healthcover*, February–March, pp. 33–9.

Walton, M 1998, *The Trouble with Medicine: Preserving the Trust Between Patients and Doctors*, Allen & Unwin, Sydney.

Ward, M, Daniels, SA, Walker, GJ and Duckett, SJ 2007, 'Connecting funds with outcomes in healthcare: A blueprint for a clinical practice improvement payment', *Australian Health Review*, vol. 31, suppl. 1, S54–S58.

Waterford, J 1982, 'The Aboriginal medical service—A uniquely Australian phenomenon', *Aboriginal Health Project Information Bulletin*, vol. 2, p. 16.

Weber, M 1978, 'Basic categories of social organisation', in WG Runciman (ed.), *Selections in Translation*, Cambridge University Press, Cambridge.

Wen, SW & Naylor, CD 1995, 'Diagnostic accuracy and short-term surgical outcomes in cases of suspected acute appendicitis', *Canadian Medical Association Journal*, vol. 152, pp. 1617–26.

Wennberg, DE & Wennberg JE 2003, 'Addressing variations: Is there hope for the future?', *Health Affairs* (web exclusive, 10 Dec.), accessed 10 July 2009, <www.content.healthaffairs.org/cgi/content/full/hlthaff.w3.614v1/DC1>.

Wennberg, JE 1988, 'Improving the medical decision-making process', *Health Affairs*, vol. 7, pp. 99–106.

Wennberg, JE, Bunker, JP & Barnes, B 1980, 'The need for assessing the outcome of common medical practices', *Annual Review of Public Health*, vol. 1, pp. 277–95.

Wennberg, JE, McPherson, K & Caper, P 1984, 'Will payment based on diagnosis-related groups control hospital costs?', *New England Journal of Medicine*, vol. 31, no. 1, pp. 295–300.

Wennitong, M 2002, *Indigenous Male Health*, Commonwealth of Australia, Canberra.

Whelan, A, Mohr, R & Short, S 1992, *Waving or Drowning? Evaluation of the National Secretariat, Healthy Cities Australia: Final Report*, Australian Community Health Association, Sydney.

White, KL 1986, *Independent Review of Research and Educational Requirements for Public Health and Tropical Health in Australia 1988*, Commonwealth Department of Health, Canberra.

WHO—see World Health Organization

Wiesner, D 1989, *Alternative Medicine: A Guide for Patients and Health Professionals in Australia*, Kangaroo Press, Sydney.

Wildavsky, A 1979, *Speaking Truth and Power: The Art and Craft of Policy Analysis*, Little, Brown, Boston.

Willcox, S 1991, *A Healthy Risk? Use of Private Insurance*, Background Paper no. 4, National Health Strategy, Melbourne.

Willcox, S 2001, 'Promoting private health insurance in Australia', *Health Affairs*, vol. 20, no. 2, pp. 152–61.

Willcox S 2005, 'Buying best value health care: Evolution of purchasing among private health insurers', *Australia and New Zealand Health Policy*, vol. 2, accessed at <www.anzhealthpolicy.com/content/2/1/6>.

Williams, A 1985, 'Economics of coronary artery bypass grafting', *British Medical Journal*, vol. 291, pp. 326–9.

Williams, P 1997, *Progress on the National Drug Strategy: Key National Indicators*, Commonwealth Department of Health and Family Services, Canberra.

Willis, E 1989, *Medical Dominance: The Division of Labour in Australian Health Care*, 2nd edition, Allen & Unwin, Sydney.

Wilson, D, Wakefield, MA, Esterman, A & Baken, CC 1987, '15's: They fit in everywhere—especially the schoolbag: A survey of purchases of packets of 15 cigarettes by 14 and 15 year olds in South Australia', *Supplement to Community Health Studies*, vol. xi, pp. 16s–20s.

Wilson, RM, Runciman, WR, Gibberd, RW, Harrison, BT, Newby, L & Hamilton, JD 1995, 'The quality in Australian health care study', *Medical Journal of Australia*, vol. 163, p. 469.

Windschuttle, K 1984, *The Media*, Penguin, Melbourne.

Women's Health Policy Review Committee (New South Wales) 1985, *Women's Health Services in New South Wales*, NSW Government Printing Service, Sydney.

World Health Organization 1978, *The Declaration of Alma Ata*, WHO, Geneva.

World Health Organization 1980, *International Classification of Impairments, Disabilities and Handicap*, WHO, Geneva.

World Health Organization 1981, *Global Strategy for Health for All by the Year 2000*, WHO, Geneva.

World Health Organization 1986, *The Ottawa Charter for Health Promotion*, WHO, Copenhagen.

World Health Organization 1997, *The Jakarta Declaration on Leading Health Promotion into the 21st Century*, WHO, Geneva.

World Health Organization 1998, *AIDS Epidemic Update: December 1998*, WHO, Geneva.

World Health Organization 1999, *The World Health Report 1999: Making a Difference*, WHO, Geneva.

World Health Organization 2005, *The Bangkok Charter for Health Promotion in a Globalised World*, WHO, Geneva.

World Health Organization 2006, *The World Health Report 2006: Working Together for Health*, WHO, Geneva.

World Health Organization 2007, *World Health Statistics*, WHO, Geneva.

World Health Organization 2008a, *Status of the Global HIV Epidemic*, WHO, Geneva.

World Health Organization 2008b, *Epidemiological Fact Sheet on HIV and AIDS: Australia*, WHO, Geneva.

World Health Organization 2008c, *The World Health Report 2008: Primary Health Care (Now More Than Ever)*, WHO, Geneva.

World Health Organization 2008d, *Closing the Gap in a Generation: Health Equity through Action on the Social Determinants of Health*, WHO, Geneva.

World Health Organization 2010a, *Health Systems Financing: The Path to Universal Health Coverage*, WHO, Geneva.

World Health Organization 2010b, *The World Health Organization Global Code of Practice on the International Recruitment of Health Personnel*, WHO, Geneva.

World Health Organization Regional Office for Europe 1998, *Social Determinants of Health: The Solid Facts*, WHO, Copenhagen.

Websites

Australia

Commonwealth government
<www.australia.gov.au>

State and territory governments
Australian Capital Territory
<www.act.gov.au>
New South Wales
<www.nsw.gov.au>
Northern Territory
<www.nt.gov.au>
Queensland
<www.qld.gov.au>
South Australia
<www.sa.gov.au>
Tasmania
<www.tas.gov.au>
Victoria
<www.vic.gov.au>
Western Australia
<www.wa.gov.au>

Health-related links
Australian Bureau of Statistics (ABS)
<www.abs.gov.au>
Australian Institute of Health and Welfare (AIHW)
<www.aihw.gov.au>
Department of Health (Australian Government)
<www.health.gov.au>
Department of Human Services (Australian Government)
<www.humanservices.gov.au>
Private Health Insurance Administration Council (PHIAC)
<www.phiac.gov.au>
Public Health Association of Australia (PHAA)
<www.phaa.net.au>

National

Canada
Health Canada
<www.hc-sc.gc.ca>
New Zealand
Ministry of Health
<www.moh.govt.nz/moh.nsf>
UK
Department of Health
<www.dh.gov.uk>
USA
Department of Health and Human Services (HHS)
<www.hhs.gov>
Centers for Medicare and Medicaid Services
<www.cms.gov>
National Centre for Health Statistics (NCHS)
<www.cdc.gov/nchs>
Office of Technology Assessment US Congress Publications (archive)
<www.princeton.edu/~ota>

International

Organisation for Economic Co-operation and Development (OECD)
<www.oecd.org>
World Bank
<www.worldbank.org>
World Health Organization (WHO)
<www.who.int/en>

Index